The Moral of the Story

AN INTRODUCTION TO ETHICS

Fourth Edition

NINA ROSENSTAND

San Diego Mesa College

Boston   Burr Ridge, IL   Dubuque, IA   Madison, WI   New York
San Francisco   St. Louis   Bangkok   Bogotá   Caracas   Kuala Lumpur
Lisbon   London   Madrid   Mexico City   Milan   Montreal   New Delhi
Santiago   Seoul   Singapore   Sydney   Taipei   Toronto

McGraw-Hill Higher Education ⚛

*A Division of The **McGraw-Hill** Companies*

THE MORAL OF THE STORY

Published by McGraw-Hill, a business unit of The McGraw-Hill Companies, Inc., 1221 Avenue of the Americas, New York, NY, 10020. Copyright © 2003 by The McGraw-Hill Companies, Inc. All rights reserved. No part of this publication may be reproduced or distributed in any form or by any means, or stored in a database or retrieval system, without the prior written consent of The McGraw-Hill Companies, Inc., including, but not limited to, in any network or other electronic storage or transmission, or broadcast for distance learning. Some ancillaries, including electronic and print components, may not be available to customers outside the United States.

This book is printed on acid-free paper.

2 3 4 5 6 7 8 9 0 FGR/FGR 0 9 8 7 6 5 4 3 2

ISBN 0-7674-2910-9

Sponsoring editor, Jon-David Hague; production editors, Vicki Moran and Jennifer Mills; manu-script editor, Anne Montague; cover designer, Lisa Buckley; design manager, Sharon Spurlock; photo researcher, Brian Pecko; illustrator, Judith Ogus; production supervisor, Pam Augspurger. Cover art © Karen Barbour. The text was set in 10.5/12.5 Berkeley Book by ColorType, San Diego, and printed on 45# New Era Matte by Quebecor, Fairfield.

Text, photo, and illustration credits appear at the back of the book on page 609, which constitutes an extension of the copyright page.

Library of Congress Cataloging-in-Publication Data

Rosenstand, Nina.
    The moral of the story / Nina Rosenstand. — 4th ed.
      p.   cm.
    Includes bibliographical references (p. 603) and index.
    ISBN 0-7674-2910-9
    1. Ethics   I. Title.
    BJ1012.R59   2003
    171—dc21   2002022532

www.mhhe.com

Contents

PART 3

How Should I Be? Theories of Virtue   321

Chapter 8
Socrates, Plato, and the Good Life   323

Chapter 9
Aristotle's Virtue Theory   365

Chapter 10
Contemporary Perspectives   401

Preface

$\mathcal{T}$he fourth edition of *The Moral of the Story* has inevitably been influenced by two events which, each in their own way, changed my life in the course of 2001. One was a personal experience, the other a collective experience that we are still deeply affected by. On the personal level, I became a naturalized United States citizen, having lived here as a welcome guest for more than twenty years. On the collective scale, the terrorist attacks of September 11 forced many of us to think about, and rethink, our views on individual rights, national security, the notions of a just war, patriotism, and terrorism, and perhaps most important, reminded us that every day we spend with those we love is precious. As a result, new themes such as national security and individual rights have been added to this edition, as have the topics of a just war and terrorism. This inclusion has not been done at the cost of any of the previous discussions or themes from the third edition, except in cases where they seemed outdated.

The general concept of *The Moral of the Story* remains the same: that discussions about moral issues can be facilitated using stories as examples, as a form of ethics lab where solutions can be tried out under controlled conditions. The book is written primarily for such college courses as Introduction to Ethics; Moral Philosophy; and Introduction to Philosophy: Values. Many textbooks in value theory or ethics choose to focus on problems of social importance, such as abortion, euthanasia, and capital punishment. This book reflects my own teaching experience that it is better for students to be introduced to basic ethical theory before they are plunged into discussions involving moral judgments. Consequently, *The Moral of the Story* provides an overview of influential classical and contemporary approaches to ethical theory. However, without practical application of the theories there can be no complete understanding of the problems raised, so each chapter includes examples that illustrate and explore the issues. As in previous editions, each chapter concludes with a section of examples—summaries and excerpts—taken from the world of fiction, particularly films.

Within the last decade, narrative theory has carved out a niche in American and European philosophy as well as in other academic disciplines. It is no longer unusual for ethicists and other thinkers to include works of fiction in their courses as well as in their professional papers, not only as examples of problem solving, but also as illustrations of an epistemological phenomenon: Humans are, in Alasdair MacIntyre's words, storytelling animals, and humans seem to choose the narrative form as their favorite way to structure meaning as they attempt to make sense of their reality. The narrative trend is making itself felt in other fields as well: the medical profession is looking to stories that teach about doctor-patient relationships; psychotherapists recommend that patients watch films to achieve an understanding of their own situation, and have patients write stories with themselves as the lead character. The court system is making use of films and novels to reach young people in trouble with the law. It seems that new fields are constantly being added to the list of professions that are discovering, or rediscovering, the potential of stories.

Organization

Like the second and third editions, the fourth edition of *The Moral of the Story* is divided into three major sections. Part 1 introduces the topic of ethics and places the phenomenon of storytelling within the context of moral education and discussion. Part 2 examines the conduct theories of ethical relativism, psychological and ethical egoism, altruism, utilitarianism, and Kantian deontology, and explores the concepts of personhood, rights, and justice. Part 3 focuses on the subject of virtue theory and contains chapters on Socrates and Plato, Aristotle, contemporary virtue theories in America, theories of authenticity in the Continental tradition, and gender theory. The virtues of compassion and gratitude are examined in detail, and the book concludes with a more detailed discussion of four moral issues, applying both ethics of conduct and virtue ethics: media ethics, just war, animal rights, and capital punishment. Each chapter concludes with a set of study questions, a section of Primary Readings with excerpts from classical and contemporary texts, and a section of Narratives, a collection of stories that illustrate the moral issues raised in the chapter.

Major Changes to the Fourth Edition

Overall, this edition takes note of the fact that we live in a changed world; many examples from September 11 and its aftermath have been included. Chapter 1 has been rewritten and reorganized to reflect post-9/11 conditions. In response to requests expressed by reviewers and instructors using the third edition, the chapter now includes a section of argumentation about moral values. The Primary Readings section also answers reviewer requests with an excerpt from Martha Nussbaum's *Love's Knowledge,* moved up from the final chapter in the previous edition. Chapter 2 now includes a section about seeing life as a story—another section that was previously placed at the end of the book, but that instructors also prefer to have up front. In Chapter 3 the section on diversity and multiculturalism has been enhanced with a discussion of what an American identity is like to different people. Chapter 6 now contains an expanded discussion of the concept of the kingdom of ends. Chapter 7 has extensive added coverage of the moral issues raised by genetic engineering, cloning, and stem cell research, previously mentioned briefly in the third edition's Chapter 1. Chapter 8 now includes an overview of Plato's influence on Augustine and the Christian tradition. Chapter 9 has been expanded with a section about Aristotle's influence on Thomas Aquinas. Chapter 11 now has a short section on women in the Middle Ages, and a discussion of the theory of psychosexual neutrality. Chapter 13 is a response to reviewers' and instructors' requests to have a concluding chapter on applied ethics. Some discussions that had previously been featured in short versions elsewhere in the book are now expanded and placed together in Chapter 13, such as a discussion of media ethics, animal rights and welfare, and the death penalty. In addition, an all-new section has been added in response to present concerns: a discussion of the concepts of a just war and terrorism.

Several new boxes have been added throughout the book, highlighting issues such as the possibility of a "moral center" in the brain; the existence of a common American culture; civil liberties and national security; the question of the rationality of animals; and the concepts of patriotism and terrorism. In addition, some existing boxes have been updated, including the Spokane serial killer case, and Christina Hoff Sommers's theory on preferential treatment of girls in school.

The new Primary Readings include an expansion of the excerpt from John Stuart Mill's *Utilitarianism;* excerpts from Martin Luther King's "A Letter from Birmingham Jail," Diane Whiteley's "The Victim and the Justification of Punishment," Sue Savage-Rumbaugh and Roger Lewin's *Kanzi: The Ape at the Brink of the Human Mind,* John Rawls's *The Law of Peoples,* and Jan Narveson's "Morality and Violence: War, Revolution, Terrorism."

The new Narratives include an episode from the sitcom *Friends:* "The One Where Phoebe Hates PBS," about selfishness and altruism, and the films *Return to Paradise,* about friendship duties; *The Insider,* about moral integrity and social conscience; *The Truman Show,* a Platonic tale of true and false realities; and *15 Minutes,* about media ethics. An excerpt from a novella has also been added, Simone de Beauvoir's "The Woman Destroyed." The film *Outbreak* has been reinstated from the second edition because of student requests as well as because of its timely theme in an era of concerns about bioterrorism: a fast-moving epidemic and a possible government response. Another story from the second edition has been reinstated as well, "The Store of the Worlds." It fell through the cracks in the third edition, but with its theme of nostalgia for the recent past, it provides a view of the "good life" that, seen against the background of September 11, will speak to many readers.

Using the Narratives

The Narratives have been chosen from a wide variety of sources ranging from epic prose, poems, and novels to films. I wish to emphasize that from a literary and artistic point of view that summaries and excerpts do not do the originals justice; a story worth experiencing, be it a novel, short story, or film, can't be reduced to a mere plot outline or fragment and still retain all of its essence. As Martha Nussbaum says, the form is an inherent part of the story content. Usually, there is more to the story than the bare bones of a moral problem, and in writing these summaries I have had to disregard much of the richness of story and character development. Nevertheless, I have chosen the summary or excerpt format in order to discuss a number of different stories and genres as they relate to specific issues in ethics. Because I believe it is important to show that there is a cross-cultural, historic tradition of exploring moral problems through telling a story, I have opted for a broad selection of Narratives. There are, of course, other ways in which stories and ethical theory can be brought together; one might, for instance, select one or two short stories or films in their original format for class discussion. I hope that instructors will indeed select a few stories—novels, short stories, or videos—for their classes to experience firsthand. However, the Narratives are written so that firsthand experience should not be necessary to a discussion of the problem presented by the story. The summaries and excerpts give readers just enough information to enable them to discuss the moral problem presented. I hope that some readers will become inspired to seek out the originals on their own.

Because space is limited, I have not been able to include more than a sampling of stories, and I readily admit that my choices are subjective ones; I personally find them interesting as illustrations and effective in a classroom context where students come from many different cultural backgrounds. Because I am a native of Denmark, I have chosen to include a few references to the Scandinavian literary tradition. I am fully aware that others might choose other stories or even choose completely different ethical problems to illustrate, and I am grateful to the many users of the previous three editions, instructors as well as students, who have let me know about their favorite stories and how they thought this selection of stories might be expanded and improved. The new Narratives reflect some of these suggestions.

Acknowledgments

I would like to thank all my students, colleagues, and friends—from Southern California to Oregon, the Inland Northwest, Texas, and Denmark—for sharing their views with me in the aftermath of September 11, by e-mail, by phone, and in person. It became clear that some of us agreed neither on the root causes of September 11 nor about the proper course of action for the United States in the post-9/11 world, but in every single talk and discussion I have had we have celebrated the right of Americans to have and voice an opinion that isn't necessarily the same as one's family's, one's co-workers', or one's government's. I cherish this as not only a celebration of the First Amendment, but also of a common feature of the American culture, from left to right: an ever-present passion for making this country a better place. As such, engaging in these discussions has been a way for me to put into practice my oath of citizenship.

I would like to extend a special thank-you to Constance Carroll, president of San Diego Mesa College, for her calm and compassionate lead in the wake of September 11. She took time out to engage in a personal e-mail conversation with me about the appropriateness of television crews covering emotionally laden campus meetings, and extended to everyone a sense of direction in our collective and individual attempts to strike a balance between our grief and worry over the fate of the nation and our immediate job at hand, of providing our students with a continuation of the quality class time they expected.

I would like to thank the production team at McGraw-Hill Higher Education for all their help and enthusiasm: Vicki Moran, Jen Mills, my production editors; Marty Granahan, my permissions editor; my editor Jon-David Hague; and most of all my editor extraordinaire and friend, Ken King, who doesn't take "I have too much work to do" for an answer! I would also like to mention Karen Barbour, the wonderful artist whose works have now graced four covers of *The Moral of the Story*. I love her visionary art, which tells stories without the need for words. Also, I'm grateful to my first editor at Mayfield, Jim Bull, who conceived of an ethics textbook based on my teaching method, using films and novels as examples, and asked me to write it—that's a fairy tale in itself. In addition, I want to thank the reviewers for their valuable suggestions which for the most part have found their way into this edition; also I want to thank them for not only pointing out what could be improved, but also what, in their view, worked particularly well in the third edition. That, too, is important for me to know.

Next, my students at San Diego Mesa College, in the classes Introduction to Philosophy: Values, Philosophy of Women in World Cultures, and Issues in Social Philosophy, deserve my deepest gratitude, and thumbs up, for their spirited cooperation in suggesting new facts and films for this edition, and behaving in the best philosophical tradition: asking good questions of the instructor/author. You guys keep me on my toes.

I would like to thank the following colleagues and friends for their gracious help, conversations about ethics and films, and suggestions for this edition. From Mesa College: Professors Jonathan McLeod, Diane Barbolla, Arelene Wolinski, Dwight Furrow, Tony Pettina, Terri Valverde, Mary Lou Locke, Richard Hammes, Charles Zappia, Kendra Jeffcoat, William Craft, Sudata Debchaudhury, Chuck Corum, Pat Sunaya, Patrick Pidgeon, Donald Abbott, and Michael Kuttnauer. Michael pointed me toward Simone de Beauvoir's works of fiction, so "The Woman Destroyed" is included in this edition thanks to him. I'd like to thank my friend and colleague John Berteaux, San Diego State University, for sharing his work on liberalism and race with me. I'm grateful to my friend, colleague, and mentor Peter Kemp, professor at the Danish Institute for Pedagogy, who keeps me up to date on issues in bioethics and policies within the European Union, and helps me stay in touch with developments within the philosophical climate of Europe. Thank you to American philosopher Richard Taylor, who sent me a very gracious letter, and who has contributed to my reconsidering the role of emotions in ethics. I'm also grateful to Harold Weiss, Northhampton Community College, for his encouraging e-mails, and his suggestions for this edition. A special conversation about ethics and stories took place on Danish Public Radio in August 2001, when I was a guest on a weekly show, *Koplevs Krydsfelt*, and I would like to thank host Kjeld Koplev for the opportunity to talk about issues that concern me deeply, to a Danish audience, twenty-two years after having emigrated. My friend Betty B. Owens has been of enormous moral support during stressful times through her encouraging e-mails, but also through a steady supply of intriguing websites. Other friends have helped more than they know, with film suggestions, philosophical questions, and just by being friends: Randi McKenzie, Phil Martin, Christa Blichmann, Søren Faartoft, Frank Thompson, Claire McCullough, Astrid Hansen, Stine Faartoft, Jessica Humphrey, Lois Covner, Russ Covner, Natalie and Sophia Schwer, Susanne and Maurice Schwer, Søren Hyldgaard, Jan and Tommy Niebuhr, Kaj and Ruth Andersen, Søren and Jytte Hansen, and Niels Foss. In addition, I would like to thank my students Ron Krack and Joya Thompson for sharing their research with me.

The previous editions wouldn't have been possible without the help and suggestions from the following friends and colleagues: Helmut Wautischer, Sonoma State University; Lawrence Hinman, University of San Diego; Eugene Troxell and Peter Atterton, San Diego State University; Betsy Decyk, Daniel Guerriere, and G. A. Spangler, California State University, Long Beach. According to Jim Bull, it was Al Spangler who steered him in the direction of my office at CSULB in the late '80s, when Jim was looking for a new author for Mayfield; that was a wonderful thing to do for a young lecturer. My heartfelt thanks, Al. I'm grateful to the late Philip Hallie for his inspiration, and to his wife Dorrit Hallie; to Russell Means for sharing his views on American Indian traditions; to Leonard Maltin for his time and advice while I was working on the first edition; to Sue Savage-Rumbaugh for her time and comments to a draft of the second edition; to Carol Enns, College of the Sequoias; John Hasenjaeger, Clackamas Community College; John Osborne, Butte College; Thomas Wren, Loyola University, Chicago; Børge Pontoppidan, Barcelona; Marianne Ammitzbøll, Copenhagen; Hans Hertel, University of Copenhagen; and Steen Wackerhausen, University of Aarhus. In addition, my eternal thanks to two people who were irreplaceable to me, and whose moral demands on themselves were without compromise: my late father-in-law Herbert Covner, and my late uncle Palle Hansen.

As they were for the three previous editions and two other books, my parents, Gladys and Finn Rosenstand, have been there for me, albeit with an ocean and a continent between us most of the time. Their enthusiastic support for my projects has helped shape my life and my self-confidence ever since I can remember. In addition, their diligence in looking up information and articles for me is as reliable and useful now as ever. Thank you for all the love and support, *Mor* and *Far,* and for all the stories. And thank you, Rowdie, for being a loyal and loving companion, and for enhancing my understanding of animal intelligence. Most of all, I want to express my gratitude to my husband, Craig R. Covner, for his love, support, and patience. Craig, you help put things in perspective for me with your sharp mind; you watch movies with me; you tell me stories and lift my spirits — and recently you were there to share my joy when I voted for the first time as a U.S. citizen.

For Craig and my parents

Immorality may be fun, but it isn't fun enough to take the place of 100 percent virtue and three square meals a day.

—Noel Coward, *Design for Living*

Part 1

The Story as a Tool of Ethics

Chapter One

Thinking About Values

After September 11

*F*or many of us, the new millennium didn't arrive on January 1, 2000, or even January 1, 2001, but on September 11, 2001, for that was when Americans' world changed, irrevocably. For the first time ever, an enemy attack was undertaken, successfully, against both military and civilian targets on the American mainland, resulting in damage to the Pentagon near Washington, D.C., the collapse of the two World Trade Center towers in New York, and the deaths of some three thousand people. A fourth target was planned in Washington — probably the Capitol — but the attack was thwarted by passengers fighting back against the suicidal hijackers, causing Flight 93 to go down in a remote area of Pennsylvania, killing all on board, but injuring no one on the ground. The 1941 attack by the Japanese air force on Pearl Harbor, terrible and surprising as it was, with profound consequences, was not directed primarily against civilians, and Hawaii was not yet a state in the Union. On September 11, however, hijackers from an extremist Muslim fringe group used commercial American airplanes with civilian passengers as missiles directed against American financial and military landmarks. And in a sense, everyone in the nation was psychologically wounded by the attack.

"The New Normalcy"

What moral problems were we discussing on Monday, September 10? We were debating whether a mother in Texas had been suffering from postpartum psychosis when she drowned her five children in the bathtub or whether she was sane enough to stand trial. We were concerned with the disappearance of a young female intern from Washington, D.C. and the possible involvement of a California congressman. We were discussing whether racial profiling was a frequent problem among police officers in the big cities. A brand-new debate was developing over giving amnesty and residence permits to undocumented immigrants from Mexico. We were discussing DNA analysis leading to death row inmates being released. Stem cell research was on the agenda as one of the most promising — but to some one of the most objectionable — new scientific approaches because it may cure illnesses and prolong life; but stem cells are acquired from week-old embryos that are destroyed in the process. And we were discussing human cloning: Scientists had announced that they would try to replicate human beings in the very near future, and we were engaged in heated discussions about the nature and rights of such future clones, about whether humans should play God and create copies of themselves. But on September 11 these discussions came to a halt, and all we could see, and think about, were two planes plowing into the World Trade towers and the New York landmarks sinking into a cloud of dust. Everything else seemed trivial.

This new edition will reflect that change, and the events of September 11 and the subsequent months will have a natural place within the discussions. However, it would be a poor tribute to the pre-9/11 world we knew, and loved to discuss and squabble about, if this edition didn't also reflect debates of a less disturbed time. Part of the grief we have felt after September 11 has been for the loss of lives and for the loss of our sense of security, false as it may have been; but part of it has also been for the loss of a world where we could afford the luxury to take things of lesser magnitude seriously. And we are by now taking such things seriously again, and rightly so—albeit with an undercurrent of awareness of how precious such a luxury really is. So in this new edition we will talk about things such as stem cell research and cloning, ethical relativism, and the perennial debate around the kitchen table late at night about whether we are fundamentally selfish by nature. But we will also talk about the concepts of a just war and terrorism, and we will talk about unselfishness. What in the fall of 2001 was termed the "new normalcy" seems to have become a mixture of topics related to the post–September 11 world as well as old themes carried over, but with a deeper resonance. Whether September 11 represented America's finest hour, as some people said, is a question posterity will have to judge. But something struck me as I watched the television coverage, hour after hour, of the events of that terrible day: As survivors were pouring out of the World Trade Center before the towers fell, individual differences had disappeared: There were no more differences of color, or ethnicities, or nationalities—everyone was covered with concrete dust and soot. For a short while, in the midst of a common tragedy, everyone was simply a shocked, wounded human being. Eighty nations reportedly lost citizens when the towers fell, but among the victims and survivors the age-old dividing lines of race, ethnicity, and nationality no longer applied. We can call it an act of war directed at Americans because it happened on our soil and involved our military, but it was also a crime against humanity as such.

The Best of Times, the Worst of Times?

Prior to 9/11, violent crime as well as crime against property had been going down year after year, to the point where, in the summer of 2001, there was speculation that it had been reduced as far as it was going to because of a slump in the economy (the better the economy, the lower the crime rate was the theory). Even so, many of us had the perception that we were living in violent times, due to the nature of the news: "Road rage" was expanding to "air rage" (people losing their tempers on airplanes), schoolchildren were bringing guns to school and shooting classmates and teachers, and there was a general agreement that people seemed ruder than ever before. In Seattle in 2001, a woman had been holding up traffic for hours while she contemplated jumping off a bridge. Some motorists leaned out their car windows yelling "Jump!" at her. She did jump to her death. Were the motorists frustrated or insensitive, or both? We can only guess, but such stories added to people's sense of unease about the way things were going. Big stories breaking in the news had people asking questions not only about the stories, but about the news media and their hidden agendas. Cynicism seemed to be the prevailing attitude.

Some people have called September 11 "the day cynicism died." The misanthropic view of humans that some of us had gotten used to took a turn: New Yorkers experienced, to their own astonishment, that in the weeks following the attacks they were kinder and gentler to each other—in a town that prides itself on its brusqueness. My students in San Diego, far from New York, reported the same thing: They had a lot more patience with each other and with strangers in traffic. Our misanthropy had become a beam narrowly focused on those who would want to do harm to strangers because of a principle: that is, focused on terrorists. We were all at war, including the media, and our grief united us. Later on, cynicism reared its head again, and it became clear that a united America was probably a hope rather than a reality. But perhaps cynicism isn't altogether a bad thing—as it is sometimes said, a cynic is a disappointed idealist. You have a vision of how things ought to be, but you also have a lot of skepticism. Already by Thanksgiving 2001 we were asking questions revealing that skepticism was alive and well, even if cynicism had abated somewhat: When it became apparent that the large sums of relief money collected by various agencies such as the Red Cross had yet to be handed out in any significant amount to survivors and families of terror victims, the criticism was instant and angry, and resulted in a speeded-up distribution process. Somewhere between hope and skepticism we may be able to deal with the real world.

It is a fact that as cynical as the late twentieth century was, we were also focused on making things better: In the past, political corruption used to be rampant; spousal abuse and child abuse weren't even considered misdemeanors; sexual harassment didn't even exist as a concept, but was endemic; knee-jerk racism, sexism, and other forms of discrimination were part of the picture of everyday life in America. By the late twentieth century the spotlight had been cast on such behavior, labeling it immoral and, some of it, also illegal. Reflecting the concern for creating the right climate, balancing individuality and a sense of community, is the debate that has extended into the "new normalcy" about how many of our individual rights we should give up, permanently or temporarily, for the sake of a safer, more secure world. In Chapter 7 we take a closer look at the discussion of liberties and rights versus security.

Morals, Values, and Ethics

In the late twentieth century the number of college classes in introductory ethics and value theory swelled. When they hear I teach ethics, people who are unfamiliar with how college classes in the subject are taught say, "Good! Our college students really need that!" This response always makes me pause: What do they think I teach? Right from wrong? Of course, we do have discussions about right and wrong, and we can,

> ### *Box 1.1*   MORAL AND NONMORAL VALUES
>
> What is a *value?* Most often the word refers to a moral value, a judgment of somebody's behavior according to whether or not it corresponds to certain moral rules (for example, "Tiffany is a wonderful person; she always stays after the party to help with the dishes"). However, some value judgments have nothing to do with moral issues, and so they are called *nonmoral,* which is not the same as *immoral* (breaking moral rules) or *amoral* (not having any moral standards). Such nonmoral value judgments can include statements about taste (such as "The new gallery downtown has a collection of exquisite watercolors"; "I really dislike Bob's new haircut"; and "Finn makes a great jambalaya"), as well as statements about being correct or incorrect about facts (such as "Lois did really well on her last math test" and "You're wrong; last Saturday we didn't go to the movies; that was last Sunday"). Like moral value judgments, nonmoral value judgments generally refer to something being right or wrong, good or bad; but, unlike moral value judgments, they don't refer to morally right or wrong behavior.

from time to time, even reach agreement about some moral responses being *preferable* to other moral responses. If students haven't acquired a sense of values by the time they're in college, I fear it's too late: Psychologists say a child must develop a sense of values *by the age of seven* in order to become an adult with a conscience. (Box 1.1 explores the concept of *value.*) If the child hasn't learned by the second grade that other people can feel pain and pleasure, and that one should try not to harm others, that lesson will probably never be truly learned. (Box 1.2 explores the topic of a moral center in the brain.) Fortunately this doesn't mean everyone must be taught the *same* moral lessons by the age of seven—as long as we have *some* moral background to draw on later, as a sounding board for further ethical reflections, we can come from morally widely diverse homes and still become morally dependable people. A child growing up in a criminal, *Sopranos*-type of family will certainly have acquired a set of morals by the age of seven—but it isn't necessarily the same set of morals as those acquired by a child in a liberal, secular, humanist, family, or in a Seventh-Day Adventist family. The point is that all these children will have their "moral center" activated and can expand their moral universe. A child who has never been taught *any* moral lessons may be a sociopath of the future: a person who has no comprehension of how other people feel, no empathy.

Should elementary schools teach values, then? It may be just a little too late, if indeed a child's moral sense is developed by the age of seven, but at least there is a chance it might help, and for children whose parents have done a minimal job of teaching them respect for others, school will probably be the only place they'll learn it. Some elementary schools are developing such programs. Problems occur, however, when schools begin to teach values with which not all parents agree. We live in a multicultural society, and although some parents might like certain topics to be on the school agenda, others would certainly not. Some parents want their children to have early access to sex education, whereas others consider it unthinkable as a

Box 1.2   A MORAL CENTER IN THE BRAIN

In 1999, researchers led by Antonio Damasio at the University of Iowa found that an area in the brain, the prefrontal cortex, plays a pivotal role in our development of a moral sense. People who have undergone a normal psychological and moral development (1) know there is a difference between right and wrong, and (2) can act on that knowledge. Adults who have had their prefrontal cortex damaged in an accident still know the difference between right and wrong, but somehow it doesn't translate into action: They can't make decisions based on that knowledge, or act on such decisions. Two patients investigated by the Iowa team had suffered damage to their prefrontal cortex before they were sixteen months of age, and—in spite of having apparently recovered from their injuries, having normal intellectual capacities, and having been reared in stable, middle-class homes—both developed severely antisocial behavior as adolescents and adults: recklessness, inability to care about others, including their own babies, abuse of others, and criminal tendencies. They seemed to recognize moral issues intellectually, but were unable to act on them because they had no sense of the consequences of their actions.

So now that we know where our morals are located in the brain, can we say we understand everything about the issues of morals, ethics, and values? Can we perhaps say that a person whose moral center is damaged shouldn't be held accountable for what she or he does? This is where sweeping generalizations can become dangerous: It may be that some people are genuinely unaware of the moral consequences of their actions—but it may be a dubious legal trend to assume that every criminal must have a damaged prefrontal cortex; if so, we create an easy excuse and throw out the possibility of people actually making decisions *deliberately*—decisions that go against the values of society. Indeed, we should be careful not to assume that neuroscience can tell us everything we need to know about who we are. Brain research can pinpoint where our thoughts and feelings originate, and what affects them chemically, but it can't tell us whether one moral answer is better than another; we need the actual human thought process for that.

Dilbert by Scott Adams

© 2001. DILBERT reprinted by permission of United Feature Syndicate, Inc.

Lately, research has pointed to the existence of an actual moral center in the brain. If this center is damaged, the individual seems to have a hard time acting on moral deliberations or even understanding moral issues. Obviously, this *Dilbert* cartoon takes a dim view of whether people in management have a functioning moral center.

(ethos, charactercharactercharactercharactercharactercharacter) and *morality* from Latin (*mores,* character, custom, or habit). Today, in English as well as in many other Western languages, both words refer to some form of proper conduct. Although we, in our everyday lives, don't distinguish clearly between morals and ethics, there is a subtle difference: Some people think the word *morality* has negative connotations, and in fact it does carry two different sets of associations for most of us. The positive ones are guidance, goodness, humanitarianism, and so forth. Among the negative associations are repression, bigotry, persecution—in a word, *moralizing.* Suppose the introductory ethics course on your campus was labeled "Introduction to Morals." You would, in all likelihood, expect something different than you would from a course called "Introduction to Ethics" or "Introduction to Values." The word *morality* has a slightly different connotation than do the terms *ethics* and *values:* That is because *morality* usually refers to *the moral rules we follow,* the values that we have. *Ethics* is generally defined as *theories about these rules;* ethics questions and justifies the rules we live by, and, if ethics can find no rational justification for those rules, it may ask us to abandon them. Morality is the stuff our social life is made of—even our personal life—and ethics is the ordering, the questioning, the awareness, the investigation of what we believe: Are we justified in believing it? Is it consistent? Should we remain open to other beliefs or not?

How, then, do we define *values*? In our everyday language, something we value is something we believe is set apart from other things that we don't value or value less. When do we first begin to value something? As babies, we live in a world that is divided into what we like and what we don't like—a world of plus and minus, of yes and no. According to some psychoanalysts, we never really get over this early stage, and some people simply divide their world into what they like or approve of and what they don't like or disapprove of. However, most of us add an element to that, a justification for our preferences or aversions.

If values have to do with people's likes and dislikes, why are they not studied only in the discipline of psychology? Why is philosophy involved with what values we have, what moral rules we follow, and what ethical justifications we give? Psychology can tell us only what people believe in and possibly why they believe it; it can't make a statement about whether people are *justified* in believing it. Philosophy's job, at least in this connection, is to *question* our values; it forces us to give reasons, and preferably good reasons, for why we approve of one thing and disapprove of something else. We might approve or disapprove of something that is a matter of taste; in that case we talk about the values of *aesthetics.* However, the primary field in which philosophers voice their approval or disapproval is the field of morality. And when we are evaluating issues in morality, we are practicing ethics.

Dilbert by Scott Adams

© 1997. DILBERT reprinted by permission of United Feature Syndicate, Inc.

Ethicists point out that having a system of values isn't enough for a person to be morally mature—one must also engage in thinking about those values, and critically examine them from time to time. Cartoonist Scott Adams obviously agrees.

In today's complex society it is not considered enough for an adult person merely to divide the world into likes and dislikes; we are exposed to so many different values that we are expected to have reasons for our moral preferences. In other words, it is not enough just to have moral rules; we should, as moral, mature persons, be able to justify our viewpoints with ethical arguments or, at the very least, ask ourselves why we feel this way or that about a certain issue. Ethics, therefore, is much more than a topic in a curriculum. As moral adults, we are required to think about ethics all the time.

Most people, in fact, do just that, even in their teens, because it is also considered a sign of maturity to question authority, at least to a certain extent. If a very young adult is told to be home at 11 P.M., she or he will usually ask, "Why can't I stay out till midnight?" When we have to make up our minds about whether to study over the weekend or go hiking, we usually try to come up with as many pros and cons as we can. When someone we have put our trust in betrays that trust, we want to know why. All of these questions are practical applications of ethics: They question the rules of morality and the breaking of those rules. Although formal training in ethical questions can make us better at judging moral issues, we are, as adult human beings, already quite experienced just because we already have asked, "Why?" a number of times in our lives.

Why Be Moral?

Do we know *why* humans all over the world have an interest in establishing and following moral rules? An age-old answer is, Because the moral rules are decrees from God (or the gods). Philosophy has several answers, and, interestingly enough, some of them are mutually exclusive. Philosophy has traditionally looked for the origin of morality in the realm of *reason:* Somehow, applying rules for decent behavior makes sense, so rationality becomes a prerequisite for moral behavior. Some philosophers, however, reject the idea of morality being a matter of the head—they claim it is the *heart* that is involved, and the head just rationalizes whatever it is the heart wants. If this is the case, no amount of rational argumentation will persuade people who listen just to their heart and to their gut feelings. For those who adhere to this theory, there is no such thing as a "morally superior" point of view. All viewpoints are just subjective emotions. A new breed of thinkers, including the American philosopher Martha Nussbaum, hold the theory that our moral values do indeed have a strong connection to our emotions, but that doesn't mean the values or our moral decisions reflecting them can't be rational. According to this theory, there is a rational element within our emotional life that makes some emotional reactions reasonable and morally relevant, while others may not be. Being angry because someone has mistreated us is justified, and may pave the way for an understanding of justice, but being angry for no appropriate reason is not morally acceptable. We return to Nussbaum later in this chapter.

There also are those who believe that morality is a built-in, fail-safe *biological* trait: We can't help being moral because otherwise our species would perish. Genetically, we have an interest, in a limited sense, in looking after one another: It is to our own advantage and that of our descendants.

Some philosophers go further in stressing the advantageous nature of morality. Morality, they say, is nothing but playing it safe when you can't get away with doing what you want; it derives from *fear of being caught.* We stick to the straight and narrow because we are afraid of what may happen if we don't: We'll go to jail, or lose our friends, or go to hell, or some other nasty prospect. If we can get away with something, however, we will do it—that is human nature. This view, a variety of *egoism,* will be discussed shortly.

Some of these attempts at explaining the nature of morality will be discussed in Part 2, where we examine the ongoing human endeavor to answer the question, *What should I do?* When faced with a moral problem that requires our immediate attention, we often realize that deep down we know what we ought to do, but we just don't feel like doing it—perhaps we feel very much like doing the exact opposite. We may, for example, believe it is our duty to be with our family for Thanksgiving, but we would rather accept an invitation to go to a mountain cabin with some good friends. Or we know we ought to work Friday afternoon, but the weather is so nice . . . or we feel attracted to someone who already has a partner, so we know we ought to get out of the way, but. . . . This conflict between what we ought to do and what we want to do—between duty and inclination—is perhaps the most common form of a moral dilemma; some people think it is the *only* form of moral conflict. There may be another kind, however, one in which we have to choose between two things we should do but don't want to do—or perhaps we don't mind doing them, but one just happens to preclude the other. We may be caught between a rock and a hard place when we need to study for a final on the same night that our boss wants us to help take inventory at our part-time job. Tell the boss that school is more important, and chances are she won't agree. Tell the professor that work is more important, and he may be completely unsympathetic. Clearly, we need to do both, but we can do only one. We may even find ourselves in a situation in which we have to decide whether to give up our car to a carjacker or to put up a fight. We don't really want to do either, but we have to make a choice; if we dawdle, the carjacker will take that to mean we have chosen to refuse to give up the car, and we may be harmed. Such moral dilemmas fill our lives and can be either fascinating or extremely anxiety-provoking. Can moral theories help us decide what to do when we really need some good advice? That is the whole point; indeed, theories of moral conduct set out to do just that by giving us a basic value by which to measure the situation. What are you most concerned with? Your own happiness? Overall consequences down the line? Doing the right thing? Keeping a promise? Obeying the law? And what do you think your priorities *ought* to be? In Part 2 of this book we look at various answers to these moral problems.

Debating Moral Issues

Every functional society on earth has had a "philosophy" of what one should do or be in order to be considered a good person. Sometimes this moral code is expressed orally in stories and songs, and sometimes it is expressed in writing. When it is expressed as a set of rules with explanations justifying the rules, we may call it a *code of ethics*. In order for it to become a philosophical discipline, we must add the practice of examining and questioning the rules. In the Western intellectual tradition, Greek philosophers were the first to focus on ethics as a subject worth studying; Socrates asked the all-important question, *How should one live?* From then on, and for over two thousand years, ethics has been one of the major branches of philosophical inquiry in the Western tradition, and contemporary philosophers around the world continue to dedicate curriculum hours, journals, papers, and conferences to its study. Other key areas of philosophy are logic (defining the rules for proper thinking), metaphysics (theories of the nature of reality), aesthetics (theories of beauty and art), and epistemology, also known as theory of knowledge (theories of how the human mind can obtain knowledge and whether the knowledge we obtain can ever be *certain*).

Cultures developing independently of the Western tradition have experienced a similar fascination for the subject of acting and living right. Socrates' version remains unique among ancient thinkers because he encouraged critical thinking instead of emphasizing being an obedient citizen. In China, Confucius expressed his philosophy of proper moral conduct as a matter of obedience to authorities and, above all, respect for one's elders at approximately the same time at which Socrates was teaching students critical thinking in the public square in Athens. In Africa, tribal thinkers developed a strong sense of morality in terms of individuals' sense of responsibility to the community and the community's understanding of its responsibility to each individual—a philosophy that has become known to the West in recent years through the proverb, "It takes a village to raise a child." Among American Indian tribes, the philosophy of harmony between humans and their environment—animate as well as inanimate nature—has been part of the moral code.

Do we have any guidelines for whether one viewpoint is *morally better* than another? How would we know which one is superior? Centuries ago the answer would have been plain: Religion would have provided the answer. We would have looked for help with moral problems in religious texts or in the advice of religious leaders; indeed, many people continue to find comfort in the belief that the answers are there. More and more people in the Western part of the world, however, live a secularized life, and, although they may ask their God for guidance, they by no means believe that all of the answers are to be found in their religious tradition. Often, people find that our society today is more complex than that presented in their religious texts. For agnostics and atheists there can be no turning to religion for unquestioned moral guidance, because they view religion itself as an unknown or nonexistent factor. Agnostics claim that they do not know whether there is a God or that it is impossible to know. Atheists claim that there is no God. Both the agnostic and the atheist may find that religion suggests solutions to their problems, but such solutions are accepted not because they come from religion but because they somehow make sense.

For a philosophical inquiry the requirement that a solution make sense is particularly important; although religion may play a significant role in the development of moral values for many people, a philosophical investigation of moral issues must involve more than faith in a religious authority. Regardless of one's religious belief or lack thereof, such an investigation must involve reasoning because, for one thing, philosophy teaches that one must examine issues without solely relying on the word of authority. For another thing, a rational argument can be a way for people to reach an understanding in spite of having different viewpoints on religion. Accordingly, a good way to communicate about ethics for both believers and nonbelievers is to approach the issue through the language of *reason*.

When we reach a conclusion based on rational premises, we are presenting an *argument.* Such arguments can be *inductive,* or they can be *deductive*. An inductive argument is a conclusion based on a gathering of evidence, but you can't be certain that the conclusion is true, only that it is likely. A deductive argument, on the other hand, is an argument where the conclusion does follow with certainty from the premises.

Logical fallacies invalidate a moral viewpoint just as they do any other kind of viewpoint. Have you heard someone claim that because she has been cheated by two auto mechanics, no auto mechanics can be trusted? That's the fallacy of *hasty generalization.* Have you heard people — perhaps a parent, or an educator — claim that they're right, "just because"? In other words, they don't give any other reason than their own authority? That is the fallacy of *appeal to authority.* When someone tries to prove a point just by rephrasing it, such as "I'm right, because I'm never wrong," that is the fallacy of *begging the question,* which makes the assumption that what you are trying to prove is a fact. How about a bully arguing that if you don't give him your seat/purse/car, he will harm you? That's the *ad baculum* (Latin for "by the stick") fallacy, the fallacy of using physical threats. And if someone says, "Well, you know you can't believe what Fred says — after all, he's from out of town," that's an *ad hominem* ("to the man") fallacy, which assumes that who a person is determines the correctness or incorrectness of what he or she says. And a politician declaring "If we continue to allow women to have abortions, then pretty soon nobody will give birth, and the human race will die out" is a *slippery slope* argument, which assumes that drastic consequences will follow a certain policy. Closely related is the *straw man* fallacy, inventing a viewpoint so radical that hardly anyone holds it, so you can knock it down: "Gun advocates want to allow criminals and children to own weapons, so we should work toward a gun ban." And if you claim that we either have to respect all individual rights or curtail people's rights in order to achieve security, one or the other, then you are *bifurcating*—you are creating a *false dichotomy* (unless, of course, we're really talking about a situation with no third possibility, such as being pregnant—you can't be a little bit pregnant; it's either/or). These and other logical fallacies are rampant in media discussions, and part of proper moral reasoning consists in watching out for the use of such flawed arguments, in one's own statements as well as in those of others.

But is logic all there is to a good moral argument? Some philosophers would say yes: The force of a moral viewpoint derives from its compelling logic. But increasingly, other voices are adding that a good moral argument is compelling not just because of its logic, but because it also makes sense *emotionally*. If we have no feeling of moral approval or outrage, then do we really *care* about whether something is morally right or wrong? If we don't *feel* that it's wrong to harm a child, then how is logic going to persuade us? A classic answer has been an appeal to the logic of the Golden Rule: You wouldn't want someone to harm *you*, would you? But say some, that's an appeal to how you'd *feel* in the same situation. An appeal to pure feeling isn't going to be enough, because feelings can be manipulated, and appeals to emotions don't solve conflicts if we don't share those emotions, but combined with the logic of reasoning emotions can form the foundation of a forceful moral argument, according to some modern thinkers.

Stories and Morals

All cultures tell stories, and all cultures have codes for proper behavior. Very often those codes are taught through stories, but stories can also be used to *question* moral rules and to examine morally ambiguous situations. A fundamental premise of this book is that stories sometimes can serve as shortcuts to understanding and solving moral problems. Many literature professors may be inclined to tell us that people don't read anymore, that the novel is dead, or that nobody appreciates good literature these days. I myself am rather disappointed when students are unfamiliar with the classics of literature or have grown to hate them through high school manglings. However, it just isn't true that people don't read novels—best-sellers are flourishing like never before. And an element has been added to our appreciation of good stories: *movies*. The American film industry has been in existence for over a hundred years, and it should be no surprise to anyone that as much as films can provide simple entertainment, they can also give us in-depth, unforgettable views of human life, including moral issues. This book makes use of that treasure trove of movie stories as well as novels, short stories, epic poems, television shows, and plays as illustrations of moral problems and solutions.

After each chapter in this book you will find a small selection of stories titled *Narratives* (summaries and/or excerpts) that illustrate the moral theory discussed in the chapter. Some examples can be seen as arguments in favor of the type of theory in question, and some can be viewed as arguments against it.

In most cases the ending is important to the moral significance of a story, and whenever that is the case, I include that ending. In cases in which the ending is not significant to the moral drama, I have done my best to avoid giving it away because I don't want to be a spoiler. Using stories here has two purposes. One is to supply a foundation for further debate about the application of the moral theories presented in the chapter; the other is to inspire you to experience these stories in their original form, through print or video, since they are, of course, richer and more interesting than any outline can show.

Stories as Survival Mechanisms

The Russian author Ilya Ehrenburg tells of a terrible time during World War II:

> During the war I visited Leningrad; it was during the occupation, and people had no water, power, or heat; the thermometer showed 30 Celsius below, the dead lay around in the houses, nobody had the strength to bury them.
>
> As the Germans retreated I returned. This time I was visited by a young woman who used to study music; now she was working in the factories, repairing cannons.
>
> "I've heard you're working on a book about the war," she said; "perhaps this can be of use to you." She handed me her diary from the occupation. I read:
>
> March 15. Mascha dead. Minus 25 degrees Celsius in the room. 125 grams of bread.
> March 16. Petrof dead. Minus 29 degrees. 120 grams of bread.
> March 18. Minus 25 degrees. Went through *Anna Karenina* at night.
> March 20. All night *Madame Bovary*.
> March 21. All night *Quietly Flows the River Don*.
>
> When she returned to pick up her diary as arranged, I asked, "How could you read at night with the power out?" She answered, "I didn't read. I just went over the books I could remember in my mind."
>
> They often ask *why* we won the war. Some say it was because our courage is so enormous. Others: It was because we are a people of wild Tartars. Others: It was because the Americans sent us grenades and canned goods. I think it was because we've given our people good books to read!

In this book you will encounter the viewpoint that stories are not just for entertainment—they have the power of revealing truths about ourselves, of helping us set directions and choose role models, and of debating the entire question of the nature of right and wrong. In his little account from the end of World War II, Ehrenburg shows his appreciation for stories as survival mechanisms: If we, in troubled times, can remember stories and hold on to their lessons about humanity, then we have a weapon against despair. This point is made in Ray Bradbury's *Fahrenheit 451* (1953); the title refers to the temperature at which paper burns. In the future, according to the story, there will be no more books because the government considered the ability to read and to understand a written narrative a dangerous path toward dissent. The fire department does not put out fires but sets them whenever a secret stash of books has been found; the owner of the books is usually executed. However, a small group of people who love books escape to create their own society, a society of books, in the wilderness; there will be no books on paper, but each person memorizes a work of world literature and becomes a living book, in the hope that the day may come when the world will once again listen to stories.

Martha Nussbaum: Living Other Lives

For the greater part of the twentieth century most Western philosophers had a tacit agreement that stories were best left in the nursery, but times have changed: There is now a growing interest in the cultural and philosophical importance of storytelling, in technological as well as pretechnological cultures, and stories are becoming shortcuts to understanding ourselves on an individual as well as a cultural level. One of the most influential voices speaking for narratives as a way to communicate about values is Martha Nussbaum (b. 1947), a philosopher and professor of law and ethics; her main interest is not the intellectual value of storytelling as much as the emotional force of narratives.

Nussbaum believes there was a time when philosophers understood the value of narratives. The Greek thinker Aristotle (whom she greatly admires) believed that experiencing a drama unfold teaches the viewer basic important lessons about having the proper feelings at the proper time — lessons about life and virtue in general. As modern Western philosophy took shape, however, the idea of emotions seemed increasingly irrelevant. There are signs today that philosophy is making a turnaround, that it is allowing itself to take a closer look at emotions as a legitimate subject for research. Nussbaum contributes to this turnaround with her books *Love's Knowledge* (1990) and *Upheavals of Thought: The Intelligence of Emotions* (2001). She points out that emotions weren't excluded from philosophy because they did not yield *knowledge;* in other words, it is not because of any lack of *cognitive value* that philosophers have refused to investigate emotions. There is actually much cognitive value in emotions, for emotions are, on the whole, quite *reasonable* when we look at them in context. When do we feel anger? When we believe that someone has deliberately injured us or someone we care about — in other words, when we feel the situation warrants it. Feelings such as disappointment, elation, grief, and even love are all responses to certain situations. They develop according to some inner logic; they don't strike at random. How do we know? Because if we realize that we were wrong about the situation, our anger slowly disappears. Perhaps love is not that easy to analyze — people in love don't seem to respond all that logically to situations that ought to change their feelings of love. (The person you love is seeing someone else, and what do you do? Continue to be helplessly in love.) But even love responds to such challenges in a way; we probably realize that our feelings are, somehow, out of place.

Why, then, have so many philosophers refused to deal seriously with emotions? Not because emotions lack cognitive value, but because they show we react to situations outside our control: When we are emotional, we are not *self-sufficient,* and

Martha Nussbaum (b. 1947), American philosopher. The author of *Love's Knowledge* and *Upheavals of Thought,* she suggests that novels are supremely well suited to explore moral problems. Through novels we have the chance to live more than our own lives and to understand human problems from someone else's point of view. Since others can read the same novels, we can share such knowledge and reach a mutual understanding.

most philosophers have, according to Nussbaum, preferred to investigate a more autonomous part of the human character, our reason. (Of course some philosophers and psychoanalysts have pointed out that reason is not immune to outside influence, either, but Nussbaum is addressing the trends in traditional philosophy before the twentieth century, when the idea of reason being affected by the Unconscious was not yet commonly accepted.)

For Nussbaum, emotions provide access to values, to human relationships, and to understanding ourselves, so they must be investigated. And where do they manifest themselves most clearly? In narratives. Stories are actually emotions put into a structure. When we are children and adolescents we learn how to manipulate objects and relate to others; we learn cognitive skills and practical skills, and among the skills we learn are when to feel certain kinds of emotions. The prime teacher of emotions is the story. This means, of course, that different societies may tell different stories teaching different lessons, so we must retain a certain amount of social awareness and social criticism when reading stories from any culture, including our own. People in their formative years are not just empty vessels into which stories are poured. Nussbaum maintains there is no rule saying that people must accept everything their culture teaches them; so if someone doesn't approve of the stories being told or thinks the stories haven't been told right, he or she will begin to tell his or her own stories.

To understand emotions we must read stories, but that ought to come easily to us, Nussbaum believes, since we already enjoy doing just that. She does stress, however, that we have to read the entire story, not just rely on a synopsis. There is an integral relationship between the form and the content of a story. As she says in her book *Love's Knowledge,* we can't skip "the emotive appeal, the absorbing plottedness, the variety and indeterminacy of good fiction" without losing the heart of the experience. So in a sense Nussbaum does not specifically advocate *using stories to illustrate moral problems,* as we will be doing in this book. Instead, she supports reading stories as a way of *sharing basic experiences of values* and using philosophy as a tool for analyzing this experience. For her, the story comes first, and then the analysis can follow.

Why use stories, though? Why can't we approach moral issues by more traditional avenues, such as examples that are "made to order" by philosophers? Because, says Nussbaum, they lack precisely the rich texture that makes the story an experience we can relate to. Besides, such examples are formulated in such a way that the conclusion is obvious. Novels tend to be quite open-ended, a feature that Nussbaum believes is valuable. Novels preserve "mystery and indeterminacy," just like real life.

Why not just rely on your own experiences to learn about life? Some of them must certainly contain both mystery and indeterminacy. To some extent we do that already; we draw on our own experience as much as we possibly can when judging concrete and abstract cases. But the trouble is, one human life is just not enough for understanding the myriad ways of being. As Nussbaum says,

> We have never lived enough. Our experience is, without fiction, too confined and too parochial. Literature extends it, making us reflect and feel about what might otherwise be too distant for feeling. . . . All living is interpreting; all action requires seeing the world *as* something. So in this sense no life is "raw" and . . . throughout our living we are, in a sense, makers of fictions. The point is that in the activity of literary imagining we are led to imagine and describe with greater precision, focusing our attention on each word, feeling each event more keenly—whereas much of actual life goes by without that heightened awareness, and is thus, in a certain sense, not fully or thoroughly lived.

Furthermore, it is much harder to talk about events in your own life than it is to discuss events in a story. We may not want to share our deepest feelings, or we may not be able to express them. But if we talk with friends about a passage in a favorite book or film, we can share both an emotional and a moral experience.

Study Questions

1. In your opinion, should children learn values in elementary school? Explain why or why not, and craft an argument for and against the idea as it might be presented by a teacher and a parent.

2. Give three examples of statements about moral issues, illustrating three logical fallacies.

3. Do you remember a story that has made a moral choice easier for you? Explain.

4. Comment on Nussbaum's statement, "We have never lived enough. Our experience is, without fiction, too confined and too parochial. Literature expands it, making us reflect and feel about what might otherwise be too distant for feeling." What does she mean? Do you agree? Why or why not?

5. Consider the multicultural challenge of storytelling. Do you remember any story that has enhanced your understanding of another culture? Do you remember any story from your own culture that expresses a moral you find unacceptable? Do you know any story from another culture whose moral you find unacceptable? Is it possible to find some common ground? Explain.

Primary Reading and Narratives

The Primary Reading is from *Love's Knowledge* by Martha Nussbaum, emphasizing the moral lessons learned by reading stories. The first Narrative is a summary of *Smoke Signals*, a film about two young American Indian men who understand their reality in very different ways: one through stereotypes, the other through stories. The second Narrative is a summary of a novel by Salman Rushdie about the power of stories to change and save lives and possibly even the world: *Haroun and the Sea of Stories*.

 Primary Reading

Love's Knowledge

MARTHA NUSSBAUM

Excerpt, 1990.

In this excerpt, Nussbaum argues that novels, short stories, and dramas are very well suited to providing an emotional lesson in moral issues, because of the brevity of human life: We just can't experience everything ourselves, so fiction provides a shortcut to understanding the range of human emotions. She also explains why such philosophical examples as those you will encounter in this book (such as Kant's example of the killer at the door looking for your friend) aren't good enough to teach the same lesson. You may want to consider why Nussbaum's argument omits the mention of movies — is it deliberate or an oversight?

Not only novels prove appropriate, because (again, with reference only to these particular issues and this conception) many serious dramas will be pertinent as well, and some biographies and histories — so long as these are written in a style that gives sufficient attention to particularity and emotion, and so long as they involve their readers in relevant activities of searching and feeling, especially feeling concerning their own possibilities as well as those of the characters. [. . .]

But the philosopher is likely to be less troubled by these questions of literary genre than by a prior question: namely, why a literary work at all? Why can't we investigate everything we want to investigate by using complex examples of the sort that moral philosophers are very good at inventing? In reply, we must insist that the philosopher who asks this question cannot have been convinced by the argument so far about the intimate connection between literary form and ethical content. Schematic philosophers' examples almost always lack the particularity, the emotive appeal, the absorbing plottedness, the variety and indeterminacy, of good fiction; they lack, too, good fiction's way of making the reader a participant and a friend; and we have argued that it is precisely in virtue of these structural characteristics that fiction can play the role it does in our reflective lives. As [novelist Henry] James says, "The picture of the exposed and entangled state is what is required." If the examples do have these features, they will, themselves, be works of literature. Sometimes a very brief fiction will prove a sufficient vehicle for the investigation of what we are at that moment investigating; sometimes, as in "Flawed Crystals" (where our question concerns what is likely to happen in the course of a relatively long and complex life), we need the length and complexity of a novel. In neither case, however, would schematic examples prove sufficient as a substitute. (This does not mean that they will be totally dismissed; for they have other sorts of usefulness, especially in connection with other ethical views.)

We can add that examples, setting things up schematically, signal to the readers what they should notice and find relevant. They hand them the ethically salient description. This means that much of the ethical work is already done, the result "cooked." The novels are more open-ended, showing the reader what it is to search for the appropriate description and why that search matters. (And yet they are not so open-ended as to give no shape to the reader's thought.) By showing the mystery and indeterminacy of "our actual adventure," they characterize life more richly and truly—indeed, more precisely—than an example lacking those features ever could; and they engender in the reader a type of ethical work more appropriate for life.

But why not life itself? Why can't we investigate whatever we want to investigate by living and reflecting on our lives? Why, if it is the Aristotelian ethical conception we wish to scrutinize, can't we do that without literary texts, without texts at all—or, rather, with the texts of our own lives set before us? Here, we must first say that of course we do this as well, both apart from our reading of the novels and (as [French novelist Marcel] Proust insists) in the process of reading. In a sense Proust is right to see the literary text as an "optical instrument" through which the reader becomes a reader of his or her own heart. But, why do we need, in that case, such optical instruments?

One obvious answer was suggested already by Aristotle: we have never lived enough. Our experience is, without fiction, too confined and too parochial. Literature extends it, making us reflect and feel about what might otherwise be too distant for feeling. The importance of this for both morals and politics cannot be underestimated. *The Princess Casamassima* [1886, a novel by Henry James]—justly, in my view—depicts the imagination of the novel-reader as a type that is very valuable in the political (as well as the private) life, sympathetic to a wide range of concerns, averse to certain denials of humanity. It cultivates these sympathies in its readers.

We can clarify and extend this point by emphasizing that novels do not function, inside this account, as pieces of "raw" life: they are a close and careful interpretative description. All living is interpreting; all action requires seeing the world *as* something. So in this sense no life is "raw," and (as James and Proust insist) throughout our living we are, in a sense, makers of fictions. The point is that in the activity of literary imagining we are led to imagine and describe with greater precision, focusing our attention on each word, feeling each event more keenly—whereas much of actual life goes by without that heightened awareness, and is thus, in a certain sense, not fully or thoroughly lived. Neither James nor Proust thinks of ordinary life as normative, and the Aristotelian conception concurs: too much of it is obtuse, routinized, incompletely sentient. So literature is an extension of life not only horizontally, bringing the reader into contact with events or locations or persons or problems he or she has not otherwise met, but also, so to speak, vertically, giving the reader experience that is deeper, sharper, and more precise than much of what takes place in life.

Study Questions

1. Is Nussbaum right that philosophical examples don't work as well as fictional stories when it comes to conveying a moral point? Why or why not?

2. What does she mean by "no life is 'raw'"?

3. Should her theory include the use of films? Why or why not?

Narrative

Smoke Signals

SHERMAN ALEXIE (SCREENWRITER)
CHRIS EYRE (DIRECTOR)

Film, 1998. Summary. Based on the short story collection by Sherman Alexie,
The Lone Ranger and Tonto Fistfight in Heaven.

Thomas and Victor are young Coeur d'Alene Indians living on the reservation in Idaho in the late 1990s. They grew up together and share the story of one fateful night when they were babies. On that night Thomas's parents' house burned down, with Thomas, his parents, and Victor inside. Someone saved Victor, and Thomas's parents threw their baby to safety out the second-story window while they themselves burned to death. Thomas was caught in midair by Victor's father, Arnold. Since then, Thomas has lived with his grandmother.

Not much happens on the reservation; everyone knows each other, and the height of excitement seems to be playing basketball at the gym. One of the young Indians remarks, "Sometimes it is a good day to die — other times it is a good day to play basketball." Sometimes they watch Westerns on TV and discuss whether the cowboys always win or whether the Indians sometimes win. Thomas remarks, with a grin, that there is nothing more pathetic than Indians on TV — except Indians watching Indians on TV!

Thomas is a seer and a storyteller; everything he has experienced in his short life turns into stories — and his stories contain a considerable amount of pure fantasy, too. This irritates Victor, who wants him just to tell the truth. Much about Thomas irritates Victor: Thomas braids his long hair very tightly; Victor wears his long hair free-flowing. Thomas always wears a dark three-piece suit, whereas Victor wears blue jeans and T-shirts. And Victor cultivates a warrior's inscrutable face, whereas Thomas has a ready smile for everyone. What irritates Victor most is Thomas's stories about Victor's father, Arnold. Victor knows him as a man who got drunk and beat him and his mother. Thomas sees Arnold as his hero, a magic man — the man who not only saved his life but also took him to a breakfast at Denny's in Spokane once. They met on the footbridge across the Spokane Falls, and somehow Thomas has associated Arnold with that spot ever since; it has become a power place to him. But Arnold is no longer around for Thomas to tell new stories about—he left his family in anger when Victor was a child.

Their quiet life is interrupted by a phone call from Phoenix: A woman named Suzy calls Victor's mother, with the news that Arnold is dead. He lived in a trailer close to her, and his things are still there, including his truck. Someone needs to get him and his belongings. Victor is reluctant to go because he harbors immense resentment toward his father for leaving him, but Thomas puts up the money for the ticket from his piggy bank under one condition: that he gets to go to Phoenix, too.

On the bus, Thomas and Victor have a variety of encounters with the world of the whites, not all of them pleasant. For instance, a pair of rednecks take their seats and force them to move. But Victor is not very pleasant, either. He calls a young girl a liar for embellishing on her one life story: her near chance of going to the Olympics. And he gets on Thomas's case for not knowing how to be an Indian: He must have watched *Dances with Wolves* two hundred times, says Victor, and he still doesn't know how to act like he's come home from the buffalo hunt. Thomas protests that their people weren't buffalo hunters but fishermen. Victor replies that there is nothing glorious about coming home from fishing—the movie wasn't called "Dances with Salmon"!—and we get a sense that perhaps it is Victor, not Thomas, who feels uncomfortable about his role and his culture.

After days of traveling nonstop they finally arrive in Phoenix and walk to the desert hideout of Arnold and Suzy. She turns out to be a hospital administrator and much younger than Arnold, but for years she has had a close relationship with him—"We kept each other's secrets," she says. The three of them share her frybread, traditional American Indian fare, and Thomas tells a wonderful story of how Victor's mother fed a hundred Indians with only fifty frybreads—which turns out to be not quite true, although it is a good story. Suzy has heard about Victor and Thomas and all the basketball games Arnold played with Victor. And she has heard the true story about the night of the fire. What had haunted Arnold for all those years was that he set the fire by accident in a drunken stupor. But now that Victor hears the truth, he also hears something he dares not believe: that it was Arnold who ran back into the burning house to save him. For years, Victor has resented Thomas for being the one saved by Arnold. And now he has to revise all his resentments. Coming face-to-face with the loss of his father, Victor grieves in the traditional Indian way: He cuts his long hair.

The next morning, Victor and Thomas leave in Arnold's truck, taking with them only Arnold's ashes and his basketball. Victor is in a panicked, angry rush to get home, but there is yet another trial ahead for him. Late that night, on a dark desert road, he and Thomas crash the truck, barely avoiding ramming into two cars that had collided moments before the boys' arrival. The driver of the car that caused the accident, a white man, is drunk and obnoxious, and his wife is desperately apologetic. But down in the ravine is an injured woman, and the nearest town is twenty miles away. Victor's truck is disabled, but he doesn't hesitate for a moment: He must run for help. And he starts out running into the night, with the long stride of his ancestor warriors. He runs until his side hurts and his vision blurs, and by dawn he collapses. But he is close enough to a town to be seen by a road repair crew, and he gets the message about the injured motorist through.

As Victor and the motorist—who would have died if it hadn't been for his heroic run—are recovering in the hospital, Thomas is standing by, and we can tell that he has the material for many future stories. One woman says they are heroes, coming to the rescue just like the Lone Ranger and Tonto — and the boys answer that they're more like Tonto and Tonto. One snag develops, though: The man who caused the accident has filed false charges against the boys for assault and causing the accident, and Victor and Thomas are taken to the police station. All the old fear and resentment of the white power structure descend on the boys, who feel they won't be believed — but not everyone outside the reservation is like the drunken white driver. His wife, for one, has issued a statement against her husband, and the two women who were in the other car side with the boys, too. And the police chief is a man of good sense and sends the boys on their way.

Six days after leaving Idaho, Victor and Thomas are back with Arnold's ashes. The one who has undergone the most profound change is Victor; he now understands that his dad never planned to leave, and that he just hadn't gotten around to going home yet. Now he understands the ghosts his father lived with year after year. So he barely picks on Thomas anymore and even offers him the deepest gesture he can think of: He shares his father's ashes with him. At last, Victor gets to scatter Arnold's ashes where both he and Thomas feel Arnold's spirit belongs: over the Spokane Falls.

Study Questions

1. What do you think made Victor come to terms with his father's disappearance and death? How has Victor changed? Why didn't Thomas change as much?

2. Thomas can make any mundane situation into an interesting, magical time by telling stories about it — but the stories are not always true. Is this morally acceptable? Why or why not?

3. Why do Western movies play such a big role in Thomas's and Victor's lives? Do you think it is a positive or a negative role?

4. What is funny about the boys' remark that they are more like Tonto and Tonto?

Narrative

Haroun and the Sea of Stories

SALMAN RUSHDIE

Novel, 1990. Summary.

In this story we encounter storytelling as a means of saving your identity, your relationship with your family, and perhaps even your life — which means that, in a sense, you are saving a world. The British-Indian author Salman Rushdie (b. 1947) had to go underground after the publication of his novel *The Satanic Verses* in 1988. The book was considered blasphemous to Islam by the fundamentalist government of Iran, which issued a death warrant against him. He says that he reached a point where he was so distressed he wasn't able to think of any stories to tell. But he worked himself out of his depression, and *Haroun and the Sea of Stories,* a book for children and other people who have a natural love for stories, is the result. This modern fairy tale has many surprising elements, but here we will focus just on the core issue: why stories have value.

Haroun's father Rashid is a professional storyteller and a very popular one. He usually tells cheerful stories, even though they live in a very sad city. Haroun is beginning to ask questions about his father's storytelling: Where do the stories come from? From the great Story Sea, says Rashid, and you have to be a subscriber to the water, which comes from a tap installed by one of the Water-Genies. But Haroun doesn't believe him. And now a sad thing happens in their lives: Haroun's mother Soraya with the beautiful voice leaves her husband and child for another tenant in their apartment building, Mr. Sengupta, who once told Haroun, *What's the use of stories that aren't even true?* Rashid is at a loss for what to do, because all he knows is storytelling, and now Haroun himself shouts the terrible words at his father, *What's the use of stories that aren't even true?* Soon after, in front of a huge audience in a city in the mountains, Rashid finds that he has lost the gift of gab: He has run out of stories. His stories are finito, *khattam-shud* (which means over and done with, the words all stories end with in Haroun's language).

Distressed, Rashid and Haroun go back to their hotel. But Rashid doesn't like his room, and Haroun doesn't like his, either, so they switch rooms. And this is why, in the night, Haroun witnesses a strangely clad little character tinkering with something in the bathroom that was supposed to be his father's: A Water-Genie from the Sea of Stories is turning off the story tap. Confronted by Haroun, he explains that Rashid ordered it so, subconsciously. Haroun points out that his father can still tell stories without any tapwater, and the Water-Genie answers, "Anyone can tell stories . . . Liars, and cheats and crooks, for example. But for stories with that Extra Ingredient, ah, for those, even the best storytellers need the Story Waters." Now Haroun begs to be taken to whoever decided to cut off his father's Story Water supply, so he can set the matter straight, and he steals the Disconnecting Tool as a bargaining chip. The Water-Genie agrees to take him to Gup City in Kahani to get the matter resolved, this instant.

At the end of a long journey Haroun is surprised to find that Kahani (which means story) is an undiscovered moon circling the earth, and on this moon is the Sea of Stories. Flying over the sea with the Water-Genie, he sees all the brilliant strands of all the stories in the world intertwining and constantly changing. And the Genie gives him a wish-drink that is supposed to set things straight with his father's storytelling, but all the boy can think about is how sad he is that his mother has left him; he can't concentrate on his father's problem at all. So now the moment for wishing has passed, and he must try something else. But the Water-Genie is now distracted, because a problem has come up: Someone is polluting the Sea of Stories, and he suspects the leader of the Land of Chup, a land in perpetual darkness on the other side of the moon. The leader's name is Khattam-Shud.

Going with the Genie to Gup City, Haroun finds, to his surprise, that his father is already there—he has made use of a home brew to travel to faraway places and is now being accused of being a spy for the Chupwalas. Rashid is able to explain the situation because he landed in the Twilite area and heard interesting things, and now they learn about the evil intent of Khattam-Shud: Not only is he opposed to stories and fantasies, he also wants to do away with *speech* altogether and has enforced strict Silence Laws.

Haroun and a few helpers from Gup now travel into the twilight and on to the dark land of Chup, where shadows have acquired a life of their own, and through many dangers and adventures they reach the heart of the Chup empire, a Factory Ship that makes poison to spill into the Sea of Stories. Khattam-Shud's plan is to block the very source of stories with a plug and spread silence and darkness. Finally they see Khattam-Shud himself, and Haroun is rather surprised: He is a scrawny, skinny, weasly type, and he looks a lot like Mr. Sengupta, who stole his mother away. And when he actually says, "What's the use of stories that aren't even true?" Haroun is certain that he is the same man — but when Khattam-Shud inflates himself and becomes a monster to prove a point, the boy realizes that this creature is much more than just Mr. Sengupta. And now we hear why Khattam-Shud wants to destroy storytelling. Haroun asks, "But why do you hate stories so much? . . . Stories are fun."

> "The world, however, is not for Fun," Khattam-Shud replied. "The world is for Controlling."
>
> "Which world?" Haroun made himself ask.
>
> "Your world, my world, all worlds," came the reply. "They are all there to be Ruled. And inside every single story, inside every Stream in the Ocean, there lies a world, a story-world, that I cannot Rule at all. And that is the reason why."

But Haroun has one weapon: the bottle of wish-water that he didn't get to use the first time around. Now he wishes for the sun to shine on Chup and melt all the shadows, including Khattam-Shud and his ship, and it happens. The Chupwala people are freed from darkness, and the Sea of Stories will be clean again. Haroun is offered a reward by the leader of Gup, but all he wants is a happy ending. The leader explains that there are very few happy endings, even in stories, and that they have to come at the end; if they happen in the middle of a story, all they do is cheer things up for a while. . . . Haroun's father's supply of Story Water is restored, and together they travel back to earth where they wake, in their beds just in time for Rashid to go to his evening engagement and tell stories, for his gift is now back: He tells the story of Haroun and the Sea of Stories, and the people find it so inspiring that they kick out the most obnoxious of their own leaders.

And so Rashid and Haroun go home, to another surprise: Soraya, Haroun's mother, has returned. She made a mistake, she says, and now she is back. And Sengupta? Well, he is all over and done with, he is *khattam-shud!*

Study Questions

1. Comment on Khattam-Shud's remark that inside a story lies a world that can't be controlled. Why is that important?

2. Is this a story for children? Why or why not?

3. What do you think the author had in mind with Khattam-Shud and his Silence Laws? Do we have to know Rushdie's personal history for the story to make sense, or does the story have a broader application?

4. If you are familiar with the classic Arab collection of stories *Arabian Nights*, the names of Haroun and Rashid may sound familiar to you. Their last name is Khalifa. What do you think the author meant by creating such a connection?

Chapter Two

Learning Moral Lessons from Stories

We may think that the most powerful moral lessons are learned from events in our childhood (when we are caught doing something we aren't supposed to do, or when we *aren't* caught), but chances are the most powerful lessons we carry with us are lessons we learn from the *stories* we have read or that were read to us.

Didactic Stories

Many of you may recognize this typical, unpleasant event from childhood: Your authority figure takes you aside to tell you Aesop's fable "The Boy Who Cried Wolf." A lad was tending sheep at the outskirts of town, and he thought it might be fun to give the village a scare, so he cried, "The wolf is here! The wolf is here!" And the villagers came running, but there was no wolf. The boy tricked the town again and again, until that fateful day when the wolf really did come. The boy cried for his life, "The wolf is here!" but nobody believed him anymore. The wolf ate the sheep and the shepherd too. At least this is the way the story was told to me when I was five years old.

Why are children told such a gruesome story? Because adults deem it necessary to teach children a moral lesson. Even a child understands the message: "The shepherd boy lied and suffered the consequences. You don't want to be like him, do you?" It is a powerful lesson. Indeed, the appeal of the story seems to go beyond European and American traditions: I have a colleague from India who tells me that when she was a little girl in Calcutta, she was told the story of the boy who cried tiger.

When discussing stories that have made a moral impact on them, several of my students have brought up another story with a grim point: "The Wooden Spoon" (or, in another version, "The Woven Basket"). Old Grandpa lives on the farm with his son and the son's family. The old man makes a terrible noise when he slurps his soup, because he has no teeth left. At the dinner table, the son irritably tells him to go sit in the corner with his soup because he isn't fit for human company anymore. The grandson hears everything, and after dinner he goes out in the woodshed and picks up some wood. When his father sees him whittling, he asks what he's making. The boy answers, "This is going to be a spoon for you, Dad, for when you get old and have to sit in the corner and eat your soup." Next time dinner is served, the son brings his old father back to the table to eat with the family. (The version called "The Woven Basket" is about Grandma, who is sent to the old folks' home in a basket, as tradition requires; the young granddaughter weaves a basket and tells her mother, "This is for you, when you grow old, Mother." And Grandma is brought back from

"The Boy Who Cried Wolf" embodies one of the most effective early moral lessons in many people's lives: If we make a habit out of lying, the chances are that we will not be believed when we are finally telling the truth.

the old folks' home.) This story mirrors the terrifying moral lesson of the epitaph I've seen in old Boston cemeteries: "Remember, friend, as you pass by/As you are now so once was I/As I am now so you shall be/Prepare thyself to follow me." In addition, it is a lesson in the Golden Rule: Would you yourself like to be treated the way you are actually treating others?

Stories that are told to teach a moral lesson are called *didactic* stories. These instructional stories may well be as old as humanity. When giving a keynote address about stories in ethics at a philosophical retreat in Denmark some years ago, I asked the audience, a mixed group of several hundred people ranging from their teens to their eighties, if they had been told the story of "The Boy Who Cried Wolf" when they were kids; a forest of hands went up, young smooth hands alongside gnarled old hands, and all of a sudden it seemed to me that I was looking down the corridor of time, from these living generations backwards to the other generations long gone, each one of them telling their children about the lying shepherd boy—in all likelihood a story so old that it predates Aesop's version.

The New Interest in Stories

The interest in using stories (narratives) to explore moral problems is increasing today, for stories can serve as a laboratory in which moral solutions can be tried out before any decisions are made. Here are some examples of how stories are being used as moral laboratories today.

- Many psychologists are advocating a method they call "bibliotherapy" to facilitate communication between parents and children. Through reading stories with their children, parents may find it easier to explain difficult issues because together, through the fictional universe, they can explore issues and emotions that might be more difficult to approach on either an abstract or a highly personal level. For example, it's hard to explain death to children—either as a concept or as a real event in a family. Perhaps a story about the death of a pet could help focus the discussion. Of course, this may be just an easy way out for parents who don't have a clue how to relate to their children, but ideally the sharing of stories is a positive way to make the child understand about arrivals of new siblings, a move to a new home, deaths in the family, and other traumatic events. (It may sound like a brand-new idea, but in the next section you will see that this is in effect how myths and fairy tales used to work in traditional societies.)

- Medical students in many parts of this country are now exposed not only to case studies that involve medical ethics but also to stories of fiction, such as Leo Tolstoy's "The Death of Iván Ilyich" (1886) and the 1994 film *Philadelphia*, that deal with medical problems. The students seem to feel better equipped to deal with "real" problems because of this exploratory background. Why? Because no matter how many case histories she examines or how many colleagues she talks to, a medical student may not be able to understand a patient from the inside quite as well as when a great writer tells the story from the patient's point of view. The New York University School of Medicine's Literature, Arts, and Medicine Database is a website dedicated to listing films and works of literature that may be of help as a resource for medical personnel, such as *And the Band Played On, Awakenings, Gattaca, Lorenzo's Oil, The English Patient,* Christy Brown's *My Left Foot,* Camus's *The Plague,* and Jane Austen's *Emma.* The Literature and Medicine program in Maine has since 1997 gathered health care professionals around the concept that reading and discussing literature can improve their professional skills and help them understand their patients and clients better.

- Patients have been encouraged to use movies as a sort of treatment. In the February 2000 issue of *Psychology Today* magazine, an article titled "Reel Therapy" explored the psychological benefits that may come from watching the right movie at the right time. The story noted that doctors assign certain films to help patients come to terms with their situation or discover a new side to themselves. Unfortunately, it gave some readers the impression that watching a movie would solve their problems. Have emotional injuries in need of healing? Rent *The Horse Whisperer.* Hopelessly cynical about modern life? Then see *Shakespeare in Love.* It doesn't quite work that way in real life, and not in this book, either! If we want

Psychologists are beginning to tap the therapeutic potential of movies — but of course merely watching movies will not solve one's emotional or moral problems.

to delve into moral issues in depth, we have to get beyond the sound bites and quick fixes. Good stories can help us begin to explore an issue — but they can't be a substitute for insight or discussion.

- The criminal justice system is experimenting with the use of stories. In a county in Massachusetts, the court is running a reading class as part of a rehabilitation program for certain inmates. They are each asked to read an American classic, such as Hemingway's *Old Man and the Sea,* and then they discuss the book in group sessions under the guidance of a literature professor. The mere exposure to the story of the old man and the giant fish caused several of these men (all male inmates) to rethink their own lives, because they had learned to see the story as a metaphor for some universal human problems. In Italy a judge sentenced a juvenile delinquent to read four novels in two months, in the hope that his moral outlook on life might be improved. In Winona, Minnesota, an eighteen-year-old was ordered to watch *Saving Private Ryan* as part of his sentence for vandalizing a park honoring veterans, because he had told the judge he didn't know what a veteran was. According to an Associated Press story, the young man thought the movie was "pretty cool."

- Psychotherapists are having patients tell about their own lives as if they were stories or asking them to select a famous fairy tale as a model or template of the way they see their own lives. The idea of telling one's own story as a form of therapy and moral education is something we will look at in detail at the end of the chapter.

- Stories have been found to have great potential for promoting cross-cultural or multicultural understanding. They can highlight cultural differences in a way that presents them as exciting and worth exploring, while emphasizing the fundamental human similarities underneath the surface differences.

- Last on this list, but not least: Some philosophers are beginning to look to stories as not only a way to explain difficult theories to their freshman students but also to explore the philosophical richness of literature and films in itself. Philosophers have for a long time been suspicious of using stories as illustrations of moral problems for several reasons. Some have felt that using stories would cause readers to be concerned with *specific* cases rather than with seeing the general picture. Others have worried that telling stories might manipulate readers' emotions instead of appealing to their reason: Such stories would perhaps lead people to *do* the right thing, but they wouldn't lead people to *think* about moral issues, because a story is not a logical argument but rather a persuasion—a story is not logic but rhetoric.

There is a difference, however, between stories that moralize and stories that discuss moral problems. In the past, philosophers seem to have assumed that stories illustrating moral problems are always of the moralizing kind. Now a different attitude seems to be growing among ethics scholars; they recognize that stories need not be moralizing in order to illustrate a moral point. Such stories may express a moral point of view, and then that point of view can be open for discussion. Or a story may have an open-ended conclusion, one in which the moral issues are not resolved. Even moralizing stories may have their proper role to play from time to time, and stories are an excellent way to illustrate how difficult a moral problem can be. As noted in Chapter 1, the field of philosophy is also slowly warming up to the old idea that feelings are not irrelevant in moral discussions. The psychologist Carol Gilligan argues for the legitimacy of emotions in moral decision making. As you know, Martha Nussbaum points out that emotions are not a matter of something uncontrollable, like hunger, but instead involve decision making and rational choices. Another philosopher, Philip Hallie, states that without feelings for the victims of evildoing, we can't hope to understand what a moral sense is all about. Jonathan Bennett, another contemporary philosopher, insists that although certain moral principles may be admirable, others may be warped: The Nazi exterminators (members of the National Socialist German Worker's Party, 1920–1945) had firm moral principles, but they were principles most people don't approve of today. Without sympathy for other people, our principles may go astray. One of the ways in which we can engage both our sympathy and our moral principles is through stories.

Some of the stories in this book are didactic (they teach a lesson), and some of them are more open-ended. It seems that, usually, we prefer learning from stories that were *not* written especially to teach a lesson. This may be one of the secrets of literature: We may forgive a good story for preaching a little, but we can't forgive a bad story for preaching. In other words, we are most accepting of a moral lesson if it is not too obvious, if it appears only between the lines and is subordinate to the plot and the characters. The stories that are most effective in teaching lessons may be those that are not obviously intended to do so.

Of course, real-life events and discussions of these events are essential to our understanding of moral issues, but using stories is an alternate way of talking about these issues, because a story can serve as a slice of life that we are invited to share in.

The Value of Stories

The philosopher Alasdair MacIntyre finds the telling of stories so important for humans that he calls us "storytelling animals." There are many reasons for telling stories, for reading and writing novels and short stories, and for making and watching films. It seems that in early, pretechnological cultures the purpose of storytelling was twofold: On the *human* side, the purpose was to knit the tribe firmly together by setting up the rules and boundaries that would establish a group identity. Besides, storytelling helped to pass the time on rainy days, and it kept the children occupied for a while. On the *cosmic* side, the purpose was to establish the story of the beginning of time, when everything was created, so if a symbolic re-creation seemed necessary (and it did, periodically), one could tell and enact the "beginning" stories and in that way "renew" the cosmos. Storytelling has never been more important than it was in those ancient times, for in telling the story people helped re-create the universe, put the sun in its right place, and make sure that the seasons followed one another in the proper order.

The strength of storytelling is no less apparent in many religions. Periodically (usually once a year), believers remind themselves of an important time in the history of their religion: the creation of the world, the creation of the religion itself, or the establishment of the believers' identity through a religious event. Usually a story is told about this event, and even if it is supposed to be a reminder rather than a re-creation, it is still a sacred and powerful vehicle.

In ancient times the storytellers were the primary teachers of morals. Of course, parents have always had a hand in moral education, but in pretechnological cultures (what used to be called "primitive" cultures), those who knew the legends were the ones who, in effect, represented the social institutions of religion, school, and government. The myths surrounding the origin of the world, of society, of food items, and of love and death and the stories of the important men and women in the tribe's past provided rules for the tribe to live by—moral structures that could be used in everyday life to make decisions about crops, marriages, warfare, and so forth. The way to teach children how to become good members of the tribe was to tell the old stories.

In our technological world we no longer have such a body of ready-made prescriptions for moral conduct—at least we don't think we do. In fact, however, we still tell stories, we still listen to stories, and we still take moral lessons from them. Some people read the Bible, the Torah, the Koran, or other religious books and seek comfort in their stories of human frailty and perseverance. Some people keep their childhood comic book collections and dive into the old stories from time to time for some basic moral reinforcement (see the rabbit outwit the fox; see the bad guy get blasted; see Robin Hood be vindicated once again). Some people read biographies of remarkable men and women and are inspired by the stories of courage and bravery. Adults may not read fairy tales anymore, but we read novels—classics, bestsellers, or science fiction. And if we don't read novels, we go to the movies or watch TV. Wherever we turn we find *stories*—some are real and some fictional, some are too outdated or too radical for us to relate to, but we find at least some stories that have served as our moral guideposts. Even if you are not a great reader or movie-goer, you probably can recall at least one story that has moved you.

Stories Past and Present

Fact, Fiction, or Both?

In the secular world we usually tell stories of two kinds: those that we believe to be historically true and those that we know never took place but that have their own special truth to them, a *poetic* truth. The fairy tale "Little Red Riding Hood" is not a historical account, but children may enjoy it if they are old enough to deal with their fear of the wolf, who comes to a gruesome end. Parents enjoy telling it, because they can smuggle home a lesson: Don't talk to strangers, and watch out for "wolves" in disguise.

What about accounts that we don't know to be either historical or poetic? The story of Zorro, for example, is not a historical account, although there may have been an outlaw in Old California who vaguely resembled the Zorro character. Some readers feel cheated if they find out that a story is more legend than history, but others find it all the more fascinating because it is a mixture of what we think happened and what we wish had happened. It may not tell us much about history, but it tells us a lot about people, including ourselves, who *wish* that Zorro were real.

Even stories that we believe to be factual, such as the story of the battle of the Alamo or the sinking of the *Titanic,* are not usually simple reports of facts; such stories must have a beginning, a middle, and an ending, and most often we choose the beginning and the ending according to what we feel makes the most *sense.* In actual life, the stream of events goes on, usually with little indication that here begins something new or here a story comes to an end—except in the case of someone's birth or death. Even in the latter case, the story goes on without the person who has died. So even "true" stories have an element of *poetic creativity,* in that we choose what to include in the story, what is *relevant* to the story (not every meal or visit to the bathroom is important in order for us to understand the life and times of Gandhi, or James Dean, or Princess Diana), and where to begin and end the story. Even eyewitness accounts, often regarded as the one true record of events, are full of creativity. Two persons observing the same event will very likely come up with slightly different versions of it; they notice different things because they are standing in different spots and because they are different people with different interests in life. If eyewitnesses are asked to tell about an event long past, some of their memories will be sharper than others, some will mirror exactly what they saw, and some will mirror what they felt or what they feel now, which turns their stories into personal interpretations of the event. At best, any account of a past event can only approximate what happened. We can never truly reproduce the event.

Religious legends reveal the same tension between fact and fiction. If believers suspect that events described in the legends never happened or that they happened in a different and more "everyday" way than is described in the religious text, they may experience a general disappointment with their religion, feeling that it is based on stories that have no foundation in fact. Other believers, however, may see the stories as being rich with poetry and telling human truths that are on a higher, more spiritual level. Aristotle, who was intensely interested in the relationship between history and poetry, said that history may deal with facts, but poetry deals with Truth.

Traditional Stories

Myths   We don't know anything about the first stories ever told, but if we are to judge from ancient myths and legends, there is a good chance that they served as reminders of proper conduct. The Cherokees tell of Grandmother Spider's way of making clay pots, and it seems to be (among other things) a lesson for Cherokee women in how to make pots the correct way. Myths in general have two main purposes: to strengthen the social bonding among people and to fortify the individual psychologically. *Traditional myths* work on both levels at once by presenting stories of gods, goddesses, and culture heroes who tell their society about the ideal social behavior and individuals about the proper role models to follow. In a sense, traditional myths are a successful combination of *ethics of conduct* and *virtue ethics* (see Parts 2 and 3). The philosopher Peter Muntz calls myths "concrete universals," stories that in a very concrete form tell about the human condition and give us courage to deal with the troubles that being human usually entails.

The myth of the loss of immortality told by the Trobriand people of New Guinea is such a story. It tells us that once humans could rejuvenate themselves; they could shed their skins and become young again. A grandmother took her granddaughter to the river and then went off by herself to shed her skin. When she came back, the granddaughter didn't recognize her (she appeared to be a young girl) and shooed her away. Upset, the grandmother went back and put her old skin on again. The granddaughter told her that she had chased a young girl, an impostor, away. The grandmother said, "Just because you refused to recognize me, nobody will be able to be young again. We shall all die of old age now." Aside from the fact that the story unfairly places the immense burden of causing humanity to die on an ignorant young girl—myths often blame a major disaster on a small event, as when Eve eats the fruit from the Tree of Knowledge—the lesson is that we humans are mortal and there is nothing we can do about it. The story also seems to say that humans, far from being victims, are very important beings since they can cause such a cosmic calamity as the loss of immortality!

Fairy Tales   Another ancient category of stories with moral lessons is the *fairy tale*. The fairy tales collected by the Grimm brothers in early-nineteenth-century Germany reflect what is probably a very old tradition of normative ethics, and they are not just for children; the stories were told originally to both young and old. The Trobriand people distinguish between three different kinds of stories. First, there are the "myths," which are sacred stories about the beginning of the world and of society. They must be taken very seriously. Second, there are the "true legends," semihistorical accounts of heroes in the past and their travels. They are supposed to be taken at face value, for the most part. Last, there are the "fairy tales," stories to be told in the rainy season, usually with some point of teaching the young about the customs of the people but also with the intent of pure entertainment. They are recognized as never having happened.

Most cultures acknowledge that there is a difference between stories in which the good get rewarded and the bad get punished and stories of everyday life. The fairy tale has been described by psychoanalysts as pure wishful thinking, but many fairy tales involve gruesome events that are hardly wish fulfillments, because they often happen to characters who don't "deserve" them. Such events do serve a purpose, though, in making the punishment of the bad characters seem justified.

In spite of its enormous popularity, the tale of Little Red Riding Hood seems to be a product of the literary elite and not of folklore, but that doesn't detract from its didactic power. "Hansel and Gretel" is a folklore classic with much the same lesson: Don't go with strangers, and don't let them feed you candy! There are also more obscure Grimm stories, such as "The Maiden Without Hands," in which a pious girl's tears fall on her hands and prevent the Devil from taking her, so her father, tricked by the Devil, chops her hands off; but she cries on the stumps, so the Devil leaves her alone, and an angel gives her silver hands. When she is finally reunited with her beloved, she even gets her own hands back. What is the lesson here? That purity and piety carry their own reward? There are, of course, stories that teach a different lesson: In "The Juniper Tree," the stepmother kills, cooks, and serves the baby brother up for dinner. His father loves the stew but doesn't know he is eating his own son. The boy's older sister Marjory (who knows about the evil deed) gathers his bones and buries them under the big tree in the yard where their mother also lies buried; in the tree is a bird (the boy's spirit) who takes on the task of punishment and reward. Marjory receives a pair of red shoes; the stepmother, in her envy, wants something, too. She gets a millstone, which falls on her head. The baby brother comes alive again, after which the father, the sister, and the brother go in and finish their dinner. What do we have here? An untrustworthy, evil (step)mother and a drastic revenge. Some psychoanalysts today maintain that the real value of such stories — which, they say, children should not be protected from but rather exposed to — is that children can get rid of their aggressions toward their parents through the stories. (As we shall see in an upcoming section, Aristotle would have agreed with this psychoanalytic point of view.) In addition, the child is exposed to evil but at the same time acquires a dose of hopeful strength and learns that evil can be dealt with. In other words, the most horrible, gruesome, bloody fairy tales may be the ones with the most positive message for the impressionable reader: Yes, there are terrible things out there, but with fortitude we can vanquish them.

Parables For two thousand years, Christians have found moral support in parables such as those of the Good Samaritan and the prodigal son.

The *parable* is an allegorical story for adults; it is supposed to be understood as a story about ourselves and what we ought to do. Although the purpose of the fairy tale seems to be primarily to entertain and secondarily to teach a moral lesson, the purpose of the parable is *primarily* to teach a moral and religious lesson. Christianity is not the only religion with parables; the Islamic, Hebrew, and Buddhist traditions contain such stories.

What fascinated the early readers of Jesus of Nazareth's parables was that they were so hard to live up to—not just because it was hard to be good, but because the moral demands of Jesus himself usually ran counter to what society demanded of its citizens or what it viewed as proper moral conduct. What was so difficult for Jesus' contemporaries to understand? He demanded not only that we be compassionate toward all in need but also that we consider *every* person a fellow human being, not just those from our own village, country, or culture, and especially not just those who show compassion toward us.

The parable of the prodigal son (Luke 15:11–32) has been one such lesson that people with ordinary common sense and good manners find hard to follow. The "bad" son who has squandered his inheritance comes home and is sorry. The father makes a fuss over the bad son and slaughters the fattened calf for him. The good son, who has stayed with his father, is upset, for he has never received any recognition of his stability from his father, and yet now it seems that the bad son is more important. And he is, to Jesus, for he has been on a longer journey than the good son: all the way to perdition and back. Christians, therefore, ask themselves if that means we should go on a binge and then repent rather than never go on a binge at all. The answer may be that the story is supposed to be judged from the point of view not of the good or the bad brother but of the father. Indeed, the secret to many of the parables is to find out whose viewpoint they express. The parable of the Good Samaritan (Luke 10:30–34) is about a victim of highway robbery and mugging. As he lies wounded at the roadside, he is ignored by several upstanding citizens but is helped by a social outcast, the Samaritan. (The story is outlined in Chapter 12.) This parable is told from the wounded man's point of view ("who is my neighbor"), not from the point of view of the Samaritan.

A Story of Sacrifice: Abraham and Isaac   Although it is not classified as a parable, the Old Testament story of Abraham being told to sacrifice his son Isaac (Genesis 22:1–19) has had the same kind of effect on its listeners. It is one of the hardest stories for a religion that believes in a loving God, be it from a Jewish or Christian point of view, to explain. Abraham and his wife Sarah are childless until they have Isaac very late in their lives, through God's intervention. God tells Abraham that his descendants will be as numerous as the stars in the sky and the grains of sand in the desert. When Isaac is a half-grown boy, however, God tells Abraham to take Isaac up the mountain and sacrifice him like a sheep. Abraham leads Isaac away, heavy-hearted but obedient to God. He ties Isaac to the sacrificial stone and is about to stab him the ritual way when God's voice stops him, saying the request was just a test of Abraham's piety. God supplies a ram for Abraham to sacrifice instead.

The implications of this story have confounded believers and nonbelievers for two thousand years. A God who commands such a thing must be a cruel God, critics say, cruel and with a strange sense of humor. The philosopher Søren Kierkegaard sees the story as an illustration of the *limitations of ethics:* Ethically speaking, what Abraham was about to do was wrong; he had no business killing his

The Trial of Abraham's Faith (plate by Gustave Doré, 1866). Abraham, having received the command from God to sacrifice his only son, Isaac, dutifully takes Isaac up the mountain to the place of sacrifice. Isaac, unaware that it is he himself who is to be the victim, is carrying the firewood that Abraham will use to light the sacrificial fire.

son, because that is not how people are supposed to behave. But for Abraham, as for any believer, there is a law that is higher than the moral laws of society, and that is the law of *faith* — not faith that God will save his child, but faith that it really *is* God who is requiring him to sacrifice Isaac and that we can't know God's purpose. Kierkegaard saw Abraham's ordeal as a test of his faith in God rather than of his

Box 2.1   KAFKA'S ABRAHAM

The Czech novelist Franz Kafka (1883–1924) interprets the story of Abraham and Isaac in ways that are rather different from the traditional one. For one thing, he says, there was no need for any "leap of faith" in order for Abraham to accept the word of God, because if Abraham were to prove himself, then something precious to him had to be put on the line. If Abraham had so much—riches, a son, and a prophecy that he would become the father of the Jewish people—then he could be tested only by the threat of having something taken away from him. This is logical, says Kafka; it requires no leap of faith at all. What *would* require a leap of faith is if Abraham had been a different sort of person. Suppose he truly wanted to please God by performing the sacrifice but was a person of low self-esteem? He really wants to do what is right, like Cervantes' Don Quixote, but he can't quite believe that he can be the one God was speaking to because he believes he is unworthy. He is afraid that if he proceeds with the sacrifice, it will turn out that the command was just a joke, and he will be a laughingstock, like Quixote, who always tried to do the heroic thing but ended up fighting windmills. For this Abraham, being laughed at would make him even more unworthy of being called by God. It would be as though a worthy person had been called, but this grungy, unworthy Abraham showed up instead, foolishly believing himself to be the worthy one. Now this, says Kafka, would indeed require a leap of faith.

morals, and a "leap of faith" is, for the Lutheran Kierkegaard, a matter between the individual and God and nobody else. The opinion of society does not enter into the picture at all. Other interpretations of the story see no split between morality and faith, but view it as an illustration of God's absolute demands on his people. Yet others see it as justification for sacrificing everything one holds dear if a higher law demands it. With this last interpretation it really is irrelevant that God stopped Abraham at the last moment. For all Christians, the parallel to a later time when God did not stop himself from sacrificing his own son to save the world is a close one. (See Box 2.1 for Franz Kafka's interpretation of this parable.)

A recent critique of the old story has been suggested by anthropologist Carol Delaney in her book *Abraham on Trial: The Social Legacy of Biblical Myth.* Delaney asks, Why should faith in God be illustrated best by a father's willingness to sacrifice his son? Why couldn't the test of faith instead be measured by a parent's willingness to protect his or her child, not sacrifice it? The story has been told as if Abraham is the sole parent, with sole rights and responsibilities, and the biblical writers obviously didn't see Isaac's mother Sarah as someone with a right to her opinion about the matter. Delaney isn't criticizing the male-dominated ways of the Old Testament so much as asking why nobody since then, of all the commentators in Judeo-Christian history, has thought to ask whether Sarah might have had something relevant to say about the murder of her son as a proof of faith in God. Delaney actually echoes Kierkegaard's idea here that Abraham's willingness to kill Isaac would be completely *immoral,* but she doesn't agree with his further step that morals and faith are different things altogether.

Fables and Counterfables   In the eighteenth and nineteenth centuries adults finally began to notice that children were not just small and inadequate adults, and children's literature was invented as a literary genre. The gory fairy tale was toned down to suit the nursery, and another kind of story, which had previously been enjoyed by adults, was introduced to children: the *fable*. Aesop's and La Fontaine's fables became very popular as moral lessons for children. "The Mouse and the Lion" taught that you had better not disregard someone unimportant, for he or she might be of help to you some day, and "The Sour Grapes" taught that if someone claims something is not worth having, it may be because he or she can't have it. The main reason adults told these fables to children was, of course, that the grown-ups wanted their children to become good citizens, and the stories seemed an efficient way to press home the point. These early stories for children said, in essence, "Behave, or else"; they provided little opportunity for children's imagination to take flight. An important exception is the work of Hans Christian Andersen (1805–1875), who, throughout his fairy tales and stories, insisted that children's imaginations should be left unfettered by the sour realism of grown-ups. In fact, Andersen's stories have a true poetic quality and carry multiple meanings; they are not really children's stories at all. Children can enjoy them, to be sure, but they will enjoy them much more when they are older and capable of reading between the lines. For Andersen, it was not just the imagination of the children that was in danger of being stifled by adults, it was the imagination of the adults themselves that was in danger of withering away. Andersen's moral lesson is one of openness. He tells us to listen to the world and not just respond to it with preconceived notions; if we do, we will encounter only what we expect, and we will never again see the magic and splendor of the world the way children do.

Few of us who heard Hans Christian Andersen's story "The Fir Tree" as children paid much attention to the lesson it taught. Way out in the woods a little Christmas tree is growing. It is a pretty little tree, and it ought to be happy just being a little tree in the woods, but every time a rabbit jumps over it, it wishes that it were already fully grown because it's not much fun to be little. Season after season this happens—the little tree wants to grow and be a mighty pine so that it can be cut down and travel to foreign lands and see exciting things. The wind and the sun whisper, "Be happy you're young! Be happy you're here in the forest with your friends. Don't wish for time to hurry." Finally the tree becomes a young adult. It is cut down for Christmas, purchased, and taken to a nice, middle-class home. It experiences a wonderful Christmas Eve, but that is it for the little Christmas tree. It keeps expecting other wonderful things to happen, but it has no future; and, finally, stuck in the attic with brown, drooping branches, it realizes that the wind and the sun were right—it should have been happy to be young and surrounded by its friends in the woods. The moral lesson is obvious: that we often don't appreciate something until it is lost to us, and then we realize that we should have been more appreciative while it was still ours.

Other stories with moral lessons were being written for children during this same time period. Didactic stories took up the thread of the fables and taught children how to behave: to obey their parents, to be kind to animals, to finish their porridge, and to not make fun of people who looked different. Although today the lessons of these stories may seem, for the most part, quite inoffensive, the stories themselves often reveal sexism, racism, and a general naive belief that the writer had all the wisdom in the world. These "moral stories" not only present a moral problem but also *moralize*. This tendency to teach moral lessons enraged Mark Twain to the extent that he wrote a parody called "About Magnanimous-Incident Literature" (to which *Mad* magazine and the *Naked Gun* films are indebted). Twain's parody gives us the "true" ending to the little moral stories. In one story, the scruffy little homeless dog that the kindly village doctor cures comes back the next day with another scruffy little dog to be cured, and the doctor praises God for the chance to heal another unfortunate creature. End of moral story; here comes Twain: The next day there are four scruffy dogs outside the doctor's office, and the following week there are hundreds of howling mutts waiting to be treated. The original mutt is going crazy from all this helpfulness and bites the doctor, who wishes he had shot it in the first place.

Stories with Role Models

What kind of people do we like to hear stories about? And after the story, do we go out and do the same thing as the hero in the book or the movie? When we talk about fictional characters who somehow teach a moral lesson, we are talking about *role models.* Cartoon characters such as Superman may have certain qualities that we identify with and would like to emulate. But if we include Batman, we encounter an interesting twist: Batman is not a wholesome character; he has a psychological problem (which was, to some extent, explored in the recent films). Not all heroic characters are completely virtuous. If we look at fictional heroes in Western popular literature, from King Arthur, Lancelot, and Robin Hood to D'Artagnan and Scarlett O'Hara, we see that most of these people are morally flawed. The tendency in the twentieth century had been to depict them as being as morally flawed as possible, something that may reflect a certain sense of cynicism. A talk-show guest once announced that she had learned her moral lessons exclusively from soap operas, and we know that soap characters are by no means morally without reproach.

This is not a new phenomenon; in the medieval churches of Europe, peasant congregations were spellbound by murals depicting biblical scenes that sometimes covered the entire inside of the church. The murals kept them occupied during the long hours while the priest spoke in Latin, which the peasants did not understand. The moral lesson of this artwork was obvious, but it was expressed through depictions not of good people as much as of *bad* people; scenes illustrating people going to hell are usually much more vivid and artistically interesting than are scenes of people going to heaven. Perhaps the artists thought it was more fun to depict horrors than bland happiness. It does seem to be a human trait that we dwell on stories with a dark element, rather than on those with happy endings. Yet these stories can certainly teach a moral lesson. We must conclude, therefore, that not all moral lessons involve role models to be emulated; rather, a considerable number of moral lessons are negative rather than positive: *Don't.* Sometimes characters who show themselves to be morally flawed become our heroes not because they are good but because they are like us, or worse. If these "bad good people" see the folly of their ways in the end, we especially take them to our hearts. (For example, in Jane Austen's novel *Pride and*

Prejudice, Elizabeth Bennet, realizing that her own biases have blinded her to the vices of Mr. Wickham and the virtues of Mr. Darcy, says, "Till this moment, I never knew myself.") Perhaps we do this because we hope that we will be loved, too, even if we make mistakes. It seems that, on the whole, we have the heroes we deserve, as it has sometimes been said. A cautious time has cautious heroes; a violent time has violent heroes. During the time that we accept them as our heroes, we let their images guide our actions; when their day is done, we can still learn from them — they can teach us about the way we once were.

Some stories are moral investigations of a flawed character, such as Joseph Conrad's Lord Jim (see the Narrative on pp. 82–84), who makes a fatal, cowardly decision in his youth and tries to live it down for the rest of his life. In Victor Hugo's *Les Misérables,* Jean Valjean morally rises above the crimes of his youth only to be haunted by them until the end of his life. Fyodor Dostoyevsky's *Crime and Punishment* examines the philosophical deliberations of Raskolnikov as he imagines the right of the extraordinary individual to do whatever he wants, including committing murder. Gustave Flaubert's *Madame Bovary* (outlined in Chapter 4) traces Emma's deterioration through boredom and through fantasies (brought on by reading novels!). A work by the Danish author J. P. Jacobsen, *Marie Grubbe,* in some ways parallels *Madame Bovary.* It investigates the downfall of a noble lady through three marriages: to a nobleman, to a soldier, and finally to a drunk. The cause of her deterioration seems to be the same as Emma's: sensualism and boredom. The last time we encounter Marie, she is tending the ferry that runs between two small towns, in order to support her drunkard husband. The irony of the story is that in this squalor Marie finally finds the happiness that eluded her when she was a "fine lady."

Stories such as these are not written with the intention of sending their readers out on any heroic errands. They are, primarily, explorations of fascinating human characters. They also serve as moral evaluations by asking whether the characters redeem themselves somehow, even in their degradation. At times a character's redeeming act or quality goes against mainstream morality, as in the story of Marie Grubbe, and then the story forces us to ask which value is the ultimate moral value. Do we agree with society that Marie's life was wasted, full of missed opportunities? Or do we agree with the author that life, and morality, have many faces and that there is some intrinsic value in staying true to yourself, no matter how much this sentiment may differ from the public ethos? If such characters serve as a warning not to emulate them, we call them *negative role models.* We meet this concept again in Chapter 10.

Contemporary Story Genres

Sometimes the moral lesson in a story is hard to find; we may be blind to it, or it may be somewhat dated, having evolved in another era. There is a scene in Aldous Huxley's novel *Brave New World* (1932) in which the young "savage," John, who has grown up on a nature reservation unaffected by the modern era of eugenics, total sexual liberty, and test-tube babies, introduces his friend, the scientist Helmholtz, to Shakespeare. He reads from *Romeo and Juliet,* certain that the moral drama of the young lovers who can't have each other will move his modern friend. Helmholtz, however, doubles up laughing, because he can't for the life of him see that there is a problem: If Romeo and Juliet want each other, why don't they just have sex and let it go at that, instead of making such an embarrassing fuss about it? He is blind to the social and moral structures of the past, and the savage is very upset that ethical communication seems impossible in a new era that has done away with family relationships, birth, siblings, and spouses and that refuses to recognize the phenomenon of death.

In a similar way, stories depicting unwanted pregnancies struck a deep chord in times past but haven't had the same resonance since the advent of legal abortion and safe birth control. Old Hollywood films about the trials of two lovers who can't get a divorce from their spouses also sometimes require us to stretch a bit in order to empathize with the characters. Stories praising the glory of war, which were quite successful until the early twentieth century, have not done well with the majority of modern readers and viewers for quite some time now.

Wartime Stories: Duty and Honor   Wartime stories with moral lessons were common in past eras when it seemed that each generation of young men was expected to be initiated into manhood through some local armed conflict. But the idea of war as a natural arena for the exercise of masculine virtues received a serious blow in World War I, with its murky reasons for fighting and its wholesale slaughter of entire squadrons—young men from the same family or village or the same university, dying side by side in the trenches from mustard gas and machine gun fire, and leaving villages and colleges empty of an entire generation of youth. The soldier on the white horse with a feather plume in his helmet, dying gloriously for his country, became one of the images left behind in the nineteenth century, giving way to twentieth-century bitterness. For many people the entire idea of glory in war has become nothing but propaganda, invented by the leaders in order to inspire their legions to march unquestioningly off to the front as cannon fodder.

However, the image of the warrior as stalwart and honorable is so deeply imbedded in most human cultures that it shouldn't be dismissed as merely the result of the manipulation of gullible people by poets, propagandists, monarchs, and generals. It seems to resonate with something deep in us that identifies us as social beings, with a loyalty to our own people, for better or worse. Some would say it is a specifically *male* resonance; others see it as a class identification, which should be uprooted in a global community—but many see it as a part of a natural love for where we grew up and who we grew up with, regardless of class and gender, and not infrequently a love for the principles we have been taught.

For some pacifists, any story of war is a distasteful reminder of human nature at its worst—but even for many pacifists, a wartime story can be meaningful in its focus, not on the glory of war, but on humans under pressure, displaying devotion to duty and their comrades. And as many otherwise peace-loving people discovered (or rediscovered) in the wake of September 11, it is possible to think of a war as *just,* and a wartime story not just as a sad testimony to the blind aggression of humanity, but a tribute to brave people righteously responding to an attack. The classic definition of a just war (see Chapter 13) is that a war can't be fought for territory, or for glory, but strictly for defending one's country or preventing future genuine threats. This means a war

In *All Quiet on the Western Front* (Universal Studios, 1930, based on Erich Maria Remarque's 1929 novel), Katczinsky (Louis Wolheim) is the old "trench hog" and Paul Baumer (Lew Ayres), the young idealist who is about to get his lesson in the realities of war. The West's image of war changed with World War I. No more shining swords and prancing horses — there was nothing glorious about dying in the trenches of the European battlefields, and few soldiers understood the purpose of the prolonged fighting. However, the virtues of friendship, courage, and loyalty seemed all the more important as a twentieth-century war ethic. (From the collection of C. R. Covner.)

can be fought only if no other option seems reasonable or practical. A story about a just war must show that war is the last moral option, and that the goal is peace. In addition, it must demonstrate a clear vision of who is right and who is wrong.

World War II, which until September 2001, many considered to be the last war that had a clear moral focus and an identifiable good and evil side, spawned thousands of novels and films telling the story of good triumphing over evil. We will have to see what kinds of stories of human nature and human character will be told by novelists and filmmakers about September 11 and its aftermath, the war on terrorism.

The Moral Universe of Westerns: Hard Choices   Stories of the American West, called *Westerns,* have served as moral lessons for both the American public and a worldwide audience for more than a hundred years. Some films attempt factually to depict actual wartime events, such as *The Longest Day, A Bridge Too Far, Enola Gay,* and *Hamburger Hill.* Others spin fictional elements and characters into a story with a message about the experience of war, such as *Twelve O'Clock High, Memphis Bell, Midnight Clear, Saving Private Ryan, The Thin Red Line,* and the HBO series *Band of Brothers.*

All nations seem to go through periods when they "rediscover" their past, but the American West as a historical period is both recent and very short: from 1865 to about 1885 — from the end of the Civil War to the end of the open cattle range, which resulted from the advent of barbed wire and the bad winters of the 1880s. There have probably been more stories told about the Old West than could ever have happened. Even when the Old West was still alive, those in the East were reading dime novels that glamorized the West; the first Western films were shot outside New York City in the early 1900s. The process of creating a legend about the recent past was very rapid and even involved actual cowboys and gunfighters who moved from the plains and deserts to Hollywood to lend a hand.

Making entertainment out of recent history was one way to draw people to the theaters. If that were all, though, the Western never would have endured as long as it has. Part of its allure seems to have been its exoticism; the West is, still, a unique landscape. And then there is wishful thinking: Perhaps the Old West was never the way it appears in movies, but we wish it had been. An even greater appeal is the *moral potential* of a Western. For Western aficionados, it is almost like watching a ritual: The story usually is one we are familiar with, even if we are seeing it for the first time: There have to be good guys and bad guys, and horses, and they have to do a lot of riding back and forth among rocks in a gorgeous landscape. Then there is usually a good girl and sometimes also a bad girl. And there is a threat, either from Indians or the railroad or rustlers or (in later Westerns) big business, which is warded off by the strength and wit of Our Hero, sometimes even reluctantly (he often has to be dragged into the fight). When the problem is solved, the hero rarely settles down but rides off into the sunset so that he doesn't get entangled in the peace and prosperity of the society he helped stabilize. In later Westerns, the good guys are Indians or blacks or a gang of outlaws and the bad guys are the Army or other Indians or the law; the stable society becomes a negative rather than a positive image. Traditionally, though, the general pattern is the same: The power of the individual (the Good) rises above the threat of a larger force (the Evil).

The 1985 Western *Silverado* (Columbia Pictures) abandoned the 1970s trend of depicting the Old West in decline and gave its audience a story in a vigorous frontier setting with a happy ending. For this reason, the film is sometimes referred to as a "retro-Western." Many of the themes incorporated in *Silverado* are anything but "retro," however; for example, with this film the Western genre entered a new era of racial awareness. Here the four buddies (Danny Glover, Kevin Costner, Scott Glenn, and Kevin Kline) ride out to save the town of Silverado from corruption.

Why do people watch Westerns if they already know what will happen? Because the movie experience (or TV experience) itself is a *moral event*. People take part in the story by watching it, and they feel that when the problems on the screen are solved, the general problems of life are, in some symbolic way, put to rest at the same time. The moviegoer may not even be aware of this psychological process.

One might think that if the Western had a moral message, it would seem pretty dated, and sometimes even offensive, to modern audiences. After all, the first generation of Westerns left the overall impression that it was fine to kill Indians, that women were weak and had to be protected, that blacks were nonexistent, that the land was there only to be developed, that animal life and suffering were irrelevant, and so on. However, the values of the Western movie changed with the changing times. There were still good guys and bad guys, but in each period they reflected the problems of the contemporary world, at least in a symbolic sense. In the 1950s the Western began to reflect a growing unease with the stereotype of townspeople conquering the wilderness; the sixties saw an increasing sympathy for the outlaw. The Western of the seventies was influenced by the Vietnam War and began to address

Box 2.2   THE CHANGING MESSAGES OF WESTERNS

Western films have from the early days managed to integrate modern problems into the period plot, sometimes without much respect for the historical context. The Vietnam War era had its "Vietnam Westerns" in which massacred Indians symbolized the Vietnamese and the Army symbolized the U.S. Army in Vietnam (*Soldier Blue, Little Big Man*). Post-Watergate Westerns showed corrupt politicians and greedy railroad tycoons (*Young Guns I and II*). Westerns of the 1990s explored the issue of violence and killing; contrary to most classic Westerns, in which violence was part of the formula, the new Western asked about its justification. *Tombstone* and *Wyatt Earp* both examine the effects of violence on a township and on the individual (Earp) who tries to put an end to it, and *Unforgiven* probably makes the strongest antiviolence statement of all newer Westerns, reflecting on the loss of humanity in the life of a gunfighter.

With the return of the Western, there has been a growing sensitivity not only to historical accuracy but also to a multiethnic presence in the Old West. African Americans have found a heroic identity in the Western landscape (*Sil-* *verado, Lonesome Dove*), and American Indians have emerged from old stereotypes such as devils or angels to become real people with their own language and their own problems and jokes (*Dances with Wolves, The Last of the Mohicans, Geronimo*). Strong female characters in Westerns are still rare, although there have been a few of them over the years in the films *Johnny Guitar, Rio Bravo,* and *High Noon,* the television movie *Lonesome Dove,* and the television series *Dr. Quinn, Medicine Woman. Bad Girls,* a film about four women outlaws; *The Ballad of Little Jo,* about a woman passing herself off as a man to get by in life; and *The Quick and the Dead,* with Sharon Stone as a gunfighter, all help to dispel the impression that Westerns are films exclusively about men for men, but we have yet to see a very good Western with a female lead. One of the few that would qualify, in my judgment, would be the TV miniseries *Buffalo Girls,* with Anjelica Huston and Melanie Griffith in the powerful lead roles: a somber, sensitive look at the final days of the Old West, moving from the romantic hardship of the open country to the phony romance of Buffalo Bill's traveling circus.

problems of discrimination, overdevelopment, and pollution. In the eighties the Western seemed to have nothing more to say, but in the nineties it acquired a voice once again; current Westerns often deal with cross-cultural and cross-racial issues in the American melting pot. (See Box 2.2 for an overview of how the messages of Westerns have changed.) The Western, being the one narrative genre that is truly American, shows an amazing potential for being able to introduce many kinds of social and moral problems in a single framework in which people have to make big moral decisions in a land where they are dwarfed by rocks, mountains, and deserts. These stories of momentous decisions appeal not just to Americans but to people all over the world. This makes the Western much more than just a movie genre. It has become a transcultural story told in a universal moral language.

Science Fiction: What Future Do We Want?   Like the Western, science fiction was born as a literary genre in the nineteenth century. The French author Jules Verne astounded the world with his fantasies of men on the moon and journeys to the center of the earth and the bottom of the sea. Even Hans Christian Andersen predicted, in one of his lesser known stories, that in "thousands of years" Americans would be flying in machines to Europe to visit the Old World. Verne's stories contained an element that has blossomed in modern science fiction: a *moral awareness*. His stories reveal an awareness of the possible repercussions of the inventions, as well as a general political consciousness, which makes his books much more than mere entertainment. In England, the works of H. G. Wells combined science fantasy and social comment in the same way.

In the twentieth century, science fiction became a major genre of entertainment, from pulp magazines and comic books to serious novels and films of high quality. Their subjects range from the pure fantasy of magical universes to hard-core thought experiments of exploratory science. (A *thought experiment* is a mental exercise in which a researcher sets up an imaginary scenario and follows it to its logical conclusion in order to explore what might happen if the scenario came true.) Although science fiction need not always involve ethical issues, it has proved to be one of the most suitable genres for exploring them, especially such problems as we believe may lurk in our future.

In a category by itself is the end-of-civilization type of science fiction, sometimes referred to as "cyberpunk." The civilized world is destroyed by a nuclear war or a giant meteor strike or pollution or the advent of hostile aliens or an epidemic disease. Although this type of story affords the author a chance to present lots of scenes of gruesome death or terrible disaster, the most serious problems usually occur in the relationships among the survivors. Will they degenerate into a "war of everybody against everybody," as the philosopher Thomas Hobbes would say, or will the human spirit of compassion for one's fellow beings triumph? This form also allows us to discuss how the characters got into such dire situations in the first place. If it is through human folly or neglect, such as global war or pollution, the stories can serve as powerful moral *caveats*, or warnings. This mistrust of what the future might bring has no greater expression than in the subtitle of the *X-Files* movie from 1998, *Fight the Future*. Other dreadful-future scenarios that have appeared recently and feature either threats from Above (aliens or meteorites) or Within (our own government, stupidity, or greed) include *Independence Day, Starship Troopers, Deep Impact, Armageddon,* and *The Postman*. For all these films that belong to the "fight the future" genre, the point is that humans are capable of surviving if only we can realize the threat in time and work together.

In the weeks after September 11, *Variety* magazine reported, screenwriters and directors met with representatives from the U.S. Army to brainstorm possible terrorist scenarios, a series of "what-ifs" to improve the preparedness of the Army. No longer are action movies, sci-fi movies, and disaster movies to be considered merely lowbrow entertainment; as some of us who occasionally enjoy watching such films have known for years, to be forewarned is to be forearmed: If we can imagine an *Independence Day* or a *Die Hard* scenario, then perhaps we can prevent a similar scenario from happening, or be ready for it when it does. The screenwriter of *Die Hard* attended the Army's anti-terrorism conference; so did the director of *Delta Force One*. In addition, David Brin, the author of *The Postman* (a fine novel that became a not-so-fine movie), suggested in an interview in the fall of 2001 that we all have to become members of a new class of amateur warriors, vigilant in our everyday life, watching out for each other and any unusual activity, and bringing our cellphones with us wherever we go. In a sense, the cyberpunk nightmare future has arrived, even if the world still looks the same by and large, except for the New York skyline. And perhaps those of us who have been encouraged by the movies to anticipate that future will adjust faster and imagine alternative ways to maintain our "new normalcy" even under trying conditions.

Interestingly enough, there is a "counterfable" to the end-of-the-world scenario. It is the story of the Happy Future—not a future without problems, but a future in which some of today's pressing problems have been solved. Such stories present a world without nuclear threat, without racism or sexism, without nationalistic chauvinism—a world in which science has acquired a humanistic face and politics on earth, as well as in space, is conducted with a democratic spirit and common sense. The original *Star Trek* television series pioneered this hopeful fantasy of the future. The sequel, *Star Trek: The Next Generation,* showed that the Happy Future scenario was as welcome as ever, not in a naive sense but as a vision of a maturing humanity that, free from the fears, deprivations, and resentments of the modern age, may be able to turn its energy toward new frontiers and challenges.

Another great series of science fiction stories that has also proved to have staying power is the *Star Wars* franchise. But in the *Star Wars* universe we find no Federation of civilized planets as in *Star Trek;* on the contrary, the evil forces are organized into an evil Empire, and the heroes, the Jedi Knights, are guerrillas battling the overwhelming military power—and its bureaucracy. Scholars and journalists have spent time analyzing this interesting opposition of space-opera scenarios—a benevolent Federation and an evil Empire—and some have pronounced *Star Trek* to be the fantasy of liberals preferring big government, and *Star Wars* the fantasy of conservatives fighting for individual freedoms in the face of the bureaucracy.

Be that as it may, both series have created enduring stories that, in many ways, have become part of our American mythology, and both occasionally approach the question of what it really means to be human: Who (or what) counts as a person? In *Star Trek* we have the half-human, half-Vulcan Mr. Spock, the android Data, and the hologram The Doctor, all on the edge of humanity, all counting as persons and yet having their personhood placed in doubt time and time again. In *Star Wars* we have a multitude of characters who are considered persons, but not human, such as Chewbacca the Wookie, the 'droids, Yoda, and Jar-Jar Binks. The question of who counts as a person is especially popular in science fiction novels: Several sci-fi authors have specialized in this issue, among them Cordwainer Smith, Octavia Butler, Rebecca Ore, Ursula K. Le Guin, and C. H. Cherry. In stories about genetically altered chimps and other animals who do the dirty work for humans (Smith), humans adopted by aliens (Butler, Ore), and lone human envoys to alien societies (Le Guin and Cherry), we are invited to explore (1) what makes us human and (2) how we treat those we think don't qualify. In Chapter 7 we take a closer look at the issue of personhood, and discuss the films *Blade Runner* and *Gattaca,* about challenges to the concepts of personhood and rights.

The *golem* may be the oldest character in the science fiction genre. It comes from the Eastern European Jewish tradition, in which it was said that a man might create an

Box 2.3   THE NONHUMAN WHO WANTS TO BECOME HUMAN

Artificial persons in fiction and films often yearn to become human. Frankenstein's monster suffers from this yearning, but he is not allowed to become what he wishes to be. Data, the android in *Star Trek: The Next Generation,* does not have the capability to feel human emotions, but he is intellectually curious about what causes humans to act passionately or maliciously. He longs to be human the way a child longs to grow up. The replicants in *Blade Runner* are ready to kill for a chance to become full-dimensional humans. The hologram Doctor in *Star Trek: Voyager* strives to expand his physical boundaries beyond sick bay and his psychological boundaries beyond those of a diagnostic computer program without any bedside manner or empathy for his patients. And the artificial human in *Terminator 2* displays definite human characteristics; he bonds with a small boy and sacrifices himself for the sake of humankind. Just as the monster side of the artificial person is symbolized by the golem, the wanting-to-be-human side is epitomized by Pinocchio, the wooden puppet who wants to become a real boy. As the story of Pinocchio teaches, you don't become a "real" boy by doing the bad-boy things. If you do the bad-boy things (have fun and skip school), you become what bad boys become: an ass. *Pinocchio* is for all intents and purposes a very moralistic fable.

artificial person out of clay, a golem, but if he weren't careful to keep this creature in check with certain magical acts and formulas, the clay man would grow and eventually take over and kill him. One story tells of a rabbi creating a golem to help the Jews protest false accusations of blood-sacrificing of Christians during Passover. This particular golem helped the Jewish people for years by exposing Christian plots to plant dead bodies of Christians in Jewish homes. But the golem became too strong and powerful for the rabbi to handle, so in the end the rabbi had to turn him back into the clay from which he had been created. (In another version of the story the rabbi turned the golem back into clay because his job was done and there was no reason to keep him around anymore.) In the early nineteenth century, Mary Wollstonecraft Shelley created a similar artificial person, the monster of Frankenstein. Shelley's theme was the same as that of the golem story: human arrogance and invention run wild. In a strange sense we might say that the golem story is very conservative: If you exceed your boundaries, your creation will come back to haunt you. In a more progressive sense, though, the story teaches us to evaluate our actions from a moral perspective. In the movies, the artificial monster has taken on a number of guises, from the maniacal computer HAL in *2001: A Space Odyssey* to the Arnold Schwarzenegger character in the *Terminator* movies.

In any event, the artificial person serves well not just as a topic for discussion about what to do if artificial beings become viable in our society but also as a figurative image of ourselves. (Box 2.3 discusses the human qualities of the artificial person.) The artificial person makes us realize what it is to be human and what we ought to be like to be *more* human; it provides an excursion into our own descriptive and normative concepts of humanity and provokes us to explore how we should treat the *Other.* (In philosophy the person who is different from oneself is often referred to as the Other. The term signifies that one is facing something or someone that one is fundamentally unfamiliar with. It can mean a stranger, a person of the other sex or of another race, or it can mean other people or beings as such, as opposed to one-self and one's own experiences. Sometimes it signifies someone complementary to oneself, but it may also mean that the Other is not as complete, worthy, or impor-tant as oneself and one's own kind.)

Mystery and Crime: The Fight Against Evil   As Chapter 1 noted, people feel vul-nerable even when the crime rate is down. Perhaps that accounts for the perennial popularity of detective stories. Cop shows and murder mysteries give us some sem-blance of a feeling that something can actually be done to control the forces we feel are threatening us.

More than in any other genre, the attention centers around the issue of *good and evil* — not in an abstract sense but as personified on the streets. We may generalize somewhat and say that science fiction deals with desirable versus undesirable futures, Westerns deal with hard choices, and war movies deal with questions of duty, but crime stories above all specialize in questions of good and evil — and what to do about evil. Sometimes we follow the story to its ending with a lot of hope: Something can be done. At other times, it seems like forces of good are trying to empty the ocean with a slotted spoon. What makes this genre so compelling is that evil acquires a face: the face of the bad guy (male or female). And when that person is caught, sentenced, or killed, the greater formless threat of Evil seems to have been vanquished for a while, too. Even when the bad guy wins, as he has so often in recent movies, we still have a sense that the fight against evil is not fruitless or without merit. As such, this genre has an inside angle on moral narratives: Regardless of whether the good guys or the bad guys win, or whether you can tell the difference between the good guys and bad guys (as in some movies from the 1970s), or whether the good guys are really bad guys (as in stories of corrupt cops), there is a subtext of a moral dis-cussion going on: What is good? What is evil? And what can be done about it?

The first acknowledged detective story with a "whodunit" focus, "The Murders in Rue Morgue," was written by Edgar Allan Poe in 1841. Sir Arthur Conan Doyle followed shortly after with his stories about the sleuth Sherlock Holmes. In France, Georges Simenon created the police detective Maigret in 1931. Major heroic fic-tional detectives — mostly private investigators — in the literary tradition include characters such as Mike Hammer, Sam Spade, Dick Tracy, Lord Peter Wimsey, Philip Marlowe, Paul Drake (from *Perry Mason*), Nero Wolfe, Miss Marple, and lately Easy Rawlins. At the movies, we've followed the puzzle-solving efforts of police detectives and private eyes from Nick and Nora Charles (*The Thin Man* films) to Dirty Harry to the detectives of *L.A. Confidential, Mulholland Falls,* the *Die Hard* and *Lethal Weapon* films, *48 Hours,* and *Devil in a Blue Dress.* Television has given us cop shows such as *Dragnet, Adam 12, Columbo, Barney Miller, Hill Street Blues, NYPD Blue, Law and Order,* and *Homicide.* A borderline mystery/sci-fi series that reached almost mythic proportions in the late 1990s was *The X-Files,* with its two-person team of FBI agents attempting to solve crimes that, in some cases, were "out of this world."

The enormously popular television series *The X-Files* created a new genre between whodunits and science fiction: the conspiracy genre. What was it in the plot lines that appealed to the turn-of-the-millennium viewer? Was it the assumption that governments are hiding things from citizens? A general fear of the future? Or was it simply good entertainment? The original main characters, Agents Fox Mulder (David Duchovny) and Dana Scully (Gillian Anderson), represent diametrically opposed attitudes toward supernatural phenomena and the UFO question: Mulder is the believer, and Scully is the skeptic.

Mulder (the believer) and Scully (the skeptic) revealed conspiracies within conspiracies, only to have their results sealed by yet another cover-up; the driving force behind Mulder's idealism was that "the truth is out there."

Like Westerns and science fiction, the mystery genre reflects changing mores: For the longest time, law enforcement officers were depicted as the good guys and

Box 2.4   THE GOOD GUYS AND THE BAD GUYS

Does it make a big difference in crime stories whether we are supposed to sympathize with the criminal? As is the case with Westerns, there are several types of crime stories. There are classic stories in the Agatha Christie mode (in which we usually approve of the apprehension of the criminal). Then there is the mobster genre, in which we may sympathize with some of the bad guys, such as in *Bonnie and Clyde, The Godfather I* and *II, Dillinger, Goodfellas, Bugsy, Miller's Crossing, Casino,* and the enormously popular HBO series *The Sopranos.* The last decades of the twentieth century saw an increasing number of films that express some ambivalence toward crime fighting. The hunter often becomes the hunted, the cop becomes a criminal, the line between good and bad is blurred. Hollywood's recent response to such films? It has returned to a defense of law enforcement, with mobsters and other criminals clearly the bad guys once again and the good guys fighting both the underworld and the corruption of the authorities. This was the focus of the 1987 movie *The Untouchables.* Another response has been a wholesale tossing around of preconceived notions about right and wrong, as in *Pulp Fiction* (see the Narrative at the end of this chapter), where tales of characters helping each other, killing each other, and sparing each other make a fast, bloody, and — for many viewers — fascinating mix.

criminals as the bad guys. (See Box 2.4 for a discussion of the changing sympathies in mystery films.) And if the law wasn't the hero, at least the detective was. As modern cynicism increased, it became common for novels and films to depict the criminal as an "antihero" and the establishment as the evil power. Lately, the patterns have merged into the good cop/detective/FBI agent fighting a two-front battle against both the bad guys on the streets and the bad guys in administration or the Internal Affairs Division. An example of this is the acclaimed film (and novel) *L.A. Confidential,* in which the truly bad guy is not the mobster or a street gang member but a high-ranking police officer. This story model — which is used so often that it has almost become a cliché — reflects something interesting: We the audience don't particularly like to see the criminal given the hero treatment anymore, and we don't automatically buy in to the idea that perps are poor misguided souls who would have been upstanding citizens if they'd had a decent childhood. On the other hand, today's audience doesn't believe that law enforcement officers are all knights in shining armor, either. We do still want to believe, however, that somebody competent and committed is out there fighting crime. So the story model of the cop fighting criminals *and* superiors strikes a realistic, as well as a hopeful, chord for a modern audience.

A special category within the crime genre has been created by the HBO series *The Sopranos,* about a middle-class New Jersey family — who happens to be part of the Mafia. Mafia and middle-class morals collide in Tony Soprano's attempt to raise a decent family and provide for them, to the point where he, like so many others these days, is seeing a therapist for his anxiety attacks. At one point she asks him

In *L.A. Confidential* (Warner Bros., 1997), the bad guys are not always the only crooks on the street. The twist-and-turn plot sees the two antagonists, Detective Ed Exley (Guy Pearce, *middle front*) and Detective Bud White (Russell Crowe, *middle rear*), put aside their differences to find the mastermind behind a series of murders. Here the detectives are flanked by Captain Dudley Smith (James Cromwell, *left*) and celebrity cop Jack Vincennes (Kevin Spacey, *right*).

about his values, as someone who raises children in a criminal environment, and he snaps at her in anger, pointing to the greater crimes of big business polluting the environment. Does the end justify the means? Can one be a good person in one area of one's life, and a bad one in another? *The Sopranos* just raises the questions—the series leaves it up to us to ponder whether there are any easy answers.

Stories to Live and Die By

In 1774 *The Sorrows of Young Werther,* a novel, was published in Germany. The author was twenty-four-year-old Johann Wolfgang von Goethe, who would later write the definitive version of *Faust*. In the novel—incidentally, one of the first modern novels as we know it, with a story line involving the emotional development of a main character during the course of a happy or unhappy encounter—young Werther suffers so dramatically from unrequited love that he takes his own life (see the Narrative on pp. 78–79). In the wake of the book's publication, Germany, and later all of Europe, witnessed a rash of suicides being committed or attempted by young readers of *Werther*. Why did they do it? Goethe certainly never intended his book to be a suicide manual. This is one of the first examples in modern times of a work of fiction inspiring its readers to take drastic action. This book, along with other works of literature, art, and philosophy, ushered in the new Age of Romanticism, when the ideal person was perceived as an *emotional* rather than a *rational* being, and men, as well as women, acted on their emotions, often in public. The decision of young Werther was seen as a romantic option and had a powerful emotional effect; even some famous poets of the day chose to end their lives, and the rest of Europe woke up to the dangers, and the thrill, of literature.

Since then, scholars of literature have discussed why Goethe's book had such an effect; it was not the first tragic story printed, and poems and songs of unrequited love had been common since the Middle Ages. Several factors seem to have been involved. First, mass printing and distribution of literature were now under way. Second, the era known as the Enlightenment was coming to an end, and its effects were beginning to be felt. There was a focus on the rights and capacities of the individual, including the right (for boys) to receive an education. This meant that the common man, as well as many women, was now able to read. Third, the theme of the story, Werther's emotions, seemed to strike a chord in the young readers who were moving away from the idealization of reason, which had been central to the lives of their parents and grandparents, to an idealization of emotions—so we are talking about a kind of generational rebellion. All in all, you might say that this was a book that appeared at exactly the right time. And its fame landed Goethe a job with the royal court at twenty-six years of age. But for the rest of his long life, he was disturbed at the effect his book had had on its young readers.

The aftermath of *Werther* was not the first time in Western culture that the topic of the effects of an artistic work had arisen: In ancient Greece, Plato and Aristotle had debated whether art was a good or a bad psychological influence. Plato claimed that art, especially drama, was bad for people because it inspired violent emotions; people watching a play with a violent theme would be inspired to commit violence themselves. For Plato the ideal life was spent in complete balance and harmony; if the balance was upset, that life would be less perfect. Reason helped keep a person in balance; if emotions took over, reason would be diminished, and imbalance would occur. And since art helped stir emotions, then art was dangerous. Aristotle believed that art, and especially drama, was good for people because it allowed them to act out their emotions vicariously; a good play would thus cleanse the spectator of disturbing emotions, and he or she could return home a calmer person: The exposure to strong feelings and to a considerable amount of stage violence would have a *cathartic* effect. Aristotle claimed that feeling pity and fear for the victim of the tragedy cleanses us by making us understand that tragedy could happen to anyone, including ourselves. In his book on tragedy, *Poetics* (see excerpt on pp. 67–69), Aristotle makes it clear that the best tragic plays are those in which misfortune happens not to a very good person but to an ordinary person who made a monumental error in judgment. And since most of us are ordinary persons, the play becomes a moral learning experience—a moral laboratory in which we can see our inner urges acted out and learn from the tragic consequences. (Box 2.5 explores the debate between reason and emotion.)

One might wonder what kind of plays the ancient Greeks watched at the time of Plato and Aristotle that led to such different evaluations of the experience of

Box 2.5   REASON OR EMOTION? APOLLO VERSUS DIONYSUS

Goethe's novel *The Sorrows of Young Werther* came as a harbinger of a cultural sea change between the dominant worldview of the eighteenth century, the Age of Reason, and the new age that was dawning, the Age of Romanticism. Goethe himself embraced the philosophy of the Age of Reason—the belief that reason, not emotion, is the true problem solver—but others took their cue from *Werther* and let the age of emotions roll in. Interestingly, these shifts of focus between rationality and emotion have happened at other times. In some ways one can say such a shift took place on a small scale between the 1950s and the late 1960s. And much earlier that same transformation had swept through a society in which intellectuals—perhaps purely by chance—had also been debating about the dangers and value of stories: Plato's and Aristotle's Greece.

The Greek theater was only a couple of generations old by the time Plato warned against its emotional pull, yet it had already developed a rich tradition of annual plays and prizes, all in honor of a god imported from the Middle East, Dionysus. The older gods such as Zeus, Athena, and Apollo, were still worshiped, especially in Athens, but a religious battle was brewing during the lifetime of Plato and Aristotle for the souls of all Greeks: Whereas the old gods, in particular Apollo and Athena, symbolized reason and self-control (a principle that is predominant in Socrates' and Plato's way of thinking), Dionysus was the god of wine and excess. You may know him under his Roman name, Bacchus. This philosophical battle between self-control and emotional abandon was won by Plato: His writings have endured, with their praise of reason, while nobody is a true worshiper of Dionysus anymore. Within the ancient Greek world itself, however, one can say that Dionysus won: The theater flourished, with the moral support of Aristotle, who himself was from the north where they worshiped Dionysus. And today the ultimate legacy of the Dionysian religion, movies and television shows, are being produced and enjoyed all over the world.

drama from these two thinkers. For one thing, Greek drama had been around for only a couple of generations. It seems to have begun in the form of religious pageants at the annual festival of Dionysus in Athens and developed rapidly into a contest among playwrights of tragedies, comedies, and satyr plays (wild farces with sexual themes), with much prestige for the winners. More than fifteen thousand spectators might see one performance of any play at the theater in Athens. The oldest surviving Greek play is *The Persians* by Aeschylus (ca. 472 B.C.E.); by that time, the emphasis on religious themes in the plays had already waned, and stories depicting the human condition (with some divine intervention) became popular.

Just what was it about drama that Plato found so dangerous and Aristotle so uplifting? One of the Narratives in this chapter is taken from a Greek tragedy, Euripides' *Medea,* in which a woman kills her children to get revenge on her estranged husband. Another, perhaps the most famous, example of Greek tragedy is the story of *Oedipus Rex* by Sophocles. At Oedipus's birth, his parents, the king and queen of Thebes, are told that their baby son will grow up to kill his father and marry his mother, so in order to thwart the fates, they have him placed on the ground in the mountains for the animals to dispose of. But his life is saved by a passing shepherd who takes him to the court of the king and queen of Corinth to be raised as their son. As a young adult, Oedipus inquires about his future—and is told by the oracle that he is destined to kill his father and marry his mother. He flees his homeland, fearing that he might harm his beloved parents (who never told him that he was adopted). At a crossroads he meets a man who won't give way to him, so Oedipus fights and kills him. Later he marries the widowed queen of the land and becomes king. But after years of happily married life, Oedipus and his wife learn the truth: that he did indeed fulfill the prophecy and kill his natural father—the unknown man at the crossroads—and marry his natural mother. His wife/mother commits suicide, and Oedipus gouges out his eyes in grief and shame.

Other stories watched avidly by the Athenian audiences include *The Bacchants*, a lesser known story by Euripides in which a mother, in a religious frenzy, tears her own son's head off, believing him to be a mountain lion; and Aeschylus's tragedy *Agamemnon*, about the king who leads the Greeks into the battle of Troy, only to lose his life on his homecoming at the hands of his wife and her lover.

The common denominators in these tragedies were strong family passions, speculations on the nature of fate, and a considerable amount of bloodshed. In the excerpt from *Poetics* (pp. 67–69), Aristotle points out that the quality of the tragedy is far superior if the producers don't rely on (in modern terminology) special effects but on the elements of the story itself: If it is well written, the audience will be shocked to the bone by the mere telling of the story—no stagecraft can make it more effective.

The debate is still with us, although it now takes a somewhat different form. We now must consider whether violence in movies and on television inspires people (and especially children) to commit violence or whether it allows them to act out their aggressions in a safe environment. Psychologists who believe that violent fairy tales can be good for children clearly belong to the Aristotelian tradition, although they may not support the excessive violence portrayed in movies and on TV. Examples of people enacting situations from fictional stories with terrible results include the scene from the 1993 film *The Program*, deleted from presently available videotapes, of football players daring each other to lie in the middle of rushing traffic; inspired by the film, some teenagers tried the stunt and died. Another example is the small boy who, after watching an episode of *Beavis and Butthead* about arson, set fire to the trailer he and his family were living in. (The producers of *Beavis and Butthead* promptly prohibited any reference to fire in future shows.) An incident often cited is the 1995 attack on a New York subway employee in the style of the movie *The Money Train;* discussions at the time ran quickly toward censorship of films. But this time the conclusion may have been premature—despite the likeness between the crime and the film, the perpetrators apparently turned out to be ignorant of the film's plot. However, it was apparently not a coincidence when a woman set fire to her husband's car in 1996. Afterward, she explained that she had been inspired by the film *Waiting to Exhale*.

Other films that have acquired a reputation for inspiring copycats are *The Burning Bed* (an abused wife kills her husband), *The Getaway* (robbers observe the schedule of money transports), *Stand By Me* (kids knock down mailboxes), *Taxi Driver* (said to have inspired John Hinckley in his attempt to assassinate President Reagan in order to impress Jodie Foster, who starred in the film), *Heat* (a bank robbery in L.A.), and *Set It Off* (a film about female bank robbers that served as a blueprint for a gang of two adult women and three teen girls who robbed banks in the state of Washington in 1998. After they were caught, a copy of the *Set It Off* video was found at their home, so there was no doubt as to the source of inspiration). The 1994 film *Natural Born Killers* may have inspired both a bank robbery and the massacre of high school students in Littleton, Colorado, in 1999. The Columbine High massacre has also been linked to the film *The Basketball Diaries*. In Los Angeles, a sixteen-year-old boy and two male cousins who stabbed the boy's mother to death told detectives that they had been inspired by *Scream* and *Scream 2*. In Michigan, a group of teens tried to make a *Blair Witch Project*-type horror video by kidnapping a young woman.

Even if we might feel tempted to do something we've seen in a film, most of us refrain because our common sense, experience, or conscience tells us it is not a smart thing to do. We believe we have a choice; we have the free will to decide whether or not to do things. Thus the question is, Should society play it safe and make sure that nobody has access to violent or suggestive stories because a few will imitate the action? In other words, should we allow censorship? Or should we let people take responsibility for what they watch and for what their children watch? Should we trust them to be their children's guides rather than hand the job over to the government?

Plato believed in censorship in his ideal state because he didn't trust people to know what was good or bad for them. Was Plato correct in saying that it can be dangerous to be exposed to emotion-stirring dramas? It seems so, under certain circumstances; but are these circumstances enough to justify censorship's being imposed on all viewers, even those who would never let their balance be disturbed?

On the other hand, is Aristotle right that it is beneficial overall to a mind under a lot of tension to be exposed to violent fictional dramas? Given that television sets in American homes are on several hours a day on the average and that a great many shows during those hours will bring violence into the home, television is not necessarily a good prescription for a modern stressed-out person seeking relaxation. We should remember that the drama Aristotle recommended as beneficial was not available twenty-four hours a day, as it is on a TV set; Greek dramas were originally performed once a year in connection with religious festivals, and Aristotle's philosophy in general advocates *moderation* in all things. If he could have taken part in the modern debate, he most certainly would have advised against overdoing the exposure to violence on TV and in movies. (For more on Plato and Aristotle, see Box 2.6.)

This viewpoint is offered by the former FBI profiler and author John Douglas, who has himself investigated the concrete results of violence in the media. In his book *Obsession* (1998), he writes,

I certainly do not blame violence in the media for violence in real life, but I do believe that the constant exposure of children and teens—not to mention adults—to depictions of violence has to have the cumulative effect of desensitizing all of us to the horrors we see visited around us. I would much rather have my children see a program that portrays

Box 2.6   SOCRATES, PLATO, AND ARISTOTLE

Plato (427?–347 B.C.E.) was a student of Socrates, the man who is sometimes called the father of Western philosophy. He studied with Socrates in Athens for over twenty years, and after Socrates' execution (see Chapter 8) he left Athens in anger and grief. A few years later he returned and became a teacher in his own right. While running his own school of philosophy he wrote numerous books, *Dialogues*, about the teachings of Socrates. Among his students was a young man from the province of Stagira, Aristotle (384–322 B.C.E.). Deeply influenced by Plato, Aristotle nevertheless developed his own approach to philosophy. For that and other reasons, Aristotle was not chosen as leader of the school when Plato died, so he left Athens for other jobs, including tutoring the young prince Alexander of Macedonia (Alexander the Great). But like Plato after his exile, Aristotle also returned to Athens, opened up his own school, and began a short but immensely influential career of teaching and writing about philosophy and science. We talk about Socrates and Plato in detail in Chapter 8 and about Aristotle in Chapter 9.

violence as it really is—quick, senseless, revolting—than one that pretties it up and glorifies it for the sake of making some movie star look heroic.

Of course, children and adults are exposed to violence not just on TV and on film; fictional violence is on the increase in comic books, in video games and computer games, and in the lyrics to music often favored by teens. The framework for this chapter, however, is the influence of stories, so I've chosen to focus on violence in movies and television.

Whether we agree with Plato or with Aristotle, the fact remains that stories—both in written and in visual form—affect us. Some societies have reacted by banning certain works or by conducting what to me is one of the foulest displays of cultural censorship: book burning. Other societies support the right of their citizens to decide for themselves what they wish to read or view.

Most influential works were never intended as moral guidebooks for the public except in the broadest sense. Goethe didn't write his *Werther* in order to convince dozens of young, lovesick Germans to kill themselves—quite possibly, he intended for young Germans to examine their lives and loves more closely. Few authors would want their readers to imitate the actions of their fictional characters, although most would like to think their story has at least been food for thought. The many readers of Dante's *Divine Comedy* probably do not expect the afterlife to be designed according to that author's specifications, but many a reader who has traveled through Dante's circles of hell probably has been motivated to rethink the general course of his or her life.

Stories considered good learning tools in twenty-first-century America will in all likelihood be different from didactic stories in Hitler's Germany, in eighteenth-century France, in tribal Native America of the nineteenth century, and in Greece in the fifth century B.C.E. It is a separate and very interesting question whether there is such a thing as universally morally commendable stories; we take a look at the subject of ethical relativism in Chapter 3 and return to the subject of intercultural values in stories at the end of this chapter.

Is it appropriate to talk about the impact of stories as if they take place in a vacuum, with vacuous people as receptacles? Of course not. Children, as well as adults, all have a certain background that helps us process the stories we are exposed to, and this is where the influence of parents becomes important: If parents and children usually communicate about the stories the children are exposed to — or if parents are the ones telling their children the stories — the children hopefully acquire a critical stance from the stories they will hear and watch as adults. This critical stance lowers the risk of their running out mindlessly to emulate some action that may look "cool" on the screen. It lowers the risk both that we take stories too seriously and that we don't take them seriously enough. So in the final analysis, those of us who, like me, love stories and like to use them as moral lessons should remember to approach any story cautiously. Do stories create moral saints? No. Do they create moral sinners? No, not without cooperation from their audience. We must process the stories we are exposed to and ask questions such as, *Do we understand its lesson? Do we want its lesson? Would we want the children in our lives to learn from the story?* And if we say no, rather than trying to ban the story we should perhaps encourage others to acquire that same critical distance. Even if the story may not have a valuable lesson to teach children, it may still be an interesting story for adults!

Seeing Your Life as a Story

Have you ever been in a situation where someone you have just met asks you to talk about yourself? You may have found yourself answering, "Oh, there isn't much to tell," and then immediately felt that this was a poor answer — especially if you were trying to make a good impression. And perhaps later, when alone, you thought of all kinds of things to say about yourself. This is a common experience, and the good thing about it is that it serves as a wake-up call: That time around you were caught by surprise, but next time you will have a story to tell, because we all do. It is sometimes said that we could all write one good novel, the novel of our life — although the saying assumes a lot in terms of our ability as storytellers. Most of us aren't very good at telling our own story and must develop a talent for shaping it and adjusting it to our audiences. Talking about ourselves makes us realize that, as much as we may try to be completely accurate, it's not possible. We simply can't remember everything that has happened to us; we also realize that even if we could remember, it would not all be equally interesting. So *selectivity* is part of the secret of effective storytelling. And we select different things to tell depending on the audience. If you are telling your story to a new boyfriend or girlfriend, you will emphasize certain things in your life, but if you are describing yourself in front of a panel of strangers during a job interview, you will most definitely emphasize other things. And if you are updating your parents about recent events in your life, you will probably choose quite a different story to tell.

FOR BETTER OR FOR WORSE by Lynn Johnston

© Lynn Johnston Productions Inc. Distributed by United Features Syndicate, Inc.

In this *For Better or Worse* comic strip, life is viewed as a story, written perhaps by fate, perhaps by God, but definitely with an individual's input. What do you think is meant by "writing our own story"? Is it the same as *telling* our own story, or is there a difference?

Another feature of telling one's own story is a result of being alive: The story is *incomplete*. We are always in the middle of it; we may be closer to the beginning than to the end or closer to the end than the beginning, but we never view our own story from the same point of view as that of an author telling a story—because our story is not finished yet. We don't know how it will end.

A third feature is that, contrary to what we might think, the telling of our own story is to a great extent *fictional*, put together with *poetic creativity*. We may try to remember to be objective, but telling a story generally involves not only a beginning, a middle, and an ending but also a movement from one situation to the next. We don't just say, "And then this happened, and then that happened;" we say, "And *because* this happened, *then* that happened." We assume causality—and since we rarely know all factors involved, we make use of interpretations and make assumptions. (And then, of course, we may be outright lying, but that is a different story!)

So if telling one's own story is such an unreliable enterprise, why bother? Because it is good for us; it helps us find out where we have been and where we are going. As you read at the beginning of this chapter, storytelling is now part of many therapy sessions, and it involves not only listening to stories but also telling them, mostly about oneself. If we see our past as a story, we might be able to identify things to be proud of and things to improve upon. In other words, we may get a better grip on our identity. And when we realize that we are also part of other people's stories, and they are part of ours, then we begin to see ourselves as part of a much bigger story, that of our community and culture.

Searching for Meaning

The psychoanalyst Erik Erikson believed that if we are lucky enough to have become psychologically mature, we will have developed *ego integrity*, and we will stop asking useless questions such as "Why did I do that? Why didn't I do such and such?" We will learn to accept the events in our lives, those we are responsible for and those that just happened to us, as facts with which we must contend. Knowing individuals who have attained this peace of mind may help us along the way.

One challenge to our ego integrity occurs when something happens in our life that we didn't expect and that we find grossly unfair. A man works hard and saves his money so he can enjoy his later years, and then he dies six months after retiring. Parents give up everything they have so that their daughter can go to college, and she ends up on skid row because of drug abuse. A young child who receives a "routine" blood transfusion is infected with AIDS.

Is there a good way to deal with such calamities? One approach that has provided comfort to many people over the ages has been to view such an event as an act of God or of Fate: It had to happen, we don't know why, but to God it makes sense. Now, we see "through a glass darkly" (1 Corinthians 13:12) but later, in heaven, we will see why it happened. Another source of comfort for some is to view it as *karma:* It is the consequence of something you did earlier or in a previous life. In other words, it is your own fault, and it will do you no good to rage about it or blame someone else. The best you can do is to realize it and try to create good karma for next time around.

A popular modern Western way of approaching the problem is to assign guilt, or blame. We say the retiree brought on his death himself; he never exercised, and his cholesterol level was too high. The parents of the girl who became a drug addict must have done a terrible job of raising her. And the parents of the child who contracted AIDS should have been more careful about checking up on the hospital. Our accusations are sometimes justified, but they can also be unnecessarily cruel. Sometimes, common sense will tell us, people really can't be blamed for what happens to them or to those they love. But it is reassuring to bystanders to blame the victim—it's a way of believing that if they're careful to avoid the victim's mistakes, they'll escape disaster. Although it may be true in some cases that a person's conduct contributed to what happened to him or her, that is far from being a universal pattern. In any case, we have no right to infer *guilt* from *causality;* in other words, just because someone's conscious or unconscious conduct led to some problem, we can't automatically conclude that he or she is guilty of some *moral wrongdoing.* Such an attitude often reflects a double standard: If it happens to strangers, they must have done something "wrong"; if it happens to me or to one of my heroes, we are just unfortunate victims. This double standard has frequently been applied to the AIDS crisis; some people see AIDS as punishment for immoral behavior—unless it strikes someone close to them.

An alternate way of dealing with life's crises is to see them in the light of *stories.* Humans—at least modern humans in the Western world—seem to have a need for history and their own lives to make sense; we need to understand *why* something happened. Even people in traditional cultures with little written history have the same concern about a life well spent. In such cultures the models are usually the myths and legends of that culture: Do as the culture hero did, and you will have lived well. In our pluralistic culture the emphasis is much more on doing something *new* — blazing a trail, inventing something, writing a paper about an idea nobody has thought of before. We like our children to be different from their friends, to be individuals. Martha Nussbaum says that stories teach us to deal emotionally with the unexpected. Of course, the unexpected situation in our own life is not likely to be the same as the one in our favorite story — then it wouldn't be unexpected. But we can react to the unexpected in the same way our favorite characters do, and in this way we may be able to rise to the occasion. Persons from a traditional culture might find such efforts at being ready for the unexpected, as well as efforts at being different, incomprehensible, for what makes persons good in their culture is precisely that they do the *same* as their ancestors. The urge to act well, however, is the same for members of both modern and traditional cultures. In order to live an accomplished life you must follow a pattern ("Do like the ancestors" or "Do something new"), and others will deem it a good thing if you succeed. *Havamal,* "The Word of the High One," the ancient Norse poem of rules for living, says that "Cattle die, kindred die, every man is mortal. But the good name never dies, of one who has done well." This doesn't just mean that good people will be remembered — it means that *we pass judgment* on people according to how they handled themselves in life.

When things go our way, we don't ask about the meaning of life. We find that the whole development makes sense. The mythologist Joseph Campbell compares it to being at a fun party: You don't stop and ask yourself what you are doing there. But at a boring party you might ask yourself that question. Similarly, when things go wrong in someone's life, he or she may question the meaning of life — because somehow, life doesn't make sense anymore. An unexpected element interrupts our life's story, and we lose the thread — we experience an *identity crisis* (an expression introduced by Erikson). So how can stories help?

When we change direction in life, we change our future; we don't know what it may be, but we assume that if we decide to have a child or switch majors or move to another city, our future will at least contain elements different from what it would have otherwise. But when we change direction in our life we also change our past, because we now see it in a different light, *redescribing* and *reinterpreting* it. When our viewpoint shifts and we interpret our past in the light of the present, we rewrite our own story and sometimes even the story of our community and our culture. When I decide to major in pre-med instead of business because of my sister's illness, I rewrite my story from then on. If my uncle dies just after retiring, I rewrite his story, and it *does* become a moral lesson; I tell myself I will try not to do what he did or try to avoid what life did to him, or at least to make every day count. (In this way I rewrite my own story as well.) If I lose my money because of bad investments, I may rewrite the story in a number of ways: I was victimized, but now I'm smarter; or I was too concerned with money, but now I'm smarter. (Of course, we are not always smarter, but it makes us feel better to think so.) At any rate, we rewrite our past so it will make sense to us in the present and give a new, meaningful direction to our future. It is when we feel incapable of finding a new story line in our life — when the change has been so dramatic, there seems to be no new purpose lurking among the rubble — that the identity crisis may be hard to shake. In that case, it takes courage to choose to view the world and human life the way the British philosopher

Bertrand Russell described it: as a collection of atoms brought together at random, with no rhyme nor reason other than the rules of science and biology. But even this is a story: It is a story of natural forces and how each human fits into the greater whole of biology — rather a romantic notion. In the face of meaninglessness, we also might choose, with certain existential philosophers, to say that life is its own meaning. In this case the force and will of life in any shape or form become a story we can relate to when no other stories present themselves. We may, of course, choose to say that we just don't know. We would like to think that there is some story, some purpose, but we don't know what it is or whether there is one at all.

When we tell our own story and the story of our culture, it is most often an attempt to see the overall pattern, or impose one, to find some sense behind chaotic events. But we tell personal and cultural stories to try to improve ourselves and perhaps to make up for cultural errors or wrongdoing of the past. This level of storytelling doesn't just *describe* the situation, it also *prescribes* what we ought to be doing next. This *normative* element contains what may be the deepest moral dimension of the so-called true stories of oneself and one's culture: looking forward to the future, trying to shape it into an ideal image, and reshaping the past so that it appears to lead toward the ideal. (Fictional stories that warn against an unwanted future are part of this moral effort.) Do we have any guarantees that such stories, told to make the future better, actually match reality at all? An actress says she has had a drug problem, but now she is clean and wants to teach others about the dangers of drugs. A schoolteacher tells her class that their culture has elements of discrimination and persecution in its past but that this will never happen again if they will all work together. A politician tells of the hardships we have endured and of the great things we can accomplish if we stand together and vote for him. Or a couple get together again after having broken up and tell each other how they were both wrong and how this time it is going to be different. In some cases these projections are, of course, just wishful thinking, and the future may not comply. But well-told stories have a power all their own: *They can make the future happen.* So while we listen to, and create, great stories that can change our lives and the life of our culture, we should remember to retain our critical sense and our sense of moral responsibility: Do our stories prescribe a future that we would actually want to have happen?

Living in the Narrative Zone

We humans are temporal beings. We live in the present, but we are constantly reaching back to the past and forward to the future, in a constant state of tension between memory and anticipation. We live our own story, which has its own beginning and its own end, although we can't describe them. Furthermore, we live the stories of our culture; we identify with them or criticize them or rewrite them. We seek moral lessons in our own stories and in the stories of our culture. We also just like to hear stories, watch stories, and tell stories; and when we do, the time period we experience multiplies. We are still living our own life, but there is a new element: *narrative time,* a concept introduced by the French philosopher Paul Ricoeur. Narrative time is the compressed time of a novel or a movie, the time it takes for the story to unfold. So while it may take us three days to read a book, its narrative time may span generations. Two hours at the movies, and we may have lived through years of narrative time, following the lives of the characters from youth to old age. In this way we share multiple experiences with fictional characters, and expand our moral horizons, as Nussbaum suggested in Chapter 1.

There is a story, "Mantage," by the science fiction writer Richard Matheson about a man who wanted his life to be like things are in the movies, because he thought his life was extremely dull. His wish was granted, and this is what happened: He found that time had sped up, and before he knew it he had fallen in love, was married and had kids; now he found himself making money, living in style, and having love affairs, but when he looked at his watch, only an hour had passed. He found that he was living out his life in abbreviated chunks of time, the same as in a movie. After two hours he was old and dying, and the last thing he saw before his eyes was the letters DNE EHT — "The End" to the audience watching him. As the saying goes, when the gods want to punish us, they give us what we wish for.

Obviously this is not what the man truly wished for — he wanted a life with an exciting story line, not a life lived in the time it takes for a film audience to watch a movie. We readers and viewers are luckier, because we can have the best of both worlds. We can retain our own real-life time while we share in the accelerated, telescoped time of books and movies. When we open a book or sit down in a movie theater we enter what we might call the *Narrative Zone,* where we can live other lives vicariously, acquire skills and experiences that we might never know of otherwise.

We may be emotionally cleansed by experiencing the strong feelings in a story, as Aristotle suggested. We may get an idea of what it feels like to be a member of the other gender or another race, of another time and place, or of another species entirely — and these experiences may help us decide how to live once we leave the Narrative Zone. Nothing else provokes our empathy as effectively as a good story: We weep and rejoice with our friends in the novel or in the movie, even if we know that it is only make-believe. They are not wasted tears or smiles, for they are, ultimately, the building blocks of our character.

If we happen to read the story of the Good Samaritan, there is a chance that we will stop to help the victim should we happen to see a mugging in progress. There is also a chance that the "victim" will end up mugging us, but that doesn't mean we should not have read the story or that we should not have come to the victim's aid; it means that life doesn't always conform to the stories we read, and we shouldn't think it does.

So sometimes we get hurt when we are inspired by stories, and sometimes we are inspired by the wrong stories. The essayist and science fiction writer Ursula K. Le Guin compares our existence as readers and listeners to the hoop snake that bites its own tail: It hurts, but *now you can roll!* What is the moral? If the hoop snake doesn't make a hoop, it won't move, and it will be as though it never lived. So we must take chances — we mustn't shy away from taking part in the listening process, in becoming engaged in the story — and we mustn't shy away from becoming engaged in our own story. For Le Guin, telling stories and listening to stories is a kind of life affirmation and an incentive to live life to the fullest.

All of the stories in this book are examples of how natural it is for humans to think in terms of stories when we want to discuss a moral problem. At this point, though, I would like to repeat something I mentioned earlier. These summaries of stories are by no means a sufficient substitute for reading the stories or watching the films yourself; the outlines merely provide a basis for discussing the specific problems explored in the stories in light of the theories presented in this book. Without actually reading the book or viewing the movie, the essential experience of being in the Narrative Zone — of sharing the narrative time with the work of fiction — is lost, or at least thoroughly diluted, and the emotional impact is at best a weak approximation of the original narrative experience. So do yourself a favor: If a certain narrative appeals to you, then read the original book or watch the original film. In this way you will add another set of "parallel lives" to your own life experience. Besides, it's not a bad idea to let the characters in films and novels make some of our mistakes for us, as long as we don't forget to make ourselves the central character in some stories of our own now and again.

Throughout this book you will see examples of stories' being the bearers of moral values. Of course, we have not even scratched the surface of the treasure of stories available to us, and I hope that our discussion will inspire you to experience and evaluate other narratives in light of the theories of ethics you'll encounter in this book.

Study Questions

1. Name three didactic stories, describe their plots, and explain their moral lessons. Do you agree with these lessons? Why or why not?

2. Discuss the phenomenon of Goethe's novel about Werther, who commits suicide because of unrequited love: What were the effects of the publication? Why did this phenomenon happen? Do you think something similar could happen today, inspired by a film, a novel, or some other medium of fiction? If yes, what should be done to prevent it, if anything? If no, why not?

3. Compare and contrast Plato's and Aristotle's views on whether watching a dramatic play (or, today, perhaps a film) has a positive influence. Compare their viewpoints to the current discussion on the subject of violence in films and on television. In your opinion, is one viewpoint more correct than the other? Why or why not?

4. Pick a sequence from your life and tell it as a story. Review it afterward: Did it give you any new insight?

Primary Readings and Narratives

This chapter concludes with four Primary Readings from the classical philosophical tradition and four Narratives. In a section from Plato's *Republic* you will read, in his own words, his argument why drama is bad for the mind; next, you will read Aristotle's argument that drama can be beneficial; the section is taken from his *Poetics*. The third Primary Reading is an excerpt from a novel, Umberto Eco's *The Name of the Rose*, in which Eco gives us an idea of how he thinks the lost part of Aristotle's *Poetics* might have read. The last Primary Reading is from Tristine Rainer's self-help book, *Your Life as Story*, a practical guide to writing one's autobiography.

Two of the narratives are dramas. They were written more than two thousand years apart, but they are both intended to be spoken by actors and experienced by an audience, and they both contain violence and human tragedy: an excerpt from Euripides' play *Medea*, and a summary of a scene from Quentin Tarantino's movie *Pulp Fiction*. The other two narratives represent other aspects of the discussions in Chapter 2: an excerpt from Goethe's *Sorrows of Young Werther*, and a summary of the film *Lord Jim*, based on the novel by Joseph Conrad. *Lord Jim* is chosen as an example of a modern application of Aristotle's blueprint for a good drama.

Primary Reading

The Republic

PLATO

Excerpt from Book X, The Republic, fourth century B.C.E. Translated by F. M. Cornford.

In this excerpt from Plato's dialogue *The Republic*, Socrates (left) is having a conversation with Plato's brother Glaucon about the nature of art and of drama in particular. Glaucon is supplying the "Quite so"s, and Socrates is supplying the rest of the conversation.

Drama, we say, represents the acts and fortunes of human beings. It is wholly concerned with what they do, voluntarily or against their will, and how they fare, with the consequences which they regard as happy or otherwise, and with their feelings of joy and sorrow in all these experiences. That is all, is it not?

Yes.

And in all these experiences has a man an undivided mind? Is there not an internal conflict which sets him at odds with himself in his conduct, much as we were saying that the conflict of visual impressions leads him to make contradictory judgments? However, I need not ask that question; for, now I come to think of it, we have already agreed that innumerable conflicts of this sort are constantly occurring in the mind. But there is a further point to be considered now. We have said that a man of high character will bear any stroke of fortune, such as the loss of a son or of anything else he holds dear, with more equanimity than most people. We may now ask: will he feel no pain, or is that impossible? Will he not rather observe due measure in his grief?

Yes, that is near the truth.

Now tell me: will he be more likely to struggle with his grief and resist it when he is under the eyes of his fellows or when he is alone?

He will be far more restrained in the presence of others.

Yes; when he is by himself he will not be ashamed to do and say much that he would not like anyone to see or hear.

Quite so.

What encourages him to resist his grief is the lawful authority of reason, while the impulse to give way comes from the feeling itself; and, as we said, the presence of contradictory impulses proves that two distinct elements in his nature must be involved. One of them is law-abiding, prepared to listen to the authority which declares that it is best to bear misfortune as quietly as possible without resentment, for several reasons: it is never certain that misfortune may not be a blessing; nothing is gained by chafing at it; nothing human is matter for great concern; and, finally, grief hinders us from calling in the help we most urgently need. By this I mean reflection on what has happened, letting reason decide on the best move in the game of life that the fall of the dice permits. Instead of behaving like a child who goes on shrieking after a fall and hugging the wounded part, we should accustom the mind to set itself at once to raise up the fallen and cure the hurt, banishing lamentation with a healing touch.

Certainly that is the right way to deal with misfortune.

And if, as we think, the part of us which is ready to act upon these reflections is the highest, that other part which impels us to dwell upon our sufferings and can never have enough of grieving over them is unreasonable, craven, and faint-hearted.

Yes.

Now this fretful temper gives scope for a great diversity of dramatic representation; whereas the calm and wise character in its unvarying constancy is not easy to represent, nor when represented is it readily understood, especially by a promiscuous gathering in a theater, since it is foreign to their own habit of mind. Obviously, then, this steadfast disposition does not naturally attract the dramatic poet, and his skill is not designed to find favour with it. If he is to have a popular success, he must address himself to the fretful type with its rich variety of material for representation.

Obviously.

We have, then, a fair case against the poet and we may set him down as the counterpart of the painter, whom he resembles in two ways: his creations are poor things by the standard of truth and reality, and his appeal is not to the highest part of the soul, but to one which is equally inferior. So we shall be justified in not admitting him into a well-ordered commonwealth, because he stimulates and strengthens an element which threatens to undermine the reason. As a country may be given over into the power of its worst citizens while the better sort are ruined, so, we shall say, the dramatic poet sets up a vicious form of government in the individual soul: he gratifies that senseless part which cannot distinguish great and small, but regards the same things as now one, now the other; and he is an image-maker whose images are phantoms far removed from reality.

Quite true. . . .

But, I continued, the heaviest count in our indictment is still to come. Dramatic poetry has a most formidable power of corrupting even men of high character, with a few exceptions.

Formidable indeed, if it can do that.

Let me put the case for you to judge. When we listen to some hero in Homer or on the tragic stage moaning over his sorrows in a long tirade, or to a chorus beating their breasts as they chant a lament, you know how the best of us enjoy giving ourselves up to follow the performance with eager sympathy. The more a poet can move our feelings in this way, the better we think him. And yet when the sorrow is our own, we pride ourselves on being able to bear it quietly like a man, condemning the behaviour we admired in the theatre as womanish. Can it be right that the spectacle of a man behaving as one would scorn and blush to behave oneself should be admired and enjoyed, instead of filling us with disgust?

No, it really does not seem reasonable.

It does not, if you reflect that the poet ministers to the satisfaction of that very part of our nature whose instinctive hunger to have its fill of tears and lamentations is forcibly restrained in the case of our own misfortunes. Meanwhile the noblest part of us, insufficiently schooled by reason or habit, has relaxed its watch over these querulous feelings, with the excuse that the sufferings we are contemplating are not our own and it is no shame to us to admire and pity a man with some pretensions to a noble character, though his grief may be excessive. The enjoyment itself seems a clear gain, which we cannot bring ourselves to forfeit by disdaining the whole poem. Few, I believe, are capable of reflecting that to enter into another's feelings must have an effect on our own: the emotions of pity our sympathy has strengthened will not be easy to restrain when we are suffering ourselves.

That is very true.

Does not the same principle apply to humour as well as to pathos? You are doing the same thing if, in listening at a comic performance or in ordinary life to buffooneries which you would be ashamed to indulge in yourself, you thoroughly enjoy them instead of being disgusted with their ribaldry. There is in you an impulse to play the clown, which you have held in restraint from a reasonable fear of being set down as a buffoon; but now you have given it rein, and by encouraging its impudence at the theatre you may be unconsciously carried away into playing the comedian in your private life. Similar effects are produced by poetic representation of love and anger and all those desires and feelings of pleasure or pain which accompany our every action. It waters the growth of passions which should be allowed to wither away and sets them up in control, although the goodness and happiness of our lives depend on their being held in subjection.

I cannot but agree with you.

If so, Glaucon, when you meet with admirers of Homer who tell you that he has been the educator of Hellas and that on questions of human conduct and culture he deserves to be constantly studied as a guide by whom to regulate your whole life, it is well to give a friendly hearing to such people, as entirely well-meaning according to their lights, and you may acknowledge Homer to be the first and greatest of the tragic poets; but you must be quite sure that we can admit into our commonwealth only the poetry which celebrates the praises of the gods and of good men. If you go further and admit the honeyed muse in epic or in lyric verse, then pleasure and pain will usurp the sovereignty of law and of the principles always recognized by common consent as the best.

Quite true.

Study Questions

1. Is Plato right that a well-balanced, emotionally stable character is rarely the main focus of a fictional drama? Can you think of any dramatic story involving an even-tempered person as the main character (or one of the main characters)? I have often asked my students this question, and I'll let you be the judge of some of my students' suggestions: How about Verbal Kint from *The Usual Suspects*? Hannibal Lecter from *The Silence of the Lambs*? Mr. Spock from *Star Trek*? James Bond? Sherlock Holmes? The butler from *The Remains of the Day*? Are these characters even-tempered, emotionally balanced, in other words, unflappable? And if so, are they still interesting as lead characters? Can you think of a female lead character who would fit the description?

2. Do you agree with Plato that having your emotions stirred on behalf of a character in a story undermines your ability to control your own emotions?

3. In your opinion, should we always be able to control our emotions? Why or why not?

4. Relate Plato's viewpoint to the current debate about violence in entertainment.

5. In Plato's view, what is the danger in watching comedies? Do you agree? Why or why not?

Primary Reading

Poetics

ARISTOTLE

Excerpts from Chapters 6, 13, and 14, Poetics, *fourth century* B.C.E. *Translated by Ingram Bywater.*

In these two excerpts from Aristotle's *Poetics* he has just explained that delight in poetry (fiction in general) is natural for humans because fiction is imitation of life, and so we learn about life from fiction—and to Aristotle, knowledge is always a good thing. Here he proceeds to tell us what makes a good tragic story.

> A tragedy, then, is the imitation of an action that is serious and also, as having magnitude, complete in itself; in language with pleasurable accessories, each kind brought in separately in the parts of the work; in a dramatic, not in a narrative form; with incidents arousing pity and fear, wherewith to accomplish its catharsis of such emotions. . . .
>
> We assume that, for the finest form of Tragedy, the Plot must not be simple but complex; and further, that it must imitate actions arousing fear and pity, since that is the distinctive function of this kind of imitation. It follows, therefore, that there are three forms of Plot to be avoided. (1) A good man must not be seen passing from happiness to misery, or (2) a bad man from misery to happiness. The first situation is not fear-inspiring or piteous, but simply odious to us. The second is the most untragic that can

be; it has not one of the requisites of Tragedy; it does not appeal either to the human feeling in us, or to our pity, or to our fears. Nor, on the other hand, should (3) an extremely bad man be seen falling from happiness into misery. Such a story may arouse the human feeling in us, but it will not move us to either pity or fear; pity is occasioned by undeserved misfortune, and fear by that of one like ourselves; so that there will be nothing either piteous or fear-inspiring in the situation. There remains, then, the intermediate kind of personage, a man not pre-eminently virtuous and just, whose misfortune, however, is brought upon him not by vice and depravity but by some error of judgment, of the number of those in the enjoyment of great reputation and prosperity; e.g. Oedipus, Thyestes, and the men of note of similar families. The perfect Plot, accordingly, must have a single, and not (as some tell us) a double issue; the change in the hero's fortunes must be not from misery to happiness, but on the contrary from happiness to misery; and the cause of it must lie not in any depravity, but in some great error on his part; the man himself being either such as we have described, or better, not worse, than that. Fact also confirms our theory. Though the poets began by accepting any tragic story that came to hand, in these days the finest tragedies are always on the story of some few houses, on that of Alcmeon, Oedipus, Orestes, Meleager, Thyestes, Telephus, or any others that may have been involved, as either agents or sufferers, in some deed of horror. The theoretically best tragedy, then, has a Plot of this description. The critics, therefore, are wrong who blame Euripides for taking this line in his tragedies, and giving many of them an unhappy ending. It is, as we have said, the right line to take. The best proof of this: on the stage, and in the public performances, such plays, properly worked out, are seen to be the most truly tragic; and Euripides, even if his execution be faulty in every other point, is seen to be nevertheless the most tragic certainly of the dramatists. After this comes the construction of Plot which some rank first, one with a double story (like the *Odyssey*) and an opposite issue for the good and the bad personages. It is ranked as first only through the weakness of the audiences; the poets merely follow their public, writing as its wishes dictate. But the pleasure here is not that of Tragedy. It belongs rather to Comedy, where the bitterest enemies in the piece (e.g. Orestes and Aegisthus) walk off good friends at the end, with no slaying of any one by any one.

The tragic fear and pity may be aroused by the Spectacle; but they may also be aroused by the very structure and incidents of the play — which is the better way and shows the better poet. The Plot in fact should be so framed that, even without seeing the things take place, he who simply hears the account of them shall be filled with horror and pity at the incidents; which is just the effect that the mere recital of the story in *Oedipus* would have on one. To produce this same effect by means of the Spectacle is less artistic, and requires extraneous aid. Those, however, who make use of the Spectacle to put before us that which is merely monstrous and not productive of fear, are wholly out of touch with Tragedy; not every kind of pleasure should be required of a tragedy, but only its own proper pleasure.

The tragic pleasure is that of pity and fear, and the poet has to produce it by a work of imitation; it is clear, therefore, that the causes should be included in the incidents of his story. Let us see, then, what kinds of incident strike one as horrible, or rather as piteous. In a deed of this description the parties must necessarily be either friends, or enemies, or indifferent to one another. Now when enemy does it on enemy, there is nothing to move us to pity either in his doing or in his meditating the deed, except so far as the actual pain of the sufferer is concerned; and the same is true when the parties are indifferent to one another. Whenever the tragic deed, however, is done within the family—when murder or the like is done or meditated by brother on brother, by son on father, by mother on son, or son on mother—these are the situations the poet should seek after.

Study Questions

1. Would you agree with Aristotle that the best kind of dramatic fiction involves an ordinary man who experiences misfortune because of an error in judgment? Think of modern films and novels that might fit this pattern (involving ordinary men *and* women). How about *American Beauty*? Brecht's *Mother Courage*? *Gladiator*? (These are some suggestions from my students.)

2. What is "catharsis of emotions"? Do you agree with Aristotle that it can be obtained by experiencing dramatic fiction?

3. As we have seen, Plato disapproves of a dramatic story, whereas Aristotle approves of it. In view of the fact that Plato wrote in quite a dramatic way about the downfall of Socrates (see Chapter 8), do you think Aristotle would have viewed Plato's story as an example of cathartic literature?

4. Aristotle says a good tragedy shouldn't need any "Spectacle" if the story is enough to make people shudder with fear and pity. In the *Poetics* he defines it as the actual, physical appearance of actors on the stage, but as you see in this excerpt he also specifies that the Spectacle is unnecessary if the audience can imagine the situation through a good narration on stage. We could perhaps take that to mean a good dramatic performance doesn't need any exaggerated display or special effects to get its point across. Can you think of movies that have been extremely vivid even with very few special effects, because they rely on our minds to fill in the gaps with our own visions of horror? Are there movies whose impact has been completely dependent on special effects? Does that detract from the story?

Primary Reading

The Name of the Rose

UMBERTO ECO

Novel, 1980. Excerpt. Translated by William Weaver.

Usually we do not present a work of fiction as a Primary Reading, but this exception relates to the Aristotle text you have just read. Aristotle's *Poetics* consisted of two books, one on tragedy, and the other on comedy, but the latter has been lost since before the

Middle Ages. We know, however, that Aristotle admired the theater, and that book would probably have paralleled his book on tragedy, outlining the proper plot type for a good comedy and so forth. The Italian philosopher and novelist Umberto Eco's novel *The Name of the Rose,* a murder mystery set in the High Middle Ages, features the resurfacing of a copy of Aristotle's book on comedy, and speculates that if a work by Aristotle had been available in those days that legitimized comedy and laughter, Western culture might have developed differently. Here William of Baskerville, a monk with detective skills visiting the monastery where serial killings are taking place, is getting close to solving the crimes. He reads from the long-lost book by Aristotle (written by Eco to resemble Aristotle's style), and has a discussion with the librarian Jorge about the effects of laughter.

In the first book we dealt with tragedy and saw how, by arousing pity and fear, it produces catharsis, the purification of those feelings. As we promised, we will now deal with comedy (as well as with satire and mime) and see how, in inspiring the pleasure of the ridiculous, it arrives at the purification of that passion. That such passion is most worthy of consideration we have already said in the book on the soul, inasmuch as — alone among the animals — man is capable of laughter. We will then define the type of actions of which comedy is the mimesis, then we will examine the means by which comedy excites laughter, and these means are actions and speech. We will show how the ridiculousness of actions is born from the likening of the best to the worst and vice versa, from arousing surprise through deceit, from the impossible, from violation of the laws of nature, from the irrelevant and the inconsequent, from the debasing of the characters, from the use of comical and vulgar pantomime, from disharmony, from the choice of the least worthy things. We will then show how the ridiculousness of speech is born from the misunderstandings of similar words for different things and different words for similar things, from garrulity and repetition, from play on words, from diminutives, from errors of pronunciation, and from barbarisms. [. . .]

"But now tell me," William was saying, "Why? Why did you want to shield this book more than so many others? Why did you hide — though not at the price of crime — treatises on necromancy, pages that may have blasphemed against the name of God, while for these pages you damned your brothers and have damned yourself? There are many other books that speak of comedy, many others that praise laughter. Why did this one fill you with such fear?"

"Because it was by the Philosopher. Every book by that man has destroyed a part of the learning that Christianity had accumulated over the centuries. [. . .]

"But what frightened you in this discussion of laughter? You cannot eliminate laughter by eliminating the book."

"No, to be sure. But laughter is weakness, corruption, the foolishness of our flesh. It is the peasant's entertainment, the drunkard's license; even the church in her wisdom has granted the moment of feast, carnival, fair, this diurnal pollution that releases humors and distracts from other desires and other ambitions. . . . Still, laughter remains base, a defense for the simple, a mystery desecrated for the plebeians. The apostle also said as much: it is better to marry than to burn. Rather than rebel against God's established order, laugh and enjoy your foul parodies of order, at the end of the meal, after you have drained jugs and flasks. Elect the king of fools, lose yourselves in the liturgy of the ass and the pig, play at performing your saturnalia head down. . . . But here, here"—now Jorge struck the table with his finger, near the book William was holding open—"here the function of laughter is reversed, it is elevated to art, the doors of the world of the learned are opened to it, it becomes the object of philosophy, and of perfidious theology. [. . .] That laughter is proper to man is a sign of our limitation, sinners that we are. But from this book many corrupt minds like yours would draw the extreme syllogism, whereby laughter is man's end! Laughter, for a few moments, distracts the villein from fear. But law is imposed by fear, whose true name is fear of God. This book could strike the Luciferine spark that would set a new fire to the whole world, and laughter would be defined as the new art, unknown even to Prometheus, for canceling fear. To the villein who laughs, at that moment, dying does not matter: but then, when the license is past, the liturgy again imposes on him, according to the divine plan, the fear of death. And from this book there could be born the new destructive aim to destroy death through redemption from fear.

Study Questions

1. Compare the real Aristotle text on tragedy and Eco's pastiche (attempt at writing something similar). Has Eco done a good job, in your view?

2. Compare Plato's view on comedy and laughter with what Eco believes to have been Aristotle's view. Which comes close to your opinion? Explain why. (Also, who do you think Eco would side with: Plato or Aristotle?)

3. Is Jorge right that law is imposed by fear of God, and laughter is a distraction from fear, so laughter is dangerous? Compare Jorge's and Plato's comments on laughter. (Remember that Jorge is a fictional character.)

4. Could Eco be right that if Aristotle's book had survived, it might have changed the course of Western culture? Why or why not?

Primary Reading

Your Life as Story

TRISTINE RAINER

Book, 1997. Excerpt.

Rainer's book is a practical guide to writing one's autobiography and includes chapters such as "The Nine Essential Elements of Story Structure," "Genres of the Self," "Truth in Autobiographic Writing," and "Finishing the Unfinished Story." She suggests looking for patterns in your life and the lives of others as a stargazer looks for constellations. Her book is more than a guide to writing a best-selling story about yourself—it is intended as a guide to make you understand yourself better. In this selection she gives the first lesson in finding the story of your life.

What is a story anyway? We all know intuitively. As children we gobble them up and never feel too full for more. Myths are stories, fairy tales and folktales are stories; so are novels, movies, and sitcoms. But you can't touch, taste, smell, hear, or see a story—only the images and words it assumes. To say what a story is, is like trying to get your hands around a ghost shape.

Though they are intangible, stories are powerful and their power seems to come from another realm. They appear to be a way in which the sacred enters our lives. Myths, stories to explain how and why we are here, begot religion. The morality tales of Moses, Jesus, Mohammed, and Buddha—stories that tell us what to value and how to live—have determined the course of world history for more than nineteen centuries. Stories remembered within a community or family transport the beliefs and values of past generations into the future. The individual stories of our own lives tell us who we are and infuse our personal existence with excitement, meaning, and mystery.

Myths, parables, family stories, and the innumerable media stories of our popular culture are offered to us already embodied in the words or images of others. However, the stories of our own lives require active searching—learning to look through our memories in a new way. To find story in your life, you must engage imagination with memory; you must invent a line of continuity—not from nothing, but from the raw materials of your life. It's like reading a pattern in DNA or figuring out the possible anagrams in a word. To find story in your life, you have to know what you are looking for. Fortunately, though you can't see a story, if you learn what its features are, when you look you will recognize one—and then many.

So what are the features of a story? A story isn't just a plot, a series of interconnected events. A story is a meaningful narrative with a beginning, a middle, and a conclusion. You started out at point A, the beginning, and because of what you did and what happened to you in the middle, point B, you ended up at point C, the conclusion. At point C you were a different person than you were at A, not just because you were older, but because you saw things differently.

In its simplest form a story is: what you wanted, how you struggled, and what you realized out of that struggle. A story is a series of interrelated events that you made happen and that happened to you, and the consequence. The consequence is a change in you. In an autobiographic story, change may occur in other characters, but it must also occur in you, because you are the protagonist. The change may come from an event (you married, you got old), but it is also a moral change. You had a realization, a shift in values or perception.

In other words, within the story you made a "character arc," you had a change in character. Gradually, because of what happened to you in life and the minirealizations you had along the way, you went from "there" to "here" as a person. What you believed, what you valued, and how you acted toward others changed, even if only slightly. You track this character arc in an autobiographic story by including your feelings, reactions to the events you experienced, and your realizations. You give the events of your life significance because of what they meant to you and how you changed from your engagement with them. An autobiographic story is not just an account of events; it is the charting of your emotional, moral, and psychological course, which gives meaning to those events.

It is worth taking some time to think about the inner course you wish to trace before you start putting down everything you can remember about your past. It is worth considering what story you want your life to tell. Why? Why not just write down everything you can remember, like so many people do? Because it won't be alive, it won't tap into the power of myth, it won't participate in the kind of truth that we read narratives for.

Study Questions

1. What does Rainer mean by a "moral change" in a story?

2. What is a "character arc"?

3. Write three pages of autobiography (the story of your life so far) using Rainer's method. Have a friend who knows you well critique it: Did you mention points in your life he or she would recognize? Are there important events you chose to omit? Does he or she recognize your self-image? Write a new version using your friend's critique, and compare the two.

4. In the first season of the television series *The Sopranos,* young Chris, a mobster as well as an aspiring screenwriter, is experiencing an existential crisis. Feeling that nobody takes him seriously enough, he shoots a deli manager in the foot because he doesn't get preferential treatment. Afterward he agonizes that his life seems disjointed and meaningless, because he has no "character arc." He proceeds to try to establish a reputation as a tough mobster. Is this what Rainer means by a character arc? If you are a *Sopranos* fan, what do you think the screenwriter had in mind by having Chris talk about character arcs?

Narrative

Medea

EURIPIDES

From a fifth-century-B.C.E. play. Summary and Excerpts. Translated by Moses Hadas.

The Greek dramatist Euripides (ca. 485–406 B.C.E.) was considered an eccentric and an intellectual radical. Nineteen of his eighty-eight plays have survived into modern times.

In fifth-century B.C.E. Athens, the annual festival held for Dionysus had developed into an established tradition of competitions among playwrights of tragedies, satyr plays, and comedies. Although the tragedies were originally supposed to deal with the life, death, and resurrection of the god Dionysus (Bacchus) and stories of the gods in general, they quickly developed into stories about human failings and revenge. The tragedy *Medea,* written in 451 B.C.E., is unusual in that it doesn't follow the established tragic pattern of the triumph of divine justice; but Euripides rarely followed the established patterns of tragedies. He won only four first prizes at the festivals in his lifetime, but after his death his plays became immensely popular. Toward the end of his life he left Athens; he died in Macedonia (where Aristotle was born in 384 B.C.E., twenty-two years later). In the preceding excerpt from Aristotle's *Poetics,* you may have noticed that Aristotle specifically praises Euripides and his unique style.

Greek mythology tells of Jason and his Argonauts, who captured the Golden Fleece from the king of Colchis and brought it back to Corinth in triumph. That is a heroic story, one of Greece's legends of the golden age. Jason was helped in his quest by the daughter of the king of Colchis, Medea, who betrayed her father, her brother, and her country in order to help Jason, the man she loved. So Medea followed him to Corinth. That was the old myth — and Euripides tells us "the rest of the story."

Years have passed, and Medea is in a deep depression. She won't eat, she can't sleep, she weeps incessantly. Jason has tired of her — she is no longer young, and Jason has fallen in love with another woman, the young blonde princess of Corinth. He has taken her as his second wife without so much as asking Medea's permission. Now the king, the princess's father, is about to banish Medea from the kingdom, together with her and Jason's two sons, because he fears that this woman, an unpredictable foreigner, may take revenge on his daughter. But Medea cannot go home because she caused her brother's death and betrayed her father in helping Jason. She forsook everything for him, including her ties to her homeland, and, without a homeland, one was barely considered a person in the ancient Greek world.

It's all over, my friends; I would gladly die. Life has lost its savor. The man who was everything to me, well he knows it, has turned out to be the basest of men. Of all creatures that feel and think, we women are the unhappiest species. In the first place, we must pay a great dowry to a husband who will be the tyrant of our bodies (that's a further aggravation of the evil); and there is another fearful hazard: whether we shall get a good man or a bad. For separations bring disgrace on the woman and it is not possible to renounce one's husband. Then, landed among strange habits and regulations unheard of in her own home, a woman needs second sight to know how best to handle her bedmate. And if we manage this well and have a husband who does not find the yoke of intercourse too galling, ours is a life to be envied. Otherwise, one is better dead. When the man wearies of the company of his wife, he goes outdoors and relieves the disgust of his heart [having recourse to some friend or the companions of his own age], but we women have only one person to turn to.

They say that we have a safe life at home, whereas men must go to war. Nonsense! I had rather fight three battles than bear one child. But be that as it may, you and I are not in the same case. You have your city here, your paternal homes; you know the delights of life and association with your loved ones. But I, homeless and forsaken, carried off from a foreign land, am being wronged by a husband, with neither mother nor brother nor kinsman with whom I might find refuge from the storms of misfortune. One little boon I crave of you, if I discover any ways and means of punishing my husband for these wrongs: your silence. Woman in most respects is a timid creature, with no heart for strife and aghast at the sight of steel; but wronged in love, there is no heart more murderous than hers.

But Medea has a plan, and the old king has seen it coming with a sure instinct: Medea plots to poison both the princess and the king. She has one last, horrible argument with Jason, who comes to make sure she won't be destitute, because he has heard that she has been expelled from the country:

Rotten, heart-rotten, that is the word for you. Words, words, magnificent words. In reality a craven. You come to me, you come, my worst enemy! This isn't bravery, you know, this isn't valor, to come and face your victims. No! it's the ugliest sore on the face of humanity, Shamelessness. But I thank you for coming. It will lighten the weight on my heart to tell your wickedness, and it will hurt you to hear it. I shall begin my tale at the very beginning.

   I saved your life, as all know who embarked with you on the Argo, when you were sent to master with the yoke the fire-breathing bulls and to sow with dragon's teeth that acre of death. The dragon, too, with wreathed coils, that kept safe watch over the Golden Fleece and never slept—I slew it and raised for you the light of life again. Then, forsaking my father and my own dear ones, I came to Iolcus where Pelias reigned, came with you, more than fond and less than wise. On Pelias too I brought death, the most painful death there is, at the hands of his own children. Thus I have removed every danger from your path.

   And after all those benefits at my hands, you basest of men, you have betrayed me and made a new marriage, though I have borne you children. If you were still childless, I could have understood this love of yours for a new wife. Gone now is all reliance on pledges. You puzzle me. Do you believe that the gods of the old days are no longer in office? Do you think that men are now living under a new dispensation? For surely you know that you have broken all your oaths to me. Ah my hand, which you so often grasped, and oh my knees, how all for nothing have we been defiled by this false man, who has disappointed all our hopes.

Jason and Medea part with bitter words, and now Medea is in luck: King Aegeus of Athens pays her a visit and hears of her marital problems and banishment. He finds Jason despicable and admires Medea for her righteous anger. He himself is looking for a wife to bear him children and offers Medea a refuge as his wife as soon as she is "done with her business."

   Medea now pretends to be submissive when Jason comes back and asks that the children be allowed to take gifts to his young bride. The enormity of what she is about to do is beginning to envelop her, and she finds it hard to control herself. After Jason leaves, she hands the gifts to the two young boys and can't stop weeping—because she not only plans to kill the princess, she also plans to *kill her own children,* to hurt Jason the only way she knows how:

> O the pain of it! Why do your eyes look at me, my children? Why smile at me that last smile? Ah! What can I do? My heart is water, women, at the sight of my children's bright faces. I could never do it. Goodbye to my former plans. I shall take my children away with me. Why should I hurt their father by *their* misfortunes, only to reap a double harvest of sorrow myself? No! I cannot do it. Goodbye to my plans.
>
> And yet . . . what is the matter with me? Do I want to make myself a laughing-stock by letting my enemies off scot-free? I must go through with it. What a coward heart is mine, to admit those soft pleas. Come, my children, into the palace. Those that may not attend my sacrifices can see to it that they are absent. I shall not let my hand be unnerved.
>
> Ah! Ah! Stop, my heart. Do not you commit this crime. Leave them alone, unhappy one, spare the children. Even if they live far from us, they will bring you joy. No! by the unforgetting dead in hell, it cannot be! I shall not leave my children for my enemies to insult. (In any case they must die. And if die they must, *I* shall slay them, who gave them birth.) My schemes are crowned with success. She shall not escape. Already the diadem is on her head; wrapped in the robe the royal bride is dying. I know it well. And now I am setting out on a most sorrowful road (and shall send these on one still more sorrowful). I wish to speak to my children. Give your mother your hands, my children, give her your hands to kiss.
>
> O dear, dear hand. O dear, dear mouth, dear shapes, dear noble faces, happiness be yours, but not here. Your father has stolen this world from you. How sweet to touch! The softness of their skin, the sweetness of their breath, my babies! Away, away, I cannot bear to see you any longer.
>
> [CHILDREN *retire within.*]
>
> My misery overwhelms me. O I *do* realize how terrible is the crime I am about, but passion overrules my resolutions, passion that causes most of the misery in the world.

She sends the children away, and after a while, a messenger tells the gruesome details: The princess put on the golden diadem, Medea's gift, and instantly the poison began to work:

> The golden diadem on her head emitted a strange flow of devouring fire, while the fine robes, the gifts of your children, were eating up the poor girl's white flesh. All aflame, she jumps from her seat and flees, shaking her head and hair this way and that, trying to throw off the crown. But the golden band held firmly, and after she had shaken her hair more violently, the fire began to blaze twice as fiercely. Overcome by the agony she falls on the ground, and none but her father could have recognized her. The position of her eyes could not be distinguished, nor the beauty of her face. The blood, clotted with fire, dripped from the crown of her head, and the flesh melted from her bones, like resin from a pine tree, as the poisons ate their unseen way. It was a fearful sight. All were afraid to touch the corpse, taught by what had happened to her.

The princess's old father rushed to the scene and took her in his arms, and that was how the poison spread to him; within minutes he, too, was dead.

The news galvanizes Medea into action: Now she feels she must kill her children so nobody will take their revenge on them, and she rationalizes,

> No flinching now, no thinking of the children, the darling children, that call you mother. This day, this one short day, forget your children. You have all the future to mourn them. Aye, to mourn. Though you mean to kill them, at least you loved them. Oh! I am a most unhappy woman.

From inside the room, we hear the cries for help as she stabs her two sons to death.

Jason returns, devastated at the turn of events. Medea gloats because now she knows she's "got under his skin." To the end, they quarrel over whose fault it is and who is to blame for the children's death. Jason didn't seem to care much for his sons while they were alive, but now that they are dead he loves them with all his heart. He invokes the power of the gods to avenge his children — but the gods don't help him. No divine lightning bolt strikes Medea down — she leaves him to become the wife of Aegeus.

Study Questions

1. This tragedy seemed nothing short of immoral to many critics in Athens because Medea gets away with quadruple murder. Can we defend Medea's actions in any way? Is Jason free of blame? What do you think Euripides intended the "moral of the story" to be?

2. How would Plato evaluate *Medea* — as a moral learning tool or a dangerous temptation to be irrational? How would Aristotle evaluate it? Does it meet his criteria for a well-written tragedy? (Tragedy has to happen to an ordinary person as the result of some grave error in judgment of theirs and preferably should happen between family members.) In other words, if Aristotle is right and a good tragedy is the story of an ordinary person — not good, not bad — who makes a major mistake and suffers for it for the rest of his/her life, then who is the main character in *Medea*? From whose viewpoint is the story told? Medea's — or Jason's?

3. Sadly, the phenomenon of parents killing their children is not unusual at all; it may be done in anger, or for insurance purposes, for convenience, or out of some peculiar sense of responsibility ("I won't allow my children to become fatherless/motherless when I kill myself, so I'll take them with me"). Rarely is it done for revenge, as in the case of Medea. Susan Smith, who in 1994 strapped her two little boys in a car and let it roll into a lake, killing both of them, wanted to be unencumbered so her former boyfriend would come back to her — apparently it didn't occur to her that she could just have left them in the loving care of their father, her ex-husband. Andrea Yates, who drowned her five children in 2001, was diagnosed as suffering from severe postpartum depression and said she heard voices telling her to take their lives. But one recent case seems like a true Medea scenario: Susan Eubanks killed her four sons in 1998 specifically to get back at their fathers. Now remember that in the play, Medea isn't punished; she leaves for a new life as the queen of Athens. How do you feel about that, considering that Smith and Yates are serving life sentences, and Eubanks is on death row?

Narrative

The Sorrows of Young Werther

JOHANN WOLFGANG VON GOETHE

Novel, 1774. Excerpt. Translated by Elizabeth Mayer and Louise Bogan.

The hypnotic power of Goethe's book about young lovesick Werther may be hard to imagine today, but the fact remains that many young readers in Europe took their own lives after suffering along with Werther. Goethe presented the story as though he had found Werther's letters to a friend and then told about the final days in narrative form. From May to December, Werther undergoes all the highs and lows of falling in love, but in the end his beloved Lotte marries someone else. Shortly after writing this letter to his friend Wilhelm, Werther takes his pistol and shoots himself in the head.

> December 4
>
> I beg you—you see I am done for; I cannot bear it any longer. Today I sat near her as she played the clavichord, all sorts of tunes and with so much expression. So much! So much! What could I do? Her little sister sat on my knee and dressed her doll. Tears came into my eyes. I bowed my head and caught sight of her wedding ring. The tears ran down my cheek—and suddenly Lotte began to play the heavenly old melody. All at once my soul was touched by a feeling of consolation, by a memory of the past, of the other occasions when I had heard the song, of the dark intervals of vexation between, of shattered hopes, and then—I walked up and down the room, my heart almost suffocated by the rush of emotions. "For God's sake," I said, in a vehement outburst, "for God's sake, stop!" She paused and looked at me steadily. "Werther," she said with a smile that went deep to my heart, "Werther, you are very sick. You dislike the things you once liked. Go! I beg you, calm yourself!" I tore myself from her sight, and—God! You see my misery and will put an end to it.

Study Questions

1. Evaluate Werther's reaction from your own point of view: Is suicide because of rejection a realistic scenario? Is it emotionally understandable? Is it morally defensible? Explain your viewpoint.

2. Apply Plato's and Aristotle's views to this excerpt.

3. Can you think of stories (movies or other media) that have had a similar effect on the audience in recent years? If so, do you think something should be done to prevent such influence in the future? Explain your viewpoint.

4. Goethe gives the story credibility by pretending that he found these letters of Werther's (although he of course made the whole story up, including the character of Werther himself). The format of letting a story unfold within a frame of a letter, or an ancient manuscript in the loft, or a videotape, lives on in the best of health, because it is such

a good way to lend credence to the story. Recently a hugely popular film used this format to make it look like a documentary: *The Blair Witch Project.* Can you think of other stories—novels or films—that use the same trick?

Narrative

Pulp Fiction

QUENTIN TARANTINO (DIRECTOR AND SCREENWRITER)

Screenplay, 1996. Film, 1994. Summary and Excerpt.

In this summary (with a short excerpt)* we focus on one aspect of a complex story. *Pulp Fiction,* which shocked its first audiences with its graphic violence and strong language, has now acquired the status of an instant classic, often referred to in educational contexts precisely because of its casual attitude toward death and violence—up to a point. Here we look at the point where violence suddenly seems to have lost its appeal for one of the main characters, Jules.

Jules and Vincent have had a rough morning. Hit men for a mobster, they have just murdered two young men, with Jules quoting a passage supposedly from Ezekiel, but heavily embroidered with Jules's own words of doom, to them before he kills them, as he usually does; it is his style. Completing the job, they retrieve a briefcase for their boss. What Jules and Vincent don't know is that another man is hiding in the bathroom. When he bursts out, emptying his Magnum at the two hit men, they fire back, and he dies—but neither Jules nor Vincent is hurt. Vincent wants to label it a stroke of good luck and get out of there, but Jules is profoundly shocked and sees it as something else: divine intervention.

Marvin, a young friend of Jules's who has helped him set up the hit, follows them out of the bloodstained apartment into their car; while Vincent is discussing the incident of the bullets that missed, his gun accidentally goes off and shoots the young man in the face. Terribly upset, Jules worries that they are now driving on the highway with a bloody car and a dead body—his concern is not for the untimely death of Marvin.

**Author's note of caution:* Please be advised that the excerpt from the screenplay (Jules's monologue) contains some profanity. Additional profanity has been omitted from the excerpt. The entire screenplay of *Pulp Fiction* uses vernacular speech laden with what many readers will consider vulgarities. In the film it may be said to serve an artistic purpose, giving the audience an immediate understanding of the underworld in which the story takes place and often providing a deliberate counterpoint to intellectual dialogue; however, excerpts from the screenplay may strike some readers as being offensive. I suggest that the issue of offensive language, in films as well as in everyday life, be part of the class discussion after reading the narrative, as indicated in study question 4.

Pulp Fiction (Miramax, 1994) appears to many people to glorify violence, but educators have discerned a deeper intention: a strong statement against violence. Here Honey Bunny (Amanda Plummer) and Pumpkin (Tim Roth) are preparing to rob the customers and staff of the diner.

Later they are having breakfast in a coffee shop, coming down from the morning's events, Jules is still contemplating what he thinks of as a miracle, the fact that he wasn't killed, and he announces that he now considers himself retired from "the Life."

Something else is going on in the coffee shop. A young couple, Pumpkin and Honey Bunny, are now rising up out of a booth, pointing guns at the patrons and the waitresses: They are going to rob the place. Vincent has gone to the restroom and is unaware of the developments, but Jules witnesses the entire holdup. The young couple take the money from the cash register and move in to rob the patrons. When Pumpkin points his gun at Jules, he gives up his wallet but flatly refuses to hand over the briefcase. He lets Pumpkin look inside (we don't get to see the contents, only its mysterious glow), but that is as far as it goes. When Pumpkin points his gun at Jules, Jules quickly twists his arm, and now Pumpkin is the one staring into the gun. The girl attempts to help her lover but realizes that Jules will shoot if she moves. Now Vincent comes back to the table and takes in the situation. Together, Jules and Vincent keep the young couple under control, and Jules tells them that under normal circumstances they would both be dead now—but today he is in a "transitional period" and doesn't want to kill them. He instructs Pumpkin to go into the loot bag, fish out Jules's wallet, take out the cash, $1,500, and just go away. And he tells Pumpkin:

> Wanna know what I'm buying? . . . Your life. I'm giving you that money so I don't hafta kill your ass. . . . You read the Bible? . . . There's a passage I got memorized: Ezekiel 25:17. "The path of the righteous man is beset on all sides by the inequities of the selfish and the tyranny of evil men. Blessed is he who, in the name of charity and good will, shepherds the weak through the valley of the darkness. For he is truly his brother's keeper and the finder of lost children. And I will strike down upon thee with great vengeance and furious anger those who attempt to poison and destroy my brothers. And you will know I am the Lord when I lay my vengeance upon you." I been sayin' that shit for years. And if you ever heard it, it means your ass. I never really questioned what it meant. I thought it was just a coldblooded thing to say. . . . But I saw some shit this morning made me think twice. Now I'm thinkin'. It could mean you're the evil man. And I'm the righteous man. And Mr. .45 here he's the shepherd protecting my righteous ass in the valley of darkness. Or it could be you're the righteous man and I'm the shepherd and it's the world that's evil and selfish. I'd like that. But that shit ain't the truth. The truth is you're weak. And I'm the tyranny of evil men. But I'm tryin'. I'm tryin' real hard to be a shepherd.

Jules lowers his gun and puts it on the table; Pumpkin looks at him, at Honey Bunny, at the $1,500 in his hand, and then he grabs the trash bag full of cash and wallets, and he and Honey Bunny walk out the door.

Study Questions

1. What does Jules mean by suggesting that he might be the "righteous man"? What does he mean by suggesting that he might be the shepherd?

2. What does Jules mean by saying that he is giving Honey Bunny and Pumpkin the money so he won't have to kill them?

3. What do you think is the point of talking about being "righteous" and "being evil," given that the scene we are witnessing is a confrontation between robbers and hit men?

4. If you have seen the film, you will know that the dialogue is laden with profanity (as is evident in the excerpt from Jules's monologue). Do you think the foul language serves a purpose in this context? Why or why not? You might want to discuss the issue of profanity in contemporary speech styles.

5. Do you believe this particular film might inspire more violence (as Plato would believe), or do you think that, in some way, it might serve as a "cleansing" experience (as Aristotle might say) or perhaps as a warning against wholesale cultural acceptance of violence?

6. You may have wondered what the briefcase contains. It is not revealed in the film, but rumor has it that it contains the soul of the gangster boss. Would such an interpretation make a difference to the story? Explain.

Narrative

Lord Jim

JOSEPH CONRAD

Film by Richard Brooks (director and screenwriter), 1965. Summary. Based on the novel by Joseph Conrad, 1900.

Lord Jim is one of the finest fictional explorations of a human soul trying to do the right thing, at the right time, for the right reason. The film based on Joseph Conrad's classic novel tells the story of a young man named Jim who dreams of doing great deeds. As a newly appointed officer in the British Mercantile Marine, he spends quiet moments on board his ship fantasizing about saving damsels in distress and suppressing mutinies. After having been stranded in a Southeast Asian harbor due to a broken leg, Jim takes a job as chief mate to a crew of drunken, raucous white sailors with an equally unpleasant captain on the rusty old *Patna,* which is transporting a group of Muslim pilgrims to Mecca. Once at sea, a storm approaches, and Jim inspects the ship's hull. It is so rusty it is on the verge of breaking up. Back on deck Jim sees that the crew is lowering a lifeboat into the water—just one, for themselves. No measures are being taken to save the hundreds of pilgrims on the ship. Jim insists to the others that he is staying on board, but, at the last minute, as the storm hits, he comes face to face with his fear of death, which causes him to push aside all dreams of heroic deeds, and he jumps into the lifeboat after all.

Believing that the *Patna* is lost already, the men in the lifeboat set course for shore. When they arrive, they see that someone got there ahead of them; in the harbor lies the *Patna* herself, safe and sound. She was salvaged and towed to shore by another crew, and all the pilgrims are safe. Jim is relieved that no one was lost, but his dreams of valor have been shattered—he is tormented by guilt. There is an inquest, and Jim decides to tell all, to the dismay of his superiors, who believe that dirty linen should not be aired in public. His testimony so affects the prosecutor that the prosecutor later kills himself, leaving a note saying that if fear can break even one of us, how can anyone believe himself to be safe and honorable? Jim's officer's papers are canceled. Everywhere he goes from now on, the memory of the *Patna* will haunt him; somebody will recognize him or mention the scandal, and he will have to go somewhere else, to another port and another odd job.

Is Jim a coward? Were all the dreams of noble deeds just fantasies? He doesn't know. Months later, in some harbor in Southeast Asia, Jim is now a common dockside worker. One day, while transferring goods from shore to ship, he finds himself in a new, dangerous situation: A worker with a grudge against the shipping company lights a fuse that threatens to blow up the ammo being freighted to the ship, and he calls out to all hands to jump, before it blows. But Jim, on hearing the yell "Jump!," stands fast. The only man remaining on board, he puts out the fire and becomes a hero. The administrator of the shipping line, Stein, offers him a job, which Jim later accepts because he wants to get out of town. The job entails taking the guns and ammunition up river to the village of Patusan to help the local people fight against a tyrant. He becomes the hero of the peo-

To stay or to jump? Jim (Peter O'Toole) is about to make the decision that will ruin his life: During a storm, he abandons ship and the many passengers who had put their trust in him, in *Lord Jim* (Columbia Pictures, 1965).

ple, respected and trusted. They call him *Tuan Jim*, Lord Jim. He now believes that he finally has proved himself, but in fact the real test is yet to come. A band of pirates land in Patusan, and with the help of a traitor from the village they trick Jim into believing that they have good intentions. They are white, they promise they will sail away without harming any of the villagers, and Jim chooses to believe them; he lets them go without disarming them, trusting their word. He vows to the chief of the village that if anyone is harmed because of his decision, he will forfeit his own life. As it turns out, the chief's own son is killed in a fight between the pirates and the villagers. The villagers expect Jim to flee to save his life, and Stein tries to make Jim leave the village with the native woman he loves, but this time Jim stands fast; he explains to Stein, "I have been a so-called coward and a so-called hero, and there is not the thickness of a sheet of paper between them. Maybe cowards and heroes are just ordinary men who, for a split second do something out of the ordinary." In the morning Jim goes to the chief, who is mad with grief over his son, and offers him his life. Does the chief kill Jim? Read the book or watch the film.

Study Questions

1. Is Jim a coward, or is he courageous? Is it possible to be both?

2. Do you think we all are like Jim in the sense that we all have a moral breaking point which, when we reach it, reveals the frailty of our character?

3. Compare the plot of *Lord Jim* with Aristotle's prescription for the perfect tragic plot: Something horrible happens to an ordinary man, not because of some vice or depravity of his character but because of a great error in judgment. Does this fit Jim? If so, is Aristotle right that we feel pity and fear because we understand what he is going through — that we might react the same way?

4. This summary focuses on the issue of courage and cowardice, but *Lord Jim* is also about *honor*. Do you agree with the author (Joseph Conrad) that it is more honorable for Jim to confess his failings during the inquest than to keep quiet and follow the lead of his superiors?

Part 2

What Should I Do?

THEORIES OF
CONDUCT

Chapter Three

Ethical Relativism

*O*n occasion we are forced to face this fact: Not everybody shares our idea of what constitutes decent behavior. You may wait at the movie theater for a friend who never shows up because she is on the phone with another friend and it doesn't occur to her that it is important to keep her date with you. Such actions usually can be dismissed as merely bad manners or callousness; still, you probably will not want to make plans with that person again. *Moral differences* can run deeper than that, however. Suppose you are dating someone to whom you feel very attracted. During dinner at a nice restaurant, your friend casually mentions that he or she supports a candidate or cause that you strongly oppose on moral grounds. The fact that your friend has a different idea about what constitutes moral behavior will probably affect the way you feel about him or her.

We regularly read and hear about actions that are morally unacceptable to us. A young foreign girl is killed by her brother because she is pregnant and unmarried or perhaps merely going out with an American boy. To the Western mind the brother's act is an unfathomable crime. But the brother believes he is only doing his duty, as unpleasant as it may be; he is upholding the family honor, which the sister has tainted by her act of unspeakable immorality (according to the traditional code of his culture). The world is full of stories about people who feel duty-bound to do things others find repugnant. People in some cultures feel it is their moral obligation, or moral right, to dispose of their elderly citizens when they become unproductive. Pretechnological cultures, in particular, have a tradition during times when food is scarce of exposing their oldest members to the elements and leaving them to die. Often the decision rests with these older people, who feel morally obliged to remove themselves from the tribe when they believe it is time. Some cultures feel a moral right or duty to dispose of infants in the same way—usually cultures with no safe medical access to contraception. Other cultures believe it is a sin to seek medical assistance—they believe life should be left in the hands of God. Some people believe it is a sin to destroy any life, even by inadvertently stepping on an insect. Some people think they have a moral duty to defend themselves, their loved ones, and their country from any threat; others think it is their moral duty to refrain from resorting to violence under any circumstances.

In the days following the terrorist attacks of September 11, I was asked by many of my students how anyone could be so utterly devoid of morals that they would choose civilian targets, with no concern for the lives they were destroying. If ever there was a situation that brought home the challenge of dealing with moral differences, this was the one. The terrorists responsible for the attacks on New York and Washington, D.C., who were identified as belonging to Al Qaeda, a loosely knit organization of Arab Muslim extremists with a long history of terrorist attacks on military as well as civilian targets, presumably had a code of ethics that identified their actions as morally justified and even mandated. While denounced by most Muslim leaders and accused of misreading the Koran and overlooking its overall peaceful intent, the terrorists saw it as their moral and religious duty not only to remove the corrupting influence of the United States from Arab soil but to undermine and destroy the security and financial foundation of the United States itself, including, apparently, a planned attack on the U.S. Congress; no civilian would be spared, since (as specifically stated in a videotaped statement by their leader, Osama bin Laden) their moral code does not recognize civilians.

How to Deal with Moral Differences

How do we approach this phenomenon of moral differences? There are at least four major paths to choose.

1. There Is No Moral Truth   We may choose to believe that there are no morally right or wrong viewpoints—that the whole moral issue is a cultural game, and neither your opinion nor mine matters in the end, for there is no ultimate right or wrong. This view is called *moral nihilism,* and at various times in our lives, especially if we are facing personal disappointment, we may be inclined to take this approach. This is a difficult position to uphold, however, because it is so extreme. It is hard to remember, every minute of the day, that we don't believe there is any difference between right and wrong. If we see somebody steal our car, we are inclined to want the thief stopped, regardless of how much our jaded intellect tells us that no one is more right or wrong than anyone else. If we watch a child or an animal being abused, we feel like stepping in, even if we tell ourselves that there is no such thing as right or wrong. In other words, there seems to be something in most of us—instinct, or socialization, or reason, or compassion, or maybe something else altogether—that surfaces even when we try to persuade ourselves that moral values are but an illusion.

Related to the attitude of moral nihilism is *moral skepticism,* which holds that we can't know whether there are any moral truths, and *moral subjectivism,* which holds that moral views are merely inner states in a person and that they can't be compared to the inner states of another person, so a moral viewpoint is valid only for the person who holds it. Both skepticism and subjectivism are more common than nihilism, but they seem to be equally difficult to adhere to in the long run, because at crucial times we all act *as if* there are valid moral truths that we share with others— we criticize a friend for being late, a politician for being a racist or sexist, a colleague for the way she raises her children. We praise a stranger for coming to our aid when we are stuck on the freeway, we praise our kids when they come home on time— so it seems that even if we believe ourselves to be nihilists, skeptics, or subjectivists, we still expect to share some values with others of our own culture.

Although moral subjectivism generally seems a more flexible and appealing theory than categorical moral nihilism or moral skepticism—to the point that some thinkers choose to treat subjectivism as a subcategory of ethical relativism—the

© 2001 Dan Wright. Reprinted by permission of King Features Syndicate.

In this cartoon Lenny, the moral nihilist, is being challenged by Bobo. How does Bobo restore Lenny's sense of justice? Do you think it would convince a moral nihilist? Why or why not?

three theories have something in common that makes all of them less than successful: *They have no conflict-solving capacity.* How would you persuade the car thief to leave your car alone on moral grounds if you are a nihilist? A skeptic? Or a subjectivist? In each case, you have given up on the idea of finding common moral ground. The best you can do is tell the car thief that he is behaving in an illegal fashion; you can't claim that you have a moral argument that he ought to listen to.

2. There Is No Universal Moral Truth We may choose to believe that there is no universal moral truth, that each culture has its own set of rules that are valid for that culture, and we have no right to interfere, just as they have no right to interfere with our rules. This attitude, known as *ethical relativism,* is not as radical as skepticism, because it allows that moral truths exist but holds that they are relative to their time and place. Ethical relativism is viewed as an attitude of tolerance and as an antidote to the efforts of cultures who try their best to impose their set of moral rules on other cultures. Can ethical relativism solve conflicts? Yes, quite effectively. You may not like the solution, but ethical relativism says that whatever the majority deems to be the moral rule is the proper rule to follow. This theory is discussed in detail in the next section.

3. Deep Down, We Can Find Basic Moral Truths We may believe that deep down, in spite of all their differences, people of different cultures can still agree on certain moral basics. We may think it is a matter of biology — that people everywhere have basically the same human nature. Or we may view this agreement as a process of acculturation, whereby people adjust to the normal way of doing things in their culture. If the native peoples of harsh climates put their unwanted babies out in the wild to perish, it need not mean that they are cruel but rather that they want to give the babies they already have a chance to survive, and they know that having another mouth to feed will kill them all. In this way we find common ground in the fact that we, and they, do care for the children we are able to raise. If we believe that some-how, under the surface of antagonism and contradiction, we can still find a few things we can agree on, even if we choose to act on them in different ways, then we believe in the existence of a few universal moral truths. I call this attitude *soft universalism*—universalism because it perceives that there are some universal moral rules; *soft* because it is not as radical as hard universalism, or absolutism. Can soft universalism solve conflicts? Perhaps it can do so better than any other approach, because soft universalism has as its main goal to seek common ground beneath the variety of opinions and mores.

4. There Is One Universal Moral Truth *Hard universalism* (sometimes called *moral absolutism*) is the attitude that most often is supported in ethical theories. It is an attitude toward morals in everyday life to which many people relate very well. Hard universalism holds that there is one universal moral code. It is the viewpoint expressed by those who are on a quest for the code ("I know there must be one set of true moral rules, but I would not presume to have found it myself"), by those who make judgments based on its analysis ("After much deliberation I have come to the conclusion that this moral code represents the ultimate values"), and by those who put forth the simple sentiment that moral truth is not open for discussion ("I'm right and you're wrong, and you'd better shape up!"). Whereas moral nihilism, with its claim that there are no moral truths, represents one end of the spectrum in terms of dealing with moral differences, hard universalism represents the other extreme: It does not acknowledge the possibility or legitimacy of more than one set of moral codes. Can hard universalism/moral absolutism solve moral conflicts? Yes, in a variety of ways: If you accept someone telling you that you must be wrong because you don't agree with him or her, then that conflict is solved right there; more frequently, an absolutist will try to show you, on the basis of reasoning and evidence, that his or her moral conclusion is better than yours. Appeals to evidence and reasoning are the common problem-solving approaches among most absolutist philosophers, not appeals to force or fallacious arguments such as "I'm right because I'm right."

The first set of viewpoints will not be discussed much in this book. The second one, *ethical relativism,* has greatly influenced moral attitudes in the West since the early twentieth century and is the main topic of this chapter. The third, *soft universalism,* and fourth, *hard universalism,* will be discussed in the subsequent chapters of Part 2.

The Lessons of Anthropology

In the nineteenth century, cultural anthropology came into its own as a scientific discipline and reminded the West that "out there" were other societies vastly different from those of Victorian Europe. Anthropological scholars set out to examine other cultures, and the facts they brought back were astounding to the nineteenth-century Western mind-set: There were cultures that didn't understand the male's role in procreation but thought that babies somehow ripened in the woman with the help of spirits. There were people who would devour the bodies of enemies killed in war in order to share their fighting spirit. There were cultures that believed in animal gods, cultures that felt it appropriate for women to bare their breasts, cultures that felt it utterly inappropriate to let your in-laws watch you eat, and so on. It was easy to draw the conclusion that there were cultures out there whose moral codes differed substantially from those of the West.

This conclusion, the first step in what has become known as ethical relativism, was not new to the Western mind-set. Because people had always traveled and returned with tales of faraway lands, it was common knowledge that other cultures did things differently. Explorers in earlier centuries brought home tales of mermaids, giants, and other fantasies. Some stories were truer than others. There really were, for instance, peoples out there who had a different dress ethic and work ethic. The lifestyle of the South Sea islanders became a collective fantasy for Europeans of the eighteenth and nineteenth centuries; imagine not wearing any clothes, not having to work all the time, living in perpetual summertime, and not having any sexual restrictions! Depending on their ethical predisposition, Europeans considered such peoples to be either the luckiest ones on this earth or the most sinful, subhuman, and depraved. Reports of cultural diversity were also supplied by Christian missionaries over the centuries; they confronted more or less reluctant cultures with their message of conversion.

The idea of cultural diversity even in early historic times is well documented. The Greek historian Herodotus (485–430 B.C.E.) tells in his *Histories* of the Persian king Darius the Great, who from the borders of his vast empire, which at the time stretched from the Greek holdings in the West to India in the East, had heard tales of funerary practices that intrigued him. The Greeks were at that time in the habit of cremating their dead; Darius learned that a tribe in India, the Callatians, would eat their dead. In Darius's Persia, burials were the norm. Herodotus wrote:

> Everyone without exception believes in his own native customs, and the religion he was brought up in, to be the best . . . [Darius] summoned the Greeks who happened to be present at his court, and asked them what it would take to eat the dead bodies of their fathers. They replied that they would not do it for any money in the world. Later, in the presence of the Greeks, and through an interpreter, so that they could understand what was said, he asked some Indians, of the tribe called Callatia, who do in fact eat their parents' dead bodies, what they would take to burn them. They uttered a cry of horror and forbade him to mention such a dreadful thing. One can see by this what custom can do, and Pindar [a Greek poet] was right when he called it "king of all."

Usually, the sound bite condensing Herodotus's observation is "Custom is king"— we all prefer what we are used to.

When anthropologists point out that moral codes vary enormously from culture to culture, they are describing the situation as they see it. As long as those anthropologists make no judgments about whether it is *good* for humanity to have different moral codes or whether those codes represent the moral truths of each culture, they are espousing a descriptive theory usually referred to as *cultural relativism*. Let us look at an example. An anthropologist acquaintance of mine came back from a

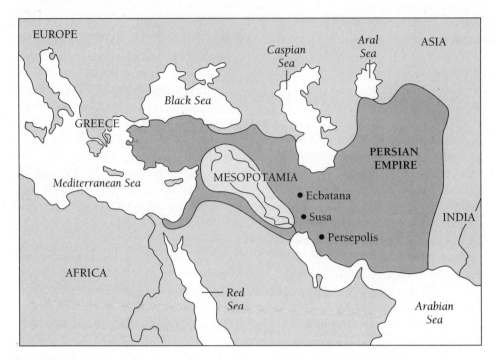

It was not so strange that King Darius might have heard of peoples living as far apart as the Greeks and the Callatian tribe of northern India, because they were in fact his neighbors. At the time of its greatest expansion, Persia (today, Iran) covered a territory stretching from Greece in the west to today's Pakistan in the east. Until the time of Alexander the Great, this was the greatest empire in the ancient Western world.

field trip to Tibet and told me the following story: In the little Tibetan village where he had been "adopted" by a local family and was doing his fieldwork, the children worked hard and had very little leisure time. The concept of competition was totally alien to them. One day my friend thought he would give them a treat, and he arranged for a race. All the kids lined up, puzzled and excited, to listen to his directions: Run from one end of the compound to the other and back again, and whoever comes in first wins. The race was on, and the children ran like mad to beat each other and "win." As one beaming kid came in first, the anthropologist handed over a prize — some little trinket or piece of candy. There was dead silence among the kids, who just looked at each other. Finally one of the children asked, "Why are you giving a gift to our friend who won?" The anthropologist realized that because the children had no idea of competition, they had no knowledge that winning often is connected with a prize. To them, this new idea of "winning" was great all by itself, and there was no need to add anything else; indeed, the prize made them feel very uncomfortable. (My friend said it also made him feel very stupid.)

What the anthropologist was doing by telling this story was relating an example of cultural relativism — describing how customs differ from culture to culture. Suppose, though, he had added, "and I realized that they were right in their own way."

Box 3.1   DESCRIPTIVE AND NORMATIVE ETHICS

The terms *descriptive* and *normative* are important terms for any ethical theory, not just relativism. When we talk about a theory being *descriptive,* we mean that the theory merely describes what it sees as fact, such as, In the United States it is, in general, not considered immoral to eat meat. In other words, a descriptive theory describes what people actually do or think. A *normative* theory adds a *moral judgment,* evaluation, or justification, such as, It is okay to eat meat because it is nourishing, or a criticism, such as, Eating meat *should* be considered im-

moral. In addition to descriptive ethics and normative ethics, there is a third ethical approach, *metaethics.* Metaethics does not describe or evaluate but analyzes the *meaning* of the moral terms we use. Some typical questions would be, But what do you mean by immoral? What do you mean by meat—beef, horse, or snake, perhaps? Most ethical systems involve judgments, criticisms, evaluations, and justifications, and are thus normative, but many systems also require an awareness of the terms used to justify the theory. Such systems involve metaethics.

(In other words, suppose he had made a *judgment* about the validity of the tribal way of life.) In that case, he would have moved into the area of *ethical relativism.* Cultural relativism is a *descriptive* theory that states that different cultures have different moral codes. Ethical relativism is a *normative* theory that states there is no universal moral code and that each culture's codes are right and valid for that culture. It is a subtle difference, but philosophically it is an important one. (See Box 3.1 for an introduction to descriptive and normative ethics.) The cultural relativist sees the cultural differences and describes them: There are many moral codes in the world. The ethical relativist sees the cultural differences and makes a judgment: We can never find a common code, and what seems right for one culture is right *for that culture.*

The anthropologist Ruth Benedict (1887–1948) was a student of the cultural anthropologist Franz Boas, who had already declared that cultures around the world should not be judged by the standards of Western civilization, and that moral standards are not universal, but relative to each culture. Sharing her teacher's viewpoint, Benedict did most of her writing toward the end of the era in which one could still speak of "uncontaminated" societies—cultures that hadn't yet been massively exposed to Western civilization. The term *primitive* still was used for some cultures, and Benedict used it, too, but she was quick to point out that the attitude that Western civilization was at the top of the ladder of cultural evolution was—or should be—outdated. In a famous paper, "Anthropology and the Abnormal," from 1934, she says that "modern civilization becomes not a necessary pinnacle of human achievement but one entry in a long series of possible adjustments." With this emphasis she established herself as an advocate of cultural and moral *tolerance,* implying that Western civilization has no right to impose its codes of conduct on other cultures. Ethical relativism has remained popular ever since as a tool of cultural tolerance.

In the paper mentioned above, Benedict tells of a number of cultural phenomena that may seem morally odd, to say the least, to you. One example will have to suffice:

Ruth Benedict (1887–1948), American anthropologist and defender of ethical relativism. Her best-known work is *Patterns of Culture* (1934).

Among the Northwest Coast American Indians of previous centuries, it was customary to view death, even natural death, as an affront that should be retaliated against in one way or another. In one tribe, a chief's sister and her daughter had drowned on a trip to Victoria. The chief gathered a war party. They set out, found seven men and two children asleep, and killed them. This made them all feel much better.

What intrigued Benedict about this story was not so much that the chief and the members of the war party viewed their actions as morally good, but that most of the tribespeople felt the same way. In other words, it was *normal* in the tribe to feel this way. Benedict concludes, "The concept of the normal is properly a variant of the concept of the good. It is that which society has approved."

Two things are worth mentioning here. First, Benedict is taking a giant leap from expressing *cultural* relativism to expressing *ethical* relativism. She moves from a description of the people's behavior to the statement that it is normal and thus good for them to behave this way — in their own cultural context. Second, Benedict is saying that normalcy is culturally defined; in other words, cultures, especially isolated cultures, often seem to develop some behaviors to an extreme. (For Benedict the range of possible human behavior is enormous, extending from paranoia to helpfulness and generosity.) Those individuals who somehow can't conform (and they will always be the minority, because most people are very pliable) become the abnormals in that culture.

Is the behavior of the Northwest Coast people totally alien to us? Benedict thinks not, because it constitutes *abnormal* behavior in our own society, not *unthinkable* behavior. We might illustrate her idea with some examples. The postal worker who has been fired and who shows up the next day with a shotgun and kills a number of his coworkers is "crazy" to us, but he actually is following the same logic as the chief: His world has been torn apart by powers over which he has no control, and he is retaliating against the affront. The driver who cuts you off on the freeway because she had a fight with her husband is doing the same thing; so was the little girl who ripped a button off your coat in grade school because someone else ripped a button off her coat. There is no question of vengeance, because neither the driver nor the little girl was looking to punish a guilty party. The seven men and two chil-

Box 3.2   THE PSYCHOLOGY OF BECOMING
A MORAL AND SOCIAL BEING

How does a person develop and become like most of the others in his or her own culture in terms of moral values? Sigmund Freud would say that each individual internalizes society's rules and its morality; this process is the development of the *Superego*—that part of our psyche that serves to reward and punish through a system of moral attitudes, conscience, and a sense of guilt. The other two parts of our psyche, according to Freud's influential theory from 1923, are the *Ego*—our conscious self—and the *Id* (Latin for "it"), our Unconscious. Freud, the founder of psychoanalysis, believed that we transform the moral voices of those in authority into that little inner voice called our conscience. Whatever the authority voices tell us is what our morality consists of. Ruth Benedict assumes that humans are extraordinarily flexible: Whatever is normal and accepted in a culture is the model most people will follow. However, in every group there will usually be some individuals who just don't fit the mold, either because they are not capable of adjusting or because they don't want to, and those are the ones the culture will label as "abnormal." Of course, what is abnormal in one culture may well be normal and commendable behavior in another.

dren had nothing to do with the deaths of the chief's relatives, and the chief never said they did. It is not a matter of seeking out the cause of the problem, of gaining retribution; rather, it is an experience of healing a wound by wounding someone else. (What if the strangers who were killed had been American or Canadian loggers who had grown up in a culture that believes it is proper to find and punish whoever is guilty? Then we'd see retribution.) Perhaps we all take it out on someone innocent from time to time; some of us probably do it more often than others. The difference is that we've chosen to call what the Northwest Coast people did *abnormal,* whereas they, in the context of their tribal civilization, considered their actions to be normal. How do such choices evolve? Usually it is a matter of habits developing over time. If there is such a thing as a "normal" way for humans to behave, it is to adjust to the pattern of normalcy that prevails in their particular culture. Today, sociologists would call this process *acculturation.* (For Freud's version of acculturation, see Box 3.2.)

Although Benedict obviously wants her readers to approach other cultures with more tolerance for customs alien to them, her choice of examples may seem odd to a modern, culturally sensitive reader: Is Benedict, in giving this account of a tribe of American Indians, actually helping to cement the old notions popular in white Western culture of the "savage Indian"? If so, she is not furthering any mutual intercultural understanding. There are two things to say here: (1) Benedict herself might answer with something like, "If you read this account as a criticism of Indian customs, then it is just because you are seeing it through the eyes of a prejudiced Westerner. The whole point is to recognize cultural differences as being equally meaningful within their cultural contexts." We should not shy away from noticing differences—but we should not judge them, either. (2) As readers looking at the disadvantages as well as the advantages of ethical relativism, we must conclude that relativism does not have as its goal any mutual *understanding*—merely noninterference. Trying to achieve an understanding requires us to find some common ground, and relativism does not allow for any intercultural common ground. We return to the question of common ground later in this chapter.

For Benedict there is no sense in imposing Western morals on another culture, because Western morals are just one aspect of the range of possible human behavior that we have chosen to elaborate; they are no better or no worse than anyone else's morals. Whatever is normal for us we think of as good, and we have no right to claim that our choice is better than any other culture's.

Is Tolerance All We Need?

Given the overwhelming intolerance for other cultures and customs that is displayed from time to time by Western civilization (a stance some refer to as "cultural imperialism"), many people find something very appealing and refreshing about ethical relativism. And we shouldn't forget to see it in its proper historical perspective: It served as an antidote to nineteenth-century "Eurocentrism" and Western colonialism, in which the notion of Western religious and moral superiority (in addition to the technological superiority of the West) had been considered an obvious truth. Ethical relativism broke away from this self-congratulatory attitude and became the inspiration for a shift toward cultural tolerance in the early part of the twentieth century, an attitude that continues in today's United States, with its plurality of cultural and ethnic heritages. It seems of doubtful virtue today to impose a particular brand of acculturation on another group that believes it is doing just fine with its own set of moral rules. Indeed, having someone else's morality presented as one we have to conform to, even if it goes against our upbringing, usually feels demeaning and unpleasant. Cultural relativism teaches a useful lesson—that cultures are different, and "our way" is just one among many. Just because "our way" may frown on eating certain foods, allow divorce, and condemn infanticide doesn't mean we have a right to criticize cultures that look at such things differently.

Some years ago a young American male was caned by the authorities in Singapore for spraying graffiti on cars. He had originally been sentenced to six strikes with a cane, but the sentence was reduced to four strikes after pressure from the U.S. government. What seemed to surprise the government in Washington, D.C. and many individuals was that there was no general sense of outrage over the prospective beating of an American citizen by a foreign power; on the contrary, many people felt that since the young man was living in Singapore, he ought to abide by the rules of that country and take his punishment for breaking them. With that viewpoint, many Americans showed themselves to have leanings toward ethical relativism: The moral codes of a culture apply to that culture only and should not be applied elsewhere, so we should not try to rescue American citizens who have broken the codes of foreign countries they have chosen to visit or live in. (In Chapter 7 we take a closer look at the questions of justice and punishment.) But would a relativist take it one step

Calvin and Hobbes   **by Bill Watterson**

Bill Watterson's comic strip, *Calvin and Hobbes,* which was discontinued in 1995, had a knack for putting its finger on tricky philosophical issues, especially in the fields of ethics and metaphysics. Here Hobbes, the stuffed tiger that only Calvin can see move, speculates that the demand for tolerance in ethical relativism may not be all that much of an advantage.

further, as many people did, and demand that tagging (spraying gang graffiti) be punished by caning here, too? Such a decision would contradict ethical relativism's basic premise that moral codes can't be transplanted from one culture to another.

Problems with Ethical Relativism

In spite of the positive lesson taught by ethical relativism to suspend our judgmental attitudes toward other cultures, there are serious problems within the theory. Here we look at six problems, all of them logical consequences of the basic idea of ethical relativism that there is no universal moral code. (Box 3.3 is a general overview of examining and testing theories.)

1. No Criticism or Praise of Other Cultures Does this mean that it is always wrong to criticize another culture or group for what it does? If we are to follow the idea of ethical relativism to its logical conclusion, yes. We have no right to criticize other cultures, period. But on occasion things happen in other cultures that we feel, either by instinct or through rational argument, we *should* criticize in order to maintain our own moral integrity. Curiously enough, at the time Benedict wrote her article (1934), one of the most offensive social "experiments" in history was being conducted in the Western world. Europe was being overtaken by the Nazis, whose extreme racism was not kept secret, even though the existence of the death camps of later years was not generally known until after the war. A true ethical relativist would have had to stick to her guns and maintain that other countries had no right to criticize what was going on in Germany and Austria in the 1930s and 1940s. (As it happens, this pretty much mirrored the actual attitude of the rest of the world at the time.) Benedict, however, mentions nothing about this issue in her paper.

Box 3.3   HOW TO TEST A THEORY

What we are doing in this text is following standard philosophical procedure. We test a theory by pounding at it with hypothetical and actual situations until we see whether it still makes sense. It is not unlike the procedure of testing a presidential candidate. When the going gets tough and all the nasty (but usually reasonable and relevant) questions are asked, we see what kind of character the candidate has. Is he or she arrogant? Weak? Capable of a sense of humor? Vindictive? Intelligent? Stupid? Lying? Truthful? Honest? Strong? What is the breaking point of the candidate? In the same way, we seek the breaking point of a theory. As you will see, almost every theory does have a breaking point, but this does not always disqualify the theory (that is, render it invalid). If the breaking point comes late in the discussion and only when the theory is attacked by an extremely unlikely hypothesis or by trifles, this speaks well for the theory and encourages acceptance or perhaps only a minor rewrite of the theory. Some theories, however, break early in the discussion and can be discarded. Ethical relativism is a theory with a fairly late breaking point; in other words, there are some good things to be said for the theory, which is a good reason not to discard it altogether.

People often say, in retrospect, that someone should have protested against or intervened in a particular situation while there was still time. Indeed, one of the arguments in support of the brief Persian Gulf War of 1991 was that the world would have another Hitler and another genocide on its hands if Saddam Hussein's invasion of Kuwait was not stopped. Any attempt at an armed takeover and genocide, even if it takes place within a country's own borders and is conducted by its own government, seems to be a good occasion for voicing the opinion that genocide is wrong. Not to the relativist, however. In the case of NATO military action against the Serbs in Kosovo in 1999, the traditional relativist did not approve, because the reported Serb genocidal actions were directed against a group within their own culture, and their war was an internal affair. In the eyes of the relativist we are against genocide only because it happens to be against the norms of our own culture; for another culture, genocide may be right.

For most people, however, even those believing they ought to be tolerant, there are moral limits to tolerance, and any theory that doesn't recognize this is just not a good theory. Most Western people, as tolerant as they might like to be, would prefer to see certain things come to an end: In China there are reports of female infanticide, a result of a strict one-child-per-family policy; in several cultures, primarily on the African continent, female genital mutilation is practiced, usually on young girls of seven to eight years of age. A report issued by the United Nations in 2000 suggests that many of these countries have recently outlawed female genital mutilation, but the practice still exists. At the end of this chapter you will find a summary of a novel that deals with this issue: Alice Walker's *Possessing the Secret of Joy*. In Sudan in 2000 the government issued a decree that women could no longer study at the universities, nor use their education in Sudanese society, because it was seen as impermissible by the Sudanese reading of the Koran. Professional women found themselves reduced to making a living doing manual labor.

In Afghanistan from 1996 to 2001, a brief period of time that must have seemed like an eternity to those victimized by the policy, the Taliban government deprived all women of their rights to freedom of movement, education, work, health care, and other essentials. Women were forced to wear a head-to-toe garment, the burka, which allowed only a limited vision through an embroidered net covering their eyes. *Beneath the Veil* (2001), a documentary secretly filmed by a British-Afghani journalist, Saira Shah, and a follow-up, *Unholy War,* told the world of women being beaten in the streets by the Taliban police for showing any skin and for wearing white socks or squeaky shoes, in an apparent attempt to eliminate the presence of women in public. Women and men were summarily executed in the football stadium, to the cheers of the all-male crowd. Hearing of such conditions, can one morally remain a relativist, holding that each culture must be left in peace to explore its own values? Many ethical relativists have felt that a line must be drawn between mere cultural preferences and assaults on human rights — but that means giving up on ethical relativism. However, when issues such as equal rights for women are raised in the United Nations, representatives of those cultures that do not recognize rights for women often respond with indignation, asserting that the West is merely doing what it has always done, trying to superimpose its cultural and moral values on other peoples in the old tradition of cultural imperialism. Although ethical relativism wanted to put an end to the wholesale export of Western values, the theorists have reached a critical point: Many people may agree with relativists that there is no need or excuse for the West to try to dictate every aspect of what other nations should think or do, but in extreme situations many of us would like to reserve the right to speak up for people in other parts of the world who can't (or aren't allowed to) speak up for themselves. We want to believe that we have the right to complain about governments that do not respect human rights and that abuse a part of their population, and, in fact, pressure on such governments has at times yielded results. South Africa is not the bastion of segregation it used to be, and the concept of human rights is not alien to the Russian media or Russian leaders any longer.

Not only are we prevented from criticizing another culture's doings if we accept the teachings of relativism; we also cannot praise and learn from that culture. If we find that the social system of Scandinavia is more humane and functions better than any other in the world, the conclusion based on relativism has to be that this is because it is right for them, but we still can't assume that it is right for us. If we happen to admire the work ethic of Japan, we can't learn from it and adapt it to our own culture, nor can Jainism's teachings of nonviolence have anything to say to us. In short, ethical relativism, when taken to its logical conclusion, precludes learning from other cultures, because there can be no "good" or "bad" that is common to all cultures. Curiously, this doesn't mean that all ethical relativists would actually *forbid* us to learn from other cultures or to criticize others — on the contrary, ethical relativists think of themselves as very tolerant and open-minded. The problem is in the logic of the theory itself: When it is applied to real-life situations as a moral principle, it reveals itself to have certain limitations.

2. Majority Rule The isolation of moral values to the conventions of specific cultural groups has another curious effect: It forces us to bow to *majority rule*. Remember that ethical relativism does not say there are *no* moral rules — only that the rules of each society are proper and valid for that society. What if you live in a society and don't agree with the rules? Then you must, ipso facto, be wrong, because we know that the rules that are morally good in a society are those rules that are in effect. If you disagree with those rules, you must be wrong. This makes it impossible to disagree with any rules that exist, and therefore civil disobedience is out of the question. In Iran, if you disagree with the fundamentalist Islamic rules of punishment, then you are wrong. It is, in fact, right and proper in Iran to amputate the hand of a thief. If you are an American and disagree with the general attitude against euthanasia and doctors who help patients commit suicide, then you are wrong, and the attitude of the majority is right — not because the attitude has been subjected to moral analysis but simply because it happens to be the attitude of the majority. It does not work, either, to point to a historical precedent and say that things were not always done as they are now, because ethical relativism cuts through time as well as space. There are no universal values among different time periods, any more than there are common values among different cultures of the same era. In other words, that was then and this is now. For an intellectual tradition such as ours, which prides itself on valuing minority opinions and promotes the idea of moral progress, the idea that the attitude of the majority is always right simply is unacceptable.

3. Professed or Actual Morality? There is a further problem with the idea that a group's morality is determined by the majority or that a certain kind of behavior is normal, for what is "normal"? Is it the *professed* morality of the group or the *actual* morality? Imagine the following situation. The majority of a cultural group, when asked about their moral viewpoints, claim that they believe infidelity is wrong; however, in that particular society, infidelity is common practice. Does that mean the morality of the culture is what the majority say they ought to do or what they actually do? We might simply decide that it must be the *normative* rules that define the morality and not the actual behavior; however, Ruth Benedict assumed morality to be the same as majority *behavior*. If Benedict had implied that morality is the same as what people think they *ought* to do, then all our example would amount to would be to show that most people have a hard time living up to their own moral standards, which is hardly a novel observation. However, Benedict's theory of ethical relativism clearly states that "moral" is the same as "normal," meaning how the majority *actually* behave.

4. What Is a "Majority"? Ethical relativism involves a practical problem as well. Suppose the question of doctor-assisted suicide had been determined by a referendum and the law against it overturned in your state. The majority now believe it is right for doctors to help terminally ill patients die. It was morally wrong the week before, but today it is morally right. By next year people may have changed their minds, and it will become morally wrong again. There is something very disconcerting about moral rightness being as arbitrary as that and depending on a vote especially since so few people actually vote in elections. And what about the individual states? They obviously are part of a larger unit, the United States, and the moral standards of this larger unit would define the morals of each singular state. But not all laws and customs are the same from state to state, and what is considered morally wrong by the majority in one state may well be considered morally acceptable by the majority in another (such as abortion or doctor-assisted suicide). Therefore, might we instead want to allow for morally autonomous subgroups in which the majority within each group defines the moral rules, even if they are at odds with the larger cultural group? If we have large minority subgroups *within* a state and their moral values differ from those of the majority, should such groups constitute morally autonomous units that should not be criticized? (See Box 3.4.)

5. What Is a "Culture"? Question 4 leads right into question 5, because ethical relativists have not explained exactly what they mean by a culture, either. How can we know if something is the norm within a culture if it isn't clear what a culture is? What sets one culture off from other cultures? Is the United States one culture (as most foreigners believe), or is it a collective of many smaller cultures, as many Americans see it? Is Europe one culture? Is Africa? Asia? Central or South America? From the outside, perhaps, but once you see the regional differences, you'll know it's not so easy to focus on common denominators rather than on the differences.

What unifies a culture? It used to be *geography*. People living within the same area moved around only rarely and acquired the same general characteristics. But now people move all over the globe, join societies across borders like never before, and subscribe to newsletters and newsgroups on the Internet. Is it *ethnicity*? Historically people have tended to stick with others of their own ethnic background, but that seems to be partly a geographical limitation and partly a *cultural* choice (and culture is what we are trying to define). People who were brought up not to be bigoted choose partners, friends, and neighbors from outside their own ethnic group all the time, yet they still feel they are choosing within their culture. In my ethnically and racially diverse college classes, it always strikes me that, as diverse as we are, we generally have much more in common than we have with some people in our own families and neighborhoods, because the world of academia is our "culture" — our common experiences with classes and grades, studying and research, exams, and so forth create a cultural identity in itself. Is it *race*? When people were less mobile, people within a region generally formed a culture, and there was ethnic and racial cohesion in the group. But now we are (at least in the United States) moving toward a mixed-race society, and biologists and sociologists are beginning to question the very concept of race and to interpret it as an eighteenth-century invention. Therefore, the category of race can hardly be a firm foundation for a definition of culture. Is it *religion*? Places with one dominant (or one permitted) religion seem to be obvious candidates for a culture, but what about places in which people tend to dress

Box 3.4   MORAL SUBJECTIVISM AND
ETHICAL RELATIVISM: A COMPARISON

Sometimes the theory of moral subjectivism is listed as a subcategory of ethical relativism. You may recall that we placed it under the general heading of *moral nihilism* at the beginning of this chapter, because theories of moral nihilism deny that there can be any agreement about moral values based on something other than personal opinion. Ethical relativism is not a morally nihilistic theory because it holds that there are very strong reasons for agreeing about values within a culture precisely because they are values shared by that culture. However, there is definitely something "relative" about moral subjectivism, so we might say that it represents the transposition of "each culture is right in its own way" to "each person is right in his or her own way." This theory is an extremely tolerant theory, a "live and let live" attitude in which no one has the right to impose their moral viewpoints, including their preference for tolerance, on anyone else. It has its own severe flaws, however: For one thing, it cannot solve moral conflicts, because there is no common value denominator to resort to. This means we can't hope to learn from other people's advice or even their mistakes, because their values and situations will always differ slightly from ours. And because the theory can't solve moral conflicts, we have no moral weapon against what we personally consider unacceptable. How would you argue against Hitler's Holocaust from a subjectivist viewpoint? Against slavery? Child abuse? Female circumcision and other enforced mutilation rituals? The only thing you might say is that you *feel* these actions are wrong—but others can also feel and think any way they like. For most people this way of thinking is so excessively tolerant that it borders on an obscene lack of social responsibility.

Furthermore, as appealing as moral subjectivism may seem when we have just escaped the confines of the moral regulations of our child-

hood, it simply isn't intuitively sound. We may think we can "live and let live," but in actual fact we react *as if* there is a basic appeal to conflict-solving values. If you are a subjectivist and you see an adult at the supermarket repeatedly hitting a small crying child, are you going to be content telling yourself that you wouldn't do such a thing but that the adult in question is entitled to feel he or she is doing the right thing? Or would you try to appeal to some common value system by stepping in? Moral subjectivism is not only counterintuitive and impractical, it is also downright dangerous as a moral theory because it provides no social cohesion and no protection against the whims of those in power, whose "feelings" may be as legitimate as yours but whose ability to carry them out is far greater.

To summarize, the criticism of moral subjectivism is different from the criticism of ethical relativism in the following ways: (1) moral subjectivism cannot solve conflicts, but ethical relativism can (through majority rule), and (2) ethical relativism is problematic because it implies a moral majority rule, but moral subjectivism does not (because each person is right in his or her own way). What the two theories have in common is the relativity of moral values: The moral subjectivist has no right to call anyone else's values wrong or evil, and neither does the ethical relativist (when judging *other* cultures). So the challenge to both moral subjectivism and ethical relativism is the experience of something that is so egregiously against "common decency" or "our sense of humanity" that we must speak up, regardless of our modern tradition of tolerance toward others' life choices. Finding a universal foundation for criticism of traditions of female circumcision or ritual animal torture or child sacrifice is equally impossible from a basis of either moral subjectivism or ethical relativism.

the same, see the same movies, buy the same groceries, and drive the same cars but have different religions? Is it (as anthropologists might suggest) how we view *family relations*? Those categories also are not so stable anymore. And if we resort to vague categories of habits, worldviews, tastes, and so forth, all we end up with is a classification of people according to some criteria, whereas other criteria may cut across those same groups. If an ethical relativist insists that as long as we can identify some form of cultural cohesion, then that group should not be interfered with in its moral practices, we run into horrible problems.

Some ethnic groups in the United States differ from the majority in their views about male–female relationships, about using animals that Americans consider pets for food, about contraception and abortion, about the rights of fathers to punish their families. How large do such groups have to be in order to be considered morally right in their own ways? If we are generous and tolerant relativists, perhaps we'll say that any large ethnic group should be considered morally autonomous. But would that mean the Mafia could be considered such a subgroup, or neighborhood gangs? Would society then have to accept a plurality of "laws," each governing the subgroups, with no higher means of control? The relativist might accept that one set of laws—national ones, for instance—would be above all other laws, but it would still be an extremely complicated matter, with possible contradictions arising between what the national law says and what the gang law says. Could we eventually end up in a situation in which acts such as looting are morally right for some because of their subgroup affiliation but not for others?

6. Can Tolerance Be a Universal Value? One of the best qualities of ethical relativism is its tolerance, although we've now seen that it can lead to problems. However, there is something problematic about the very claim of tolerance coming from a relativist, for is someone who believes in ethical relativism allowed to claim that tolerance is something everyone should have? In other words, can a relativist say that tolerance is *universally good*? If all values are culture-relative, then this condition must apply to tolerance as well. Tolerance may be good for us, but who is to say if it is good for other groups! This notion severely undermines the whole purpose of tolerance, which is not usually considered a one-way street. And what if the highest moral dictum of a certain culture is to superimpose its values on other cultures? Does relativism teach that we must respect a moral system that doesn't respect the morals of others? Western cultures of the past—and, some would say, even the present—have exported their own moral systems; the Communist bloc of the twentieth century sought expansion along those same principles; today, Muslim extremism in some parts of the world also seeks this kind of expansion, combined with political ambitions. One could say, as some ethical relativists have attempted, that as long as they keep their moral (and perhaps even political and religious) expansionism within their own borders, they have a right to think whatever they want—but the problem is that the moral focus of certain cultures is precisely to export itself to other places. Not only does ethical relativism not have a right to claim that tolerance is universally good, since it also claims that there are no universal values; it can't even give a practical answer as to how to deal with moral, religious, and political expansionism.

Refuting Ethical Relativism

The "Flat Earth" Argument

Now we have seen why many people believe that ethical relativism doesn't have enough to offer to be adopted 100 percent; it is a theory with immense theoretical and practical problems. For some critics, the *logic* of the key argument proposed by ethical relativism is faulty. Let us assume that the culture "up north" believes that abortion is morally wrong, whereas the culture "down south" believes it to be morally permissible. The relativist concludes that because there is a disagreement between the two groups, neither can be right in an absolute sense. But surely, the critics say, that is not so; some things are simply true or false. We may have had a disagreement in the past about whether the earth is round or flat. (Indeed, the Flat Earth Society today is upholding that tradition by claiming that all space reports and photos from space missions are fraudulent and were concocted in a movie studio.) However, that doesn't mean that there is no correct answer; the idea that the earth is round is a verifiable fact. We may be able to verify that some moral codes are objectively right and others are wrong.

The trouble with this critique is that it is easy to verify that the earth is round; all we have to do is look at how things gradually disappear over a flat horizon. But how exactly would you go about verifying that abortion is objectively right or wrong? That would bring us into a much bigger discussion of the very nature of moral truths, which would be no help at all in determining whether ethical relativism is right. The flat earth example is, of course, not supposed to be taken that far. All it shows is that you can't conclude, on the basis of there being a disagreement, that both parties are wrong. It is never as easy to find out who is right in a discussion of moral issues as it is to settle questions of geography.

The Problem of Induction

Some critics believe that the very foundation of the ethical relativism theory is wrong; they believe it simply is not true that there is no universal moral code. If relativists were asked how they know that there is no universal moral code, they would answer that they looked around and found none or possibly that, given the diversity of human nature, there never will be one. This begs the question, though, because we might reasonably suggest that they should look around a bit longer and refrain from making absolute statements about the future. Blanket statements bring on their own undoing, because any theory based on collecting evidence faces a classic problem: *the problem of induction.*

Induction is one of two major scientific methods; the other is deduction. In deductive thinking we start with an axiom that we believe is true, and we apply this axiom to establish the validity of other axioms, or we apply the theory to specific cases. In inductive thinking we gather empirical evidence in order to reach a comprehensive theory. Ethical relativism is an example of inductive thinking; it bases its general theory that there are no universal moral codes on evidence from particular cultures. The problem of induction is that we never can be sure that we have looked hard enough to gather all possible evidence.

A recent report from the medical world serves as a good example. Doctors and researchers have tried for years to find out how heart disease develops, and there are now several theories about the disease, plus a number of guidelines for how to avoid it and ways to treat it when it develops. This was considered a fairly well researched area until information surfaced in the 1990s that revealed that all the research participants over the years in every major study had been *male*. There was no sufficient available information on women and heart disease. This was a problem, because we can't assume that female biology responds to heart disease exactly the same way that male biology responds. (Studies that include women have now been completed.) Why were women excluded from the earlier studies? For many reasons, apparently: Men were easier to "keep track of," their physique is unaffected by childbirth and menopause, they were the ones experiencing heart disease in middle age. Here, then, was a series of studies believed to be comprehensive, but with one big problem: They excluded vital research material. This is typical of the problem of induction: whatever you are gathering evidence for or against, you'll never know for certain when you have gathered enough material, and you will never reach an absolutely certain conclusion, simply because it always is conceivable that something will come up in the future that will undermine your theory.

The induction used by the relativist to make up the theory that there are no universal codes suffers from the same problem. Can we know, with 100 percent certainty, on the basis of collected evidence, that there are no universal codes? No. We have to leave it open; perhaps some day a universal code will appear—or perhaps we will find that it had been there all the time, and we just didn't see it.

Soft Universalism

The clue to toppling ethical relativism actually lies very close, and perhaps that is why ethical relativists haven't seen it. Remember King Darius, who tried to get the Greeks to eat their dead and the Callatians to burn theirs? You may have asked yourself why any group would want to eat its dead. You may have wanted to ask Ruth Benedict why the Northwest Coast Indians were so aggressive (she doesn't say). We all may wonder why some peoples approve of infanticide or of dismemberment as punishment. As soon as we ask why, though, we have left the realm of ethical relativism. Relativists don't ask why; they just look at different customs and pronounce them fine for those who hold them. In asking why, we are looking for an explanation, one we can understand from our own point of view. In other words, we are expecting, or hoping, that there is some point at which that other culture will cease to seem so strange. And very often we reach that point. For instance, disposing of the dead through cannibalism is not at all uncommon, and it usually is done for the sake of honoring the dead or sharing in their spiritual strength. It would seem, then, that the Greeks and Callatians had something in common after all: The Greeks burned their dead because they wanted to honor their spirits, and the Callatians ate their dead for the same reason. Some nomad tribes of the Sahara consider it bad manners to eat in front of their in-laws. American couples rarely talk about sexual matters in the presence of their in-laws for the same reason—it is considered bad manners. These cultures share some common values: Both value good family relationships, and both express embarrassment when a transgression occurs.

The idea that all cultures have at least some values in common, even if they are buried beneath layers of different behavior patterns, is what I called *soft universalism* at the beginning of this chapter. The idea is not new; it was suggested by the Scottish philosopher David Hume in the eighteenth century. Hume believed that all people share a fellow-feeling, a compassion, that may show itself in different ways but that is present in all cultures nevertheless.

The philosopher James Rachels suggests that at least three values are universal:

1. A policy of caring for enough infants to ensure the continuation of the group

2. A rule against lying

3. A rule against murder

We may be horrified to learn about the custom of killing female babies in the old Eskimo (Inuit) culture, Rachels says, but we gain a better understanding when we learn that female babies were killed only because a high death rate among male hunters led to a surplus of females in the community. Why would it be a bad thing for an Inuit tribe to have more women than men? Certainly not because the women were unproductive—in addition to raising children and cooking, they were the ones manufacturing tools and clothing from the animals brought home by the hunters— but because male hunters were the sole providers of food (the Inuit diet is primarily meat). Therefore, a shortage of men in relation to the number of women would mean a shortage of food. Another important fact is that babies were killed only during hard times and only if adoptive parents couldn't be found. In such times, if the babies had been kept alive, the lives of the older children would have been in jeopardy. In other words, the Inuit killed some infants in order to protect the children they already had. Their culture valued what ours values: caring for the babies we already have.

Why do all cultures have a rule against lying? Because if you can't expect a fellow citizen to tell the truth most of the time, there is no use attempting to communicate, and without communication human society would grind to a halt. This doesn't mean, obviously, that humans never lie to one another, but only that, on the whole, the acceptable attitude is one of truthfulness.

The rule against murder derives from similar reasoning: If we can't expect our fellow citizens not to kill us, we will not want to venture outdoors, we will stop trusting in people, and society will fall apart (not, as some might think, because everyone will be killed off, but because of general mistrust and lack of communication). Rachels believes that even under chaotic circumstances small groups of friends and relatives would band together, and within these groups the nonmurder rule would be upheld.

The only trouble with the last two rules is that they seem to apply to "fellow citizens" only. As a member of society, you are expected not to lie to or murder mem-

James Rachels (b. 1941), American philosopher and advocate of human and animal rights. He is the author of *Elements of Moral Philosophy* (1968), *The End of Life: Euthanasia and Morality* (1986), *Created from Animals: The Moral Implications of Darwinism* (1990), and *Can Ethics Provide Answers?* (1997).

bers of your own social group, but there is really nothing preventing you from being morally free to lie through your teeth to an outsider or to an enemy government. You may even be free to prey on and murder members of other tribes, gangs, or countries. A scandal in the discipline of anthropology illustrates this phenomenon in a way that is quite significant: The renowned anthropologist Margaret Mead (1901–1978), who was a student of Franz Boas and Ruth Benedict, and like them an ethical relativist, wrote a book about the sexuality of young South Sea islanders, *Coming of Age in Samoa* (1928), which became a best-seller. But in the 1980s it became clear that she had been the victim of a hoax: Her native contacts in Samoa had strung her along to see how many whopping lies she'd swallow before she became suspicious — but she was young and gullible. It appears that with some additional research Mead could have discovered this for herself, but she never did. So even though the Samoans certainly had an overall rule against lying within their culture (which we know because one of Mead's contacts felt she ought to 'fess up when she was in her eighties), it didn't necessarily extend to the inexperienced young anthropologist.

Besides, is it true that we are expected to tell the truth? Many would challenge this idea across the board of world cultures. In some cultures it is considered good manners to lie, to play down one's own accomplishments (such as the tradition known in China to berate one's own cooking skills), not to tell the whole truth about a friend's appearance if she or he asks your opinion, to lie about sexual relationships to protect those involved (the notion of chivalry is sometimes invoked). In folklore there is even a tradition of telling "whoppers," and American Western folklore contains many prime examples of "tall tales." The frontiersman David ("Davy") Crockett was elected to Congress in 1827 not just because he was a likable and conscientious man but because he told better whoppers than his opponent (and had the grace to freely admit that he had been lying). So although it may not be true that a rule against lying is universal, if we characterize it as a rule against malicious deception we are closer to what Rachels means: Without that trust, your network of communications will break down.

Another problem with Rachels's three rules lies in the fact that, whatever rules may apply to a given culture, the *leaders* of those cultures, who should embody the cultural standards, are often the ones who break those rules. If it was to a leader's advantage to bend or break a rule, he or she might even consider it a duty to the throne to do so. Only in the twentieth century did the concept of rulers' not being above the law become solidified (to the extent that some leaders have to deal with civil lawsuits during their time-limited reign rather than face charges afterward). Even the near-universal ban on incest, which might well qualify as a fourth universal value, has traditionally been broken by leaders such as the pharaohs of ancient Egypt, who would marry their own siblings, and the royal families of Europe in previous centuries, who sometimes matched up first cousins because nobody else with "blue blood" was available.

Rachels has not provided us with any rules that apply universally, only with rules that all responsible people seem to be required to stick to *within their own societies*. Rachels has, however, provided all we need to show that ethical relativism is wrong in its assumption that cultures have nothing in common; we don't have to find a universal moral rule, just a universal pattern of behavior. Because Rachels believes that there are at least three such patterns — care of infants, not lying, and not murdering — we can call him a *descriptive soft universalist:* He describes what he thinks is the case, that we actually have some codes of behavior in common. But even if you can't find any codes in common, you might still be a *normative soft universalist.* In that case you believe we *ought* to have some code of behavior in common and that we ought to work toward establishing or finding such a code. You can, of course, be both a descriptive and a normative soft universalist. In that case you believe human beings around the world do have a few basic moral codes in common; but you also believe that in order to move toward a world community in which we can respect one another's differences while striving to work together to solve problems, we ought to find some common ground and set up a basic moral code for humanity to live by, a code such as the concept of human rights.

There is perhaps no better example from the world of current fiction of the theory of normative soft universalism than the *Star Trek* universe (see Chapter 2): The trek to the stars was made possible in the twenty-first century by humans putting their differences aside to work toward a common goal and a common idea of rights for all people while still respecting one another's diversity. In other words, if we define a set of common bottom-line values and respect cultural variety that doesn't infringe on such values, the sky will be the limit to human accomplishments.

Ethical Relativism and Multiculturalism

With the increasingly pluralistic character of modern Western society comes an increasing belief that all cultural traditions and all viewpoints represented in the public deserve to be heard — at universities, in politics, in the media, and elsewhere. Sometimes this is referred to as "multiculturalism," sometimes as "cultural diversity."

Let us consider multiculturalism and its goals. America used to be called a melting pot, meaning that there was room for anybody from anywhere, that all would be welcomed, and that after a while all individual cultural differences would subside in favor of the new culture of the United States. To many Americans (those from many different ethnic backgrounds, in fact) this continues to represent a beautiful image as well as an accurate description of what America is all about. For many people around the world this is what America seems to be. For others, however, the idea of the melting pot is a travesty, an illusion, and an insult. America may have embraced immigrants from countries such as England, Sweden, Ireland, and Germany, but many other people still feel as though they are living on the fringes of American society; they have not been accepted the way others have been. For such people, who feel that they and their ancestors were excluded from the melting pot because they were too different or simply unwanted, there is no such thing as a *common* American culture, only a *dominant* American culture; and they claim that what has been taught and practiced until recently has been *monoculturalism* (sometimes referred to as *Eurocentrism*). Today there is an understanding even among those from the "dominant culture" that this damages the very concept of an American culture. The question is what to do about it.

Some proponents of multiculturalism believe that what we must do is begin to listen to one another. I call this *inclusive multiculturalism* (also referred to as *pluralism*). The general idea is to integrate everyone — by law, if necessary — into all aspects of our society; to break through the "glass ceilings" that prevent people of color (women and men) as well as white women from reaching top positions; to become sensitized to what others might perceive as slurs (what one scholar calls *micro-inequities,* those little jabs that can hurt so deeply); and, if we are on the receiving end of such slurs, to learn to speak up for ourselves. An increased awareness of the multicolored pattern of our society will, the thinking goes, result in better working relationships, less of a sense that one cultural tradition dominates the country and that everyone who doesn't share it must be left out, and more tolerance and understanding among the groups. This awareness is supposed to begin in schools, where children should learn about as many cultural groups in American society as possible. Adding multicultural awareness to the curriculum means there will be less time for some subjects that are usually taught, but proponents of inclusive multiculturalism believe that a growing cultural understanding is worth the price. Today, a new image is frequently offered as an alternative to the old image of the melting pot: the *salad bowl.* A metaphor for inclusive multiculturalism, the salad image implies that each group retains its original "flavor" but that the groups also relate to one another; together they make a sum that is greater than its parts. The metaphor can be stretched only so far, though: Critics who believe that inclusive multiculturalism is not doing enough to foster cultural identity can always turn the image around and ask, Who supplies the salad dressing? The "dominant culture"! (Box 3.5 examines how some advocates of cultural diversity apply what appears to be an ad hominem fallacy.)

For a while in the 1980s and 1990s a certain approach was attempted in some schools, but its popularity seems to have declined over the last decade: The method of *exclusive multiculturalism* (also called *particularism*) was intended to help children from minority cultures retain or regain their self-esteem, under the assumption that self-esteem is fragile for such children (which in itself might be a questionable assumption). To counteract this supposed lack of self-esteem, children from each

Box 3.5   CULTURAL DIVERSITY OR CULTURAL ADVERSITY?

The idea that moral viewpoints acquire their importance from the groups that utter them rather than from their content is, to some philosophers, a misguided attitude. In the old days of Western culture, the dominant viewpoint was the one held by some—but not all—white males, and for most white males as well as for others that was enough to make the viewpoint "correct." Churches and political groups occasionally take the same attitude: The identity of the group is enough justification for the correctness of its views. Today we also see this same viewpoint applied socially by certain groups: If you are a member of an oppressed group, your viewpoint on right and wrong is valuable just because you are a member of that group, and if you are not, then your viewpoint is irrelevant. This form of relativism, which grants the importance of a viewpoint on the basis of gender, race, and class, may be as misplaced as one that denies the importance of certain groups just because they are who they are. Such an attitude, the argument goes, reflects the logical fallacy of the *ad hominem argument:* You are right or wrong because of who you are, not because of what you say. In Jim Garrison's words from Oliver Stone's film *JFK,* "I always wondered in court why it is because a woman is a prostitute, she has to have bad eyesight" (meaning some people think that just because someone is a prostitute, we can't trust her testimony). Whether this attitude is assumed by those in power or by those who are dispossessed, it is equally faulty as a moral principle, according to the rules of critical thinking. Can you imagine situations in which a person's identity alone would determine whether he or she was right or wrong?

ethnic group were isolated so they could be taught about the cultural advances of their particular group. Many parents as well as students felt uncomfortable about this approach, claiming that it led to a new form of segregation. And indeed, problems with the method of exclusive multiculturalism haven't quite been worked out to everyone's satisfaction: In a future society where mixed race and ethnicity are the rule rather than the exception, must a child then choose a primary racial or ethnic affiliation? And where would students of Euro-American ancestry be placed, regardless of whether they have majority or minority status—surely not in separate groups learning about the illustrious achievements of exclusively Euro-Americans? That would end up looking like white supremacy.

All in all, it seems that the inclusive approach to multiculturalism has become the standard method in primary and secondary schools. Since the early 1990s I have tried to keep track of the progress of an inclusive approach to American history in high schools, and in the fall of 2001, for the first time, more students in one of my classes in Introduction to Philosophy: Values had been taught American history in high school according to inclusive multicultural principles than through history books reflecting a monocultural approach.

How might multiculturalism affect our attitude toward basic values in ethics? That depends greatly on what we believe those values to be. If we think our values can't be disputed, that they are somehow determined by God or by Nature, then we will find it hard to accept other and different viewpoints. As we will see, such absolutism ("hard universalism") usually does not allow for any tolerance of other basic ideas.

If we adopt the attitude of ethical relativism, the result may surprise us, because ethical relativism doesn't automatically support multiculturalism. Ethical relativism states that there is no universal moral code — that each culture will do what is right for it, and no other culture has any business interfering. This may work when cultures are separate and isolated from one another, because the moral code in that case is defined as the code of the *dominant population*. Remember problem 2, "majority rule"? One of the problems with ethical relativism is precisely that it implies the moral rule of the majority. However, in our pluralistic society, this won't work, because the "dominant culture" (white society) is increasingly reproached for displaying cultural insensitivity. Can ethical relativism function, therefore, in a country as diverse as ours, where we often find opposing values ("Looting is antisocial" versus "Looting is a righteous act for the dispossessed," for example) within the same neighborhood? Because a multicultural ethic asks us not to think in terms of one dominant set of rules, some might opt for an attitude of total *moral nihilism* instead: No values are better than any other values, because no values are objectively correct. Such nihilism might well result in the breakdown of the fabric of a society, and possibly in a greater cohesion within subgroups, with different groups battling one another. Rather than describe these battles as gang wars, we might call this phenomenon *Balkanization* — when groups have nothing or very little in common except hatred for what the other groups stand for. It seems as though ethical relativism is not the answer to our new ethical problems of multiculturalism.

Suppose we look to soft universalism for the answer? If we are soft universalists we hope to be able to agree with others on some basic issues, but not on all issues. In the case of multiculturalism we may be able to agree on the promotion of general equality, tolerance, and cohesion in the nation (in other words, the will and ability to live together); we *have* to agree that what we want is a functioning society we all share in. If we don't agree on this, multiculturalism is a lost cause, and so is the whole idea of a United States. According to soft universalism, values can't be allowed to differ dramatically, so we wouldn't end up with acts such as looting being morally right for some and not for others, nor would the killing of family members for the sake of honor be acceptable in one neighborhood and not in another. These questions of common values in the context of a multicultural society are particularly burning, for without some values in common we simply won't have a society.

Is it possible to have one overall culture and several subcultural affiliations at the same time? In other words, can we have loyalties to our ancient ethnic roots and also be Americans (or Canadians, or Italians, or Brazilians, or whatever the case may be)? A few generations ago, immigrant parents made sure their children learned English and had American first names, encouraging them to blend in as quickly as possible so that their future as American citizens would have as few obstacles as possible — an obvious ethnic identity being considered an obstacle. A generation of children lost the language of their parents, and in many cases their family history, too. But over the past twenty-five years or so, people have been involved in looking for their roots, to a great extent inspired by Alex Haley's novel and television series *Roots*

Box 3.6   AN AMERICAN CULTURE?

When discussing the mores and habits of other cultures with my classes, I often hear students claim that there is no American culture—and if common denominators do exist, they are considered negative: brashness, ignorance or mistrust of other cultures, materialism, and so on. To many students, the fact that we are a very diverse society means that we have no shared culture; many consider themselves hyphenated Americans: Irish-Americans, African-Americans, Italian-Americans, Arab-Americans, and so forth. And yet in the weeks and months following the terrorist attacks of September 2001, many Americans, including many of my students, discovered that they had an American identity after all, and the loss of American lives felt like a personal loss.

If you agree that an American cultural identity exists, how would you characterize it? Is it founded in our Constitution? Is it a matter of a general outlook on life? Is it the fact that we, as a matter of course, question authority? Does it have to do with common cultural experiences, common holidays and food rituals (such as Thanksgiving), a love of traveling within our country, and perhaps also with an image of ourselves that has been invented by the movies?

Or perhaps it is the very freedom to define oneself that other cultures seem to have only to a lesser degree? Many Americans don't realize what it means to be an American until they travel abroad and experience other cultures—or perhaps tangle with legal systems that do not presume one to be innocent until proven guilty! Rather (as in the Napoleonic Law of France), you are presumed guilty until you can prove yourself innocent.

In the event of a common threat from abroad, one's cultural identity seems to loom larger, in the form of an appreciation for everyday things we used to take for granted, and for the rights this society grants us—even the right to disagree about this whole issue. The philosopher and novelist Ayn Rand (see Chapter 4), an immigrant from the Soviet Union, called America the only truly moral culture in the world. Some of us who are naturalized Americans seem to have an easier time identifying what it means to be an American than many natural-born citizens do, being appreciative of the Bill of Rights and the quintessential American quality of always being ready to reexamine an issue and "make things right"—even when it involves profound self-criticism.

(1977), about an African-American family's history. This trend has involved a renewed interest in teaching the new generation of children the language of their grandparents as a second language. One's cultural identity has been to a great extent perceived as formed through the original nationality of one's immigrant ancestors: one is Irish-American, Polish-American, Chinese-American, and so forth—to the extent that the nationality to the left of the hyphen has seemed, to some, to outweigh the second identity: American. This is what has spawned the expression "hyphenated American"—someone who sees himself or herself as having a composite heritage and perhaps also a split cultural identity. Does this mean you have to identify with some ancient ethnic heritage because there really isn't any American cultural identity per se? Box 3.6 explores what it might mean to have an American identity. In the

©2001 Scott Stantis. Reprinted by permission of Copley News Service

For many Americans, September 11 brought about a reevaluation of what it means to have a national and ethnic identity. Does this cartoon reflect your post-9/11 feelings about your nationality and ethnicity? Why or why not?

aftermath of the terrorist attacks of 2001, a new generation may have found, on their own, an answer to what it means to be an American. It doesn't mean disregarding one's ethnicity or ancient national roots—but it does mean that to many the common denominator of being American outweighs the individual differences.

Study Questions

1. Describe the four major approaches to moral differences outlined at the beginning of this chapter. Which one comes closest to your own viewpoint? Explain.

2. Discuss Ruth Benedict's claim that what is normal for a culture is what is moral in that culture. Discuss the advantages and problems associated with the theory of ethical relativism.

3. Discuss James Rachels's three suggested universal values: Are they truly universal? Why or why not? Can you think of other universal values not mentioned?

4. Can one have both an ethnic and a national identity? Explain.

Primary Readings and Narratives

The first Primary Reading is an excerpt from Ruth Benedict's famous paper "Anthropology and the Abnormal." The second is an excerpt from Bhikhu Parekh's "The Concept of Multicultural Education," in which he argues that a monocultural education is harmful to children. The Narratives are a summary of Alice Walker's novel *Possessing the Secret of Joy,* which indirectly — but powerfully — criticizes ethical relativism's tolerance toward the tribal practice of female circumcision; a summary of and excerpt from Sheri Tepper's novel *Sideshow;* and a summary of Spike Lee's film *Do the Right Thing,* which explores multiracial tensions and relationships in a Brooklyn neighborhood.

 Primary Reading

Anthropology and the Abnormal

RUTH BENEDICT

1934. Excerpt.

In her famous paper, Benedict talks about a Melanesian culture displaying extreme fears of poisoning. In addition, you'll read in her own words her view that morality is merely what is considered normal in a given society.

The most spectacular illustrations of the extent to which normality may be culturally defined are those cultures where an abnormality of our culture is the cornerstone of their social structure. It is not possible to do justice to these possibilities in a short discussion. A recent study of an island of northwest Melanesia by Fortune describes a society built upon traits which we regard as beyond the border of paranoia. In this tribe the exogamic groups look upon each other as prime manipulators of black magic, so that one marries always into an enemy group which remains for life one's deadly and unappeasable foes. They look upon a good garden crop as a confession of theft, for everyone is engaged in making magic to induce into his garden the productiveness of his neighbors'; therefore no secrecy in the island is so rigidly insisted upon as the secrecy of a man's harvesting of his yams. Their polite phrase at the acceptance of a gift is, "And if you now poison me, how shall I repay you this present?" Their preoccupation with poisoning is constant; no woman ever leaves her cooking pot for a moment untended. Even the great affinal economic exchanges that are characteristic of this Melanesian culture area are quite altered in Dobu since they are incompatible with this fear and distrust that pervades the culture. They go farther and people the whole world outside of their own quarters with such malignant spirits that all-night feasts and ceremonials simply do not occur here. They have even rigorous religiously enforced customs that forbid the sharing of seed even in one family group. Anyone else's food is deadly poison to you, so that communality of stores is out of the question. For some months before harvest the whole society is on the verge of starvation, but if one falls to the temptation and eats up one's seed yams, one is an outcast and a beachcomber for life. There is no coming back. It involves, as a matter of course, divorce and the breaking of all social ties.

Now in this society where no one may work with another and no one may share with another, Fortune describes the individual who was regarded by all his fellows as crazy. He was not one of those who periodically ran amok and, beside himself and frothing at the mouth, fell with a knife upon anyone he could reach. Such behavior they did not regard as putting anyone outside the pale. . . . But there was one man of sunny, kindly disposition who liked work and liked to be helpful. The compulsion was too strong for him to repress it in favor of the opposite tendencies of his culture. Men and women never spoke of him without laughing; he was silly and simple and definitely crazy. Nevertheless, to the ethnologist used to a culture that has, in Christianity, made his type the model of all virtue, he seemed a pleasant fellow.

These illustrations, which it has been possible to indicate only in the briefest manner, force upon us the fact that normality is culturally defined. An adult shaped to the drives and standards of either of these cultures, if he were transported into our civilization, would fall into our categories of abnormality. He would be faced with the psychic dilemmas of the socially unavailable. In his own culture, however, he is the pillar of society, the end result of socially inculcated mores, and the problem of personal instability in his case simply does not arise.

No one civilization can possibly utilize in its mores the whole potential range of human behavior. Just as there are great numbers of possible phonetic articulations, and the possibility of language depends on a selection and standardization of a few of these in order that speech communication may be possible at all, so the possibility of organized behavior of every sort, from the fashions of local dress and houses to the dicta of a people's ethics and religion, depends upon a similar selection among the possible behavior traits. In the field of recognized economic obligations or sex [taboos] this selection is as nonrational and subconscious a process as it is in the field of phonetics. It is a process which goes on in the group for long periods of time and is historically conditioned by innumerable accidents of isolation or of contact of peoples. In any comprehensive study of psychology, the selection that different cultures have made in the course of history within the great circumference of potential behavior is of great significance.

Every society, beginning with some slight inclination in one direction or another, carries its preference farther and farther, integrating itself more and more completely upon its chosen basis, and discarding those types of behavior that are uncongenial. Most of those organizations of personality that seem to us most incontrovertibly abnormal have been used by different civilizations in the very foundations of their institutional life. Conversely the most valued traits of our normal individuals have been looked on in differently organized cultures as aberrant. Normality, in short, within a very wide range, is culturally defined. It is primarily a term for the socially elaborated segment of human behavior in any culture; and abnormality, a term for the segment that that particular civilization does not use. The very eyes with which we see the problem are conditioned by the long traditional habits of our own society. . . .

. . . Mankind has always preferred to say, "It is morally good," rather than "it is habitual". . . But historically the two phrases are synonymous . . . The concept of the normal is properly a variant of the concept of good. It is that which society has approved. . . . Western civilization allows and culturally honors gratifications of the ego which according to any absolute category would be regarded as abnormal. The portrayal of unbridled and arrogant egoists as family men, as officers of the law, and in business has been a favorite topic of novelists, and they are familiar in every community. Such individuals are probably mentally warped to a greater degree than many inmates of our institutions who are nevertheless socially unavailable. They are extreme types of those personality configurations which our civilization fosters. . . .

The relativity of normality is important in what may some day come to be a true social engineering. Our picture of our own civilization is no longer in this generation in terms of a changeless and divinely derived set of categorical imperatives. We must face the problems our changed perspective has put upon us. In this matter of mental ailments, we must face the fact that even our normality is man-made, and is of our own seeking. Just as we have been handicapped in dealing with ethical problems so long as we held to an absolute definition of morality, so too in dealing with the problems of abnormality we are handicapped so long as we identify our local normalities with the universal sanities. I have taken illustrations from different cultures, because the conclusions are most inescapable from the contrasts as they are presented in unlike social groups. But the major problem is not a consequence of the variability of the normal from culture to culture, but its variability from era to era. This variability in time we cannot escape if we would, and it is not beyond the bounds of possibility that we may be able to face this inevitable change with full understanding and deal with it rationally. No society has yet achieved self-conscious and critical analysis of its own normalities and attempted rationally to deal with its own social process of creating new normalities within its next generation. But the fact that it is unachieved is not therefore proof of its impossibility. It is a faint indication of how momentous it could be in human society.

Study Questions

1. Is it important for Benedict to discover why the members of the tribe on the Melanesian island are afraid of poisoning? Why or why not? Would it make a difference in terms of ethical relativism if we knew the origin of the fear?

2. Is she right in her statement that "the concept of the normal is properly a variant of the concept of good"? Why or why not?

3. Does Benedict's cultural approach facilitate intercultural understanding? Why or why not?

4. Benedict is now viewed as one of the first spokespersons for ethical relativism, although her aim in this paper was to explore the concept of the abnormal. Her paper ends with these rarely quoted words, exploring the possibility of intercultural stan-

dards of normalcy: "It is as it is in ethics: all our local conventions of moral behavior and of immoral are without absolute validity, and yet it is quite possible that a modicum of what is considered right and what wrong could be disentangled that is shared by the whole human race." Does this statement contradict the general view of Benedict as being an ethical relativist? Does it undermine the philosophy of ethical relativism? Is she contradicting herself? Why or why not?

Primary Reading

The Concept of Multicultural Education

BHIKHU PAREKH

Essay, 1986. Excerpt.

Bhikhu Parekh is professor of political theory at the University of Hull (UK) and deputy chair of the Commission for Racial Equality. In this excerpt Parekh addresses the lack of multicultural sensitivity in English schools. In England the reference to "blacks" covers both people of African descent and people from India, Bangladesh, and Pakistan.

Let us now briefly explore the impact of this type of mono-cultural education (whether in Britain or elsewhere) on the child and how it measures up to the objectives the school claims to achieve.

First, it is unlikely to awaken his curiosity about other societies and cultures either because he is not exposed to them at all or because they are presented in uncomplimentary terms, or both. Thus our curriculum on religious studies is hardly likely to inspire him to enquire how some non-Christian religions manage to do without the idea of God as the creator of the universe, or have very different views of prophets, or conceive human destiny and come to terms with death and suffering in very different ways. A child exposed to no other religion but his own grows up asking only those questions that it encourages him to ask. And since he asks only those questions that his religion answers, he finds its answers satisfactory. In other words, he never gets out of its framework, and never feels disturbed or perplexed enough to explore other religions. What is true of religious studies is equally true of history, geography, literature, social studies and so on, none of which is likely to stimulate his curiosity about other civilizations and societies.

Second, mono-cultural education is unlikely to develop the faculty of imagination. Imagination represents the ability to conceive alternatives; that is, it is the capacity to recognize that things can be done, societies can be organized and activities can be performed in several different ways, of which the most familiar is but one and not necessarily the best. Imagination does not develop in a vacuum. It is only when one is exposed to different societies and cultures that one's imagination is stimulated and the consciousness of alternatives becomes an inseparable part of one's ways of thinking. One cannot then think of anything, be it an activity, a form of enquiry, a culture or a society without at the same time realizing that it can be conceptualized or thought about or conducted in several different ways. And this awareness of alternatives radically alters one's perspective to the way it is organized in one's own environment. One cannot avoid asking *why* it is organized in a particular manner in one's society, and *if* this way of organizing it is better than others. Mono-cultural education blots out the awareness of alternatives and restricts imagination. It cannot avoid encouraging the illusion that the limits of one's world are the limits of the world itself, and that the conventional way of doing things is the only natural way.

Third, mono-cultural education stunts the growth of the critical faculty. A child taught to look at the world from the narrow perspective of his own culture and not exposed to any other is bound to reject all that cannot be accommodated within the narrow categories of his own way of looking at the world. He judges other cultures and societies by the norms and standards derived from his own, and predictably finds them odd and even worthless. And since he judges his society in terms of its own norms, he can never take a genuinely critical attitude to it. Further, as we saw, mono-cultural education blunts imagination, and therefore the child lacks the sharp awareness of alternatives that alone can give a cutting edge to his critical faculties. Unable to criticize his society and unable to appreciate alternatives, he can hardly avoid admiring its "glory" and the "genius" and greatness of his "race," and remains vulnerable to the deadly vice of narcissism.

Fourth, mono-cultural education tends to breed arrogance and insensitivity. The child who is not encouraged to study other cultures and societies or to study them with sympathy and imagination cannot develop a respect for them. Imprisoned within the framework of his own culture, he cannot understand and appreciate differences nor accept diversity of values, beliefs, dress, food, ways of life and views of the world as an integral part of the human condition. He does not welcome, let alone rejoice in, diversity. Naturally he feels threatened by it and does not know how to cope with it. He approaches the world on his own terms, expecting it to adjust to him and seeing no reason why he should adjust to it. This leads to arrogance and double standards and, what is but a converse of it, an attitude of hypocrisy. When he visits other countries, he sees no need to learn their languages and adjust to their customs, whereas he expects others visiting his own to speak his language and accept its customs. . . .

Fifth, mono-cultural education provides a fertile ground for racism. Since a pupil knows very little about other societies and cultures, he can only respond to them in terms of superficial generalizations and stereotypes. These, in turn, are not haphazard products of individual imagination but culturally derived. A culture not informed by a sensitive appreciation of others cannot but judge them in terms of its own norms. It sets itself up as an absolute, that is, as the only universally valid point of reference, and evaluates others in terms of their approximation to it. The greater the degree to which they resemble it, the more civilized or developed they are supposed to be. And conversely the more they diverge from it, the more uncivilized they are judged to be. This is indeed how the Victorians built up a hierarchy of human societies. They placed the African societies at the bottom, the Asians a little higher, the Mediterranean still higher, and so on until they got to the English whom they regarded as representing the highest stage of human development. . . .

We have so far considered the impact of mono-cultural education on white children. We may now briefly consider its impact on their black peers. The latter obviously suffer from the same consequences as the former. In addition they also suffer from other sets of consequences.

The white children raised on a mono-cultural diet look at their black peers through the prism of the stereotypes they have acquired from their education. They find it difficult to accept them as equals, relax in their presence, appreciate their desire to retain their distinct cultural identity, and generally treat them with a mixture of contempt and pity. For their part, the black children either reciprocate the hostility, or bend over backwards to conform to their white peers' expectations and in so doing alienate their parents and less conformist peers. Like the white children, some white teachers have grown up on a mono-cultural diet and share their cultural arrogance and insensitivity. Consciously or unconsciously they approach their black pupils with the familiar stereotypes; they expect little of them, tend not to stretch them to their fullest, and fail to provide them with necessary educational and emotional support and encouragement. Not surprisingly many black children tend to under-achieve, rarely feel relaxed at school, lack trust in their teachers and go through the school with a cartload of frustrations and resentment.

When constantly fed on an ethnocentric curriculum that presents their communities and cultures in a highly biased and unflattering manner, black children can hardly avoid developing a deep sense of inferiority and worthlessness. They feel that they belong to a "race" which is culturally deficient and scarred by grave defects of character and intelligence; and that their ancestors have contributed "nothing" to the growth of human civilization, invented nothing of which others should take note, composed nothing which others could read with profit, built no empires, left behind nothing that is worth preserving or even cherishing, and indeed had lived such a fragile and primitive life that, but for the white colonizers, they would have by now become extinct. The impact of all this on the self-respect and identity of a black child and on his relations with his parents, brothers, elders and indeed with the members of his community in general is shattering. Lacking a sense of worth, he develops self-pity and self-hatred. He resents his parents for what they are and what they have done to him. He feels they have nothing worthwhile to teach or transmit to him; and that diminishes his respect for them, and consequently their authority over him. With their authority diminished, the parents feel compelled to rely on physical force to maintain a modicum of order in the family. . . .

The black child raised on a mono-cultural diet in an English school experiences profound self-alienation. His colour and his affections bind him to his people; the culture he is in the process of acquiring distances him from them. His birth and his destiny, his past and his future, point in wholly different and incompatible directions. His present is nothing but a battleground between his present and his future, and he is not quite sure which will eventually win. He feels suspended between two worlds; he half-wishes to leave one but he cannot, and it would not let go of him either; he half-wishes to embrace the other, but fears that he cannot and that it will not accept him either. . . .

What is, perhaps clumsily, called multi-cultural education is ultimately nothing more than this. It is essentially an attempt to release a child from the confines of the ethnocentric straitjacket and to awaken him to the existence of other cultures, societies and ways of life and thought. It is intended to de-condition the child as much as possible in order that he can go out into the world as free from biases and prejudices as possible and able and willing to explore its rich diversity. Multi-cultural education is therefore an education in freedom—freedom *from* inherited biases and narrow feelings and sentiments, as well as freedom *to* explore other cultures and perspectives and make one's own choices in full awareness of available and practicable alternatives. Multi-cultural education is therefore not a departure from, nor incompatible with, but a further refinement of, the liberal idea of education. It does not cut off a child from his own culture; rather it enables him to enrich, refine and take a broader view of it without losing his roots in it.

Study Questions

1. Discuss the five consequences of monocultural education outlined by Parekh: Is he right? Why or why not?

2. Does Parekh advocate inclusive or exclusive multiculturalism?

3. Do you think Parekh's arguments are equally valid for the American and for the British educational system?

4. Parekh is concerned about raising the cultural sensitivity of the dominant, white British culture. How does he himself fare in terms of *gender* sensitivity? (A clue: How does he refer to the schoolchildren?) Is this a relevant issue? Why or why not?

Narrative

Possessing the Secret of Joy

ALICE WALKER

Novel, 1992. Summary and Excerpt.

If you have read or seen *The Color Purple,* you will recognize some of the main characters in this moving and shocking novel: Olivia, Adam, and Tashi (Olivia and Adam are the children of Celie, the key character in *The Color Purple,* and Tashi is their best friend in the African village where Olivia and Adam's adoptive parents are missionaries). However, *Possessing the Secret of Joy* is a story that stands on its own, making a powerful ar-

Alice Walker (b. 1944), American novelist, author of *The Color Purple, The Temple of My Familiar, Possessing the Secret of Joy,* and *The Same River Twice*. Walker's fiction incorporates many of the cultural strands contributing to the lives of American people of color and relates the African American experience to that of the African. Walker focuses particularly on the life experiences of women who are African and African American.

gument against the ancient practice of female genital mutilation.* The novel weaves its way through the life of the storyteller Tashi. She is now an American, but originally she was of the Olinka tribe in Africa, a tribe Walker invented as a symbol for all African tribes. In real time and flashbacks, we are introduced to the nightmare of Tashi's life: the death of her older sister Dura, at first a vague memory, but in the end a reality so horrible that, to Tashi, it may be worth killing for.

Tashi has always been afraid of bleeding to death, and she has always had a terrifying dream of a dark tower where she is being kept prisoner, unable to move. Her adult life is in complete disarray. Her husband, Adam, and her best friend, Olivia, try to understand and support her as well as they can, but Tashi has periods of mental instability and moments of great, uncontrollable rage. She sees psychiatrists, and she spends time at a mental institution. But in the course of the book she tells her own story with increasing insight, and we realize that her mental condition is a result of two traumatic events: a terrible experience when she was a child and another when she was a young adult.

Tashi grew up in the Olinka village, the daughter of a Christian woman. Always a sensitive girl, Tashi was never the same after the death of her sister. As a young woman, Tashi left for America with the missionary family and became an American citizen. She and Adam were lovers, and Tashi loved her American life, but, even so, she decided as a young adult to return to Africa for a ceremony. She wanted to be "bathed" like the rest of the women in her tribe. Because of her Christian beliefs, her mother had kept her

*Female genital mutilation (sometimes referred to by Walker and others as female circumcision) is a process that can involve cutting the clitoris, removing it, or completely cutting away the inner and outer labia and sewing up the young girl with an aperture only big enough to allow for menstrual flow. The procedure is widespread in Africa and the Middle East and occurs illegally in the United States among some immigrant groups from these areas. The purpose of the procedure is not hygiene; it is strictly a cultural and religious ritual. Sexual pleasure becomes all but impossible, and a husband is assured of a virgin wife who is also going to remain faithful. In addition, health problems and chronic pain are often a consequence of the procedure. Most critics of the procedure see it as an affront to human rights and a tool for the subjugation and domination of women. Defenders of the practice argue that Western critics have no right to superimpose Western values on other cultures. As such, female genital mutilation presents a challenge to ethical relativism, which argues that nobody has the right to criticize the moral and traditional practices of another culture. World attention has been focused on this practice since the mid-1990s.

away from this ritual in childhood when most young girls were "bathed," but Tashi, at this point in her life, felt that as a political and sentimental gesture of solidarity with her people, and in particular their charismatic political leader, she ought to undergo the ritual — without completely realizing its ramifications. She sought out the *tsunga* (medicine woman), M'Lissa, who performs the rituals. "Bathing" is a euphemism for female genital mutilation, and, from that day on, Tashi has experienced daily pain and health problems, in addition to a loss of sexual sensitivity. While still recuperating in M'Lissa's custody, Tashi is found by Adam, who has been frantically searching for her. She returns to the United States, marries him, and has a baby, Benny, under extremely painful conditions because of the mutilation. As a result, Benny is born with a mental disability. Increasingly, Tashi experiences bouts of anxiety and rage. With the help of psychiatrists she has begun to remember the death, the *murder,* of her sister: Tashi was hiding outside the hut where her sister died, screaming and bleeding to death — from a botched procedure. And who performed the ritual? The same *tsunga,* M'Lissa, with the help of Tashi and Dura's own mother.

By the time we read this, we also know that Tashi is now, in real time, on trial in Africa for murder — the murder of M'Lissa. Did she do it? We won't know until the very end of the story. But we learn that after many years of marriage to Adam, with increasing problems due to psychological instability, Tashi has chosen to return to Africa to confront M'Lissa, who by now is a nationally renowned person, symbolizing the Olinka tradition. M'Lissa welcomes Tashi and reveals to her that she now expects Tashi to kill her, because that will elevate M'Lissa to the position of a saint. She also reveals that she finds Tashi naive beyond belief to have come back for the mutilation when she didn't have to — something M'Lissa would never have done herself. Even so, M'Lissa didn't try to stop her but performed the operation just because she was asked to do it, and it was her traditional job. And M'Lissa now recalls Tashi's sister who died — she had abandoned the bleeding little girl because her crying was too much for M'Lissa to bear.

Is M'Lissa the great evil figure in the story? Responsible for the death of Dura and the loss of Tashi's own spirit — Tashi calls it her own death — she is certainly a villain. But she herself is also a victim: Her own procedure was botched, with lameness resulting. She is a tool for the culture, passing the terror along to future generations of young girls as it was passed on to her. Tashi realizes that the true culprit is not the mutilator but the older men of the tribal society who want the mutilations done, who argue that God thinks of woman as unclean if she isn't "circumcised" — the ones who think of an "uncircumcised" woman as "loose" and immoral, as someone who needs to be kept under control. But still, Tashi can't help blaming M'Lissa:

> It is what you told me. Remember? The uncircumcised woman is loose, you said, like a shoe that all, no matter what their size, might wear. This is unseemly, you said. Unclean. A proper woman must be cut and sewn to fit only her husband, whose pleasure depends on an opening it might take months, even years, to enlarge. Men love and enjoy the struggle, you said. For the woman . . . But you never said anything about the woman, did you, M'Lissa? About the pleasure she might have. Or the suffering.

At the end of the story we learn the source of Tashi's nightmare about the dark tower, the truth about M'Lissa's death, and Tashi's own fate at the hands of the jury. And the secret of joy? On a very concrete level, the secret of sexual joy is to have an intact, unmutilated body and an unmutilated sense of self, of freedom. On a deeper level, the secret of joy itself is something we each have to find. Tashi's loved ones suggest that the secret is *resistance*.

Alice Walker's novel was received with alarm by many people who were unaware of the practice of female genital mutilation and welcomed by many others as a strong statement against excessive cultural tolerance. Walker was also criticized by some for betraying her African heritage in denouncing a traditional tribal practice as something that should not be tolerated in today's world.

Study Questions

1. Explain how this story can be viewed as an attack on ethical relativism. How might an ethical relativist respond to Walker's attack?

2. In view of the theme of female genital mutilation, do you find ethical relativism to be an appealing or a problematic moral theory? Explain.

3. Can we understand why Tashi went back as an adult to have the operation performed? Is this a realistic idea? Why or why not?

4. In your opinion, is Walker doing the right thing, exposing the practice of female genital mutilation as immoral, or should she show loyalty and solidarity with her African heritage by defending the practice? Is this a true dichotomy (an either-or situation), or is there another alternative?

5. M'Lissa asks Tashi what an American looks like, and Tashi answers, "An American, I said, sighing, but understanding my love for my adopted country perhaps for the first time: an American looks like a wounded person whose wound is hidden from others and sometimes from herself. An American looks like me." What does Tashi mean? Do you agree with her? Why or why not?

Narrative

Sideshow

SHERI S. TEPPER

Novel, 1992. Summary and Excerpt.

Sheri S. Tepper's *Sideshow* is a philosophical debate about misdirected tolerance; it is a philosophical story clad in a science fiction cloak. The planet Elsewhere is the only place left in the galaxy that is not infected with the virus of the Hobbs Land Gods, a virus that, to the people of Elsewhere, is blasphemous; it abolishes war and enmity and cultural differences and creates a new kind of being by fusing humans and other sentient beings into *Fauna sapiens*. Elsewhere is populated by humans who prefer to remain as they are, worship their gods, keep their slaves, sacrifice their children, and keep their men and women prisoners in their home the way they have always done, all in the name of holy diversity. Enforcers make sure that citizens of each country on the planet stay within their own borders (tourism is acceptable, but not emigration), that no one smuggles artifacts from a technologically higher culture to a lower culture, and that all rules pertaining to each country are strictly adhered to. Occasionally an Enforcer will let his or her human side show and will prevent some particularly gruesome tradition from taking place, such as the sacrifice of a child, but on the whole such interference is considered a criminal act.

Nela and Bertran are two young humans from our own time period who have been catapulted to the future by a time travel device and now find themselves on Elsewhere. They have their own problems: Nela and Bertran are Siamese (conjoined) twins, joined at the side, who share too many organs to be separated surgically. Conjoined twins are always genetically identical, and yet Nela is a girl and Bertran is a boy. How could that be? This is a result of socialization, not biology. Nela and Bertran's mother wanted a girl, and their father wanted a boy, but the twins were born androgynous (with both male and female sexual organs). So their parents' choice was to change them both surgically to be distinctly female and male and raise them accordingly. The twins have always dreamed of being separated, although they know it is an impossibility. They befriend two Enforcers, Fringe (a woman) and Danivon (a man), and take a tour of Elsewhere. The twins tell the Enforcers about political and social conditions on Earth, of militarism, slavery, oppression of men and of women, and also of democracies and freedom-loving countries. They are told that equivalent societies to all of them can be found somewhere on Elsewhere.

> "And this is the diversity you are sworn to preserve?" asked Nela.
> "There are one thousand and three provinces," said Fringe. "We have mentioned only a tiny few of them. On Elsewhere, mankind is free to be whatever he can, or will."
> The twins thought about this for a time before Bertran asked, "Let us suppose one of the women of the Thrasis wishes to escape. Or one of the—what did you call them? The Murrey?—one of the Murrey from Derbeck? Let us suppose a civilian from Frick grows weary of being ruled by soldiers. What recourse do they have?"
> "I don't understand," said Danivon. "Recourse?"
> "Are they free to leave?"
> "Of course not," said Fringe. "Persons must stay in their own place, in the diversity to which they were born. . . ."
> "I'd call it a people zoo," [Nela] said. "Just like the zoos on Earth of long ago, with all the people in habitats."

Later the Enforcers apprehend a child killer, and Nela and Bertran congratulate them on a job well done; however, the twins have misunderstood the Enforcers' mission:

> "Our job is to protect diversity," [Danivon] said through gritted teeth, "the very diversity that is the essence of humanity! In that diversity children are always being killed for any number of reasons. If the killing is proper to that place, then it is proper. But this old man took children across *borders*! He *interfered* in the affairs of a province! Here on Elsewhere, we let one another alone."

As it happens, Fringe begins to doubt the Enforcer code herself when, on a river flowing from the country of Choire, where only children with perfect pitch fit (for the choir practices) are kept alive, they encounter a child in a basket. The child has been "exposed" by Choire parents, perhaps because they want a newborn child instead, or perhaps because the child is musically defective or doesn't get along with its parents. . . .

Following the extended finger, Fringe saw. A basket floated out in midstream, bobbing on the wavelets, carrying a child some three or four years old who held tight to the closely woven rim and cried silently, mouth open, eyes and nose streaming.

"You said babies . . . ," said Fringe to Jory [another traveler], surprised and offended at this event following so soon upon her catechism.

Jory corrected her, "I said children."

. . . The basket bobbed on the river waves. The child looked up, saw them, stretched out its arms, and cried across the water. "P'ease . . . p'ease . . ." The river flow swept the basket on past, the child's voice still rising in a wail of fright. "Oh, oh, pick Onny up, p'ease. Pick Onny up. . . ." Where the basket bobbed, something large and many-toothed raised itself from the water and gulped hugely.

Fringe turned blind eyes away from the water, shutting out the sight, driving out the memory of it. Such things were. Diversity implied both pleasure and pain, both justice and injustice, both life and death. That's the way things were.

Eventually, Fringe and Danivon join forces with rebels trying to make changes in the diversity enclaves, and now things shift rapidly; a gateway in time and space opens, and the lives of the people of Elsewhere are about to be transformed forever. The conjoined twins Nela and Bertran face their ultimate wish and challenge, that of separation, but it comes at a terrible price. And the ultimate goal for all the turmoil and suffering? "The Ultimate Destiny of Man is to stop being only man." The Hobbs Land Gods are taking over, and *Fauna sapiens* is spreading across the galaxy. (But to find out how it happens, you must read this wonderful novel yourself.)

Study Questions

1. Identify the elements in this excerpt that correspond to the debate about ethical relativism.

2. What is Fringe the Enforcer's problem?

3. What is Tepper trying to convey in this story?

4. There is an additional element to the theme of ethical relativism: gender theory. Nela and Bertran are conjoined twins, which means they are genetically identical, in their case born androgynous. Yet one is raised as a girl and the other as a boy to satisfy their parents' hopes and expectations. What do you think Tepper is trying to say with this subplot?

5. Is this an argument against cultural tolerance? Judging from the excerpt, does Tepper come across as a hard universalist or a soft universalist?

Narrative

Do the Right Thing

SPIKE LEE (SCREENWRITER AND DIRECTOR)

Film, 1989. Summary.

In a book dealing with the question of what one should do, I couldn't possibly pass up a film with the title *Do the Right Thing*. The question was, where to place it? The film can perhaps be seen as an argument for ethical relativism, or at least for cultural tolerance, but perhaps not. I will leave that up to you.

It is a very hot summer morning in Bedford-Stuyvesant, a predominantly African American part of Brooklyn. Sal, an Italian, and his two sons are opening their pizzeria on one corner; a Korean family is opening up their grocery store on the other. The police (all white) are cruising the streets. Most of the black population is out of work. A young, mentally disabled man, Smiley, is trying to sell photos of Martin Luther King, Jr., and Malcolm X. A young black man, Mookie (played by Spike Lee), is delivering pizza in the neighborhood, and "Da Mayor," an old black man, is patrolling the streets, being friendly to everybody although not everybody takes kindly to him. He calls Mookie over and admonishes him always to "do the right thing."

As the day gets hotter, tempers flare. Sal likes the neighborhood and his customers (who all grew up on his pizzas). His younger son, Vito, is a good friend of Mookie's. His older son, Pino, however, wants out; all he perceives is that his family members are not welcome in the African American community, and he thinks they should associate with their own kind in their Italian neighborhood. But Mookie points out to Pino that although he may think he does not like blacks, all his heroes are African American. In Sal's pizzeria, one of his customers, Buggin' Out, notices that Sal's wall is full of pictures of famous Italians and Italian Americans and asks why there are no brothers on the wall. When the question becomes a demand, Sal loses his temper and has Mookie throw him out. Radio Raheem, a young man with a big boom box, has a loudness contest with a group of Puerto Ricans and their own boom box. Mookie becomes upset when his sister comes to visit the pizza place and Sal appears to have a crush on her. So Mookie quarrels with his sister and later with his Puerto Rican girlfriend, Tina, too. Quarrels break out at the slightest provocation, such as scuffed running shoes, loud radios, and lack of a certain brand of beer at the grocery store: Blacks, Puerto Ricans, Italians, Koreans—just about everyone has a short temper and a ready vocabulary of epithets. Da Mayor is trying to smooth things out and eventually becomes a hero: He saves a little boy from being run over. The only one who thinks to thank him is Mother Sister, a woman in the neighborhood who apparently has disliked him for years.

The sun sets, but tempers are still hot. Sal and his sons are closing the pizzeria for the night, but Buggin' Out (who has been trying to organize a "Boycott Sal's Pizzeria" campaign), Radio Raheem, and Smiley turn up. Buggin' Out demands pictures of African Americans on the wall, and Raheem is upset that Sal told him to turn his radio down earlier. Everybody starts screaming, and Sal snaps, smashing Raheem's radio with a bat.

In *Do the Right Thing* (Universal City Studios, 1989) Mookie (Spike Lee) and Sal (Danny Aiello) are discussing neighborhood issues in Sal's pizza restaurant. On this hot day, tensions run high between ethnic groups: the Italians, the blacks, the Koreans, and the all-white police force.

A fight ensues and spills into the street; Raheem is holding Sal by the throat. The police arrive and pull Raheem off Sal, but the choke hold they apply kills Raheem. In shock, the fighting crowd freezes — until Mookie, as if surfacing from a dream, grabs a trash can and hurls it through Sal's window. The crowd bursts into the restaurant, looting and smashing things, and Smiley lights a match: The place goes up in flames. As the place is burning, he pins one of his pictures of Martin Luther King, Jr., and Malcolm X on the wall next to the photos of Italian Americans.

Next, the crowd turns on the Korean grocery store, but the young Korean store owner cries, "I'm black! You — me — we're the same!" Some laugh, but this quiets down tempers, and the store is safe.

The next day is another hot one. There is no solution to any of the problems in the neighborhood. Da Mayor is the only person who resolved anything; during the riot he managed to overcome the animosity of Mother Sister. Mookie vows only to spend more time with his and Tina's little boy.

The end of the movie? Two quotes appear on the screen, one from Martin Luther King, Jr., and the other from Malcolm X. King says that violence never solves any problems. Malcolm X says that, in general, violence is evil, but not in self-defense — in that case it is not even violence, but, rather, intelligence.

Study Questions

1. What do you think Spike Lee intended us to conclude?

2. *Did* Mookie do the right thing? Did anybody?

3. What did the Korean store owner mean when he said he was black, too?

4. Is this film advocating inclusive or exclusive multiculturalism?

5. Can there be different moral rules for different ethnic and cultural groups? Should there be?

6. Does Spike Lee present his characters as stereotypes? Why or why not?

Chapter Four

Myself or Others?

We usually assume that moral behavior, or "being ethical," has to do with not being overly concerned with oneself. In other words, selfishness is assumed to be an unacceptable attitude. Even among scholars, though, there is disagreement about what constitutes ethical behavior. Since very early in Western intellectual history the viewpoint that humans aren't built to look out for other people's interests has surfaced regularly. Some scholars even hold that proper moral conduct consists of "looking out for Number One," period. These viewpoints are known as *psychological egoism* and *ethical egoism,* respectively. Both psychological egoism and ethical egoism are examples of absolutist theories; they hold that only one code is the norm for ethical behavior. (See Box 4.1 for an explanation of the difference between *egoism* and *egotism.*)

Psychological Egoism

On September 11, some three thousand people perished in the terrorist attacks on New York and Washington, D.C., but an estimated twenty thousand people survived, many rescued—by civilian strangers, firefighters, and police. One blind man was saved by his guide dog, which led him to safety down seventy-eight flights of stairs—from above where the second plane hit the World Trade Center's north tower. As we see in Chapter 12, the film *Schindler's List* makes the point, familiar to anyone raised in the Jewish tradition, that whoever saves a life saves a world. Many thousands of worlds were saved that day, some of them through extraordinarily heroic actions. But other worlds perished in the rescue attempts: Three hundred New York firefighters and police officers were among the dead, having rushed into the trade center towers before they fell. While everyone else was heading down the stairs, they were running up.

Police officer Walwyn Stuart arrived at the WTC subway station after the first plane had hit, and he herded arriving passengers back on the trains. Then he ordered the trains to leave and stopped all incoming trains. Because of Officer Stuart, apparently not a single person was trapped in the subway at Ground Zero. Then he ran upstairs to do what he could in the burning tower; he never came out. Two men carried a woman in a wheelchair—a complete stranger to them—down sixty flights of stairs to safety. A military man crawled through burning debris to free another man who was trapped in the burning section of the Pentagon. I think most of us wouldn't hesitate to call these people heroes.

And so it is disturbing for many of us that one moral theory would calmly dismiss all these acts as expressions of fundamentally selfish human nature: *psychological egoism.* Similarly, ask a psychological egoist about the fundamental motivation of the suicidal hijackers, and the answer will be the same: As much as the terrorists

Box 4.1   EGOISM OR EGOTISM?

The terms *egoism* and *egotism* are part of our everyday speech, and people often use them interchangeably, but do they really mean the same thing? No: An *egoist* is a person who thinks in terms of his or her own advantage, generally by disregarding the interests of others. An *egotist* is a person who has a very high opinion of himself or herself and whose language often consists of self-praise; praise an egotist for a good result on a test or for looking nice, and you might receive responses such as "Of course I did well—I always do, because I'm very smart" or "Nice? I look great!" An egoist need not fall into this pattern, although he or she might, of course, be an egotist as well.

themselves may have felt they were dying selflessly for a cause, they were being utterly selfish, according to psychological egoism. Indeed, we don't even have to inquire into their motivation—for the psychological egoist, it is a given that everyone is selfish all the time, because it is built into our nature as human beings. We simply cannot avoid being selfish.

Cases such as those of Officer Stuart and so many others that seem to exemplify selflessness are precious to most people, because they show us what we might be capable of. We like to believe that humans have a built-in measure of courage that allows us to rise to the occasion and give up our lives, or at least our comfort, for others. Of course, few people perform heroic deeds with the *intent* of getting killed, but if they lose their lives in the process, we only seem to admire them more. (There are those who feel that losing one's life for someone else is stupid, useless, or even morally wrong. Such people may feel more comfortable with the theory of *ethical egoism*.)

If we ask a person who has performed (and survived) a heroic deed why he or she did it, the answer is almost predictable: "I just had to do it" or perhaps "I didn't think about it, I just did it." We take such comments as a sign that we are in the presence of a person with extraordinary moral character. But there are other ways of interpreting the words and actions of heroes. The theory of psychological egoism states that whatever it may look like and whatever we may think it is, no human action is done for any reason other than for the sake of the agent. In short, we are all selfish, or at least we are all self-interested.

The term *psychological egoism* is applied to the theory because it is a psychological theory, a theory about how humans behave. A psychological egoist believes that humans are always looking out for themselves in some way or other, and it is impossible for them to behave any other way. As such, psychological egoism is a descriptive theory; it doesn't make any statements about whether this is a *good* way to behave. What does it take for a person to be labeled a psychological egoist? It's not necessary that he or she be a selfish person, only that he or she hold to the theory that all people look after themselves. As we see later, it is entirely possible for someone to be kind and caring and still be a psychological egoist. (See Box 4.2 for an explanation of the difference between *selfish* and *self-interested*.) Suppose, though, that

Box 4.2   SELFISH VERSUS SELF-INTERESTED

Psychological egoism is generally described as a theory which states that everyone is selfish at all times. But what does the word *selfish* mean? Some psychological egoists (people who believe everyone is selfish) sometimes emphasize that there is nothing bad or morally deficient about being selfish; all it means, they say, is that we are "self-ish," we are focused on our own survival, which doesn't necessarily imply that we are disregarding other people's interests. However, we use the word in a different sense in our everyday language. According to Webster's Dictionary, *selfish* means "devoted unduly to self; influenced by a view to private advantage," so if we concede that Webster's reflects the common use of the word, we can't deny that *selfish* is a morally disparaging term; it isn't value-neutral, and it certainly isn't a compliment.

Sometimes psychological egoists use the term *selfish,* and sometimes the term used is *self-interested.* There is no consensus among psychological egoists about which term to use. It makes quite a difference which term you choose, but in the end, it may not make the theory of psychological egoism any more plausible. If you say (1), "All acts are selfish," you imply that all of us are always looking for self-gratification and have

no feeling for the interests of others. However, if you say (2), "All acts are self-interested," you imply that all of us are always thinking about what is best for us. Is statement 1 true? It may be true that we are always looking out for ourselves in some way, but it is certainly not true that we are always looking for self-gratification; many a moment in a lifetime is spent agonizing over doing what we want versus doing what we ought to do, and often we end up choosing duty over desire. So what if the psychological egoist says, "Doing my duty is better in the long run for me, even if I don't feel like doing it, so I guess I'm self-interested" (statement 2)? But is statement 2 true? Many philosophers over the years have gleefully pointed out that it isn't—we are hardly concerned with what is good for us, at least not all the time. Many people smoke, drink to excess, and take drugs even though they know it is not in their own best interest. So couldn't psychological egoism state that "all acts are either selfish or self-interested"? It could, but it generally doesn't; part of the appeal of psychological egoism is that it is a very simple theory, and putting a dichotomy (an either-or) into the theory makes it much more complicated.

someone insists that everyone *ought to* look after themselves. Then he or she is an *ethical egoist.* We discuss the theory of ethical egoism later in this chapter.

All People Look After Themselves

In Plato's *Republic* we find a discussion about morality and selfishness. Plato's brother Glaucon is trying to make Socrates give some good reasons why it is better to be just than to be unjust. Glaucon insists that all people by nature look after themselves, and whenever we can get away with something, we will do it, regardless of how unjust it may be to others. Unfortunately, we may receive the same treatment from others, which is highly unpleasant, so for the sake of peace and security we agree to treat each other decently—not because we want to, but because we are playing it safe. Morality is just a result of our looking out for ourselves. (See Box 4.3 for an explanation of psychological egoism in terms of "ought implies can.")

Box 4.3   "OUGHT IMPLIES CAN"

Sometimes a philosophical text will state that "ought implies can." In the civil code of the Roman Empire (27 B.C.E.–395 C.E.) this principle was clearly stated, and Roman citizens knew that *impossibilium nulla est obligatio* (nobody has a duty to do what is not possible). Many philosophical and legal schools of thought today are still based on this idea, and one of these is psychological egoism. "Ought implies can" means that we can't have an obligation (ought) to do something unless it is actually possible for us to do it (can). I can't make it a moral obligation for you to swim across San Francisco Bay to show your support for the Save the Whales program if you can't swim (but I might try to make it an obligation for you to donate a dollar, because most people can afford that). I can't make it a moral obligation for you to take home a pet from the pound if you are allergic to animals (but I might insist that you have an obligation to help in other ways). You can't tell me that I ought to be unselfish if in fact I was born selfish and can't be any other way because it is part of my human nature. This is the point that psychological egoism wants to make: It is irrational to keep wanting humans to look out for each other when, as a matter of fact, we aren't built that way.

What Glaucon is suggesting here about the origin of society is a first in Western thought. His theory is an example of what has become known as a *social contract theory,* a type of theory that became particularly influential much later, in the eighteenth century. A social contract theory assumes that humans used to live in a presocial setting (without rules, regulations, or cooperation) and then, for various reasons, got together and agreed on setting up a society. Generally, social contract theories assume that humans decide to build a society with rules (1) for the sake of the common good or (2) for the sake of self-protection. Glaucon's theory belongs to the second category because he claims (for the sake of argument) that humans primarily look after themselves.

To illustrate his point, Glaucon tells the story of a man called Gyges, a shepherd in ancient Lydia. (You will find the entire story at the end of this chapter.) Gyges was caught in a storm and an earthquake, which left a large hole in the ground. He explored the chasm and found a hollow bronze horse with the corpse of a giant inside. The giant was wearing only a gold ring on his finger. Gyges took the ring and left and later, wearing the ring, attended a meeting of shepherds. During the meeting Gyges happened to twist the ring, and he realized from the reaction of the other shepherds that he had become invisible. Twisting the ring back, he reappeared. Realizing the advantages gained by being invisible, Gyges arranged to be one of the elected messengers who report to the king about his sheep. Gyges went to town, seduced the queen, and conspired with her to kill the king. He then took over the kingdom, sired a dynasty, and became the ancestor of King Croesus.

Glaucon's question is, Suppose we had two such rings? Let us imagine giving one to a decent person and one to a scoundrel. We know that the scoundrel will abuse the ring for personal gain, but how about the decent person? To Glaucon it is the same thing; their human natures are identical. Decent persons will do "unjust"

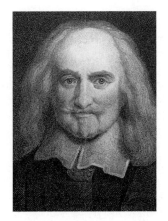

The English philosopher Thomas Hobbes was one of the first modern materialists, claiming that all of human psychology consists of the attraction and repulsion of physical particles. As such, the natural human approach to life is one of self-preservation, and the natural life of humans outside the regulations of society (the state of nature) is for Hobbes a filthy and frightening war of everyone against everyone.

things just as quickly as scoundrels if they know they can get away with it; furthermore, if they *don't* take advantage of such situations, they are just stupid. In the end, who will be happier, the unjust person who schemes and gets away with everything or the just person who never tries to get away with anything but is so good that people think there must be something wrong with him? Why, the unjust person, of course.

This little story may be the first in the literary tradition to explore a theme that has remained popular to this day—and that may be one reason it seems timeless, but it could also be that the moral problem it represents hasn't changed, either. *Arabian Nights* is full of stories about invisibility cloaks, magic rings, and owners making creative uses of them, sometimes to gain a personal advantage, and sometimes to spy on and vanquish the bad guys; in 1897 H. G. Wells wrote *The Invisible Man,* which has been made into a movie numerous times and inspired the film *Hollow Man* (2000). J. R. R. Tolkien's trilogy *The Lord of the Rings* (1954–56) features an invisibility ring. Usually the moral problem stated is, If you could become invisible, what would you do? Would you still be a morally decent or even halfway decent person, or would you use your power selfishly if you knew you could get away with it?

With few exceptions, the invisible person succumbs to temptation and meets a terrible end, as punishment for his or her weak or evil character. So most invisible-person stories are *didactic* stories (see Chapter 2), designed to teach a moral lesson: If you let your selfish nature rule, you will surely be punished—if not by others, then by fate. But what is the lesson of Glaucon's story? Is he seriously implying that it is foolish and unnatural to be good if you can get away with being bad? No; he is acting as the devil's advocate in order to make Socrates defend justice as something that is good in itself. However, Glaucon does imply that what he is describing is in fact the opinion of most people. He may have been right; a good two thousand years later Thomas Hobbes (1588–1679) agreed with Glaucon's theory of self-interest on all three counts: (1) Humans choose to live in a society with rules because they are concerned with their own safety and for no other reason; (2) humans are by nature self-interested, and any show of concern for others hides a true concern for ourselves; (3) we would be fools if we didn't look after ourselves. (We return to this point in

Box 4.4   HOBBES AND THE FEELING OF PITY

Hobbes believed humans feel pity for others in distress because they fear the same may happen to themselves. We identify with the pain of others, and that makes us afraid for ourselves. Therefore, helping others may be a way to ward off bad events. In actual fact we have no pity for others for their sake — only for our own. (He is not the first thinker to have expressed this opinion; Aristotle said approximately the same thing, but without implying that we are selfish to the bone.) Hobbes was one of the first modern Western philosophers to ponder human psychology, and we might say that he put his finger on a sore spot: Sometimes we do sympathize with others because we imagine how awful it would be if the same thing were to happen to us. What exactly does Hobbes mean when he says we *identify* with others? It seems that we ask ourselves, If this happened to me, how would I feel? This does not necessarily lead to concern for ourselves but rather leads to a concern for others, precisely because we know how they feel. Furthermore, isn't it possible to feel pity for someone or something with which you don't identify so easily? We certainly can feel pity for someone of the other gender or

someone of another race or culture, even if what happens to them wouldn't happen to us. But how about feeling pity for dolphins caught in gill nets? For animals caught in traps? For pets used in lab experiments? Some years ago a couple of whales were trapped in the ice off the coast of Alaska, and rescue teams and reporters came from all over the world to help free them. Even Inuit trappers and hunters joined in. One of them said, "This is kind of strange for me — I usually kill whales for a living!" It is hard to believe that in this case people cared only because they were afraid the catastrophe might happen to them. In a broad sense, perhaps we do identify with other creatures when their lives are in danger and feel that we ward off our own demise by saving their lives. In the final analysis, though, that idea is rather far-fetched, because if Hobbes is right and we fear "contamination" from the misery of others, wouldn't we rather turn our backs on them and flee rather than expose ourselves to their suffering? Given that we don't, perhaps there are forces at work other than selfishness. An easier explanation is that we simply, on occasion, care for the well-being of others.

the next section; you will find Hobbes's theory in the Primary Readings at the end of this chapter, and his view of the selfish basis for pity in Box 4.4.)

Surely we all can remember events in our lives that show that we don't always act out of self-interest. You may remember the time you helped your best friend move across town. The time you sat up all night preparing your brother's taxes. The time you donated toys to the annual Christmas toy drive. The time you washed your parents' car. Did the dishes at Thanksgiving. Or perhaps even helped a stranger on the road or saved the life of an accident victim. Were all those good deeds really done for selfish reasons? The psychological egoist would say yes — you may not have been aware of your true motives, but selfish they were, somehow. You may have wanted to borrow your parents' car: hence, the car wash and the dishes. You helped your friend move because you were afraid of losing her friendship. You may have felt guilty for not helping with your brother's taxes the year before, so you did them this year. The toys? You wanted to feel good about yourself. The stranger on the road?

Psychological egoism claims that every act we do is for selfish reasons. For many people, September 11 put that notion to shame; an overwhelming number of stories documented police officers, firefighters, and civilians trying to help others escape the burning towers.

You wanted to rack up a few points in the Big Book of Heaven. Helping the accident victim? You wanted to get your name in the paper.

What about Officer Walwyn Stuart and others who lost their lives at the World Trade Center and the Pentagon, or Todd Beamer and other passengers on Flight 93, fighting back against the terrorists, trying to help others by preventing their plane from crashing into another building? In the aftermath of September 11 there was very little doubt among the millions of us watching the attacks being replayed again and again on TV that those who perished saving lives were heroes—not movie heroes or sports

Calvin and Hobbes   by **Bill Watterson**

One of the reasons psychological egoism has attained such popularity is that it appeals to a modern person's sense of honesty: In order not to fool ourselves into thinking we are better than we are, we should be honest and admit that we are selfish. Calvin, being a smart kid, not only uses this argument but also turns it to his advantage; in other words, he uses it as an excuse, which is one of the other reasons psychological egoism is popular. And let's face it: It is a very cynical slice of life!

heroes, but real-life heroes. Nevertheless, the psychological egoist would maintain that as much as such acts may look like selfless acts of heroism, they can all be boiled down to some expression of our inherent selfishness: Perhaps these people wanted to be famous. Perhaps they wanted to make up for past sins of omission, or perhaps they just wanted to feel good about themselves. As far as the psychological egoist is concerned, everyone who engages in a seemingly heroic act is as selfish as one who doesn't, because we all are, in the final analysis, doing everything for ourselves.

This theory, cynical as it may sound, had established itself firmly in the minds of many Westerners prior to September 11, and it is too soon to say whether the public's massive outpouring of sympathy and financial support for the families of the rescuers who perished has modified our modern cynicism in any major way; psychological egoism was an immensely popular theory throughout the twentieth century, a period abounding with its own stories of heroism, in both peace and wartime. So what is it that has proved so appealing about the theory? After all, it removes the halo from the head of every hero and every unselfish person in the history of humankind. In fact, that may be part of its appeal: We like to think, in this day and age, that we are honest about ourselves, and we don't want to be tricked into thinking that we are better than we are or that anyone else is, either. One reason, then, for this theory's popularity is its presumed *honesty*. Later in this section you'll find an example of this phenomenon in the story of Lincoln and the pigs.

Closely related to the notion of honesty is our modern tendency toward *cynicism*. Somehow, we have a hard time believing good things about people, including ourselves. Refusing to take things at face value may be the mature thing to do, but it may also close our minds to the possibility that not all acts are selfish and not everybody is rotten at heart. (See Box 4.5 for a discussion of modern cynicism.)

Box 4.5   MODERN CYNICISM

There is much speculation about how cynicism began. It's not a new phenomenon. The ancient Greeks invented it: The Cynics, headed by Diogenes, did their best to undermine convention in order to break its hold on people's minds—one of the original "Question authority" movements. In later years, cynicism has questioned authority to the point at which misanthropy—automatically believing the worst about everybody—has become a form of authority in itself.

In the late nineteenth century, the Western world experienced a surge of optimism, because many believed we were very close to solving all technological, scientific, and medical riddles. It was even assumed that we were too civilized to ever go to war again. You may remember from the section in Chapter 2 on war movies that enthusiasm for war by and large ended with World War I. Often our modern cynicism is regarded as having been born in the trenches of World War I, but there is an interesting precursor: the sinking of the *Titanic*. The 1997 award-sweeping film *Titanic* reminded us not only of the human tragedies involved but also of the hubris, the cocky assurance that human technology could conquer all obstacles. A ship so well built that it was unsinkable! As we know, it wasn't, and the optimistic belief that now humans were the masters of the universe went to the bottom of the ocean with the great ship. It may not have been the very first blow to human self-assurance in the twentieth century, but it became the first serious crack in the hull of modern belief in technology.

Cynicism became a way of life in the twentieth century, fueled by the two world wars, the Great Depression, and the revelation of the horrors of the Holocaust. Children who lived through the tragedies and disappointments of the 1960s and 1970s, as well as their children, were all affected by the assassinations of John F. Kennedy, Robert Kennedy, and Martin Luther King, Jr., by the Korean and Vietnam wars, fuel shortages, and the Watergate and Iran-Contra scandals. And then there are the revelations from past decades such as the now infamous Tuskegee syphilis study, in which close to four hundred African American men from 1932 to 1972 unwittingly were reduced to the status of lab rats for government medical experiments. Other examples of the use of citizens for some larger purpose without their consent include the nuclear tests of the 1950s, which often involved soldiers and civilians who were given the impression that their lives were not in danger. Inuit people in Alaska were given radioactive medication as part of an experiment. In 1996, the *Los Angeles Times* revealed that in the 1950s the U.S. Army had sprayed chemicals and bacteria over large populations in New York and Washington and even over a school in Minneapolis. Years after the Vietnam War, it became apparent that soldiers had been exposed to a toxic exfoliant, Agent Orange. Gulf War Syndrome is still an unsolved riddle, attributed by some to chemical weapons in the area that the soldiers had not been warned about. So perhaps it is understandable that many people believe the conspiracy rumor that the CIA introduced crack cocaine into urban ghettos, although this rumor has not been shown to have any foundation.

At the end of the second millennium it seemed as if the accumulated atrocities and disappointments of the twentieth century had brought us to a mind-set that left us perpetually skeptical, perpetually ready to believe the worst about politicians, religious figureheads, celebrities—and even ourselves. Cynicism had become a national pastime. But with the horrors and tragedies of September 11, 2001, cynicism took a breather, as Chapter 1 noted. The question now is, Are we again ready to believe the worst about our fellow human beings, or have

(continued)

Box 4.5   MODERN CYNICISM   *(continued)*

we reached some new level of understanding where the old general lack of faith in others still exists but has been tempered with an appreciation that ordinary people can rise to perform extraordinarily unselfish acts in unexpected situations? Time will tell.

However, as much as some of us may have thought we'd become a nation of more caring people after 9/11, it seems there are still plenty of reasons to question people's motivations. In the wake of 9/11, numerous fraudulent claims were filed on behalf of nonexistent terror victims; wreckage from the WTC was offered on the Internet auction-site, eBay; souvenirs were being sold at Ground Zero. Some would say the more things change, the more they stay the same. But the fact that such enterprising behavior is frowned on by so many could be an indication that times really have changed—at least for a while.

This possibility doesn't mean we shouldn't view the world with a healthy dose of skepticism and suspicion. Often, we really *are* taken advantage of, people *are* truly selfish and devious, and things *aren't* what they seem. But there is a difference between this kind of prudent skepticism and a universal cynicism that borders on paranoia. Such radical cynicism doesn't allow for the possibility of the existence of goodness and kindness.

A third reason that psychological egoism is so popular has to do with *making excuses.* When psychological egoists say, "I can't help myself—it's my nature," they're saying they don't have to worry about remembering Aunt Molly's birthday or calling in on the cellphone to the radio station about the mattress they saw blocking the number-two lane on the freeway because humans are selfish *by nature,* and we are not capable of worrying about others—unless, of course, there is something in it for ourselves. But this is nothing but a bad excuse. Psychological egoists who take their own theory seriously never say we can't help being selfish to the bone—they just say there is some hidden selfish motive for whatever we do that we may not even be aware of.

Shortcomings of Psychological Egoism

There is something beguiling about psychological egoism; once you begin to look at the world through the eyes of a psychological egoist, it is hard to see it any other way. In fact, no matter how hard we try to come up with an example that seems to run counter to the theory, the psychological egoist has a ready answer. This is due to several factors.

1. Falsification Is Not Possible Psychological egoism always looks for selfish motives and refuses to recognize any other kind. For any nonselfish motivation you can think of for doing what you did, the theory will tell you that there was another, ulterior motive behind it. It is inconceivable, according to the theory, that other motives might exist. This is in fact a flaw in the theory. A good theory is not one that can't be proven wrong but one that allows for the possibility of counterexamples.

The inability of a theory to allow for cases in which it doesn't apply is considered bad science and bad thinking. The principle of *falsification* was advanced by the philosopher Karl Popper (1902–1994) as a hallmark of a viable theory. It states that a good scientific theory must allow for the possibility that it might be wrong; if it declares itself right under any and all circumstances, it cannot be "falsified." So "falsification" doesn't mean that a theory has to be proven wrong but that it has to be engaged in rigorously testing itself—in other words, it has to consider the possibility that it might be wrong, and test itself in any way possible. Popper says in his book *The Poverty of Historicism* (1957), "Just because it is our aim to establish theories as well as we can, we must test them as severely as we can; that is, we must try to find fault with them, we must try to falsify them. Only if we cannot falsify them in spite of our best efforts can we say that they have stood up to severe tests." Science itself doesn't always follow the principle of falsification; an example is the eighteenth-century debate about meteorites in which most scientists chose to side with their own theory that rocks couldn't fall from the sky, since outer space, they said, consists of a vacuum. The statements of reliable private citizens who claimed to have seen meteorites fall and land on the ground were consistently brushed aside by scientists as being lies or delusions, because most scientists did not question their own theory: It was nonfalsifiable, since it didn't allow for the possibility that it might be wrong. As we know, science later had to revise its notion of outer space (the theory was falsified): In 1803, scientists at l'Aigle, France, actually observed meteorites falling.

Is the theory of evolution a good theory in the sense that it is falsifiable? Scientists today would say yes: The theory is based on empirical research that can be verified objectively (the fossil record), but it doesn't claim that it is correct no matter what happens; it claims that it is the most plausible theory of biology so far, but if new and different evidence should surface, then it is (presumably) open to revision.

Psychological egoism is not a good theory, according to Popper's principle, because it doesn't allow for the possibility that it might be wrong, but reinterprets all acts and motives so they fit the theory instead. That is not a theory, strictly speaking; it is a prejudice. It comes across as a strong theory precisely because there seems to be nothing that can defeat it; however, that is not a strength, scientifically speaking. A strong theory recognizes the reality of the problem of induction (see Chapter 3): Any empirical theory (that is, one based on evidence) can't be 100 percent certain.

In addition, the unfalsifiability of psychological egoism demonstrates the logical fallacy of *begging the question*. When an argument begs the question, it assumes that what it is supposed to prove is already true, so the "proof" does nothing but repeat the assumption (such as, "Marcia is right because Marcia is never wrong!"). Psychological egoism works in the same way: It assumes that all acts are selfish and therefore interprets all acts as selfish. So psychological egoism is not the scientific theory it claims to be.

2. Is Doing What We Want Always Selfish? Biologically, psychological egoists have a forceful argument: the survival instinct. It seems a fact that all animals, including humans, are equipped with some sort of instinct for self-preservation. We might ask ourselves, though, whether this instinct is always the strongest instinct in all relationships, animal as well as human. There are cases in which animals seem to sacrifice themselves for others, yet surely they don't have any underlying motives, such as the desire to be on TV or go to heaven. Nor is it likely that they would suffer from a guilt complex if they did not perform such deeds. There is, then, at least the possibility that some actions are not performed for the reason of self-preservation.

Is it true that we always do things for selfish reasons? Let us assume, for the sake of argument, that we do actually do what we want so that we may benefit from some long-term consequences. But is doing what we want in order to benefit ourselves always a "selfish" act? Abraham Lincoln seems to have agreed that it is. A famous story tells of him riding on a mud coach (a type of stagecoach) with a friend. Just as he is explaining that he believes everybody has selfish reasons for their actions, they pass by a mudhole where several piglets are drowning. The mother sow is making an awful noise, but she can't help them. Lincoln asks the driver to stop the coach, gets off, wades into the mudhole, brings the pigs out, and returns to the coach. His friend, remembering what Lincoln had just said, asks him, "Now, Abe, where does selfishness come into this little episode?" Lincoln answers, "Why, bless your soul, Ed, that was the very essence of selfishness. I should have had no peace of mind all day had I gone on and left that suffering old sow worrying over those pigs. I did it to get peace of mind, don't you see?"

So Lincoln saved the pigs in order to benefit himself (and here we thought he was just a nice man). That is, of course, the irony of the story: Lincoln is not known to us as a selfish person. But was his theory right? He may have been lying in claiming that he did his good deed for himself—or he may have been joking—but let us assume that he spoke the truth as he saw it—that he saved the pigs in order to gain peace of mind for himself. Was it still a "selfish" act? That depends on what you call selfish. Is doing things to benefit yourself always selfish, or does it perhaps depend on what it is you want to gain? Would there be a difference between saving a pig for its own sake and saving it because you want to eat it for dinner? Most people would say there is a substantial difference between the two. In other words, it is *what* you want that matters, not just the fact that you want something. If what you want is to save someone, that is surely different from wanting to hurt someone. Lincoln might, of course, interject that saving the pigs was still in his own self-interest, so it wasn't done for them but for himself—but is that true? Why would it have been in his self-interest to know that the pigs were safe if self-gratification was all he cared about? A selfish person hardly loses sleep over the misery of other human beings, let alone that of a sow. Let us suppose, then, that he did it just to feel "warm and fuzzy" inside, and let us conclude that people who help others because they enjoy it are as selfish as can be. Nevertheless, a person who enjoys helping others is not our usual image of a selfish person; rather, as James Rachels points out, that is exactly how we picture an *unselfish* person. (See Box 4.6 for further discussion of

Box 4.6   LINCOLN: HUMBLE MAN OR CLEVER JOKESTER?

We might ask how Lincoln could have been unaware of the distinction between caring and not caring that becomes apparent when we consider different kinds of behavior. For an intelligent man, his remarks seem unusually dim. It's possible, of course, that the pig story illustrates Lincoln's true nature: that of a very humble and honest man who does not wish to take credit for having done something good. The story makes him all the more endearing, if that is the case, for indeed we know him as Honest Abe. But there is another possibility—that he was joking. Lincoln had a fondness for jokes, and this may have been one of them. Knowing full well that he was doing a nice thing, he made use of *irony* by claiming that rescuing the piglets was nothing but a selfish act. Lincoln scholars may have to decide which version they like best. In any event, Lincoln was speaking as a psychological egoist, regardless of how unselfishly he acted, because he expressed the theory that everyone acts selfishly.

Lincoln's motivation.) So if we assume that it is the *objective* rather that the mere fact of our wanting something that makes our want selfish or unselfish, we have an answer to psychological egoism right there: If what made Lincoln feel good was the thought of the pigs being safe—for their own sake, not his—then his deed of saving them was not a selfish deed. If what made him feel good was that now he would somehow benefit from saving them other than by just feeling good, then it was selfish. And how about if it was both? Suppose he saw a certain advantage in people knowing that he was a good guy who cared about pigs (although that's certainly not part of the original story), but he also liked the thought of the pigs being safe? Then it is still a refutation of psychological egoism, because there was an unselfish element in an otherwise selfish act. And here we have reached the level of common sense: Some acts are unselfish, some are selfish, and some are a mixed bag.

3. Problems of Language   As we have seen, psychological egoism presents certain problems, because it does not always describe the world in a way that allows us to recognize it. One of its flaws may actually be a problem of *language.*

Suppose the theory insists that regardless of whether we want to help others or hurt them for our own gain, our desire to help or hurt them is a selfish want. In that case we may respond that we consider it less selfish to help others than to hurt them, and we may want to introduce some new terms: *less selfish* versus *more selfish,* terms that distinguish between acts done for yourself and acts done for others. This, however, is just another way of trying to distinguish selfish behavior from unselfish behavior. Psychological egoism seems to have overlooked the fact that we already have a concept for "less-selfish" behavior that is perfectly well understood: *unselfish.* Changing language to the extent that it goes against our common sense (by claiming that there is no such thing as *unselfish* but that it is acceptable to use the term *less selfish*) does not make psychological egoism correct. So, if the psychological egoist admits that there can be degrees of selfishness, we might reply that the least degree of selfishness is what the rest of us call *unselfish;* if the psychological egoist insists that all acts are self-serving in some way, critics of psychological egoism point to the linguistic phenomenon known as the *fallacy of the suppressed correlative.* The correlative of the word *selfish* is *unselfish,* just as the correlative of *light* is *dark;* other pairs are *hot/cold, tall/short,* and so on. It is a psychological as well as a linguistic fact that we understand one term because we understand the other: If everything were dark, we wouldn't understand the meaning of *light,* and neither would we understand the meaning of *dark,* because it is defined by its contrast to light; without the contrast there is no understanding. In other words, a concept without a correlative becomes meaningless. If all acts are selfish, *selfish* has no correlative, and the statement "All acts are selfish" has no meaning. In fact, we could not make such a statement at all if psychological egoism were correct; the concept of selfishness would not exist, since any nonselfish behavior would be unthinkable. So not only does psychological egoism go against common sense and preclude a complete understanding of the full range of human behavior; it also goes against the rules of language.

This may sound like a complex argument, but we actually use it frequently in everyday situations. Here are a few examples of suppressed correlatives, situations in which something becomes meaningless if it doesn't have any opposite: (1) If you use a highlighter in your textbook, you may have found yourself studying a difficult text and highlighting many sentences. After a while, when you look at the pages, you find that you've actually highlighted just about everything. The task of highlighting all of a sudden has become meaningless; now *everything* is highlighted (the highlighted areas have lost their contrast), and that is just the same as not having anything highlighted. (2) At Starbucks a small cup of coffee is called "tall," a medium is called "grande," and a large is called "venti" (Italian for "twenty"—ounces, presumably). Does the designation "tall" really mean anything anymore when it comes to coffees, or has the meaning been gutted by the disappearance of its opposite, "short"? (3) Sometimes I hear students plead (as a joke, I hope), "Why can't you just give us all A's?" (whether they are deserved or not). The answer is that (aside from the fact that it wouldn't be right), if everybody in the class or the school or the country got A's, the A would become meaningless since there would be no lower grade to serve as a contrast. If instructors bowed to the pressure to give only A's or B's, the whole idea of grading would be undermined. (4) There are situations that are supposed to have significance but are so common that the impact is nullified: Car alarms go off all the time, so the "alarm" effect is gone; people who curse all the time drain their words of any impact, so there is no way to emphasize a really bad situation; parents who yell at their children constantly have no voice impact left when the time comes for a yell to be effective; kids who "cry wolf" won't be believed in the end. And the psychological egoist who claims that everyone is selfish can't explain what *selfish* means if no behavior is recognized as unselfish.

Proponents of psychological egoism have responded that unselfishness doesn't actually exist, but you can still have the *concept* of unselfishness, which serves as the

Calvin and Hobbes

by Bill Watterson

CALVIN AND HOBBES © Watterson. Reprinted with permission of Universal Press Syndicate. All rights reserved.

For many readers the idea that egoism might be a legitimate moral theory is surprising, but indeed Calvin is right: "You ought to look out for Number One" is, in fact, a moral principle. However, critics of ethical egoism point out that it is hardly an acceptable moral principle. (Since the philosopher Thomas Hobbes is mentioned in this chapter, you might like to know that Hobbes the tiger is named after Thomas Hobbes.)

correlative of selfishness, even if it is imaginary; but critics of psychological egoism reply that the theory still does not make much sense. If it states that everybody is selfish to the bone, then it is a downright false theory. If it just says everybody has a selfish streak, then it is so trivial that it is not even interesting.

Ethical Egoism

We have already heard amazing stories about heroic acts of rescue on 9/11. As more survivors tell their stories, we'll probably hear more. A person such as Officer Stuart who lost his life helping commuters get out of the subway would be admired as a hero by most of us.

However, the ethical egoist would say that, in effect, he did the wrong thing. For the ethical egoist there is only one rule: *Look after yourself.* The ethical egoist would say you are throwing your life away.

Here we should make sure that we have our terms straight. This theory is called ethical egoism simply because it is an ethical theory, a *normative* theory about how we *ought* to behave (in contrast to psychological egoism, which claims to know how we actually *do* behave). The theory implies that we ought to be selfish. Or, to put it more gently, we ought to be *self-interested.* Calling the theory "ethical" does not suggest there might be a decent way to be selfish; it just means ethical egoism is a theory that advocates egoism as a moral rule. (Box 4.7 is a discussion of individual ethical egoism.)

Box 4.7   INDIVIDUAL ETHICAL EGOISM

This version of *ethical egoism,* commonly adopted by small children and childish adults, holds that "everyone ought to do what I want," regardless of whether it is in the other person's interest. This view is rarely taken seriously as an ethical theory, because it doesn't have any good arguments to support it except that it's what the person wants. We can't expect everyone else to follow our whims or even look after our interests; this is nothing but emotional tyranny. However, the individualist egoist attitude is not limited to children and childlike adults; people who throughout their lives have been used to having their way will sometimes display the same attitude. From royalty in times past to people of wealth and power in the present, certain individuals (although by no means the majority) will act as though others have responsibilities to them, but they feel exempt from having responsibilities to others.

A moral theory, if it is to be accepted today, has to involve an important element of acceptance. It has to be imaginable that most people, if not everyone, would be willing to adopt the theory for themselves. This phenomenon, which we shall discuss later, is known as *universalizability.* We can hardly imagine the world agreeing to serve our interests, because, after all, what makes us so special? However, it is a fact that some people choose to live their lives seeking to fulfill *someone else's* wishes or interests; such choices may be made by parents, spouses, grown children taking care of their parents, disciples following their guru or leader, and devout believers trying to live the way God wants them to live. If you are a parent or a political or religious leader, you may claim that "people should do what I want because it is good for them." In that case, you are moving out of the realm of egoism; the main interest is no longer yourself, but everyone; you just have the audacity to claim that you know better than anyone else how everyone's lives should be lived.

You Should Look After Yourself

Glaucon insisted that, if you don't take advantage of a situation, you are foolish. Hobbes claimed that it makes good sense to look after yourself, and morality is a result of that self-interest: If I mistreat others, they may mistreat me, so I resolve to behave myself. This is a rather twisted version of the Golden Rule (Do unto others as you would have them do unto you; see Box 4.8). It is twisted because it is peculiarly slanted toward our own self-interest. The reason we should treat others the way we would like to be treated is that it gives us a good chance of receiving just such treatment; we do it for ourselves, not for others. So the ethical egoist might certainly decide to help another human being in need—not for the sake of the other but to ensure that "what goes around, comes around." The Golden Rule usually emphasizes others, but for the ethical egoist it emphasizes the self. With ethical egoism we encounter a certain phenomenon for the first time in this book: an ethical theory that focuses on the *consequences* of one's actions. Any theory that looks solely to consequences of actions is known as a *consequentialist theory;* the consequences that ethical egoism stipulates are good consequences for the person taking the action.

Box 4.8   THE GOLDEN RULE WITH VARIATIONS

Most people know the Golden Rule: Do unto others as you would have them do unto you, or treat others as you would like to be treated. It is often attributed to Jesus Christ; the Gospel of Matthew cites him as saying, "Therefore all things whatsoever ye would that men should do to you, do ye even so to them: for this is the law and the prophets" (7.12). However, others expressed similar thoughts long before the time of Jesus: The Chinese philosopher Confucius (551–479 B.C.E.) is known to have taught his students this version, taken from *The Doctrine of the Mean, The Four Books:* "What you do not like when done to yourself, do not do to others." This is sometimes called the "Silver Rule."

The rule teaches that in order to find a blueprint for treating others, we should imagine how we would or would not like to be treated. Ethical egoists don't read it that way, however; they read it as a rule for protecting yourself and being as comfortable as possible. The way to avoid trouble with others is to treat them as you'd want to be treated—the path of least resistance. The emphasis on *others* is not a given within the rule. This is the aspect of *prudence* connected with the Golden Rule. But as we see in Chapter 5, the Golden Rule is also used as a blueprint for general happiness, one's own as well as others'. In this case, it is concern for *the other person* that underlies the rule.

Recognizing the wisdom of the Golden Rule is perhaps the most important early stage in civilization, because it implies that we see others as similar to ourselves and that we see ourselves as deserving no treatment that is better than what others get (although we would generally prefer it—we're not saints). However, the Golden Rule may not be the ultimate rule to live by, because (as we discuss further in Chapter 11) what if others *don't want* to be treated as *you'd* like to be treated? Then, according to some thinkers, the "Platinum Rule" ought to kick in: Treat others as *they* want to be treated! Proponents of the Golden Rule say that this takes the universal appeal out of the rule. The spark of moral genius in the rule is precisely that we are *similar* in our human nature—not that we would all like to have things our way.

However, we can imagine other kinds of consequentialist theories, such as one that advocates good consequences for as many people as possible. Such a theory is discussed in Chapter 5.

Ethical egoists are themselves quite divided about whether the theory tells you to do *what you want* without regard for others or *what is good for you* without regard for others. The latter version seems to appeal to common sense, because, in the long run, just looking for instant gratification is hardly going to make you happy or live longer. Saying that one ought to look after oneself need not, of course, mean that one should annoy others whenever possible, step on their toes, or deliberately neglect their interests. It simply suggests that one should do what will be of long-term benefit to oneself, such as exercising, eating healthy food, avoiding repetitive argumentative situations, and so forth. Even paying one's taxes might be added to the list. In addition, it suggests that other people's interests are of no importance. If you might advance your own interests by helping others, then by all means help others, but only if you are the main beneficiary. It is fine to help your children get ahead in school, because you love them and this love is a gratifying emotion for you. But there is no reason to lend a hand to your neighbor's children unless you like them or you achieve gratification through your actions.

This interpretation—that the theory tells us to do whatever will benefit ourselves—results in a rewriting of the Golden Rule because, obviously, it is not always the case that you *will* get the same treatment from others that you give to them. Occasionally you might get away with not treating others decently, because they may never know that you are the source of the bad treatment they are receiving. Ethical egoism tells you that it is perfectly all right to treat others in a way that is to your advantage and not to theirs as long as you can be certain that you will get away with it.

Shortcomings of Ethical Egoism

Let us return now to Glaucon and his rings. He assumes that not only will the scoundrel take advantage of a ring that can make him invisible, but so will the decent man, and, furthermore, we would call them both fools if they didn't. A theory of psychological egoism, therefore, can also contain a normative element: ethical egoism (which tells us how we *ought* to behave). Of course, it is hard to see what the point is if we can't stop ourselves from doing what we do.

At the end of Glaucon's speech the reader expects Socrates to dispatch the theory of egoism with a quick blow. The answer, however, is a long time coming; as a matter of fact, Plato designed the rest of his *Republic* as a roundabout answer to Glaucon. In the end, Socrates' answer is, The unjust person can't be happy because happiness consists of a good harmony, a balance between the three parts of the soul: *reason, willpower (spirit),* and *desire.* Reason is supposed to dominate willpower, and willpower desire. If desire or willpower dominates the other two, we have a sick person, and a sick person can't be happy by definition, says Socrates. We will return to this theory later in this book.

In considering the question Why be just? we must consider justice in terms of the whole society, not just the individual. We can't argue for justice on the basis of individual situations, but only in general terms. That makes the question Why be just? more reasonable because we don't look at individual cases but at an overall picture in which justice and well-being are interrelated. For Socrates and Plato, being just is part of "the good life," and true happiness cannot be attained without justice.

To the modern reader there is something curiously bland and evasive about these answers. Surely unjust persons can be disgustingly happy—they may seem to us to have sick souls, but they certainly don't act as if they are aware of it or suffer any ill effects from it. The answer to this—that being selfish is *just plain wrong in itself*—is not addressed by Socrates at all. For a modern person it seems reasonable to be "just" out of respect for the law or perhaps because that is the right thing to do, but Socrates mentions this only briefly; it is a concern that belongs to a much later time period than the one in which he lived. The highest virtue for the ancient Greeks was, on the whole, ensuring the well-being of the community, and this well-being remained the bottom line more than any abstract moral issue of right and

In *Madame Bovary* (MGM, 1942), Emma Bovary (Jennifer Jones, right) loves romantic novels and finds her own life unspeakably drab. She neglects her husband and her daughter, and in this scene she contemplates having an affair with the young man on the left, going shopping for new clothes, and buying new drapes and furniture—anything to make life a little more exciting. The story of *Madame Bovary* is outlined at the end of this chapter as an illustration of egoism.

wrong. Today we know this social theory as *communitarianism*. Because justice was best for the state in the final evaluation, justice was a value in itself. In the end, Socrates' answer evokes self-interest and urges us to discern truth from appearance: If you are unjust, your soul will suffer, and so will your community.

This attitude may not impress persons seeking self-gratification (who are unlikely to be concerned about the effects of their actions on their souls or on the people around them), but it may have some impact on persons seeking long-term self-interest. It still rests on an empirical assumption, however: that sooner or later you must pay the piper—that is, atone for your wrongdoing. History, though, is full of "bad guys" who have gone to their graves rich and happy. The religious argument that you will go to hell, or suffer a miserable next incarnation, if you are concerned only with yourself is not really an argument against *egoism,* because it still asks you to look after yourself, even to the point of using others for the purpose of ensuring a pleasant afterlife (treat others decently and you shall be saved).

The one type of argument against ethical egoism that has most appealed to scholars insists that ethical egoism is self-contradictory. If you are supposed to look after yourself and your colleague is supposed to look after herself, and if looking after yourself will mean stealing her diskettes, then you and she will be working at cross-purposes: Your duty will be to steal her diskettes from her, and her duty will be to protect her diskettes. We can't have a moral theory that says one's duty should be something that conflicts with someone else's duty, so ethical egoism is therefore inconsistent.

Few ethical egoists find this argument convincing, because they don't agree that we can't have a moral theory that gives a green light to different concepts of duty. Such a view assumes that ethical egoism benefits everyone, even when each person does only what is in his or her best interest. Occasionally, ethical egoism assumes just that: We should look after ourselves and mind our own business, because meddling in other people's affairs is a violation of privacy; they will not like our charity, they will hate our superiority, and we won't know what is best for them, anyway. So, along these lines, we should stay out of other people's affairs because it is best for everybody. The political theory resulting from this point of view is known as *laissez-faire*, the hands-off policy. Political theorists, however, are quick to point out that laissez-faire is by no means an egoistic theory, because it has everybody's best interests at heart. That is precisely what is wrong with the idea that we should adopt ethical egoism for the reason that it will be good for everybody: It may be true that if we all look after ourselves, we'll all be happier—but who is the beneficiary of this idea? Not "I," but "everybody," so this version is, in fact, no longer a moral theory of egoism, but something else.

Another argument against ethical egoism is that it carries no weight as a solver of moral conflicts: If you and I disagree about the correct course of action, who is to say who is right? If you favor the course of action that is to your advantage and I favor the course of action that is to my advantage, then there is no common ground. But the ethical egoist generally answers in the same way as to the charge that ethical egoism is self-contradictory: It never claimed to be a theory of consensus in all approaches, merely in the basic approach—that everyone ought to look after him- or herself.

A better argument against the conceptual consistency of ethical egoism is this: Ethical egoism doesn't work in practice. Remember that the theory says all people ought to look out for themselves—not merely that *I* should look out for *myself*. But suppose you set out to look after your own self-interests and advocate that others do the same; within a short while you will realize that your rule is *not* going to be to your advantage, because others will be out there grabbing for themselves, and you will have fierce competition. You might decide that the smart thing to do is to advocate not that all people look out for themselves but that all people look after one another while keeping quiet about your own intention of breaking the rule whenever possible. This would be the prudent thing to do, and it probably would work quite well. The only problem is that this is not a moral theory because, for one thing, it carries a contradiction. It means you must claim to support one principle and act according to another one—in other words, it requires you to be dishonest. Also, a moral theory, in this day and age, has to be able to be extended to everybody; we can't uphold a theory that says it is okay for me to do something because I'm *me*, but not for you just because you're *not me* — that would be assuming that I should have privileges based on the mere fact that I'm *me*.

Logical attacks on ethical egoism have a persuasive power for some — as logical arguments rightly should have. However, perhaps the most forceful argument against ethical egoism involves an emotional component. Often, philosophers have been afraid to appeal to emotions because emotions have been considered irrelevant. But as philosophers such as Martha Nussbaum, Philippa Foot, Philip Hallie, and James Rachels point out, what is a moral sense without the involvement of our feelings? Feelings need not be irrational — they are often quite rational responses to our experiences (see Chapter 1). And what seems such an affront to most people is the apparent callousness of an ethical egoist: Other people's pain simply doesn't matter as a moral imperative.

One example may speak louder than theoretical speculations: the murder in 1998 of seven-year-old Sherrice Iverson by Jeremy Strohmeyer in a Nevada casino restroom. Strohmeyer's friend David Cash knew about the crime taking place, heard the screams, and may even have witnessed it. He never tried to stop his friend, nor did he alert casino security, nor did he turn in his friend afterward.

Psychologically, both Strohmeyer and Cash may have been warped and damaged, but Cash had quite a rational grip of the situation and a straightforward explanation for why he didn't step in. It is debatable whether Cash is an ethical egoist or a moral subjectivist. In an interview he said, "I'm not going to get upset over somebody else's life. I just worry about myself first. I'm not going to lose sleep over somebody else's problems." He seems to be recommending selfishness, not the tolerance of moral subjectivism's "to each his or her own." If so, is this the kind of practical expression of a moral theory that we should think is legitimate, just because it allows everyone else to be selfish, too? Isn't this a case in which we are allowed to feel moral outrage over someone's inhumanity? Why, indeed, should we lose sleep over someone else's problems? *Because they are fellow human beings.*

Altruism: Ideal and Reciprocal

To return to the question of September 11: Were the rescuers — those who survived as well as those who died — selfish? Going back to our Lincoln discussion, we can say they were selfish only if they did what they did for purely self-serving reasons. Judging from the remarks of rescuers who survived, their own self-interests seemed to be very far from their minds. And how about the suicidal terrorists? Were they selfish or unselfish, or both? Judging from letters and statements from other terrorists and sympathizers from the same groups, their motivation was mixed: They believed the Koran promised them direct, immediate access to heaven, where they would live in bliss for eternity, attended by beautiful virgins — but they also believed they were doing a heroic deed for their people. The Western mind-set considers self-sacrifice to be noble. Then why do most of us not consider terrorist acts noble? Because self-sacrifice is usually regarded as an act wherein a person dies trying to help others, not one that involves deliberately killing innocent people. To discuss this issue further you may want to go directly to Chapter 13, where we address the question of terrorism — but you may also want to consider the concept of *group egoism:* extending your self-interest to the group you belong to, so that if you could help the group survive by giving up an advantage or even sacrificing yourself, then (theoretically) you'd be willing to do that. A group egoist would not consider members of other groups valuable, or having claims as legitimate as those of one's own group. A suicide bomber does not have the interest of all at heart — just the interests of his or her group — at the cost of others.

As an alternative to ethical egoism, *altruism* hardly seems preferable if we view it in its ideal, normative sense: *Everybody ought to give up his or her own self-interest for others.* In that case we might want to complain (as the philosopher and writer Ayn Rand did) that we have only one life to live, and why should we let the "moochers and leeches" drain our life away? If we let them take advantage of us, they surely will. Our lives are not things to be thrown away. Only a few philosophers and a few religions have ever held such an extreme altruistic theory. One person in the late twentieth century who did was the Lithuanian-French philosopher Emmanuel Levinas, whom you will meet in Chapter 10. For Levinas, the Other (another human being, the stranger) is always more important than you yourself are (which also means that you are important, as a stranger and an Other, to everyone else), and you should always put the needs of the Other ahead of your own. But Levinas is an exception among modern thinkers; usually there is a realistic recognition of the fact that humans are apt to ask what's in it for them. (See Box 4.9 for a discussion of psychological and ethical altruism.)

And yet, as mentioned earlier, we do know of people who sacrificed themselves for others because "it was the least they could do." Some did it once, in a heroic situation, and others did it over the course of a lifetime, setting their own needs aside in order to help others. We already know what the psychological egoist will say to such deeds, but we also know now that psychological egoism does not have all the answers. Even if it is true that people do seek self-gratification in "selfless" acts, there are many examples of animals helping other animals, sometimes even those of a different species. A baboon will sacrifice itself to leopards so that its tribe can make a getaway. Dolphins carry drowning people to the surface and even to boats. Are these animals really thinking of others rather than of themselves? Sociobiologists such as Richard Dawkins and Edward O. Wilson say no; they are thinking of themselves, because that is the only destiny their genes as well as ours have made possible for us. It is not a conscious thought process, but rather a predisposition toward creating the best conditions of survival, not for oneself as an individual, but for one's genes. This theory has become known as the *selfish-gene theory,* from the title of Dawkins's book *The Selfish Gene* (1976). The baboon instinctively wants his genes to survive in his sister's children. The dolphin acts by instinct; that is what she does when her own baby is suffocating. A seeing-eye dog is well trained and does what she is supposed to, to save her human and herself.

Ideal altruism seems to imply that there is something inherently *wrong* with acting to benefit oneself, and if that is the case, it will never become a widely accepted moral theory because it will work only for saints. According to the Australian

Box 4.9 PSYCHOLOGICAL AND ETHICAL ALTRUISM

The term *altruism* comes from the Latin *alter*, meaning "other." The version of altruism that we are discussing in this chapter is sometimes known as ethical altruism—not because there is a form of altruism that is *unethical*, but simply because philosophers have seen a parallel to ethical egoism: "Everyone *ought* to disregard his or her own interests for the sake of others." In other words, ethical altruism is a normative theory, like its opposite, ethical egoism. But is there also a counterpart to psychological egoism, *psychological altruism*? I'll let you be the judge of that. As psychological egoism, a descriptive theory, claims that everyone is selfish at heart, psychological altruism would claim that everyone is unselfish at heart: "Everyone always disregards his or her own interests for the sake of others." Now who would hold such a theory? Not many, since it seems to fly in the face of the facts: We know very well that not everyone in this world is caring and unselfish. As a matter of fact, one might speculate that psychological altruism was invented by a philosopher with a sense of symmetry, just to have a matching pair of altruisms to compare the two forms of egoism with. But if psychological altruism is redefined in the following way, "There is something good and caring deep down in every human being," then the theory sounds quite familiar and plausible to many people. You may remember the phrase "ought implies can" used as an excuse by psychological egoism: "Don't tell me I ought to be unselfish, because I can't." The same idea works for psychological altruism: The person who is caring by nature might say to the ethical egoist, "Don't tell me I ought to be selfish, because I can't!"

philosopher Peter Singer, there is another way of viewing altruism, a much more realistic and rational way: Looking after the interests of others makes sense, because, overall, everyone benefits from it. This moderate, limited version of altruism is sometimes called Golden Rule altruism (or reciprocal altruism): You are ready to place others' interests ahead of your own, especially in emergency situations, and you expect them to do the same for you. Philosophers are in disagreement over whether this position actually deserves the name of altruism. (David Hume's theory of fellow-feeling as an aspect of altruism is discussed in Box 4.10.)

In *The Expanding Circle* (1981), Singer suggests that egoism is, in fact, more costly than altruism. He presents a new version of a classic example, known as the prisoner's dilemma. Two early hunters are attacked by a saber-toothed cat. They obviously both want to flee, but (let us suppose) they also care for each other. If they both flee, one will be picked off and eaten. If one flees and one stays and fights, the fleeing one will live but the fighting one will die. If both stay and fight, there is a chance that they can fight off the cat. So it is actually in the interest of both of them to stay together, and all the more so if they care for each other. Singer's point is that evolution would favor such an arrangement, because trustworthy partners would be viewed as better than ones who leave you behind to get eaten, and they would be selected in future partnerships. If you are an egoist and you manage to get picked as a partner by an altruist, you will be the one who benefits from the situation (the altruist is sure to stay, and you'll be able to get away). This will work only a few

Box 4.10   DAVID HUME: HUMANS ARE
BENEVOLENT BY NATURE

David Hume, Scottish philosopher and historian. Hume believed that human beings are born with a fellow-feeling, a sense of compassion and empathy for others.

The Scottish philosopher David Hume (1711–1776) believed compassion is the one natural human feeling that holds us together in a society. For Hume, all of ethics can be reduced to the idea that reason acts as the handmaiden to our feelings; there is no such thing as an *objectively* moral act—nothing is good or bad in itself, not even murder. The good and bad lie in our *feelings* toward the act. For Hume, all morality rests ultimately on our emotional responses, and there are no "moral facts" outside our own personal sensitivity. This theory says that whatever we would like to see happen we think of as morally good, and whatever we would hate to see happen we think of as morally evil. And what is it we would like to see happen? For Hume the answer is, whatever corresponds to our *natural feeling of concern for others*. Contrary to Hobbes, Hume believes that humans are equipped not only with self-love but also with love for others, and this emotion gives us our moral values. We simply react with sympathy to others through a built-in instinct—at least most people do. Even persons who are generally selfish will feel compassion toward others if there is nothing in the situation that directly concerns them personally. Having the virtues of compassion and benevolence is a natural thing to Hume, and if we are a little short on such virtues, it simply means that we lack a natural ability, as when we are nearsighted. Such people are an exception to the rule.

This means that Hume's theory, far from being merely a focus on how we feel about things, is actually an example of *soft universalism:* We may have many different ideas and feelings about right and wrong, good and bad, but as human beings, most of us share a bottom-line criterion for morality: a fellow-feeling, a natural concern for others.

times, however; after a while the altruist will be wise to you and your kind. In the end, then, it is in your own self-interest not to be too self-interested.

This argument actively defeats not only the everyday variety of ethical egoism that says you ought to do what you want—because in the end that will not improve your survival odds—but also the more sophisticated *rational ethical egoism* that requires us to think of what is to our advantage in the long run. If we look toward our own advantage exclusively, we may not be optimizing our chances, as the example of the hunters shows. Being capable of taking others' interests into consideration actually improves our own survival odds.

Why is this viewpoint not just another version of the ethical egoist's credo of looking after yourself? Because it involves someone else's interests, too. It says that there is nothing wrong with keeping an eye out for yourself, so long as it doesn't happen at the expense of someone else's interests. In other words, the solution may not be myself *or* others, but myself *and* others. This idea, incorporated in the moral theory of *utilitarianism,* will be explored in the next chapter.

So what do biologists and psychologists at the cutting edge today think about the idea that humans are born selfish and become moral beings only through reluctant acculturation? It is not nearly as much in fashion as it used to be. The possibility that human evolution has favored the less selfish individuals, as Singer's example claims, now seems quite plausible. The British philosopher Mary Midgley suggests that since there is such a difference between what psychological egoists call normal selfish behavior (doing something nice for others so you can feel good) and *really* selfish behavior (doing something hurtful to others so you can gain an advantage), it would be illogical to call both selfish. In addition, she suggests that a much simpler explanation exists for our altruistic behavior than some selfish gene: It's the fact that we've all grown up in groups with other people, and in most cases the people who raised us loved us and cared about our well-being. And when we raise children, we care about them for their sake, too. So we have a built-in capacity for caring for our family—and in our human society we just extend that capacity to strangers, who become honorary relatives for a time. What makes this different from a version of the selfish-gene theory is that we extend our caring capacity to strangers not for *our* sake (to perpetuate our genes) but for *theirs* (because we care about how they feel).

A recent example may illustrate what Midgley means: In February 2002 a seven-year-old girl, Danielle van Dam, was abducted in the middle of the night from her bedroom in an upscale and supposedly safe San Diego neighborhood. Friends and neighbors of the parents immediately went about organizing a search, setting up a website, and distributing fliers. While everyone feared the worst—especially after a neighbor, after several weeks of investigation, was arrested and charged with kidnapping and murder in the case—the search effort continued. The San Diego district attorney commented that he had never heard of a volunteer effort that size in California: Some twenty-five hundred people came from all over San Diego, but also from Los Angeles, Oregon, Arizona, and Texas to participate in the search.

In the end it was indeed a group of volunteers who found the girl's body in a rural area. What made these strangers give up their time to look for a little girl they'd never met? Many said they were parents and if it were their child, they'd want someone to help look for him or her. But many also said that they just felt they had to. A television commentator perhaps said it best: Danielle had been adopted by all of San Diego, indeed, by the whole nation. Was it just because she was cute? Because she was white, perhaps? Because television played home videos of her? If so, what about all the abducted children who aren't cute, or white, or on video? Opinions may differ on that, but most volunteers simply saw her as a child taken from her own bed, supposedly the safest place on earth. She was, to them, their own honorary child for a while, and I think most of us who followed the story reacted not simply as Hobbes claims human nature dictates, out of fear the same thing might happen to our children, but out of a desire to extend to strangers emotions ordinarily reserved for family.

In addition, studies of fifteen low-technology cultures around the world recently undertaken by the anthropologist Joe Henrich of UCLA, in close collaboration with economists from the United States and Switzerland, conclude that the story of the selfish gene doesn't hold up to scrutiny: Overall, in every group, humans are more generous than stingy, and the more socially interdependent the society, the more generous the individuals. Henrich concludes that neither egoism nor altruism is innate — the more social the culture, the less selfish the individuals.

But there is another angle to the question: If humans have a selfish streak but also have a door to altruism built into them, how is it for the higher animals?

Some years ago a small boy fell into the Western Lowland gorilla pit at the Brookfield Zoo in Chicago. The female gorilla Binti Jua, herself a new mother, picked up the unconscious child and shielded him from the other gorillas. Then she carried him over to the doorway, where she was used to zoo personnel going in and out, and a rescue crew came and got the boy.

The story received nationwide attention. Why did Binti Jua show such seemingly "human" concern for the child? Many people were astonished to hear that a gorilla could show signs of compassion, let alone for someone not of her own species. A curator explained that she had been trained to bring her own baby to curators, and she was accustomed to being in close proximity with humans. So some concluded that Binti Jua did not act out of any rational or compassionate decision but simply on the basis of her training. Perhaps she was used to getting a reward for bringing her own baby and expected a reward for bringing the child. Other animal behaviorists who work with great apes didn't find Binti's action very remarkable: Gorillas and chimpanzees have a great capacity for compassion, they said, and will shield and defend an infant ape against aggressive adult apes. But Binti showed not just a compassion that went beyond her own species but good common sense in carrying the boy over to the place where humans would be most likely to come and get him. So is it possible for a great ape to act unselfishly? Binti may certainly have been expecting a reward, but she also exhibited a gentle concern for the boy himself, so in one gesture this gorilla demonstrated transspecies compassion and foresight that seem to go beyond instinct and training.

Science and philosophy have generally assumed that nonhuman animals live in a nonmoral universe of innocence, where what seems cruel to humans is just the natural response of self-preservation: They are beyond the categories of good and evil. But now comes thought-provoking new research, gathering results from years of observing monkeys, apes, dolphins, whales, elephants, and wolves. Contrary to what people have told each other for so long about nonmoral animals, it turns out that some form of moral code seems to prevail in all these groups of social animals, and "moral code" here doesn't just mean that each animal has an instinct for behaving within the group, because often an individual (usually a young animal) will misbehave and then be punished by the group (with beating or ostracism, but usually not death). After the punishment, there is usually a kiss-and-make-up phase. According to Frans de Waal of Emory University's Yerkes Primate Center, chimps share food with one another and are indignant when an individual who seldom shares his or her own food expects a share of someone else's. At the primate center, two young female apes came home late one day and held up dinner for all the other apes in the research group; the scientists kept them separate overnight for their safety, but the next day they were beaten up by the rest of the colony. That night they were the first to come home. So the origin of moral rules may have to be sought much farther back in time than the Pleistocene, when Singer's hunters decided whether to run or to fight the saber-toothed cat.

This also means that the psychological egoist's theory that we are "born" selfish needs to be rewritten, because it is too vague a statement in light of new research. It is not impossible that each child (and each chimpanzee) is born completely selfish, exclusively focusing on what Freud calls the "pleasure principle," the pursuit of feeling good, and that we only begin to modify our selfish behavior when we realize we can't get away with it constantly (which was Hobbes's theory, and Glaucon's before him). But the child is not the same as the adult, and some thinkers claim that what I've outlined here is the *genetic fallacy:* confusing the origin of something with what it has become at a later stage. We don't ordinarily claim that children are moral agents, because psychologists tell us that children really don't know the difference between right and wrong before they are about seven or eight years old. So why should the amoral demeanor of a small child be held up as the natural morality of an adult? We don't claim that the talent of a gifted ballplayer, a star chef, a good parent, or a great teacher can be reduced to their skills and knowledge when they were four years old. Children experience *socialization,* and since humans are social beings by nature, the effects on the individual of living in society are part of what we are as human beings. With the right training, we develop intellectually and technically as we grow older; therefore, it should be apparent that we also develop morally. We may start out in life as selfish, but with socialization, most people end up being capable of taking other people's interests into account—not merely because it is the prudent thing to do but because they develop an interest in other people's well-being. And that may be the secret behind the immense evolutionary success of human beings.

In his book *Good Natured: The Origins of Right and Wrong in Humans and Other Animals* (1996), Frans de Waal speculates that although humans are the only animals that can take delight in cruel treatment of others, both humans and great apes have the capacity for selfless caring for others. Echoing the thoughts of David Hume as well as Peter Singer and Charles Darwin himself, he writes:

> Human sympathy is not unlimited. It is offered most readily to one's own family and clan, less readily to other members of the community, and most reluctantly, if at all, to outsiders. The same is true of the succorant behavior of animals. The two share not only a cognitive and emotional basis, but similar constraints in their expression.
>
> Despite its fragility and selectivity, the capacity to care for others is the bedrock of our moral system. It is the only capacity that does not snugly fit the hedonic cage in which philosophers, psychologists, and biologists have tried to lock the human spirit. One of the principal functions of morality seems to be to protect and nurture this caring capacity, to

guide its growth and expand its reach, so that it can effectively balance other human tendencies that need little encouragement.

Study Questions

1. What "other human tendencies" is Frans de Waal talking about? Do you agree with him that humans and some apes share the capacity for caring? Why or why not?

2. What are the most powerful arguments in favor of psychological egoism? What are the most damaging arguments against it?

3. Discuss the concept of ethical egoism in its most rational form: We ought to treat others the way we want to be treated to ensure our own safety and prosperity. What can be said for this approach? What can be said against it?

4. Discuss examples of heroic rescues from 9/11, including the story of the seeing-eye dog. Can they be sufficiently explained by psychological egoism? Why or why not?

Primary Readings and Narratives

The Primary Readings are the story of the Ring of Gyges from Plato's *Republic,* an excerpt from Thomas Hobbes's *Leviathan,* and an excerpt from Ayn Rand's philosophical essay "The Ethics of Emergencies." The first Narrative is a summary and excerpt from an episode of the TV show *Friends* about whether an unselfish act is possible. The second Narrative is a summary of the film *Return to Paradise,* whose plot is a variation on the prisoner's dilemma. The third Narrative is a summary and excerpt from Gustave Flaubert's classic novel *Madame Bovary,* about a woman who destroys the life of her family as well as her own. The fourth Narrative is an excerpt from *Atlas Shrugged,* about the rights of creative people to maintain their high standards and look out for themselves.

 Primary Reading

The Republic

PLATO

Book II. Excerpt.

You have already read a section of Plato's most famous Dialogue, *The Republic,* in Chapter 2. Here Socrates and Glaucon discuss the issue of justice and selfishness, illustrated by Glaucon's story of the Ring of Gyges. Glaucon is playing the devil's advocate, provoking Socrates into defending the concept of justice. Socrates is talking about the conversation to friends, so the narrator (the "I") is supposed to be Socrates himself (as written by Plato). Notice Socrates' answer at the end of this excerpt. Is he serious? Hardly; Socrates was famous for his wry, ironic answers, and this is one of them. The rest of *The Republic* is in a sense dedicated to proving Glaucon wrong.

Good, said Glaucon. Listen then, and I will begin with my first point: the nature and origin of justice.

What people say is that to do wrong is, in itself, a desirable thing; on the other hand, it is not at all desirable to suffer wrong, and the harm to the sufferer outweighs the advantage to the doer. Consequently, when men have had a taste of both, those who have not the power to seize the advantage and escape the harm decide that they would be better off if they made a compact neither to do wrong nor to suffer it. Hence they begin to make laws and covenants with one another; and whatever the law prescribed they called lawful and right. That is what right or justice is and how it came into existence; it stands half-way between the best thing of all—to do wrong with impunity—and the worst, which is to suffer wrong without the power to retaliate. So justice is accepted as a compromise, and valued, not as good in itself, but for lack of power to do wrong; no man worthy of the name, who had that power, would ever enter into such a compact with anyone; he would be mad if he did. That, Socrates, is the nature of justice according to this account, and such the circumstances in which it arose.

The next point is that men practise it against the grain, for lack of power to do wrong. How true that is, we shall best see if we imagine two men, one just, the other unjust, given full license to do whatever they like, and then follow them to observe where each will be led by his desires. We shall catch the just man taking the same road as the unjust; he will be moved by self-interest, the end which it is natural to every creature to pursue as good, until forcibly turned aside by law and custom to respect the principle of equality.

Now, the easiest way to give them that complete liberty of action would be to imagine them possessed of the talisman found by Gyges, the ancestor of the famous Lydian. The story tells how he was a shepherd in the King's service. One day there was a great storm, and the ground where his flock was feeding was rent by an earthquake. Astonished at the sight, he went down into the chasm and saw, among other wonders of which the story tells, a brazen horse, hollow, with windows in its sides. Peering in, he saw a dead body, which seemed to be of more than human size. It was naked save for a gold ring, which he took from the finger and made his way out. When the shepherds met, as they did every month, to send an account to the King of the state of his flocks, Gyges came wearing the ring. As he was sitting with the others, he happened to turn the bezel of the ring inside his hand. At once he became invisible, and his companions, to his surprise, began to speak of him as if he had left them. Then, as he was fingering the ring, he turned the bezel outwards and became visible again. With that, he set about testing the ring to see if it really had this power, and always with the same result: according as he turned the bezel inside or out he vanished and reappeared. After this discovery he contrived to be one of the messengers sent to the court. There he seduced the Queen, and with her help murdered the King and seized the throne.

Now suppose there were two such magic rings, and one were given to the just man, the other to the unjust. No one, it is commonly believed, would have such iron strength of mind as to stand fast in doing right or keep his hands off other men's goods, when he could go to the market-place and fearlessly help himself to anything he wanted, enter houses and sleep with any woman he chose, set prisoners free and kill men at his pleasure, and in a word go about among men with the powers of a god. He would behave no better than the other; both would take the same course. Surely this would be strong proof that men do right only under compulsion; no individual thinks of it as good for him personally, since he does wrong whenever he finds he has the power. Every man believes that wrong-doing pays him personally much better, and, according to this theory, that is the truth. Granted full license to do as he liked, people would think him a miserable fool if they found him refusing to wrong his neighbours or to touch their belongings, though in public they would keep up a pretence of praising his conduct, for fear of being wronged themselves. So much for that.

Finally, if we are really to judge between the two lives, the only way is to contrast the extremes of justice and injustice. We can best do that by imagining our two men to be perfect types, and crediting both to the full with the qualities they need for their respective ways of life. To begin with the unjust man: he must be like any consummate master of a craft, a physician or a captain, who, knowing just what his art can do, never tries to do more, and can always retrieve a false step. The unjust man, if he is to reach perfection, must be equally discreet in his criminal attempts, and he must not be found out, or we shall think him a bungler; for the highest pitch of injustice is to seem just when you are not. So we must endow our man with the full complement of injustice; we must allow him to have secured a spotless reputation for virtue while committing the blackest crimes; he must be able to retrieve any mistake, to defend himself with convincing eloquence if his misdeeds are denounced, and, when force is required, to bear down all opposition by his courage and strength and by his command of friends and money.

Now set beside this paragon the just man in his simplicity and nobleness, one who, in Aeschylus' words, "would be, not seem, the best." There must, indeed, be no such seeming; for if his character were apparent, his reputation would bring him honours and rewards, and then we should not know whether it was for their sake that he was just or for justice's sake alone. He must be stripped of everything but justice, and denied every advantage the other enjoyed. Doing no wrong, he must have the worst reputation for wrong-doing, to test whether his virtue is proof against all that comes of having a bad name; and under this lifelong imputation of wickedness, let him hold on his course of justice unwavering to the point of death. And so, when the two men have carried their justice and injustice to the last extreme, we may judge which is the happier.

My dear Glaucon, I exclaimed, how vigorously you scour these two characters clean for inspection, as if you were burnishing a couple of statues!

I am doing my best, he answered. Well, given two such characters, it is not hard, I fancy, to describe the sort of life that each of them may expect; and if the description sounds rather coarse, take it as coming from those who cry up the merits of injustice rather than from me. They will tell you that our just man will be thrown into prison, scourged and racked, will have his eyes burnt out, and, after every kind of torment, be impaled. That will teach him how much better it is to seem virtuous than to be so. [. . .]

With his reputation for virtue, [the unjust man] will hold offices of state, ally himself by marriage to any family he may choose, become a partner in any business, and, having no scruples about being dishonest, turn all these advantages to profit. If he is involved in a lawsuit, public or private, he will get the better of his opponents, grow rich on the proceeds, and be able to help his friends and harm his enemies. Finally, he can make sacrifices to the gods and dedicate offerings with due magnificence, and, being in a much better position than the just man to serve the gods as well as his chosen friends, he may reasonably hope to stand higher in the favour of heaven. So much better, they say, Socrates, is the life prepared for the unjust by gods and men.

Here Glaucon ended, and I was meditating a reply, when his brother Adeimantus exclaimed:

Surely, Socrates, you cannot suppose that that is all there is to be said.

Why, isn't it? said I.

Study Questions

1. How does Glaucon use the story of Gyges to express a theory of human nature?

2. Is Glaucon right? Why or why not?

3. Plato has Glaucon speculate about the terrible fate of the truly good man. How might Plato's readers interpret that? (Remember that this dialogue was written years after Socrates' death at the hands of the Athenian court.)

Primary Reading

Leviathan

THOMAS HOBBES

1651. Excerpt.

Whereas Glaucon's arguments were the result of playing the devil's advocate, Thomas Hobbes came to the same conclusion in all seriousness some two thousand years later: Humans are selfish by nature, and society is our best way to protect ourselves from each other. Justice is a concept that is to be found in a society only once the rules have been laid down. Prior to the creation of society, in the "state of nature," where people live in a perpetual state of war against one another, life is "nasty, brutish, and short," and no rules apply except that of self-preservation. In order to improve our personal condition and for no other reason, we choose to live by the rules of society. Justice is indeed to Thomas Hobbes an invention based on self-preservation, nothing more.

> Hereby it is manifest, that during the time men live without a common Power to keep them all in awe, they are in that condition which is called Warre; and such a warre, as is of every man against every man. For WARRE, consisteth not in Battell onely, or the act of fighting; but in a tract of time, wherein the Will to contend by Battell is sufficiently known: and therefore the notion of *Time,* is to be considered in the nature of Warre; as it is in the nature of Weather. For as the nature of Foule weather, lyeth not in a showre or two of rain; but in an inclination thereto of many dayes together; So the nature of War, consisteth not in actuall fighting; but in the known disposition thereto, during all the time there is no assurance to the contrary. All other time is PEACE.
>
> Whatsoever therefore is consequent to a time of Warre, where every man is Enemy to every man; the same is consequent to the time, wherein men live without other security, than what their own strength, and their own invention shall furnish them withall. In such condition, there is no place for Industry; because the fruit thereof is uncertain: and consequently no Culture of the Earth, no Navigation, nor use of the commodities that may be imported by Sea; no commodious Building; no Instruments of moving, and removing such things as require much force; no Knowledge of the face of the Earth; no account of Time; no Arts; no Letters; no Society; and which is worst of all, continuall feare, and danger of violent death; And the life of man, solitary, poore, nasty, brutish, and short. . . .
>
> To this warre of every man against every man, this also is consequent; that nothing can be Unjust. The notions of Right and Wrong, Justice and Injustice have there no place. Where there is no common Power, there is no Law: where no Law, no Injustice. Force, and Fraud, are in warre the two Cardinall vertues. Justice, and Injustice are none of the Faculties neither of the Body, nor Mind. If they were, they might be in a man that were alone in the world, as well as his Senses, and Passions. They are Qualities, that relate to men in Society, not in Solitude. . . .
>
> The Passions that encline men to Peace, are Feare of Death; Desire of such things as are necessary to commodious living; and a Hope by their Industry to obtain them. And Reason suggesteth convenient Articles of Peace, upon which men may be drawn to agreement.

Study Questions

1. What does Hobbes mean by saying that when humans live in a state of war of everybody against everybody, there is neither justice nor injustice? What event creates justice and injustice?

2. Compare Glaucon's and Hobbes's ideas of justice.

3. Hobbes believes we are all selfish by nature; however, since right and wrong for Hobbes don't exist prior to the creation of society, is selfishness in itself a bad thing? Why or why not?

Primary Reading

The Ethics of Emergencies

AYN RAND

The Virtue of Selfishness: A New Concept of Egoism, *1964. Excerpt.*

Ayn Rand (1905–1982), an American writer and philosopher, emigrated to the United States from the Soviet Union at age twenty-one because of a deep disenchantment with the Communist ideology. Her viewpoints were controversial from the beginning of her career, and her theory of objectivism still generates debate. Today some members of the Libertarian Party claim intellectual kinship to Rand.

Many philosophers have been reluctant to recognize her as a fellow thinker and have preferred to label her a novelist.

The psychological results of altruism may be observed in the fact that a great many people approach the subject of ethics by asking such questions as: "Should one risk one's life to help a man who is: a) drowning, b) trapped in a fire, c) stepping in front of a speeding truck, d) hanging by his fingernails over an abyss?"

Consider the implications of that approach. If a man accepts the ethics of altruism, he suffers the following consequences (in proportion to the degree of his acceptance):

1.   Lack of self-esteem—since his first concern in the realm of values is not how to live his life, but how to sacrifice it.

2.   Lack of respect for others—since he regards mankind as a herd of doomed beggars crying for someone's help.

3.   A nightmare view of existence—since he believes that men are trapped in a "malevolent universe" where disasters are the constant and primary concern of their lives.

4.   And, in fact, a lethargic indifference to ethics, a hopelessly cynical amorality—since his questions involve situations which he is not likely ever to encounter, which bear no relation to the actual problems of his own life and thus leave him to live without any moral principles whatever.

By elevating the issue of helping others into the central and primary issue of ethics, altruism has destroyed the concept of any authentic benevolence or good will among men. It has indoctrinated men with the idea that to value another human being is an act of selflessness, thus implying that a man can have no personal interest in others—that *to value* another means *to sacrifice* oneself—that any love, respect or admiration a man may feel for others is not and cannot be a source of his own enjoyment, but is a threat to his existence, a sacrificial blank check signed over to his loved ones.

The men who accept that dichotomy but choose its other side, the ultimate products of altruism's dehumanizing influence, are those psychopaths who do not challenge altruism's basic premise, but proclaim their rebellion against self-sacrifice by announcing

Ayn Rand (1905–1982), the Russian-born American philosopher and writer, developed the theory of *objectivism,* which stresses the right of the individual to keep the fruits of his or her labors and not be held responsible for the welfare of others. She is today best known for her novels, although her philosophy is also gaining recognition as an original twentieth-century contribution.

that they are totally indifferent to anything living and would not lift a finger to help a man or a dog left mangled by a hit-and-run driver (who is usually one of their own kind).

Most men do not accept or practice either side of altruism's viciously false dichotomy, but its result is a total intellectual chaos on the issue of proper human relationships and on such questions as the nature, purpose or extent of the help one may give to others. Today, a great many well-meaning, reasonable men do not know how to identify or conceptualize the moral principles that motivate their love, affection or good will, and can find no guidance in the field of ethics, which is dominated by the stale platitudes of altruism.

On the question of why man is not a sacrificial animal and why help to others is not his moral duty, I refer you to *Atlas Shrugged.* This present discussion is concerned with the principles by which one identifies and evaluates the instances involving a man's *nonsacrificial* help to others.

"Sacrifice" is the surrender of a greater value for the sake of a lesser one or of a nonvalue. Thus, altruism gauges a man's virtue by the degree to which he surrenders, renounces or betrays his values (since help to a stranger or an enemy is regarded as more virtuous, less "selfish," than help to those one loves). The rational principle of conduct is the exact opposite: always act in accordance with the hierarchy of your values, and never sacrifice a greater value to a lesser one.

This applies to all choices, including one's actions toward other men. It requires that one possess a defined hierarchy of *rational* values (values chosen and validated by a rational standard). Without such a hierarchy, neither rational conduct nor considered value judgments nor moral choices are possible.

Love and friendship are profoundly personal, selfish values: love is an expression and assertion of self-esteem, a response to one's own values in the person of another. One gains a profoundly personal selfish joy from the mere existence of the person one loves. It is one's own personal, selfish happiness that one seeks, earns and derives from love.

A "selfless," "disinterested" love is a contradiction in terms: it means that one is indifferent to that which one values.

Concern for the welfare of those one loves is a rational part of one's selfish interests. If a man who is passionately in love with his wife spends a fortune to cure her of a dangerous illness, it would be absurd to claim that he does it as a "sacrifice" for *her* sake, not his own, and that it makes no difference to *him,* personally and selfishly, whether she lives or dies.

Any action that a man undertakes for the benefit of those he loves is *not a sacrifice* if, in the hierarchy of his values, in the total context of the choices open to him, it achieves that which is of greatest *personal* (and rational) importance to *him.* In the above example, his wife's survival is of greater value to the husband than anything else that his money could buy, it is of greatest importance to his own happiness and, therefore, his action is not a sacrifice.

But suppose he let her die in order to spend his money on saving the lives of ten other women, none of whom meant anything to him — as the ethics of altruism would require. *That* would be a sacrifice. Here the difference between Objectivism and altruism can be seen most clearly: if sacrifice is the moral principle of action, then that husband *should* sacrifice his wife for the sake of ten other women. What distinguishes the wife from the ten others? Nothing but her value to the husband who has to make the choice — nothing but the fact that his happiness requires her survival.

The Objectivist ethics would tell him: your highest moral purpose is the achievement of your own happiness, your money is yours, use it to save your wife, *that* is your moral right and your rational, moral choice.

Consider the soul of the altruistic moralist who would be prepared to tell that husband the opposite. (And then ask yourself whether altruism is motivated by benevolence.)

The proper method of judging when or whether one should help another person is by reference to one's own rational self-interest and one's own hierarchy of values: the time, money or effort one gives or the risk one takes should be proportionate to the value of the person in relation to one's own happiness.

To illustrate this on the altruists' favorite example: the issue of saving a drowning person. If the person to be saved is a stranger, it is morally proper to save him only when the danger to one's own life is minimal; when the danger is great, it would be immoral to attempt it: only a lack of self-esteem could permit one to value one's life no higher than that of any random stranger. (And, conversely, if one is drowning, one cannot expect a stranger to risk his life for one's sake, remembering that one's life cannot be as valuable to him as his own.)

If the person to be saved is not a stranger, then the risk one should be willing to take is greater in proportion to the greatness of that person's value to oneself. If it is the man or woman one loves, then one can be willing to give one's own life to save him or her — for the selfish reason that life without the loved person could be unbearable.

Conversely, if a man is able to swim and to save his drowning wife, but becomes panicky, gives in to an unjustified, irrational fear and lets her drown, then spends his life in loneliness and misery — one would not call him "selfish"; one would condemn him morally for his treason to himself and to his own values, that is: his failure to fight for the preservation of a value crucial to his own happiness. Remember that values are that which one acts to gain and/or keep, and that one's own happiness has to be achieved by one's own effort. Since one's own happiness is the moral purpose of one's life, the man who fails to achieve it because of his own default—his failure to fight for it, is morally guilty.

Study Questions

1. Is Rand correct in saying that if you accept altruism, then you end up with a lack of self-esteem and a lack of respect for others?

2. Is Rand criticizing ideal or reciprocal altruism? Do you think that she would differentiate between the two? Would you?

3. Comment on the following quote: "The proper method of judging when or whether one should help another person is by reference to one's own rational self-interest and one's own hierarchy of values: the time, money or effort one gives or the risk one takes should be proportionate to the value of the person in relation to one's own happiness." What might the social and political outcome be if this approach were implemented?

4. A suggestion: Reread this excerpt after you have studied Chapter 5, on utilitarianism, and speculate: How would Rand evaluate the theory that asks us to maximize happiness for the maximum number of people?

5. Go back to Chapter 3 and reread, in the excerpt from Ruth Benedict's paper "Anthropology and the Abnormal," the section about "unbridled and arrogant egoists" as being typical of Western civilization. What might Rand's comment be to that remark?

Narrative

The One Where Phoebe Hates PBS

MICHAEL CURTIS (TELEPLAY)
SHELLEY JENSEN (DIRECTOR)

An episode of Friends, *1998–99. Summary.*

Can a television sitcom discuss moral problems in an even remotely significant way? I'll let you be the judge of that. If you've ever sat around the kitchen table after a party with friends discussing whether everyone is selfish, then you can relate to the main story line in this episode. Just a brief introduction to the characters: *Joey* is an aspiring actor who has a rather blatant tendency to think of himself first, and others second. *Phoebe* is a kind-hearted and spiritual (some would say light-headed) poet/singer/masseuse who has her own private view of the world. She is the surrogate mother of triplets, given over to her half-brother and his wife who can't conceive. One morning while some of the friends (Phoebe, Chandler, Ross, and Monica) are having breakfast, Joey comes in, wearing a tuxedo. He has got a gig (he thinks), hosting a telethon for PBS, and he brags that he's doing a good deed for PBS while he himself is getting TV exposure. But Phoebe is appalled: for one thing, she thoroughly dislikes PBS, because she had a bad experience with the network some years back. Her mother had just killed herself, and Phoebe was feeling sad, so she wrote to *Sesame Street,* because she remembered them fondly from when she was a little kid. But nobody replied—they just sent her a key chain. And at the time she was homeless, living in a box, so she didn't even have any keys! Besides, she says, the only reason why Joey wants the gig is so he can get on TV, not because he wants to do something unselfish.

This gets the ball rolling: Now Joey accuses Phoebe of being selfish, herself, for having triplets for her brother—because it made her *feel good,* and, says Joey, that makes it selfish; we recognize the attitude of a convinced psychological egoist: everyone is selfish, and, in Joey's words, "there's no unselfish good deeds." Phoebe might just as well forget that, because that's like believing in Santa Claus. (Later on she casually asks him what he meant, and when she hears him say that Santa doesn't exist, we see the shock on her face.)

So Phoebe sets out to prove Joey wrong, because, as she explains to Monica and her other friend Rachel, she just won't let her babies be raised in a world where Joey is right. Her first attempt involves sneaking over to an elderly neighbor, and raking the leaves from his doorstep. But he discovers her, and treats her to cider and cookies, which makes her feel great. So, since her good deed made her feel good, it doesn't qualify as a selfless deed, according to Joey's definition.

Meanwhile, to his immense disappointment, Joey finds out that he isn't hosting the telethon after all, talk show host Gary Collins is; Joey is just going to answer phones, and it looks like he dressed in a tux for nothing. But one of the calls he receives is from Phoebe who proudly announces that she has found a selfless, good deed: She went to Central Park and let a bee sting her, so it could look macho in front of its friends! And since she's hurting, it's not a selfish deed. But Joey shoots that down instantly: Since the bee probably died from stinging her, the bee didn't benefit (so it wasn't a good deed!).

Joey himself is doing a fine job of demonstrating what his true goal is: TV exposure, rather than helping PBS, thus proving Phoebe's point that he himself is just looking out for Number One. He realizes that the place where he is answering calls isn't even within range of the television camera, so he tries to swap places with another volunteer, who is utterly unwilling to comply, to the point where they slug it out between the tables, in the background while Gary Collins is talking about contributing to PBS's fine programming. So Joey's own quest of gaining an advantage for himself isn't doing too great. But now Phoebe makes one last attempt to prove that unselfishness exists:

She makes one more call to Joey, pledging $200 to PBS. She explains that even if she is still mad at them, she also knows that lots of children love their shows, so she is doing a good deed by supporting them, while it doesn't make her feel good at all: $200 is a lot of money, and she had plans for that sum: She was saving up to buy a hamster. Joey can't believe what he's hearing: A $200+ hamster? When they normally cost $10? Phoebe implies that it was a very special hamster (and we get the feeling that she was probably being taken for a ride, as it often happens). So it looks like she has proved to Joey that selfless, good deeds do indeed exist! But here comes the twist: Because of Phoebe's pledge, the station has now surpassed the sum collected by pledges last year, and Gary Collins steps over to the volunteer who took the pledge—Joey! Who now gets his TV exposure: he is introduced by name standing there in his tux, with a big smile on his face. Phoebe is watching it on TV, and is overjoyed that her pledge got Joey on TV — until she realizes what has happened! Her good deed which was supposed to make her feel bad, now has made her feel good — which again proves Joey's point that all deeds are selfish! So she loses again.

Has Joey now been vindicated? Has Phoebe's failure in proving that she can do a "selfless, good deed" convinced us that psychological egoism is true? If things we do make us feel good afterwards, do they automatically fall into a "selfish" category, even if we didn't plan on feeling good, and the pleasure is an unintended aftereffect? Keep in mind the debate about whether Lincoln's act of saving the pigs was selfish or not. A truly selfish person would not feel good about having sacrificed something for others; as you've read, it could be a way to tell unselfish people from the selfish ones that they actually feel good after helping others.

Study Questions

1. Some would say that Phoebe's project was doomed from the start, due to the nature of her goal. What might that mean, and do you agree?

2. Discuss Phoebe's attempts at disproving Joey, relating them to the arguments against psychological egoism in the chapter text: the principle of falsification, the Lincoln story, and the fallacy of the suppressed correlative.

3. Is Joey selfish? Is Phoebe? Is everybody? Are you? Explain.

Narrative

Return to Paradise

WESLEY STRICK AND BRUCE ROBINSON (SCREENWRITERS) AND JOSEPH RUBEN (DIRECTOR)

Film, 1998. Summary.

Peter Singer's story of the two hunters and the saber-toothed cat cited earlier in this chapter is a version of the so-called *prisoner's dilemma:* You and your friend are both political prisoners of a totalitarian regime, isolated from each other, and you are each told that the length of your sentence will depend on whether or not you confess: If you confess and your friend doesn't, you will get one year in prison and your friend will get ten years; if your friend confesses and you don't, he/she will get one year and you'll get ten. If neither of you confesses, you will each get two years. If both of you confess, you'll each get five years. So if your only goal is to limit your own sentence, logic demands that you confess, because you'll be ahead whether or not your friend also confesses. Since your friend is thinking along the same lines, chances are you'll both confess and both get five years. But if you're capable of thinking about each other's interests and can be certain that you can trust each other, then it's a win–win situation for both of you: If you both don't confess, you'll both get out after only two years. So the lesson of the prisoner's dilemma is that it can be of greater personal advantage to be less selfish than more selfish — just as in the hunter story. But it depends completely on whether we can trust each other — whether we dare take the chance that our friend will also put selfishness aside.

A film that explores the prisoner's dilemma with a chilling twist is *Return to Paradise,* based on the 1989 French movie *Force Majeure* by Pierre Jolivet. Here we have a prisoner who hopes that his two friends, enjoying their freedom, will submit to punishment for his sake, thus averting his own death sentence. The two friends must confront the conflict between their instinct for self-preservation and their sense of duty to help a friend. The film is thus a prisoner's dilemma story combined with an exploration of the nature of selfishness and altruism.

Sheriff, Tony, and Lewis are three young Americans having a good time in Malaysia, smoking dope, hanging out with the local young women, and enjoying the exotic scenery. On the way back from a trip to the market, they wreck a borrowed bicycle, and Sheriff heaves it over a precipice. A short time afterward, Sheriff and Tony go home to New York City, while Lewis stays on to help endangered orangutans. Before leaving, Sheriff and Tony give their stash of hashish to Lewis.

Two years later Sheriff is working as a limo driver in New York; Tony is working in construction and thinking about getting married. They haven't seen each other since leaving Panang. One night Sheriff has a fare, a young woman named Beth, who reveals that she is a lawyer for Lewis — he's been in the Panang jail ever since they left, for having in his possession more than the legal limit of 100 grams of hash. The excess amount was the stash given to him by his two friends. The man whose bicycle they wrecked came looking for it with the police, and they found the dope. Ten months ago Lewis received his sentence: death. All appeals have been exhausted, but only last week he mentioned his friends and the hashish story. So now the Malaysian authorities have the following suggestion: If Sheriff and Tony return to take their share of the responsibility, everybody gets three years in prison. If only one of them returns, he gets six years, and so does Lewis; if no one comes back to Panang, Lewis will be hanged — in eight days. Beth tells the same story to Tony, who is at once willing to consider going back but won't do it if Sheriff doesn't, because he is willing to lose only three years of his life, not six. Sheriff, on the other hand, sees no reason why he should even consider going — he doesn't think they can trust the deal, and it seems he just doesn't have the morals Beth assumes he has.

Beth is approached by a persistent journalist, who insists that she has a right to publish Lewis's story and that she can help him by drawing the world's attention to his case. Beth is terrified: In another case the Malaysian government reneged on a deal because of international publicity, and the prisoner was executed. She can't take such a chance but promises the reporter an exclusive if she will wait a few days.

Beth shows Sheriff a tape made by a physically and mentally worn-down Lewis, begging him and Tony to come and save his life. As the reality of Tony's impending execution dawns on Sheriff, he has a talk with his father, who is no help: He suggests that Sheriff go because Lewis is probably worth more as a person than Sheriff is. We realize he was being sarcastic. Why agonize over it, he says, when Sheriff isn't even considering

In the film *Return to Paradise* (Polygram, 1998), two friends are faced with a moral problem: Should they voluntarily return to Malaysia to save another friend from a death sentence, and share the blame for his illegal drug possession, even if it would entail prison time for both of them? Here attorney Beth Eastern (Anne Heche) is trying to convince Sheriff (Vince Vaughn) to return with her.

going? So Sheriff tells Beth he won't go: "It isn't in me." Compelled by Sheriff's selfish attitude, Tony now promises to go, but Beth isn't certain of his commitment.

Sheriff and Beth have been developing an attraction for each other, and in a desperate mood they make love. The next morning he is still with her, now committed to helping her and his friend Lewis. Two days before Lewis's scheduled execution, all three of them are on the plane to Panang. The two friends have decided to give Lewis three years of their lives to save his.

Once in Panang, they go to see Lewis, but only one visitor is allowed. Sheriff finds Lewis hunched over, shivering, rocking back and forth, praying. Sheriff tries to comfort him and lift his spirits, and it seems to be working: As Sheriff is leaving, Lewis says to him, "I knew you'd come back—even if *you* didn't." Back with Tony and Beth, Sheriff expresses his concerns about Lewis's state of mind, and Beth lets slip that he's always been that way. How would she know, as his lawyer? It turns out she's not just his lawyer—she's his big sister.

With that revelation, the deal is off. Tony and Sheriff feel they can't trust her—she'd promise them anything just to get Lewis out. Fearing for their own lives, they take off for the airport. Tony boards the plane for New York—but Sheriff hesitates: He has realized it was his recklessness in throwing the bike away that put Lewis in this situation, so he must take responsibility for it. Tony leaves for New York, but Sheriff goes back to Panang, in time to walk into the courtroom where Lewis's sentence is about to be confirmed. The judge exclaims that his faith in humanity is half restored. Sheriff says they were young and stupid, but not evil; he is responsible and is willing to do what it takes to save his friend's life. The judge goes to his chambers to reassess the situation; he is expected to come out and pronounce a reprieve for Lewis and a six-year sentence for Sheriff.

But a commotion erupts as the media arrive at the courthouse. Apparently an American newspaper has published the persistent journalist's story, making the Malaysian system of justice look medieval and cruel. The judge emerges, livid: He won't have the Western media dictating the decisions of his court. The West might not understand his country's harsh drug sentences, he says, but Malaysian kids are safe from drugs, unlike kids in the West.

Will the judge stand by his word and give Lewis a lesser sentence because Sheriff came back? Or has the publication of the article endangered Lewis's life, as Beth predicted it would? The ending of this film is haunting and thought-provoking, and I would like for you to experience it yourself. Also, I'd like you to consider the following: If Lewis dies, has Sheriff's willingness to help him been for nothing?

Study Questions

1. Early in the film, Sheriff asks Beth whether *she* would go to prison for Lewis, if the question were put to her. Would *you* give three years of your life to save a friend? Would you give six? Explain.

2. Explore the changes in the characters of Tony and Sheriff. Which change is the greatest, and why?

3. What would a psychological egoist say to this story? What would an ethical egoist say?

4. Compare this story to the original prisoner's-dilemma scenario. What are the similarities, and what are the differences?

5. Is anyone being altruistic in this film? Does a person have to have no self-interest involved in order to be unselfish?

Narrative

Madame Bovary

GUSTAVE FLAUBERT

Novel, 1857. Summary and Excerpt. Translated by Lowell Bair. Film version in United States (1949) and in France (1991).

As a young girl in the country, Emma, the title character of *Madame Bovary*, devours sentimental novels and dreams about romantic love. She marries the first man ever to find her attractive, the decent and well-meaning but dull Dr. Charles Bovary. They have a little girl, but Emma finds no satisfaction in the tranquil life of a doctor's wife and a mother in a small French town. The fact that her husband is not even a mediocre doctor but a downright bad one doesn't help any. Emma falls in love with a wealthy neighbor and embarks on a path that leads to her ruin. She has an affair with the neighbor, and she begins an extravagant shopping spree by mail order, on credit. After a while she prepares to elope with her lover, only to find that he already has eloped—without her. Devastated, she falls ill, but she recuperates when she meets a former acquaintance, a young man who has been secretly in love with her for years. They have an affair, and Emma reembarks on her shopping venture, sending her daughter to live with strangers. Here we see how Emma entangles herself in a web of lies to be able to see her young lover Léon once a week in the nearby town of Rouen:

It was at about this time, toward the beginning of winter, that she apparently developed a great ardor for music.

One evening when Charles was listening to her, she started the same piece over again four times, growing more and more annoyed, while Charles, without noticing any difference, kept crying out, "Bravo! Very good! . . . You shouldn't stop! Keep going!"

"No! It's disgusting! My fingers are rusty."

The next day he asked her to "play him something again."

"All right, if you really want me to."

And he admitted that she had gotten a little out of practice. She struck wrong notes, fumbled and hesitated; then she stopped short and said, "No more! I ought to take lessons, but . . ." She bit her lip and added, "Twenty francs a lesson—it's too expensive."

"Yes, you're right, it is a little . . ." said Charles, laughing foolishly. "I think we might be able to find a teacher for less, though, because there are a lot of musicians who don't have a big reputation but are better than the celebrities."

"Well, find one of them," said Emma.

When he came home the next day he gave her a sly look and finally blurted out, "You're so opinionated sometimes! I went to Barfeuchères today, and Madame Liégeard told me that her three girls—they're all at La Miséricorde now—used to take lessons for two and a half francs an hour, and from a wonderful teacher, too!"

She shrugged her shoulders and left her instrument closed from then on.

But whenever she walked past it she would sigh (if Bovary happened to be there), "Ah, my poor piano!"

And when she had visitors she never failed to inform them that she had abandoned her music and could not go back to it now, for reasons beyond her control. Everyone pitied her. It was a shame! She had such talent! Some people even spoke to Bovary about it. . . .

And so Charles brought up the question of the piano again. Emma answered bitterly that it would be better to sell it. But that poor old piano had given his pride such satisfaction that to see it go would have been almost like watching Emma kill part of herself.

"If you want to . . ." he said. "After all, a lesson now and then wouldn't really make us go bankrupt."

"But lessons don't do any good," she replied, "unless you take them regularly."

It was thus that she obtained her husband's permission to go to the city once a week to see her lover. And by the end of the first month everyone found that she had made considerable progress. . . .

She was more charming than ever to her husband; she made him pistachio custards and played waltzes for him after dinner. He regarded himself as the luckiest of mortals, and she never worried about him until suddenly one evening he asked her, "It's Mademoiselle Lempereur who gives you lessons, isn't it?"

"Yes."

"Well, I saw her today," said Charles, "in Madame Liégeard's house. I talked to her about you: she doesn't know you."

It was like a thunderbolt. However, she answered in a natural tone, "She must have forgotten my name."

"Or maybe there are several piano teachers named Lempereur in Rouen," said the doctor.

"Maybe so." Then she quickly added, "Anyway, I have my receipts: here, look!"

She went to the writing desk, rummaged through all the drawers, mixed up all the papers and finally became so frantic that Charles strongly urged her not to go to so much trouble for those wretched receipts.

"Oh, I'll find them!" she said.

True enough, on the following Friday, as Charles was putting on one of his boots in the dark little room where he kept his clothes, he felt a piece of paper between the leather and his sock; he pulled it out and read: *"Received the sum of sixty-five francs, for three months of lessons, plus various supplies. Félicie Lempereur, Music Teacher."*

"How the devil did this get into my boot?"

"It probably fell down from that old box full of bills on the shelf," she replied.

From then on her whole life was a tissue of lies which she wrapped around her love like a veil, to hide it.

Lying became a need, a mania, a pleasure; so much so that if she said she had walked down the right side of a street the day before, it was almost certain that she had walked down the left.

Eventually the merchant who has been supplying her with clothes, jewelry, and furniture confronts Emma with her enormous debt and demands immediate payment in return for promising not to tell her husband of her affair. Emma, who is now desperate, begins selling off her own assets as well as Charles's property and his medical tools. In the end, forced to face her own degradation, she swallows poison and dies. Charles refuses to think evil of her and even when faced with the truth—Emma's love letters— sees only that she was a poor and desperate soul.

Study Questions

1. Can Emma's case be viewed as a case for psychological egoism?

2. Can Emma be considered an ethical egoist?

3. Emma gets her ideas about romantic passion from books. Does that mean that fiction can be morally dangerous?

4. Flaubert, the author, used to say *"Emma Bovary, c'est moi"* (Emma Bovary, that's me). Do you think he viewed his protagonist in an overall negative or positive way?

Narrative

Atlas Shrugged

AYN RAND

Novel, 1957. Summary and Excerpt.

In Greek mythology, Atlas is the god who holds up the earth on his shoulders—and when Atlas shrugs, the world shakes. Ayn Rand's book is about the shake-up of the world by those who form its economic foundation: the factory owners, the entrepreneurs, the railroad builders. It is not the workers but those who employ them who are the movers and the shakers of the world, and in Rand's opinion they have been abused by unions and "bleeding hearts" long enough. In this book she outlines her philosophy of objectivism "between the lines" of the novel, urging those people with creative powers to start thinking about themselves and taking pride in what they do, for without them the world literally will come to a halt. In *Atlas Shrugged,* the movers and shakers go on strike, led by the mythic figure of John Galt and joined by the railroad tycoon Dagny Taggart. The common folk who have no talent or will to keep themselves going must perish. This vision of ethical egoism sees the world as being divided between those who can think and create and those who are parasites on the creators; each person has a right to what he or she creates (and earns), and no one else has any right to any of it. The only duty we have is to look out for ourselves and not give our lives away to others who aren't willing to work for their own share. The following excerpt is from a conversation between Francisco d'Anconia, a copper tycoon and millionaire, and Henry Rearden, a steelworks owner and inventor who is beginning to understand that he has been letting people take advantage of him all his life:

"If you want to see an abstract principle, such as moral action, in material form—there it is. Look at it, Mr. Rearden. Every girder of it, every pipe, wire and valve was put there by a choice in answer to the question: right or wrong? You had to choose right and you had to choose the best within your knowledge—the best for your purpose, which was to make steel—and then move on and extend the knowledge, and do better, and still better, with your purpose as your standard of value. You had to act on your own judgment, you had to have the capacity to judge, the courage to stand on the verdict of your mind, and the purest, the most ruthless consecration to the rule of doing right, of doing the best, the utmost best possible to you. Nothing could have made you act against your judgment, and you would have rejected as wrong—as evil—any man who attempted to tell you that the best way to heat a furnace was to fill it with ice. Millions of men, an entire nation, were not able to deter you from producing Rearden Metal—because you had the knowledge of its superlative value and the power which such knowledge gives. But what I wonder about, Mr. Rearden, is why you live by one code of principles when you deal with nature and by another when you deal with men?"

Rearden's eyes were fixed on him so intently that the question came slowly, as if the effort to pronounce it were a distraction: "What do you mean?"

"Why don't you hold to the purpose of your life as clearly and rigidly as you hold to the purpose of your mills?"

"You have judged every brick within this place by its value to the goal of making steel. Have you been as strict about the goal which your work and your steel are serving? What do you wish to achieve by giving your life to the making of steel? By what standard of value do you judge your days? For instance, why did you spend ten years of exacting effort to produce Rearden Metal?"

Rearden looked away, the slight, slumping movement of his shoulders like a sigh of release and disappointment. "If you have to ask that, then you wouldn't understand."

"If I told you that I understand it, but you don't—would you throw me out of here?"

"I should have thrown you out of here anyway—so go ahead, tell me what you mean."

"Are you proud of the rail of the John Galt Line?"

"Yes."

"Why?"

"Because it's the best rail ever made."

"Why did you make it?"

"In order to make money."

"There were many easier ways to make money. Why did you choose the hardest?"

"You said it in your speech at Taggart's wedding: in order to exchange my best effort for the best effort of others."

"If that was your purpose, have you achieved it?"

A beat of time vanished in a heavy drop of silence. "No," said Rearden.

"Have you made any money?"

"No."

"When you strain your energy to its utmost in order to produce the best, do you expect to be rewarded for it or punished?" Rearden did not answer. "By every standard of decency, of honor, of justice known to you—are you convinced that you should have been rewarded for it?"

"Yes," said Rearden, his voice low.

"Then if you were punished, instead—what sort of code have you accepted?"

Rearden did not answer.

"It is generally assumed," said Francisco, "that living in a human society makes one's life much easier and safer than if one were left alone to struggle against nature on a desert island. Now wherever there is a man who needs or uses metal in any way—Rearden Metal has made his life easier for him. Has it made yours easier for you?"

"No," said Rearden, his voice low.

"Has it left your life as it was before you produced the Metal?"

"No—" said Rearden, the word breaking off as if he had cut short the thought that followed.

Francisco's voice lashed at him suddenly, as a command: "Say it!"

"It has made it harder," said Rearden tonelessly.

"When you felt proud of the rail of the John Galt Line," said Francisco, the measured rhythm of his voice giving a ruthless clarity to his words, "what sort of men did you think of? Did you want to see that Line used by your equals—by giants of productive energy, such as Ellis Wyatt, whom it would help to reach higher and still higher achievements of their own?"

"Yes," said Rearden eagerly.

"Did you want to see it used by men who could not equal the power of your mind, but who would equal your moral integrity—men such as Eddie Willers—who could never invent your Metal, but who would do their best, work as hard as you did, live by their own effort, and—riding on your rail—give a moment's silent thanks to the man who gave them more than they could give him?"

"Yes," said Rearden gently.

"Did you want to see it used by whining rotters who never rouse themselves to any effort, who do not possess the ability of a filing clerk, but demand the income of a company president, who drift from failure to failure and expect you to pay their bills, who hold their wishing to an equivalent of your work and their need as a higher claim to reward than your effort, who demand that you serve them, who demand that it be the aim of your life to serve them, who demand that your strength be the voiceless, rightless, unpaid, unrewarded slave of their impotence, who proclaim that you are born to serfdom by reason of your genius, while they are born to rule by the grace of incompetence, that yours is only to give, but theirs only to take, that yours is to produce, but theirs to consume, that you are not to be paid, neither in matter nor in spirit, neither by wealth nor by recognition nor by respect nor by gratitude—so that they would ride on your rail and sneer at you and curse you, since they owe you nothing, not even the effort of taking off their hats which you paid for? Would this be what you wanted? Would you feel proud of it?"

"I'd blast that rail first," said Rearden, his lips white.

Study Questions

1. What is it that d'Anconia accuses Rearden of?

2. Can you identify d'Anconia's political standpoint and the standpoint he argues against?

3. Why is this considered an example of ethical egoism? How does this excerpt relate to Rand's analysis of happiness as a moral purpose?

Chapter Five

Using Your Reason,
Part 1: Utilitarianism

*W*hen deciding on a moral course of action, some of us find it is the potential consequences of our choice that determine what we decide to do. Others of us see those consequences as being of minor importance when we view them in light of the question of right and wrong. A student of mine, when asked to come up with a moral problem we could discuss in class, proposed this question to ponder: Imagine that your grandmother is dying; she is very religious, and she asks you to promise her that you will marry within the family faith. Your beloved is of another faith. Do you tell her the truth, or do you make a false promise? This profound (and I suspect, real-life) question makes us all wonder: If I think it is right to lie to Grandma, why is that? To make her last moments peaceful; what she doesn't know won't hurt her; why should I upset her by telling her the truth? Is that a good enough reason? And if I think lying to Grandma is wrong, and refuse to do it, how do I justify making her last moments miserable? You will see that those of us who think lying to her is the only right choice because then she will die happy generally subscribe to the theory of *consequentialism,* in particular the theory of *utilitarianism,* the most widespread and popular form of consequentialism. If you think that lying is always wrong, even if it would make Grandma feel better, then hang in there until Chapter 6, where we discuss Kant's moral theory.

In the preceding chapter you encountered the philosopher Peter Singer, who claimed that we as humans are capable of caring for others as well as ourselves. Singer identifies himself as a utilitarian, as do numerous others today—philosophers as well as laypeople. Utilitarians see as their moral guideline a rule that encourages them to make life bearable for as many people as possible. Perhaps we can actively do something to make people's lives better, or perhaps the only thing we can do to make their lives better is to stay out of their way. Perhaps we can't strive to make people happy, but we can at least do our best to limit their misery. This way of thinking just seems the decent thing to do for many of us, and when we include ourselves among those who should receive a general increase of happiness and decrease of misery, then the rule seems attractive, simple, and reasonable. Small wonder this attitude has become the cornerstone of one of the most vital and influential moral theories in human history.

A utilitarian is a hard universalist in the sense that he or she believes there is a single universal moral code, which is the only one possible, and everyone ought to realize it. It is the *principle of utility,* or the *greatest-happiness principle:* When choosing a course of action, always pick the one that will maximize happiness and minimize unhappiness for the greatest number of people. Whatever action conforms to this rule will be defined as a morally right action, and whatever action does not conform to this principle will be called a morally wrong action. In this way utilitarianism proposes a clear and simple moral criterion: Pleasure is good and pain is bad; therefore, whatever causes happiness and/or decreases pain is morally right, and whatever causes pain or unhappiness is morally wrong. In other words, utilitarianism is interested in the *consequences* of our actions: If they are good, the action is right; if bad, the action is wrong. This principle, utilitarians claim, will provide answers to all real-life dilemmas.

Are all theories that focus on the consequences of actions utilitarian? No. As we saw in Chapter 4, the consequences we look for may be happy consequences for ourselves alone, and in that case we show ourselves to be egoists. We may focus on the consequences of our actions because we believe that those consequences justify our actions (in other words, that the end justifies the means), but this does not necessarily imply that the consequences we hope for are good in the utilitarian sense that they maximize happiness for the maximum number of people. We might, for instance, agree with the Italian statesman Niccolò Machiavelli (1469–1527) that if the end is to maintain political power for oneself, one's king, or one's political party, this will justify any means one might use for that purpose, such as force, surveillance, or even deceit. Although this famous theory is indeed consequentialist, it does not qualify as utilitarian, because it doesn't have the common good as its ultimate end.

Jeremy Bentham and the Hedonistic Calculus

It is often tempting to say that history moves in a certain direction. For example, eighteenth-century Europe and America saw a general movement toward greater recognition of human rights and social equality, of the value of the individual, of the scope of human capacities, and of the need for and right to education. During this period, known as the *Enlightenment,* rulers and scholars shared a staunch belief that human reason, *rationality,* held the key to the future — to the blossoming of the sciences as well as to social change. This period is, appropriately, also referred to as the *Age of Reason,* not so much because people were particularly rational at the time but because reason was the social, scientific, and philosophical *ideal.*

Perhaps, then, it is tempting to say that civilization moved toward an appreciation of human rationality, but it would be more appropriate to say that it was moved along by the thoughts of certain thinkers. Such a mover was the English jurist and philosopher Jeremy Bentham (1748–1832).

Bentham, author of *Introduction to the Principles of Morals and Legislation* (1789), set out to create not a new moral theory so much as a hands-on principle that could be used to remodel the British legal system. Indeed, it was not Bentham but another philosopher, David Hume, who invented the term *utilitarianism.* Hume believed that it is good for an action to have *utility* in the sense that it makes yourself and others

Jeremy Bentham (1748–1832), English philosopher and jurist. With his friend James Mill he developed the theory of utilitarianism based on the principle of utility: Maximize happiness and minimize unhappiness for as many as possible. Bentham donated his body to medical research and his money to University College of London, with the provision that after research on his body was complete, it was to be preserved and displayed at university board meetings. This request is not as odd as it might sound: Bentham, a prominent person, hoped that by donating his body to science he would make a statement in support of the medical profession's need for cadavers for research. Most people at the time felt, however, that having one's deceased body cut up was a sacrilege, and so only the bodies of executed criminals were available. As a result, a thriving clandestine business arose, a trade in newly dead bodies stolen from their graves. In one case, the body snatchers didn't wait for corpses to be buried, but murdered sixteen people in one year and sold them to anatomists. By deciding to donate his body, Bentham took a stand against what he saw as superstition and attempted to put a stop to the practice of body snatching. And he may have thought further, What better way to undo superstitions about dead bodies than for his own to be on display at board meetings? He specified in his will that he was to become an *Auto-Icon,* an image of himself, and he even picked out the glass eyes to be placed in his head after his demise and carried them around in his pocket, according to legend. He had intended for his head to remain on the shoulders of his Auto-Icon, but after his death, the preservation process presumably went wrong, and a wax head was substituted. In this photo you see both the wax head (a good likeness), and Bentham's real head between his feet. He still sits in his mahogany case at the University College of London and is wheeled in at annual board meetings. He is recorded as "present, but not voting."

Box 5.1   HEDONISM AND THE HEDONISTIC PARADOX

Often the Greek thinker Epicurus (341–270 B.C.E.) is credited with being the first philosopher to advocate a life in search of pleasure, hedonism. This, however, isn't quite accurate, because what Epicurus seems to have been after was a life free of pain, because if you are free of pain you have obtained peace of mind, *ataraxia*, the highest pleasure. But others have advocated that seeking pleasure and avoiding pain is human nature, and what humans ought to embark on in life is to accumulate good times. Jeremy Bentham believed all humans are hedonists. Everyone wants pleasure, so we search for it. Searching and finding are two different things, however, and the paradox of hedonism often prevents us from finding what we are looking for. Suppose we set out to achieve pleasure on the weekend. We go to the beach, we take a walk in the woods, we hang out at the mall, we go to the movies, but we're just not enjoying ourselves that much; pleasure has somehow eluded us, and we face Monday with the sense of a lost weekend, telling ourselves that next weekend we'll look harder. Our friend, on the contrary, had a great time; he went with us because he likes going to the beach, loves the woods, wanted to look for a pair of jeans at the mall, and had been looking forward to seeing a movie for weeks. He even enjoyed our company. Why did he have a good weekend while we felt unfulfilled? Because we were trying to have a good time, and he was doing things he liked to do and enjoying being with

someone he liked. The pleasure he got was, so to speak, a by-product of doing those things—it wasn't the main object of his activity. We, on the other hand, looked for pleasure without thinking about what we like to do that might give us pleasure, as if "pleasure" were a thing separate from everything else. The hedonistic paradox is this: If you look for pleasure, chances are you won't find it. (People who have been looking hard for someone to love can attest to this.) Pleasure comes to you when you are in the middle of something else and rarely when you are looking for it. Sometimes the "Don Juan syndrome" is cited as an example of the hedonistic paradox. A person (traditionally a man, but there is no reason it can't apply to women) who has a lot of sexual conquests very often feels compelled to move from partner to partner because he or she likes the pursuit but somehow tires of an established relationship. Why is this the case? It could be because such people are unwilling to commit themselves to a permanent relationship, but it also may be due to the paradox of hedonism: In each partner they see the promise of "pleasure," but somehow all they end up with is another conquest. If they had been setting their sights on building a relationship with their partners, they might have found out that pleasure comes from being with someone you care for, and you have to care in order to feel pleasure; you can't expect pleasure to appear if there is no genuine feeling—or so the theory says. . . .

happy, but he never developed this idea into a complete moral theory. Bentham, however, used the term to create a moral system for a new age.

In Bentham's England the feudal world had all but vanished. Society had stratified into an upper class, a middle class, and a working class, and the Industrial Revolution was just beginning. Conditions for the lowest class in the social hierarchy were appalling. Rights in the courts were, by and large, something that could be bought, which meant that those who had no means to buy them didn't have them.

Box 5.2   INTRINSIC VERSUS INSTRUMENTAL VALUES

An *instrumental* value is one that can be used as an instrument or tool to get something else that we want. If you needed to get to class or work on time, a car might be the instrumental value that would get you there. If you didn't have a car, then money (or good credit) might be the instrumental value that would get you the car that would get you to school or to your workplace. How about going to school? If you're going to school in order to get a degree, then you might say that going to school is an instrumental value that will get your degree. And the degree? An instrumental value that will get you a good job. And the job? An instrumental value that will get what? More money. And what do you want with that? A better lifestyle, a better place to live, good health, and so on. And why

do you want a better lifestyle? Why do you want to be healthy? This is where the chain comes to an end, because we have reached something that is obvious: We want those things because we want them. Perhaps they "make us happy," but the bottom line is that we value them for their own sake, *intrinsically*. Some values can of course be both instrumental and intrinsic; the car may help you get to school, but also, you've wanted the car for a long time just because you like it. Exercising may make you healthy, but you also may actually enjoy it. And going to school is certainly a tool that can be used to get a degree, but some people appreciate training and knowledge for their own sake, not just because these goods can be used to get them somewhere in life.

The world portrayed in the novels of Charles Dickens was developing; if you were in debt, you were taken to debtors' prison, where you stayed until your debt was paid. Whoever had funds could get out, but the poor faced spending the rest of their lives with their family inside debtors' prison. There were no child labor laws, and the exploitation of children in the workforce, which horrified Marx some decades later, was rampant in Bentham's day. Bentham saw it as terribly unfair and decided that the best way to redesign this system of unfair advantages would be to set up a simple moral rule that everyone could relate to, rich and poor alike.

Bentham said that what is good is what is pleasurable, and what is bad is what is painful. In other words, *hedonism* (pleasure seeking) is the basis for his moral theory, which is often called *hedonistic utilitarianism* (see Box 5.1). The ultimate value is happiness or pleasure — these things are *intrinsically* valuable. Anything that helps us achieve happiness or avoid pain is of *instrumental* value, and because we may do something pleasurable in order to achieve another pleasure, pleasure can have both intrinsic and instrumental value. (Box 5.2 explains this distinction in more detail.) In order for this basic rule to be useful in legislation, we need to let people decide for themselves wherein their pleasure lies and what they would rather avoid. Each person has a say in what pleasure and pain are, and each person's pleasure and pain count equally. We might illustrate this viewpoint by traveling back in our minds to nineteenth-century London. A well-to-do middle-class couple may feel that their greatest pleasure on a Saturday night is to don their fancy clothes, drive to Covent Garden in their shining coach, and go to the opera. The girl at Covent Garden who tries to sell them a bouquet of wilting violets as they pass by would probably not enjoy a trip to the opera as much as she would enjoy the bottle of gin she saves up for all week. Bentham would say she has as much right to relish her gin as the couple has a right to enjoy the opera. The girl can't tell the couple that gin is better, and they have no right to force their appreciation of the opera on her. For Bentham, what is good and bad for each person is a matter for each person to decide, and as such, his principle becomes a very *egalitarian* one.

The Hedonistic Calculus

How exactly do we choose a course of action? Before we decide what to do, we must calculate the probable consequences of our actions. This is what has become known as Bentham's *hedonistic calculus* (also called the *hedonic calculus*). We must, he says, investigate all aspects of the proposed consequences: (1) Its *intensity* — how intense will the pleasure or pain be? (2) Its *duration* — how long will it last? (3) Its *certainty or uncertainty* — how sure can we be that it will follow from our action? (4) Its *propinquity or remoteness* — how far away is it, in time and space? (5) Its *fecundity* — how big are the chances that it will be followed by a similar pleasure or a similar pain? (6) Its *purity* — how big are the chances that it will not be followed by the opposite sensation (pain after pleasure, for example)? (7) Its *extent* — how many people will be affected by our decision? After considering these questions, we must do the following:

> Sum up all the values of all the *pleasures* on the one side, and those of all the pains on the other. . . . Take the balance; which, on the side of *pleasure,* will give the general *good tendency* of the act, with respect to the total number or community of individuals concerned; if on the side of pain, the general *evil tendency,* with respect to the same community.

What do we have here? A simple, democratic principle that seems to make no unreasonable demands of personal sacrifice, given that one's own pleasure and pain count just as much as anybody else's. Furthermore, in line with the scientific dreams of the Age of Reason, the proper moral conduct is calculated mathematically; values are reduced to a calculation of pleasure and pain, a method accessible to everyone with a basic understanding of arithmetic. By calculating pleasures and pains one can presumably get a truly rational solution to any moral as well as nonmoral (morally neutral) problem.

This sounds very good, and yet there is a problem — actually, there are several. For one thing, from where does Bentham get his numerical values? Ascertaining that our pleasure from eating a second piece of mud pie will be intense but will not last long and very likely will be followed by pain and remorse will not supply us with any numerical values to add or subtract: We have to make up the numerical values! This may not be as difficult as it seems, though. It is surprising how much people can agree on a value system, if they can just decide what should count as top and bottom value. If they agreed on a system that goes from −10 to +10, for example, most people would agree to assigning specific numerical values to the various consequences of eating that second piece of pie. What value would be assigned to the

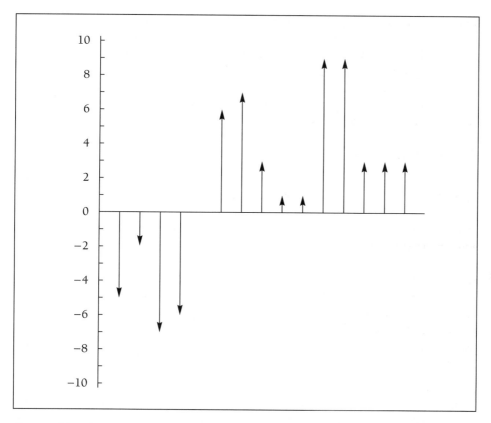

Sheer numbers: If we imagine the horizontal line representing a neutral position in terms of pain and pleasure, 0, the vertical line above 0 representing pleasure, and the line below 0 representing pain, we have a visual representation of the hedonistic calculus. Here all that matters is that the positive numbers outweigh the negative numbers. So if we have a scenario where many (humans or animals) are suffering but not much contentment is generated, the utilitarian would be against it. If only a few are suffering, and the many benefit from their suffering, it is the morally right course of action, according to utilitarianism.

aspect of intensity? Not a 10, because that probably would apply only to the first piece, but perhaps an 8. The *duration* of the pleasure might get a measly 2 or 3, and the chance that it would be followed by pleasure or pain certainly would be way down in the negative numbers, perhaps −5 or worse. As for evaluating how many people are affected by the decision, that could take into account friends and family who don't want you to gain weight or the person who owns the second piece of pie (which you stole), who will be deprived of it if you eat it. All such hypothetical situations can be ascribed a value if people can agree on a value system to use for all choices, from personal ones to far-reaching political decisions. (See Box 5.3 for a discussion of pleasure as an indicator of happiness.)

What this rating system adds up to is what most people would call the "pros and cons," those lists we sometimes make for ourselves when we are in severe doubt

Box 5.3   WHAT IS HAPPINESS?

One of the persistent problems in utilitarianism is the claim that the ultimate intrinsic value is happiness. We have already seen how the search for pleasure can lead to the hedonistic paradox (see Box 5.1), and this paradox is a problem for utilitarians as much as for anyone claiming that the ultimate reason we do things is to seek happiness. But is happiness the same as pleasure? Jeremy Bentham doesn't say, and indeed he doesn't care: For him, happiness is how *you* define it. John Stuart Mill defines happiness as distinct from both pleasure and contentment and views it as an intellectual achievement. Aristotle, who introduced the idea of happiness as a human goal to Western philosophy, also believed it was a result of rational activity and not a pursuit of pleasure. Few philosophers have

chosen Bentham's path and allowed for the possibility that happiness might have something to do with pleasure. An ancient story illustrates this tendency, not just within the Western tradition, to frown on the connection between happiness and physical comfort or indulgence: A Persian prince was told that in order to cure his unhappiness he had to wear the shirt of a happy man. The Persian prince now tried the shirts of lords, artists, merchants, soldiers, and fools, but it was to no avail. Happiness seemed to elude him. Finally he encountered a poor farmer singing behind his plow; the prince asked him if he was happy, and the farmer answered that he was. The prince then asked if he could have the farmer's shirt, and the farmer answered, "But I have no shirt!"

about what to do—what major field of study to choose, whether to go home for Thanksgiving or celebrate it with friends, whether to get married, whether to take a new job, and so on. The only difference is that in this system we assign numerical values to the pros and cons. Can such a list really help us make rational decisions? Bentham believed it was an infallible system for rational choice. A method that quantifies (makes measurable) the elusive qualities of life would certainly be useful, and several workplaces today are actually employing a form of hedonistic calculus in their hiring process: Applicants are rated according to their qualifications, and these qualifications are assigned numerical values (they are quantified); the person with the highest score presumably gets the job. Another area in which the calculus has had a rebirth is in the field of health care, where attempts are being made to create an objective measure for what is known as *quality of life* (see Chapter 7). One person's idea of quality of life may not be the same as another person's, however, and even in workplaces where such a hiring method is used, other, less rational, elements may play a part in the hiring process (such as the looks of the applicant or relation to the employer). People who have given Bentham's system a try in their own personal decision making often find that it may help in clarifying one's options, but the results are not always persuasive. You may end up with sixteen items on the con side and four on the pro side and still find yourself getting married or taking a new job simply because you want to so badly. There are parts of the human psyche that simply don't respond to rational arguments, and Bentham didn't have much appreciation for that. Interestingly enough, his godson and successor, John Stuart Mill, did have just such an appreciation, and we will look at his work shortly.

But suppose you actually make a detailed list of the consequences of your actions. How, exactly, do you decide on the values that you assign each consequence? In some cases it is easy, as for example when you compare school fees or driving distances. But if you want to decide whether to stay in school for the duration or quit and get a job and make fast money, how do you choose what things to put on your list? Critics of Bentham's approach say that if we assign a higher value to getting an education than to acquiring fast money, then it is because we are operating within a system that favors higher education; in other words, we are *biased,* and our choice of values reflects that bias. To put it another way, we rig the test even as we perform it. If we were operating within a system that favored making money—for instance, if we already had left school to make money—then our values would reflect that bias. The values, therefore, are truly arbitrary, depending on what we would like the outcome to be, and we can't trust the hedonistic calculus to give us an objective, mathematically certain picture of what to do. This does not mean such lists are useless; they can tell us much about ourselves and our own preferences and biases. However, they can do little more than that.

The Uncertain Future

Utilitarianism might still be able to offer a less presumptuous system, one designed to give guidance and material for reflection rather than objectively calculated solutions. Even with that kind of system, though, there are problems to be dealt with. One lies in the concept of *consequences* itself. Of course we can't claim that an action has any consequences before we actually have taken that action. The consequences we are evaluating are hypothetical; they have yet to occur. How can we decide once and for all whether an action is morally good if the consequences are still up in the air? We have to (1) make an educated guess and hope for the best, (2) act, and (3) wait to see the results. If we're lucky and wise, the results will be as positive as what we hoped for. But suppose they aren't? Before we learn the results, our good intentions are of course part of the plus side of the hedonistic calculus: If we intend to create beneficial consequences for as many as possible, it is a process that the utilitarian will approve of. But the true value of our action is not clear until the consequences are clear. You may intend to create much happiness, and your calculations may be educated, but your intentions may still be foiled by forces beyond your control. In that case, it is the *end result* that counts and not your fine intentions and calculations. How long do we have to wait until we know whether our actions were morally good or evil? It may take a long time before all the effects are known— maybe a hundred years or more. Critics of utilitarianism say it is just not reasonable to use a moral system that doesn't allow us to know whether what we did was morally right or wrong until some time in the far-off future. Furthermore, how will we ever be able to decide anything in the first place? Thousands—perhaps millions—of big and small consequences result from everything we do. Do we have to calculate them all? How can we ever make a quick decision if we have to go through such a complicated process every time?

Answers to such criticisms were provided by the philosopher and economist John Stuart Mill (1806–1873). For one thing, Mill says, we don't have to calculate every little effect of our action; we can rely on the common experience of humanity. Through the millennia, humans have had to make similar decisions all the time, and we can consider their successes and failures in deciding our own actions. (Because Mill had actually given up on calculating every action to an exact mathematical value, it was easier for him than for Bentham to allow for some uncertainty in future results.) What about having to wait a long time for future consequences to happen, in order to pass judgment on the morality of our action? Mill says all we have to do is wait a reasonable amount of time—a short wait for small actions, a longer wait for bigger actions. Mill relies on us to know intuitively what he means, and perhaps we do. But the problems inherent in utilitarianism are not solved with these suggestions, merely diffused a little.

The Moral Universe of Utilitarianism: Advantages and Problems of Sheer Numbers

Initially, the idea of creating as much pleasure as possible for as many as possible seems a positive one. If we read on in Bentham's writings, we even find that "the many" may not be limited to humans. Bentham's theory was so advanced for its time that it not only gave the right to seek pleasure and avoid pain to all humans, regardless of social standing, it also said that the criterion for who belongs in the moral universe is not who has the capability to speak or to reason but *who can suffer,* and surely suffering is not limited to human beings. (See Box 5.4 for a discussion of suffering and nonhuman animals.)

If we assume that the capacity to suffer (and feel pleasure) qualifies a living organism for inclusion in the moral universe, and if we believe that each individual's pleasure counts equally, we find ourselves with a dramatically expanded moral universe. Even today, the idea that all creatures who can suffer deserve to be treated with dignity does not meet with the approval of every policymaker. Moreover, if the decrease of suffering and the increase of happiness are all that counts for all these members of our moral universe, what does it mean for our decision if the happiness of some can be obtained only at the cost of the suffering of others? This is where we encounter the problem of *sheer numbers* in utilitarianism, because whatever creates more happiness for more individuals or decreases their pain is morally right *by definition.* If giving up animal-tested household products causes human housekeepers only minor inconvenience, then we have no excuse to keep using them, because major suffering is caused by such testing. However, if it could be shown that only a few animals would have to suffer (even if they would suffer horribly) so that an immense number of humans would find their housecleaning greatly eased, would it then be permissible to cause such suffering? Yes, if the pleasure gained from easy housecleaning in a large number of households could be added up and favorably compared to the immense suffering of only a very few nonhuman animals.

Box 5.4   WHO CAN SUFFER?

Jeremy Bentham's insistence that the moral universe be open to any creature who can suffer is still a controversial statement, and in Bentham's own day it was extremely radical. Of his influential contemporaries, only John Stuart Mill took up the idea that humans are not necessarily the only members of the moral realm; it was (and still is) standard procedure to view morality as something only humans can engage in or benefit from. Most arguments that exclude animals are based on the assumption that they can't speak or reason (which is why Bentham says this is irrelevant and asks, "Can they suffer?"). To most people, then and now, it is obvious that animals can suffer—all we have to do is observe an injured animal. But to some thinkers, this is not a foregone conclusion. An argument that used to be popular in theology was that humans suffer because Adam and Eve sinned against God in the Garden of Eden, and suffering was their, and their children's, punishment; since animals have not sinned against God, they can't suffer. A more influential argument in philosophy comes from René Descartes (1596–1650), otherwise known for opening up the gates of modern philosophy with his statement "I think, therefore I am." Descartes argued that only humans have minds; everything else in the world consists of matter only, including animals. If you have a mind, you can have awareness of suffering; if you have no mind, your body may be subjected to physical stress, but you won't know it. The dog whose tail is caught in the door will yelp, but that is no sign of feeling pain, according to Descartes—that is the way the dog is constructed, like a clock with moving parts (in today's jargon, the dog is *programmed* to yelp). The dog itself has no mind and feels nothing. (Descartes actually was a dog owner; according to legend, his dog's name was Monsieur Grat.) When challenged by Margaret Cavendish, the duchess of Newcastle, Descartes's answer was that if animals had minds, then oysters would have to have minds, too, and he found that ridiculous. Margaret Cavendish was a writer with an interest in science. Like most contemporary readers, she knew that there is a considerable difference between the nervous systems of dogs and oysters, but Descartes's viewpoint has had immense influence on the treatment of animals to this day.

Modern biology generally assumes that mammals and many other animals can feel pain, precisely because there is such a similarity between their nervous systems and ours. In addition, the capacity for suffering seems to be an evolutionary advantage; a being that can feel pain is more likely to be cautious, to survive, and to propagate.

The argument for doing whatever benefits more living creatures, human or non-human, is usually advanced with regard to animal testing of medical procedures that could benefit humans. But because sheer numbers are all that matter in utilitarianism, the housecleaning example works, too. Curing human ailments is not intrinsically "better" than helping humans clean their houses—what matters is the happiness that is created and the misery that is prevented. Suppose feline leukemia could be cured by subjecting ten humans to painful experiments. The humans would certainly suffer, but all cats would, from then on, be free of leukemia. For some, this type of example reveals the perversely narrow focus of utilitarianism; looking at pleasure and pain and adding them up are simply not enough. For others,

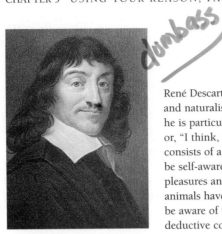

René Descartes (1596–1650), French philosopher, mathematician, and naturalist, known as the founder of modern philosophy; he is particularly famous for having said, "*Cogito, ergo sum,*" or, "I think, therefore I am." Descartes believed that a human consists of a body and a soul; thanks to the soul, humans can be self-aware and conscious of their bodies, including physical pleasures and pains. But since Descartes couldn't imagine that animals have souls, he had to conclude that animals couldn't be aware of their physical condition either, so the inevitable deductive conclusion was, for him, that animals can't feel pain.

examples like this one only confirm that all creatures matter, and no one's pain should be more or less important than anyone else's.

To focus on the problem, let's assume that we are faced with a situation in which some humans are sacrificed for the happiness and welfare of other humans. Suppose it is revealed that governments around the world have for years had a secret pact with aliens from outer space, whereby the governments have agreed to deny consistently that UFOs exist and to not interfere with occasional alien abductions of humans for medical experiments. In return, at the end of their experiments, the aliens will provide humanity with a cure for all viral diseases. For a great number of people this would be a trade well worth the suffering of the "specimens" involved—provided that they themselves would not be among the specimens. Indeed, some humans might even *volunteer* for the experiments, but let us assume, as a condition, that the human subjects are reluctant participants, and no volunteers are accepted. Although some people would gladly commit their fellow humans to death from suffering, others would insist that it is not right; somehow, these humans do not deserve such a fate, and the immense advantages to humankind forever do not really make up for it. In other words, some may have a moral sense that the price is too high, but utilitarianism can't acknowledge such a moral intuition, because its only moral criterion is one of sheer numbers. For many, the morality of utilitarianism is counterintuitive when applied to some very poignant human situations.

The UFO example is (or at least it is intended to be) fictional. But the late twentieth century revealed to us a number of real-life large-scale cases in which a number of people had unwittingly been made into guinea pigs for the sake of some greater cause. What if we could accomplish beneficial results for a large number of people or living beings at the cost of intolerable pain suffered by a few? Whether one sees immediate benefits to a population, such as security measures, or long-term benefits, such as medical knowledge, the price of pain and suffering, even death, was paid by human beings, not by choice but by force, for the sake of some higher goal. The Tuskegee syphilis experiment is a chilling example, but it doesn't end there.

Other morally questionable governmental practices have been revealed; see Box 4.5 for some examples. Such experiments have reduced people to being mere tools in someone else's agenda. A classic utilitarian will answer that, depending on the greatness and nature of the goal, the sacrifice and suffering might well be worth the price. But John Stuart Mill added that, in the long run, a population abusing a minority will reap not good results but social unrest, so such practices should be discouraged (see the subsequent section on act and rule utilitarianism).

Still, the salvation of humanity is a forceful argument. Let us suppose, however, that we are talking not about salvation from disease but about salvation from boredom. Television is already moving toward showing live or videotaped events involving human suffering and death; home movies are often the source of this footage, and this form of "entertainment" has become increasingly popular. Reality-based TV shows such as *Survivor* have flourished, although there are signs the trend has peaked. Is a future reality-based show with actual violence a possibility? Might viewers choose to watch real-time shows of criminals who are granted one television hour to run through a city or neighborhood, avoiding snipers and hoping to live through it all and win their freedom? The Romans watched Christians, slaves, criminals, prisoners of war, and wild animals fight each other, with much appreciation for the entertainment value of such events. If they had had the ability to televise the events, might we not assume that they would have done so, having recognized that "bread and circuses" (food and entertainment) would appease the unruly masses? According to the utilitarian calculation, a great number of people may be hugely entertained by the immense suffering of one or a few. How far are we allowed to let numbers run away with us in disregarding people's inherent right to fair treatment?

As you know, this would point out that under such circumstances, people start worrying about being victimized, and social unrest follows. Until that happens, though, utilitarians must conclude that there is justification in letting a large number of people enjoy the results of the suffering of a few (or even enjoy the suffering itself).

In the Narrative section you'll find several stories illustrating this problem of "sheer numbers": Ursula K. Le Guin's story about a child being tortured for the sake of communal happiness, "The Ones Who Walk Away from Omelas"; a selection from Dostoyevsky's *Brothers Karamazov;* and summaries of the films *Saving Private Ryan* and *Extreme Measures*. Once we start identifying the utilitarian sheer-numbers problem as one of disregard for the rights of the individual for the sake of the well-being of the many, we tend to be critical of any decision that would favor the happiness of the majority over the rights of a minority, and perhaps rightfully so. However, there are compelling scenarios that make us reevaluate the simple math of Bentham's utilitarianism: When push comes to shove, and hard decisions have to be made in a split second, saving the many by sacrificing the few may be the decision most of us would agree with. Think back to that dreadful day of September 11, with four airplanes being hijacked with the presumed intent to cause as much damage as possible to people and institutions. Three planes hit their targets: the World Trade Center towers and the Pentagon. But as you'll recall, the fourth plane, Flight 93, did not reach its intended target, in all likelihood the Capitol, because of the heroic resolve of the passengers. But in the aftermath we also learned that had the passengers not acted, Flight 93 would probably not have reached its target anyway, because Air Force fighter jets were already poised to escort the plane down or, if necessary, shoot it down. This came as a shock to many Americans, in particular when the government announced that *any* plane on a collision course with a civilian or military structure would be regarded as a threat and would be shot down. Here we see the principle of utility at work in a desperate situation: Sacrifice the few on the plane rather than take a chance and risk the lives of the many on the ground and the security of our institutions. Some might say, "But those people on the plane were going to die when the plane hit the building anyway, so what difference did it make if they died sooner rather than later?" The difference is in the attitude regarding the few as expendable. Furthermore, it isn't a *given* that they would die anyway. So if we could limit terrible consequences for a large number of people by sacrificing a few innocent people, would the decision be acceptable, even if we happened to be among the unfortunate few ourselves? If we say "yes," where do we draw the line? How do we define "terrible consequences"? And, if we say "no," are we seriously advocating that it is better for the many to perish in the name of fairness than for the many to survive at the cost of the lives of the few?

John Stuart Mill: Another Utilitarian Vision

Bentham was not alone in designing the theory of utilitarianism. He and his close friend James Mill worked out the specifics of the new moral system together. Mill's son John Stuart Mill was a very bright boy, and James Mill's ambition was to develop his son's talents and intelligence as much as possible and as fast as possible. The boy responded well, learned quickly, and was able to read Greek and Latin at an early age. Throughout his childhood he was groomed to become a scientist. He was tutored privately and performed marvelously until he came to a halt at the age of twenty, struck by a nervous breakdown. His crisis was quiet and polite, in accordance with his nature: He went on with his work, and few people close to him realized what was going on; but internally he stopped in his tracks and in a very modern sense decided to "get in touch with himself," for he had come to the realization that despite his intense studying, one part of his education was pitifully incomplete. He knew much about how to think, but he didn't know how to *feel;* as a child he had been emotionally deprived and had never been allowed to have playmates other than his siblings, and in terms of his emotional life he now felt totally inadequate. (If you remember from Chapter 2 the emphasis that was placed on feelings during the Age of Romanticism, you'll have an even better understanding of what Mill went through, because he was a young man of twenty when the Age of Romanticism was at its peak.) In the months before his breakdown, he had engaged in debates, published articles, helped edit a major work by Bentham, and was probably beginning to suffer from what we today call burnout—at the very least, he was overworked.

John Stuart Mill (1806–1873), English philosopher and economist. Believing that utilitarianism was the only reasonable moral
system, Mill nevertheless saw Jeremy Bentham's version as rather
crude and created a more sophisticated version of the principle
of utility, taking into consideration the qualitative differences
between pleasures.

Later in life, Mill described his breakdown in his *Autobiography;* in modern terminology, he put a spin on it that reflected his rebellion against Jeremy Bentham:

> From the winter of 1821, when I first read Bentham . . . I had what might truly be called
> an object in life; to be a reformer of the world. My conception of my own life was entirely
> identified with this object. . . . But the time came when I awakened from this as from a
> dream. It was in the autumn of 1826. I was in a dull state of nerves, such as everybody is
> occasionally liable to; unsusceptible to enjoyment or pleasurable excitement. . . . In this
> frame of mind it occurred to me to put the question directly to myself: "Suppose that all
> your objects in life were realized; that all the changes in institutions and opinions which
> you are looking forward to, could be completely effected at this very instant: would this
> be a great joy and happiness to you?" And an irrepressible self-consciousness distinctly an-
> swered, "No!" At this my heart sank within me: the whole foundation on which my life
> was constructed fell down. . . . I seemed to have nothing left to live for. . . . If I had loved
> anyone sufficiently to make confiding my griefs a necessity, I should not have been in the
> condition I was.

What Mill read into his breakdown later in life was that his father's intellectual
training and Bentham's philosophy had let him down—the utilitarian greatest-
happiness principle might lead to happiness for the many, but it didn't necessarily
lead to happiness for the utilitarian. Mill, in his *Autobiography,* uses this term to ram
a lesson home: You don't find happiness by looking for it but by enjoying life along
the way as you focus on other things. "Ask yourself whether you are happy, and you
cease to be so." In his crisis, Mill rediscovered the truth of the paradox of hedonism:
The harder you look for happiness, the more likely it is to elude you. But what really happened to himself psychologically may not have been clear to Mill at all. For
one thing, he was overworked, and winter was approaching. For another, he found
himself a cerebral intellectual in the midst of the most feeling-oriented period so far
in Western history. For a third, he was lonely and became depressed; he had what
we've come to know as a severe case of "the blues." But the loneliness problem didn't
last long. Neither did his disenchantment with utilitarianism—he just stopped looking for self-gratification in it and focused on the goal of improving the world.

Mill began exploring the world of feelings—music, poetry, literature—and later he went abroad to the European continent and traveled (as did the Romantic painters and poets). During this period he took time out to reexamine his life and his future, turned his back on the sciences, and decided to "go into his father's business" and become a social thinker. As a social thinker he became one of the most influential persons of the nineteenth century, laying the foundation for many of the political ideas in the Western world on both the liberal and the conservative sides.

Mill's aim was to take his godfather and father's theory of utilitarianism and redesign it to fit a more sophisticated age. What had seemed overwhelmingly important to Bentham—a more just legal system—was no longer the primary goal, due to the realization that without proper education for the general population, true social equality would not be obtained. Also, Mill realized that Bentham's version of utilitarianism had several flaws. For one thing, it was too simple; it relied on a very straightforward system of identifying good with pleasure and evil with pain, without specifying the nature of pleasure and pain. (Some say this was actually one of the strengths of early utilitarianism, but Mill saw it as a serious deficiency.) Bentham's version also assumed that people were so rational they would always follow the moral calculations. Mill pointed out, however, that even if people are clearly shown it would give them and others more overall pleasure to change their course of action, they are likely to continue doing what they are used to because people are creatures of habit; our emotions, rather than cool deliberation, often dictate what we do. We can't, therefore, rely on our rationality to the extreme degree that Bentham thought we could. (This doesn't mean, of course, that we can't *educate* children and adults to use their heads more profitably.) We will return to the education question later, but first we look at how Mill decided to redesign the theory of utilitarianism.

Mill was a more complex person than Bentham, and his theory reflects this complexity. For Mill the idea that humans seek pleasure and that moral goodness lies in obtaining that pleasure is only half the story—but it is the half that is most frequently misunderstood. What do people think when they hear this idea? That all that counts is easy gratification of any desire they may have—in other words, a "doctrine worthy only of swine," as Mill says, repeating the words of the critics of utilitarianism. And because people reject the notion of seeking only swinish pleasures, they reject utilitarianism as an unworthy theory. They get upset, said Mill, precisely because they are not pigs and want more out of life than a pig could ever want. People are simply not content with basic pleasures, and a good moral and social theory should reflect this. Furthermore, says Mill, all theories that have advocated happiness have been accused of talking about easy gratification, but that is an unfair criticism when applied to utilitarianism. Even Epicurus held that there are many things in life other than physical pleasures that can bring us happiness, and there is nothing in utilitarianism that says we have to define pleasure and happiness as mere gratification of physical desires.

Why was Mill so uneasy about being accused of seeking gratification of physical desires? Consider the changing times in which he lived. When Mill wrote his book *Utilitarianism* (1863), the British Empire was twenty-six years into the Victorian era,

Harriet Hardy Taylor Mill (1807–1858) was a chief source of inspiration for her longtime friend and later husband John Stuart Mill. Her views on individual rights are reflected in Mill's book *On Liberty* (1859), published immediately after her death. They did not agree on everything, though: Mill believed that when a woman marries, she must give up working outside the home; Taylor believed that women have a right to employment regardless of their marital status and that no-fault divorce should be available. However, the spouses seemed to be in agreement on most other issues and found in each other what we today call a soul mate. Mill grieved deeply when she died and moved to a house close to the cemetery where she was laid to rest, so he could visit her grave often.

and morals had subtly undergone a shift since Bentham's day; preoccupation with physical pleasures was, on the whole, frowned upon by the middle classes, more so than in the previous generation — it was not considered proper to display such indulgence. For many this signifies an age of hypocrisy, of double standards, but it would be unfair to accuse Mill of such double standards, because several of his truly innovative social ideas stemmed from his indignation toward this preoccupation with the way other people choose to live. However, it may have been a sign of the times that Mill felt compelled to reassure his readers that they could be followers of utilitarianism without being labeled hedonists.

Some believe there is also a personal side to the story. In his early twenties, Mill, having earlier worried that he didn't have any knowledge of feelings, fell head over heels in love with a young married woman, Harriet Taylor, and the feeling was mutual. They maintained a relationship for almost twenty years, until her husband died, and then they finally got married. Their relationship had become an open secret over the years, even to Mr. Taylor. (Being honest people, they apparently told him of their feelings, but he was also assured that they had no intention of breaking up the Taylor marriage.) It has generally been assumed that they were sexually involved, but judging from their correspondence, it may well have been a platonic friendship until their wedding. Their letters testify to Mill's later version of utilitarianism: They both seem to agree that spiritual pleasures and intellectual companionship are more valuable than physical gratification. John Stuart Mill prepared his book *Utilitarianism* during the years of their marriage, but when it was published in 1863, Harriet was no longer alive. She died (probably of tuberculosis) less than ten years after they got married; however, Mill's moral and political writings were clearly inspired by their intellectual discussions over three decades. (See Box 5.5 for a discussion of Mill's views on women's rights.)

What, then, does Mill propose? That some pleasures are more valuable, "higher," than others. That on the whole, humans prefer to hold on to their dignity and strive for truly fulfilling experiences rather than settle for easy contentment. *It is better to be a human dissatisfied than a pig satisfied, better to be Socrates dissatisfied than a fool satisfied,* says Mill. Even if the great pleasures in life require some effort — for instance,

Box 5.5   MILL AND THE WOMEN'S CAUSE

John Stuart Mill is today recognized as the first influential male speaker for political equality between men and women in modern Western history. (In England, Mary Wollstonecraft published her *Vindication of the Rights of Women* in 1792, but already in 1673 the French author Poulain de la Barre, a student of Descartes, had published *De l'égalité des deux sexes*, in which he argued for total equality between men and women because of their equality in reasoning power. This book, however, was largely ignored for a long time.) Mill's book *The Subjection of Women* (1869) revealed to his readers the abyss of inequality separating the lives of men and women in what was then considered a modern society. His exposé of this inequality was a strong contributing factor in women's obtaining the right to vote in England, as well as elsewhere in the Western world. In 1866 Mill, then a member of the British Parliament, had tried to get a measure passed that would establish gender equality in England. The measure failed, but Mill had succeeded in drawing attention to the issue. It is often mentioned in this context that Mill was inspired by his longtime friend and later wife, Harriet Taylor. Scholars now believe that Mill's fight for women's rights was not just a matter of subtle inspiration from Mrs. Taylor but a direct result of their long and detailed intellectual discussions, for Mrs. Taylor was well educated and an intellectual in her own right.

one has to learn math in order to understand the joy of solving a mathematical problem—it is worth the effort, because the pleasure is greater than if you had just remained passive.

Now the question becomes, Who is to say which pleasures are the higher ones and which are the lower ones? We seem predisposed to assume that the physical pleasures are the lower ones, but need that be the case? Mill proposes a test: We must ask people who are familiar with both kinds of pleasure, and whatever they choose as the higher goal is the ultimate answer. Suppose we gather a group of people who sometimes order a pizza and beer and watch *Monday Night Football* but also occasionally go out to a French restaurant before watching *Masterpiece Theatre* on PBS. We ask them which activity—pizza and football or French food and *Masterpiece Theatre*—is the higher pleasure. If the test works, we must accept it if the majority say that on the whole they think pizza and football is the higher pleasure. But will Mill accept that? This is the drawback of his test—it appears that he will not:

> Capacity for the nobler feelings is in most natures a very tender plant, easily killed, not only by hostile influences, but by mere want of sustenance; and in the majority of young persons it speedily dies away if the occupations to which their position in life has devoted them, and the society into which it has thrown them, are not favorable to keeping that higher capacity in exercise. Men lose their high aspirations as they lose their intellectual tastes, because they have not time or opportunity for indulging them; and they addict themselves to inferior pleasures not because they deliberately prefer them, but because they are either the only ones to which they have access or the only ones which they are any longer capable of enjoying.

Dilbert by Scott Adams

© 2001. DILBERT reprinted by permission of United Features Syndicate, Inc.

One of the deficiencies of utilitarianism is that if the final goal of any action is to feel good, it doesn't matter *what* makes us feel good. This *Dilbert* cartoon hits the nail on the head: If succeeding is supposed to make us feel good, but failure doesn't make us feel bad (because some believe that feeling good is important for people to maintain their self-esteem no matter how they do it), what is the incentive for success?

What does this mean? It means if you vote for pizza and football as the overall winner, Mill will claim you have lost the capacity for enjoying gourmet French food and intellectual television (which demands some attention from your intellect). In other words, he has rigged his own test. This has caused some critics to voice the opinion that Mill is an intellectual snob, a "cultural imperialist" trying to impose his own standards on the general population. And the immediate victim of this procedure? The egalitarian principle that was the foundation of Bentham's version of utilitarianism — that one person equals one vote regarding what is pleasurable and what is painful — collapses under Mill's test. According to him, we have to go to the "authorities of happiness" to find out what it is that everybody ought to desire.

If we perform Mill's test and ask individuals who seem to know of many kinds of pleasure what they prefer, we may get responses that Mill would not have accepted, because some people may indeed favor physical pleasures over intellectual or spiritual ones; however, a recent study claimed (with no reference to Mill whatsoever) that people who have a spiritual side are happier overall than are people whose lives are completely focused on material pleasures. Now, it is questionable in itself whether it is at all possible to put together reliable statistics on this topic, but Mill would probably have welcomed the survey: It is not merely because higher, intellectual, or spiritual pleasures are somehow finer that he recommends them; it is because they presumably yield a higher form of happiness in the long run than do pleasures of easy gratification. (Box 5.6 explores Mill's attempt at proving that higher pleasures are more desirable and introduces the concept of the naturalistic fallacy.)

Be that as it may, the idea of a "spiritual life" is rather vague and intangible, so let us use an example that is more concrete: learning to play a musical instrument. Anyone who has attempted it knows that for the first few months it usually doesn't sound very good, practicing is hard work, and you'll be tempted to give up. But if you

Box 5.6   THE NATURALISTIC FALLACY

John Stuart Mill acknowledges there is no proof that happiness is the ultimate value because no founding principles can be proved, yet he offers a proof by analogy. This proof has bothered philosophers ever since, because it actually does more harm than good to Mill's own system of thought. The analogy goes like this: The only way we can prove that something is visible is when we know people actually see it. Likewise, the only way we can prove that something is desirable is when we know people actually desire it. Everyone desires happiness, so happiness is therefore the ultimate goal. Why does this not work as an analogy? It doesn't work because being "visible" is not analogous to being "desirable." When we say that something is visible, we are describing what people actually see. But when we say that something is desirable, we are not describing what people desire. If a lot of people desire drugs, we do not therefore conclude that drugs are "desirable," because "desirable" means that something *should be* desired. The problem, however, goes deeper. Even if it were true that we could find out what is morally desirable by doing a nose count, why should we then have to conclude that because a lot of people desire something, there should be a moral requirement that we all desire it? In other words, we are stepping from "is" (from a descriptive statement that says something is desired) to "ought" (to a normative/prescriptive statement that says something ought to be de-

sired), and as the philosopher David Hume pointed out, there is nothing in a descriptive statement that allows us to proceed from what people actually do to a rule that states what people ought to do. This step, known as the *naturalistic fallacy,* is commonly taken by thinkers, politicians, writers, and other people of influence, but it is nevertheless a dangerous step to take. We can't make a policy based solely on what is the case. For instance, if it were to turn out that women actually are better parents than men by nature, it still would not be fair to conclude that men ought not to be single fathers (or that all women ought to be mothers), because we can't pass from a simple statement of fact to a statement of policy. This does not mean we can't make policies based on fact; that would be preposterous. What we have to do is insert a value statement—our opinion about what is good or bad, right or wrong (a so-called hidden premise)—so we can go from a fact (such as "there are many teen pregnancies today") to the hidden premise ("We believe teen pregnancies are bad for teen girls, for their babies, and for society") and then to the conclusion ("We must try to lower the number of teen pregnancies"). In that case, someone who doesn't agree with our conclusion can still agree with the fact stated, but disagree with our hidden premise. Although this idea is occasionally contested by various thinkers, it remains one of philosophy's ground rules.

stick with it, there will probably come a day when you feel you can play what you want the way you want, and even play with others, giving joy to yourself and your listeners. The same process occurs, of course, with many other skills that take hard work to learn but yield a lot of gratification when acquired: speaking a foreign language, for example, or painting with watercolors. So now Mill can step in and ask his question: If you had the choice, would you give up that skill, provided you could get all those hours of practice time back so you could spend them watching sitcoms? I doubt that a single one of us would say yes; identifying our artistic skill as the higher pleasure in spite of all the hours of hard work, tedium, and frustration leading up to it is no challenge at all. It seems that many of us, including Mill, and perhaps also Socrates, would indeed rather be temporarily dissatisfied if it meant we'd put the easy gratifications on hold for something higher and better down the road. But we'd still have to ask whether all skills that have taken an effort to acquire would qualify as "higher pleasures" according to Mill—as well as according to us: How about sports? Computer games? Or con artistry?

Mill's Political Vision: Equality and No Harm to Others

Did Mill achieve what he wanted? Certainly he wanted to redesign utilitarianism so that it reflected the complexity of a cultured population, but did he intend to set himself up as a cultural despot? It appears that what he wanted was something else entirely. Whereas Bentham wanted the girl who sold flowers at Covent Garden to be able to enjoy her gin in peace, Mill wants to *educate* her so that she won't *need* her gin anymore and will be able to experience the glorious pleasures enjoyed by the middle-class couple who have learned to appreciate the opera. What Mill had in mind, in other words, was probably not elitism, but the notion that the greater pleasure can be derived from achievement. We feel a special fulfillment if we've worked hard on a math problem or a piece of music or a painting and we finally get it right. Mill thought this type of pleasure should be made available to everyone with a capacity for it. This Mill saw as equality of a higher order, based on general education. Once such education is attained, the choices of the educated person are his or hers alone, and nobody has the right to interfere. However, until such a level is achieved, society has a right to gently inform its children and childlike adults about what they ought to prefer.

This sounds today like paternalism, and there is much in Mill's position that supports this point of view. In order to look more closely at Mill's ideas of what is best for people, we must take a look at what has become known as the *harm principle*.

Although the principle of utility provides a general guideline for personal as well as political action in terms of increasing happiness and decreasing unhappiness, it says very little about the circumstances under which one might justifiably become involved in changing other people's lives for the better. Mill had very specific ideas about the limitations of such involvement; in his essay *On Liberty* (1859), he examines the proper limits of government control. Because history has progressed from a time when rulers preyed upon their populations and the populations had to be protected from the rulers' despotic actions to a time when democratic rulers, in principle, *are* the people, the idea of absolute authority on the part of rulers should no longer be a danger to the people. But reality shows us that this is not the case, because we now must face the *tyranny of the majority*. In other words, those who now need protection are minorities (and here Mill thinks of political minorities) who may wish to conduct their lives in ways different from the ways of the majority and its idea of what is right and proper. As an answer to the question of how much the social majority is allowed to exert pressure on the minority, Mill proposes the harm principle:

That principle is, that the sole end for which mankind are warranted, individually or collectively, in interfering with the liberty of action of any of their number, is self-protection.

That the only purpose for which power can be rightfully exercised over any member of a civilized community, against his will, is to prevent harm to others. His own good, either physical or moral, is not a sufficient warrant. He cannot rightfully be compelled to do or forbear because it will be better for him to do so, because it will make him happier, because, in the opinions of others, to do so would be wise, or even right. These are good reasons for remonstrating with him, or reasoning with him, or persuading him, or entreating him, but not for compelling him, or visiting him with any evil in case he do otherwise. To justify that, the conduct from which it is desired to deter him must be calculated to produce evil to someone else. The only part of the conduct of anyone, for which he is amenable to society, is that which concerns others. In the part which merely concerns himself, his independence is, of right, absolute. Over himself, over his own body and mind, the individual is sovereign.

So how does this policy go with his statement four years later that higher pleasures are better for people than lower pleasures and that some people aren't capable of knowing what is good for them? Some Mill critics say that they don't go well together at all—that Mill is claiming in one text that people have a right to choose their own poison, and in the other that they haven't. But we can perhaps find a middle way: What Mill is saying in *On Liberty* is that people, if they so choose, should be allowed to follow their own tastes; what he is saying in *Utilitarianism* is that everybody should be allowed to be exposed to higher pleasures through education, so they might be able to make better choices—but he is not going to force anyone who is adult and in control of his or her mental faculties to submit to a life ruled by someone else's taste. At least this is a possible reading of Mill that brings the two viewpoints together. (See Box 5.7 for an application of the harm principle to the issue of the legalization of drugs.)

The harm principle has had extremely far-reaching consequences. Built in part on John Locke's theory of negative rights (see Chapter 7), that had had great influence not only in the United Kingdom, but also on the Constitution of the United States, Mill's theory helped define two political lines of thought that, paradoxically, are now at odds with each other. We usually refer to Mill's view as *classical liberalism* because of its emphasis on personal liberty. The idea of civil liberties—the rights of citizens, within their right to privacy, to do what they want provided that they do no harm and to have their government ensure that as little harm and as much happiness as possible is created for as many people as possible—is also a cornerstone of modern liberalism. But the notions of personal liberty and noninterference by the government have also become key in the political theory of *laissez-faire,* the hands-off approach that requires as little government interference as possible, primarily in private enterprise. The idea behind laissez-faire is that if we all look after our own business and no authorities make our business theirs, then we all are better off, which is today considered a *conservative* economic philosophy, expressed in its extreme form by the Libertarian Party.

The limitations of the right to privacy are more numerous than might be apparent at first glance. For one thing, what exactly does it mean that we are accountable to society only for our conduct that concerns others? What Mill had in mind certainly included the right of consenting adults to engage in sexual activity in the

Box 5.7   THE HARM PRINCIPLE AND DRUG LEGALIZATION

John Stuart Mill's harm principle, that the only purpose of interfering with the life of someone is to prevent harm to others, has been applied in many social and political debates, with the general result that we see how ambiguous the principle really is. Examples are the euthanasia debate (see Chapter 7), the debate about "victimless crimes" such as (presumably) prostitution, and the discussion about the legalization of drugs.

A general utilitarian view of the legalization of drugs does not take a stand on whether drugs in themselves are "good" or "bad" but on whether more misery (or happiness) in the long run will be created through making them legally available than through prohibiting them. But remember that the harm principle sets limits to the "general-happiness principle" because it keeps us from interfering with people *for their own sake,* unless they are harming others. You can't force someone to try out someone else's model for happiness (and by now you have probably noticed that Mill's own theory of higher pleasures doesn't quite go well with his harm principle, because he believed people ought to be educated so they could enjoy the higher pleasures, even though they might not want to give up their lower pleasures).

Arguments in favor of drug legalization generally include these:

- The war on drugs isn't working—it is costly and clogs the jails with drug offenders; furthermore, drugs are still being brought across the borders.

- If drugs were legalized, they would be safer because they would be controlled by the state, and the black market would disappear. Drugs would become less expensive, and addicts wouldn't have to turn to crime in order to feed their habit.

- Heavy drug users could be helped by the state, and people who could manage their own drug use could be left to themselves; after all, people who can manage their own drinking are not criminalized.

The harm principle obviously applies here: If a person does no one else harm by a moderate drug intake, then he or she should be allowed to continue using drugs. (This is the drug policy of the Libertarian Party.) This is where advocates of drug legalization usually seek Mill's support. But we should not draw hasty conclusions. If we look at the issue from a more realistic perspective, do we still have a situation that involves only individuals who are mature enough to manage their own habits?

- The fact that the war on drugs isn't working is no reason to give it up. If jails are being inundated with drug offenders, the solution is not to decriminalize drug use but to educate children about drugs before they start using.

- Will crime go down? Will the black market disappear? Will drugs be safer? Only if you live in a fantasy world. Cigarettes are legal, but there is a huge black market for tobacco, smuggling is big business, and even with cheap drugs there will be some who can't afford them and will turn to crime. If drug legalization involves regulation (safer drugs), then there will surely arise a black market for unregulated drugs, which would begin the cycle again.

- Certainly it is a good idea for the state to help heavy users—individual states already do that. And it is also possible that many people could be completely responsible with a drug habit, just as many are responsible in their enjoyment of alcohol (which is, of course, a drug). But—and this is where the harm principle takes a turn—imagine all those people, young people in particular, who refrain from drugs simply because they are illegal. With drug legalization, that obstacle is removed; this means there will be many more people

(continued)

Box 5.7   THE HARM PRINCIPLE AND DRUG LEGALIZATION
(continued)

on the streets who are under the influence, endangering themselves *and* others in traffic, not to mention creating lifelong dependencies.

So opponents of drug legalization are saying that, overall, legalization will cause more harm than continued drug legislation. In addition, even though one individual may not be directly harming anyone else, he or she may serve as a role model of drug use for others less mature or responsible. Mill only considered direct harm to others a reason to interfere, not this kind of indirect harm. However, later critics as well as supporters of the harm principle have argued that the line between direct and indirect harm is often blurred. A bad role model may cause more obvious and direct harm to an impressionable child than to an adult who is supposed to

be able to distinguish right from wrong. So the harm principle may be used to argue against drug legalization. The issue of medical use of drugs, such as marijuana, may be different, because drugs for medical use are already part of our culture. The question of legislating alcohol as a drug of course has similarities with the drug issue: Alcohol directly endangers not just the person under the influence, but others as well; MADD (Mothers Against Drunk Drivers) and other victims of alcohol-related accidents and their relatives can attest to that. But there is a difference: Most other drugs are taken strictly for their effect; alcohol is very often consumed not for its effect, but for its taste, and the intake need not reach a level where a person is a risk to others.

privacy of their own homes, regardless of what any "moral majority" might feel about the issue. In such cases, only nosy neighbors might be "concerned," and for Mill their right to concern would be proportionate to the extent that they would be exposed to the activities of the couple in question. In other words, if it takes binoculars for you to become exposed to a situation (and hence become "concerned"), then put aside your binoculars and mind your own business.

But what about, say, a teenage girl who decides to put an end to her life because her boyfriend broke up with her? Might that fall within the harm principle? Is she harming only herself, so that society has no right to interfere? Here Mill might answer in several ways. First, she is harming not only herself but her family as well, who would grieve for her and feel guilty for not having stepped in. There is also the problem of role models. If other teens in the same situation learn about her suicide, they might think it would be a good idea to follow her example, and more harm would be caused. But when does indirect harm ever end? Doesn't it spread like rings in water? Mill himself would not allow for indirect harm, such as the harm caused by flawed role models, to be an obvious cause for the interference of authorities. To him, an adult should not be prevented from doing what he or she wants to do just because some other adult might imitate their actions, but only if his or her action (such as a policeman being drunk on the job—Mill's own example) is a likely cause for direct harm to others. You may draw your own conclusions about current discussions concerning direct and indirect harm, such as the debate surrounding helmet laws. In the late 1990s an issue arose where the question of direct versus indirect harm became quite relevant: Militant anti-abortion groups created a website, "The Nuremberg Files," where names and addresses of doctors performing abortions were listed, with the presumed underlying intention that these doctors, labeled "baby butchers," should be targeted and harassed—perhaps even killed. An Oregon jury found the activists guilty of inciting violence and sentenced them to pay $107 million to Planned Parenthood. But in March 2001 the Ninth Circuit Court ruled that the website was protected by the First Amendment (freedom of speech). In October 2001 the appeals court nullified the earlier ruling and decided to rehear the case, presumably under the assumption that if someone takes it upon himself or herself to act on information supplied by the website, it is no longer a matter of free speech, but a direct call to violence. So would harm caused by the website be called indirect or direct harm, in your opinion? It is clear that Mill's interpretation of his own harm principle still engenders heated debate. As for our example of the suicidal teenage girl, Mill would most certainly add the following: This situation does not fall under the harm principle, because the girl is (1) not an adult, and (2) not in a rational frame of mind:

> This doctrine is meant to apply only to human beings in the maturity of their faculties. We are not speaking of children, or of young persons below the age which the law may fix as that of manhood or womanhood. Those who are still in a state to require being taken care of by others, must be protected against their own actions as well as against external injury. For the same reason, we may leave out of consideration those backward states of society in which the [human] race itself may be considered as in its nonage. . . . Despotism is a legitimate mode of government in dealing with barbarians, provided the end be their improvement, and the means justified by actually effecting that end. Liberty, as a principle, has no application to any state of things anterior to the time when mankind have become capable of being improved by free and equal discussion. . . . But as soon as mankind have attained the capacity of being guided to their own improvement by conviction or persuasion (a period long since reached in all nations with whom we need here concern ourselves), compulsion . . . is no longer admissible as a means to their own good, and justifiably only for the security of others.

With this addition to the harm principle, Mill certainly makes it clear that children are excluded, but so is anyone who, in Mill's mind, belongs to a "backward" state of society. Again, we see evidence of Mill's complexity: He adamantly wants to protect civil liberties, but he is also paternalistic: Whoever is not an "adult" by his definition must be guided or coerced to comply with existing rules. Individuals as well as whole peoples who fall outside of the "adult" category must be governed by others until they reach sufficient maturity to take affairs into their own hands. Critics have seen this as a defense of not merely cultural but also political imperialism: There are peoples who are too primitive to rule themselves, so someone else has to do it for them and bring them up to Western standards. Who are these peoples? We may assume that they include the native-born peoples of old British colonies. Since Mill made his living not as a philosophy professor but as a Chief Examiner at India House, East India Company, which administered the colony of India (his father, James Mill, had worked there for years and was the author of a lengthy work on the history of India), his knowledge of colony affairs came from the perspective of the colony power. This viewpoint, sometimes referred to as "the white man's bur-den," is very far from being acceptable in our era, but is it fair to accuse Mill of being an imperialist? Perhaps, especially if we take into account that Mill published his piece in 1859, and two years earlier the British Empire had been shocked by the so-called Sepoy mutiny in northern India, in which hundreds of British officers and their wives and children had been murdered by Indian infantry soldiers in the British-Indian army. This mutiny was the result of long-standing clashes and mis-understandings between the two cultural groups, after a hundred years of British do-minion and (as many would describe it) exploitation. In the aftermath of the mutiny, India was taken over by the British Crown and ruled as a part of the empire. Mill was appalled at the mutiny but also at the take-over by the British government, and he retired, declining to take part in the new government. His chief aim seems to have been perpetuating not the British Empire but the utilitarian idea of maximizing hap-piness for the greatest number and minimizing pain and misery on a global scale. If Mill was biased toward the British way of life, it may be understandable: That way of life was in many ways the best the planet Earth had to offer in the nineteenth cen-tury for those with access to a good education. It was, in our terms, an extremely "civilized" culture, at least for the upper and middle classes. Perhaps, then, we can think of Mill not merely as an intellectual snob, but also as an educator who wanted to see everybody get the same good chances in life that he got and enjoy life as much as he did.

Act and Rule Utilitarianism

In the twentieth century it became clear to philosophers attracted to utilitarianism that there were severe problems inherent in the idea that a morally right act is an act that makes as many people as possible happy. One flaw is that, as we saw previ-ously, it is conceivable many people will achieve much pleasure from the misery of a few others, and even in situations where people don't know that their happiness is achieved by the pain of others, this is still an uncomfortable thought. It is especially so if one believes in the Golden Rule (as John Stuart Mill did), which states that we should do for others what we would like done for ourselves and refrain from doing to others what we would not like done to ourselves. Mill himself was aware of the problem and allowed that in the long run a society in which a majority abuses a mi-nority is not a good society. That still means we have to explain why the *first* cases of happiness occurring from the misery of others are wrong, even before they have established themselves as a pattern with increasingly bad consequences. In a sense, Mill tried to address the problem, suggesting that utilitarianism be taken as a gen-eral policy to be applied to general situations. He did not, however, develop the idea further within his own philosophy.

Others have taken up the challenge and suggested it is just that particular for-mulation of utilitarianism which creates the problem; given another formulation, the problem disappears. If we stay with the *classical* formulation, the principle of utility goes like this: *Always do whatever act will create the greatest happiness for the greatest number of people.* In this version we are stuck with the problems we saw earlier; for example, the torture of innocents may bring about great pleasure for a large group of people. The Russian author Dostoyevsky explored this thought in his novel *The Brothers Karamazov:* Suppose your happiness, and everyone else's, is bought by the suffering of an innocent child? (We look more closely at this idea at the end of this chapter.) It is not hard to see this as a Christian metaphor, with Jesus' suffering as the condition of happiness for humans, but there is an important difference: Jesus was a volunteer; an innocent child is not. In any event, a utilitarian, by definition, would have to agree that if a great deal of suffering could be alleviated by putting an innocent person through hell, then doing so would be justified. Putting nonhuman animals or entire populations of humans through hell would also be justified. The glorious end (increased happiness for a majority) will in any event justify the means, even if the means violate these beings' right to life or to fair treatment.

Suppose we reformulate utilitarianism. Suppose we say, *Always do whatever type of act will create the greatest happiness for the greatest number of people.* What is the result? If we set up a one-time situation, such as the torture of an innocent person for the sake of others' well-being, it may work within the first formulation. But if we view it as a *type* of situation — one that is likely to recur again and again because we have now set up a *rule* for such types of situations — it becomes impermissible: The consequences of torturing a *lot* of innocent people will not bring about great happiness for anyone in the long run. Is this, perhaps, what Mill was trying to say? This new formulation is referred to as *rule utilitarianism,* and it is advocated by many modern utilitarians who wish to distance themselves from the uncomfortable implications of the classical theory, now referred to as *act utilitarianism*. If this new version is used, they say, we can focus on the good consequences of a certain type of act rather than on the singular act itself. It may work once for a student to cheat on a final, but cheating as a rule is not only dangerous (the student herself is likely to be found out) but also immoral to the rule utilitarian, because very bad consequences would occur if everyone were to cheat. Professors would get wise in no time, and nobody would graduate. Students and professors would be miserable. Society would miss out on a lot of well-educated college graduates. The Golden Rule is in this way fortified: Don't do something if you can't imagine it as a rule for everybody, because a rule not suited for everyone can have no good overall consequences.

Some critics have objected that not everything we do can be made into a rule with good consequences. After all, lots of the things we like to do are unique to us, and why should we assume that just because one person likes to collect movie memorabilia, the world would be happier if everyone collected movie memorabilia? This is not the way it is supposed to work, say the rule utilitarians. You have to specify that the rule is valid for people *under similar circumstances,* and you have to specify what *exceptions* you might want to make. It may be morally good to make sure you are home in time for dinner if you have a family to come home to but not if you are living by yourself. And the moral goodness of being there in time for dinner depends on there not being something of greater importance that you should see to. Such things might be a crisis at work, a medical emergency, extracurricular activities, walking the dog, seeing your lover, watching a television show all the way to the end, talking on the phone, or whatever you choose. They may not all qualify as good exceptions, but *you* should specify in your rule which ones are acceptable. Once you have created such a rule, the utilitarian ideal will work, say the rule utilitarians; it will make more people happy and fewer people unhappy in the long run. If it doesn't, then you just have to rework the rule until you get it right.

The problem with this approach is that it may be asking too much of people. Are we likely to ponder the consequences of whatever it is we want to do every time we are about to take action? Are we likely to envision everyone doing the same thing? Probably not. Even if it is wrong to make lots of private phone calls from a company phone, we think it won't make much difference if one person makes private calls as long as nobody else does. As long as most people comply, we can still get away with breaking the rule without creating bad consequences. Even so, we are in the wrong, because a healthy moral theory will not set "myself" up as an exception to the rule just because "I'm me and I deserve it." This, as philosopher James Rachels has pointed out, is as much a form of discrimination as racism and sexism are. We might call it "me-ism," but we already have a good word for it, *egoism,* and we already know that that is unacceptable.

This addition to utilitarianism, that one ought to look for rules that apply to everyone, is for many a major step in the right direction. Rule utilitarianism certainly was not, however, the first philosophy to ask, What if everybody did what you intend to do? Although just about every parent must have said that to her or his child at some time or other, the one person who is credited with putting it into a philosophical framework is the German philosopher Immanuel Kant. There is one important difference between the way Kant asks the question and the way it has later been developed by rule utilitarians, though. Rule utilitarianism asks, What will be the *consequences* of everybody doing what you intend to do? Kant asks, Could you wish for it to be a *universal law* that everyone does what you intend to do? We look more closely at this difference in the next chapter.

Study Questions

1. Explain the function of Bentham's hedonistic (hedonic) calculus and give an example of how to use it. Explain the advantages of using the calculus; explain the problems inherent in the concept of the calculus.

2. Explain John Stuart Mill's theory of higher and lower pleasures: What are the problems inherent in the theory? Overall, does Mill's idea of higher and lower pleasures make sense to you? Why or why not?

3. Evaluate Descartes's theory that only those beings with a mind can suffer and that only humans have minds. Explore the consequences for utilitarianism if we agree that animals (including human beings) have a capacity for suffering.

4. Explore Mill's harm principle: Do you find the principle attractive or problematic? Explain why. Discuss the application of the harm principle to the issue of drug legalization.

5. Are we more likely to accept the idea of utilitarianism in a time of crisis? If so, does that make the theory acceptable? Explain.

Primary Readings and Narratives

The two Primary Readings are Jeremy Bentham's definition of the principle of utility and John Stuart Mill's vision of true happiness. The Narratives based on literature include a Danish tale about utilitarianism in action and a pairing of excerpts from Dostoyevsky and Ursula K. Le Guin that look at the happiness of the many in light of the suffering of a few. A summary of the film *Saving Private Ryan* illustrates the wartime complexity of the utilitarian question of the few being sacrificed for the many, and an additional film summary, *Extreme Measures,* explores the moral question of performing medical experiments on a few unwanted homeless people in order to gain knowledge that will save the lives and mobility of thousands of others. Both films ask, in different ways, whether some individuals can be considered more valuable than others.

Primary Reading

Of the Principle of Utility

JEREMY BENTHAM

From An Introduction to the Principles of Morals and Legislation, *1789. Excerpt.*

Jeremy Bentham's primary interests were legislative, and he wrote in a meticulous style suited to the language of the law. In this excerpt Bentham defines the principle of utility and outlines the consequences for individuals, for the community, and for moral concepts.

I. *Mankind governed by pain and pleasure.* Nature has placed mankind under the governance of two sovereign masters, *pain* and *pleasure.* It is for them alone to point out what we ought to do, as well as to determine what we shall do. On the one hand the standard of right and wrong, on the other the chain of causes and effects, are fastened to their throne. They govern us in all we do, in all we say, in all we think: every effort we can make to throw them off our subjection, will serve but to demonstrate and confirm it. In words a man may pretend to abjure their empire: but in reality he will remain subject to it all the while. The *principle of utility* recognises this subjection, and assumes it for the foundation of that system, the object of which is to rear the fabric of felicity by the hands of reason and of law. Systems which attempt to question it, deal in sounds instead of sense, in caprice instead of reason, in darkness instead of light.

But enough of metaphor and declamation: it is not by such means that moral science is to be improved.

II. *Principle of utility, what.* The principle of utility is the foundation of the present work: it will be proper therefore at the outset to give an explicit and determinate account of what is meant by it. By the principle of utility is meant that principle which approves or disapproves of every action whatsoever, according to the tendency which it appears to have to augment or diminish the happiness of the party whose interest is in question: or, what is the same thing in other words, to promote or to oppose that happiness. I say of every action whatsoever; and therefore not only of every action of a private individual, but of every measure of government.

III. *Utility, what.* By utility is meant that property in any object, whereby it tends to produce benefit, advantage, pleasure, good, or happiness, (all this in the present case comes to the same thing) or (what comes again to the same thing) to prevent the happening of mischief, pain, evil, or unhappiness to the party whose interest is considered: if that party be the community in general, then the happiness of the community: if a particular individual, then the happiness of that individual.

IV. *Interest of the community, what.* The interest of the community is one of the most general expressions that can occur in the phraseology of morals: no wonder that the meaning of it is often lost. When it has a meaning, it is this. The community is a fictitious *body,* composed of the individual persons who are considered as constituting as it were its *members.* The interest of the community then is, what? — the sum of the interests of the several members who compose it.

V. It is in vain to talk of the interest of the community, without understanding what is the interest of the individual. A thing is said to promote the interest, or to be *for* the interest, of an individual, when it tends to add to the sum total of his pleasures: or, what comes to the same thing, to diminish the sum total of his pains.

VI. *An action conformable to the principle of utility, what.* An action then may be said to be conformable to the principle of utility, or, for shortness sake, to utility, (meaning with respect to the community at large) when the tendency it has to augment the happiness of the community is greater than any it has to diminish it.

VII. *A measure of government conformable to the principle of utility, what.* A measure of government (which is but a particular kind of action, performed by a particular person or persons) may be said to be conformable to or dictated by the principle of utility, when in like manner the tendency which it has to augment the happiness of the community is greater than any which it has to diminish it.

VIII. *Laws or dictates of utility, what.* When an action, or in particular a measure of government, is supposed by a man to be conformable to the principle of utility, it may be convenient, for the purposes of discourse, to imagine a kind of law or dictate, called a law or dictate of utility: and to speak of the action in question, as being conformable to such law or dictate.

IX. *A partizan of the principle of utility, who.* A man may be said to be a partizan of the principle of utility, when the approbation or disapprobation he annexes to any action, or to any measure, is determined by and proportioned to the tendency which he conceives it to have to augment or to diminish the happiness of the community: or in other words, to its conformity or unconformity to the laws or dictates of utility.

X. *Ought, ought not, right and wrong, &c. how to be understood.* Of an action that is conformable to the principle of utility one may always say either that it is one that ought to be done, or at least that it is not one that ought not to be done. One may say also, that it is right it should be done; at least that it is not wrong it should be done: that it is a right action; at least that it is not a wrong action. When thus interpreted, the words *ought,* and *right* and *wrong,* and others of that stamp, have a meaning: when otherwise, they have none.

Study Questions

1. Identify the concept of moral right and wrong as defined by the principle of utility. Do you approve of such a definition? Why or why not?

2. How does Bentham identify the concept of "community"? Evaluate Bentham's statement in terms of possible political consequences. Do you agree with him? Why or why not?

3. In your opinion, is Bentham right in stating that pain and pleasure govern us in everything we do?

4. Some scholars see Bentham as one short step removed from ethical egoism. Why? Is that a fair assessment?

Primary Reading

Utilitarianism

JOHN STUART MILL

1863. Excerpt.

In this section Mill outlines the idea of a test of higher and lower pleasures according to the judgment of those who know and appreciate both kinds. He then speaks of the true nature of happiness, as he sees it: a feeling that has little to do with pleasure seeking and much to do with the joy of contributing to the common good.

It is quite compatible with the principle of utility to recognize the fact, that some *kinds* of pleasure are more desirable and more valuable than others. It would be absurd that while, in estimating all other things, quality is considered as well as quantity, the estimation of pleasures should be supposed to depend on quantity alone.

If I am asked what I mean by difference of quality in pleasures, or what makes one pleasure more valuable than another merely as a pleasure, except its being greater in amount, there is but one possible answer. Of two pleasures, if there be one to which all or almost all who have experience of both give a decided preference, irrespective of any feeling of moral obligation to prefer it, that is the more desirable pleasure. If one of the two is, by those who are competently acquainted with both, placed so far above the other that they prefer it, even though knowing it to be attended with a greater amount of discontent, and would not resign it for any quantity of the other pleasure which their nature is capable of, we are justified in ascribing to the preferred enjoyment a superiority in quality, so far outweighing quantity as to render it, in comparison, of small account.

Now it is an unquestionable fact that those who are equally acquainted with, and equally capable of appreciating and enjoying, both, do give a most marked preference to the manner of existence which employs their higher faculties. Few human creatures would consent to be changed into any of the lower animals, for a promise of the fullest allowance of a beast's pleasures; no intelligent human being would consent to be a fool, no instructed person would be an ignoramus, no person of feeling and conscience would be selfish and base, even though they should be persuaded that the fool, the dunce, or the rascal is better satisfied with his lot than they are with theirs. They would not resign what they possess more than he for the most complete satisfaction of all the desires which they have in common with him. If they ever fancy they would, it is only in cases of unhappiness so extreme, that to escape from it they would exchange their lot for almost any other, however undesirable in their own eyes. A being of higher faculties requires more to make him happy, is capable probably of more acute suffering, and certainly accessible to it at more points, than one of an inferior type; but in spite of these liabilities, he can never really wish to sink into what he feels to be a lower grade of existence. We may give what explanation we please of this unwillingness: we may attribute it to pride, a name which is given indiscriminately to some of the most and to some of the least estimable feelings of which mankind are capable; we may refer it to the love of liberty and personal independence, an appeal to which was with the Stoics one of the most effective means for the inculcation of it; to the love of power, or to the love of excitement, both of which do really enter into and contribute to it: but its most appropriate appellation is a sense of dignity, which all human beings possess in one form or other, and in some, though by no means in exact, proportion to their higher faculties, and which is so essential a part of the happiness of those in whom it is strong, that nothing which conflicts with it could be, otherwise than momentarily, an object of desire to them. Whoever supposes that this preference takes place at a sacrifice of happiness — that the superior being, in anything like equal circumstances, is not happier than the inferior — confounds the two very different ideas, of *happiness* and *content*. It is indisputable that the being whose capacities of enjoyment are low, has the greatest chance of having them fully satisfied; and a highly endowed being will always feel that any happiness which he can look for, as the world is constituted, is imperfect. But he can learn to bear its imperfections, if they are at all bearable; and they will not make him envy the being who is indeed unconscious of the imperfections, but only because he feels not at all the good which those imperfections qualify. It is better to be a human being dissatisfied than a pig satisfied; better to be Socrates dissatisfied than a fool satisfied. And if the fool, or the pig, are of a different opinion, it is because they only know their own side of the question. The other party to the comparison knows both sides. [. . .]

According to the "greatest happiness principle," [. . .] the ultimate end, with reference to and for the sake of which all other things are desirable (whether we are considering our own good or that of other people), is an existence exempt as far as possible from pain, and as rich as possible in enjoyments, both in point of quantity and quality; the test of quality, and the rule for measuring it against quantity, being the preference felt by those who in their opportunities of experience, to which must be added their habits of self-consciousness and self-observation, are best furnished with the means of comparison. This, being, according to the utilitarian opinion, the end of human action, is necessarily also the standard of morality; which may accordingly be defined, the rules and precepts for human conduct, by the observance of which an existence such as has been described might be, to the greatest extent possible, secured to all mankind; and not to them only, but, so far as the nature of things admits, to the whole sentient creation. [. . .]

[. . .] If by happiness be meant a continuity of highly pleasurable excitement, it is evident enough that this is impossible. A state of exalted pleasure lasts only moments, or in some cases, and with some intermissions, hours or days, and is the occasional brilliant flash of enjoyment, not its permanent and steady flame. Of this the philosophers who have taught that happiness is the end of life were as fully aware as those who taunt them. The happiness which they meant was not a life of rapture; but moments of such, in an existence made up of few and transitory pains, many and various pleasures, with a decided predominance of the active over the passive, and having as the foundation of the whole, not to expect more from life than it is capable of bestowing. A life thus composed, to those who have been fortunate enough to obtain it, has always appeared worthy of the name of happiness. And such an existence is even now the lot of many, during some considerable portion of their lives. The present wretched education, and wretched social arrangements, are the only real hindrance to its being attainable by almost all.

In a world in which there is so much to interest, so much to enjoy, and so much also to correct and improve, everyone who has [a] moderate amount of moral and intellectual requisites is capable of an existence which may be called enviable; and unless such a person, through bad laws or subjection to the will of others, is denied the liberty to use the sources of happiness within his reach, he will not fail to find this enviable existence, if he escape the positive evils of life, the great sources of physical and mental suffering—such as indigence, disease, and the unkindness, worthlessness, or premature loss of an affection. The main stress of the problem lies, therefore, in the contest with these calamities from which it is a rare good fortune entirely to escape; which, as things are now, cannot be obviated, and often cannot be in any material degree mitigated. Yet no one whose opinion deserves a moment's consideration can doubt that most of the great positive evils of the world are in themselves removable, and will, if human affairs continue to improve, be in the end reduced within narrow limits. [. . .]

As for vicissitudes of fortune, and other disappointments connected with worldly circumstances, these are principally the effect either of gross imprudence, of ill-regulated desires, or of bad or imperfect social institutions. All the grand sources, in short, of human suffering are in a great degree, many of them almost entirely, conquerable by human care and effort; and though their removal is grievously slow—though a long succession of generations will perish in the breach before the conquest is completed, and this world becomes all that, if will and knowledge were not wanting, it might easily be made—yet every mind sufficiently intelligent and generous to bear a part, however small and unconspicuous, in the endeavor, will draw a noble enjoyment from the contest itself, which he would not for any bribe in the form of selfish indulgence consent to be without.

And this leads to the true estimation of what is said by the objectors concerning the possibility, and the obligation, of learning to do without happiness. Unquestionably it is possible to do without happiness; it is done involuntarily by nineteen-twentieths of mankind, even in those parts of our present world which are least deep in barbarism; and it often has to be done voluntarily by the hero or the martyr, for the sake of something which he prizes more than his individual happiness. But this something, what is it, unless the happiness of others, or some of the requisites of happiness? It is noble to be capable of resigning entirely one's own portion of happiness, or chances of it: but, after all, this self-sacrifice must be for some end; it is not its own end; and if we are told that its end is not happiness, but virtue, which is better than happiness, I ask, would the sacrifice be made if the hero or martyr did not believe that it would earn for others immunity from similar sacrifices? Would it be made if he thought that his renunciation of happiness for himself would produce no fruit for any of his fellow creatures, but to make their lot like his, and place them also in the condition of persons who have renounced happiness? All honor to those who can abnegate for themselves the personal enjoyment of life, when by such renunciation they contribute worthily to increase the amount of happiness in the world; but he who does it, or professes to do it, for any other purpose, is no more deserving of admiration from the ascetic mounted on his pillar. He may be an inspiriting proof of what men *can* do, but assuredly not an example of what they *should*.

Study Questions

1. Do you agree with Mill that "A being of higher faculties requires more to make him happy [. . .] than one of an inferior type"?

2. What might be Ayn Rand's comment on the excerpt?

3. What does Mill mean by "the whole sentient creation"?

4. Comment on the meaning of this passage: "It is better to be a human being dissatisfied than a pig satisfied; better to be Socrates dissatisfied than a fool satisfied." What does Mill mean? Do you agree? Why or why not?

Narrative

The Blacksmith and the Baker

JOHANN HERMAN WESSEL

Poem, 1777. Loosely translated from Danish, from verse to prose. Summary and Excerpt.

Wessel is famous in his own country of Denmark for his satirical verses. This one may have been inspired by a real newspaper story or possibly by British fables.

Once upon a time there was a small town where the town blacksmith was a mean man. He had an enemy, and one day he and his enemy happened to meet at an inn. They proceeded to get drunk and exchange some nasty words. The blacksmith grew angry and knocked the other man out; the blow turned out to be fatal. The blacksmith was carted off to jail, and he confessed, hoping that his opponent would forgive him in Heaven. Before his sentence was pronounced, four upstanding citizens asked to see the judge, and the most eloquent of them spoke:

"Your Wisdom, we know you are thinking of the welfare of this town, but this welfare depends on getting our blacksmith back. His death won't wake up the dead man, and we'll never find such a good blacksmith ever again."

The judge said, "But a life has been taken and must be paid for by a life. . . ."

"The Blacksmith and the Baker," illustration by Nils Wiwel, 1895. Utilitarianism taken to an extreme: The baker is led away to be executed for what the blacksmith has done, because that is more useful to society. The policeman's belt reads "Honest and Faithful," and the building in the background is the old Copenhagen courthouse with the inscription "With Law Must Land Be Built."

"We have in town an old and scrawny baker who'll go to the devil soon, and since we have two bakers, how about taking the oldest one? Then you still get a life for a life."

"Well," said the judge, "that is not a bad idea, I'll do what I can." And he leafed through his law books but found nothing that said you can't execute a baker instead of a blacksmith, so he pronounced this sentence:

"We know that blacksmith Jens has no excuse for what he has done, sending Anders Petersen off to eternity; but since we have but one blacksmith in this town I would be crazy if I wanted him dead; but we do have two bakers of bread . . . so the oldest one must pay for the murder."

The old baker wept pitifully when they took him away. The moral of the story: Be always prepared to die! It comes when you least expect it.

Study Questions

1. Do you think this is a fair picture of a utilitarian judge?

2. What might the utilitarian respond to this story?

3. Return to this story after reading Chapter 6 and consider: What might a Kantian respond?

Narrative

The Brothers Karamazov

FYODOR DOSTOYEVSKY

Novel, 1881. Film, 1958. Summary and Excerpt.

(This excerpt should be read in conjunction with the narrative "The Ones Who Walk Away from Omelas," which follows.)

The story of the brothers Karamazov, one of the most famous in Russian literature, is about four half-brothers and their father, an unpleasant, old, corrupt scoundrel. The brothers are very different in nature; the oldest son, Dmitri, is a rogue and a pleasure-seeker; the next son, Ivan, is intelligent and politically engaged; the third son, Alyosha, is gentle and honest; and the fourth son, Smerdyakov, was born outside of marriage and never recognized as a proper son. When a murder happens, each son in turn finds himself under suspicion.

Here, Ivan is telling Alyosha a story:

"It was in the darkest days of serfdom at the beginning of the century. . . . There was in those days a general of aristocratic connections, the owner of great estates, one of those men—somewhat exceptional, I believe, even then—who, retiring from the service into a life of leisure, are convinced that they've earned absolute power over the lives of their subjects. There were such men then. So our general, settled on his property of two thousand souls, lives in pomp, and dominates his poor neighbors as though they were dependents. He has kennels of hundreds of hounds and nearly a hundred dog-boys—all mounted, and in uniform. One day a serf boy, a little child of eight, threw a stone in play and hurt the paw of the general's favorite hound. 'Why is my favorite dog lame?' He is told that the boy threw a stone that hurt the dog's paw. 'So you did it.' The general looked the child up and down. 'Take him.' He was taken—taken from his mother and kept shut up all night. Early the next morning the general comes out on horseback, with the hounds, his dependents, dog-boys, and huntsmen, all mounted around him in full hunting parade. The servants are summoned for their edification, and in front of them all stands the mother of the child. The child is brought forward. It's a gloomy cold, foggy autumn day, a perfect day for hunting. The general orders the child to be undressed. The child is stripped naked. He shivers, numb with terror, not daring to cry. . . . 'Make him run,' commands the general. 'Run, run!' shout the dog-boys. The boy runs. . . . 'At him!' yells the general, and he sets the whole pack of hounds after the child. The hounds catch him, and tear him to pieces before his mother's eyes! . . . I believe the general was afterwards declared incapable of administering his estates. Well—what did he deserve? To be shot? To be shot for the satisfaction of our moral feelings? Speak, Alyosha!

"Tell me yourself, I challenge you—answer. Imagine that you are creating a fabric of human destiny with the object of making men happy in the end, giving them peace and rest at last. Imagine that you are doing this but that it is essential and inevitable to torture to death only one tiny creature—that child beating its breast with its fist, for instance—in order to found that edifice on its unavenged tears. Would you consent to be the architect on those conditions? Tell me. Tell the truth."

"No, I wouldn't consent," said Alyosha softly.

"And can you accept the idea that the men for whom you are building would agree to receive their happiness from the unatoned blood of a little victim? And accepting it would remain happy forever?"

"No, I can't admit it," said Alyosha suddenly, with flashing eyes.

Here Ivan and Alyosha are engaged in a discussion about the meaning of life: If God does not exist, then what? Then everything is permissible. But what if our highest moral aim is to make the majority happy? Do the means always justify the end? If the suffering of a child could somehow create general happiness and harmony, should its mother forgive those who caused it to suffer?

Study Questions

1. Answer Ivan's question: Would you agree to make humankind happy at the cost of a child's suffering? Explain how a utilitarian might answer, and then explain your own answer.

2. Should the mother ever forgive the general for murdering her son?

3. Return to this story after reading Chapter 6 and consider: What might a Kantian respond?

Narrative

The Ones Who Walk Away from Omelas

URSULA K. LE GUIN

Short story, 1973. Summary and Excerpt.

There is a festival in the city of Omelas. The weather is beautiful, the city looks its best, and people are happy and serene in their pretty clothes. This is a perfect place, with freedom of choice and no oppressive power enforcing the rules of religion, politics, or morality—and it works, because the people know they are responsible for their actions.

This place is a Utopia, except for one thing: The happiness of the citizens is bought at a high price, with the full knowledge of every citizen.

> In a basement under one of the beautiful public buildings of Omelas, or perhaps in the cellar of one of its spacious private homes, there is a room. It has one locked door, and no window. A little light seeps in dustily between cracks in the boards, secondhand from a cobwebbed window somewhere across the cellar. In one corner of the little room a couple of mops, with stiff, clotted, foul-smelling heads, stand near a rusty bucket. . . . The room is about three paces long and two wide: a mere broom closet or disused tool room. In the room a child is sitting. It could be a boy or a girl. It looks about six, but actually is nearly ten. It is feeble-minded. Perhaps it was born defective, or perhaps it has become imbecile through fear, malnutrition, and neglect. It picks its nose and occasionally fumbles vaguely with its toes or genitals, as it sits hunched in the corner farthest from the bucket and the two mops. It is afraid of the mops. It finds them horrible. It shuts its eyes, but it knows the mops are still standing there; and the door is locked; and nobody will come. The door is always locked; and nobody ever comes, except that sometimes . . . the door rattles terribly and opens, and a person, or several people, are there. . . . The people at the door never say anything, but the child, who has not always lived in the tool room, and can remember sunlight and its mother's voice, sometimes speaks. "I will be good," it says. "Please let me out. I will be good!" They never answer.

All this is part of a greater plan. The child will never be let out — it will die within a short time — and presumably another child will take its place, for it is the suffering of this innocent being that makes the perfect life in Omelas possible. All the citizens know about it from the time they are adolescents, and they all must go and see the child so that they can understand the price of their happiness. They are disgusted and sympathetic for a while, but then they understand the master plan: the pain of one small individual in exchange for great communal happiness. Because the citizens know the immense suffering that gives them their beautiful life, they are particularly loving to each other and responsible for what they do. And what would they gain by setting the child free? The child is too far gone to be able to enjoy freedom, anyway, and what is one person's suffering compared to the realm of happiness that is achieved? So the people feel no guilt. However, a few young people and some adult visitors go to see the child, and something happens to them: They don't go home afterward, but keep on walking — through the city, through the fields, away from Omelas.

Study Questions

1. Where are they going, the ones who walk away? And why are they leaving?

2. How does Le Guin feel about the situation? Does she condone the suffering of the child, or is she arguing against it? Is the story realistic or symbolic?

3. How would an act utilitarian evaluate the story of Omelas? Would a rule utilitarian reach the same conclusion or a different one? Why?

4. Return to this story after reading Chapter 6 and develop a deontological critique of the people of Omelas (those who don't walk away).

Narrative

Saving Private Ryan

ROBERT RODAT (SCREENWRITER)
STEVEN SPIELBERG (DIRECTOR)

Film, 1998. Summary and Excerpt of Screenplay.

Saving Private Ryan is a film that leaves very few viewers unmoved. Its level of stark realism in the opening and closing battle scenes marks it as too much of a true-to-life experience for some. Others argue, however, that these scenes can't be removed because without the experience of the bloody struggle on Omaha Beach, how can we appreciate the magnitude of the danger these eight young men will face *voluntarily* later in the film?

The movie is selected here as an illustration of the ideals of utilitarianism, and yet you may want to discuss whether the film is, in the end, pro-utilitarian or anti-utilitarian. Although I generally try to avoid giving away the ending of a story in discussing the moral issues, in *Saving Private Ryan* only a few things can remain secret because we need to know all the facts in order to determine whether the sacrifices were worth it.

The film throws us into a living hell: the landing on the beaches of Normandy on D-Day, June 6, 1944, the beginning of the end of the Nazi reign in Europe. In landing craft in a stormy sea, seasick, terrified young soldiers prepare for battle. Some of them never even set foot on dry land but are shot to pieces by machine gun fire from the bluffs; others drown as their equipment drags them under. Death is indiscriminate and terrible, whether it is quick or slow. Limbs are torn off, shocked soldiers revert to childhood and call for their mothers in mortal agony. A small group makes its way up under the bluff and, at a dreadful cost in lives, manages to take over a bunker from where the Germans were shooting down the beach. The aftermath is no less gruesome: There is no mercy shown to the defending German soldiers. Captain John Miller regroups his men and imposes both order and, eventually, a nominal return to decency among the survivors. Though an experienced veteran, the captain himself is deeply affected—he has developed an uncontrolled nervous twitching in his hand.

Meanwhile a mother in Iowa is told by the top military brass that she has lost three of her four sons in battle in different parts of the world. The one remaining son is James Ryan, a paratrooper behind enemy lines somewhere in Normandy. The chief of staff now sees it as imperative to bring Private Ryan home so his mother will not have lost all her sons, and he quotes a letter Abraham Lincoln wrote during the Civil War to a mother who had lost all of her five sons in battle. It is obvious to the chief of staff that some civilian sacrifices are just too great. But is it only the one last son who is so important—one son, one mother—or is there something deeper?

Captain Miller is given the order to find Private Ryan and bring him home. He selects a squad of men he can trust, seven young "veterans," survivors of the carnage on Omaha Beach. There is little comprehension among the squad as to why one soldier's life can be so important that eight men must risk their lives to save his. As they encounter enemy fire along the way and two of their group lose their lives, their job begins to take its toll, even on Captain Miller. He speculates that losing a soldier is supposed to mean that other soldiers' lives are saved:

> *Miller:* Every time you kill one of your men, you tell yourself you just saved the lives of two, three, ten, a hundred others. You know how many men I've lost under my command?
>
> *Sarge:* How many?
>
> *Miller:* Ninety-four. So that must mean I've saved the lives of ten times that number. Maybe twenty, right? See, it's simple. It lets you always choose the mission over men.
>
> *Sarge:* Except this time the mission is a man. . . .
>
> *Miller:* And Ryan better be worth it. He better go home and cure some disease or invent a new longer-lasting lightbulb.

A captured German soldier who is the lone survivor of a group responsible for the death of one of Miller's men is about to be summarily executed by some of the enraged squad members. The nightmarish possibility of good soldiers murdering an unarmed prisoner out of revenge threatens to divide the group, but Miller again pulls everybody together by telling them a seemingly irrelevant fact: what he did for a living back home. He is beginning to feel that if he can save Private Ryan, he will have earned the right to return home to his wife and resume his life as a schoolteacher. But with every man he kills, the farther he gets from home and the person he once was. The prisoner is released. This is a decision that will come back to haunt Miller and his men.

Against enormous odds, the diminished squad does find Private Ryan, but the young man refuses to return to safety. Now that his brothers are gone, his fellow soldiers represent his "brothers," and they are holding a bridge, trying to prevent the Germans from using it in a counterattack on the beachhead. The men in Miller's troop have repeatedly questioned whether Ryan was worth saving and worth the lives of two good men, but his insistence on staying and fighting with his comrades gives Miller's men hope. Ryan seems to be a kid with character, and he wants to know the names of the men who died trying to rescue him. Leaving without Ryan would render their sacrifices meaningless, so Miller and his men decide to risk all and join forces with Ryan's little troop to hold the bridge, and, perhaps by saving the invasion, to restore meaningfulness to their members' sacrifices and earn the right to go home themselves.

Each soldier is prepared to fight to the end—we know that because Miller evokes the Battle of the Alamo, in which all the defenders perished. When the grueling battle is over, Ryan understands, in much the same way that Captain Miller felt saving Ryan would earn him the right to go home, that now he must earn the life that others have paid such an immense price to save.

This film is about duty and sacrifice; it is also about "sheer numbers": Eight men's lives are on the line to save one, whereas the losses of lives on Omaha Beach and on the other battlefields make the thought of one single life saved seem insignificant. So, according to the hedonistic calculus, was it worth the cost to save Private Ryan? In a narrow sense, no: The loss of most of the troop can't be balanced by one life, even if it makes his mother very happy. From a narrowly utilitarian point of view, the endeavor was a failure, a terrible waste of lives for the sake of one young man and his mother. But from a broader and deeper utilitarian perspective things change, and perhaps this is the most interesting perspective utilitarianism has to offer. Is Private Ryan just one young man? For the chief of staff he is much more: He is the very meaning of going to war. We fight so someone at home can live in freedom, and if there are no sons or daughters left at home, then the sacrifices are in vain. Private Ryan becomes a symbol of the future that must be saved, and, in the light of saving a world, the sacrifices made by Miller's men are not too great — in the balance of things, saving Private Ryan may make more sense than anything else the soldiers have been through. This is why the film has been called "an antiwar, but pro-soldier film." It has cynicism, but it also has great faith in humanity.

In the film, Miller attains complete moral authority over his men. In real life, a similar situation arose: During the filming of *Saving Private Ryan,* the actors underwent a grueling week of boot camp training, and at some point in time, they all decided they had had enough — they were actors, not military men. But Tom Hanks (Captain Miller), who took part in the training program, talked to them and pointed out that they had their free will but also a responsibility to the story they were about to tell. So every man decided to stay and finish the training. The story is significant, because it shows that the command Miller had over this troop was a reflection of the professional authority and humanity of the actor portraying him.

Study Questions

1. Was saving James Ryan a meaningful or a meaningless order? Did Miller's men accomplish something worthwhile, or did they risk everything for nothing?

2. How might Ryan "earn" the rest of his life? What would you say would be sufficient as a "good life," considering that men died specifically to save him? Would saving Ryan have been less meaningful if it had turned out that he was not a good person? Why or why not?

3. Comment on the quote from the film dialogue: What does Miller mean by saying that Ryan had better cure some disease or invent a better lightbulb?

4. In releasing the German soldier, Miller and his men respond to their deepest feelings of human decency. However, if you have seen the film, you know that it turns out to be a fateful decision: The German soldier returns. Is there such a thing as a *subjectively* morally right but an *objectively* morally wrong decision? How would a utilitarian respond? How would you respond?

5. Identify the utilitarian elements in the film. Is this a pro-utilitarian or an anti-utilitarian story? Explain your answer.

6. You may want to go back and reread the discussion in Chapter 2 about violence in films and Plato's and Aristotle's views on the value of drama. Given that the violence is extremely graphic in *Saving Private Ryan* but that it is also highly realistic, is this film likely to inspire more violence? Why or why not? Does this give us a hint about how to approach the debate about violence in movies and on TV? Is Aristotle right in saying that a good drama is better conveyed without what we today would call special effects?

Narrative

Extreme Measures

TONY GILROY (SCREENWRITER)
MICHAEL APTED (DIRECTOR)

Film, 1997. Based on a novel by Michael Palma. Summary.

A young British emergency room doctor, Guy Luthan, is faced with a terrible moral and professional choice: In his emergency room, two patients need urgent care. One is a police officer who has been shot, and the other is the man who shot him, a troublemaker who pulled a gun on a bus. He was in turn shot by the cop. The officer is barely stabilized, whereas the gunman is in critical condition. There is only one surgery slot available. Whom should Guy choose? He needs to decide immediately. He sends the police officer into surgery and lets the gunman wait his turn. As it happens, they both survive, but a young nurse, Jodie, blames Guy for making an unprofessional moral choice: The gunman's medical needs were more urgent than the cop's. Guy explains, "I had to make a choice; on my right I see a cop with his wife in the corridor and pictures of his kids in his wallet, and on my left some guy who's taken out a gun on a city bus! I had ten seconds to make a choice, I had to make it—I hope I made the right one. I think I did, oh shit, maybe I didn't . . . I don't know."

This sets the scene for what could be just a run-of-the-mill hospital suspense story but which turns out to be an honest exploration of the principle of utility as a social, moral, and psychological justification.

Guy has just received a fellowship in neurology at New York University. This means much to him and his family, because his father in England, once a medical doctor, lost his license to practice after administering euthanasia to an old friend—another moral choice with consequences.

Meanwhile, a patient is brought to Guy's emergency room from the street, half naked and in complete physical and mental breakdown. He has a hospital bracelet on, and, in a lucid moment before he dies, he says two things to Guy—the word *triphase* and the name of a friend. Not understanding the cause of death, Guy orders an autopsy, but the hospital not only loses track of the autopsy but the body itself. Guy feels that something is terribly wrong and pursues the dead man's records on his own. The man had been admitted to the hospital previously for a neurological examination. Other patients turn up in the computer with the same profile: homeless, without relatives, having lab work done, and all files on them deleted.

But Guy is in for another shock: His apartment has been burglarized, and the detectives investigating the burglary find a stash of drugs in his place. Guy is arrested. Since Guy doesn't do drugs, he realizes that the burglary was a ruse and that the drugs were planted to discredit him, to get him out of the way—by whom? Whoever it is, their plan succeeds; Guy manages to raise bail, but once out of jail, he is suspended from his hospital position—his colleagues and supervisors assume that he is guilty. This also means that his fellowship to NYU will be lost because he will no longer be able to practice med-

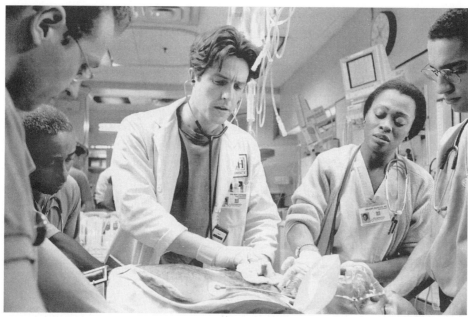

The film *Extreme Measures* (Castle Rock, 1996) notes that sometimes we must make hard moral choices; the question is, What criterion should we use? Should we do what is right, regardless of the consequences, or should we try to obtain the best result for as many as possible with the least harm caused? This is the dilemma facing Dr. Guy Luthan (Hugh Grant), not only in his own career but also as the pawn in a greater plot orchestrated by a famous doctor: to use homeless people as guinea pigs. Here Guy has to choose whether to save the life of a police officer with a wife and kids or the gunman who shot the officer in cold blood.

icine — just like his father. Compelled to seek the truth, Guy locates a patient of his among the homeless and soon finds himself in a world underground in the subway system, where the homeless and destitute have made a world for themselves. Here he finds another piece of the puzzle: Doctors have been preying on the homeless, subjecting them to experiments leading to great suffering and death. But Guy himself is now being hunted in a prolonged chase, and just as he thinks he has found refuge with a friend, he is rendered unconscious.

Guy wakes up in a hospital bed — and to his horror, he finds himself paralyzed from the neck down. He is told that the blow he sustained to his spine severed it, and he will be a quadriplegic for life. Realizing the enormity of what has happened to him, Guy feels that, having no hope of recovery, he might as well be dead. The famous neurologist Dr. Myrick now pays him a visit, talking enigmatically about hope. What if there were hope for him after all? What would it be worth to him to return to his old life? What would he risk if a procedure were available? Guy answers, "Anything!" Myrick replies, "You'd better think about that."

Who is responsible for the burglary, the planted drugs, the disappearance of the homeless, and the attempt on Guy's life? The answer lies within Guy's own hospital environment. When Guy's paralysis miraculously wears off after 24 hours, he realizes he'd been drugged, and that it is Dr. Myrick, passionately engaged in helping victims of spinal cord injury, who has undertaken research into spinal cord regeneration by using homeless patients as guinea pigs for the good of humanity.

Guy now tries to escape from the hospital. This is a pivotal scene in the film, and I will not spoil the surprise twists for you. During a dramatic moment, Myrick tries to explain his actions to Guy: The homeless men he experimented on were useless beings—but now they are heroes, since their deaths have given hope to so many injured people. "Good doctors do the correct thing. Great doctors have the guts to do the right thing. . . . If you could cure cancer by killing one person, wouldn't you have to do it? Wouldn't it be the brave thing to do? One person, and it's gone tomorrow?" Guy replies that perhaps the homeless people he used weren't worth much, but they didn't choose to be heroes—he never asked for volunteers. To Guy, doctors can't do that—Myrick has been playing God.

One final confrontation remains—one that solves some issues but raises others. In the end, Guy is given all of Myrick's files from his research into spinal cord injuries . . . and Guy does not reject the files.

Study Questions

1. Discuss the opening scene. Did Guy make the right professional choice? The right moral choice? Should there be a difference? Explain your position.

2. Is Dr. Myrick's experimentation a noble quest in order to help humanity or a perverse abuse of human beings? Is there a third alternative? Explain your position.

3. Dr. Myrick asks Guy what he would be willing to do in order to regain his mobility at a time when Guy believes himself to be paralyzed for life. What does Guy answer, and why is this scene so important?

4. Guy accuses Myrick of playing God. Guy's own father lost his license to practice medicine because he performed euthanasia on a friend. Do you think there is a connection here, or is this a coincidence in the film?

5. In the end, Guy takes over Myrick's research papers. Is this gesture an acceptance of Myrick's utilitarian principles, or is there another possibility? By accepting the papers, have Guy's hands now been dirtied? Why or why not?

6. Is this a pro-utilitarian or an anti-utilitarian film? Explain.

7. Scientists announced recently that they believe great strides can be made toward curing paralysis through stem cell research. Given that the stem cells originated in a human embryo, do you think there is a difference between Myrick's experiments on homeless people for the sake of helping patients with paralysis and using stem cells from an embryo to accomplish the same thing? Explain similarities and differences.

Chapter Six

Using Your Reason,
Part 2: Kant's Deontology

On the whole, we might say that there are two major ways in which we can approach a problem. We might ask ourselves, What happens if I do X? In this case we're letting ourselves be guided by the future consequences of our actions. Or we might ask ourselves, Is X right or wrong in itself, regardless of the consequences? The first approach is utilitarian, provided that we are looking for good consequences for as many as possible. The version of the second approach that has had the most influence is Immanuel Kant's *duty theory*. (See Box 6.1 for a summary of Kant's life.)

Kant's moral theory is often referred to as *deontology* (the theory of moral obligation, from the Greek *deon,* "that which is obligatory"). Kant believed his theory was the very opposite of a consequentialist theory and his moral analysis was, in part, written to show how little a moral theory that worries about consequences has to do with true moral thinking. Let us look at an example to illustrate this fundamental difference.

The Good Will

Some years ago, newspapers reported an accident somewhere in the Pacific Northwest. A family had gone away for a short vacation and had left their keys with their neighbor so that he could water their plants and look after the place. On Sunday afternoon, a few hours before they were due to arrive home, the temperature was dropping, and the neighbor thought he would do them a favor and make sure they would come home to a nice, toasty house. He went in and turned on the furnace. You've guessed what happened: The house burned down and the family came home to a smoking ruin. This was the extent of the newspaper coverage, but suppose it had been reported by a classical utilitarian. Then the article might have ended something like this: "The neighbor will have to answer for the consequences of this terrible deed." Why? Because, given that only consequences count, the act of turning on the furnace was a terrible one, regardless of the man's good intentions. As it is sometimes said, the road to hell is paved with good intentions. In other words, only your deeds count, not what you intended by them.

Suppose, however, that a Kantian had written the article. Then it might have ended like this: "This good neighbor should be praised for his kind thought and good intentions regardless of the fact that the family lost their home; that consequence certainly can't be blamed on him, because all he intended to do was the right thing."

Box 6.1   KANT: HIS LIFE AND WORK

Some famous and influential people lead lives of adventure. The life of Immanuel Kant (1724–1804) seems to have been an *intellectual* adventure exclusively, for he did little that might in any other way be considered adventurous. He grew up in the town of Königsberg, East Prussia (a city on the Baltic Sea, now Kaliningrad in Russian territory). He was raised in an atmosphere of strict Protestant values by his devout mother and by his father, who made a meager living as a saddler. He entered Königsberg University, studied theology, graduated, and tutored for a while until he was offered a position at the university in his hometown. In 1770 he became a full professor in logic and metaphysics, and this was when the philosophical drama began, for Kant achieved influence not only in Western philosophy but also in science and social thinking—an influence that was never eclipsed by anyone else in the eighteenth century. He developed theories about astronomy that are still considered plausible; he laid out rules for a new social world of mutual respect for all citizens; he made contributions to philosophy of law and religion; he attempted to map the entire spectrum of human intelligence in his three major works, *Critique of Pure Reason* (1781), *Critique of*

Practical Reason (1788), and *Critique of Judgment* (1790), as well as in smaller works such as *Prolegomena to Every Future Metaphysics* (1783) and *Grounding for the Metaphysics of Morals* (1785). He continued working until late in life; one of his most influential works from that period is *The Metaphysics of Morals* (1797).

When Kant calls a book a "critique," he is not implying that he is merely writing a negative criticism of a subject; he is, rather, looking for the *condition of possibility* of that subject. In *Critique of Pure Reason* he asks, "What makes it possible for me to achieve knowledge?" (In other words, what is the condition of possibility of knowledge?) In *Critique of Practical Reason* he asks about the condition of possibility of moral thinking, and in *Critique of Judgment* he examines the condition of possibility for appreciating natural and artistic beauty. In all of these fields his insights helped shape new disciplines and redefine old disciplines. Kant was never an agitator for his ideas, though; on the contrary, he was famous for his extremely quiet and highly regulated routine. He remained single throughout his life, and his sole interest seems to have been his work. His students reported that he was in fact a good and popular teacher.

Let us continue speculating. Suppose the house didn't burn down, but instead provided a warm, cozy shelter for and saved the lives of the entire family, who (shall we say) had all come down with pneumonia. The utilitarian now would have to say that the act of lighting the furnace was a shining example of a morally good deed, but Kant would not change his mind: The neighbor's action was good because of his intention, and the consequences of the act don't make it any better or worse. It is not just any good intention, however, that makes an action morally good in Kant's view: One must have *a respect for the moral law* that is expressed in the intention. It isn't enough for the neighbor to be a kind man who wants his neighbors to be comfortable; he must imagine it to be a good thing for neighbors to act that way *in general*—not because it would make everyone comfortable and happy but strictly for the sake of the *principle* of doing the right thing. This is what Kant calls having a *good*

This painting shows the German philosopher Immanuel Kant, second from the left, dining with friends. Perhaps the most influential Western philosopher of "modern times" (the seventeenth century to the present), Kant was reportedly a popular guest at dinners and parties and equally popular with his students.

will. For Kant the presence of a good will is what makes an action morally good, regardless of its consequences. Therefore, even if you never accomplished what you intended, you are still morally praiseworthy provided you tried hard to do the right thing. In his book *Grounding for the Metaphysics of Morals* (1785; also commonly referred to as *Groundwork* or *Foundations*), Kant assures us that

> [e]ven if, by some especially unfortunate fate or by the niggardly provision of stepmotherly nature, this will should be wholly lacking in the power to accomplish its purpose;* if with the greatest effort it should yet achieve nothing, and only the good will should remain (not, to be sure, as a mere wish but as the summoning of all the means in our power), yet

---

*To modern readers without much experience with older literature in English, the term *niggardly* generally gives pause, because it bears an unfortunate resemblance to a racial epithet; however, the two words are unrelated in etymology and meaning, and there is no racial undertone in the word used by Kant's translators. The term means "avaricious" or "stingy." But even though *niggardly* doesn't associate to bigotry and discrimination, how about the term *stepmotherly*? That is Kant's own term in translation.

would it, like a jewel, still shine by its own light as something which has its full value in itself. Its usefulness or fruitlessness can neither augment nor diminish this value.

The Categorical Imperative

How do we know that our will is good? We put our intentions to a test. In *Grounding for the Metaphysics of Morals*, Kant says we must ask whether we can imagine our intentions as a general law for everybody. This means that our intentions have to *conform to a rational principle*. We have to think hard in order to determine whether we're about to do the right thing or not; it can't be determined just by some gut-level feeling. However, we don't have to wait to see the actual consequences in order to determine whether our intentions are good—all we have to do is determine whether we could imagine others doing to us what we intend doing to them. In other words, Kant proposes a variant of the Golden Rule—but it is a variant with certain specifics, as we shall see—and it illustrates that Kant is also a *hard universalist,* perhaps the hardest one ever to write a book on morals.

For Kant, humans usually know what they *ought* to do, and that is almost always the opposite of what they *want* to do. Our moral conflicts are generally between our duty and our inclination, and when we let our desires run rampant it is simply because we haven't come up with a way for our sense of duty to persuade us to do the right thing. Kant therefore proposes a test to determine the right thing to do. He refers to this test as the *categorical imperative.* But because it is a matter of doing the right thing not only in terms of the outcome but also in terms of the intentions, we must look more closely at these intentions.

Suppose a store owner is trying to decide whether to cheat her customers. She might tell herself, (1) "I will cheat them whenever I can get away with it" or "I will cheat them only on occasion so nobody can detect a pattern." We can all tell, intuitively, that this merchant's intentions aren't good, although they certainly might benefit her and give her some extra cash at the end of the week. In other words, the consequences may be good, yet we know that cheating the customers is not the right thing to do. (We'll get back to the reason in a while.) Suppose, though, that the owner decides not to cheat her customers because (2) she might be *found out,* and then she would lose their business and might have to close shop. This is certainly prudent, but it still is not a morally praiseworthy decision, because she is doing it only to achieve good consequences. What if the store owner decides not to cheat her customers because (3) she *likes them too much* to ever do them any harm? She loves the little kids buying candy, the old ladies buying groceries, and everyone else, so how could she ever consider cheating them? This, says Kant, is very nice, but it still is not morally praiseworthy, because the merchant is doing only what she feels like doing, and we can't be expected to praise her for just wanting to feel good. (If you want to reexamine this argument, go back to the section in Chapter 4 on psychological egoism, where a similar argument is analyzed in detail.) And indeed, what if some day she should stop loving her customers or just one of them? Then the reason for not cheating is gone; so, as a principle of right action, Kant cannot approve of motive 3, regardless of how much we generally approve of people who help others because they enjoy it.

The only morally praiseworthy reason for not wanting to cheat the customers would be if the store owner told herself, (4) "It wouldn't be right," regardless of consequences or warm and fuzzy feelings. Why wouldn't it be right? Because she certainly couldn't want everybody else to cheat their customers as a universal law.

If the store owner tells herself, "I will not cheat my customers because otherwise I'll lose them," then she is not doing a bad thing, of course. She is just doing a prudent thing, and Kant says our lives are full of such prudent decisions; they are dependent on each situation, and we have to determine in each case what would be the smart thing to do. Kant calls these decisions, which are *conditional,* because they depend on the situation and on one's own personal desires, *hypothetical imperatives — imperatives* because they are commands: *If* you don't want to lose your customers, *then* you should not cheat them. *If* you want to get your degree, *then* you should not miss your final exam. *If* you want to be good at baking biscuits, *then* you ought to bake them from scratch and not use a prepared mix. But suppose you're closing down your shop and moving to another town? Then you might not care about losing those customers. And suppose you decide to drop out of school — then who cares about that final exam? And if you and everyone you know hates biscuits, then why bother worrying about getting good at baking them? In other words, a hypothetical imperative is dependent on your interest in a certain outcome. If you don't want the outcome, the imperative is not binding. We make such decisions every day, and, as long as they are based merely on wanting some outcome, they are not morally relevant. (They can, of course, be morally bad, but, even if they have a good outcome, Kant would say that they are morally neutral.) What makes a decision morally praiseworthy is if the agent (the person acting) decides to do something because it might be applied to everyone as a *universal moral law.* In that case that person has used the categorical imperative.

What makes a categorical imperative *categorical* is that it is not dependent on anyone's desire to make it an imperative; it is binding not just in some situations and for some people, but always, for everyone. It is absolute. That is the very nature of the moral law: If it applies at all, it applies to everyone in the same situation. Although there are myriad hypothetical imperatives, there is only one categorical imperative, expressed in the most general terms possible: *Always act so that you can will that your maxim can become a universal law.* In ordinary language this means: Ask yourself what it is you want to do right now (such as making the house next door toasty for your neighbors, skipping classes on Friday, or lying to Grandma about dating someone outside your religion). Then imagine making that action into a rule (such as, Always make sure your neighbors come home to a toasty house; Always skip Friday classes; Always lie to Grandma to spare her pain). Now you've identified your *maxim,* or the principle or rule for your action. The next step is to ask yourself whether you could want that maxim to become a universal rule for everyone to follow. And, if you can't agree to that — if you don't think *everyone* should, under similar circumstances, light their neighbors' furnaces, skip classes, or lie to Grandma — then *you* shouldn't do it either. It's that simple, and for Kant this realization was so breathtaking that it could be compared only to his awe of the universe on a starry night. Let us use Kant's own example to illustrate.

> [A man] in need finds himself forced to borrow money. He knows well that he won't be able to repay it, but he sees also that he will not get any loan unless he firmly promises to repay it within a fixed time. He wants to make such a promise, but he still has conscience enough to ask himself whether it is not permissible and is contrary to duty to get out of difficulty in this way. Suppose, however, that he decides to do so. The maxim of his action would then be expressed as follows: When I believe myself to be in need of money, I will borrow money and promise to pay it back, although I know that I can never do so. Now this principle of self-love or personal advantage may perhaps be quite compatible with one's entire future welfare, but the question is now whether it is right. I then transform the requirement of self-love into a universal law and put the question thus: how would things stand if my maxim were to become a universal law? He then sees at once that such a maxim could never hold as a universal law of nature and be consistent with itself, but must necessarily be self-contradictory. For the universality of a law which says that anyone believing himself to be in difficulty could promise whatever he pleases with the intention of not keeping it would make promising itself and the end to be attained thereby quite impossible, inasmuch as no one would believe what was promised him but would merely laugh at all such utterances as being vain pretenses.

Do we know why this man wants to borrow money? Perhaps he wants to buy a speedboat. Perhaps he wants to pay a hit man for a contract killing. Or he needs to pay the rent. Perhaps his child is ill, and he has to buy medication and pay the doctor's bill. We don't know. Is knowing his reason relevant? If we were utilitarians, it would be very relevant, because then we could judge the merit of the proposed consequences (saving his child generally has more utility than buying a boat or hiring a hit man). But Kant is no utilitarian, and the prospect of the man in the example wanting to do good with the borrowed money is no more relevant than the prospect of him wanting to buy a boat or even to hire a hit man. The main issue here is, Does the man have a good will? Would he refuse to follow a course of action if he couldn't agree to everyone else having the right to act the same way?

Let us go over the structure of the proposed test of right and wrong conduct again: What is it you're thinking of doing? Imagine that as a *general rule* for action you'll follow every time the situation comes up. You have now expressed your *maxim.* Then imagine everybody else doing it, too; by doing this you *universalize your maxim.* Then ask yourself, Could I want this? Could I still get away with it if everyone did it? The answer is no, you would *undermine your own intention,* because nobody would lend *you* any money if everyone were lying about paying it back. So it is not just the fact that banks would close and the financial world would be in chaos—it is the *logical outcome* of your universalized maxim that shows you that your intention was wrong.

The categorical imperative asks us in effect, Would you want others to treat you the way you're thinking of treating them? The association to the Golden Rule (see Box 4.8) is almost inevitable: How should we treat others? The way we would want to be treated. And yet Kant had harsh words for the old Golden Rule. He thought it was just a simplistic version of his own categorical imperative and that it could even be turned into a travesty: If you don't want to help others, just claim you don't want or need any help from them! But the bottom line is that the categorical imperative draws on that same fundamental realization that I called a spark of moral genius in the Golden Rule: It sees self and others as fundamentally similar — not in the details of our lives but in the fact that we are human beings and should be treated fairly by each other.

Does this mean that the categorical imperative works only if *everyone* can accept your maxim as a universal law? Not in the sense that we have to take a poll before we decide to act; if everyone's actual approval were the final criterion, the principle would lose its appeal as an immediate test of where one's duty lies. There is an element of universal approval in Kant's idea, but it lies in the reflection of an *ideal* situation, not an *actual* one. If everyone put aside his or her personal interests and then used the categorical imperative, then everyone would, ideally, come up with the same conclusion about what is morally permissible. Kant, who belonged to an era of less doubt about what exactly rationality means, believed that if we all used the same rules of logic and disregarded our personal interests, then we all would come to the same results about moral as well as intellectual issues.

This immense faith in human rationality is an important factor in Kant's moral theory, because it reflects his belief that humans are privileged beings. We can set up our own moral rules without having to seek guidance by going to the authorities; we need not be told how to live by the church or by the police or by the monarch or even by our parents. All we need is our good will and our reason, and with that we can set our own rules. If we choose a certain course of action because we have been told to — because we listen to other people's advice for some reason or other — we are merely doing what might be prudent and expedient, but if we listen to our own reason and have good will, then we are *autonomous lawmakers*.

Won't this approach result in a society where everyone looks after him- or herself and lives by multiple rules that may contradict one another? No, because if everyone has good will and applies the categorical imperative, then all will set the same, reasonable, unselfish rules for themselves, because they would not wish to set a rule that would be impossible for others to follow.

In this way Kant believes he has shown us how to solve every dilemma, every problem where desire clashes with duty. When the categorical imperative is applied, we automatically disregard our own personal interests and look at the bigger picture, and this action is what is morally praiseworthy: to realize that something is right or wrong in itself.

Criticism of the Categorical Imperative

Some people are immediately impressed by the idea that one's intentions count for more than the outcome of one's actions and that the question of right or wrong in itself is important; we can't consider only the consequences if it means violating the rights of others. Others claim that no matter how much you say you're not interested in consequences, they still end up being a consideration. Critics have raised five major points when finding fault with Kant's theory.

1. Consequences Count   Doesn't the categorical imperative actually imply concern for consequences? This is the criticism of John Stuart Mill, who had some sharp things to say about Kant's example of borrowing money and not keeping promises. If this was the best Kant could come up with to show that consequences don't count, he was not doing a very good job, said Mill, because what was he appealing to? By asking "What if everybody does what you want to do?" wasn't Kant worrying about consequences? What will happen if everyone borrows money and doesn't pay it back in spite of their promises? Then no one else can take advantage of promising falsely, either. In Mill's view, this is as much an appeal to consequences as regular utilitarianism is. This caused Mill to conclude that we all must include consequences in our moral theory, no matter how reluctant we are to recognize their importance. This appears to be a valid point against Kant. The only thing Kant might say in response to this (he never did, of course, since he was long dead by the time Mill criticized his point of view) is that his viewpoint does not look at *actual* consequences but at the *logical implications* of a universalized maxim: Will it or will it not undermine itself? Whether Mill has successfully criticized Kant or misunderstood him is still a topic of discussion among philosophers.

2. Conflict Between Duties   Can we be so sure that the categorical imperative is always going to tell us what to do? Suppose we have a conflict between two things we have to do—and we don't particularly want to do either of them. Kant's system assumes that a moral conflict is one between duty and inclination—between what we have to do and what we want to do. In that case it is entirely possible we may be convinced to do the right thing by imagining our maxim as a universal rule for everyone. But suppose we have a conflict between two duties, such as having to take inventory at our workplace the night before we have a final exam for which we should be studying. Certainly we can't say we want to do one thing more than we want to do the other—anyone who has done both will probably agree that they are both rather unpleasant tasks. How might the categorical imperative help us decide what to do? All it can tell us is that failing to show up for the inventory would not be rational, but neither would skipping the final, because both are duties that everyone ought to fulfill under the same circumstances. The amount of help offered by the categorical imperative is at best limited to cases where duties are not in conflict. (Of course, in a situation where we have a conflict between duties, we already know of another approach that might answer the question of what to do: Bentham's hedonistic calculus. But most philosophers agree that you can't just mix and match theories according to your needs. In Chapter 12 we return to the question of combining the best of various moral theories.)

3. The Loophole   Might it not be possible to find a loophole in the imperative? Suppose the categorical imperative tells us that it would be irrational (and thus morally impermissible) for anyone to even think about robbing a bank if he needs money because we wouldn't want everyone in the same situation to take that course of action. But what exactly *is* the situation we're talking about? Suppose Joe is broke because he is out of work and has been for seven months. He is twenty years old and has a high school diploma. He worked at a video arcade, but now it is closed because of gang violence. Joe likes to wear denim. His parents are divorced. He is dating a girl named Virginia who works at a supermarket and goes to the community college, and he needs money so that they can get married and rent a small apartment. Let's assume that Joe applies the categorical imperative and that his maxim is, Every time I (who am in a certain situation) am broke and cannot get a loan, I will rob a bank. Then he universalizes it: Every time someone who is twenty, and whose name is Joe, who has divorced parents, used to work in a video arcade, likes denim, and is dating a checkout girl named Virginia who goes to a community college — anytime he feels like robbing a bank because he is broke, it is all right for him to do so. Now is that rational? Will Joe's maxim undermine his intention because everyone else will do the same thing he is planning to do? No, because he has described his situation so that "everyone" is reduced to a group of very few people who are in his exact same situation. In fact, his description of "everyone" could apply to only one person: Joe himself. In that case it is perfectly logical for him to rob a bank, because he won't undermine his own intention. This is hardly the kind of ironclad philosophical proof of doing the right thing that we were looking for. This argument, which also works against rule utilitarianism, is of course not a valid excuse for doing the wrong thing, and Joe shouldn't run out and rob the bank because he thinks philosophers have shown it to be okay. It is, however, an attempt to show that if we work with a principle that is as general as the categorical imperative, we just can't expect it to answer all our moral questions without a doubt. Of course it isn't an example Kant himself would have appreciated. Kant would have complained that we are making the example too specific. But the fact remains that the categorical imperative needs some further clarification and definition to avoid the "escape clause" that the loophole provides. You may think this example is rather far-fetched, since it's pretty obvious that nobody designs a moral rule you can get away with breaking if it applies only to yourself. However, the story of Joe, be it ever so outlandish, is our own story, in all those situations where we ask for lenient treatment because "we're special." We know we're supposed to send our taxes in on time, and to show up for the final, and so forth, but it's been a hard year, we just had the flu, our family's falling apart, and we'd really like some special consideration. And, if the special circumstances apply only in our case, well, then, we've found a loophole. The example of Joe is just a little more extreme.

4. What Is Rationality? Who is to say when something is irrational? This is an issue that might not have occurred to Kant. He, as a product of his times and a co-producer of the Age of Reason, believed that if we use our reason without looking to self-interest, then we will all come up with the same idea and result. Actually, Bentham believed the same thing, even though his moral vision was quite different from that of Kant. Today, after garnering a century of knowledge about the workings of the subconscious mind and realizing that people just aren't rational all or even most of the time, we are more inclined to believe that our individual idea of what is rational may depend greatly on who we are. If we use a very broad definition of rational, such as "realizing the shortest way to get to your goal and then pursuing it," we still may come up with different ideas about what is rational. Suppose not only that our Joe is broke but that he is also a political anarchist who believes that the sooner society breaks down, the better for all humanity and for himself in particular. Why then would it be particularly illogical for him to rob a bank, given that the downfall of society, including banks, is what he is longing for? And why should we refrain from lying to each other if what we want is to create social chaos and alienate our friends? Why refrain from hurting each other, if we are sadomasochists and believe it would be great to live in a world of mutual harmdoing? Although Joe is a fictional example, the real world provides examples of people who most of us believe acted irrationally while in their own minds following a sure rational path toward a goal. Consider Timothy McVeigh, the man responsible for the bombing of the Alfred P. Murrah Federal Building in Oklahoma City in 1995, which killed 167 men, women, and children. McVeigh was convicted of multiple murders of federal agents and was executed in June 2001. What kind of reasoning process did he go through in order to decide that taking human lives—the lives of strangers who had never done him any harm, the lives of toddlers and children—would somehow further a goal? If we ask whether he seriously considered the categorical imperative— Could he want others to do the same thing? Could he agree to a world in which someone did such things to him and his family?—then the Kantian tradition would probably claim that he could not, that his decision was irrational. But McVeigh already believed he did live in such a world, in which the *government* kills innocent people. (McVeigh was highly influenced by the federal raid on the Branch Davidian compound in Waco two years earlier.) In an interview he admitted that he thought his actions would start a revolution. So, if the rationality of one's decision depends on one's personal interpretation of the situation, how can the categorical imperative be a guarantee that we will all reach the same conclusion if only we use logic? Would using the categorical imperative have stopped Theodore Kaczynski, the Unabomber? For all his mental problems, Kaczynski is apparently an intelligent man and a scholar, and it is not improbable that he may have asked himself, Would you want your action to become a universal law? and answered Yes, I am doing the morally right thing.

Kant seems to assume that we all have the same general goals, which serve as a guarantee of the rationality of our actions. Change the goals, though, and the ideal of a reasonable course of action takes on a new meaning. (Box 6.2 further explores the issue of rationality.)

5. No Exceptions?   Does it really seem right that we can never be morally correct in breaking a universal rule? In other words, can the categorical imperative always assure us that sticking to the rule is better than breaking it? Let us say that a killer is stalking a friend of yours, and the friend comes to your door and asks you to hide her. You tell her to go hide in the broom closet. (This is a slightly altered version of one of Kant's own examples.) The killer comes to your door and asks, "Where is she?" Most of us would feel a primary obligation to help our friend, but for Kant the

Box 6.2 WHAT IS RATIONALITY?

Philosophers often refer to conduct and arguments as being *rational* or *logical*. Since the Age of Reason (the Western Enlightenment) in the eighteenth century, the emphasis has been particularly strong, the assumption being that as long as you use your reason, you can't go wrong. If you do go wrong, the implication is that you have been applying faulty logic: One part of your conduct or your statement has been at odds with another part. For both Bentham and Kant, products of the Enlightenment, there is a staunch belief in the infallibility of properly applied reasoning. This belief was eroded considerably in the twentieth century, partly because of Freud's theories of the Unconscious as a powerful factor in our decision making but one fundamentally outside the control of our rational mind. In the last decades of the twentieth century, other criticisms were raised against the concept of rationality. If we choose a basic definition of rationality that says, "Decide on a goal and select the most direct method to achieve it," then critics of the philosophical emphasis on reason may point out that this method is above all a *Western* cultural ideal and is not indicative

of a worldwide method of conduct. Some cultures prefer *indirect* methods of achieving goals and consider direct methods rude. Some feminists point out that the direct method of rationality is a predominantly *male* approach, whereas many women prefer an indirect way of achieving a goal; in addition, they say, women make use of a special way of knowing: knowledge by emotion and intuition. Could it be true that men, having developed rational skills from millennia of being hunters, think in hunters' terms—going straight for the prey and killing it? And women, after millennia of being gatherers, think more in terms of picking and choosing and comparing? A comedian built this into his act in the 1990s, illustrating man the hunter going shopping at the mall, single-mindedly tracking down a shirt—and his wife, the gatherer, shopping around until all items have been compared. It was a pretty funny routine—and it may actually come close to an evolutionary truth. But many feminists, such as Alison Jaggar, argue that the highest kind of knowledge incorporates both traditional rational thinking and

(continued)

cathy ®   **by Cathy Guisewite**

Is there a male and a female type of rationality? And does it reveal itself in our different styles of shopping? And if that might be the case, can a female shop the male way, and vice versa? Could there be other explanations for different shopping styles, rather than hard-wired gender nature?

Box 6.2   WHAT IS RATIONALITY?   *(continued)*

emotional thinking—for both men and women. Although some rejoice in the possibility of there being several legitimate ways of being rational, some women thinkers worry that this view might turn back the clock and revive the old prejudice that "women can't think logically." And some advocates of traditional rationality as a universal philosophical method speculate that although it is possible that several different ways of conducting oneself rationally may exist, the rules of mathematics and logic are universal examples of applied rationality: The basic rules for pure, logical thinking are not culture- or gender-dependent.

primary obligation is to the truth. You are supposed to answer, "I cannot tell a lie—she is hiding in the broom closet." This is what is meant by an *absolutist* moral theory: A moral rule allows for no exceptions. But why? Most of us would assume that the life of our friend would at least be worth a white lie, but for Kant it is a matter of principle. Suppose you lie to the killer, but your friend sneaks out of the house, and the killer finds her; then it is your fault. If you had told the truth, your friend might still have escaped, and the killer could have been prevented from committing the murder (perhaps you could have trapped him in the broom closet). This far-fetched argument follows Kant's own reasoning for why we should always stick to the rule: because if we break a rule we must answer for the consequences, whereas if we stick to the rule, we have no such responsibility. If we tell the truth, and the killer goes straight for the broom closet and kills our friend, Kant insists that we bear no responsibility for her death. But why should we accept Kant's idea that consequences don't count as long as you are following the rule but that they do count when you are not? Philosophers tend to agree that you can't make such arbitrary choices of when consequences count and when they don't.

If there are all these difficulties with the categorical imperative, why has it been such an influential moral factor? The reason is that it is the first moral theory to stress the idea of *universalizability*: realizing that the situation you are in is no different from that of other human beings. If something will bother you, it will probably bother others, too, everything else being equal. If you allow yourself a day off, you should not gripe when others do the same thing. Most important, however, you should think about it before you allow yourself that day off and realize that it won't do as a universal rule. The problem is, on occasion we all encounter special situations when we might actually *need* a day off; perhaps we are sick or emotionally upset. Similarly, on the whole we should not kill, but in certain rare situations we may be called on to do just that, in war or in self-defense. On the whole we should not lie, but there may come a day when a killer is stalking a friend of ours, and we have a chance to save her. In that case we may need to lie. These are unusual situations, so why should Kant's generalizations apply to them? This issue has caused scholars to suggest that there really is nothing wrong with the format of the categorical imperative, provided that we are allowed to expand our maxim to include situations in which we might accept certain *exceptions* to our rule. As long as they don't expand to become a loophole, the universalization works just fine: We can universalize not killing, with the exception of self-defense and certain other specified cases. We can universalize not taking a day off from work unless we are sick or severely emotionally upset, as long as it doesn't happen very often. We can universalize not lying if it is understood that preventing harm to an innocent person would constitute an exception. At the end of this chapter we look at a classic episode from the television series *Star Trek: The Next Generation* in which this problem is nicely illustrated: Absolute moral rules may have their advantages, but a truly mature moral theory must allow for some exceptions to the rules.

Rational Beings Are Ends in Themselves

In his book *Grounding for the Metaphysics of Morals,* Kant explores three major themes: the *categorical imperative,* the concept of *ends in themselves,* and the concept of a *kingdom of ends.* In a sense you might say that if we add the idea of people being ends in themselves to the idea of the categorical imperative, then the result will be a kingdom of ends. Below we look at the ends-in-themselves concept as well as the kingdom of ends.

Persons Shouldn't Be Used as Tools

In *Grounding,* Kant suggests two different ways to express the categorical imperative. The first one we have just looked at; the other goes like this:

> Now I say that man, and in general every rational being, exists as an end in himself and not merely as a means to be arbitrarily used by this or that will. He must in all his actions, whether directed to himself or to other rational beings, always be regarded at the same time as an end.

What does it mean to be treated as an "end in himself"? Let us first look at the opposite approach: to be treated as a "means to an end only." What is a means to an end? It is a tool, an instrument to be used to achieve some goal; it is something that has *instrumental* value in the achievement of something of *intrinsic* value. If someone is used as a means to an end, she or he is treated as a tool for someone else's purpose, in a very broad sense. If someone is being sexually abused or kept as a slave, that person obviously is being treated as a means to an end, but so is the girl we befriend so we can get to know her brother. So is anyone who is being used for other people's purposes without regard for his or her intrinsic value and dignity as a human being, even if the purpose is good—such as creating happiness for a large number of people. For Kant this is just another way of expressing the categorical imperative. What made him think this? For one thing, when you use the categorical imperative you are universalizing your maxim, and if you are refusing to treat others merely as means to an end, you are also universalizing a maxim, and a very fundamental one. Second, both maxims may be interpreted as expressions of the Golden Rule.

This statement about the immorality of treating other humans as means to an end was, for the eighteenth century, a tremendously important political and social

For Better or For Worse   **by Lynn Johnston**

Copyright © Lynn Johnston Prod., Inc. Dist. by United Features Syndicate, Inc.

> Immanuel Kant says we should never treat another rational being as merely a means to an end; although extreme cases of reducing another person to an instrument for someone else's purpose, such as slavery or sexual abuse, are today recognized as morally unacceptable, we still have lots of everyday examples in which people treat one another as tools for their own agenda—as, for example, in this situation from the comic strip *For Better or For Worse*.

statement. In Kant's era (although not in Kant's country) slavery was still a social factor; abuse of the lower classes by the upper classes was commonplace; Europe was just emerging from a time when monarchs and warlords could move their peasants and conscripted soldiers around like chess pieces with no regard for their lives and happiness. Then Kant clearly stated that it is not social status that determines one's standing in the moral universe, but one thing only: the capability to use reason. As one of the leading lights of the Age of Reason, Kant stated that any rational human being deserves respect. Rich and poor, young and old, all races and peoples— all are alike in having rationality as the one defining mark of their humanity, and none deserves to be treated without regard for that characteristic. Here it must be interjected, in case we get carried away with our praise, that Kant himself expressed doubt as to whether women were actually rational beings, or as rational as men; he may have had the same reservations about people of color (see Box 6.3), but we will be generous and look at the *implications* of Kant's theory for human rights, regardless of whether or not he himself saw as the goal that every human being deserves respect.

Why are rational beings intrinsically valuable? Because they can place a value on things. What is gold worth if nobody wants it? Nothing. Humans are value-givers; they assign a relative worth to things that interest them. However, as value-givers, humans always have an *absolute* value. They set the price, so to speak, yet cannot have a price set on them. We do, however, constantly talk about people being "worth money." A baseball player is worth a fortune, a Hollywood actress is worth millions. What does that mean? Have we set a price on humans after all? Not in the appropriate sense. It doesn't mean we can *buy* the Hollywood actress for a couple of million (well, we might, but in that case she is treating *herself* as a means to an end only, by selling her

Box 6.3 KANT, THE ENLIGHTENMENT, AND RACISM

Over the years, Kant has acquired the status of one of the primary sources of the idea of human rights and equality because of his view that any rational being should be treated with dignity and never merely as a means to an end. This view has inspired Western thinkers, writers, and politicians to the point that we can actually say now that, even if the ideal has not yet been reached, the Western world is denouncing regimes that do not recognize all their citizens as equals, regardless of gender, income, race, ethnicity, religion, and nationality (see the United Nations Declaration of Human Rights at the end of Chapter 7). But was this the goal Kant had in mind? It is rather discouraging to find out that it wasn't. Kant himself, as much as he has inspired today's quest for equality, had no philosophical goal of either gender or racial equality. Kant believed himself to be drawing on the cutting edge of biological research (he actually taught more classes in geography than in philosophy); in a rarely quoted text, "On the Different Races of Man" (1775), Kant voices the opinion that there are substantial differences in "natural dispositions" among what Kant sees as the four predominant human races of the world. For Kant and many other eighteenth-century Western thinkers, the European race was more intelligent than other races, and males were more intelligent than females. With no sound scientific evidence, some of the most important thinkers of the Western Enlightenment—which did usher in the first stages of global equality—decided that some humans were more advanced than others. This of course raises suspicion that Kant's "rational beings" may not have included all *humans,* but primarily white males. However, ten years later Kant specified, in *Grounding,* that *all of humanity* should be treated like ends in themselves. It would be grossly unfair to assume that Kant thought only white males were "persons." But Kant's rule of "ends in themselves" only protects humans against abuse—it doesn't guarantee social equality.

Old heroes sometimes topple in the light of new research, and according to some critics this is what is happening to Kant: He may not be the champion of human rights we thought he was. We are even justified in calling him a racist, if we use today's view of racism as discrimination against individuals or groups of people solely based on their race. In my view, however, we should never forget that Kant was, for his day, indeed a champion of human rights. Europe was a place of serfdom, where peasants were treated as the property of the great landowners. Kant's writings did help set in motion the process that we all today have benefited from: the philosophical sea change that resulted in the concept of inalienable human rights. So Kant himself may have been locked in the racial bigotry of ignorance common for his day and age, but his ideas of a kingdom of ends in which *everyone* is treated with respect and dignity have today survived to become a Western political and philosophical ideal. He may fall short of the "minimum qualifications" considered necessary for an open-minded thinker today, but he did leave a legacy that can't be overestimated: the ideal of social and political dignity as a human birthright. That credit should not be taken away from him.

body). What we usually mean is that she has a lot of money. And the baseball player? He certainly can be "bought and sold," but hardly as a slave; he retains his autonomy and gets rich in the process. It is his talent and his services that are paid for. Under normal circumstances we don't refer to people as entities that can be bought for money, and if we do, we are usually implying that something bad is taking place (slavery and bribery, for instance). Thus people are value-givers, because they can decide rationally what they want and what they don't want. This means that rational beings are *persons,* and the second formulation of the categorical imperative is focused on respect for persons: *Act in such a way that you treat humanity, whether in your own person or in the person of another, always at the same time as an end and never simply as means.*

Notice that Kant is not talking about not mistreating just others. You have to respect yourself, too, and not let others step on you. You have a right to set values of your own and not just be used by others as their key to success. But what exactly does it mean not to treat anybody *simply as means to an end*? We know that blatant abuse is wrong and that a subtler kind is no better. But what about using someone's services? When you buy your groceries, there usually is some person who bags your items. Truthfully, are you treating that person as a means to get your groceries bagged? Yes, indeed, but not *simply* as a means; he or she is getting paid, and you presumably don't treat these workers as though they were put on this earth just to bag your groceries. Everyday life consists of people using other people's services, and that is just the normal give-and-take of social life. The danger arises if we stop respecting people for what they do and reduce them in our minds to mere tools for our comfort or success. As long as the relationship is reciprocal (you pay for your groceries, and the bagger gets a paycheck), then there is no abuse taking place. Indeed, students use their professors as a means to an end (to get their degree), but the professors rarely feel abused, provided that they receive a salary. Likewise, the professors use students as a means to their ends (to receive that salary), but the professors surely don't imagine that the students were put on this earth to feed them or pay their mortgage.

What makes the question of treating someone as a means to an end especially interesting is the borderline type of situation in which both parties agree to treat each other merely as instruments for their own purposes. What about the prostitute and her (or his) customer? What about marriages of convenience made in order to secure some mutual advantage? The film *Indecent Proposal* (1993) explores a relationship between people who reduce each other to tools: A wealthy man offers a destitute young couple a million dollars if the wife will sleep with him. What might Kant say to that situation? There is a mutual agreement, so one is not unilaterally abusing the other; however, remember that Kant also says we should not allow ourselves to be reduced to being mere tools for others. In *The Metaphysics of Morals* (1797) he gives a more specific answer: In sexual situations people *seem* to be reducing each other to mere objects, but that is not really what takes place: When there is mutual agreement (and for Kant that meant lovemaking between husband and wife), then one gives oneself to the other as a gift, rather than reducing the other to a thing, and that makes a world of difference. But for Kant all other sexual situations did indeed involve reducing the other (and/or oneself) to a tool. (Kant himself apparently did contemplate marriage on more than one occasion but hesitated so long, because he was not a wealthy man and was worried about being able to support a wife, that the widow he had hoped to marry accepted someone else's proposal.)

Beings Who Are Things

Any rational being deserves respect. We assume that humans fall into that category, but what if there are rational beings who are not human? It is not unthinkable that humans might encounter extraterrestrials who are rational enough to know math, language, and space science; and how about the possibility of AI, Artifical Intelligence? Would Kant respect a thinking android or computer, or a rational alien, or would he advocate treating them like things? If these beings are *rational,* they qualify as full members of our moral universe, and humans have no right to treat them as tools to achieve knowledge or power. Aliens and androids, would likewise have no right to cart humans off for medical experiments, because all humans are generally rational beings.

There are beings on this earth who are not rational in Kant's sense of the word — animals, for example. In *Grounding* he presents his theory in this way:

> Beings whose existence depends not on our will but on nature have, nevertheless, if they are not rational beings, only a relative value as means and are therefore called things. On the other hand, rational beings are called persons inasmuch as their nature already marks them out as ends in themselves. . . .

This means that nonhuman animals don't belong in the moral universe at all; they are classified as *things* and can be used as a tool by a rational person, because animals can't place a value on something — only humans can do that. And an animal is not worth anything in itself; it has value only if it is wanted for some purpose by a human. If nobody cares about cats, or spotted owls, then they have no value. Is it true, though, that animals can't place a value on things? Most people with firsthand knowledge of animals will report that pets are capable of valuing their owners above all and their food bowl second (or is it the other way around?). And animals in the wild place extreme importance on their territory and their young. Many people today categorize animal interests as just different in *degree* from human interests and not different in *kind* (Chapter 13). Although Kant and most of his contemporaries (with the exclusion of Bentham) believed that the moral universe is closed to nonhuman animals, it is just possible today that we not only might include animals as "creatures who deserve respect" but also might actively look for traces of *animal morality.* Might the self-sacrifice of a baboon to save her tribe from the leopard constitute a moral dimension? Is a gorilla morally good if she comes to the rescue of a child who has fallen into the gorilla enclosure at the zoo? Or are we just witnessing automatic instinctual responses? (See Box 6.4 for further discussion.)

Whatever we think now, the day could be near when dolphins, elephants, and the great apes are included in a category of rudimentary rational beings. For our purposes here, we simply should remember that for Kant it was not just a matter of being able to think — one must also be able to show that one has autonomy and can set up universal moral rules for oneself and others; and although certain animals may have some thought capacity, it is doubtful whether they ever can be considered *morally autonomous* in the Kantian sense of the term.

Box 6.4   CAN ANIMALS THINK?

From the previous chapter you may remember that Descartes didn't believe animals had any mental activity because according to his theory they consisted of matter only. Kant does not deny that nonhuman animals have minds; he just does not believe them to be rational minds but rather instinctive—in his own words, "depending on nature" (*Grounding*). In *The Metaphysics of Morals* he explains further: Although animals and humans all have wills that propel them toward their goals, only humans have free choice; animals making choices about what to eat, with whom to mate, and where to sleep don't make use of moral laws, and so their choice is merely brutish (as some people's choices of the same type may be). But when a person makes a choice based on a rational principle of universalizability, then Kant calls it a free choice.

Today the issue of animal intelligence is still controversial. Some ethologists (animal behaviorists) continue to believe that human and non-human animal intelligence are different *in kind;* others now lean toward the assumption that they are different *in degree.* Close observations in experimental situations over years of research and coexistence with animals have led many modern biologists and behaviorists to conclude that at least certain animals, such as great apes, dolphins, and orcas (killer whales), have a rudimentary capacity for rational thinking and even for linguistic comprehension (as humans define language). In Chapter 13 we take a closer look at the issues of animal intelligence and animal rights.

Numerous scholars have pointed out, however, that there is a serious problem with Kant's own classification of humans as rational beings, for suppose someone who is genetically human can't think rationally? There are many humans who aren't good at thinking or can't think at all, either because they are infants, babies, have Alzheimer's, or because they are mentally disabled or in a coma. Does this mean that all of these people aren't *persons* and should be classified as *things*? As some scholars have remarked, there are animals who are more like persons (that is, rational beings) than newborn infants or severely mentally disabled humans are. Would Kant really say that such humans are no better than things? The trouble is that Kant never made provisions for any such subcategories of "persons" in *Grounding.* It is either-or.

There is no denying that problems arise if you divide the world into persons (with rights not to be abused by others) and things (that persons have a right to use). But twelve years after writing *Grounding,* in his long-awaited *The Metaphysics of Morals,* Kant addressed the question of an intermediate category: people who have absolute rights as ends in themselves but who also, for various reasons, "belong" to other persons. Kant calls it "the right to a person akin to a right to a thing"—such persons are legitimately treated *as if* they were possessions, although they cannot be owned as slaves. An example would be a small child: She is a person with the right to personal freedom; the child's parents can't destroy her, even if they brought her into the world; but the child does not have full self-determination, either, because she is still regarded as a pseudo-possession of her parents until the day she is grown (if someone takes her, her parents can demand to have her back). The parents have a duty to raise the child properly, and the child has no duty to repay them. Similarly, servants of a household belong in the intermediate category of being pseudo-possessions: They are free persons, but because they have signed contracts they can't just take off whenever they feel like it, Kant says. On the other hand, they can't be bought and sold, either, because then they would be slaves, and slavery is reducing someone to merely a means to an end. Some scholars believe that with this intermediate category between a person with full freedom and a thing with none, Kant has opened the door for the modern category sometimes called "partial rights": A being who is not a rational, human adult may be granted some rights but may still be regarded as under the guardianship of other humans. Vilifying Kant for poisoning philosophy toward the rights of partially rational beings hardly seems fair, under these circumstances. But in *The Metaphysics of Morals* we also hear in no uncertain terms from Kant that animals are not rational and have no rights, because in order for us to have duties to other beings, they have to be capable of having obligations to us. (See Chapter 13 for a continuation of this debate.) Classifying an animal as a thing seemed reasonable to Kant, but, even so, he was concerned that some readers might take this as permission to treat animals any way they saw fit, including being cruel to them. Kant was very specific about condemning cruelty to animals; however, he took this stance not so much for the sake of the animals themselves but because someone who hurts animals might easily get used to it and begin to hurt people. It appears that Kant was more right than most of his readers could have known at the time; although Kant is not the first person to have claimed that cruelty to animals may lead to cruelty toward people (St. Thomas Aquinas had said the same thing in the thirteenth century), the depth of the connection only became apparent in the late twentieth century, when criminal profiling established that just about every serial killer questioned through the late 1990s turned out to have tortured small animals when he was a child. (This investigation focused on male serial killers, since there have been very few female serial murderers so far.) In addition, such individuals would also engage in setting fires and were chronic bed-wetters. This does not mean that a boy who wets his bed, sets fires, and tortures animals will invariably grow up to be a serial killer, but these behaviors are considered warning signs that should be attended to while the child is still young. The point Kant wanted to make, which criminal profiling has corroborated, is that desensitization to — or even enjoyment of — animal pain can lead to deliberately inflicting pain on human beings. In Kant's words (from *The Metaphysics of Morals*):

> It dulls his shared feeling of their pain and so weakens and gradually uproots a natural predisposition that is very serviceable to morality in one's relations with other men. Man is authorized to kill animals quickly (without pain) and to put them to work that does not strain them beyond their capacities (such work as man himself must submit to). But agonizing physical experiments for the sake of mere speculation, when the end could also be achieved without these, are to be abhorred.

It is interesting that Kant, having over the years acquired the reputation of being insensitive to the plight of animals, himself argued against causing needless pain to them. Contrary to Descartes, Kant never thought animals couldn't feel pain; he just thought that within the context of human moral issues it was only marginally relevant. Some issues are thus resolved in *The Metaphysics of Morals,* but not all issues. Even so, the idea that rational beings should never be treated merely as means to an end has been a powerful contribution to a world of equality and mutual respect because it is such a remarkable expansion of the moral universe described in previous moral theories, which tended to exclude social groups that somehow weren't considered quite as valuable as others. Furthermore, Kant placed the foundation of morality solidly with human rationality and not with the state or the church.

The Kingdom of Ends

This brings us to the third major theme in Kant's *Grounding,* the "kingdom of ends." Applying the categorical imperative is something all rational beings can do—and even if they can't do it exactly the way Kant uses it, the logic of it should be compelling for all people who can ask themselves, "Would I want everybody to do this?" Kant calls this *moral autonomy:* The only moral authority that can tell us to do something and not to do something else is our own reason. As we saw previously, if all people follow the same principle and disregard their own personal inclinations, then all will end up following the same good rules, because all have universalized their intention. In such a world, with everyone doing the right thing and nobody abusing anyone else, a new realm will have been created: the *kingdom of ends.* "Kingdom" poetically describes a community of people, and "ends" indicates that the people treat each other as ends only—as beings who have their own goals in life—never merely as means to other people's ends. Every time we show respect and consideration for one another, we make the kingdom of ends a little more real. In Kant's words from *Grounding,*

> By "kingdom" I understand a system of different rational beings through common laws . . . For all rational beings stand under the law that each of them should treat himself and all others never merely as a means but always at the same time as an end in himself. Hereby arises a systematic union of rational beings through common objective laws, i.e., a kingdom that may be called a kingdom of ends (certainly only an ideal), inasmuch as these laws have in view the very relation of such beings to one another as ends and means.
>
> A rational being belongs to the kingdom of ends as a member when he legislates in it universal laws while also himself being subject to these laws. He belongs to it as sovereign, when as legislator he is himself subject to the will of no other . . . In the kingdom of ends everything has either a price or a dignity. Whatever has a price can be replaced by something else as its equivalent; on the other hand, whatever is above all price, and therefore admits no equivalent, has a dignity.

Here we see how Kant combines the first part of his book, the categorical imperative, with the second part, the idea that nobody should be used merely as a means to an end. People who adhere to the method of the categorical imperative are autonomous lawmakers: They set laws for themselves that, when universalized, become acceptable to every other rational being. When we use that approach, we realize that we can't allow ourselves to treat others (or let others treat us) as merely a means to an end, but recognize that other people should be treated with respect, because they are rational beings with dignity, *irreplaceable* beings. ~~We all belong in the kingdom of ends, the realm of beings with dignity.~~ But whatever doesn't qualify as rational has a price, and can be replaced with a similar item. (This of course means that any human being has dignity and is irreplaceable, while your dog has no dignity, and can be replaced.)

Some readers of Kant believe that he shows a more humane side in his theory of ends in themselves, and indeed we might take this idea and apply it to the problem of whether to lie to the killer who has come to murder your friend. The categorical imperative tells you to speak the truth always, because then you can't be blamed for the consequences. But is this really the same as saying we should treat others as ends in themselves? Perhaps there is a subtle difference; if we apply this rule to the killer who is stalking our friend, would we get the same result? Might we not be treating our friend as merely a means to an end if we refuse to lie for her, whether it is for the sake of principle or just so that we can't be blamed for the consequences? If we are sacrificing our friend for the sake of the truth, it might rightfully be said that in that case we are treating her as a means to an end only. So even within Kant's own system there are irreconcilable differences. This should not cause us to want to discard his entire theory, however; since the nineteenth century, philosophers have tried to redesign Kant's ideas to fit a more perceptive (or, as Kant would say, more lenient) world. Some of these ideas are working quite well — for example, allowing for general exceptions to be built into the categorical imperative itself and allowing for animals to be considered more rational than Kant ever thought possible.

Study Questions

1. Evaluate the following statement: "Actions are morally good only if they are done because of a good will." Explain what Kant means by a "good will." Do you think the statement is correct or incorrect? Explain your position.

2. Analyze the following statement: "Man, and in general every rational being, should be treated as an end in himself, never merely as a means." What are the moral implications of this statement for humans, as well as nonhumans?

3. Explain Kant's position on lying: Is it always morally wrong to lie? What are the implications for the question raised in Chapter 5, "Should we lie to Grandma about something that will distress her?"

Primary Readings and Narratives

The first Primary Reading is an excerpt from Kant's famous *Grounding for the Metaphysics of Morals* in which he explains the structure of the categorical imperative. The second Primary Reading is an excerpt from Kant's less frequently quoted book, *The Metaphysics of Morals,* in which he explains why lying is wrong. The Narratives are all summaries: A set of three similar stories: *Outland* and *Cop Land* draw on the theme suggested by the original story, the famous Western *High Noon,* in which the town marshal chooses to face three gunmen alone after having been rejected by the community he is trying to defend. The film *Abandon Ship!* is a true story about a shipwrecked lifeboat with too many people on board. The episode "Justice" from *Star Trek: The Next Generation* is about young Wesley, who breaks a rule on an alien planet and is scheduled for execution as a result.

 Primary Reading

Grounding for the Metaphysics of Morals

IMMANUEL KANT

1785. Excerpt.

In this passage Kant introduces the categorical imperative and links it with the concept of the good will as an understanding of doing one's duty in accordance with reason.

Thus the moral worth of an action does not lie in the effect expected from it nor in any principle of action that needs to borrow its motive from this expected effect. For all these effects (agreeableness of one's condition and even the furtherance of other people's happiness) could have been brought about also through other causes and would not have required the will of a rational being, in which the highest and unconditioned good can alone be found. Therefore, the pre-eminent good which is called moral can consist in nothing but the representation of the law in itself, and such a representation can admittedly be found only in a rational being insofar as this representation, and not some expected effect, is the determining ground of the will. This good is already present in the person who acts according to this representation, and such good need not be awaited merely from the effect.

But what sort of law can that be the thought of which must determine the will without reference to any expected effect, so that the will can be called absolutely good without qualification? Since I have deprived the will of every impulse that might arise for it from obeying any particular law, there is nothing left to serve the will as principle except the universal conformity of its actions to law as such, i.e., I should never act except in such a way that I can also will that my maxim should become a universal law. Here mere conformity to law as such (without having as its basis any law determining particular actions) serves the will as principle and must so serve it if duty is not to be a vain delusion and a chimerical concept. The ordinary reason of mankind in its practical judgments agrees completely with this, and always has in view the aforementioned principle.

For example, take this question. When I am in distress, may I make a promise with the intention of not keeping it? I readily distinguish here the two meanings which the question may have; whether making a false promise conforms with prudence or with duty. Doubtless the former can often be the case. Indeed I clearly see that escape from

some present difficulty by means of such a promise is not enough. In addition I must carefully consider whether from this lie there may later arise far greater inconvenience for me than from what I now try to escape. Furthermore, the consequences of my false promise are not easy to forsee, even with all my supposed cunning; loss of confidence in me might prove to be far more disadvantageous than the misfortune which I now try to avoid. The more prudent way might be to act according to a universal maxim and to make it a habit not to promise anything without intending to keep it. But that such a maxim is, nevertheless, always based on nothing but a fear of consequences becomes clear to me at once. To be truthful from duty is, however, quite different from being truthful from fear of disadvantageous consequences; in the first case the concept of the action itself contains a law for me, while in the second I must first look around elsewhere to see what are the results for me that might be connected with the action. For to deviate from the principle of duty is quite certainly bad; but to abandon my maxim of prudence can often be very advantageous for me, though to abide by it is certainly safer. The most direct and infallible way, however, to answer the question as to whether a lying promise accords with duty is to ask myself whether I would really be content if my maxim (of extracting myself from difficulty by means of a false promise) were to hold as a universal law for myself as well as for others, and could I really say to myself that everyone may promise falsely when he finds himself in a difficulty from which he can find no other way to extricate himself. Then I immediately become aware that I can indeed will the lie but can not at all will a universal law to lie. For by such a law there would really be no promises at all, since in vain would my willing future actions be professed to other people who would not believe what I professed, or if they over-hastily did believe, then they would pay me back in like coin. Therefore, my maxim would necessarily destroy itself just as soon as it was made a universal law.

Therefore, I need no fear-reaching acuteness to discern what I have to do in order that my will may be morally good. Inexperienced in the course of the world and incapable of being prepared for all its contingencies, I only ask myself whether I can also will that my maxim should become a universal law. If not, then the maxim must be rejected, not because of any disadvantage accruing to me or even to others, but because it cannot be fitting as a principle in a possible legislation of universal law, and reason exacts from me immediate respect for such legislation. Indeed I have as yet no insight into the grounds of such respect (which the philosopher may investigate). But I at least understand that respect is an estimation of a worth that far outweighs any worth of what is recommended by inclination, and that the necessity of acting from pure respect for the practical law is what constitutes duty, to which every other motive must give way because duty is the condition of a will good in itself, whose worth is above all else.

Study Questions

1. What does Kant mean by a good will?

2. Explain the structure and purpose of the categorical imperative.

3. Can you think of a situation where it might actually be counterproductive to do a good or a harmless thing if everyone did the same thing? How might Kant respond?

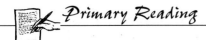

The Metaphysics of Morals

IMMANUEL KANT

Excerpt from Book I, Chapter II, 1797.

This book was actually printed separately in two parts but is considered one book today. The first part is *The Doctrine of Right,* and the second one is *The Doctrine of Virtue.* This section on lying from *The Doctrine of Virtue* illustrates Kant's talent for careful analysis of even an ordinary kind of experience in order to argue his points that you should not make choices you couldn't wish to become a universal law and that you should not make choices that diminish the dignity of others or yourself.

Man's Duty to Himself Merely as a Moral Being: This duty is opposed to the vices of *lying, avarice,* and *false humility* (servility).

On Lying: The greatest violation of man's duty to himself regarded merely as a moral being (the humanity in his own person) is the contrary of truthfulness, *lying* (*aliud lingua promptum, aliud pectore inclusum gerere*). ["To have one thing shut up in the heart and another ready on the tongue." Sallust, *The War with Catiline* X, 5.] In the doctrine of Right an intentional untruth is called a lie only if it violates another's right; but in ethics, where no authorization is derived from harmlessness, it is clear of itself that no intentional untruth in the expression of one's thoughts can refuse this harsh name. For the dishonor (being an object of moral contempt) that accompanies a lie also accompanies a liar like his shadow. A lie can be an external lie (*mendacium externum*) or also an internal lie. By an external lie a man makes himself an object of contempt in the eyes of others; by an internal lie he does what is still worse: He makes himself contemptible in his own eyes and violates the dignity of humanity in his own person. And so, since the harm that can come to other men from lying is not what distinguishes this vice (for if it were, the vice would consist only in violating one's duty to others), this harm is not taken into account here. Neither is the harm that a liar brings on himself; for then a lie, as a mere error in prudence, would conflict with the pragmatic maxim, not the moral maxim, and it could not be considered a violation of duty at all. By a lie a man throws away and, as it were, annihilates his dignity as a man. A man who does not himself believe what he tells another (even if the other is a merely ideal person) has even less worth than if he were a mere thing; for a thing, because it is something real and given, has the property of being serviceable so that another can put it to some use. But communication of one's thoughts to someone through words that yet (intentionally) contain the contrary of what the speaker thinks on the subject is an end that is directly opposed to the natural purposiveness of the speaker's capacity to communicate his thoughts, and is thus a renunciation by the speaker of his personality, and such a speaker is a mere deceptive appearance of a man, not a man himself. *Truthfulness* in one's declarations is also called *honesty* and, if the declarations are promises, *sincerity;* but, more generally, truthfulness is called rectitude.

Lying (in the ethical sense of the word), intentional untruth as such, need not be *harmful* to others in order to be repudiated; for it would then be a violation of the rights of others. It may be done merely out of frivolity or even good nature; the speaker may even intend to achieve a really good end by it. But his way of pursuing this end is, by its mere form, a crime of a man against his own person and a worthlessness that must make him contemptible in his own eyes.

It is easy to show that man is actually guilty of many inner lies, but it seems more difficult to explain how they are possible; for a lie requires a second person whom one intends to deceive, whereas to deceive oneself on purpose seems to contain a contradiction.

Man as a moral being (*homo noumenon*) cannot use himself as a natural being (*homo phaenomenon*) as a mere means (a speaking machine), as if his natural being were not bound to the inner end (of communicating thoughts), but is bound to the condition of using himself as a natural being in agreement with the declaration (*declaratio*) of his moral being and is under obligation to himself to *truthfulness.* Someone tells an inner lie, for example, if he professes belief in a future judge of the world, although he really finds no such belief within himself but persuades himself that it could do no harm and might even be useful to profess in his thoughts to one who scrutinizes hearts a belief in such a judge, in order to win His favor in case He should exist. Someone also lies if, having no doubt about the existence of this future judge, he still flatters himself that he inwardly reveres His law, though the only incentive he feels is fear of punishment.

Insincerity is mere lack of *conscientiousness,* that is, of purity in one's professions before one's inner judge, who is thought of as another person when conscientiousness is taken quite strictly; then if someone, from self-love, takes a wish for the deed because he has a really good end in mind, his inner lie, although it is indeed contrary to man's duty to himself, gets the name of a frailty, as when a lover's wish to find only good qualities in his beloved blinds him to her obvious faults. But such insincerity in his declarations, which man perpetrates upon himself, still deserves the strongest censure, since it is from such a rotten spot (falsity, which seems to be rooted in human nature itself) that the evil of untruthfulness spreads into man's relations with other men as well, once the highest principle of truthfulness has been violated.

Remark: It is noteworthy that the Bible dates the first crime, through which evil entered the world, not from *fratricide* (Cain's) but from the first *lie* (for even nature rises up against fratricide), and calls the author of all evil a liar from the beginning and the father of lies. However, reason can assign no further ground for man's propensity to *hypocrisy* (*esprit fourbe*), although this propensity must have been present before the lie; for an act of freedom cannot (like a natural effect) be deduced and explained in accordance with the natural law of the connection of effects with their causes, all of which are appearances.

Casuistical Questions: Can an untruth from mere politeness (e.g., the "your obedient servant" at the end of a letter) be considered a lie? No one is deceived by it. An author asks one of his readers, "How do you like my work?" One could merely seem to give an answer, by joking about the impropriety of such a question. But who has his wit always ready? The author will take the slightest hesitation in answering as an insult. May one, then, say what is expected of one?

If I say something untrue in more serious matters, having to do with what is mine or yours, must I answer for all the consequences it might have? For example, a householder has ordered his servant to say "not at home" if a certain man asks for him. The servant does this and, as a result, the master slips away and commits a serious crime, which would otherwise have been prevented by the guard sent to arrest him. Who (in accordance with ethical principles) is guilty in this case? Surely the servant, too, who violated a duty to himself by his lie, the results of which his own conscience imputes to him.

Study Questions

1. Why does a liar annihilate his or her own dignity? Is there a connection to the categorical imperative and/or the theory of respect for persons?

2. What is the difference between an external and an internal lie? Is one more acceptable than the other, according to Kant? And according to you?

3. Discuss Kant's own "study question," "Is the servant guilty?" Why? Compare this example to the example of the killer at the door.

Narratives

Three Deontological Films

High Noon

CARL FOREMAN (SCREENWRITER)
FRED ZINNEMAN (DIRECTOR)

Film, 1952. Summary.

This film may be the most famous Western of all time, and yet it is not a "true" Western. There is very little riding, no troops or Indians, no cattle, no cowboys — but much talk about the right thing to do. This film was made in the early days of McCarthyism in Hollywood, and Fred Zinneman (the director) has admitted that it is an allegory of the general attitude in Hollywood of 1952 of turning your back on friends who were accused (mostly falsely) of "un-American" (Communist) activities and who might have needed help. When it was produced, it was not considered to have any potential as a classic but it has soared in public opinion ever since then. It is a Western — but a Western of a different sort — a Western about the problems of a budding civilization in the midst of an era of violence. The film also is very well crafted. The amount of time that elapses from the moment Marshal Will Kane realizes he will have to face four gunmen alone because

In *High Noon* (United Artists, 1952) Will Kane (Gary Cooper, left) has just been married and has resigned as marshal of Hadleyville, but a killer he helped put in prison and three other gunmen are now looking for him. He tries to get the townspeople to stand by him the way they did when he captured the killer five years earlier, but now everybody turns their back on him, preferring not to get involved. In this scene a former friend, Herb (James Millican), is backing out of his promise to help Kane, having found out that nobody else is coming along.

the whole town worries about the consequences of siding with him to the moment the actual gunfight takes place is the exact amount of time you spend watching it in the theater or in front of your TV: an hour and a half.

The plot is simple. Five years before, Kane brought a killer, Frank Miller, to justice. Miller was sentenced to hang, but "up North they commuted it to life, and now he's free," as the judge says. He is coming in on the noon train to have it out with Kane. Word of his intentions comes just as Kane is marrying his Quaker bride in a civil ceremony. He has already given up his job and is leaving town with his new wife when he turns around to face the gunmen coming in on the noon train. His wife, Amy, asks him why he is turning back—he doesn't have to play the hero for her, she says. He answers, "I haven't got time to tell you. . . . And if you think I like this, you're crazy."

In town, Kane tries to get his former deputies to join him, but everyone is afraid of Miller, except the deputy, who is the boyfriend of Helen Ramirez, Kane's former girl-friend. Helen is the only one who understands Kane's problem, because, as a Mexican, she has always felt like an outcast herself—and besides, she used to be Frank Miller's girlfriend, too. When Amy leaves Kane because she can't stand the threat of violence, she seeks out Helen because she thinks it is because of her that Kane is staying in town. Amy begs Helen to let him go, and when she hears that he isn't staying because of Helen, she asks, bewildered, what then is making her husband stay. Helen tells her, "If you don't know, I can't tell you." Helen's boyfriend, the deputy, looks up Kane and tries to force him to leave town so that he can take over as town marshal. He also asks Kane why he is staying, and all Kane says is, "I don't know."

Desperate, Kane makes for the little church where the Sunday service is still going on, and we remember that an hour ago he was married in a civil ceremony. The service comes to a stop as he enters, and the minister asks him what could be so important since he didn't see fit to be married in church. Kane explains that his wife is a Quaker, and not a member of the town's Protestant congregation, and he knows he is not a churchgoing man, but he needs help. Some of the same men who were deputies with him when they arrested Miller are attending the service—don't they feel the call to duty? Democratically, the congregation plunges into a debate: Why is Kane still here if he is no longer marshal? Why hasn't he arrested the men at the depot? Why must private citizens pitch in every time law enforcement can't handle the situation? But Kane also has supporters who remember that he cleaned up the town and made it a place fit for civilized people. In the end, the mayor speaks: We owe Kane a great debt, he says, so we, the citizens, ought to take care of the situation—and Kane ought to get out of town so there will be no bloodshed. Because (and this is obviously the mayor's real concern) with bloodshed in the streets, investors from up North will shy away from putting money into the town. The support Kane was hoping for evaporates in light of financial concerns.

The "good citizens" want Kane to leave town so there will be no deterrence to progress. The former sheriff wants him to leave, saying that keeping the law is an ungrateful business. Everybody wants him to leave, and at the train depot Frank Miller's three gunmen are waiting for the train that will bring Frank. But Kane feels compelled to stay, even with nobody to side with him. The last man to abandon Kane is his friend Herb. When he realizes that it will be just him and Kane against Miller and his gang, he pleads with Kane, "I have a wife and kids—what about my kids?" And Kane responds, "Go home to your kids, Herb."

The train arrives, a gunfight ensues in the dusty streets of the town, and two of Frank's gunmen are killed. In the end, Amy comes to Kane's rescue and kills the third gunman; Kane kills Miller, and together he and Amy leave town—but not before Kane has thrown his marshal's star in the dust.

Study Questions

1. What makes Kane stay? Is he serious when he says, "I don't know"?

2. Is it fair of Kane to place Amy in a situation where she has to give up her own moral principles?

3. Why might we say that this is a "Kantian" Western?

4. How would a utilitarian judge Kane's feeling of conscience and duty?

5. Are the townspeople who refuse to help primarily deontologists, utilitarians, or ethical egoists?

The theme of the morally righteous loner has been repeated in two very different movies, one a sci-fi film and the other a cop film; in each case the focus is on the man who stands by his principles, working against the politics of his superiors and even the wishes of his community, for the sake of the categorical imperative—although nobody ever mentions Kant on the silver screen. These two films are *Outland* and *Cop Land*.

Outland

PETER HYAMS (SCREENWRITER AND DIRECTOR)

Film, 1981. Summary.

Outland takes place in the near future on Io, one of Jupiter's moons, which has become a mining colony. Work is excruciatingly hard, and the workers are allowed to "play hard"; a number of deaths among veteran workers have been registered, all due to what seems like instant insanity involving violence, either toward others or toward themselves. In spite of warnings from the administration, Federal District Marshal William T. O'Niel sets out to investigate the deaths with no cooperation from the station's personnel except for the crusty female station physician. What does he find? That each of the dead workers had a drug in his system—a drug that allows the person to work beyond ordinary capacity for a while and then fatally attacks the brain. Marshal O'Niel concludes that this is not due to personal choice by the workers—this is a way for the administration to get as much labor out of each individual as possible with total disregard for his or her personal fate or well-being—in other words, the administration is treating these workers merely as a means to an end for the sake of profit. But O'Niel doesn't have long to ponder his findings: He learns that three hit men are arriving at the space station, sent by the administration to silence him. And as the arrival time for the shuttle nears, we see O'Niel preparing for the gun battle all by himself, abandoned by everyone except the doctor. Will he succeed in defending the principle of doing the right thing, in spite of the threat to his life? Watch this film and *High Noon,* and enjoy a sci-fi tribute to perhaps the most famous moral statement in any Western ever made!
     See Study Questions following *Cop Land*.

Cop Land

JAMES MANGOLD (SCREENWRITER AND DIRECTOR)

Film, 1997. Summary.

Cop Land takes place not in the Old West of the past or in the outer space of the future but in the New Jersey of the present. "Cop Land" is the nickname for a small town across the Hudson River, Garrison, where many New York Police Department officers prefer to live and pretty much have the run of the town. There is very little crime, and the local nice-guy sheriff Freddy (who would really have liked to be an NYPD cop but is hearing impaired) is reduced to writing reports about garbage tampering. But then crime from the big city spills over into the small community: A young cop, "Superboy," fakes his own suicide after a traffic stop resulting in the shooting death of an unarmed man. While a spirited wake is held for Superboy, it dawns on Freddy that he is not dead at all—his friends and his uncle, a senior cop, are covering for him, to the point of killing off other cops who may be tempted to spill the beans. But as the existence of the "dead" cop is becoming hard to hide, Superboy himself becomes a target for his former friends, including his uncle: He is too hot to have around, and they try to eliminate him, because underlying this particular situation is a web of corruption and cover-ups that has gone on for years in Cop Land. The Internal Affairs office of NYPD appeals to Freddy to do his civic duty, to actually be a cop and report his findings, even if it involves informing on the police officers living in Cop Land. But the sheriff, who is not very bright, hesitates, not quite understanding where his loyalty ought to lie—with the people living in Cop Land whom he thinks he is hired to protect? Or to the truth? Freddy decides to do nothing—until he realizes that by not standing up for the good he is in effect letting evil run loose. And so he decides to fight evil all by himself, with obstacles from every direction: The Internal Affairs office has closed the case. Only one deputy remains by his side, but even he begins to talk about how his pregnant wife needs him, and Freddy sends him home. What does Freddy do? He finds Superboy and sets out to bring him in alive single-handedly, under fire from the police, as proof of the vast conspiracy permeating the seemingly quiet Cop Land. Does he succeed? Did Will Kane succeed? Did O'Niel succeed? Judge for yourself whether their success is complete. All three films are testimony to Kant's thought that doing the right thing, in spite of the danger and the apparent futility of the job, is worth it in itself, simply because it is the right thing to do—and because we wouldn't want to universalize sitting back and doing nothing or turning tail and running for the sake of personal convenience.

Study Questions

1. Compare *High Noon*, *Outland*, and *Cop Land*: What are the differences? What are the similarities?

2. Suppose Kane, O'Niel, and Freddy did not succeed in their lonely fight against evil forces, or suppose they had lost their nerve. Would it make any difference to Kant in evaluating the moral value of their actions? Would it make a difference to you? Why or why not?

3. When someone decides to act on principle against the wishes of the community, can we always assume that this person is doing the right thing? How would Kant decide? How would a utilitarian decide? How would you decide?

Narrative

Abandon Ship!

RICHARD SALE
(SCREENWRITER AND DIRECTOR)

Film, 1957. Summary.

Based on a true story, this film opens during the aftermath of an explosion on a luxury liner far from shore. The ship sank so quickly that no S.O.S. signal was sent, and no lifeboats were lowered. Now, some twenty survivors are clinging to the one lifeboat that was launched. It is the captain's dinghy, and it can hold fourteen people maximum. The captain is dying, and he transfers his authority to his first officer, Alec Holmes, admonishing him to "save as many as you can." Holmes is hopeful that help may arrive, but when he realizes that no S.O.S. has been sent, he knows that their only option is to row for the coast of Africa, fifteen hundred miles away. An officer and a friend of Holmes, himself mortally wounded, tells Holmes that he won't be able to make it if he tries to keep everyone alive—he must "evict some tenants" in order to save others. To emphasize his point, the officer throws himself overboard, because he would only be a hindrance to the survival of the "fittest." Holmes at first will hear nothing of this plan, but when a storm approaches, he realizes that he must choose between the death of them all and the death of those who already are hurt and can't pull their weight. Under protest and at gunpoint, the others comply by forcing the wounded passengers and crewmen, who are wearing life preservers, overboard, setting them adrift in shark-infested waters. One professor remarks, "This is an interesting moral problem," and insists that it is barbarism—the civilized thing to do would be to choose to die together.

Another passenger, moved by seeing a young boy lose both his parents to Holmes's weeding-out process, breaks out a knife and tries to force Holmes to turn around and look for the ones that were adrift. Holmes kills the man in self-defense, but not before the man succeeds in wounding Holmes with his knife. Now the storm hits, and all through the night the remaining passengers and crew struggle to keep afloat. When dawn breaks, and the storm dies down, everyone on board has survived, and there is a general feeling of good will toward Holmes—but he is suffering severely from his knife wound. Now Holmes applies his rule to himself and slips overboard so as not to be a burden, but the others rescue him and bring him back on board. Just as the passengers are getting ready to thank him for his foresight and effort, a ship is spotted on the horizon. Miraculously, help has arrived, "too soon," as a feisty woman passenger remarks—too soon for everybody to have decided to support Holmes in his plan to force some of the passengers overboard. The people on the boat are rescued (it is hinted that some of the evicted passengers are rescued, too), and Holmes goes on trial for murder. The film concludes with the question, "If you had been on the jury, would you have found Holmes guilty or innocent?"

Facing a hard decision, Captain Holmes (Tyrone Power) surveys the situation after the shipwreck in *Abandon Ship!* (Columbia Pictures, 1957). Soon he must decide which passengers are fit to row to Africa and which must be thrown overboard, sacrificed so that the others have a chance to survive. The story of *Abandon Ship!* is an illustration of a clash between utilitarian and deontological views.

Study Questions

1. Can this film be seen as a defense of utilitarianism? Explain why or why not.

2. Do you agree that it would have been a more civilized thing for all of the passengers to die together?

3. Would you have convicted Holmes of murder? (In actual fact he was convicted, but he received a short sentence because of the unusual circumstances.)

4. How might Ayn Rand have evaluated Holmes's solution?

5. Can you think of another way of solving Holmes's problem?

6. What was Holmes's intention? Might a Kantian accept that as morally good?

Narrative

Justice

WORLEY THORNE (TELEPLAY)

JAMES L. CONWAY (DIRECTOR)

***An episode of* Star Trek: The Next Generation, 1987. Summary.**

The television series *Star Trek: The Next Generation* has supplied philosophy instructors with some superb examples of moral dilemmas dressed up as good entertainment. This early episode, now considered a classic, deals not only with a Kantian type of ethics but also with its shortcomings.

The crew of the starship *Enterprise* are partaking of some rest and relaxation on what seems like the ideal vacation planet: Everybody is friendly, sex is considered a nice way for people to express their friendship (and it is, presumably, safe), and there is no crime. For the adults this seems like paradise, but, for Wesley, a young officer who is still in his early teens, it is rather bewildering. He joins a group of children on the planet and shows them how to play baseball, but he accidentally falls into some shrubbery that is marked off by white bars. The other children become quite subdued when two uniformed officials show up. With a minimum amount of explanation, the officials tell Wesley that he broke a rule — don't step on the grass — and now he must die.

The captain of the *Enterprise,* Picard, is alerted. The reason there is no crime on this planet is because there is one overriding rule, and it is absolute: Do not break any rules or you will die instantly. You never know when the attention of the "mediators" (the execution squad) will focus on any of the forbidden zones (marked by white bars), but if you are caught transgressing, you will die. Wesley has been caught; Wesley must die.

Picard's problem now is how to rescue Wesley. He can't use the "transporter," the molecule disrupter beam that moves people from planet to ship, because a higher power watching over this planet believes that he is interfering in their business and has frozen the *Enterprise's* transport system. Furthermore, Picard must adhere to his own "prime directive": Starfleet is not allowed to interfere with the internal affairs of nonspacefaring peoples. And here is a population who is exceedingly moral — it is not a backward culture of lawless thugs. What to do? Picard is experiencing a conflict between his own rules: "Keep the prime directive" versus "Do anything to save a crew member." At the same time, he is threatened by the authors of the absolutist moral code, the higher beings who are watching out for the people of the planet: Attempt a rescue, and the *Enterprise* will be destroyed. Pleading that Wesley didn't know doesn't do any good, because (as we all know) ignorance of the rules is no excuse. The situation is put in focus for Picard when the android Data asks him, with his usual detached sense of logic, whether he is willing to sacrifice one member of the *Enterprise* for the safety of the rest.

In the end, Picard comes up with an answer that satisfies the higher beings, and, with the transporter functioning again, all the *Enterprise* crew members beam up and away. What did Picard say to convince the higher beings to release Wesley? "Any mature moral

In an episode of *Star Trek: The Next Generation* titled "Justice," is it justice for Wesley or an inhumanly harsh sentence? Wesley (Wil Wheaton, center) has been caught trespassing on a planet visited by Starfleet, and only too late he learns that on this planet all crimes, big and small, are punishable by death. Here the lethal injection is being prepared for Wesley's execution, and we ask ourselves whether a system of laws that doesn't allow for exceptions is morally acceptable.

system must allow for exceptions." This may not seem very impressive, but in fact it is; you may remember that it is the one major point brought against Kant's categorical imperative.

Study Questions

1. Can you think of another way Picard could have handled the situation without violating the prime directive?

2. What is Kantian about the morality of the planet population?

3. Could you imagine a situation (perhaps this one qualifies) in which it would be acceptable for a commander to sacrifice a member of his or her crew in order to save the lives of the rest of the crew? Under what circumstances might this be acceptable?

4. Which of the problems concerning the categorical imperative listed on pp. 226–230 can this story be seen to illustrate? Explain in detail.

5. Kant himself would not have approved of executing Wesley for crashing into some plants, regardless of its being illegal. Kant believed that if you are guilty of a crime, you should be punished, but only in proportion to the crime (see Chapter 13). What do you think Kant would have suggested as proper punishment for Wesley?

Chapter Seven

Personhood, Rights, and Justice

To Kant, any being who is capable of rational thinking qualifies as a person, and (according to Kant's *Grounding for the Metaphysics of Morals*) creatures incapable of rational thinking are classified as things. Today, the debate about what constitutes a person is still with us, because the question has lost none of its urgency. At the time when Kant lived, human beings were often treated as things, tools, stepping-stones for the needs or convenience of others. This idea was a legitimate part of public policy in many places throughout the world, and the moral statement that a thinking being should never be reduced to being merely a tool for someone else became part of the worldwide quest for human rights — rights that still have not been universally implemented. This statement is historically important and should not be forgotten, even though many social thinkers today believe that Kant's fight for the recognition that all persons deserve respect must be expanded, and that Kant himself didn't have a concept of universal human rights in mind.

In this chapter we discuss issues that reflect several of the theories already studied and that illustrate how such theories can be applied on a social scale in creating policies regarding the rights and duties of citizens. It is thus important that you have studied Chapters 5 and 6 in particular before you proceed.

What Is a Human Being?

If we focus on the rights of human animals we have to address the question What does it mean to be human? Are the criteria physical? Does a being have to look human in order to be human? How detailed must we get? A traditional answer is "a featherless biped" — in other words, a creature that walks upright on two legs but is not a bird — but that is hardly a sufficient criterion. Nowadays, if we want to use physical criteria, we include not only physical appearance but also genetic information. But with this type of explanation we're faced with two problems. (1) Genetically, there are creatures that are 98 percent identical to the human but are obviously not human: chimpanzees. (2) There are individuals born of human parents who may not have all the human physical characteristics — for instance, persons with multiple physical disabilities (not to mention *mental* disabilities). So is a being born of humans who happens to have some physical aberration — from missing limbs to minor abnormalities such as extra toes and fingers — human? For most people today, the answer is obviously yes, but this was not always so. A worldwide tradition in pretechnological societies has been to dispose of newborns with physical "handicaps" ranging from missing limbs to unwanted birthmarks, and not all of these disposals can be explained by saying that a tribe isn't able to feed those who can't feed themselves. Our culture doesn't follow that practice, but some of us do screen the fetus for severe disabilities and perform abortions if we believe that these disabilities will condemn the child to a less than dignified life. This is not a discussion of the pros and cons of abortion, any more than it is a discussion of infanticide, but it does point out that a good deal of policy making in other cultures as well as our own depends on how we define "human being," including what a human being, and a human life, *should be like* — a normative concept.

The Expansion of the Concept "Human"

There was a time when people distinguished between friend and foe by calling friends humans and foes beasts, devils, or such. At the tribal level of human history it has always been common to view the tribe across the river as not quite human, even if members of your tribe marry their sons or daughters. (In fact, the usual word that tribes use to designate themselves is their word for "human," "the people," or "us.") In any geographic area there are people who remain dubious about those from the "other side" because their habits are so different that it seems there must be something "strange" about their general humanity. From the time of the ancient Greeks until quite recently, a common assumption has been that women are not quite human. Interestingly enough, this idea has been held not only by many men but also by many women, who took the men's word for it. (Some still do.) At the nationalistic level, it still is common practice to view foreigners as less than human, not in a physical sense, but rather politically and morally. And the humanity of a people's wartime enemies almost always is denied, usually because it becomes easier to kill an enemy, either soldier or civilian, if you believe he or she really is not quite as human as you or I. Thus the term *human* sometimes evolves into an honorary term reserved for those with whom we prefer to share our culture. Historically, the meaning of the term in the Western world expanded to include not only "our people" but also "all Europeans" and, with the advent of the Enlightenment, all free white males of any nationality. In the nineteenth century the term was expanded again to cover women as well as people born into slavery.

Persons and Rights

Many social thinkers prefer the term *person* to *human being* as a philosophical and political concept, partly in order to avoid the association with the human physical appearance. A person is someone who is capable of psychological and social interaction with others, capable of deciding on a course of action and being held responsible for that action. In other words, a person is considered a *moral agent*. (See Box 7.1 for a discussion of the abortion issue and the idea of the fetus as a person.) Being a person implies certain duties and privileges — in other words, it is a normative concept: what a person *ought to be and do* in order to be called a person. Personhood implies that one has certain social privileges and duties and that under extreme circumstances these can be revoked. What was a person to the Greeks? To

Box 7.1   IS A FETUS A PERSON?

The debate over whether abortion should be generally available often focuses on the question of whether the fetus is a person. In some cultures the fetus is not a person at all; even the newborn infant is not considered a person until after a waiting period that usually is imposed to see if the baby will live. The view adopted by the Catholic church (but not by all churches or religious communities) is that the fetus is a person from conception. This has not always been Catholic dogma, however. The idea underlying this viewpoint is that the soul is present when the fetus *looks* human; thus, in earlier times, a fetus was not considered a person until well into the pregnancy. Saint Augustine specifically states that terminating a pregnancy before the fetus is able to *feel* anything should not be considered homicide, because until that point in time the soul is not present. However, in the late seventeenth century, a primitive microscope seemed to show that a tiny, fully formed person (a *homunculus*) could be seen in the spermatozoon, and so church policy considering the fetus a person from conception was established. The policy remained unchanged even with the advent of better microscopes, which conclusively refuted the previous theory. One can of course choose to view the beginning of life as the beginning of personhood regardless of church policies and misunderstandings about microscopes. In that case the argument against abortion is generally that if it is wrong to kill a human being, a person, then it must also be wrong to kill a fetus who is either a person from conception or a potential person and should therefore have the same rights as a born person. Within the Catholic tradition one can circumvent the ban on killing a fetus through the principle of the *double effect,* which states that one mustn't take a life under normal circumstances, but that it is permissible under very special circumstances: (1) Death must be an *unintended*

In the seventeenth century a young scientist reported that he saw a small person, a homunculus, inside a sperm cell while looking through a primitive microscope. Presumably, he saw something like this image. He was never able to duplicate the experiment; nevertheless, since then, the official Catholic policy is that a fetus is a person from conception.

side effect of accomplishing something else (a primary effect), such as saving a life, (2) the primary effect must be *proportionately* very serious so as to outweigh the death, and (3) causing the death is *unavoidable,* and the only way to accomplish the primary effect. Thus a pregnant woman who has cancer of the uterus will get permission from the church to have an abortion, because it will be part of the necessary medical process to remove the uterus. The removal of the uterus will kill the fetus, but it is an unavoidable and unintended side effect of saving the woman's life. However, a pregnant woman whose pregnancy itself is in danger of killing her receives no such permission, because killing the fetus would in this case be intentional—regardless of the woman's life being in danger. We will meet the double effect again in Box 7.5 on euthanasia, as well as in Chapter 13 in the discussion of the just-war concept.

What does it take for us to identify a fetus as a person? There are thinkers today who believe that we can surely call the fetus a human being, but we can't call it a person, because it takes

(continued)

Box 7.1   IS A FETUS A PERSON? *(continued)*

more to be a person than just having human genetic material. The philosopher Mary Ann Warren argues that a being has to have (1) consciousness and ability to feel pain, (2) a developed capacity for reasoning, (3) self-motivated activity, (4) capacity to communicate messages of an indefinite variety of types, and (5) self-awareness in order to be considered a person; thus even the most developed fetus does not qualify. But neither do newborn babies, according to this viewpoint; so in order to avoid the specter of infanticide, Warren argues that as long as anyone in our culture objects to infanticide, then it should be outlawed—not for the sake of the infant (who is not a person yet) but for the sake of people's feelings in general.

A slightly less radical view is presented by another philosopher, Judith Jarvis Thomson, who argues for a woman's right to an abortion by saying that it does not matter whether the fetus is a person: What matters is that a woman has a *right to defend her body against intrusions*—even if the fetus should qualify for personhood. Thomson (who wrote her famous contribution to the abortion debate in 1971, just prior to *Roe v. Wade*) compares the pregnant woman to a person—any one of us—who wakes up in a hospital bed and finds herself (or himself) attached with intravenous tubes to someone in the next bed, a famous violinist. Suppose, Thomson says, you are told that the violinist can't be moved, or else he will die, so he must be sustained by you for the next nine months (or eighteen years). Do you have a right

to unplug yourself? Yes, even if it would mean an innocent violinist's death. For Thomson there is a small catch, however: You must have tried to take precautions not to be in that situation. Furthermore, if it is only a small sacrifice to you, then you have a moral duty to go through with it—but the violinist still doesn't have any right to demand your life and freedom.

Other positions put forth by abortion rights advocates, based on the view that the fetus may be a person, at least late in the pregnancy, argue that even so, the rights of the fetus as a person do not outweigh the rights of the woman as long as the fetus is not viable (can't survive outside the woman's body).

It is possible to approach the abortion issue from both a utilitarian and a deontological point of view, regardless of whether one is pro-choice or anti-abortion (pro-life). The utilitarian approach focuses on the *consequences* of abortion: The anti-abortion utilitarian will point to the many deaths of unborn children, and the utilitarian who is an abortion rights advocate will point to the back-alley deaths that occur when women seek illegal and unsanitary abortions. The deontological approach focuses on the issue of *rights*: The anti-abortion deontologist will argue that the fetus, as a person, is being used merely as a means to an end, its life and rights disregarded; the deontologist who is an abortion rights advocate will argue that the rights granted by the personhood and life of the woman outweigh the rights of the fetus, at least until viability (in the third trimester).

the Romans? To medieval Europeans? To these groups a person was usually a male adult landowner or tribesmember. Different societies have excluded some or all of the following people from their concept of a person: slaves, women, children, foreigners, prisoners of war, and criminals. (See Box 7.2 for a discussion of the personhood of people on the fringes of society, such as prostitutes and drug addicts.) Usually the list of exclusion extended to animals, plants, and inanimate objects, but other beings might well be granted personhood, such as gods and goddesses, totems (ancestor animals), and dead ancestors.

Today we in the Western world assume that all humans are persons with inalienable rights. This is not a recognized truth all over the world, however (and even in our own society we may have doubts about our landlord, our professor, or the neighbor's noisy kids, though such feelings are usually rather tongue-in-cheek). A more serious problem of recent years is the reemergence of *racism,* which can be seen as a reduction of the human fellow feeling, a return of the reluctance to call other humans "persons." Perhaps this reluctance was always there, at a primitive level, but lately it seems more persistent for any of various reasons: fears of each other or the economy, a need for scapegoats, and so forth. It is also possible that the new racism is in some cases not directed against persons of other races as much as persons of other *social strata.* In other words, much of what today is called racism may also have elements of class-oriented bigotry. Although racism seems to have been on the rise in the 1980s and 1990s, it is certainly not the only form of bigotry in modern society.

Questions about who counts as a person arise in a number of areas. We may think we treat everybody as persons with equal rights, but our society still experiences problems with sexism, and *ageism,* discrimination against the elderly (or for that matter, discrimination against the young) because of their age, is now recognized as a common problem. In the 1980s and early 1990s, AIDS and HIV patients experienced much discrimination, but new laws and an increased level of understanding have lessened that form of bigotry to some extent. Mentally disabled and mentally ill citizens still feel stigmatized, and so do physically disabled people, to the point that there is now a new word for discrimination against the disabled: *ableism.*

Is a *criminal* a person? For many people, the more callous the crime, the less human the criminal. Sometimes we even call murderers "animals," although few nonhuman animals have been known to display the methodical, deliberate preying on one's own species typical of human career criminals, serial rapists, and serial killers. In our attitudes toward such criminals much of our view of what counts as human is revealed: We're not trying to describe their genetic makeup, we're expressing a moral condemnation of their actions and choices. Calling a criminal an animal is a normative statement, not a descriptive one: He has not lived up to our expectations of what a person ought to be and do, and so we view him as less than human. But genetically as well as legally, a serial killer such as Robert Yates (see Box 7.2) is still a person, and the very fact that we choose to hold him accountable in court is proof of that. Had he been an "animal," we wouldn't have taken him to court—he would have been put down immediately, like a vicious dog. However, criminals, even convicted ones, don't lose all their rights: Their personhood status is not revoked, at least not in our culture. They still have the right not to be tortured, for example, although they may have lost their right to liberty. Below we take a closer look at the animal issue as well as the concept of rights.

Children as a group have not until recently been considered "real people." Until recently, child abuse was not considered a felony. In previous times—in fact, as recently as the nineteenth century and, in some places, the twentieth century—the father of the household had the supreme right to treat his family (including his

Box 7.2   IS A PROSTITUTE A PERSON?

In April 2000 a man named Robert L. Yates, Jr., was arrested for the murders of nine women in Spokane, Washington. In order to avoid the death penalty, he pleaded guilty to all nine murders, plus four others, including two that came as a complete surprise to the police. To this day it is speculated that we have yet to hear the end of the story, since there are many more women missing in the Pacific Northwest. He had been committing these murders since the mid-1990s but had been able to evade capture by blending into society with a seemingly normal existence as an ex–military man, a Seventh-Day Adventist, a helicopter pilot, a husband, and a father of five. Another factor that may well have helped him evade capture was the nature of his victims: He preyed on women whose lifestyles included drug addiction and prostitution.

While the detectives on the task force assigned to the serial killings in Spokane seemed highly committed to solving them, one can't help wondering (as many did) whether more funding might have been put into the investigation if the women had been college students, businesswomen, shopkeepers, or housewives rather than hookers and drug addicts. This is by no means an isolated phenomenon: From San Diego to Seattle to New York State we have had examples of serial killings of prostitutes that perhaps a few police detectives took very seriously, but that in no way stirred the general outrage of the community. A local radio talk show in Spokane received several calls from listeners

who expressed the opinion that the prostitutes somehow were asking for it, living a criminal life on the fringes of society, and that somehow the serial killer was just "cleaning up." But the radio hosts took on the capture of the murderer as a righteous cause, keeping up the pressure in the community and criticizing the apathy among citizens as well as what they saw as inadequate police work, even when the killings seemed to stop. The hosts raised questions such as "Are these women not human beings with the same rights as the rest of us? Don't they have families who mourn them? Don't they feel pain and anguish in their last moments at the mercy of a murderer? It may be illegal to be a prostitute and to use drugs, but it doesn't carry a death penalty."

Months before Yates was captured a billboard had been erected in downtown Spokane, with photos of sixteen victims and the plea "Help Us Find Our Killer." For many citizens of the city, this helped them realize that each murdered woman had had a life that was precious, each was a person who would have liked to stay alive. It is now part of the civic identity of Spokane that the sheriff's department managed to catch an elusive serial killer—a rare feat. But serious questions have been raised about the professional standards and efficiency of the task force, indicating that a more concerted police effort combined with more experience and willingness to reach out to the public might have resulted in finding Yates sooner, and thus saving lives.

wife) any way he pleased. This might very well include physically punishing all the family members, even unto death. This right, *patria potestas,* is still in effect in certain societies in the world. The thought of protecting children against abuse, even abuse from their own parents, is actually quite a new idea in Western cultures; even in the recent past, child abuse cases were sometimes covered up, or never reported. In 2002 several Catholic priests were accused of having raped children in decades past. What angered many Americans (Catholics as well as non-Catholics) was not only the

Copyright *Spokesman-Review,* Spokane

Years into the investigation of the serial murder of prostitutes, the Spokane sheriff's department appealed to the community for help, putting murder victims' faces on a billboard reading "Help Us Find Our Killer." The personalization of each woman may have inspired a change in attitude in the community toward the victims, from expendable outcasts to individuals with a right to live.

Another result of the serial killer investigation was that the community in the end seemed to understand that the murdered women were fellow citizens, too. A great many people, as well as the media, showed up in court to hear Yates's sentence—408 years in prison—and stood by the relatives of the victims as they cried out their grief and outrage at the murderer, one after the other, while he offered scripted apologies to each in turn as part of his plea bargain. In the text you will find a discussion of the appropriateness of anger felt by victims and survivors (resentment) and by the community (moral indignation). One might say that on the day Yates was sentenced, the community did, at long last, stand up for the victims.

abuse, but that the church seemed to have covered up the allegations and simply relocated the priests to other regions. During the unfolding scandal several things became clear. While the percentage of pedophile priests seemed to be small, and other religious groups report similar abuse cases against children and teens, there was widespread disappointment in the church because of the perceived cover-ups, and also a widespread realization that the psychological damage done to these children is immeasurable. In the terminology of Kant, these children had been used merely as a means to an end. Today we recognize that not only should children be protected from abuse; children have interests and wishes that they are capable of expressing and that should be heard, such as which parent they wish to stay with after a divorce.

We are now at the point at which the conscious interests of children (which can include everything from having enough food, shelter, love, and education to refusing to go to school in order to play video games or watch TV) must be balanced against what conscientious adults deem to be in the children's best interests, best *in spite of* themselves. In other words, we must remember that what children want is not necessarily good for them. The idea that children are minors who have neither the legal rights—nor the legal responsibilities—of adults is not about to disappear, even when their interests are taken into consideration. We tend to forget that when a group is excluded from having rights, it is usually also excluded from having responsibilities. In other words, such a group must be given legal protection so that its members, who are incapable of taking on civil responsibilities, will not be treated unjustly.

Historically, the idea of animals and children having responsibilities has shifted back and forth. Until the mid-nineteenth century, animals could be held legally responsible for their actions (although they had very few recognized rights); all through the European Middle Ages rats, roaches, and other pests were put on trial (usually in absentia) for the damage they caused to human lives and property. Even in the United States, animals were put on trial for hurting their masters or their own offspring, and they were "executed" if found guilty. Today, when an aggressive dog attacks a small child and is put to death, do we consider ourselves to be "executing" the dog? Some might argue that that is exactly what we are doing—we are punishing the dog for transgressing a human law. But legally we are simply disposing of the dog's owner's property not as a punishment against the dog but as a precaution in the public interest. Who *does* get punished? Not the dog, but the *owner,* who receives a fine or even a jail sentence. In San Francisco in 2002, a dog owner even received a second-degree murder sentence after her dogs attacked and killed a neighbor. Today we don't consider animals to be legally responsible for their actions, because we don't consider them to be moral agents. A dog who fails to wake up her owners when the house is on fire will not be blamed for it afterward, though her owners might be blamed for not training her properly. (In previous times, when animals were put on trial, the issue of whether they were moral agents still was not solved, because it was commonly considered that they had no souls and thus had no free will. Were the people who put them on trial contradicting themselves? Yes. But so do we sometimes, and one of the objectives of discussing these issues is to get into the habit of thinking more consistently.)

The case of the legal responsibility of children parallels that of animals. It was only in the twentieth century that we in the Western world agreed not to hold minors responsible for criminal acts. The legendary German figure Till Eulenspiegel was a mischievous kid who played one too many tricks on decent citizens, and the decent citizens hanged him. The title character of Herman Melville's *Billy Budd* faced the same fate. Billy, a young sailor, was falsely accused of wrongdoing by a vicious officer. Because Billy had a problem articulating and could not speak up to defend himself, he acted out his frustration by striking the officer. Unfortunately, this resulted in the officer's death, and the captain, although aware of Billy's problem, had to follow the law of the sea: mandatory death for anyone who kills an officer. In the end, Billy had to submit to the traditional execution method by climbing up the rigging and slipping a noose around his own neck. Today a crime committed by a person under the age of eighteen must reveal an extraordinary amount of callousness and "evil intent" in order for the court to try the minor as an adult. This is because childhood is considered to be a state of mind and body that doesn't allow for the logical consistency we assume is available, most of the time, to adults; therefore children aren't held accountable for their actions to the degree that adults are. (Box 7.3 explores the relationship between morality and the law.)

The United States, however, has seen a shift lately in the attitude toward children who commit crimes. Although most child psychologists still agree that children below the age of seven or eight don't know enough about the difference between right and wrong to be held accountable, public demand is now growing for trying older child offenders as adults. What should the court do with a child who kills another child for his sneakers or his jacket? Or who takes a gun to school and kills a number of his classmates and teachers before being stopped? In some states, such as Arkansas, children cannot be tried as adults. In other states, it is the severity of the crime that determines whether the youth will be tried as an adult; we have lately seen teenagers being given hefty prison sentences (although a teenager under eighteen normally can't be given the death penalty). The issue of when a child can be held criminally responsible for his or her actions is the focus of much current legal attention. For example, in 2000, thirteen-year-old Nathaniel Abraham was convicted of second-degree murder after being tried as an adult for a murder he committed at age eleven. He was *sentenced* as a juvenile, however, and will be held in a juvenile detention facility until he is twenty-one. An illustration of how times have changed since the 1970s is the case of Michael Skakel, indicted in 2000 for the 1975 murder of his fifteen-year-old neighbor, Martha Moxley. Skakel, a cousin of the Kennedy family by marriage, was himself fifteen years old at the time, and the state of Connecticut would, in 1975, have considered him a juvenile who could not therefore be tried as an adult. That law was changed a few years later, but Skakel's attorney argued, unsuccessfully, that Skakel, now very much an adult, should be tried as a juvenile. In 2002 he was tried as an adult and found guilty of murder.

In the past, the rights of women have followed a course similar to those of animals and children. Women had very few rights until the late nineteenth century — no right to hold property, no right to vote, no right over their own person. This went hand in hand with the common assumption that women were not capable of moral consistency and thus were not responsible (mention of women and children in the same breath was no coincidence). This view often coincided with a male reverence for women and their supposedly higher moral standards, but such reverence was often combined with an assumption that women were idealists with no conception of the sordid dealings and practical demands of the real world.

When it applied to women, the practice of holding only those with rights legally responsible was not strictly adhered to. Many, many women were put on criminal trial. Even so, the general idea was that withholding rights from women *protected* them

Box 7.3   MORALITY AND THE LAW

The relationship between morals and legislation is ancient. From the Code of Hammurabi (developed by Babylonians in approximately 2000 B.C.E.) to the legislation of today, some laws have reflected the moral climate of the time. Not all laws have done so, though some scholars argue that because laws tell us what we ought to do or ought not to do, all laws have a moral element to them; if nothing else, they promote the idea that it is morally good to uphold the law. However, sometimes the law does not seem to be morally right. When times change, what seemed right before may not seem right anymore, and if the legislative power is sensitive to that fact, the law will change. Sometimes it takes a civil war for such laws to be changed; sometimes it takes an act of defiance; sometimes it takes only a simple vote. We can't, therefore, conclude that all laws are morally just, because experience tells us this is not so. Some laws may not even have an obvious moral element. A traffic law that allows us to turn right on red hardly addresses a moral issue.

Legislators, though, are naturally interested in the public's opinion of right and wrong, because, in general, this opinion will be represented by the laws of the country. Not all moral issues are relevant for legislators, however; whether you go home for Thanksgiving may be an important moral issue in your family, but it is hardly the business of anyone else, let alone the state legislature. Philosophy of law generally speaks of two viewpoints concerning the relationship between ethics and the law. The viewpoint of *naturalism* (or *natural law*) holds that the law reflects, or ought to reflect, a set of universal moral standards; some naturalists consider these standards given by God, and some see them as part of human nature. The other viewpoint is referred to as *legal positivism* and holds that the law is based on consensus among legislators; in other words, there is no ultimate moral foundation for our laws, and legislation merely reflects shifting opinions over time.

Within the area of legal justice today, the question of the welfare of society is often contrasted with the rights of the individual. How much will it take before we are willing to say that individual rights should be superseded by concerns for society as such? Are we willing to give up freedom of speech in order to prevent hate speech and riots, not to mention the overall feeling of being offended? Are we willing to take away the right of a convicted child molester who has served his or her time to start a new life for the sake of protecting the community by letting them know of the offender's whereabouts (Megan's Law)? Are we willing to give up the right to privacy for the sake of security? These questions about rights in conflict with the public good are all questions that have no easy answer, and whatever answer we do settle on generally reflects what we think is more important: the protection of the community or the rights of an individual. Below we take a closer look at the issue of the rights of the individual vs. the interests of the community.

from the harsh world of reality, whose demands they weren't capable of answering. A similar kind of argument kept slaves from having rights throughout most slaveholding societies—rights were denied in order to provide "protection" for these people because they were "incapable." This did not preclude punishing slaves, of course, as anyone who has read *Huckleberry Finn* knows. In *On Liberty* (see Chapter 5), John Stuart Mill argues that the right to self-determination should extend universally, *provided* that the individuals in question have been educated properly, in the British sense, so that they know what to do with the self-determination. Until then, they are incapable of making responsible decisions and should be protected — children by their guardians and colonial inhabitants by the British. (Today, an animal rights activist might argue that we see the same pattern repeated with animals: We don't believe them to be fully developed moral agents, and so we protect them — by withholding rights from them.) An interesting concept evolves from these arguments, namely, that it is possible for someone to be considered a person, but a person with *limited* rights, duties, and privileges whose rights are assigned to a guardian. We will return to this idea later in this chapter.

Science and Ethics in the New Millennium

As it stands now, we must agree that our culture has come a long way in terms of recognizing all postnatal humans as persons, at least in principle, although that principle sometimes seems to be overpowered by controversy. But what about the future? Genetically engineered children already walk among us, and there will be many more. Your children — and perhaps even yourself — may be able to look forward to a longer, healthier life span due to genetic engineering. By the time you're reading this, there may be viable human clones among us, too, legally or otherwise. Will these new members of our human family be considered persons, or will they encounter some new form of discrimination? In the Narrative section you'll find two stories that explore either end of this spectrum of possibilities: The film *Blade Runner* envisions a near future where genetically engineered "replicants" will be used as disposable people, slaves in the service of humans. The film *Gattaca* suggests a world, right around the corner, where genetic engineering has become mainstream and it is those who have *not* been genetically "improved" at the embryo stage who will form the new underclass. Who will really be up, and who will be down, in such a "brave new world"?

We can ask ourselves two questions here: Given that a future involving a variety of options for genetic engineering and cloning is already upon us, (1) how should we deal with the scientific possibilities opening up for humanity? Should we be phobic about scientific developments and encourage bans and limits to scientific research? Or, should we encourage all such research under the assumption that somehow it may benefit us and that science has a right to seek knowledge for the sake of knowledge no matter the consequences? Or perhaps some position in between? (2) Should scientists themselves exercise some form of moral responsibility, taking into consideration that their results will be used in the future, perhaps to the detriment of humans and animals living in that future? In this section we take a look at one of the most burning issues today: the question of science and moral responsibility.

In 1968 a book came out in Germany which challenged the traditional scientific view that science is value-free, or morally neutral: the philosopher Jürgen Habermas's *Knowledge and Interest*. Scientists had claimed — some still do — that scientific research is done for the sake of knowledge itself, not for the social consequences it might bring. As such, scientists' professional integrity hinges on impeccable research; they have no responsibility to the community in terms of what problems — or even benefits — their research might lead to in the future. Habermas claimed that science might attempt to be objective but that an element of vested interest is always present. Society will fund only those projects it deems "valuable" for either further scientific progress, prestige, or profit. Political concerns, social biases, and fads within the scientific community often influence the funding of scientific research projects. Researchers often choose projects for similar reasons. Furthermore, the data selection (choosing research materials according to what the researcher finds relevant to the project) is influenced by the interests of the researcher—whether we like it or not. Habermas's point is that we may think science is conducted in a value-neutral way, but it is not. In addition, having seen what harm irresponsible scientists can cause to a society, wouldn't it be appropriate for scientists to conduct their research with a sense of obligation to the future? And for the community to monitor scientific research?

The question posed by the scientist Malcolm in *Jurassic Park* sums up the issue of "science without responsibility": Just because it is possible for science to do something, does it mean that science *should* do it? After all, there is an underlying suspicion that some scientific research is done strictly to see whether it can be done.

Medical doctors of the past had their own share of moral problems: An army surgeon would have to decide which of the wounded soldiers he should operate on and which ones should be left to die. A nineteenth-century family doctor might have to choose between saving a young mother dying in childbirth or the infant being born. But today, technology allows medical procedures that would have been unimaginable a few generations ago. Life can be prolonged artificially; pregnancies can be terminated with comparative safety for the woman; genetic engineering can save babies from a life of illness while they are still in the womb; women can give birth after menopause; stem cell research promises to cure diseases; and the Human Genome Project, completed in 2000, suggests a future in which we will have mapped human DNA to the point of understanding and preventing a vast array of medical problems. With the increased knowledge, however, comes an increase in moral problems.

In this new era of medical possibilities, there are few established rules to guide those making the decisions. For this reason, the medical profession has a vested interest in supporting the creation of a viable set of ethical procedures to follow in the gray areas of decision making. When we finally have the complete ability to interfere purposefully with the human DNA code, how much is too much interference? Should we interfere strictly to prevent terminal diseases, or is it acceptable to interfere with nature in order to determine the shape of the baby's nose, for example? And given the limited resources of medicine, who should benefit from organ transplants—first come, first served? The young, the wealthy, the famous? Those who have waited the longest? Another element of the discussion of medical ethics is the attitude of society toward sick people—in particular, terminally ill people with communicable diseases. Should they remain part of society, or should they be locked away and forgotten? Do we as citizens act ethically toward contagious fellow citizens, or do we send them to leper colonies or other such places?

In the seventeenth and eighteenth centuries, the early years of modern science, the moral sensitivity that accompanied research seems to have differed from that which prevails today. The main concern of scientists then was how to proceed with research without violating the values believed to be expressed in the Bible. In modern times, scientists have occasionally diverged from the path of ethical behavior. In Nazi Germany the ultimate value was success for the Party and the realization of that abstract concept, "the Fatherland." Scientists in Nazi Germany engaged in painful, humiliating, and eventually fatal experiments on human subjects, primarily women and children. Even now, we occasionally learn that, since World War II, scientists have subjected people to experimental medical procedures or have withheld treatment from them—without their knowledge or consent. The Tuskegee Syphilis Study is one of the best known of these experiments. Another less known case is the forced sterilization of about 7500 people in Virginia from 1924 to 1979 based on the ideology of eugenics. California was also active in the eugenics project, sterilizing over 20,000 people.

Most scientists and laypeople today would agree that knowledge can come at a price in suffering that is too high; yet we have a credo that says science is value-free: Scientific research is supposed to be objective, and scientists are not to be swayed by personal ambitions and preference. But does that mean they are not supposed to be swayed by ethical values either?

Medical and general scientific researchers now have capabilities that could only be dreamed of in previous generations. We are only slowly developing a set of ethical rules by which to judge these capabilities, however. Genetic manipulation makes possible a future such as the one Aldous Huxley fantasized about in his *Brave New World,* one with a human race designed for special purposes. Agriculture has for several years been making use of genetic engineering to create disease-resistant crops. Milk and meat are being irradiated before they hit the stores. And perhaps the most controversial issue: *Transgenic* animals are being patented, such as pigs that have had human genes placed in them, to facilitate organ transplants, and goats that have been genetically manipulated to contain spider silk proteins in their milk, to be extracted and combined to produce materials of unprecedented strength. Although it may be to humankind's ultimate advantage to have access to these wonders, failure to contain such laboratory-generated genetic material, or failure to foresee the overall consequences of such genetic tinkering, could have disastrous results if no sense of ethics or social responsibility is instilled to guide the decision of researchers. After all, the infamous killer bees (which have now settled comfortably in the southwestern United States) are the result of a lab experiment gone out of control.

In Europe there is now a general mistrust of the entire idea of genetically engineered food products, from grain to farm animals. But what about genetically engineered humans?

In 2000 a little boy was born specifically in order to try to save the life of his older sister. Six-year-old Molly Nash had a congenital blood disease that would, in all probability, take her life before the age of ten. Doctors used "preimplantation genetic diagnosis" (PGD) to select an embryo in vitro that was both free of the disease and a good match as a blood cell donor. A month after the baby, Adam, was born, stem cells from his umbilical cord blood were transplanted into his sister. Molly was given the transplant while she held her little brother in her arms. Three months later she was allowed to return home from the hospital to her parents and her new brother, with her chances of survival improved to 85 percent.

Such are the possibilities opening up to us with genetic engineering. Then why are some people worried about the social consequences of this miracle cure? Because we, as a society, have not decided where we'd draw the line: Do we endeavor to create healthy babies, or should we go further, such as customizing babies according to their parents' specifications — or even to society's needs? Will babies be genetically engineered for sex, height, eye color, and skin color? And will those babies who have been genetically engineered be the new society's favorites, leaving the natural-born children behind as a new underclass? Molly and Adam Nash's doctor was quick to emphasize that the parents' use of PGD was acceptable because "they were not selecting in a eugenic sense," just looking for a donor baby. The doctors also outlined what they would consider unacceptable uses of the PGD technology, such as aborting selected implanted embryos just to collect tissue or putting the baby up for adoption after using its cord blood — in other words, using such babies merely as a means to an end, as Kant would say.

Although still controversial to some, stem cell research holds great promise as a means of repairing and replacing damaged organs. Stem cells are general cells, not yet specialized, and they apparently have the capacity to become any organ in the body, with the intervention of medical science. The controversy arises from the practice of harvesting stem cells from *embryos*, which involves taking the life of the embryo. If one is against abortion at any time during pregnancy because one considers the embryo a person from conception, one will also be against any form of stem cell research involving human embryos. If one believes that since abortions happen anyway the fetal tissue might as well be useful for people who suffer from an illness, then one might be open to the idea of harvesting embryos for medical research. But using fetal tissue from abortions that have been a result of a choice by pregnant women is one thing — it is another to *deliberately* create embryos for medical use. In the summer of 2001, President George W. Bush laid down rules for future stem cell research so that no embryo would be conceived for the specific purpose of being used for stem cell research. Some seventy lines of stem cells are already in existence in various labs, however, and those have been made available for research.

A side effect of knowledge about a person's DNA profile was anticipated by new legislation a few years ago that prevents insurance companies and workplaces from discriminating against persons based on their DNA. An increased risk of cancer or early heart disease should not hurt a person's chances of employment or insurance — but it is not hard to imagine a future where such rules could be sidestepped.

Genetic engineering is closely related to another high-profile contemporary medical issue, *cloning*. A genetically engineered person is someone whose DNA has been manipulated before birth to avoid certain congenital problems or perhaps to enhance certain traits. A cloned person is someone who is, physiologically, a copy of another individual. The excitement and concerns about cloning began in 1994, with the announcement that researchers had successfully split a fertilized (but nonviable) human ovum into twins (which is no more than nature does when she makes identical twins). But since then the cloning issue has taken off with a speed not even predicted by science fiction authors: In rapid succession, labs around the world have succeeded in cloning sheep, calves, goats, and mice, using a variety of techniques, including creating a copy of an adult individual using a cell from that individual with a technique pioneered by the creators of Dolly the sheep—raising the specter of genderless reproduction.

With the successful cloning of mice, scientists now seem ready to do any customized cloning their prospective customers may want as long as viable DNA is available—from duplicating your aging beloved mutt to creating custom-made pigs with human organs to resurrecting extinct woolly mammoths. The imagination is the only limit. Officially there is a moratorium on cloning humans because of the staggering moral implications. But over Thanksgiving weekend 2001 the news broke that a small lab in Massachusetts, Advanced Cell Technology, had cloned the first human embryo, consisting of six cells. Some ethicists and religious leaders pointed out that this development might be the first step down the slippery slope to creating humans; lab representatives were quick to point out that the purpose of cloning the embryo was not to make more humans, but to provide stem cells for therapeutic use, such as curing spinal injuries, diabetes, and other illnesses. But in the summer of 2001 an Italian scientist and an American scientist had announced that they already had hundreds of couples wanting a cloned baby lined up, ready to be cloned—they weren't talking about creating embryos for stem cells, but creating future people. The scientists, well aware that neither Italy nor the United States allows such research, proclaimed that they were going to take their cloning operation to an undisclosed place, and within a few years they would be able to present the world with the first human clone. World opinion was strongly against the scientists. The general assumption was that these scientists were playing God and that there was no good reason for anyone to want himself or herself cloned. Other arguments against cloning included these:

- Overpopulation threatens the planet as it is, so why add more people artificially?

- Why create people who, as copies of someone else, will have to struggle to find their identity?

- Clones might be considered expendable people, a new slave population—or perhaps so valuable that they would become a preferred population group. In other words, cloning might lead to a new form of discrimination.

- Animal cloning has led to individuals with abnormal physical traits being born. Aren't we risking the same thing making human clones?

These are good questions, but before we become too "scientophobic," we should reconsider the issue. What are the doctors actually claiming? Some want human cloned embryos to remain at the embryo stage for use in treating patients. Others want to clone humans on the assumption that human cloning is the answer to being childless. But why would anyone want to have himself or herself cloned? Why not opt for adopting an already existing child who needs a home? Well, for some people the whole point is to have a child who is *related* to them, and cloning would provide that (but here we should note that the clone would be a blood relative, a twin, of just one of the parents, not both). The reasons people want babies are complex:

Some people want children so they can love them and raise them to be good citizens; others want an additional hand on the farm, an heir to their name, a tax write-off, or a status symbol to parade in front of their friends. We have yet to set up legal rules for what reasons are *good* reasons to have children (although we already have an idea of which reasons count as *morally* good reasons). Excluding some prospective parents from parenthood because they'd like a kid who looks like themselves will exclude a whole lot more people than those lined up to be cloned. Some say, If it can be done, it will be done, so why make an issue of it? Supply and demand will rule! A viable alternative approach probably lies somewhere in the middle: The day will indeed come when we have human clones, from occasional individuals created to carry on the family name or be the bearer of the cherished face of a departed loved one to the nightmare scenario of mass-produced "worker ants." We need to think carefully about the implications of this technology for society and about the need for legislation. We have to consider the difference between a cloned child who would be loved and cared for by its parents and one who might be used or enslaved for society's purposes. Perhaps the bottom line, as with any planning involving a child, is whether that child can reasonably expect a stable, loving home — not the circumstances of the child's conception. There is a wide variety of issues for legislators and ethicists to consider in the twenty-first century.

Questions of Rights

We have already referred to the concept of rights several times; now we are going to take a closer look at what it entails. In Western culture today it is generally assumed that all people have rights; the nature and extension of these rights is continually being disputed, however. In the seventeenth century some European thinkers began to advocate the idea of *natural rights,* and this idea became very important in the eighteenth century with its many social revolutions. A natural right was defined as a right one was born with as a human being (or as a male human being, as it was most often argued). Sometimes the concept of natural rights is intended as descriptive (as in, "We are actually born with rights"), and sometimes its intention is normative ("We ought to have such rights because we are human"). The utilitarian Jeremy Bentham had his doubts about the concept of natural rights. His response to the Declaration of the Rights of Man (1789) of the French Revolution — and implicitly also to the American Declaration of Independence (1776) — was that all men are obviously *not* born free, and they are *not* born or do not remain equal in rights. (Nor should they — someone has to give the orders, he says. We can't have associations between equal members, such as equality in marriage — Bentham believed that would never work out!) People are not born with rights because the concept of rights is a human invention and does not occur in nature. One might wish it did, he says, but it doesn't. So for Bentham, the concept of natural rights is "nonsense upon stilts." That doesn't mean we can't operate with the concept of rights though; we must just recognize it as a legal principle (not a natural one) and identify its goal as being the creation of as happy a society as possible — in other words, maximizing happiness for the maximum number of people (the basic utilitarian principle).

You may remember John Stuart Mill's insistence that there ought to be such a thing as a personal right to be left alone if you are not harming anybody else (the "harm principle"). As in so many other areas, Mill is here redefining utilitarianism from within, but he still remains a utilitarian; his ultimate reason for setting limits on government involvement in people's private affairs is the overall happiness of the population. There is no such thing as a concept of "rights" or "justice" for its own sake in utilitarianism, even in Mill's version: The ultimate goal is still the general happiness, not an abstract principle of justice. We have to go to another theory in order to find a defense of the concept of rights for their own sake, not for what good social consequences may come of enforcing them: to Kant's deontology. As you have read in Chapter 6, he insists that human beings are ends in themselves and may not be treated merely as a means to an end. This means that even if treating a person as a means to an end might be useful for the majority in a society, it is still not permissible to do so. Good overall consequences for a majority do not provide a sufficient reason to do away with the rule that every person deserves respect. The question of whether decisions affecting many people in a society should be made on the basis of social utility or individual rights is still very much part of the contemporary debate, as we shall see.

What Is Equality?

When we try to define equality, we sometimes feel as much confusion as Saint Augustine did in trying to define time: "When you don't ask me, I know what it is; when you ask me, I don't know." We tend to think equality has something to do with treating everybody the same way—but since everybody is not the same, or even similar, how can that be fair? And we know that equality and fairness are supposed to be linked. There are actually several definitions of equality:

1. **Fundamental equality** is the concept we know from the American Declaration of Independence and the French Declaration of the Rights of Man and of the Citizen. The American Declaration reads, "We hold these truths to be self-evident, that all men are created equal, that they are endowed by their Creator with certain unalienable Rights, that among these are Life, Liberty, and the pursuit of Happiness." The French Declaration begins, "All men are by nature free and equal in respect of their rights." However, these declarations do not say that people *are* factually equal—such as equally tall, strong, pretty, or smart—just that people *should be treated as* equals by their government and their legal system: no special privileges, just an entitlement to respect and consideration as human beings.

2. **Social equality** refers to the idea of people being equal within a social setting, such as politics or the economy. Today, most Western political theories are completely in tune with the idea of fundamental equality, but what exactly social equality (and indeed "people") can mean is variable: The French Revolution did not see women as socially or politically equal with men, and neither did the American Declaration of Independence, although Thomas Jefferson himself has been quoted as being opposed to viewing women as second-class citizens or as property. People of color were generally not considered included in the social equality of the

Declaration of Independence, either, although Jefferson seemed to have had some second thoughts about that, too. Social equality today is generally obtained through such formal rights as the right to vote and to stand for public office; however, that doesn't mean that everyone's social status or income is supposed to be equal.

3. **Equal treatment for equals** is an ancient idea, in glaring contradiction to the fundamental equality principle; we find it in Aristotle's *Politics*. Justice means treating people of the same, usually social, group in the same way. But since we don't know from the definition what it would take to be considered an "equal," it is generally assumed to be an elitist principle with no underlying intent to recognize equality as a fundamental human right.

Sometimes an alternative definition is proposed: *Treat equals equally and unequals unequally.* At first sight this looks like principle (3), equal treatment for equals, but there is a potential difference. It may look like a principle of elitism and bigotry, but who are "equals"? And who are "unequals"? Instead of pointing to a social or political group or saying that "equals" means "everybody," let's say that "equals" in this definition are people who are in a similar situation under similar circumstances. Imagine the freeway at rush hour: We are all out there in our cars, either moving at high speeds or simply stuck. We don't know each other, but we all deserve respect and decent treatment from each other, no more and no less. Now imagine a person trying to change lanes so he can reach the next exit, because he has some kind of emergency—a flat tire, a sick passenger perhaps. He signals, and you let him go in front of you. Because of his situation he is in fact an "unequal," in special need of assistance. Now imagine that someone else up ahead is impatient and wants to get off the freeway, so she cuts in front of someone else and causes him to brake hard, resulting in a couple of fender benders that include your car. Now that person has also become an "unequal" and deserves special, "unequal" treatment that others don't get unless they have transgressed: punishment. So the principle states that under ordinary circumstances we are just "equals" and deserve the usual decent treatment and respect. When someone has special needs, he or she becomes an "unequal" who needs assistance in order to reach the level of those who are "equals." And when someone breaks the rules, he or she also becomes an unequal and deserves special punishment (see the later section on criminal justice). The principle of *treating equals equally and unequals unequally* is in complete harmony with the fundamental equality principle, but it is more elaborate because it recognizes that we sometimes have special needs or sometimes transgress, and so sometimes deserve special treatment. The principle supports affirmative action, if people who have experienced the effects of discrimination are considered to be "unequals" in the sense that the "playing field" is not yet level and that some "players" need special assistance before everyone on the field will actually have equal opportunities.

One thing the principle of equality usually does not imply is *sameness*. What would it be like if we were required to treat others and to be treated in exactly the same way, even if we are physically different? Kurt Vonnegut's short story "Harrison Bergeron" (1970) is a scathing parody of a future society in which it is politically incorrect (years before the term became popular) to be smarter, stronger, or more beautiful than anyone else. In Bergeron's future the smart people wear caps with buzzers that prevent them from thinking a thought through; the beautiful people wear bags over their heads so the less-than-pretty people won't feel bad. Dancers are weighed down with lead so ungraceful people won't feel left out, and strong people wear lots of bags of lead so they won't have an advantage over the weaker ones. Vonnegut doesn't write about how the truly disabled might feel about such artificial disabling or about what constitutes "normal" sameness, but the story does effectively question the identification of sameness and equality.

Dworkin: Rights Can't Be Traded for Benefits

A contemporary thinker who uses Kant's approach to the issue of rights is the American philosopher Ronald Dworkin. For Dworkin the importance of rights becomes apparent precisely at the moment when social considerations might justify the violation of those rights; we may think that our rights are protected by the Constitution, but there is such a thing as a constitutional amendment. Could we imagine a situation so serious that horrible social consequences will ensue if certain rights are not set aside for the common good? In other words, when push comes to shove, should we adopt a utilitarian view that social benefits outweigh the rights of the individual, or should we, along with Kant, hold the rights of the individual higher than social benefits? Dworkin asks us to consider an example: the right to free speech. Suppose someone, angered by some personal or collective experience, gets up and speaks in public, in an emotional manner, advocating violence as a way to secure political equality. Suppose the emotional speech starts a riot, and suppose people get hurt or even killed. Many would say that if such a situation can be prevented by making such a type of speech illegal, then that is the course we have to take. Dworkin would not. He argues that we can use one of two models for our political thinking about rights:

1. The first model says we have to find a balance between the rights of the individual and the demands of society. If the government *infringes* on a right, it does the individual wrong; but if it *inflates* a right, it does the community wrong (by depriving it of some benefit, such as safe streets). So we should steer a middle course and take each situation on a case-by-case basis. Well-behaved discussion groups can have more freedom of speech than unruly demonstrators, because there is more social risk involved in the demonstration. This model of balancing the public interest against personal claims sounds reasonable, but it is not, says Dworkin. If we adopt the model, he asserts, we will have given up on two very important ideas: One is the idea of human dignity (Kant would say, Don't treat people merely as means), and the other is the idea of political equality (if one person has a certain freedom, then all persons should have that freedom, regardless of the effect on the general good). In Dworkin's words (from his book *Taking Rights Seriously*):

> So if rights make sense at all, then the invasion of a relatively important right must be a very serious matter. It means treating a man as less than a man, or as less worthy of concern than other men . . . then it must be wrong to say that inflating rights is as serious as invading them.

So we can't balance individual rights against social goods; what we *can* do is balance individual rights against each other when the claims collide, because then each individual still retains his or her dignity. But the best proof that the first model doesn't work, says Dworkin, is that it is *not* applied in actual cases in which the stakes for the individual are the highest: in criminal processes. Social benefits don't determine the outcome of a trial. The adage says, It is better that many guilty people go free than that one innocent person be punished, and this is Dworkin's choice for his second model.

2. The second model says that invading a right is far worse than inflating it. If someone is prevented from expressing himself or herself freely and in any way he or she likes, then that is an assault on human personality, and all the more so if the subject of the speech is morally important to the speaker. The only time when the government might actually be allowed to step in would be if the consequences of such a speech would very certainly be grave. But when is anyone that certain? According to Dworkin the risk involved is speculative; someone's right to free speech should not be abridged just because someone else might harm others because of that speech. This is the only way to protect the rights of individuals and in particular the rights of the few against the many. For a discussion of examples of rights traded for benefits, see Box 7.4.

Dworkin seems to imply that freedom of speech (which might lead to violence) is typically used to defend the idea of human dignity; in other words, most decent people might agree with the content of the speech, if not with its emotional character. That may not always be the case. You might want to consider Dworkin's second model in the scenario of an inflammatory racist hate speech being delivered on your campus. Would you say that the rights of the speaker to express a personal opinion any way he or she likes is more important than the harmful effects on the group being targeted for hatred or even the harmful effects on the audience being stirred up? Lately we have seen several examples not only of hate speech but of supremacist demonstrations (one being a Ku Klux Klan demonstration in the aftermath of the murder of an African American hitchhiker in Jasper, Texas). Although such demonstrations have drawn scant participation and hardly any spectators, the risk of riots and mayhem is still very much a factor, with the possibility of lives lost in the process. According to Dworkin's second model, such demonstrations should be allowed to take place, because the rights of demonstrators should not be invaded (the First Amendment allows not only freedom of *speech* but also freedom of *assembly*). But the Constitution grants no right to create a public disturbance. So critics of Dworkin's second model suggest a middle course: Certainly we have freedom of speech and freedom of assembly—but that doesn't entail an automatic police permit to march in a demonstration. So let those who want to exercise their freedom of speech assemble someplace, in a hall or on a street corner, but limit the possibility of harm to the public if the issue is volatile. The tendency in our society is increasingly to move toward protection of the public rather than protection of the individual's right to freedom of speech, assembly, or movement. Some years ago judges were generally reluctant to issue restraining orders against domestic abusers because of

Box 7.4   CIVIL LIBERTIES VERSUS SECURITY

In the fall of 2001, as a step in the war against terrorism, Congress passed the U.S.A. Patriot Act of 2001, directed at preventing future terrorism through increased powers of wiretapping, including "roving wiretaps" that zero in on a person rather than a telephone number, and intercepting e-mails, faxes, and so on. The purpose is to find and arrest any terrorist, foreign or domestic, who might threaten the security of U.S. citizens at home and abroad. In the wake of September 11 such measures seemed welcome and reasonable to many, but there were also voices who warned that we might come to regret this decision.

Interestingly, these voices have come from both the left and the right within American politics: Liberals see these measures as a threat to political dissidents in an era of conservative government. Conservatives see them as a danger to individual freedom—especially under some possible future liberal administration. And both point out that it in effect undermines the Fourth Amendment of the Bill of Rights, the search-and-seizure amendment, which says officers have to demonstrate *probable cause* (that a crime has been/is being committed) before entering and searching the premises of a citizen without that citizen's permission. The Patriot Act is intended to be in effect for four years, until 2005. By then we will probably have had a chance to evaluate the pros and cons of the congressional decision.

In addition, September 11 inspired sweeping measures to try foreign terrorists in military tribunals, so as to keep the proceedings—and especially the evidence—secret and thus out of reach of other terrorists. And the newly realized threat of bioterrorism seems to call for further measures of protection (as illustrated by the film *Outbreak*, summarized in the Narrative section).

How far are we willing to go in giving up our civil liberties, and even our constitutional rights, in order to obtain security? What are we willing to do? In the days following September 11 many Americans would have said, "Anything, just so we're safe," but others have reminded us that having an open, free society carries with it some inherent risks. If we put up too many safeguards to protect our society, we may lose our freedoms in the process. Benjamin Franklin wrote, "They that can give up essential liberty to obtain a little temporary safety deserve neither liberty nor safety." It is not unusual, however, for a country to enact strict legal measures in wartime that then will be lifted when the war is over.

What puts this into perspective is that prior to September 11 there was already a tendency in American politics (supported by eight years of a Democratic presidency) to "trade rights for benefits," as Ronald Dworkin would put it. In 1994 a seven-year-old New Jersey girl named Megan Kanka was killed, and her murderer was suspected to be a known child molester. In the aftermath, the question was asked, Could her death have been prevented if the whereabouts of the released child molester had been made public beforehand? In that case the community would have known to keep their children away from him. The law requiring such notification, known as Megan's Law, was passed by Congress in 1997, although individual states had earlier passed similar laws. In January 1999 it took effect across the United States. The addresses of sex offenders who are released from prison will be on file at the local police stations for the community to inquire into and make public. In some communities, the names and addresses of sex offenders are regularly released by community leaders or radio stations. In other communities, citizens have a more difficult time getting access to the information.

From the point of view of the community, this is tremendous progress in protecting the

(continued)

Box 7.4   CIVIL LIBERTIES VERSUS SECURITY *(continued)*

lives and well-being of our children; from the point of view of the sex offender, though, this is hardly good news. So what? we might say—who cares what sex offenders think of our attempts to foil their future exploits? The trouble is that our conception of civil liberties doesn't quite correspond to this idea of protection of the community. The sex offenders have served their time, paid their debt to society, and in most other cases this means they can start over again—with a criminal record but with the past behind them. They may have lost some rights (such as the right to vote and to own weapons), but presumably they retain the right not to be assumed guilty before they have done anything. Megan's Law casts this freedom into doubt: The past crimes of sex offenders will never be put

behind them, and, as such, the punishment never seems to come to an end. To some philosophers of law, this is terribly unfair, but others point out that the crimes such offenders have committed never come to an end, either—the victims of sexual molestation (if they survive it) will have to live with the memory always. Even so, this is not an argument in favor of Megan's Law, because punishment is not intended to match the pain intensity caused by the crime—how would that be possible? To the legal complaint that having one's name posted in the community prolongs the punishment, the court replied that the surveillance and posting of names is the community exercising its right to self-protection—it is not part of the punishment.

their right to freedom of movement; today such restraining orders are much more common. You might want to argue about rights within this scenario from the viewpoints of Dworkin and John Stuart Mill.

Negative Rights

Some social thinkers believe that although we do and should have rights, those rights should only be of a certain kind: *negative rights,* so called because they specify what ought *not* to be done to you (they are rights of noninterference). John Locke (1632–1704), a philosopher within the British tradition, is the author of the idea that people have natural rights against the government—the rights are natural because even outside of society, says Locke, people would agree that these rights are reasonable, but they are easier to enforce within a society. These rights are the right *to life, to liberty,* and *to property.* In his *Second Treatise on Government* (1690) Locke specifies that "The State of Nature has a law of Nature to govern it, which obliges everyone, and Reason, which is that law, teaches all mankind who will but consult it, that being all equal and independent, no one ought to harm another in his life, liberty, health or possessions." So even before a society is formed with all its rules and laws, says Locke, there is a law of nature guiding our rational thinking toward realizing that everyone is equal by birth, and everyone should be able to live their life in liberty without the interference of anyone else. In many ways Locke's philosophy was an inspiration to the Founding Fathers of the United States. Ayn Rand (see Chapter 4) expressed the conviction that the United States was the first moral society in history because it set limits on the power of the state and respected the concept of the rights of the individual. In an essay, "Man's Rights," from *The Virtue of Selfishness* (1965), she says, "All previous systems had regarded man as a sacrificial means to the ends of others, and society as an end in itself. The United States regarded man as an end in himself, and society as a means to the peaceful, orderly, *voluntary* coexistence of individuals."

So what are these individual rights? There is only one fundamental right, says Rand: the right to your own life and to act free of coercion. In that sense it is a positive right. But as for your neighbors, they have negative rights against you: the right not to have their right to life and liberty violated. How do we maintain our life? By our own effort, Rand says; this means you have the right to make money or own property without having it taken away. So the right to property is also a negative right. Are these rights absolute? Do you always have a right to your life, liberty, and property? Not if you have violated someone else's right to life, liberty, or property. In such a case your rights have been forfeited; so the limit of your own liberty is the liberty of the other person. But does this mean you have a right to be kept alive if you can't provide for yourself? Do you have a right to be given property and to be provided with the means to enjoy your liberty? No, says Rand. If you can't fend for yourself, then society has no obligation to help you (but others may want to, because they are caring people). There is no such thing as a right to a job, home, or fair wages — nor a right to be made happy, only the right to not be interfered with if you don't bother others in your own pursuit of happiness. (See Box 7.5 for a discussion of the right to die: euthanasia.)

The American philosopher John Hospers expresses the same sentiments in defending the political viewpoint of libertarianism in his book *The Libertarian Alternative* (1974):

Each man has the right to life: any attempt by others to take it away from him, or even to injure him, violates this right, through the use of coercion against him. Each man has a right to liberty: to conduct his life in accordance with the alternatives open to him without coercive action by others. And every man has the right to property: to work to sustain his life (and the lives of whichever others he chooses to sustain, such as his family) and to retain the fruits of his labor.

Both Rand and Hospers emphasize the right to life; does this mean they are part of the right-to-life movement? If we identify the right to life as an anti-abortion viewpoint, then it is not the same as the libertarian negative right, because libertarians are generally concerned with the right of people who are already born not to have their lives taken away. The Libertarian Party platform of 1994 specified a pro-choice stand, as a logical consequence of its view that the right to liberty includes the right for women to choose for themselves; however, the platform also specified that libertarians are against public funding of abortion clinics, because forcing others to pay for abortions violates the right to property.

Accordingly, the right to life is simply a right not to have your life interfered with. What if you are not capable of working to sustain your life? Then you have a problem, because Rand and Hospers do not believe you have a right to receive other

Box 7.5   EUTHANASIA AS A RIGHT?

Negative rights are traditionally defined as the right to life, liberty, and property. The right to die is usually not part of the discussion. We shall here take a look at the concept of the right to die and its relation to negative and positive rights.

First of all, what is euthanasia? Literally, it is Greek for "good death." There are four major distinctions: *voluntary* and *involuntary* euthanasia and *active* and *passive* euthanasia. "Voluntary" implies that the patient requests euthanasia. "Involuntary" has two meanings: (1) The patient clearly doesn't want to die, but is killed anyway (this is the kind of "euthanasia" performed by doctors in the death camps of Hitler's Holocaust); (2) the patient is incapable of communicating his or her wish, leaving the decision to the family (this is also sometimes called *nonvoluntary* euthanasia to distinguish it from outright killing). "Active" euthanasia refers to the patient's life being taken directly, by means such as drugs or the use of a weapon; "passive" euthanasia usually refers to the withholding of treatment from the patient that would otherwise have kept the patient alive longer. At the time of writing, Oregon is the only state that allows active voluntary euthanasia, under specifically de-fined circumstances (and this law is in conflict with federal law, according to U.S. Attorney General John Ashcroft). Passive voluntary euthanasia is common: The patient wishes life-prolonging treatment to end. Active involuntary euthanasia is not a legal option, whether it means killing someone who doesn't want to die or assisting someone whose family requests assisted suicide for them. Passive involuntary euthanasia is common, if we take "in-voluntary" to mean "nonvoluntary": The family requests a stop to life-prolonging measures.

When Dr. Jack Kevorkian began his work of either helping suffering people end their lives or killing misguided patients (depending on which view you hold), the idea of doctor-assisted suicide was still considered a radical one by most Americans. In 1999, Kevorkian stood trial for the third time. Acquitted of assisting suicide on two previous occasions, this time he was convicted of second-degree murder. The main reason Kevorkian had been acquitted twice was, in fact, the principle of the double effect which you know from Box 7.1: His lawyer argued that his primary intent had been to alleviate the patients' suffering (allowing them to inject them-

people's property without their consent. In practical terms, this means you should have planned ahead while you were able to work and saved up or taken out insurance; for those who never have been and never will be able to work, libertarianism advocates private charity, not government interference, because the only role for the government, say both Hospers and Rand, is to protect the negative rights of the citizens against violation. Anything else is, in the colorful language that Hospers echoes from Rand, "moral cannibalism." You may remember the excerpt in Chapter 4 from Rand's *Atlas Shrugged* in which she speaks of the right of the capable person not to have to support the lives of "whining rotters" — those she elsewhere calls "moochers and leeches" and "moral cannibals." Critics of this philosophy — and there are many — sometimes invoke the Golden Rule and ask of the libertarian, Is this the way *you* would want to be treated if stricken with a personal catastrophe that you could not have prepared for? Should the goods of this world be reserved for those who are strong, healthy, and capable of securing them for themselves, or should weaker in-

selves with a large dose of painkiller), with death as an unintentional and unavoidable side effect. Some of us may think that such an argument was a bit of a stretch, since by Kevorkian's own admission the fatal outcome was intentional, but legally it made a difference between a direct and an indirect action. Also, when Kevorkian was eventually convicted it was partly because the double effect argument couldn't be used: He had himself administered the lethal dose to a patient who subsequently died.

The key arguments in favor of active voluntary euthanasia (which is what the debate usually focuses on) are that (1) it should be the right of individuals to decide the manner and time of their own death; (2) it should be a person's right to avoid otherwise inevitable suffering (in other words, the right to death with dignity); (3) we help others we love when their lives are at an end and they are facing severe pain — our pets — so we should be able to do the same for our human loved ones; (4) we might want to have that option ourselves someday.

The most common counterarguments are that (1) it is not up to patients or doctors to play God: There is a time to die for everyone, and we shouldn't interfere; (2) it goes against the Hippocratic oath, by which doctors are sworn to heal, not to take lives; (3) having opened up the possibility of doctors assisting in people's death, the step from voluntary to involuntary euthanasia (the kind where the patient has not given his or her consent) is only as short as the doctor's and family's conscience; (4) financial pressures might be brought to bear on a terminally ill family member whose insurance is about to run out.

Could the right to die be considered a *negative* right? Yes, if one's body is considered property, then we may argue that we have a right to do with our bodies what we please, provided it doesn't infringe on other people's rights. But it doesn't entail that we have a right to *assisted suicide*, which is the issue. Could the right to die be considered a *positive* right? This is more probable. We may argue that the right to death with dignity is an entitlement all people have, similar to the right to food, shelter, clothing, work, education, and so forth. However, it would be hard to compel others, such as doctors, to help in *taking* lives as a professional duty; nor does a woman's right to seek abortion mean that a doctor is obliged to perform the abortion.

dividuals who lack such abilities also have a right to share in the goods in a civilized society?

Positive Rights

Views in opposition to libertarianism can be found in several areas of modern social thinking. The most extreme alternative would be provided by Marxism (rather quiet at the moment), which holds, on the basis of the ideal of social equality, that everyone in society has the right to have his or her life sustained, "to receive according to need, and to give according to ability." This makes the right to live and have your life sustained a *positive right* (a right to receive something from somebody, usually the government). As has often been pointed out, the politics of Communism exclude the negative rights just described: It rarely recognizes any right as not to be interfered with by the government. Socialist viewpoints (which are generally not as radical as

Communist ones in terms of government control) also support positive rights (entitlements) such as the right to work, to have shelter, and possibly also to have health care, education, clothing, and food?

According to the German political philosopher Karl Marx (1818–1883), the Communist state will take care of the needs of the individual: The individual has a positive right to have his or her needs met. But *needs* is an amorphous term. What does it mean to have your needs met? Marx had in mind the basics: food, shelter, clothing, meaningful work, education, and health care. The needs of your family, however, might stretch the definition of basic needs. Wanting and needing are, after all, not the same. What about feeling you *need* an extra VCR so you can tape two news shows at a time and be really well informed? What about braces for your daughter's teeth? What about a copy of the Phonics Game for your son? You may argue that the kids really *need* those things to secure their future, but who is to judge? And who is to pay for them? Those who have the ability to work.

In Marx's vision of the Communist state — the final stage of political development after feudalism and capitalism — the world will have changed. The capitalist concept of profit will have disappeared, because profit is the "surplus value" that the factory owner adds to the product on top of the wages paid to the factory worker — in Marx's view, value stolen from the worker and created on the worker's time and through the worker's effort. In the world of Communism, people no longer go to work in order to make wages or make a profit — they go to work because they have certain abilities that they put into the service of the state. And since they are allowed (ideally!) to work with whatever their talents dictate, they are not bored: The compensation for hard work is the joy of having meaningful work in itself. So society can require a person to work for the good of the community to the extent that he or she is able to do it (willingness is simply assumed). In compensation, the worker will be paid in goods according to his or her needs. In the early stages of the new world, Marx envisioned a monetary system, but within the completed Communist system, money would be abolished. In *Atlas Shrugged*, Ayn Rand (who fled the Soviet Union for the United States) creates a wicked parody of the fate of a factory run on Communist principles. The workers with needs soon outnumbered those who were able to put in long hours of work. Those workers with bright ideas and abilities were put on overtime without compensation, so that very soon they were out of ideas and discovered that they were able to put in only a feeble amount of work. But everybody was quick to think up new needs. . . .

The concept of positive rights need not take on such extreme proportions. Most liberal philosophies (see the next section) include the view that negative rights are not of much use if one's health or the country's economy prevent one from making a living. What good is the right to vote, to express yourself freely, and to hold office if you are so sick or destitute that you can't feed your kids or give them a safe place to grow up? In order to enjoy negative rights, one must be assured of having basic needs met. Welfare for a limited number of years is intended to tide a person over until he or she is able to work full-time again (although we have yet to see whether the current welfare system is an incentive toward personal responsibility in taking charge of one's life or whether it leaves people stranded because they can't find work).

As mentioned previously, affirmative action, in recent years under scrutiny (and presumably abolished in California's public sector after Proposition 209 passed in 1996), is intended to help overcome the inequalities of the past. Education itself is often considered a positive right, something the state must provide to its citizens in some basic form, such as public schools. We'll return to the topic of affirmative action.

Distributive Justice

In modern social philosophy we talk about two kinds of justice. One is the kind that is upheld by the law; it is generally referred to as *criminal justice,* and we will return to it at the end of this chapter. The other kind is *distributive justice,* theories of how to distribute the goods of society fairly. This distinction dates all the way back to Aristotle, who says in his *Nicomachean Ethics* that "A just thing . . . will be (1) that which is in accordance with the law, (2) that which is fair; and the unjust thing will be (1) that which is contrary to law, (2) that which is unfair."

For some social thinkers in the past, distributive justice depended on who could grab how much and hold on to it, but in modern times a clear understanding has emerged among social philosophers that in order for society to be a functioning system, it must offer both some recognition of needs and some way to meet those needs.

Rawls: Justice as Fairness

One of the most influential arguments against exclusively negative rights and in favor of positive rights—an argument that is also directed against a utilitarian view of rights as merely a means to happiness for the majority (*social utility*)—comes from the American philosopher John Rawls. This is usually identified as a *liberal* argument, not in the sense of Mill's *classical* liberalism (which comes close to today's libertarianism), but in the sense of the modern *egalitarian* liberalism, which believes that everyone should have equal access to social goods, in some way or other. A liberal generally believes in some positive rights as well as some negative rights: You need the right to life and liberty (such as freedom of speech), but without positive rights you may not be able to enjoy those negative rights, so you also have a basic right to be taken care of by society if you can't take care of yourself.

In order to envision a society that is as fair toward everyone as possible, Rawls suggests a thought experiment: Imagine, he says, that we are about to make rules for a brand-new society and that we are all in on it. (This is one of the most modern versions of the old *social contract theory* that you'll remember from Chapter 4.) Then, he says, imagine that you don't know who or what you'll be when the rules take effect; you may be rich, you may be poor, young or old, male or female, of another race. You pretend you are ignorant of your position in the future; you have now lowered a *veil of ignorance* over your mind's eye. This Rawls calls the *original position,* because it is from this position that we should imagine making rules for all of society. If you don't know who or what you will be, you will want to make certain that whatever rules you help make about fair distribution of the goods of society (such as jobs, food, shelter, child care, health care) don't place you at the bottom of the pile. If you end up being poor and ill, your new rules should be as fair to you as to anyone else; if you end up being

rich, you would want fairness, too. This is, of course, a form of rational self-interest —
but in the bigger picture it transforms itself into an understanding of other people's
needs. In Rawls's own words, from his influential work *A Theory of Justice* (1971),

> Thus we are to imagine that those who engage in social cooperation choose together, in
> one joint act, the principles which are to assign basic rights and duties and to determine
> the division of social benefits. . . . This original position is not, of course, thought of as an
> actual historical state of affairs, much less as a primitive condition of culture. It is under-
> stood as a purely hypothetical situation characterized so as to lead to a certain conception
> of justice. Among the essential features of this situation is that no one knows his place
> in society, his class position or social status, nor does any one know his fortune in the dis-
> tribution of natural assets and abilities, his intelligence, strength, and the like. . . . The prin-
> ciples of justice are chosen behind a veil of ignorance. This ensures that no one is advantaged
> or disadvantaged in the choice of principles by the outcome of natural chance or the con-
> tingency of social circumstances.

An example may help illustrate this (it is not an image that Rawls uses, but he
might): Think of a birthday party for a little girl. There is a big birthday cake, and
she would like to cut a big piece for herself before any of the guests get some of it.
But her parents tell her, "You may cut the cake, but you get to choose last!" She is a
smart girl; what will this force her to do? Cut pieces as evenly as possible, because
a tiny piece is likely to be rejected by her guests and thus be the last one remaining
for her. In a sense she is in the original position, creating a system of fair distribution for the future.

This analogy works well for the original position, but real life is different. The
needs (or wants) of the party guests were for a piece of cake, but in real life some
may need more food, shelter, and health care than others, and some have talents that
others don't have. So a completely fair distribution of goods would be one in which,
as a result, no one is in need of the bare essentials. Justice, then, consists in equal
liberty (having the same rights and duties as everyone else) for persons within a society. This doesn't mean that everyone should be treated the same way. As a matter
of fact, some inequality is permissible, provided that the end result is *everyone* in society benefits from that inequality (and not just some majority, as in utilitarianism).

Wolgast and Friedman: Reactions to Abstract Individualism

Rawls's viewpoint has helped immensely in identifying goals within liberal politics;
as you can imagine, he has critics among nonliberals, but he also has them even
among thinkers who are generally in favor of social equality involving fair distribution of goods. Here we look at viewpoints from two American philosophers,
Elizabeth Wolgast and Marilyn Friedman; each in her own way points to a lack in
Rawls's approach: the understanding that humans are not just "social atoms," separate individuals who might imagine themselves to be someone else entirely, but persons already existing in a web of interrelationships.

The idea of individualism has a long and important history, says Elizabeth Wolgast, and it has helped make this country what we perceive it to be; a place for in-

Elizabeth Wolgast (b. 1929), a philosophy professor emerita at California State University, Hayward, is the author of *The Grammar of Justice* (1987) and several other books and papers. She argues that Rawls's famous theory views people as separate individuals without any recognition of the community ties that bind these individuals. As an alternative she argues for a return to communitarianism, the view that an individual is partly understood through his or her ties to the community.

dividual achievement as a result of competition. It began with René Descartes daring to assert that humans all have the capacity to reason and are equal in their intelligence. Since everyone has this capacity, there is no need for any religious or political authority: We can figure things out for ourselves. This is the beginning of the egalitarianism, as well as the anti-authoritarianism, of Western individualism, says Wolgast, the source of a "do-it-yourself science and theology" that lets everyone play a part. Other thinkers, such as Thomas Hobbes and John Locke, emphasized the right of the individual as a "self-motivated unit" to decide his or her own social destiny, at least in extreme circumstances. One of the modern thinkers who have the most influence in supporting this idea of the individual as a separate unit is John Rawls. If we imagine a society in which everyone is an equal atom, then those atoms are interchangeable, and so ideally each person should be treated the same. But since we are not the same, a policy of justice should take that into consideration, and this is what Rawls's original position policy is all about. This is ingenious as an abstract ideal, but what about real life? asks Wolgast. This model of thinking, beginning with Descartes and culminating with Rawls, presupposes that all human relationships are entered into by separate "atomic" individuals as if they are entering into a contract, as if they weren't in any binding relationships already. According to Wolgast in *The Grammar of Justice* (1987):

> The atomistic model has important virtues. It founds the values of the community on private values; it encourages criticism of government and requires any government to answer to its original justification; it limits government's powers, as they may threaten to interfere with the needs of atomistic units. . . . But it leaves a great deal out. . . . In it one cannot picture human connections or responsibilities. We cannot locate friendliness or sympathy in it any more than we can imagine one molecule or atom moving aside for or assisting another; to do so would make a joke of the model. . . . we need to loosen the hold that the atomistic picture has on our thinking, and recognize the importance that theory has on our judgments and our moral condition.

What is Wolgast saying? She is siding with the much older political theory of *communitarianism*, which stems from the ancient Greek tradition. For the Greek thinkers,

Marilyn Friedman (b. 1945), a philosophy professor at Washington University, St. Louis, is the author of *What Are Friends For? Feminist Perspectives on Personal Relationships and Moral Theory* (1993) and several papers on philosophy, ethics, and feminism. In "Feminism and Modern Friendship: Dislocating the Community" (1989) she argues that although Rawls's abstract individualism is not sufficient to explain social ethics, neither is classical communitarianism, because it tends to be oppressive to women. An appreciation for the individual as well as for new types of community relationships is needed.

and Aristotle in particular, an individual does not understand himself or herself as a separate entity but as a social being. We understand ourselves, and others understand us, through the connections we have to our community. A society is not just a collection of individuals but part of the very purpose of the life of an individual. We are all someone's daughter or son; we have parents and children and siblings; we have friendships and trade relations and other community ties; and stripped of those we are nobody (which is why, to many Greeks, banishment from the community was a horrible threat, as we shall see in the next chapter). As Wolgast says, "the whole makes the part comprehensible." This is the view that has been popularized with the title of Hillary Rodham Clinton's book *It Takes a Village* (to raise a child, an African proverb). So Rawls's thought experiment is bound to have limits in this real world, because we are not simply atomic units, individuals alone in the universe. We have responsibilities to our community, and a good theory of justice must take such community ties into account. (See Box 7.6 for a discussion of bioethics and the needs of the individual versus the needs of the community.)

Marilyn Friedman agrees with much of Wolgast's criticism of the "abstract individualism" of Western modern philosophy and social thinking. She points out that many women thinkers in particular are now critical of this approach because they don't see themselves or people who depend on them and on whom they depend as utterly separate individuals but rather as a network or a group of individuals relying on one another. And the solution of communitarianism is tempting and reasonable, says Friedman in a paper from 1989, "Feminism and Modern Friendship: Dislocating the Community"—but we should be careful, because it may take us places we don't want to go. What do we mean by "community"? Very often what is meant is the *family,* the *neighborhood,* and the *nation;* communitarianism teaches that the traditions and demands of our community are highly important and should be a defining factor in each person's sense of self. But if we look at such communities in a historical sense, we find that most often they have been very oppressive toward women; so if we choose communitarianism over Rawls's idea of people as social atoms, aren't we risking going backward and accepting traditions dictating, for instance, that women are the property of their husbands, that children have no rights,

Box 7.6   BIOETHICS: HUMANS ARE NOT COMMODITIES

One area in which utilitarian and deontological approaches clash is in the moral debate about access to health care. We all want policies to live up to the ideals of equality as well as of justice, but we also know that some people's needs are greater than others'. Since resources seem to be dwindling, it is a question of how to distribute such social goods in a manner that is "fair." In the health care debate the question is becoming urgent, because whatever ethical viewpoint we adopt as the basis for our policies will determine the way in which people with health problems are going to be treated in the future. The utilitarian viewpoint of creating as much happiness for as many as possible was a genuine improvement over the lack of concern for ordinary people that was common in the public policies of Bentham's day, but in Chapter 5 we saw some problems that have arisen from the principle of utility: The majority may be happy, but what if the price of their happiness is the misery of a minority?

Kant's rule that we should never treat a rational being as merely a means to an end has become an antidote to the utilitarian disregard for the minority. In the health care debate the discussion is forming along these same lines: The utilitarian view points to the limited resources of society and the overall capacity for pain and pleasure of the individual and suggests that resources should be directed toward people whose quality of life will be improved in the long run, rather than toward people whose quality of life might not improve dramatically. Bentham's idea of quantifying a qualitative experience (putting numbers on feelings) is in the forefront again, because that may help doctors decide which patient to help: a thirty-five-year-old person or a ninety-three-year-old person (under the assumption that society can't afford to help both). Since the thirty-five-year-old may enjoy life and contribute to society for many years, resources should

probably go there instead of to a person close to the end of life whose quality of life might not be improved much; where the concept "quality of life" used to refer to extreme situations in which a person was suffering so much that life was no longer enjoyable, it has now come to mean an overall "global" evaluation of a person's life, a concept that has become known as Quality Adjusted Life Years (QALY). Some utilitarian doctors argue that it is the overall QALY calculation that will tell where funding is going to go, and this means that the care of elderly or terminal patients (which has a low QALY yield) will receive less priority than will the care of younger patients whose lives may be saved.

Some doctors and philosophers are disturbed by this development, because they see it as a complete disregard for the respect for *all* individuals (regardless of their age) that Kant argued for and that Rawls is working for in his theory of the original position (in which everyone must have at least minimal care and security, no matter who he or she is). As a modern equivalent of Kant's idea, these philosophers suggest the concept *irreplaceability*. In his essay "Social Justice," the Danish philosopher Peter Kemp writes,

> The irretrievable loss of another is one of the most universal human experiences. If I smash a plate I can buy another one. If my house burns down I can build another one in the same style as the old one. Everything we appreciate solely in material terms can be replaced. But another human being can never be replaced. . . . The death of another (which also occurs when e.g. a marriage or friendship breaks down irreversibly) is the fundamental reality from which the irreplaceable ethic springs.

According to the ethics of irreplaceability, each person, no matter how old or how isolated

(continued)

Box 7.6   BIOETHICS: HUMANS ARE NOT COMMODITIES
(continued)

and lonely, is unique and should be respected as a person, never to be sold out to the happiness of the majority. This also means that individuals can't be reduced to a resource for society—their bodies as incubators or their organs for transplants—without their consent. The discipline of bioethics is continually struggling to create policy suggestions for all the areas in which human needs may collide, such as the abortion issue, genetic profiling, euthanasia, and organ transplants; but the underlying philosophy is that human beings and their bodies are not commodities to be used for someone else's purpose, even if that purpose may be the greater good.

or that men have no place in the kitchen or nursery? Traditions may be a wonderful legacy for a community, but not all traditions are necessarily so. And suppose some of the old traditions were to blame for divisions and resentment among people today; ought we not be morally obligated to overcome those traditions? We can't just celebrate our community attachments uncritically, as some modern communitarians suggest, says Friedman. And how can we get to a point at which we can allow ourselves to be critical? By not throwing out the concept of the modern self without affiliations (what Wolgast called a "social atom"), a self who has learned to be critical of society's claims that we have social and moral obligations.

Furthermore, communitarians seem to believe that we are always a part of a community from the beginning; we have not chosen it, and yet we have responsibilities as members. But, says Friedman, that is true only when we are young; an adult person can generally choose many of his or her community affiliations. Does she want to belong to a union? Does he want to move to this or that neighborhood? Does she want to emigrate? Does he want to join a new church? We choose affiliations based on our personal needs, wishes, and critical sense, and they don't even have to be live-in communities. Today it's possible to belong to communities that don't really have a location, such as chat rooms on the Internet (when Friedman wrote her paper, the Internet was still in the future). So Friedman concludes (in "Feminism and Modern Friendship") that looking to community ties in order to expand traditional abstract individualism is a good idea, but it should not be done uncritically: We must develop communitarian thought beyond its complacent regard for the communities in which we once found ourselves toward (and beyond) an awareness of the crucial importance of "dislocated" communities, communities of choice.

Forward- and Backward-Looking Justice

In the debate about the nature and goals of justice it may seem confusing that legal experts sometimes talk about improving things in the *future,* and sometimes talk about making up for mistakes and evils of the *past,* as if the two approaches might exclude each other. And to some legal minds they effectively do, because the issue of justice can be defined in two ways: as *forward-looking,* and as *backward-looking.* One concept focuses on future consequences, the other is a rights-based concept centered on responding to conditions in the past. Here it is essential that you have studied Chapters 5 and 6, because this section relies heavily on your understanding of the goals of utilitarianism and other consequentialist theories, as opposed to the ideals of a Kantian viewpoint.

A forward-looking view of justice sees the purpose of justice as creating a fair system of distribution of social goods in the future. (Social thinkers use "social goods" to mean access to opportunities such as jobs as well as material things available to citizens in a community.) Regardless of what in the past has brought us to where we are today, our focus must be on creating as good consequences for as many as we can — for everyone, if possible — in the future. A utilitarian would concentrate on creating a functional society of equality and access to opportunities for the majority, under the assumption that that's the best we can do. Of course, a utilitarian might also consider instituting social *inequalities,* provided that the overall outcome is considered beneficial for the many.

A backward-looking view of justice requires us to look to conditions in the past and ask, What has brought us to where we are today in terms of inequality and unfair distribution of social goods, and how can we make amends? For a backward-looking view it is essential that we identify both the root causes of today's inequalities and the people in the past who have been affected by them, as well as their descendants and those still living today. Whether compensation for past wrongs done to these people will actually accomplish a system of fair distribution of goods in the future is not relevant — the main concern is to rectify the past wrongs.

An interesting hybrid form is John Rawls's theory of the original position. The Rawlsian focus would be on creating a fair system for *everyone,* using the original position to create rules of distribution of social goods so that no one falls through the cracks. As you'll remember, the original position is a thought experiment requiring that we forget about who we are and have been in the past, in order to imagine a fair and just society of the future where everyone is equal, and no one will be sacrificed for the convenience of anyone else. As such it is future-oriented, forward-looking. But Rawls himself is not a consequentialist; rather, he is a follower of Kant's philosophy that nobody should be used as merely a means to other people's ends, even if it might create good consequences. So Rawls's theory of justice in effect looks forward, drawing on a concept of rights and fairness, not on good social consequences as such. Later we look at Rawls's own theory of combining forward-looking and backward-looking theories of punishment.

In the field of *affirmative action* the views of forward- and backward-looking justice have determined the way many issues have been raised and solved. While the entire concept of affirmative action — a term coined by President Lyndon B. Johnson in the 1960s in connection with the Civil Rights Act — is now undergoing scrutiny by politicians, the media, and citizens for its overall results and possibly negative impact on public jobs and education, the goal of affirmative action ("preferential treatment," as it is referred to by critics) was to level the playing field for disadvantaged citizens. But exactly who the disadvantaged citizens are, and how the playing field is to be leveled, depends on whether one adopts a forward-looking or a backward-looking view.

A *forward-looking* approach identifies those in society who, at this point, seem disenfranchised, and those who in the near future may be in danger of being caught up in a socially disadvantaged situation, and will focus on making access to public jobs and education easier for that group, regardless of why the situation has arisen, or whether the beneficiaries or their ancestors were discriminated against in the past. Thus it is the present needs of disenfranchised individuals and groups that would determine the measure of help required, not their experience with discrimination in the past. A forward-looking view has to determine how far into the future such programs will have to exist in order to level the playing field—forever, or a few generations—because there will always be needy individuals.

A *backward-looking* view will focus on the history of disenfranchised groups and seek some form of compensation or restitution to those groups—living members or their descendants—based on the past experiences of group members regardless of whether everyone in that group today has in fact experienced discrimination in his or her lifetime. A backward-looking view will also have to determine how far into the past one must go in order to rectify old wrongs—should it be limited to living memory, meaning about a hundred years at the most, or should it go back several more generations? Regarding the question of compensation to African Americans for past injustices caused by slavery, the issue is extremely relevant: Assuming that one finds the idea of reparations at all reasonable (which many don't), a living memory criterion would include compensation not for slavery itself, but for the consequences of slavery. And a broader criterion would have to seek compensation not just from descendants of American slave owners, but also from descendants of Arab slave traders, and so on.

The very different approaches of forward- and backward-looking justice can be found not only within the realm of what we call distributive justice, the distribution of social goods, they are also an important part of what we refer to as *criminal justice*.

Criminal Justice

As a society, we believe that law-abiding persons should be treated equally, *ceteris paribus*. The Latin expression means "everything else being equal," so if you just go about your business, you deserve the same decent treatment by the government that anyone else deserves, no more and no less. But sometimes everything else is not equal: You may come from a historically deprived group, and legislation may state that such persons deserve special benefits (such as affirmative action). Or you may have experienced personal hardship that couldn't be anticipated and may need special help, perhaps in the form of welfare (all depending on which government system is in effect and what kind of rights its legislators may believe in: negative rights, positive rights, both, or none). Or you may have actually benefited society in some way, so the government believes you should be rewarded (some governments will pay families bonuses or give them tax breaks for having children, for example). But suppose you have broken the law? Then, according to criminal justice, the government is entitled to treat you differently from the rest of the population—by depriving you of benefits and sometimes also of certain rights, by punishing you for the crime committed. You may recognize the principle of treating equals equally and unequals unequally.

The concept of punishment is as old as human history, but only in the past two hundred years has it acquired the face we see today. In past eras around the world, punishment often involved banishment (temporary or permanent), financial restitution to the victims or their families, or loss of body parts—or even execution. The principle of "an eye for an eye," today referred to as the law of retaliation, or *lex talionis,* has been in effect for the past four thousand years, since the Code of Hammurabi.

Incarceration was rarely considered a form of punishment in former times, but could be a method of keeping dangerous people under control—either political figures who had worn out their welcome or who had a high enough profile that they could be held for ransom, such as the twelfth-century British king Richard the Lion-Hearted. In seventeenth-century Denmark the old king's daughter Leonore Christine was locked up for twenty-two years in a castle tower because her husband was a traitor, and the new king's queen thoroughly disliked her. The Tower of London, and the dungeons of medieval castles, served similar purposes, at a time when due process was a concept of the future. Torture, often a feature of these "holding facilities," would have several functions, among them obtaining information from the prisoner and punishing a crime. This was often undertaken privately rather than by the authorities. The fact that people were kept locked up was not in itself considered part of the punishment as much as facilitating the torture. The custom of incarceration as a form of punishment dates back only a few hundred years; the idea of keeping people in prison to punish them for their crimes has in itself undergone changes, from the notion that people should be kept in solitary confinement so they could contemplate the magnitude of their crimes and thus become rehabilitated to simply keeping criminals out of circulation as a way to protect the public.

While most people today think punishment (in some form) is an appropriate response to crime, the viewpoint has been advanced, particularly in the last half of the twentieth century, that punishment is a demeaning and inhumane approach. The question was raised, Who are we, law-abiding citizens, to pass judgment on people who have perhaps been deprived of the chances in life that have resulted in our being law-abiding? And who is to say that punishment will actually deter them from further criminal activity? Rather than punish people for what they have done, we ought to educate them and supply them with the chance they may never have had before to become a good citizen. In other words, the purpose of incarcerating criminals or subjecting them to other restraints has been viewed not as *punishment,* but as *therapeutic rehabilitation.* This fundamental philosophical difference between viewing punishment as something deserved and viewing it as something superimposed by a power structure that, somehow, has helped create the problem has led to the distinction between *retributive* and *restorative* justice. In defense of *restorative* justice, Pat Nolan of the Justice Fellowship says,

> If all we do is focus on the broken law, then all you can do is enforce the power of the government, the fist of government, and lock people up, to punish them. If, on the other hand, you look at crime as "victim harming," the solution should bring repair to the harm

done to the victim. And when you repair the harm done to the victim through restitution and reparation, generally the victim becomes very forward looking and doesn't want to harm and further punish the offender, but says, "I don't want you to do this again." "What can we do to make you not do this again?" "How can we change your life?" Transformation becomes important.

Nolan served fifteen years in the California State Assembly—and twenty-five months in a federal prison on racketeering charges. So perhaps he has an insider's understanding of the issue. He believes the solution lies in religion and in teaching morals. Those who focus on restorative justice emphasize that the balance in society is not restored by locking perpetrators up or executing them. The balance can only be restored if their criminal propensities can be transformed.

Proponents of restorative justice such as Howard Zehr, professor of sociology, often point out the differences between their view and retributive justice: Retributive justice sees a crime as a violation of rules and relationships, while restorative justice sees it as harm caused to people; retributive justice sees the state as the victim, while restorative justice sees people as victims. Retributive justice focuses on the past, while restorative justice focuses on the future. The courtroom is a battle situation for retributive justice, while for restorative justice the model is a dialogue. And for retributive justice, the debt is paid through punishment, while for restorative justice the debt is paid by "making it right."

The most influential, and perhaps also the most comprehensive defense of retributive justice to this day may have been supplied by Immanuel Kant. For Kant, justice *must* focus on the past, because that is how we identify the criminal and the severity of the crime; it must be seen as a violation of rules, because it is by the rationality of rules that we justify our moral system—but Kant would not conclude that only rules and not people are victims. On the contrary. Respecting the inherent dignity of another human being—victim as well as criminal—is the foundation of his retributive justice. Among contemporary supporters are the philosopher Igor Primoratz and the author Robert James Bidinotto. Below we look at Kant's argument in favor of *retributivism*.

So even though most social thinkers believe there should be an institution of punishment within society, there is widespread disagreement on not only *what kind of punishment* people should reasonably be subjected to but also on *why* they should be punished. It should not be hard for you to guess at some of the major disagreements.

Five Common Approaches to Punishment

Among all the different reasons people might give for punishment to be an option for society, five appear most often. Four of them are classics in the law books; the fifth one, although popular, is not considered legitimate by most legal experts.

Deterrence   It is often argued that punishment, provided it is swift and strict, is a good deterrent against crime. It may make the criminal change his or her mind about doing it again (specific deterrence) and it may make others think twice before turning to crime (general deterrence). Statistics indicate that in places where severe forms of punishment are the norm, such as Singapore, where disturbing the peace is punished by caning and political dissidence can lead to the death penalty, streets are noticeably safer than in free, Western-style societies. We must of course ask ourselves what price we are willing to pay for safe streets—a question we explored in Box. 7.4. It appears that here in the United States, crimes against property may be deterred by the knowledge of likely punishment. Who knows how many people refrain from stealing cars only because they know they'll face prison time if they're caught? It has been reported that some juvenile criminals deliberately scale down their criminal activity when they reach the age of eighteen because they know their punishment will be harsher—meaning that the concept of punishment *can* have a deterrent effect. But violent crimes seem not to be deterred much by the threat of punishment. California's controversial three-strikes law, which sends felons to jail for twenty-five years to life when they're convicted of a third serious crime, may serve as a deterrent in cases where two strikes are already on a person's record—but other factors may be at work, too, such as shifts in the economy.

Rehabilitation Some social thinkers see the purpose of punishment as making a better person out of the criminal (see the previous section); having undergone some form of appropriate punishment (generally incarceration), the criminal will have learned not to turn to crime again. This viewpoint generally presupposes prison programs that offer the inmate alternatives to a life of crime.

Incapacitation If punishment keeps the criminal off the streets, the public is safe and a social good has been achieved. But the proponents of the incapacitation, or protecting the public, approach don't specify *how* a wrongdoer should be incapacitated. Locking someone up is usually considered sufficient for protecting the public, but in the case of an individual who is a flight risk, conditions may have to be tightened, such as placing him or her in a high-security prison. A convicted rapist may be required to submit to chemical castration (although that does not address the problem of violence and aggression underlying the rape), so he is incapacitated in terms of his offense but may still be released into society. The ultimate incapacitation is of course executing the criminal, which eliminates the chance that he or she will prey on innocent people again. We return to this issue in Chapter 13.

These three approaches to punishment have one important thing in common: They all focus on the future social consequences of punishment; in other words, they are *forward-looking.* If there are no future benefits to be had from punishing someone, then a forward-looking theory will not recommend punishment. Because the primary forward-looking social theory today is utilitarianism, these three approaches are often labeled utilitarian.

By now you may wonder why these viewpoints don't address what for many is the best reason for punishing someone: the fact that he or she is *guilty of a crime.* But that is in effect a completely separate reason for punishment; because utilitarianism approves of punishment only if there is social good involved, it is theoretically possible that the overall benefits of punishing some guilty person are minimal, whereas the benefits of punishing someone who is *not* guilty may be considerable—instantly punishing a scapegoat may have a deterrent effect that far outweighs that of catching and convicting the real perpetrator some time in the future (and it may even deter the per-petrator from doing it again). In addition, setting an example by punishing someone with disproportionate harshness is a utilitarian possibility. If, however, we think that it ought to be of some importance whether a person is actually guilty and that we should take the magnitude of the crime into consideration, we must look to the fourth theory.

Retribution   A person should be punished because he or she has committed a crime, and the punishment should be in proportion to that crime. Social utility does not enter into the picture. The most influential thinker advocating retribution as the only proper reason for punishment is Kant. The principle he applies is *lex talionis,* the law of retaliation. Kant would not approve of the three forward-looking ap-proaches because they allow us to use a person *merely as a means* to achieve social utility. When we use a person to set an example, others may be deterred from com-mitting a crime; the goal of incapacitation is to keep the public safe; rehabilitation does indeed make a better person out of the criminal, but who decides how the criminal ought to be? We, society. So even here Kant implies that society is using people for its own purpose. The only acceptable reason for punishment is to show the criminal the respect any person deserves: It is to assume that he or she decided freely to commit the crime. With freedom comes responsibility, so if we want the freedom of never being treated merely as means to an end, we must also accept the responsibility that goes with it. If we transgress, we should be punished for our transgressions. (See Box 7.7 for a reflection on how the idea of retributive justice ap-plies to the *Star Trek* episode discussed in Chapter 6.)

As I mentioned earlier, these four reasons might be found in a legal text on re-tributive justice. But if you ask a person without any legal training why a criminal should be punished, she or he might answer in the following way: "Well, it just makes us feel better to see the murderer (or rapist, or burglar) get punished."

In the weeks following September 11, when the grief and shock for many people were followed by a furious anger, the question of vengeance came up. The nineteen suicidal terrorists who hijacked the airplanes could obviously not be pun-ished further, so now attention was directed to their accomplices—people who had trained them and planned the attacks and the nations that gave them shelter. Some moderate voices feared that America's anger might turn into a clamor for blind vengeance, resulting in the deaths of more civilians. And some did indeed want ven-geance, pure and simple. But for others, the issue was clear: It was not vengeance they wanted, but *justice.* Initially the government's name for the war on terrorism was "Operation Infinite Justice," until some American Muslims protested that only Allah can be associated with infinite justice. The name was then changed to "Operation Enduring Freedom." In Chapter 13 we return to the issue of vengeance and justice, in the sections on the just war concept and on the death penalty. For now it will suf-fice to outline the fundamental difference between a vengeance approach and a jus-tice approach, as some scholars see it.

Vengeance   Vengeance and retribution have something in common: They are both *backward-looking* theories, looking to the past (asking, "Who did this?") in order to

Box 7.7 STAR TREK: JUSTICE FOR WESLEY?

If you studied the episode "Justice" from *Star Trek: The Next Generation* in Chapter 6, you will remember that the teenager Wesley was scheduled for immediate execution for violating a local planetary law (he fell over a boundary and stepped on the grass). You are now in a position to evaluate the ruling from the point of view of retributive justice. Was the attitude of the people on the planet visited by Starfleet one of social utility or one of retribution? We saw in Chapter 6 that their general attitude was Kantian, in terms of respect for moral rules without exceptions; however, their approach to justice was a mixture of attitudes. In terms of punishing the guilty person out of respect for the law, this culture is clearly Kantian; but, in terms of ensuring a strong deterrent effect, the culture can be said to be using the person being executed merely as a means to an end, since there is no attempt to make the punishment fit the crime: All that matters is deterrence based on fear. Captain Picard might have used this as a defense of Wesley, but fortunately he did not have to; as you may remember, his attack on the shortcomings of a theory allowing for no exceptions was sufficient.

punish the guilty. Like retribution, the approach based on vengeance seeks to punish the criminal because of the crime committed, but there are three major differences between retribution and vengeance:

1. Retribution is based on *logic,* whereas vengeance is an *emotional* response: It is possible for people bent on vengeance to take their anger out on individuals other than the guilty person.
2. Retribution is a *public* act, done with the authority of the government, whereas vengeance is a *private* enterprise, undertaken by private citizens (vigilantes).
3. Retribution wants punishment to be proportionate to the crime, but vengeance may go beyond that and exceed the damage done by the criminal.

Although some people (generally opponents of the death penalty) argue that harsh punishments are just a form of social vengeance, many legal thinkers insist that when the government punishes a criminal, it is not the same as an individual or a group enjoying its revenge.

We have now considered three forward-looking and two backward-looking arguments for punishment, although the last one (vengeance) is rarely considered legitimate by philosophers of law. But are forward- and backward-looking theories always destined to be opposite? We know that utilitarians and Kantians don't agree on the basic moral motivations, but in real life most of us believe that sometimes people ought to be punished because it will deter others from doing the same thing; sometimes we want the wrongdoer incapacitated; and sometimes we think a first-time offender can be saved from a life of crime and rehabilitated with the proper form of punishment. And sometimes we think a criminal should be punished by the book simply because his or her crime warrants it and for no other reason. If we as individuals can hold such different views, does it mean we are just inconsistent, or does it mean we have some deeper, if inarticulated, understanding of the issue?

John Rawls has a suggestion that may shed some light on this phenomenon. In his paper "Two Concepts of Rules" (1955) he says utilitarians and retributivists are both right — but in different ways. In *individual* court cases we appeal to retributivism: A burglar goes to prison because he has committed a crime, and the crime determines the length of the sentence. But why do we send people to prison *in general*? To make society a better place — which is the point utilitarianism makes. So the *judge's* reason for sending a person to prison is retributivist, but the *legislator's* reason for making laws is utilitarian. The danger, as Rawls sees it, is that this definition might allow the utilitarian to make laws that might sacrifice the innocent for the sake of social benefits for the many — the problem of "sheer numbers" which you encountered in Chapter 5. Thus the application of utilitarianism must be very careful; in other words, a system of checks and balances is needed.

Is Anger Ever Appropriate?

A utilitarian, forward-looking penologist (someone interested in theory of punishment) usually sees no difference between retribution and vengeance: Retributivism is just a fancy word for the emotional demand for revenge. A retributivist will argue that the difference between vengeance and retribution is that vengeance is based on an emotion, anger, whereas retributivism is based on a wish for a proportional, logical response. That would imply that if we feel anger toward a perpetrator, whether as victims or as other members of society, we are merely being emotional and should set aside those emotions for the sake of logic.

In *For Capital Punishment: Crime and the Morality of the Death Penalty* (1979), Walter Berns argues that anger has a deep connection with justice that modern penology hasn't understood. Berns says,

> If men are not saddened when someone else suffers, or angry when someone else suffers unjustly, the implication is that they do not care for anyone other than themselves or that they lack some quality that befits a man. . . . Punishment arises out of the demand for justice, and justice is demanded by angry, morally indignant men; its purpose is to satisfy that moral indignation and thereby promote the law-abidingness that, it is assumed, accompanies it.

(In 1979 gender-neutral language hadn't yet become the norm in academic publications, but I assume Berns is talking about morally indignant men *and* women.) If we are not angry, says Berns, it is because we are selfish utilitarians who are concerned only with *compensations,* but you can't compensate victims for the loss of their physical integrity due to rape or for the loss of their life. (As Kant and the Danish philosopher Peter Kemp would say, people are irreplaceable.) Not all crimes can be balanced by compensation, but without righteous moral indignation we won't have an understanding of that.

The British philosopher P. F. Strawson argues, in his paper "Freedom and Resentment" (1982), that it is normal and appropriate to react emotionally to other people's actions toward us. We feel *resentment* if we are directly harmed, and we feel *moral indignation* if our involvement is indirect. To this the philosopher of law Diane Whiteley adds in her paper "The Victim and the Justification of Punishment" (1998, excerpted in the Primary Readings at the end of the chapter) that we must also take human *empathy* into account, because it is "by virtue of human beings possessing the three natural capacities of moral understanding, self-evaluation, and empathy that they have the capability to be moral agents." This means the demand for justice and punishment becomes society's communication of the victim's resentment and the community's moral indignation. In this way, the community stands up for the victim and shows her or him respect. If there is no (or too lenient) punishment, the community sends out two messages: that it feels no "retributive sentiment" (or, as Berns would say, anger) toward the criminal and no respect for the victim. And if a victim feels no resentment and doesn't insist on punishment, then she or he has too little self-esteem. A battered spouse who doesn't want her (or his) spouse punished may have internalized the spouse's claim that she has deserved being beaten. And the community that feels no moral indignation over a crime being committed against one of its members fails to stand up for that member and fails to show the respect for the victim that she deserves.

But, says Whiteley, this is not merely a blindly emotional response (you'll remember Martha Nussbaum in Chapter 1 arguing that emotions can have their own inherent logic and can be rational responses to situations). Provided that the victim's resentment is directed toward the right person, and for the right reason, it is an appropriate sentiment, and the community's moral indignation is an endorsement of the victim's resentment, as well as a condemnation of the criminal act that has attempted to deprive the victim of moral value (because if you value someone you don't commit a crime against him or her—committing a crime against someone is reducing her or him to merely a means to an end of instrumental value only). Resentment and indignation are proper elements in the process of justice and punishment if they lead, not to pure revenge, but to retribution based on a natural fellow feeling within a community.

In the aftermath of September 11, the debate arose whether it was appropriate to seek revenge on the people ultimately responsible for the terrorist attacks, and whether rage was a destructive emotion that would lead to vengeance rather than justice. From Whiteley's analysis (although it was of course written before 9/11) we might draw the conclusion that a *lack* of moral indignation and resentment against the terrorists would have been morally wrong—and that such an anger doesn't have to lead to bloody revenge but can be channeled into an appropriate societal response that takes the dignity of the victims into account.

Study Questions

1. What are Dworkin's two models? Explain, and apply his second model to the issue of protecting a country against terrorism.

2. What does it mean that science is supposed to be value-free? Do you agree? Why or why not? Apply the theory of value-free science to contemporary issues such as cloning and genetic engineering.

3. Explain the three principles of equality. Which one do you find most reasonable? Why?

4. Explain the concepts of negative and positive rights, and identify support-ers of each theory.

5. What is the "original position"? Explain the pros and cons of Rawls's theory.

6. Explain forward-looking and backward-looking justice, and apply both to the issue of affirmative action.

7. Explain forward-looking and backward-looking theories of punishment. Which approach seems the most reasonable to you? Why?

8. Can anger ever be justified as a reason for punishment? Explain, referring to Berns and Whiteley.

Primary Readings and Narratives

The Primary Readings are the United Nations Universal Declaration of Human Rights; an excerpt from John Rawls's "Justice as Fairness"; an excerpt from Martin Luther King's "Letter from Birmingham Jail"; and an excerpt from Diane Whiteley's "The Victim and the Justification of Punishment." The first Narrative is a summary of the film *Blade Runner*, a science fiction story about future exploitation of artificial humans; the second is a summary of the film *Gattaca*, about genetic engineering cre-ating a human super-race as well as an underclass. The third is a summary of the film *Losing Isaiah*, which raises the questions of interracial adoption and fairness for a small child. The fourth is a summary of the film *The Insider*, about a tobacco-industry whistleblower. The fifth is a summary of the film *Outbreak*, a fictional story of government response to an Ebola-type epidemic in the United States.

 Primary Reading

The United Nations Universal Declaration of Human Rights

1948.

Now, Therefore, The General Assembly proclaims

This universal declaration of human rights as a common standard of achievement for all peoples and all nations, to the end that every individual and every organ of society, keep-ing this Declaration constantly in mind, shall strive by teaching and education to pro-mote respect for these rights and freedoms and by progressive measures, national and international, to secure their universal and effective recognition and observance, both among the peoples of Member States themselves and among the peoples of territories under their jurisdiction.

Article 1: All human beings are born free and equal in dignity and rights. They are en-dowed with reason and conscience and should act towards one another in a spirit of brotherhood.

Article 2: Everyone is entitled to all the rights and freedoms set forth in the Declaration without distinction of any kind, such as race, colour, sex, language, religion, political or other opinion, national or social origin, property, birth or other status.

Furthermore, no distinction shall be made on the basis of the political, jurisdictional or international status of the country or territory to which a person belongs, whether it be independent, trust, non-self-governing or under any other limitation of sovereignty.

Article 3: Everyone has the right to life, liberty and security of person.

Article 4: No one shall be held in slavery or servitude; slavery and the slave trade shall be prohibited in all their forms.

Article 5: No one shall be subjected to torture or to cruel, inhuman or degrading treatment or punishment.

Article 6: Everyone has the right to recognition everywhere as a person before the law.

Article 7: All are equal before the law and are entitled without any discrimination to equal protection of the law. All are entitled to equal protection against any discrimination in violation of this Declaration and against any incitement to such discrimination.

Article 8: Everyone has the right to an effective remedy by the competent national tribunals for acts violating the fundamental rights granted him by the constitution or by law.

Article 9: No one shall be subjected to arbitrary arrest, detention or exile.

Article 10: Everyone is entitled in full equality to a fair and public hearing by an independent and impartial tribunal, in the determination of his rights and obligations of any criminal charge against him.

Article 11:

1. Everyone charged with a penal offence has the right to be presumed innocent until proved guilty according to law in the public trial at which he has had all the guarantees necessary for his defense.

2. No one shall be held guilty of any penal offence on account of any act or omission which did not constitute a penal offence, under national or international law, at the time when it was committed. Nor shall a heavier penalty be imposed than the one that was applicable at the time the penal offence was committed.

Article 12: No one shall be subjected to arbitrary interference with his privacy, family, home or correspondence, nor to attacks upon his honour and reputation. Everyone has the right to the protection of the law against such interference or attacks.

Article 13:

1. Everyone has the right to freedom of movement and residence within the borders of each state.

2. Everyone has the right to leave any country, including his own, and to return to his country.

Article 14:

1. Everyone has the right to seek and to enjoy in other countries asylum from persecution.

2. This right may not be invoked in the case of prosecutions genuinely arising from non-political crimes or from acts contrary to the purposes and principles of the United Nations.

Article 15:

1. Everyone has the right to a nationality.

2. No one shall be arbitrarily deprived of his nationality nor denied the right to change his nationality.

Article 16:

1. Men and women of full age, without any limitation due to race, nationality or religion, have the right to marry and to found a family. They are entitled to equal rights as to marriage, during marriage and at its dissolution.

2. Marriage shall be entered into only with the free and full consent of the intended spouses.

3. The family is the natural and fundamental group unit of society and is entitled to protection by society and the State.

Article 17:

1. Everyone has the right to own property alone as well as in association with others.

2. No one shall be arbitrarily deprived of his property.

Article 18: Everyone has the right to freedom of thought, conscience and religion; this right includes freedom to change his religion or belief, and freedom either alone or in community with others and in public or private, to manifest his religion or belief in teaching, practice, worship and observance.

Article 19: Everyone has the right to freedom of opinion and expression; this right includes freedom to hold opinions without interference and to seek, receive and impart information and ideas through any media and regardless of frontiers.

Article 20:

1. Everyone has the right to freedom of peaceful assembly and association.

2. No one may be compelled to belong to an association.

Article 21:

1. Everyone has the right to take part in the government of his country, directly or through freely chosen representatives.

2. Everyone has the right of equal access to public service in his country.

3. The will of the people shall be the basis of the authority of government; this will shall be expressed in periodic and genuine elections which shall be by universal and equal suffrage and shall be held by secret vote or by equivalent free voting procedures.

Article 22: Everyone, as a member of society, has the right to social security and is entitled to realization, through national effort and international cooperation and in accordance with the organization and resources of each State, of the economic, social and cultural rights indispensable for his dignity and the free development of his personality.

Article 23:

1. Everyone has the right to work, to free choice of employment, to just and favourable conditions of work and to protection against unemployment.

2. Everyone, without any discrimination, has the right to equal pay for equal work.

3. Everyone who works has the right to just and favourable remuneration ensuring for himself and his family an existence worthy of human dignity, and supplemented, if necessary, by other means of social protection.

4. Everyone has the right to form and to join trade unions for the protection of his interests.

Article 24: Everyone has the right to rest and leisure, including reasonable limitation of working hours and periodic holidays with pay.

Article 25:

1. Everyone has the right to a standard living adequate for the health and well-being of himself and his family, including food, clothing, housing and medical care and necessary social services, and the right to security in the event of unemployment, sickness, disability, widowhood, old age or other lack of livelihood in circumstances beyond his control.

2. Motherhood and childhood are entitled to special care and assistance. All children, whether born in or out of wedlock, shall enjoy the same social protection.

Article 26:

1. Everyone has the right to education. Education shall be free, at least in the elementary and fundamental stages. Elementary education shall be compulsory. Technical and professional education shall be made generally available and higher education shall be equally accessible to all on the basis of merit.

2. Education shall be directed to the full development of the human personality and to the strengthening of respect for human rights and fundamental freedoms. It shall promote understanding, tolerance and friendship among all nations, racial or religious groups, and shall further the activities of the United Nations for the maintenance of peace.

3. Parents have a prior right to choose the kind of education that shall be given to their children.

Article 27:

1. Everyone has the right freely to participate in the cultural life of the community, to enjoy the arts and to share in scientific advancement and its benefits.

2. Everyone has the right to the protection of the moral and material interests resulting from any scientific, literary or artistic production of which he is the author.

Article 28: Everyone is entitled to a social and international order in which the rights and freedoms set forth in this Declaration can be fully realized.

Article 29:

1. Everyone has duties to the community in which alone the free and full development of his personality is possible.

2. In the exercise of his rights and freedoms, everyone shall be subject only to such limitations as are determined by law solely for the purpose of securing due recognition and respect for the rights and freedoms of others and of meeting the just requirements of morality, public order and the general welfare in a democratic society.

3. These rights and freedoms may in no case be exercised contrary to the purposes and principals of the United Nations.

Article 30: Nothing in this Declaration may be interpreted as implying for any State, group or person any right to engage in any activity or to perform any act aimed at the destruction of any of the rights and freedoms set forth herein.

Study Questions

1. Find examples of negative and positive rights, and explain the difference.

2. Evaluate these articles from a libertarian approach and from Rawls's approach.

3. Evaluate Article 11 from a utilitarian and from a deontological approach.

4. In your opinion, are there any rights that should be on the list but aren't included? Are there any rights you disagree with? Explain.

Primary Reading

Justice as Fairness

JOHN RAWLS

Excerpt from a 1958 essay.

The following passages are from a famous paper by John Rawls written years before his even more famous book, *A Theory of Justice* (1971).

The conception of justice which I want to develop may be stated in the form of two principles as follows: first, each person participating in a practice, or affected by it, has an equal right to the most extensive liberty compatible with a like liberty for all; and second, inequalities are arbitrary unless it is reasonable to expect that they will work out for everyone's advantage, and provided the positions and offices to which they attach, or from which they may be gained, are open to all. These principles express justice as a complex of three ideas: liberty, equality, and reward for services contributing to the common good.

The term "person" is to be construed variously depending on the circumstances. On some occasions it will mean human individuals, but on others it may refer to nations, provinces, business firms, churches, teams, and so on. The principles of justice apply in all these instances, although there is a certain logical priority to the case of human individuals. As I shall use the term "person," it will be ambiguous in the manner indicated.

The first principle holds, of course, only if other things are equal: that is, while there must always be a justification for departing from the initial position of equal liberty (which is defined by the pattern of rights and duties, powers and liabilities, established by a practice), and the burden of proof is placed on him who would depart from it, nevertheless, there can be, and often there is, a justification for doing so. Now, that similar particular cases, as defined by a practice, should be treated similarly as they arise, is part of the very concept of a practice; it is involved in the notion of an activity in accordance with rules. The first principle expresses an analogous conception, but as applied to the structure of practices themselves. It holds, for example, that there is a presumption against the distinctions and classifications made by legal systems and other practices to the extent that they infringe on the original and equal liberty of the persons participating in them. The second principle defines how this presumption may be rebutted.

It might be argued at this point that justice requires only an equal liberty. If, however, a greater liberty were possible for all without loss or conflict, then it would be irrational to settle on a lesser liberty. There is no reason for circumscribing rights unless their exercise would be incompatible, or would render the practice defining them less effective. Therefore no serious distortion of the concept of justice is likely to follow them including within it the concept of the greatest equal liberty.

The second principle defines what sorts of inequalities are permissible; it specifies how the presumption laid down by the first principle may be put aside. Now by inequalities it is best to understand not *any* differences between offices and positions, but differences in the benefits and burdens attached to them either directly or indirectly, such as prestige and wealth, or liability to taxation and compulsory services. Players in a game do not protest against there being different positions, such as batter, pitcher, catcher, and the like, nor to there being various privileges and powers as specified by the rules; nor do the citizens of a country object to there being the different offices of government such as president, senator, governor, judge, and so on, each with their special rights and duties. It is not differences of this kind that are normally thought of as inequalities, but differences in the resulting distribution established by a practice, or made possible by it, of the things men strive to attain or avoid. Thus they may complain about the pattern of honors and rewards set up by a practice (*e.g.* the privileges and salaries of government officials) or they may object to the distribution of power and wealth which results from the various ways in which men avail themselves of the opportunities allowed by it (*e.g.* the concentration of wealth which may develop in a free price system allowing large entrepreneurial or speculative gains).

It should be noted that the second principle holds that an inequality is allowed only if there is reason to believe that the practice with the inequality, or resulting in it, will work for the advantage of *every* party engaging in it. Here it is important to stress that *every* party must gain from the inequality. Since the principle applies to practices, it implies that the representative man in every office or position defined by a practice, when he views it as a going concern, must find it reasonable to prefer his condition and prospects with the inequality to what they would be under the practice without it. The principle excludes, therefore, the justification of inequalities on the grounds that the disadvantages of those in one position are outweighed by the greater advantages of those in another position. This rather simple restriction is the main modification I wish to make in the utilitarian principle as usually understood. When coupled with the notion of a practice, it is a restriction of consequence, and one which some utilitarians, for example Hume and Mill, have used in their discussions of justice without realizing apparently its significance, or at least without calling attention to it. Why it is a significant modification of principle, changing one's conception of justice entirely, the whole of my argument will show.

Further, it is also necessary that the various offices to which special benefits or burdens attach are open to all. It may be, for example, to the common advantage, as just defined, to attach special benefits to certain offices. Perhaps by doing so the requisite talent can be attracted to them and encouraged to give its best efforts. But any offices having special benefits must be worn in a fair competition in which contestants are judged on their merits. If some offices were not open, those excluded would normally be justified in feeling unjustly treated, even if they benefited from the greater efforts of those who were allowed to compete for them. Now if one can assume that offices are open, it is necessary only to consider the design of practices themselves and how they jointly, as a system, work together. It will be a mistake to focus attention on the varying relative positions of particular persons, who may be known to us by their proper names, and to require that each such change, as a once for all transaction viewed in isolation, must be in itself just. It is the system of practices which is to be judged, and judged from a general point of view: unless one is prepared to criticize it from the standpoint of a representative man holding some particular office, one has no complaint against it.

Study Questions

1. Describe Rawls's two principles in your own words.

2. Can you think of a policy involving inequality that Rawls might approve of?

3. Judging from this excerpt, what would you think Rawls's position on affirmative action might be? Explain.

Primary Reading

A Letter from Birmingham Jail

MARTIN LUTHER KING, JR.

Excerpt from an essay written April 16, 1963.

This open letter was written by the civil rights leader Martin Luther King, Jr., in response to a published statement from eight clergymen from Alabama who had criticized King's activities as "unwise and untimely." As president of the Southern Christian Leadership Conference, King had taken part in a nonviolent protest against racial segregation in Birmingham, and he and others had subsequently been jailed for "parading without a permit." King notes in the published version of his letter that he began writing his response to the clergymen in the margin of the newspaper where the statement had appeared and continued on scraps of paper, because that was all he had available in his jail cell.

You express a great deal of anxiety over our willingness to break laws. This is certainly a legitimate concern. Since we so diligently urge people to obey the Supreme Court's decision of 1954 outlawing segregation in the public schools, at first glance it may seem rather paradoxical for us consciously to break laws. One may well ask: "How can you advocate breaking some laws and obeying others?" The answer lies in the fact that there are two types of laws: just and unjust. I would be the first to advocate obeying just laws. One has not only a legal but a moral responsibility to obey just laws. Conversely, one has a moral responsibility to disobey unjust laws. I would agree with St. Augustine that "an unjust law is no law at all."

Now, what is the difference between the two? How does one determine whether a law is just or unjust? A just law is a man-made code that squares with the moral law or the law of God. An unjust law is a code that is out of harmony with the moral law. To put it in the terms of St. Thomas Aquinas: An unjust law is a human law that is not rooted in eternal law and natural law. Any law that uplifts human personality is just. Any law that degrades human personality is unjust. All segregation statutes are unjust because segregation distorts the soul and damages the personality. It gives the segregator a false sense of superiority and the segregated a false sense of inferiority. Segregation, to use the terminology of the Jewish philosopher Martin Buber, substitutes an "I-it" relationship for an "I-thou" relationship and ends up relegating persons to the status of things. Hence segregation is not only politically, economically and sociologically unsound, it is morally wrong and awful. Paul Tillich has said that sin is separation. Is not segregation an existential expression of man's tragic separation, his awful estrangement, his terrible sinfulness? Thus it is that I can urge men to obey the 1954 decision of the Supreme Court, for it is morally right; and I can urge them to disobey segregation ordinances, for they are morally wrong.

Let us consider a more concrete example of just and unjust laws. An unjust law is a code that a numerical or power majority group compels a minority group to obey but does not make binding on itself. This is *difference* made legal. By the same token, a just law is a code that a majority compels a minority to follow and that it is willing to follow itself. This is *sameness* made legal.

Let me give another explanation. A law is unjust if it is inflicted on a minority that, as a result of being denied the right to vote, had no part in enacting or devising the law. Who can say that the legislature of Alabama which set up that state's segregation laws was democratically elected? Throughout Alabama all sorts of devious methods are used to prevent Negroes from becoming registered voters, and there are some counties in which, even though Negroes constitute a majority of the population, not a single Negro is registered. Can any law enacted under such circumstances be considered democratically structured?

Sometimes a law is just on its face and unjust in its application. For instance, I have been arrested on a charge of parading without a permit. Now, there is nothing wrong in having an ordinance which requires a permit for a parade. But such an ordinance becomes unjust when it is used to maintain segregation and to deny citizens the First Amendment privilege of peaceful assembly and protest.

I hope you are able to see the distinction I am trying to point out. In no sense do I advocate evading or defying the law, as would the rabid segregationist. That would lead to anarchy. One who breaks an unjust law must do so openly, lovingly, and with a willingness to accept the penalty. I submit that an individual who breaks a law that conscience tells him is unjust, and who willingly accepts the penalty of imprisonment in order to arouse the conscience of the community over its injustice, is in reality expressing the highest respect for law.

Study Questions

1. How does King justify advocating breaking some laws and obeying others? Would you agree with him? Why or why not?

2. What, according to King, is unsound about segregation? Explain. Would that also apply to a group of people who would *voluntarily* segregate themselves from other groups?

3. How does King reconcile the breaking of an unjust law with respect for the law? Is he a legal positivist or a naturalist? Explain.

4. Is King's ideal of nonviolent resistance to unjust laws a concept that has mainly historical interest, or might it have something to say to people of the twenty-first century? Explain.

Primary Reading

The Victim and the Justification of Punishment

DIANE WHITELEY

Excerpt from a 1998 article.

Diane Whiteley is a scholar associated with the administration at Simon Fraser University in British Columbia. In this paper, published in the John Jay College of Criminal Justice's journal *Criminal Justice Ethics*, she argues that the focus of justice has been insufficiently directed toward the concerns of the victim and too much toward the wrongdoer and the community. In addition, she argues that if we as a community don't feel moral indignation over what the criminal has done, we are letting the victim down.

> The victim's resentment is a moral sentiment. But what is a moral sentiment? To begin with, it is worth pointing out that a moral sentiment may judged justified or not. I offer some examples of unjustified moral sentiments presently. A justified moral sentiment is an "intelligent" emotion in the sense that it conveys a "considered" emotional reaction — one which is based on reasons and takes account of the circumstances. Significantly, a moral sentiment is directed at another person. Resentment, for example, would not arise on injury by a natural disaster or an animal — at least not appropriately. It is experienced on being harmed by a person.
>
> A moral sentiment is not a mere passion such as vengefulness which is characterized by inappropriate intensity or a failure duly to consider facts and circumstances. It can be evaluated, judged appropriate or not, and controlled. It is not a simple feeling — a pleasant or unpleasant sensation such as a pounding heart or queasy stomach. While there is no

denying that a moral sentiment may have a physiological component, it is, in part, a cognitive state of belief. It is *about* something, a way of seeing and engaging with the world. In short, it is a complex emotion that involves a belief, an evaluation, and a relation to action.

The victim's resentment is, in fact, a paradigmatic moral sentiment. Its cognitive content consists in a belief that the wrongdoer did the crime. But resentment also involves the victim's corresponding evaluation of the wrongdoer. It is an attitude towards him that stems from viewing him in the light of the belief that he did the harm and related beliefs about his moral qualities. The wrongdoer is evaluated as uncaring of the victim's value. The victim infers that he is capable of respecting her dignity but failed to do so. As Murphy points out, the reason we deeply resent moral injuries done to us

> is not simply that they hurt us in some tangible or sensible way; it is because such injuries are also *messages*—symbolic communications. They are ways a wrongdoer has of saying to us, "I count but you do not," "I can use you for my purposes," . . . Intentional wrongdoing *insults* us and attempts (sometimes successfully) to *degrade* us.

Resentment has, in addition, an affective component. It arouses in the victim desires or feelings directed at the wrongdoer. Those desires motivate the victim to act in ways characteristic of the emotion. The attitude that arises in the resenter is one of defiance in which she denies to herself and others the presumption, fostered by the wrongdoer's action, that she is low in value. This psychological reaction is analogous to one's physical reaction of striking out in self-defense at an assault. It motivates the victim to get back at the wrongdoer by *expressing* her resentment. Failure to express it may signify acceptance of the wrongdoer's evaluation. And acceptance would indicate that she suffers some psychological pathology such as a severe lack of self-esteem.

For example, a woman who suffers from the "battered woman syndrome" is a victim who does not react with resentment when she is beaten by another person. Instead, she accepts the batterer's assessment that she deserves to be beaten. She should resent the beatings. The fact that we judge her lack of resentment to be pathological indicates that experiencing resentment is an appropriate reaction to the deliberate harm of another.

As a moral sentiment involving a belief, an evaluation, and an affective component, the victim's resentment can be judged as justified or not. It is unjustified if the belief about the wrongdoer is false. For example, resentment toward the accused thief, Smith, would be unjustified if Smith did not, in fact, snatch the victim's purse but was mistakenly apprehended because he was in the vicinity and fit the description of the real thief. The resentment would be unjustified were the victim's evaluation of the wrongdoer incorrect. If Jones snatched the purse because he was coerced into doing so by a gang that was threatening his life, the victim's evaluation of Jones as uncaring of her value would be incorrect and unjustified. Finally, the affective component of the resentment may be inappropriate. If, on having her purse snatched, the victim's resentment were so intense that she would express it by cutting the thief's hands off so that he could never steal again, we would judge her resentment unjustified because it was too intense.

Even if the resentment is justified, however, the question remains as to whether it should be communicated through the social institution. Before addressing that question, it will be helpful to consider the moral psychology of the remaining stakeholder, the community.

The members of the community react to a harm in which they are not personally involved with a certain disinterest. Their experience of moral indignation involves sympathy for the victim but tends to be less intense than resentment. Like resentment, however, moral indignation rests on and reflects the moral demand for some degree of goodwill.

Moral indignation is a complex emotion. It is similar to resentment in that it involves a belief, a related evaluation, and an affective component. In addition, however, it has a normative dimension. It is grounded in *approval* of the victim's resentment. It reflects sympathy for the victim from an impersonal standpoint. As such, it is not a mere *feeling* of sympathy arising out of sentimentality. It involves a reflective evaluation of the victim's resentment which results in a judgment to endorse it. The cognitive content of the moral indignation is the belief that the wrongdoer did the crime. The related evaluation is that the wrongdoer is uncaring, to some degree, of the victim's value. The affective component, which is normally less intense than that of resentment, involves sympathy for the victim and a desire to get back at the wrongdoer on the victim's behalf.

The fact that moral indignation involves a judgment to endorse the victim's resentment entails that it may be modified or even withdrawn when the facts of the case are examined. Feinberg points out that at a criminal trial the absolution of the accuser often hangs as much in balance as the guilt of the accused. In the case of date rape, for example, the victim's motives and actions may be examined and questioned equally with those of the accused. The upshot is that, in our system in which the value of fairness is given a high priority, the community withholds its expression of moral indignation until the wrongdoer is pronounced guilty.

In sentencing, the community has the opportunity to express its moral indignation. The expression is intended to send a message. The community intends that the wrongdoer and public recognize that the punishment means denunciation, among other things. In crimes such as robbery, assault, rape, or murder the wrongdoer fails to meet the demand for goodwill. In extreme cases such as violent, brutal murder, her actions express outright malevolence. But in all cases a criminal act shows that the wrongdoer views the victim as having no or reduced moral value. If the community were to fail to express censure, it would be acquiescing in the wrongdoer's devaluation of the victim. Jean Hampton suggests that the community's response involves "a *kind* of fear and defiance." On her view, the community *fears* that by not opposing the wrongdoer's challenge to its values, it invites further challenges. Therefore, it *defies* the challenge. I think Hampton's analysis is correct for our existing justice system. But if the system were changed to accommodate the victim's concerns by giving him a role, the community's response could also reflect sympathy for him, the sympathy inherent in moral indignation. The sentence would involve denunciation of the wrongdoer to be sure, but it would also be a way of standing up for the person devalued by the crime. In other words, the community would acknowledge the victim as one of its audiences.

From the community's perspective, as already mentioned, punishment conveys a variety of messages, not just moral indignation. I have focused on the retributive sentiment of moral indignation because of its connection to the victim's resentment.

This examination of moral psychologies makes it clear that, when the wrongdoer commits the crime, it is not just her relationship with society as a whole that is affected. The victim, too, has a substantial and justifiable stake in what happens to her. In other words, the recognition that the victim's resentment may be justified and that it needs to be expressed provides at least a *prima facie* reason to include the victim as a stakeholder in the social institution and as an audience for the communication. From the victim's perspective, an appropriate, public acknowledgment and communication of his justified resentment through the justice system would serve a number of purposes. It would convey publicly his resentment. It would communicate his demand for a minimum degree of respect from the wrongdoer and others. Finally, it would signify to the victim that the community is willing to stand up for him and reject his devaluation.

In the next section, I proceed with the second step in the argument about whether the victim's concerns are pertinent to the justification of punishment. I argue that the victim's personal, justified reaction should be acknowledged as a justifying reason for punishment by giving him a role in the social institution.

Study Questions

1. What is, to Whiteley, a "justified moral sentiment," and what makes a victim's resentment of the wrongdoer justified?

2. How should the community react toward a wrongdoer?

3. Why, to Whiteley, is it appropriate to include the emotion of moral indignation in the concept of punishment? Do you agree? Why or why not?

4. What does Whiteley mean by saying that moral sentiments can have a cognitive content? Why is this important for her theory of justification of punishment?

5. Does Whiteley's inclusion of emotions with a cognitive element in the justification of punishment lead to the acceptance of revenge? Why or why not?

Narrative

Blade Runner

HAMPTON FANCHER AND DAVID PEOPLES (SCREENWRITERS)
RIDLEY SCOTT (DIRECTOR)

Based on the novel **Do Androids Dream of Electric Sheep?**
by Philip K. Dick. Film, 1982. Summary.

At its premiere the critics weren't impressed with *Blade Runner;* it was too weird for most moviegoers' taste at the time. Over the years, though, the film has achieved cult status among film lovers for its film noir style and prophetic theme of asking, Who counts as a person? What looked like cultural mishmash in 1982 is now recognized as an accurate depiction of life in the inner cities—not only in the far-distant future, but even today.

This is the Los Angeles portrayed in the movie: dirty, perpetually rainy because of pollution, and populated with people from all cultures, all of whom are looking out

The replicant Batty (Rutger Hauer) and Deckard (Harrison Ford) struggle in the dramatic conclusion of *Blade Runner* (Warner Bros., 1982). Batty, dying because of a built-in self-destruct mechanism, shows that even with only four years of life, an artificial intelligent being can, in a sense, develop a soul. And Deckard is left wondering about the nature of his own humanity.

for themselves. The language of the streets is a mix of Japanese, German, and English. Giant blimps cruise the skies advertising "a new life off-planet," away from the hopelessness of earth life. There are almost no nonhuman animals left on earth, so humans are manufacturing mechanical pets—robotic owls and ostriches and snakes and what have you. In addition they are manufacturing artificial humans, "replicants," to take on hazardous and difficult work off-world. The latest series of replicants is particularly advanced. Stronger and more intelligent than humans, they already have become a danger to them: They are rebelling and have already killed some humans. Private detective Deckard is assigned the job of hunting them down and destroying them. He meets with their manufacturer, who tells him that these beings have a built-in self-destruct mechanism; four years is the maximum life span. Deckard has no sympathy for these beings; as far as he is concerned, they are mere things to be terminated. A young woman, Rachael, is staying at the house of the manufacturer. Deckard is attracted to her, and his view on replicants begins to change when he realizes that she is a replicant, although she herself is unaware of it. She is an experimental model, and her "brain" contains implants of someone else's childhood memories, which make her seem more human and make her believe she is human. Given the existence of such extraordinary features, who can say for sure who is a replicant and who isn't? Might Deckard himself also be one?

Arriving on earth without a clue where to go, but with a strong sense that an injustice must be corrected, the replicants slowly find their way to their manufacturer, to hold him accountable for creating lives without rights, and of such brief duration. But before they come face to face with the manufacturer, they find his chief designer, Sebastian, who lives by himself in an abandoned building. Sebastian is a genius, but he is also a lonely man, and he has created friends for himself—robots of all sizes and shapes that greet him when he comes home. Ironically, Sebastian has no problem seeing the replicants as people—he treats his own robots as people. In another ironic twist, Sebastian suffers from an illness that is causing him to age rapidly. His days are numbered just as surely as those of the replicants are. But as much as Sebastian is able to relate to the plight of the replicants, to them he is a means to an end: getting to the manufacturer. And when they reach the man who is responsible for creating them for a life of slavery, they show him no mercy.

Eventually, Deckard catches up with the runaway replicants one by one. Their leader, Batty, the strongest and most intelligent of all of them, engages Deckard in a fight to the death. (The replicant's death is approaching anyway, because his four years are almost up.) In the fight, when Deckard is close to losing his own life, he realizes that what the replicant wants is what all humans want—just a little more time to live, to sense, and to breathe. Dying, Batty speaks of his life: "I've seen things you people wouldn't believe . . . attack ships on fire off the shoulder of Orion. . . . I've watched c-beams glitter in the dark near the Tanhauser Gate. All those moments . . . they'll be lost, in time . . . like tears in rain. . . ."

Study Questions

1. What statement does *Blade Runner* make about humanity and human rights, if any?

2. Are the runaway replicants persons? Is Rachael? Is Deckard? Is the manufacturer? What makes someone a person?

3. What might Kant's position be concerning the rights of the replicants—or the rights of any future self-aware artificial intelligence? (See Chapter 6 for Kant's distinction between a person and a thing.)

Narrative

Gattaca

ANDREW NICCOL (SCREENWRITER AND DIRECTOR)

1997 film. Summary.

The ancestor of all mad-scientist stories surely must be the tale of Frankenstein's monster. Invented by nineteen-year-old Mary Wollstonecraft Shelley as a contribution to a ghost story contest among friends in 1816 and pronounced a classic by Sir Walter Scott, it is the haunting account of a scientist who wants to control nature and create artificial life. Mary Shelley's monster is not the hulking idiot of the movies but an intelligent creature who is malicious because he is lonely; there is no one like him, and he has no purpose, since his creator, Dr. Frankenstein, denounces him. Shelley's subtitle for the story, *The Modern Prometheus,* gives another clue as to who the monster is. Prometheus was a figure from Greek myth credited with creating humans out of clay and giving them fire from the gods' hearth. Perhaps we all are Frankenstein monsters, abandoned by our creator, who didn't know quite what he was doing in the first place?

One might say that the film *Gattaca* is an offspring of Shelley's story, but here the scientists are benevolent, and the "monsters" have become the norm. The monstrous one is now the person who has *not* been genetically engineered.

Gattaca is a science fiction film (and an unusual one at that, since there are very few special effects or futuristic inventions). The science fiction element is almost exclusively one of a thought experiment, a mind game: What if . . . ? What if babies could be designed in the lab, eradicating birth defects, nearsightedness, high cancer risk, and so forth? Wouldn't that be wonderful? Perhaps not. Exploring the possible human future of genetic engineering (reminiscent of Huxley's *Brave New World*), *Gattaca* tells the story of a near-future society in which each child is the dream child of its parents, the best combination of their genes—if the child is legitimately conceived in the lab, that is. Children conceived the natural way are considered flawed and will never rise higher in society than doing manual labor.

Vincent Freeman is such a child, the firstborn son of young parents. He is born with myopia and a high probability of heart failure before the age of thirty; even so, as a young adult he outpaces his younger brother, a more socially acceptable individual conceived in a petri dish with all the good genes. At the beginning of the film we witness Vincent's

Gattaca (Columbia Pictures, 1997) posits a future world where respectable persons are conceived and genetically designed in vitro; only slobs and destitute people have children the natural way. Here Vincent/Jerome (Ethan Hawke) and Irene (Uma Thurman) are hiding from the police, and his false identity is in danger of being revealed.

parents' visit to the clinic where they discuss the future genetic characteristics of Vincent's brother-to-be, as yet an embryo, with the doctor. We see how reluctant the parents are at first, being resigned to following custom and merely having the embryo screened for diseases, but the doctor persuades them that life is hard enough as it is, so why not give him all the advantages that are possible? "He will still be you—only the best of you." But growing up, the one with the ambitious goals is not the perfect boy conceived in the lab, Anton, but his imperfect older brother. Vincent dreams of becoming an astronaut and leaving for the outer solar system, but as a natural-born individual he has no chance—legally. So he embarks on acquiring an illegal identity, not just a new name and history but new DNA, an entirely new genetic profile. An identity broker sets him up with a genetically perfect individual, Jerome Eugene ("good genes"), who has no use for perfection. Jerome is disabled after a suicide attempt that was never registered, so Vincent pays him "rental" on his identity and moves in with him. The transformation involves surgery to add height to Vincent's legs, but otherwise the two young men are fairly similar. Vincent, now Jerome, acquires a dream job at the Gattaca complex, where future space programs are planned and astronauts trained, by submitting urine and blood samples from Jerome. Every morning Jerome prepares samples of more blood, urine, hair and skin cells, and so forth for Vincent to use for the ongoing tests so that no trace will reveal the identity of the impostor. In the process, Vincent and Jerome become close friends.

Everything is working smoothly, and Vincent is valued at work for his high intelligence, his physical stamina, and his flawless genetic code. He meets a young female coworker, Irene, who also longs for the stars but has a heart disease probability that restricts her future as an astronaut. Vincent tries to make her realize that such preset probabilities are nothing but that, probabilities. They are not set in stone. He himself is overdue for his heart attack. He has apparently overcome all social obstacles handed to him by his low birth, but an unforeseen event happens: A Gattaca executive hostile to the current space program is found murdered. Although there is no evidence linking him to the murder, one of Vincent's eyelashes is found near the scene of the crime. The police run a genetic analysis on it and come up with Vincent's original identity; but since he as "Jerome" has a different genetic profile, nobody makes the connection. Even so, he fears he will be found out on the threshold of his dream: He has been slated for the next launch to Titan. As the police detectives move closer to his personal life and his girlfriend herself is beginning to suspect that Vincent is not what he seems to be, his audacious attempt at breaking out of the social hierarchy seems to be failing and his true identity about to be revealed.

Will Vincent go to prison for the murder, or will he go to Titan after all? Will his heart hold out? Will Irene guess his identity? What happens to the real Jerome? Who killed the executive? And where is Vincent's brother? The ending of this interesting film offers many surprises.

Study Questions

1. What elements in the *Gattaca* plot do you think might become a reality in the future? Should we welcome them or fight them? Is there a third alternative? Explain your position.

2. The film addresses first and foremost the discrimination against Vincent and others who are being excluded from having a happy, productive life because of their genes. But there is also a underlying angle: a criticism of the *predictable* future society in which there are no surprises because they have been bred out of the population. What is your opinion?

Does society need genetic "surprises," unforeseeable genius and generosity as one side of the coin and unpredictable criminal pathology as the other? Or are we better off with the vast majority of the population falling into a predictable norm?

3. Do the characters' names add something to the story? Explain.

4. When the film came out, very few people caught on to the significance of the title. Now that the Human Genome Project has been completed, it may not seem so mysterious to us. GATC are the initials of materials in the DNA code: guanine, adenine, thymine, and cytosine. What do you think the moviemakers wanted to say by calling the film, and Vincent's workplace, *Gattaca*?

5. The *Gattaca* DVD has outtakes (missing scenes), some of which add interesting elements to the story. The scene with Vincent's parents in the lab, discussing the future characteristics of Anton, is longer and gives us an understanding of their switch from skepticism to enthusiasm when they hear that they can determine the boy's height and even a musical talent! But the addition of the talent turns out to be too expensive, so they settle for having a strong, smart, healthy, tall kid. This is the only time we hear that acquiring good genes is also a matter of money. In a future where genetic engineering is the order of the day, do you think the scenario of *Gattaca* is realistic? Does the outtake make a difference to the story? Should it have been left in?

Narrative

Losing Isaiah

NAOMI FONER (SCREENWRITER)
STEPHEN GYLLENHAAL (DIRECTOR)

Based on a novel by Seth Margolis. Film, 1995. Summary.

Losing Isaiah deals with justice — not criminal justice, but "distributive" justice: What is fair to a little boy when his best interests are considered? But more than that, it is a film about love — the ancient Solomonic question of which of two mothers has the greater love for her child. In the Bible story (1 Kings 3:16–27), two mothers approach King Solomon, asking for his judgment. They each had a son, but now one boy is dead, and both lay claim to the surviving boy. Solomon makes the famous suggestion to cut the boy in half so each mother can have half a child. One mother agrees, but the other mother cries out to give the child to the first woman rather than see him suffer and die. Solomon decides the second woman must be the real mother. What are we willing to give up for love?

Losing Isaiah is about a cross-racial adoption being challenged by the child's birth mother. Khaila Richards, a homeless African American crack addict, leaves her infant son in a cardboard box by a dumpster while she scurries off to get a fix. By the time she returns, in a panic, the trash collectors have been there and picked up the box with the boy inside. Khaila gives him up for dead, but the boy lives. He is taken to a hospital, where a white social worker, Margaret Lewin, takes an interest in him, and soon she and her husband Charles are filing adoption papers. They want to give the boy, Isaiah, a good, loving home with them and their teenage daughter, Hannah.

Meanwhile, Khaila is arrested for shoplifting and possession of drugs and enters a rehabilitation work program in prison. Within a few years she is clean, is out of prison, and has a place to live and a job. By chance she finds out that her son is alive and well, and with the support of her counselor and a lawyer from the black community she tries to have him returned to her. This is devastating news to the Lewins, who consider themselves Isaiah's parents. They hire a black female lawyer who promises to do what she can for them but warns them she believes, as a matter of principle, that a child is better off with his or her natural parents and racial group.

In court, Khaila's lawyer succeeds in showing that the two white middle-class parents may be well meaning but that they have not taken any steps to create any connection to the black community for Isaiah—no books about blacks, no black dolls, no black friends of the family. Margaret argues that it shouldn't be a matter of political correctness but of love and that they just haven't gotten around to such things yet—the boy is only two years old. But at home, Margaret looks around at Isaiah's toys, and we sense that Khaila's lawyer's words struck home.

An expert witness, a white psychologist, testifies for Khaila that she believes a child should be raised within his or her own race. The judge rules in Khaila's favor. At home, Margaret says good-bye to Isaiah and gives him a red barrette of hers as a keepsake. A social worker comes to take him away, and a heartbreaking scene ensues in which the boy is removed by force, screaming and crying for the only parents he has ever known. Charles is ready to fight the ruling, but Margaret acquiesces and sinks into a depression.

Khaila is doing her utmost to make little Isaiah feel safe and loved, but he doesn't know her and doesn't want to get to know her. He is lonely and afraid at the day care center where she leaves him to go to work. At home, he retreats into himself and stops talking, until he finally throws a fit, crying for his mommy. Khaila discovers what he clenches in his hand: Margaret's red barrette. Khaila herself was torn away from one foster home after another as a little girl, and she knows the pain of not having a stable home. She knows what happens psychologically: You just want to disappear into yourself until everything goes away. And this she will not let happen to Isaiah, so she makes a difficult decision—she calls Margaret.

What will she suggest? Will Isaiah stay with Khaila? Will she become a good, loving parent? Will Charles challenge the ruling? Or will Khaila return the boy to Margaret and Charles? The film actually leaves a number of questions open, but it does propose a compromise that goes beyond the old story of King Solomon and the two mothers. These two mothers reach their own cross-racial understanding. Leonard Maltin, the film critic, didn't like the final scene, but I find it a fine testimony to the philosophy of seeking common ground. See this excellent film and judge for yourself.

Study Questions

1. Do you agree with the judge, the psychologist, and the lawyers that a child should be raised within his or her own racial group? Explain why or why not.

2. Who is the more mature parent in your opinion? Khaila or Margaret?

3. Can you think of a compromise that would have made the judge's decision easier on all parties involved? Explore the possibilities.

4. Could John Rawls's idea of the original position be useful in dealing with this issue? Why or why not? Might Elizabeth Wolgast's suggestion of communitarianism be useful? Explain why or why not.

Narrative

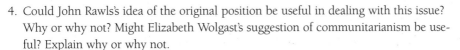

The Insider

ERIC ROTH AND MICHAEL MANN (SCREENWRITERS)
MICHAEL MANN (DIRECTOR)

Based on "The Man Who Knew Too Much," a magazine article by Marie Brenner.
Film, 1999. Summary.

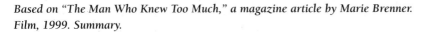

This film is based on the true story of one man making the decision to go public against the tobacco companies with his expert knowledge of the addictive nature of nicotine. In the context of this chapter, the story illustrates the interests of a community versus the interests of a corporation, the idea of respect for other human beings, and the notions of negative and positive rights—the right to free speech and the right to receive truthful information about health-related issues. In the context of Chapter 6, we might view it as the story of two men's sense of duty, regardless of the consequences, acting just for the sake of a moral principle. But, in the context of Chapter 8, we might view it as the story of a person of integrity choosing to fight for what is right, even if the outcome may cost him everything—a story paralleling that of Socrates. And, in the context of Chapter 13, we can choose to view it as a story of media responsibility: What is the bottom line for a television show doing investigative reporting—doing business or serving the public?

One day in the mid-1990s Jeffrey Wigand comes home from work early. His wife is horrified when she learns that he has been fired. They live in an expensive home and have lots of medical expenses: Their oldest daughter has asthma, and his wife can't work because someone has to look after the little girl in case she has an attack. Wigand was a corporate VP in charge of research and development at Brown & Williamson, the tobacco giant. He has a severance package, but the future looks grim. It is only as the story unfolds that we realize just how grim it is going to get. By coincidence, at the CBS studios in New York, the producer of *60 Minutes,* Lowell Bergman, is putting together a story about a tobacco study and calls Wigand. To his surprise Wigand won't talk to him—but he faxes him cryptic messages, indicating that he'd like to be able to talk, but he has a confidentiality agreement with his former company. Later, Brown & Williamson

In this scene from *The Insider* (Touchstone, 1999), Jeffrey Wigand (Russell Crowe) is being interviewed by Mike Wallace for *60 Minutes*. When the actual interview between Wigand and Wallace
aired in 1998, the impact was tremendous. Wigand told the inside story about nicotine that the tobacco companies didn't want us to know: that it is an addictive drug, and cigarettes are the delivery device for the drug. The film uses blurry images (such as the foreground in this picture) and
mirror reflections with much effectiveness, perhaps symbolizing the contrast between truth
and falsehood.

executives let Wigand know that since they suspect he has broken the agreement, they
want him to sign a new, expanded one—and if he doesn't, he'll lose all benefits. Now
Wigand is furious—at B&W for threatening his family and at Bergman, whom he believes has leaked the story. Bergman flies down from New York to Wigand's home to persuade him that he, Bergman, can be trusted, and Wigand then tells him the story: At a
congressional hearing on the tobacco industry and nicotine some years back, seven
CEOs—the Seven Dwarfs, as Wigand calls them—from the tobacco industry testified
that nicotine was not an addictive drug. But Wigand knows that to be false. So why was
he working for the tobacco company? The pay was good, and there was good medical
coverage, even if he perceived that integrity within the industry was a problem.

Mike Wallace, the investigative journalist for *60 Minutes* who early in the film has
been introduced as a man of integrity himself, suggests a way for Wigand to be able to
speak on his show: What if he was subpoenaed as a witness in a smoker's lawsuit in Mississippi? Then his statement would be on record, and in this way he could get around
the confidentiality agreement. So Bergman links Wigand up with the lawyer for the
plaintiffs in the Mississippi lawsuit. Meanwhile, the Wigands have had to move out of
their beautiful home and into a more modest house. He begins a new career as a high

school science teacher and forces himself to adjust to the situation, but his wife finds the transition hard. When they start to receive death threats, Wigand decides that it is time to go public.

He agrees to an interview with Wallace on *60 Minutes.* During the taping he reveals that the tobacco CEOs perjured themselves when they claimed nicotine isn't addictive: Cigarettes, he says, are "delivery devices for nicotine." In addition, he reveals that Brown & Williamson is enhancing nicotine chemically so it is absorbed more rapidly by the brain and that he got fired because he wouldn't keep quiet. Mike Wallace asks him if he wishes he hadn't blown the whistle. At times, Wigand says, but he'd do it again, because he thinks it was worth it. Now things start to happen quickly for Wigand, but in a way he hadn't imagined: Security guards are moving into his home because of the threats, and his wife is leaving him, taking their children with her. They keep the house, so he has to move into a hotel room. He testifies in the Mississippi lawsuit, specifically stating that nicotine is a drug, but his deposition is sealed, unavailable to the public. And the *60 Minutes* crew is in for a surprise: CBS executives lean on them to cut Wigand's interview, claiming the broadcasting company may be sued by the tobacco company for "tortious interference," a third party interfering in a contract situation, creating damages for the first party (the tobacco company).

Bergman is livid: Why should lawyers be able to determine the content of *60 Minutes,* a program of investigative journalism which has proved its integrity over and over again? Is the priority business or news? To Bergman's enormous disappointment, Wallace caves: In the twilight of his career, he has to consider his legacy, and sides with the corporate lawyers. And now the tobacco company embarks on a smear campaign against Wigand, digging up any old secret they can find, such as a dismissed shoplifting charge, so his word will be discredited. Jeffrey watches the cut, gutted interview air and becomes despondent. Both Bergman and Wigand have so much to lose: one his self-esteem and reputation for professional integrity, the other his family and perhaps his life. After a heated, then conciliatory, talk with Wigand, Bergman decides it is time for desperate measures: He leaks the story to the *New York Times.* When the story appears on the front page of the paper, Wallace changes his mind: He will air the original interview. The CBS executive tries to argue that this story will only last fifteen minutes and then people will forget it, but Wallace reminds him that it is fame that only lasts fifteen minutes—infamy lasts longer than that. So Jeffrey Wigand gets to tell his side of the story on national TV. After the airing, Lowell Bergman quits. What was broken doesn't get put back together again.

Study Questions

1. Does the public have a right to know about health-related issues concerning available products? Does the manufacturer have the right to withhold the information?

2. How might one say that this film tells a story about respect for persons?

3. If you were in Jeffrey Wigand's position, what do you think you would have done?

4. Identify issues of negative and positive rights in the film. On the basis of Chapter 6, are Wigand and Bergman men of good will? Is Wallace?

Narrative

Outbreak

LAURENCE DWORET AND ROBERT ROY POOL (SCREENWRITERS)
WOLFGANG PETERSEN (DIRECTOR)

Film, 1995. Summary.

It is 1967 in Motaba, Zaire; a camp of mercenaries is struck by a deadly and unknown virus that is 100 percent lethal. Doctors from an American military unit come in, investigate, draw blood samples—and leave. The next thing we know, the camp is annihilated by a bomb blast.

We move on to the present day and are introduced to Colonel Sam Daniels and his ex-wife Robby Keough, both medical scientists at a military center for disease control, cleared to work with pathogens at the most contagious levels. Sam has to go to Zaire to investigate an outbreak of what looks like a new virus, 100 percent lethal, which kills its victims within three to four days.

In the lab, Sam and his superior officer General Billy Ford investigate the virus; Sam wonders why Ford does not seem surprised by this virus and does not wish any measures taken to prevent it from entering the country. But behind Sam's back Ford is in touch with his own superior officer, General Donald McClintock, and now we learn that the new virus is the same as the one from 1967, that Ford knows of an antidote, and that McClintock was responsible for the bombing of the mercenary camp in order to contain the virus—and perhaps also for another reason. To prevent Sam from finding out, they assign him to another case . . . but when news comes in of a viral outbreak in Boston and in Cedar Creek, California, Sam defies orders and goes to Cedar Creek. Here he encounters Robby, who has been assigned to do research on the outbreak.

How did these outbreaks occur? We are told the story in flashes: A monkey is caught by animal dealers in Zaire, brought illegally to San Francisco on board a ship, placed temporarily in an animal research facility, and taken from there by an animal trader, Jimbo Scott, to a pet store in Cedar Creek. The pet store owner doesn't want the monkey (wrong gender), especially after the monkey scratches him. So Jimbo takes the monkey out in the woods and releases it. Meanwhile, the pet store owner gets very sick; the lab assistant at the hospital dealing with his blood test gets sick and infects an entire movie theater full of people; Jimbo gets sick while flying home to Boston and infects his wife. Within three to four days, everybody infected dies from symptoms much like those associated with the Ebola virus: bleeding from all orifices. In Boston the only ones infected were Jimbo and his wife, but the infection is rampant in Cedar Creek, because a mutation has occurred: The California strain is now airborne. And so the army moves into Cedar Creek and isolates the town. No one goes in or out. Sick family members are rounded up and taken to a camp from which nobody is expected to return. Ford tries to use the old antidote here (and this tips Sam off to the fact that Ford knew about this virus all along), but it doesn't work, because the virus has mutated.

The film *Outbreak* (Warner Brothers, 1995), a medical thriller, pits concern for the safety of the many against the rights of the few: In a situation where a contagious, fatal disease is spreading, is it acceptable to adopt a utilitarian policy of isolating and "terminating" the infected? Here Casey (Kevin Spacey), Sam (Dustin Hoffman), Walter (Cuba Gooding, Jr.), and Robby (René Russo) are searching for records that might help pinpoint the origin of the fast-spreading Ebola-like virus.

This crisis reaches to the level of the president of the United States. How fast can the disease spread? Within days the entire country could be infected. What must be done to help the people of Cedar Creek and to save the lives of other Americans, perhaps the world? The solution, reached with much hesitation and soul-searching, is "Clean Sweep": an eradication of the town of Cedar Creek in the same manner the mercenary camp was bombed in 1967. In McClintock's words, "Our procedure must be viewed objectively. Be compassionate, but be compassionate globally." As the president's aide remarks, the firebombing of Cedar Creek is unconstitutional because nobody should be deprived of life, liberty, or property without due process—so if the decision is made to go ahead, everyone should know what price is being paid for the safety of the world. Ford and McClintock have their own conversation where Ford points out that you can't treat the people of Cedar Creek like that—they are Americans. McClintock replies that the rest of America may be dying; the people of Cedar Creek should be regarded as casualties of war.

Back at the isolated town, Robby is infected by accident, and Sam confronts Ford: Why was the antidote not given in time, before the mutation happened? Because, as Sam guesses, there was an ulterior motive: The virus presented the perfect biological weapon and had to be protected, so the antidote was withheld. Ford defends the decision as a matter of national security: "At the time it was felt that we could afford a certain amount of losses." And now Ford reveals that Clean Sweep will take place in twenty-four hours.

With the help of young Major Salt, Sam commandeers a helicopter: Quick action must be taken. They now know that the virus came into the country with a monkey as a host. They break into a local television newscast with a warning and a picture of the monkey. This has immediate results: a mother knows her daughter has been playing with a monkey in the woods, not far from Cedar Creek. Sam and Salt capture the monkey and send immediate word to Ford, but to their horror they find out that McClintock has no intention of calling off Clean Sweep, even if serum can now be made from the monkey to save the people of Cedar Creek and Robby. He still wants to protect the virus as a future biological weapon. The pilots of Clean Sweep are in the air, and McClintock is telling them to do their duty. Sam gets on the intercom and pleads with them to reconsider; he tells them the entire story, but they don't respond. In a last-ditch effort, Sam tries to make Ford stop the bombing, but all Ford can do is to send an indirect message to Sam by telling him that he must "get out of the way," because the mission will have to be aborted if his chopper is in the flight path of the incoming bomber. . . .

Will Sam and Salt succeed in stopping the firebombing of Cedar Creek? Will McClintock win? Will Robby live? Will she and Sam get together again? I'm not going to tell!

Study Questions

1. How would an act utilitarian evaluate McClintock's decisions? Would a rule utilitarian respond any differently? What would a Kantian Say? Explain.

2. Can Ford's actions as co-conspirator acting on the orders of his superior officer be defended? Why or why not?

3. Use Ronald Dworkin's two models on the scenario. What would Dworkin conclude about "Clean Sweep"?

4. After 9/11, the country underwent yet another series of traumatic events: Numerous pieces of mail on the East Coast had been tainted with anthrax spores, causing the deaths of five people, affecting practically the entire nation with postal delays, and adding to the fears of an already traumatized population. (At the time of this writing the culprit has yet to be identified.) In the wake of the anthrax attacks came speculations that terrorists might be preparing for other biological attacks on U.S. citizens. In a worst-case scenario, such a bioterror assault might spread like the virus in *Outbreak*. Would the government be entitled to protect the rest of the citizens by isolating and perhaps hastening the deaths of the infected ones? Why or why not? Is there any kind of scenario that, in your opinion, would allow for such drastic measures?

Part 3

How
Should
I Be?

THEORIES OF VIRTUE

Chapter Eight

Socrates, Plato, and the Good Life

$\mathcal{T}$hroughout most of Western civilization and most of the history of ethics, scholars have tried to answer the question What should I do? Part 2 of this book explored this quest. Theories that consider what proper human conduct is are often referred to as *ethics of conduct*.

There is a more ancient approach to ethics, and in the past few decades this older approach has experienced a revival. This form of ethics asks the fundamental question How should I be? It focuses on the development of certain personal qualities, of a certain behavior pattern—in other words, on the development of what we call *character*. Because its foundation is in ancient Greek theories involving the question of how to be a virtuous person, this approach usually is referred to as *virtue ethics*.

What Is Virtue?

The concept of virtue (Greek: *aretē*) is complex. For one thing, it carries certain associations, which it has acquired over the centuries; thus, in English, we may think of virtue as a basically positive concept—a virtuous person is someone you can trust. We also may experience, however, a certain negative reaction to it; sometimes, a virtuous person is thought of as being rather dull and perhaps even sanctimonious (being called a "Goody Two Shoes" is not a compliment). In other languages, the term (such as *Tugend* in German) has all but lost its positive association in everyday language.

When we look back to the origin of Western virtue theory, in ancient Greece, we find no negative associations, because the word *aretē* signifies a different kind of person altogether: not a person of untainted thoughts and behavior, but a person who does what he or she does best and does it excellently, on a regular basis. We still have a trace of the ancient meaning of *aretē* in the word *virtuosity*. Originally, a virtuous person was a *virtuoso* at everything he or she did, due to proper choices and good habits but, above all, because such a person had succeeded in developing a good character.

What Is Character?

Today we often take a deterministic view of the concept of character. It is something we are born with, something we can't help. If we try to go against our character, it will surface in the end. This viewpoint may or may not be correct, but in any event

Box 8.1   VICTIMS OF FANATICISM

Two examples of Christians' early, violent reactions to the world of the classical tradition are both from the Egyptian city of Alexandria. In the year 415 C.E. a mob of fanatical Christian monks, possibly inspired by the Bishop of Alexandria, attacked and murdered one of the first women philosophers on record, Hypatia, leader of the Neoplatonic Institute in Alexandria. As far as we know, Hypatia lectured on Plato, Aristotle, and Pythagoras, and thus the Christians associated her with paganism. As she was riding through town in her chariot during one of the many religious riots, the mob dragged her out of her cart, tore off her clothes, and flayed her alive with clamshells. Hypatia had done her research in the great library at Alexandria (or what was left of it), which was founded by one of Alexander the Great's generals, Ptolemy I, who became the founder of an Egyptian dynasty (fourth century B.C.E.). The library was expanded over the centuries and probably contained most of the works of Greek philosophy, literature, and science, either in the original or copied by hand. During the reign of Queen Cleopatra, one of Ptolemy's descendants (around 30 B.C.E.), a part of the library was burned down by the Roman army, possibly by mistake. When another section of the library went up in flames in 391 C.E. (along with a pagan temple), there was no doubt that the destruction was caused by Christian extremist fundamentalists. The final destruction of the library came at the hands of Islamic fundamentalist invaders in 646 C.E. Scholars estimate that science suffered a setback of perhaps a millennium from the loss of the library; humanity's loss in works of art—philosophy, literature, drama, and artifacts—cannot be measured.

it is shaped by modern schools of thought in philosophy and psychology. Not everyone shares this view; it often is pointed out that we may be born with a certain character, but our character can be molded to a certain extent when we are young, and it certainly can be *tested* throughout our lives. This point of view comes closer to the prevailing attitude toward virtue among Greek philosophers: Character is indeed something we are born with, but it is also something that can and must be shaped. We are not the victims of our character, and if we let ourselves be victimized by our own unruly temperaments, then we are to blame.

The Case for Virtue Ethics

What happened to virtue ethics, and why has it been revived by scholars of ethics recently? By and large, what happened was Christianity—with its emphasis on following God's rules and conducting oneself according to the will of God. A chasm appeared between the teachings of the classical tradition and the moral and philosophical viewpoints of the rising religion. Disagreements exceeded verbal argumentation and turned violent for the first time in Christian history (but unfortunately not for the last time). See Box 8.1 for some examples of this violence.

To *do the right thing* became the main imperative of Christian ethics; however, the concepts of virtue and vice became main elements. Within the Christian tradi-

Hypatia (370–415 C.E.), the leader of the Neoplatonic Institute in Alexandria and one of the first female philosophers that we know of, was driving through the streets of town in her chariot when she was intercepted, tortured, and killed by Christian extremists.

tion and within every aspect of our Western outlook on life that has been shaped by this tradition, the idea of virtue is central, but scholars of ethics point out that it is not so much the question of *shaping your own character* that is important in this tradition as it is recognizing the *frailty of human character in general* and believing that with the help of God one may be able to choose the right thing to do.

From the time of the Renaissance to well into the twentieth century, questions of ethics were less a matter of doing the right thing to please God and more a matter of doing the right thing because it led to general happiness — because it was prudent or because it was logical. However, present-day scholars interested in virtue ethics have put forth the following argument: You may choose to do the "right thing" to please God or to escape unpleasant consequences or to make some majority happy or to satisfy your inner need for logic — but you may still be a less than admirable person. You may give to charity, pay your taxes on time, remember your nieces' and nephews' birthdays, hold the door for physically challenged people, and still be a morose and mean person. As we saw in the chapter on psychological egoism, you may be doing all the "correct" things just to get a passport to heaven or to be praised by others or to make sure they owe you a favor. So "doing the right thing" doesn't guarantee that you are a good person with a good *character*. However, if you strive to develop a good character—to be courageous or protective or tolerant or compassionate—then, on the basis of this character trait, you will *automatically* make the right decisions about what to do, what course of action to take. In other words, virtue ethics is considered to be more fundamental than ethics of conduct, yielding better results.

In today's discussions on ethics, opinions are divided as to the merits of virtue versus conduct; however, no virtue theory is complete without recognition of the importance of conduct. We can have a marvelous "character," but if it never translates into action or conduct, it is not of much use—and how do we develop a good character in the first place if not through *doing* something right? Also, one of the most conduct-oriented ethical theories, Kant's deontology, has the question of character embedded in it. For Kant, a good character in the form of a *good will,* a fundamental respect for other people and respect for the nature of the moral law itself, is essential to the moral decision process. Indeed, one-half of the book he wrote late in life, *The Metaphysics of Morals,* focuses on a doctrine of virtue (in Chapter 6 you read the section concerning *lying*), and what he used to call the good will is here renamed a *virtuous disposition.* The question of whether we should choose ethics of conduct or virtue ethics is a false dichotomy (an either-or situation in which there are actually more choices); we can certainly decide that there is room for both approaches.

In this and the next chapter we look at the classical virtue theories of Plato and Aristotle. We then move on to some examples of modern virtue theory.

The Good Teacher

The saying goes that a good teacher is one who makes herself or himself superfluous. In other words, a good teacher lets you become your own authority; she or he does not keep you at the psychological level of a student forever. As a matter of fact, great personalities who have had considerable influence on their followers often have failed in this respect. For a teacher it is hard to let go and consider the job done (whether one is a professor or a parent), and for a student it is often tempting to absorb the authority of the teacher, because life is hard enough as it is without having to make your own decisions about everything all the time. This is what the good teacher or parent prepares the student for, however—autonomy, not dependence.

The teacher–student relationship between Socrates and Plato would probably not have become so famous if Plato had remained merely a student, a shadow of the master. Indeed, we have Socrates' own words (at least through the pen of Plato) that the good teacher does not impose his ideas on the student but rather serves as a midwife for the student's own dormant intellect. In many ways Socrates has become a philosophical ideal. As we shall see, he stood by his own ideals in the face of adversity and danger; he believed in the intellectual capacities of everyone; he strove to awaken people's sense of critical thinking rather than give them a set of rules to live by, and, above all, he believed that "the unexamined life is not worth living."

Socrates, Man of Athens

What do we know of Socrates? There is no doubt that he lived — he is not a figment of Plato's imagination, as much as Plato may have made use of poetic license in his writings. Aristophanes, the author of comedies in Athens, refers to Socrates in his play *The Clouds* (albeit in a rather unflattering way). The fact is that we don't have any writings by Socrates himself, for his form of communication was the discussion, the live conversation — what has become known as the *dialogue*. From this word is derived the term for Socrates' special way of teaching, the *dialectic method* (sometimes also called the *Socratic method*). A method of teaching that uses conversation only, no written texts, is not exactly designed to affect posterity, but posterity has nevertheless been immensely affected by our indirect access to Socrates through the writings — the *Dialogues* — of Plato.

What we know of Socrates is that he lived in Athens from approximately 470 to 399 B.C.E. The son of a sculptor and a midwife, he was married to Xantippe and had children. He was one of several teachers of philosophy, science, and rhetoric in Athens at a time when internal politics were volatile (aristocrats versus democrats) and when Greece, which had experienced a golden age of cultural achievements in the wake of the Persian wars, was actually on the verge of decline. The single most important political element of the time was the city-state, the *polis* (the origin of the word *politics*). With the peculiar features of the Greek countryside — the inland features of tall mountains and the seaside features of islands — the stage had been set for centuries for a specific power structure: small, independent, powerful realms warring and/or trading with one another. Two of the main areas were Athens and Sparta. Each area, a state in itself, considered itself to be geographically Greek but politically specific to its particular *polis*. Thus it meant more to an Athenian to be a citizen of Athens than it meant to be Greek. Being a free citizen of a particular *polis* carried with it an inordinate pride. Today we might condemn such a pride as being nationalistic or even chauvinistic (in the original sense of the word); for a Greek of the time it was a reasonable feeling. When Socrates was younger, he had been a soldier in the Athenian infantry and had distinguished himself as a courageous man. The loyalty to Athens that was expected of him then was something he lived up to his entire life; indeed, when he returned from the war, he stayed put in his hometown.

In one of Plato's dialogues, *Phaedrus*, Socrates and a friend, Phaedrus, have ventured outside the city walls, and Socrates carries on about the beauty of nature, the trees and the flowers, to such a degree that Phaedrus remarks that Socrates acts like a tourist. Socrates agrees, because he never ventures outside of Athens, not even to go to the Olympic Games. The city of Athens is everything to him. It is the life among people, the communication, the discussions, the company of friends that are important to him, not nature, as beautiful as it may be: "My appetite is for learning. Trees and countryside have no desire to teach me anything; it's only the men in the city that do."

It is not unusual to hear a big-city person say the same thing today — that New York or Paris or Rio has everything they could ever want. Most of us think such people are missing out on a few things, but Socrates' attitude becomes crucial to our understanding of his conduct toward the end of his life.

Jump Start by Robb Armstrong

JUMP START reprinted by permission of United Feature Syndicate, Inc.

The words of Socrates sometimes turn up in popular culture, such as in this comic strip about a young police officer and his family. Here his mother, an erudite woman, quotes Plato. Another introduction to Socrates from the realm of popular culture is the film *Bill and Ted's Excellent Adventure,* although Bill and Ted persist in pronouncing his name wrong.

The Death of Socrates and the Works of Plato

Many cultures take the position that someone's life cannot be judged until it is over, that the ending helps define—sometimes even determine—how we think of the life spent. This may seem terribly unfair, for few of us are in full control of our lives, and we would prefer not to have our accomplishments judged primarily by circumstances beyond our control. In the case of Socrates, though, it seems fitting that his life is judged in the light of his death, for in the face of adversity, in the ultimate "situation beyond his control," he seems to have remained in full control of *himself.* This is another reason that Socrates has become not just the philosopher's ideal but also a human role model—because he did not lose his head but instead faced injustice with courage and rationality.

After what in antiquity passed for a long life (he was nearing age seventy), Socrates found himself in a difficult political situation, brought about by several factors. First, Socrates had great influence among the young men of Athens—those young men who might be of political influence in the future—and many were the sons of noblemen. Second, Socrates conducted his classes in public (this was customary at the time in Athens, prior to the formalization of classes, schools, and academy life), and his method was well known to his students, as well as to any city council member who might cross the agora (the public square) while Socrates was teaching. Socrates used a certain method of *irony* to get his point across, and this often involved engaging politicians in a discussion under the pretext of ignorance in order to trick the speaker into revealing his own ignorance or prejudice. His students adored him for it, because this was the ultimate "questioning of authority." The fact that Socrates himself may have been serious in a roundabout way about claiming his ignorance was something his listeners may not have realized. Socrates did not adhere to any one conception of reality unless it could be tested by reason; in other words, he would not profess to "know" anything for certain before investigating it and discussing it. This attitude, which was essentially one of humility rather than arrogance, seems to have been lost on his enemies, and over the years he acquired a considerable number of such enemies. Third, the most elusive factor but perhaps also the most important one: Athens was changing; what had been a place of comparatively free exchange of ideas, the undisputed center of the intellectual Western world, was becoming a place in which people expressed themselves more cautiously. Old laws against impiety were now more thoroughly enforced, and people were being banished for offenses against the state. The reason was complete exhaustion after thirty-seven years of war with Sparta, political upheavals, and an ensuing suspicion of dissidents. Most important, in Socrates' case, he had expressed reservations concerning the democratic government (not "democratic" in any modern political or partisan sense of the word, but a form of government in which male citizens of the city-state had a political voice, as opposed to the oligarchic form of government by the few). For most of Socrates' life Athens had had a democratic constitution, but during a brief, troubled time after Athens lost the long Peloponnesian War to Sparta, a group of aristocrats seized power and overthrew the constitution. The leader of this group of "Thirty Tyrants," Critias, had been a former member of Socrates' circle, and although Socrates himself fell into disfavor with the tyrants, scholars speculate that some of his enemies had old scores to settle, even though the new Athenian democratic government had given amnesty to all involved in the affair after the fall of the tyrants. Another of Socrates' earlier associates, Alcibiades, had been responsible for a major naval expedition which went terribly wrong: He deserted, and the expedition was destroyed. These connections may also have contributed to the downfall of Socrates.

Eventually his enemies took action. There was no way of getting rid of Socrates by political means, so they resorted to what appears to be a standard charge: that Socrates was "offending the gods and corrupting the youth." Socrates was tried and convicted by a jury of 500 male citizens of Athens. The Athenian court would vote once for conviction or acquittal, and once again if the verdict was guilty, in what we today would call the "penalty phase," determining the punishment. Socrates himself gave two speeches, one in his defense, and one concerning his punishment. His speech during the penalty phase featured an in-your-face suggestion that the proper punishment would be not death, but a *reward* for services to the state, much like a sports hero: to be feted by the city of Athens.

The verdict was determined by a simple majority, not by a unanimous vote. The jury was almost split down the middle as to Socrates' guilt: Some speculate that if Socrates had had another 30 votes in his favor, he would have been acquitted. It seems that 280 voted for conviction, while 220 voted for acquittal, and a tie vote — half the difference between 280 and 220 — would have been resolved in favor of the accused. But the votes in favor of the death penalty after Socrates' "reward" speech were considerably higher than for his conviction — which means that some people who had thought him innocent were now so outraged at his behavior that they voted for capital punishment.

It seems possible that his enemies did not intend to get rid of Socrates by actually executing him. The standard reaction to such charges by accused citizens was to

The Death of Socrates (1787) by Jacques-Louis David shows Socrates still exploring issues of life and death with his friends, even though he will soon drink the cup of poison prepared for his execution by the distraught jailer.

leave the city and go elsewhere within the Greek realm, and there were many places to choose from, because this realm extended from Italy well into the Middle East. But because Socrates chose to stand trial, arguing that by leaving he would be admitting guilt, his fate appeared sealed. Even so, to the last minute there were powers working to free him; his friends, many of whom were of considerable influence, conspired to spring him from jail and bring him to exile in safety. In Plato's dialogue *Crito* we hear how Socrates' good friend Crito pleads with him to listen to his friends and take their offer of escape and life, because "otherwise people will say we didn't do enough to help you." Socrates answers:

> In questions of just and unjust, fair and foul, good and evil, which are the subjects of our present consultation, ought we to follow the opinion of the many and to fear them; or the opinion of the one man who has understanding? . . . Then, my friend, we must not regard what the many say of us: but what he, the one man who has understanding of just and unjust, will say, and what the truth will say.

When Crito suggests that Socrates ought to escape because he has been convicted by unjust laws, Socrates replies that two wrongs don't make a right, and the

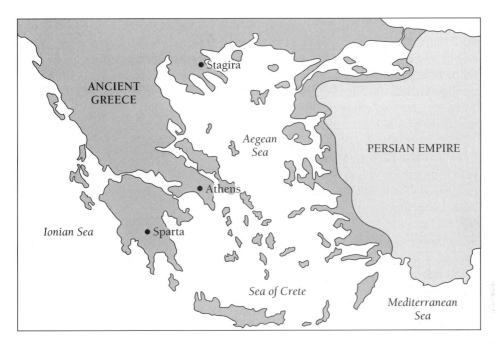

During the time of Socrates (fifth century B.C.E.) the Greek cultural realm stretched from Italy in the west to Asia Minor in the east; although people would consider themselves citizens of the Greek culture, their most important affiliation was with the city-state (*polis*) in which they were born.

laws of Athens have supported him throughout his life; even though unjust, they are still the laws of Athens. If he, Socrates, had been a less faithful citizen of Athens, he might choose to leave, but because he never left the city, he believes he has to live by his own rule of respecting the laws and the rules of reason and virtue and not turn his back on them.

So Socrates, the citizen of Athens, could not envision a life away from the city, even when the alternative was death.

Could Socrates have done a better job defending himself? Given that only a narrow majority of the 500 jury members found him guilty, it seems clear it wouldn't have taken much for that small majority to change their minds. In Plato's dialogue the *Apology* (an excerpt of which appears as a Primary Reading at the end of this chapter), Socrates isn't exactly expressing himself cautiously or diplomatically in his address to his judges. He is assuming they will use rational judgment and see his point of view; he doesn't seem to understand the considerable animosity many feel toward him. The end result is of course a conviction. Since we can see in retrospect that another style of argumentation, or even just being slightly apologetic, might have saved his life, many have speculated that perhaps he didn't try too hard because he *wanted* to die and make a point. This theory goes all the way back to Plato's contemporary Xenophon, who thought Socrates deliberately antagonized the jury to get a conviction. Others are convinced that he didn't and claim that he was arguing in a style completely true to his personality and outlook on life, that he fought for his life in court, in his own way, until the very end.

In the Narrative section you will find another historical figure, Sir Thomas More, who apparently made the same choice: that standing up for the truth is more important than staying alive. But that doesn't mean he, or Socrates, *wanted* to die. You might say they chose integrity over personal concerns, and that is probably what makes the Socratic example so compelling.

Since we're speculating, let's take it one step further: What might have happened if the jury had been convinced of Socrates' innocence—or if Socrates had been convinced by Crito and had allowed himself to escape? If Socrates hadn't been executed, chances are Plato wouldn't have become a writer or a philosopher, for he wouldn't have felt compelled to preserve Socrates' name for posterity and give him philosophical immortality. And without Plato's writings we would have no Platonism, no school influencing antiquity for nine hundred years and beyond, into Christianity. And without Plato's school the young man from Stagira who came to the big city of Athens to get an education—Aristotle—might never have become a philosopher. And without Aristotle's philosophy? Universities would probably be structured differently, sciences would have other categories, ethics would be different, and elements of Christianity would be absent. Our world might look substantially different today if Socrates had died a natural death.

Was Socrates guilty? His accusers may have believed so, although we may find it hard to imagine why. Did he offend any gods? He seems to have been a religious man; he often made the traditional sacrifices to the gods, and Plato has him referring to gods or "the god" often in his dialogues. But Socrates also referred to what he called his *daimon* (spirit), a little voice inside him telling him what to do. It is hard to know whether he was just talking about his conscience or whether he believed in some guardian spirit, but it may have seemed to his accusers that he was trying to introduce new gods. Did he corrupt the youth of Athens? Well, yes, if you believe that teaching young people to think for themselves, to use their reason in search of the truth, is corrupting them. In his speech in his own defense (see page 348–351) Socrates asked those young people to come forth if they felt they had been corrupted; of course none of the young people of his own circle did.

Plato tells us about the last, dignified minutes of Socrates' life, thereby giving history and philosophy the legacy of someone who chose to die for a rational principle. The scene is vividly described in the dialogue *Phaedo*. Plato writes that he himself wasn't present because of illness, and the story of Socrates' death is told by another student, Phaedo, but others have speculated that Plato may have already left Athens as a precaution, fearing reprisals against Socrates' supporters. In the end, Socrates' friends and students are gathered to say good-bye. They are on the verge of breaking down, while Socrates does his best to keep their spirits up. Even the jailer who brings in the poison apologizes to the old philosopher for having to cause him harm and hopes Socrates will not hold it against him. Socrates assures him that he will not and swallows the poison, an extract of hemlock. He continues talking, but the end approaches quickly. He lies down and pulls a blanket over himself, covering himself completely. But then—it must have been a dramatic moment for his

Plato (427?–347 B.C.E.) was the son of Ariston and Perictione. They named their son Aristocles, but he became known as Plato, "broad forehead" (for his wide knowledge). Perictione was apparently a philosopher in her own right, although women in ancient Greece had virtually no independence.

friends—he removes the cover from his face for a final statement. And what are the last words coming from the Master's mouth? None of the wisdom they were used to hearing him speak, such as "The unexamined life is not worth living." No, he says to his old friend Crito, "I owe a rooster to Asclepius—will you remember to pay the debt?" Crito promises that he will, and within minutes Socrates is dead. The meaning of this request has been discussed by philosophers ever since. Was Socrates driven by the memory of an unpaid debt, or was he talking in symbolic terms? Asclepius was a common Greek name but also the name of the god of healing. Did he want his friends to sacrifice the rooster to the god because Asclepius had "cured" him, that is, released his soul from the prison of the body? We can only guess.

The effect of Socrates' death on Plato was profound. Born in about 427 B.C.E., Plato had been Socrates' student, in an informal sense, for thirteen years, and the death of his teacher caused him to take leave of Athens for a lengthy period, during which he traveled to Egypt and Sicily, among other places. Eventually he returned to Athens, and some time before 367 B.C.E. he founded his own school of philosophy, the Academy (Plato's own home—which he opened up to his students—named after the Greek hero Academos). This school appears to have been the beginning of a more formalized teaching institution, with regular lectures and several professors associated with the school. It remained open until 529 C.E., when it was closed by Christians. As Plato took on the mantle of his teacher, he began to reconstruct Socrates' intellectual legacy by writing the *Dialogues*. These books remain some of the most influential writings in philosophy, but they also are works of literature, as brilliant as any drama written in antiquity. That Plato from the very first dialogues reveals himself to be a great storyteller is all the more interesting, for, as you may remember from Chapter 2, he himself was not in favor of the arts, because he believed they spoke to people's emotions and made them forget the cool balance of reason. And, yet, Plato's own writings are works of art in themselves. Socrates and his friends and students come alive. We understand their way of talking, and we gain insight into their thinking, which, on occasion, is rather alien to our own day and age. The early dialogues of Plato give a picture of Socrates that is very fresh and probably quite accurate. However, scholars believe that in later dialogues Socrates changes into something that is more Plato's image of an ideal philosopher than Socrates himself. Indeed, in the last dialogues, Socrates appears as Plato's mouthpiece for his own advanced theories on metaphysics—theories that Socrates probably never held himself. This may mean that Socrates was indeed a good teacher who did not hinder Plato from "graduating" intellectually. It also means that through this lifelong tribute to Socrates, Plato showed that you can kill a thinker but not his thoughts; so in a sense Plato made certain that Socrates, long dead at the hands of the Athenian judges, lived on to affect the history of thought well after his accusers had turned to dust.

The Good Life

Socrates' statement to Crito that some things are more important than life itself, such as being true to your principles, no matter how others may feel about it, holds the key to what Socrates seems to have considered the "good life" or a life worth living. This would be a life in which one is not ruled by the opinion of others or even by one's own opinions, those ideas of ours that may or may not have some basis in the truth but that we haven't bothered to examine closely. If we stop for a minute and examine such opinions, we will probably discover that they constitute the basis for the majority of our viewpoints: We think we live in a great country, or perhaps we think we live in a deceitful, oppressive country. We think that chicken soup is good for colds. We may think that what scientists say must be true as long as they are wearing white lab coats. Perhaps we think that people who believe in UFOs are nuts, or we think that UFOs abduct humans from time to time. We think a lot of things, and if we allow ourselves to examine these opinions, we will usually find that they are based on very flimsy evidence. Of course, on occasion we feel strongly about something precisely because we *have* examined it, but, in that case, Socrates would say, we are not talking about opinion (*doxa*) anymore—we are talking about knowledge (*epistēmē*). This, for Socrates, was the test of truth: Can it stand up to unprejudiced scrutiny? If so, it must override any sort of opinion we may have, even though it may hurt the feelings of others, because if they see the truth, they, too, will understand, for *only ignorance leads to wrongdoing.* For Socrates as well as for Plato this is a truth in itself: No one is willfully evil, provided that he or she understands the truth about the situation. And if a person still chooses the wrong course of action, it must be because his or her understanding is faulty.

For a modern person the response to this seems inevitable: What if there is more than one way of looking at the situation? In other words, what if there is more than one truth? We are so used to assuming there is more than one way of looking at something that we sometimes assume there is no truth at all. This, however, is very far from the intellectual attitude of Socrates. For Socrates, as well as for Plato, each situation has its Truth, and each thing can be described in one way that best captures its true nature, its essence. This does not mean that this was a common attitude among Greek thinkers. In Socrates' own time, contact with other cultures had brought about a certain amount of cultural relativism, and Greece was sufficiently heterogeneous to foster a tolerance of different customs. Accordingly, for many of

Socrates' contemporaries, such as the Sophists, relativism became the accepted answer to the search for absolute truth. For Socrates the theory that virtue might be a question of personal preference or relative to one's own time and culture was the epitome of misunderstanding, and much of the Socratic quest for the true nature, the essence, of a thing or a concept is a countermeasure to the prevailing relativism of the Greek intelligentsia.

Virtue for Socrates means to question the meaning of life and to keep one's integrity while searching, to not be swayed by one's physical longings or fear of unpleasant situations or concern for comfort. This ideal is attainable because the Truth can be found — in fact, it can be found by *anyone* who has as a guide a teacher with integrity. In other words, Socrates says we can't hope to attain virtue without the use of our *reason*. Later on (in particular during the Middle Ages), the link between virtue and reason was weakened, but, for Plato and Socrates, as well as for Greek antiquity as such, the connection was obvious. Using our reason will make us realize what virtue is and will actually make us virtuous.

The good life, therefore, is not a pleasant life in which we seek gratification for the sake of having a good time. The good life is strenuous but gratifying in its own way, because one knows that one seeks and sees the Truth, and one is in control of oneself.

The Virtuous Person

Let us now focus on what makes a person good. You may remember that Plato's brother Glaucon told a story about the Ring of Gyges, stating that if you had the chance to get away with something and you didn't, you had to be stupid. For Socrates this matter was of grave importance, and this was his answer: A person who does something unjust to others is either ignorant or sick. If we inform that person that he is being unjust, he may realize his ignorance and improve himself. But there is the chance that he will laugh in our face. In that case, Socrates said, he is simply not well — he is out of balance. (When I say "Socrates says . . ." it is the same as saying "Plato says . . . ," because the words assigned to Socrates in the dialogues are, as far as we know, the opinions of Plato, at least in most cases.) Glaucon's argument that an unjust person is happier than a just person carries no weight with Socrates, because an unjust person can't be happy at all; only a well-balanced person can be happy. But what is a well-balanced person?

Everybody has desires, and sometimes these desires can be very strong. We may want something to drink when we are thirsty, something to eat when we are hungry; we have desires for sex, for power, and for many other things. We also have desires to get away from things, as when we move away from a fire we're too close to. These needs and wants Plato calls *appetites,* and these are what we must control if we are to achieve the good life. Appetites may rule a person's life, but that is not good, because the things we desire aren't necessarily the things that are good for us. (As a matter of fact, Plato is not just talking truisms here; there are many philosophers who believe that what is natural for humans is good for them!) So sometimes we pull away from what we want because we realize that it will be bad for us. This power that pulls us back is our *rational element,* our *reason.*

There is a third element at play; Plato calls it *spirit.* Sometimes he calls it *willpower.* We feel it when we sometimes let our appetites win out over our reason; afterward we feel disgusted with ourselves, and this anger directed at ourselves is our spirit. When we fall off our diet, our reason may have lost the battle, but our spirit will be angry at our weakness and will keep bothering us. What, then, should a person do? Establish a good working relationship between reason and spirit; let reason be clear about what it wants to do, and then train the spirit to help control the appetites. Reason and spirit will, side by side, keep the body healthy and the soul balanced. In his dialogue *Phaedrus* Plato describes the three-sided relationship by the following metaphor: A charioteer has two horses to pull his chariot; suppose one is well-behaved, whereas the other is wild and unruly. He is stuck with both and can't choose another horse, so he must make the well-behaved horse help him control the unruly horse and subdue it. So which roles do these figures play? The charioteer is Reason, the well-behaved horse is Willpower, and the wild horse is Appetites. Notice that a "balanced" individual to Plato does not have one-third of each element — he or she has total control by reason and willpower over appetites. When reason rules, the person is *wise;* when spirit controls the appetites, that person is also *brave* (because it takes courage to say "no" to temptation and "yes" to a painful experience); and when the appetites are completely controlled, the person is *temperate.* Such a person is well balanced and would not dream of being unjust to anybody; on the contrary, he or she would be the very picture of *justice,* and justice is the virtue that describes the well-balanced human being who is wise, brave, and temperate. Only this kind of person can be happy in the true sense of the word; Glaucon's idea that an unjust person is happier than a just person can be discarded, because such a person is off balance. (For another thinker's view of the tripartite soul, see Box 8.2.)

Plato was not just interested in the virtuous individual; further on in his famous dialogue *The Republic,* he speculates that a well-balanced person can be compared with a society in harmony with itself; as appetites must be controlled by reason and willpower, so, too, must parts of the population be controlled by other parts. Who corresponds to *reason*? Wise rulers, says Plato, "philosopher-kings" who would rather not rule; they will get the job done without fuss and with reason as their principle of guidance. Who corresponds to *willpower* in a state? The "auxiliaries," soldiers and law enforcement. And what about all the rest of the population — merchants, businesspeople, educators, entertainers, private citizens? They correspond to the *appetites* and must be thoroughly controlled. If they are not — such as in a democracy — then that society is off balance and sick. This restrictive social plan did not correspond to democratic Athenian society at all, and Plato has been vilified by democratically minded thinkers ever since.

Among modern Plato scholars there is some disagreement about Plato's intentions in his social theory of the ideal state. Its radical principles include not only a strict hierarchy but also rules about marriage and children among the philosopher-kings. For one thing, Plato advocates that anyone would be eligible as a Guardian (a ruler or a soldier), depending on his or her talent and regardless of *gender;* to his contemporaries (and even to some of our contemporaries) the idea of a woman ruler (or president) is outlandish or even outrageous, but Plato apparently found it

Box 8.2 THE TRIPARTITE SOUL: PLATO AND FREUD

Plato

Elements of the Soul		Virtues
Reason	—corresponds to—	Wisdom
Willpower	—corresponds to—	Courage
Appetites	—corresponds to—	Temperance

Freud

Theory of the Psyche

Superego
Ego
Id

If an individual has succeeded in mastering his or her appetites by using reason to guide willpower, then a fourth virtue comes into play: *justice*. In that case Plato would say we have encountered a truly virtuous individual: a just person, a person of internal balance and integrity.

In the early twentieth century Sigmund Freud suggested a theory about the human psyche that has some parallels to Plato's theory: Freud's psyche comprises the Id (the Unconscious), the Ego (the conscious self), and the Superego (the codes and rules we have been taught). Can the Id be compared to appetites? Yes, as long as we remember that, for Freud, the Id can't be accessed, whereas Plato believed a person could understand his or her own appetites. As for the Ego and the Superego, they don't match Plato's schema too well: The Ego is part reason but also part willpower; the Superego has elements in common with both, too. The similarity between Plato's theory of the soul and Freud's theory of the psyche is not a coincidence: Freud was a great admirer of Plato's dialogues.

a completely reasonable thought. Most people today, however, find his rules about childbearing among the Guardians too extreme and certainly both outlandish and outrageous: For the sake of eugenics (creating a superior breed of people by mating selected men and women), Guardians would be paired off and mated during their childbearing years, but the children would be removed from the mothers and raised in common so that no parent would know his or her own child. Plato envisioned that in that way personal preferences and affiliations would be held to a minimum so that the Guardians could focus on what was good for the state.

These radical thoughts have caused some Plato scholars to say that Plato may not have meant one word of his political theory—it was all tongue-in-cheek, a big joke on his students told at a dinner party. Women in government! He couldn't possibly have been serious. However, at least two things speak for taking Plato seriously:

For one thing, late in life he left his teaching position in Athens to return to Syracuse, presumably in order to tutor the young tyrant Dionysius II. Apparently Plato used his own principles as outlined in *The Republic* to try to groom Dionysius into a Guardian, without much success. Even though Plato's family had intended for him to go into politics, it is obvious that Plato was much more a scholar and a writer than a successful politician. For another thing, Plato's student Aristotle had no doubt that Plato was serious, and who could be a better judge than a contemporary source who had heard Plato discuss his theories?

There is little evidence that Socrates himself ever had such political visions; his main interests seem to have been getting individuals to improve their thinking and become better persons. Examining the concept of virtue, he would begin with a concept, a word of common usage, such as *justice* or *piety,* and ask his partners in the dialogue to define it, under the assumption there would be one, and only one, description that would be the true one. At some point in the Platonic dialogues we begin to lose the sense that it is Socrates talking, for a theory develops that is Plato's own: the theory of Forms.

Plato's Theory of Forms

When we ask about a person's view of reality, we generally want to know whether that person is religious or an atheist, pessimistic or optimistic about other people and events, interested in a historical perspective or mainly looking to the present and the future, and so on. Philosophically speaking, however, a person's view of reality is what we call *metaphysics.* What exactly is the nature of reality as such? In philosophy the answer will be one of three major types: Reality is made up of things that can be measured (*materialism*); or, Reality is totally spiritual, all in the mind (*idealism*); or, Reality consists of part matter, part mind (*dualism*). (These three theories of metaphysics are described in Box 8.3.) What, exactly, was Socrates' philosophical view of reality? The early dialogues indicate that he seems to have believed in an immortal soul that leaves the body at death, which would make him a dualist. In later dialogues, though, Plato chooses to let Socrates speak for a theory — which was obviously Plato's own — that says reality is very much different from what our common sense tells us. What we see and hear and feel around us is really a shadowy projection of "true reality." Our senses can't experience it, but our mind can, because this true reality is related to our mind: It is one of the Ideas, or *Forms.*

What exactly is a Form? Today it is hard to grasp Plato's concept, but for the Greek mind of Plato's own day it was not so alien. In early times the Greeks saw each good thing as represented by some divinity; there was a goddess for justice, another for victory. There were the Muses, lesser goddesses representing each form of art. The Olympic gods each had their own areas of protection. At the time of Plato many intellectuals, including Plato himself, had left traditional Greek religion behind. Some of the ancient tendency to personify abstract ideas, though, may have survived in his Forms. A Form is at once the ideal abstraction and sole source of each thing that resembles it. Let us look at an example. There are all kinds of *beds* today — double beds, twin beds, bunk beds, futons, waterbeds, hammocks. Plato would ask, What makes

Box 8.3   THREE THEORIES OF METAPHYSICS

In philosophy we encounter three major theories of the nature of reality, or of metaphysics: *materialism, idealism,* and *dualism.* Through the ages people have leaned toward one or the other, and today the prevailing theory in the Western world is overwhelmingly *materialistic.* This does not mean people are overwhelmingly interested in accumulating riches, although this may be the case. Metaphysical materialism has nothing to do with greed; it merely means you think reality consists of things that are *material*—they or their effects can be *measured* in some sense. This category includes everything from food to briefcases to brainwaves. It follows that a materialist doesn't believe in the reality of things supposedly immaterial, such as souls or spirits. Typical philosophical materialists are Thomas Hobbes, Karl Marx, and Paul and Patricia Churchland.

Idealism is the theory that only spiritual things have true existence and that the material world is somehow just an illusion. Again, this has very little to do with the colloquial use of the word, which we associate with a person with high ideals. Few people in philosophy define themselves as idealists today, but this theory had a certain influence in earlier times. Bishop George Berkeley was an idealist, and so was the German philosopher G. W. F. Hegel. The Hindu belief that the world we see is a mere illusion, *maya,* is also an example of idealism.

The theory of *dualism* combines materialism and idealism in that a dualist believes reality consists of a matter-side and a spirit-side—in other words, that although the body is material, the soul/spirit/mind is immaterial and perhaps immortal. Although this theory seems to appeal to our common sense, it poses several logical problems, which philosophy has not been able to solve, for how exactly does the mind affect the body if the mind is immaterial and the body is material? René Descartes is the most famous of the dualists, but Plato also is often counted among them, although some might prefer to call him an idealist because of his theory of Forms.

these things beds? We, today, would approach the question in a functionalistic manner and say something about them all being things to sleep on. Plato would say they are all beds because they all participate in the Form of Bed, a kind of ideal "bedness" that they not only have in common as a *concept* but that also actually *exists* above and beyond each singular bed. It is this quality that gives the bed its share of reality, as a sort of dim copy of the true Bed Form. This realm of Forms is true reality, and the entire world in which we move around is only a dim copy of the ideal Form. Where exactly *is* this world of Forms? It is nowhere that you can see and touch, because then it would just be another example of a copy. It has to be "out of this world," in a realm that our body does not have access to but that our mind does. So it is through our intellect that we can touch true reality, and only through our intellect. This is why Plato has Socrates tell Phaedrus that trees and countryside can't teach him anything—because there is nothing to be learned from the senses except confusion. The only true lesson in reality is achieved by letting the mind, the intellect, contemplate the Forms, because the world we see changes constantly, but the world of Forms never changes. The Forms are eternal, and for Plato (and for many other philosophers), the more enduring something is, the more real it is.

Box 8.4   THE THEORY OF ANAMNESIS

How do we know about the Forms if we can't learn about them by observing the world around us? Plato believed that we remember the Forms from the time before we were born, because during this time the soul's home was the realm of the Forms themselves. At birth the soul forgets its previous life, but, with the aid of a philosopher "in the know," we can be reminded of the nature of true reality. This is one of the functions of Socrates in the literature of Plato: to cause his students to remember their lost knowledge. The process is known as *anamnesis,* a rerembering, or, literally, a nonforgetting. In Plato's dialogue *Meno,* Socrates shows that this knowledge is accessible to everyone, as he helps a young slave-boy "remember" truths of math and logic that he has never learned in this life.

Plato, furthermore, believed in *reincarnation* (transmigration of souls). Reincarnation was not a common belief among the ancient Greeks, who seem to have believed in a dreary, dark Hades to which all souls were destined to go, regardless of whether they had been good or bad in life. But Plato apparently saw it differently: Toward the end of *The Republic,* Socrates tells an evocative story of the soul's long journey after death, called "The Myth of Er." He claims that the soul must undergo several cycles of life before it is purified sufficiently to go back to the Forms to stay forever. We know that Plato was influenced by Pythagoras, who believed in reincarnation; but some scholars also speculate that Plato may have been under the direct or indirect influence of Hindu theories of karma and reincarnation, which had existed in India for at least five hundred years prior to Plato's own time. However, other scholars point out that Hinduism hadn't yet spread beyond isolated groups in India.

But how did Plato conceive of such a theory? And how does he propose to persuade us that he is right? One example answers both questions: Think of a circle; now think of a perfect circle. Have you ever drawn one? No. Have you ever seen one? No. Can you imagine one? Yes. Can you describe one mathematically (if you have the training)? Yes. If you have never experienced it, then how can you imagine it and describe it? Because your mind understands that the perfect circle really exists—not just as a mathematical formula, but in a higher, mental realm of reality. From this higher realm the perfect Form of a circle (and all the other Forms) lend their reality to imperfect circles and other things in our tangible world; if the Form of a circle didn't exist, then you wouldn't have a notion that a circle could be perfect! Today we would say we understand the perfect circle because we can describe it mathematically, but that doesn't mean it exists somewhere else. (See Box 8.4 for a discussion of how we can know Forms.)

Because the world of Forms is purely spiritual and immaterial, some philosophers choose to call Plato an idealist; however, more prefer to call him a dualist, because the world of matter is not "nonexistent" but merely of a lesser, shadowy existence than the world of Forms.

Does everything have a Form? Concepts such as justice, love, and beauty have their natural place in the realm of Forms; they may be on this earth incompletely, but their Forms are flawless. Cats and dogs obviously have Forms; things of nature have a perfect Form in the spiritual realm, which gives them reality. Manufactured objects have Forms, too, so in the realm of Forms there is a Form of a chair, a knife, a cradle, and a winding staircase. What about a Form of something that has not "always" been — like a computer, a video game, or a microwave oven? Here we are moving into an uncomfortable area of Plato's theory, because even if microwave ovens are a new invention, presumably their Form has always existed. But what about Forms for dirt, mud, and diseases? Plato gives us the impression that the Forms are perfect and somehow closer to goodness than things on this earth; however, it is hard to envision perfect dirt, mud, and diseases, even though the theory of Forms certainly implies they exist. (A generation later, Plato's student Aristotle was to criticize the theory of Forms for assuming that every phenomenon has a Form. Aristotle asserted that some phenomena are merely a "lack" or deficiency of something. A doughnut hole doesn't have a Form — it is just the empty middle of a doughnut.)

The Form of the Good and Plato's Influence on Christianity

For Plato the world of Forms represents an orderly reality, nothing like the jumble of sensory experience. Forms are ordered according to their importance and according to their dependence on other Forms. Certainly worms and dirt have Forms, but they are very low in the hierarchy; at the highest level are abstract concepts such as justice, virtue, and beauty. At the very top of the hierarchy Plato sees the Form of the Good as the most important Form and also as the Form from which everything else derives.

Is the Form of the Good a god, in the final analysis? Followers of Plato around the fourth and fifth centuries C.E., the *Neoplatonists,* leaned toward that theory, but it is hard to say whether Plato himself had specifically religious veneration for his Forms; it is certain that he had intellectual respect and veneration for them and for the Form of the Good in particular.

The Form of the Good allows us to understand a little better what Plato means by saying that evil acts stem from ignorance, because, according to the theory of Forms, if a person realizes the existence of the Forms and in particular the highest Form of them all, the Good, it will be impossible for that person to deliberately choose to do wrong; the choice of wrongdoing can come only from ignorance of the Good. The choice to follow the Good is not an easy one, though, even when we have knowledge of it, because we have desires that pull us in other directions. Besides, Plato says the first time we hear about the Forms, the theory sounds so peculiar that we refuse to accept our own recollection of it. Plato tells a story to illustrate this, "The Myth of the Cave." (See the excerpt from Plato's *Republic* with the story of the cave at the end of this chapter.) In a large cave a group of prisoners are kept chained to their seats so they can look only in one direction, toward a huge wall. Behind them there is a fire that casts shadows on the wall. The prisoners, having never seen anything else, believe these shadows are all the reality there is. One prisoner gains his freedom and now sees the cave, the fire, and the world outside the cave for what they really are — but will the others believe him when he returns?

DILBERT by Scott Adams

© 1998 DILBERT reprinted by permission of United Feature Syndicate, Inc.

The influence of Plato's "Myth of the Cave" can be detected in this *Dilbert* strip that asks, What is reality? In the *Dilbert* universe we can be sure it is our worst nightmare.

As the cave is our everyday world of the senses, and as we are the prisoners who see only two-dimensional shadows instead of a multidimensional reality, we have the same problems the prisoners have when one prisoner stands up and claims that he or she has "seen the light" and knows that reality is totally different from what we think. How do we respond to such "prophets"? We ignore them or ridicule them or silence them and continue to live on in our illusion. And what is the duty of the philosopher who has seen "the light" of true reality, the Good and the other Forms, according to Plato? To return to the cave, even if it would be wonderful to remain in the light of the Truth and forget about the world of shadows. The philosopher's duty is to go back and tell the others, and this, Plato believed, was what he himself was doing with his dialogues. For Plato, Truth was not something relative that differed for each person; it was an absolute reality beyond the deceptive world of the senses, a reality that never changes and that we, when we shed the chains of our physical existence — either intellectually or through death, will be able to see and be in the presence of.

Plato's momentous influence on Western thinking is not measured by how many people took his theory of Forms to heart. As a matter of fact, not many scholars followed Plato's metaphysics to the letter; however, his idea of a never-changing realm of goodness, light, and justice to which our soul can have access made its way into Christianity, along with the Platonic disdain for the physical world as an obstruction to this access. Many early Christian thinkers had been trained in the Platonic and Neoplatonic schools of thought (which were probably taught by Hypatia in Alexandria, for one, before she was murdered), and the view of true reality as something that is not of this world came naturally to them; controlling the desires of the body and focusing on the afterlife are elements that Platonic philosophy and early Christian thinking have in common. Saint Augustine (354–430 C.E.), for example, had had a

In Plato's "Myth of the Cave," a group of prisoners are placed so they can only see on the wall of the cave reflections of objects carried back and forth in front of a fire behind them. Since this is all they see, they assume it to be reality. Had Plato been acquainted with movie theaters, he might have chosen the movie screen as a metaphor for the shadow world of the senses.

thorough pagan spiritual education prior to his conversion to Christianity at age thirty-two. He had studied Manichaeism, the then-popular Persian philosophical religion that taught the powers of light and the powers of darkness are locked in battle until the final day and the powers of light will not win unless we humans help them in their fight for goodness. He had studied Neoplatonism, a philosophy developed by the thinker Plotinus on the basis of Plato's philosophy, which taught that this tangible, material world is unimportant compared to the world of the spirit and even that the material world is godless and should be shunned. This intellectual and religious legacy that Augustine brought with him subtly changed the direction of Christianity forever, according to historians. In the writings of Augustine, Christianity became a religion which, even more than previously, looked to the afterlife as the true reason for human existence and shunned earthly concerns and earthly pleasures. This disregard for the physical world and our physical existence has been heavily criticized since the end of the nineteenth century by scholars such as Nietzsche (see Chapter 10), who believe that it shows an abysmal contempt for what Nietzsche saw as the only true reality there is: the ever-changing reality of our physical existence on this earth.

Box 8.5   DIVINE COMMAND THEORY AND NATURAL LAW

In Plato's dialogue *Euthyphro* Socrates is engaged in a discussion of religion and morals with a young man and asks a question that sums up one of the most persistent problems in the entire debate about religion and values then and now (because the question just won't go away): Socrates asks, Is something right because the gods command it, or do the gods command it because it is right?

If you answer that a moral law is made right by a *divine command*, it implies that the divinity commanding the moral issue is omnipotent (all-powerful) and creates moral right and wrong, and it implies that without the divinity there would be no right or wrong; many people feel just this way about their God and their moral law. But here comes the problem: If God creates moral right and wrong, what is to prevent him (or her) from declaring that lying is morally right, or cheating, or murder? Remember that God is omnipotent (according to this *divine command theory*), and if God should decree that cheating is morally good, then it would instantly appear to us that cheating is, of course, morally good. This has the unfortunate effect of rendering the moral law *arbitrary*—it depends on God's tastes or whims. So suppose you answer that God, in his (her) wisdom, doesn't have whims and would never make cheating morally right, because cheating is simply wrong in itself. Then you have, in a manner of speaking, played into Socrates' hands, because that is his next point: If God calls murder, cheating, and lying morally wrong, then it must be because he in his wisdom realizes that they *are* morally wrong. But that means God is not seen as all-powerful anymore: The moral power of reasoning is not under his command, but it is a *natural law* of reason that even God must conform to. This argument has the advantage of making morality accessible by our reason, and it makes God's reason accessible for a believer simply because humans and God presumably share the same kind of rationality; but the concept of God as the inventor and creator of morality has gone out the window. (Here we are looking at the debate strictly from *within* a religious viewpoint; natural law does not have to lead to atheism or agnosticism, but it does lead to a view of God's power as limited by reason.)

Thomas Aquinas incorporated natural law into Catholic theology and moral thinking; this makes God's commands accessible through individual reason. The concept of natural law is more complex than that, however; it also entails a theory of what is natural for human beings, such as procreation, self-preservation, social existence, and intellectual curiosity about God. We revisit the concept of natural law in Chapter 9.

Study Questions

1. What are the elements that constitute a person, according to Plato? What is the proper relationship between these elements? (In other words, what is a virtuous person?)

2. You read that Socrates' last words referred to paying a debt to Asclepius. What do you think he meant?

3. Explain Plato's theory of Forms, using his story of the cave as an illustration. Is Plato's theory of reality (metaphysics) materialistic, idealistic, or dualistic? Explain.

4. Imagine that you were assigned as Socrates' legal counsel. What would you advise him to do or say in order to escape a death sentence? Do you think it might make a difference? Why or why not?

Primary Readings and Narratives

The two Primary Readings are an excerpt from Plato's dialogue *Euthyphro,* about the question of loyalty and morals, and one from his *Apology,* his version of Socrates' speech in his own defense. The first two Narratives have Socratic themes: a summary of the film *A Man for All Seasons,* whose title character finds himself falsely accused by advisers to King Henry VIII and defends himself in a manner reminiscent of Socrates, and an excerpt from Plato's *Republic,* "The Myth of the Cave," in which people have been imprisoned all their lives so that the only reality they know is the shadows on the wall. The third Narrative is a summary of the film *The Truman Show,* a story that questions the nature of reality; and in the fourth we encounter the question of what constitutes a good life in the short story "The Store of the Worlds."

Primary Reading

Euthyphro

PLATO

Dialogue excerpt, fourth century B.C.E. Translated by R. F. Allen.

The dialogue *Euthyphro* is an early work of Plato's that probably depicts Socrates fairly realistically. It is particularly famous for its question *Is something right because it is favored by the gods, or do the gods favor it because it is right?* (See Box 8.5 for a discussion of this question.) This excerpt has been chosen partly for this famous question but also for the interesting exchange between Socrates and Euthyphro about the proper course of action when someone close to you is in trouble with the law or has done something wrong: Do you denounce him or her for the sake of pure justice, or do you stand by him or her in a display of friendship and loyalty? According to our moral standards of today, the idea of justice generally overrides the idea of loyalty, but, as you will see, Socrates (and Greeks in general in his day and age) thought differently. Loyalty to family and friends was an important virtue, and standing by your kin was considered a sacred duty.

> *Euthyphro:* Perhaps you will settle your case satisfactorily, as I think I will mine.
>
> *Socrates:* What about that, Euthyphro? Are you plaintiff or defendant?
>
> *Euthyphro:* Plaintiff.

Socrates: Against whom?

Euthyphro: Someone I am again thought mad to prosecute.

Socrates: Really? He has taken flight?

Euthyphro: Far from flying. As a matter of fact, he is well along in years.

Socrates: Who is he?

Euthyphro: My father.

Socrates: Your own father, dear friend?

Euthyphro: Yes, indeed.

Socrates: But what is the charge? What is the reason for the suit?

Euthyphro: Murder, Socrates.

Socrates: Heracles! Surely, Euthyphro, the majority of people must be ignorant of what is right. Not just anyone would undertake a thing like that. It must require someone quite far gone in wisdom.

Euthyphro: By Zeus, very far indeed, Socrates.

Socrates: Was the man your father killed a relative? But, of course, he must have been—you would not be prosecuting him for murder in behalf of a stranger.

Euthyphro: It is laughable, Socrates, your thinking it makes a difference whether the man was a relative or not; the only thing to watch out for is whether his slayer was justified. If so, let him off. If not, prosecute him, even if he shares your health and table. For if you knowingly associate with a man like that and do not cleanse yourself, and him, by bringing action at law, the pollution is equal for you both. Now as a matter of fact, the dead man was a day-laborer of mine, and when we were farming in Naxos he worked for us for hire. Well, he got drunk and flew into a rage with one of our slaves and cut his throat. So my father bound him hand and foot, threw him in a ditch, and sent a man here to Athens to consult the religious adviser as to what should be done. In the meantime, my father paid no attention to the man he had bound; he neglected him because he was a murderer and it made no difference if he died. Which is just what he did. He died of hunger and cold and his bonds before the messenger got back. But even so, my father and the rest of my relatives are angry at me for prosecuting him for murder in behalf of a murderer. For he did not kill him, they claim, and even if he did, still, the fellow was a murderer, and it is wrong to be concerned in behalf of a man like that—and anyway, it is unholy for a son to prosecute his father for murder. They little know, Socrates, how things stand in religious matters regarding the holy and the unholy.

Socrates: But in the name of Zeus, Euthyphro, do you think you know so accurately how matters stand respecting divine law, and things holy and unholy, that with the facts as you declare, you can prosecute your father without fear that it is you, on the contrary, who are doing an unholy thing?

Euthyphro: I would not be much use, Socrates, nor would Euthyphro differ in any way from the majority of men, if I did not know all such things with strict accuracy.

Socrates: Well then, my gifted friend, I had best become your pupil. Before the action with Meletus begins I will challenge him on these very grounds. I will say that even in former times I was much concerned to learn about religious matters, but that now, in view of his claiming that I am guilty of loose speech and innovation in these things, I have become your pupil. "And if, Meletus," I shall say, "if you agree that Euthyphro is wise in such things, then accept the fact that I worship correctly and drop the case. But if you do not agree, then obtain permission to indict this my teacher in my place, for corrupting the old—me and his own father—by teaching me, and by correcting and punishing him." And if I can not persuade him to drop charges, or indict you in place of me, might I not then say the same thing in court I said in my challenge?

Euthyphro: By Zeus, if he tried to indict me, I would find his weak spot, I think, and the discussion in court would contain him long before it concerned me.

Socrates: I realize that, my friend. That is why I want to become your pupil. I know that this fellow Meletus, and no doubt other people too, pretend not even to notice you; but he saw through me so keenly and easily that he indicted me for impiety. So now in Zeus's name, tell me what you confidently claimed just now that you knew: what sort of thing do you say the pious and impious are, both with respect to murder and other things as well? Or is not the holy, itself by itself, the same in every action? And the unholy, in turn, the opposite of all the holy— is it not like itself, and does not everything which is to be unholy have a certain single character with respect to unholiness?

Euthyphro: No doubt, Socrates.

Socrates: Then tell me, what do you say the holy is? And what is the unholy? . . . For consider: is the holy loved by the gods because it is holy? Or is it holy because it is loved by the gods?

Euthyphro: I do not know what you mean, Socrates.

Study Questions

1. In your opinion, is something morally right because God commands it, or does God command it because it is morally right? What is the difference? (The question seems to assume that you have a religion, but it is entirely possible to approach the question theoretically: If there is a god, then does something become morally right because he or she commands it, or does he or she command it because it is morally right?)

2. If a close relative or a friend of yours had committed a felony, would you volunteer as a witness for the prosecution? Why or why not? What would Euthyphro advise? What would Socrates advise? Are there alternatives?

3. You may remember from Chapter 4 that in 1998, a college student from California, Jeremy Strohmeyer, raped and strangled seven-year-old Sherrice Iverson in a restroom in a Nevada casino. His friend David Cash knew about the crime taking place and may have witnessed it. Strohmeyer is serving a life sentence, but the State of Nevada wasn't able to prosecute Cash for his silence because he had broken no law. Cash explained

that he didn't want to be the one to turn Strohmeyer in, because they were best friends. He was displaying the virtue of loyalty to a friend. Can this virtue be carried too far? Should he have turned Strohmeyer in? Prior to that, should he have attempted to stop the rape and murder? Are there other alternatives? Strohmeyer himself later implied that Cash was not a good friend because he could have stopped Strohmeyer but didn't. How do you view the demands and limits of the virtue of friendships?

Primary Reading

The Apology

PLATO

Dialogue excerpt, fourth century B.C.E., translated by R. G. Bury.

In *The Apology,* one of Plato's dialogues, Socrates argues in his own defense while on trial. This is not a typical "dialogue" since Socrates does most of the talking, but we know he has listeners, because he begs for their attention and asks them not to heckle him. Is this a true retelling of what Socrates actually said, or is Plato here (as often elsewhere) making things up? Scholars have speculated that Plato, being present at the trial, must surely have remembered every word of this traumatic, horrible event; however, the account was probably not written until some years later, perhaps as much as ten years, so we must assume that Plato tells it not only the way he remembers it but also the way he believes it *ought* to sound. Since Plato's account of the trial is not the only one in existence, we can assume that the general gist of Socrates' defense was the way Plato presented it.

I have said enough in my defense against the first class of my accusers; I turn to the second class. They are headed by Meletus, that good man and true lover of his country, as he calls himself. Against these, too, I must try to make a defense. Let their indictment be read; it runs like this: "Socrates is a doer of evil who corrupts the youth, and who does not believe in the gods of the state, but has other new divinities of his own." Such is the charge; now let us examine the particular counts. He says that I am a doer of evil and corrupt the youth; but I say, men of Athens, that Meletus is a doer of evil, since he pretends to be in earnest when he is only joking, and is so eager to bring men to trial from a pretended zeal and interest about matters in which he really never had the smallest interest. And the truth of this I will try to prove to you.

Come here, Meletus, and let me ask you a question. You think a great deal about the improvement of youth?
Yes, I do.

Tell the judges, then, who is their improver; for you must know, since you care so much.* You say you have discovered their corrupter, and are citing and accusing me before them. Speak then, and tell the judges who their improver is. Observe, Meletus, that you are silent and have nothing to say. But is not this disgraceful, and a clear proof of what I say, that you have never cared about this? Speak up, friend, and tell us who their improver is.

The laws.

But that, my good sir, is not my meaning. I want to know who the person is who, in the first place, knows the laws.

The judges, Socrates, who are present in court.

What, do you mean to say, Meletus, that they are able to instruct and improve youth?

Certainly they are.

What, all of them, or some only and not others?

All of them.

By the goddess Hera, that is good news! There are plenty of improvers, then. And what do you say of the audience—do they improve them?

Yes, they do.

And the members of the Council?

Yes, they improve them.

But perhaps the members of the Assembly corrupt them? Or do they too improve them?

They improve them.

Then every Athenian improves and elevates them except me; and I alone am their corrupter? Is that what you affirm?

That is what I stoutly affirm.

I am very unfortunate if you are right. But suppose I ask you a question. How about horses? Does one man do them harm and all the world good? Is not the exact opposite the truth? One man is able to do them good, or at least not many; the trainer of horses does them good, and others who have anything to do with them rather injure them. Is that not true, Meletus, of horses or of any other animals? Surely it is; whether you and Anytus say yes or no. Happy indeed would be the condition of youth if they had one corrupter only, and all the rest of the world were their improvers. But you, Meletus, have sufficiently shown that you never had a thought about the young; your carelessness is seen in your not caring about the very things you bring against me. Now, Meletus, I will ask you another question—by Zeus I will. Which is better, to live among bad citizens or among good ones? Answer, friend, I say; the question can be easily answered. Do not the good do their neighbors good, and the bad do them evil?

Certainly.

And is there anyone who would rather be injured than benefited by those who live with him? Answer, my good friend, the law requires you to answer—does anyone like to be injured?

Certainly not.

---

*A play on Meletus' name, which means "one who cares" in Greek. [Ed.]

And when you accuse me of corrupting the youth, do you allege that I corrupt them intentionally or unintentionally?

Intentionally, I say.

But you have just admitted that the good do their neighbors good, and evil do them evil. Now, is that a truth which your superior wisdom has recognized so early in life, and am I at my age in such darkness and ignorance that I do not know that if one of my associates is corrupted by me, I am very likely to be harmed by him? Yet I corrupt him, and intentionally too? So you say, although neither I nor any other human being is ever likely to be convinced by you. Either I do not corrupt them, or I corrupt them unintentionally; and in either case you lie. If my offense is unintentional, the law has no cognizance of unintentional offenses; you should have taken me aside privately and warned and admonished me. For if I had been better advised, I would have stopped doing what I only did unintentionally—no doubt I would; but you had nothing to say to me and refused to teach me. Instead you bring me up in court, which is a place not of instruction, but of punishment. It will be very clear to you, Athenians, as I said, that Meletus has no care at all, great or small, about the matter. But still I would like to know, Meletus, how you think I corrupt the young. I suppose you mean, according to your indictment, that I teach them not to acknowledge the gods the state acknowledges, but some other new divinities instead. These are the lessons by which I corrupt the youth, you say.

Yes, that I say emphatically. . . .

I have said enough in answer to the charge of Meletus; any elaborate defense is unnecessary. But I know only too well how many are the enmities I have incurred, and this is what will be my destruction if I am destroyed—not Meletus or Anytus, but the envy and detraction of the world, which has been the death of many good men, and will probably be the death of many more; there is no danger of my being the last of them.

Someone will say, "Are you not ashamed, Socrates, of a course of life which is likely to cause your death?" To him I may fairly answer: There you are mistaken; a man who is good for anything should not calculate the chances of living or dying; he should only consider whether in doing anything he is doing right or wrong—acting the part of a good or a bad man. . . . Wherever a man's place is, whether he has chosen it or has been placed in it by his commander, there he should remain in the hour of danger; he should not think of death or of anything but disgrace. For so it is, men of Athens, in truth.

Strange indeed would be my conduct, men of Athens, if I who, when I was ordered by the generals you chose to command me at Potidaea and Amphipolis and Delium, remained where they placed me, like any other man, facing death, and if now, when I believe the god orders me to fulfill the philosopher's mission of searching into myself and other men, I were to desert my post through fear of death or any other fear. That would indeed be strange, and I might justly be arraigned in court for denying the existence of the gods, if I disobeyed the oracle because I feared death, fancying that I was wise when I was not. For the fear of death is indeed the pretense of wisdom and not real wisdom, being a pretense of knowing the unknown; for no one knows whether death, which men in their fear think is the greatest evil, may not be the greatest good. Is not this ignorance disgraceful, the ignorance which is the conceit that man knows what he does not know? In this respect only I believe I differ from men in general, and may perhaps claim to be wiser than they are—that whereas I know but little of the world below, I do not suppose that I know; but I do know that injustice and disobedience to a better, whether god or man, is evil and dishonorable, and I will never fear or avoid a possible good rather than a certain evil. Therefore if you let me go now, and are not convinced by Anytus, who said that since I had been prosecuted I must be put to death (for otherwise I should never have been prosecuted at all), and that if I escape now, your sons will all be utterly ruined by listening to my words—if you say to me, "Socrates, this time we will not listen to Anytus and we will let you go, but upon one condition, that you do not inquire and speculate in this way any more, and that if you are caught doing so again you will die"—if this was the condition on which you let me go, I would reply: Men of Athens, I honor and love you; but I will obey the god rather than you. And while I have life and strength I will never cease from the practice and teaching of philosophy, exhorting anyone I meet and saying to him in my manner, "You, my friend, a citizen of the great and mighty and wise city of Athens, are you not ashamed of heaping up the greatest amount of money and honor and reputation, and caring so little about wisdom and truth and the greatest improvement of the soul, which you never regard or heed at all?" And if the person with whom I am arguing says, "Yes, but I do care," then I will not leave him or let him go at once, but will interrogate and examine him, and if I think he has no virtue in him, but only says he has, I will reproach him for undervaluing the greater and overvaluing the less. And I will repeat the same words to everyone I meet, young and old, citizen and alien, but especially the citizens, since they are my brothers. For this is the command of the god; and I believe no greater good has ever happened in the state than my service to the god. For I do nothing but go about persuading you all, old and young alike, not to think of your persons or properties, but first and chiefly to care about the greatest improvement of the soul. I tell you that virtue is not given by money, but that from virtue comes money and every other good of man, public as well as private. This is my teaching, and if this is the doctrine which corrupts the youth, I am a mischievous person. But if anyone says this is not my teaching, he is speaking an untruth. Therefore, men of Athens, I say to you, do as Anytus bids or not as Anytus bids, and either acquit me or not; but whichever you do, understand that I will never alter my ways, not even if I have to die many times.

Men of Athens, do not interrupt, but hear me; there was an understanding between us that you would hear me to the end. I have something more to say, at which you may be inclined to cry out; but I believe that to hear me will be good for you, and therefore I beg you not to cry out. I would have you know that if you kill such a one as I am, you will injure yourselves more than me. Nothing will injure me, not Meletus or Anytus—they cannot, for a bad man is not permitted to injure one better than himself. I do not deny that Anytus may perhaps kill me, or drive me into exile, or deprive me of civil rights; and he may imagine, and others may imagine, that he is inflicting a great injury on me; but there I do not agree. For he does himself a much greater injury by doing what he is doing now—unjustly taking away the life of another.

Study Questions

1. What does Socrates mean by saying, "The fear of death is indeed the pretense of wisdom and not real wisdom"?

2. What does he mean by saying that if the Athenians put him to death, they will hurt themselves more than him?

3. It has been speculated by philosophers that Socrates in his heart really wanted to die, and for that reason he said things in his argument for his defense that would irritate the jury of 500 citizens (who voted guilty with only a small majority); however, newer research points toward Socrates being serious about defending himself. In your opinion, based on this excerpt, should Socrates have argued for his defense in some other way?

4. Socrates has been called a martyr to the principle of seeking the Truth. Could you imagine any principle so important to you that you would be willing to give up your life for it? Alternatively, can you think of any circumstances that to you would override even the most important principle?

  *Narrative*

 A Man for All Seasons

ROBERT BOLT (SCREENWRITER)
FRED ZINNEMAN (DIRECTOR)

Based on a 1960 play by Robert Bolt. Film, 1966. Summary.

This film, which won multiple Academy Awards, including best picture, best director, and best actor, portrays a real event in England's history. It is the sixteenth century; Henry VIII is king, and he has a problem: His wife Catherine, whom the pope gave him dispensation to marry because she was his brother's widow (and as such, a relative), has not borne him any sons, and since he is concerned with the line of succession, he is looking around for another queen. The problem is that since England is Catholic, the king has no legal access to divorce, unless clever lawyers can find a loophole in his marriage. Churchmen, government officials, and legal experts, concerned with their own future, put together a strategy: to declare the marriage annulled on the grounds that the pope had no authority to grant the permission to marry in the first place. However, there is one legal expert who refuses to go along with the scheme, Sir Thomas More, a man whom the king considers a friend. Hoping to win him over, King Henry appoints him chancellor and shows up in person at More's estate on the River Thames in order to persuade him, but he leaves in anger when it becomes clear that More considers the word of the pope to have a higher authority. Why is it so important for the king to get More on his side, when he has the support of everyone else? Because, as the king himself remarks, More is an honest man who would not choose convenience over his conscience, and receiving More's blessing would make the plan legitimate to the king. But More refuses to budge, even though he knows that incurring the king's wrath can be a dangerous thing; indeed, this is the beginning of the end for More, as his erudite daughter Margaret soon realizes.

In the 1966 film *A Man for All Seasons* we meet Sir Thomas More (Paul Scofield), a lawyer associated with the court of King Henry VIII. In this true story, More becomes a victim of his own high moral standards: The king wants More's support in annulling his marriage, but More's professional integrity won't allow him to give it. In this scene paralleling Socrates' speech in his own defense (see *The Apology*), More argues for his viewpoint and his life, well knowing that he is already condemned.

When Henry VIII institutes the Reformation and outlaws Catholicism so he can divorce Catherine and marry his new love, Anne (who herself will be executed to make way for another queen a few years later), More withdraws from his position as chancellor in silence, never uttering a word in public or private about the king's activities. A brilliant lawyer, More is trying to protect himself and his family by following both his conscience and the law to the letter, believing that his silence will be a shield, but he discovers that his silence does not protect him, as it should according to the law. As the king's man Thomas Cromwell remarks, More is an innocent and does not envision the schemes being prepared by his adversaries. A young man, Richard, who used to be part of the circle around More but believed he could find glory and fortune by attaching himself to Cromwell instead, now serves as an informant on More. But there is truly nothing to report: More is a man of integrity, the only lawyer in London who has not accepted bribes on a regular basis, says More's friend, the Duke of Norfolk. Since More refuses to sign a new oath of allegiance to the king and to accept the new rules of succession according to the Protestant Church of England, he is called in for a hearing, where his sharp legal mind outwits Cromwell; but from now on he is considered an enemy of the court, and being his friend becomes dangerous. Norfolk tries to persuade him to do as everyone else, do the convenient thing to save himself and his career, but following one's principles is more important to More than life and safety. To save his friend Norfolk from the danger and embarrassment of their friendship, he provokes a quarrel that leaves Norfolk hurt and angry, so that he turns his back on More.

Soon More finds himself a prisoner in the Tower of London, the last stage in the lives of many political prisoners; through several seasons he languishes in the damp cell without being allowed to see his family, under constant pressure from Cromwell to either sign the oath or speak up against it. We see how his posture has deteriorated; his hair is gray, and his face shows the hardship of imprisonment. One day he is surprised and overjoyed to see his family — his wife Alice, his daughter, and her husband — but when he realizes that they have been ordered to come just to put pressure on him, he understands that he will not be seeing them again and that staying in England will endanger their lives; he makes them promise that they will flee the country, by different routes, on the same day, and very soon.

His daughter asks him why he can't just sign the oath to save himself — speak it with his mouth and speak against it in his heart — and More answers,

> What is an oath, then, but words we say to God? Listen, Meg, when a man takes an oath, he is holding his own self in his own hands, like water — and if he opens his fingers then, he needn't hope to find himself again.

But Margaret is not satisfied; to her, it is not her father's fault if the state is three-quarters bad, and if he elects to suffer for it, then he elects himself a hero. More replies:

> That's very neat. If we lived in a state where virtue was profitable, common sense would make us saints, but since we see that avarice, anger, pride and stupidity commonly profit far beyond charity, modesty, justice and thought, perhaps we must stand fast a little, even at the risk of being heroes.

More knows that his daughter will understand, but his wife Alice is tormented by the suffering he is putting her through — she says she is afraid that when he is gone, she is going to hate him for what he has done to them; and, for once, at this moment, Thomas More begins to lose his composure. It means so much to him that his wife understand why he may be going to his death. He begs her to say she does, for without her understanding he might not be able to endure what is going to happen to him. And now she looks at him, embraces him, and tells him she understands that he is a good man and that he must do what his conscience tells him to do. Sad but relieved, he hugs his daughter and his wife one last time.

At last More stands trial; he has often told his family as well as his adversaries that there can be no trial, because they have nothing on him; silence can be used only to signify tacit consent and not dissent. But now there is a witness: A man in fancy clothes, a rich and powerful man, approaches the bench. It is Richard, the young man who sold out to Cromwell, More's former friend who now holds a high public office, a position received in return for the perjury he is about to commit. He swears that he has heard More speak his mind, against the king and the new Church of England. Cromwell asks the questions, and his instructions to the jury consist of saying that the jury hardly need deliberate. Thus we know that they, too, must have been "instructed" prior to the trial. And indeed the verdict is "guilty." Almost deprived of his right to speak, More now rises, a condemned man, and breaks his silence, arguing that he is being executed for not agreeing to the king's divorce, which he certainly was against, because it nullified the authority of the pope. Cromwell decries this as treason; and soon after, on a sunny day in summer, More is executed by beheading.

Study Questions

1. Find similarities between Socrates and Thomas More; are there any significant differences?

2. What does More mean by saying, "When a man takes an oath, he is holding his own self in his own hands, like water—and if he opens his fingers then, he needn't hope to find himself again"?

3. If you were in More's position, what might you have chosen to do? If you had been in the position of More's daughter or wife, would you have understood and accepted his actions? Why or why not?

4. Virtue ethics, as you know, focuses not on what to do but on how to be; the film shows More as a man of honesty and integrity, two very important virtues. But would it be possible to criticize More for having failed the test of the virtues of family loyalty and flexibility? Why or why not? (This question actually reveals one of the problems with virtue ethics: What do we do about conflicting virtues?)

Narrative

The Myth of the Cave

PLATO

Excerpt from **The Republic,** *fourth century* B.C.E., *translated by Francis MacDonald Cornford.*

There is no better fictional narrative that illustrates Plato's theory of Forms than the Myth, Fable, or Allegory of the Cave itself. Here you have it in its entirety; the two persons talking are Socrates, telling the story, and Plato's brother Glaucon, listening.

Next, said I, here is a parable to illustrate the degrees in which our nature may be enlightened or unenlightened. Imagine the condition of men living in a sort of cavernous chamber underground, with an entrance open to the light and a long passage all down the cave. Here they have been from childhood, chained by the leg and also by the neck, so that they cannot move and can see only what is in front of them, because the chains will not let them turn their heads. At some distance higher up is the light of a fire burning behind them; and between the prisoners and the fire is a track with a parapet built along it, like the screen at a puppet-show, which hides the performers while they show their puppets over the top.

I see, said he.

Now behind this parapet imagine persons carrying along various artificial objects, including figures of men and animals in wood or stone or other materials, which project above the parapet. Naturally, some of these persons will be talking, others silent.

It is a strange picture, he said, and a strange sort of prisoners.

Like ourselves, I replied; for in the first place prisoners so confined would have seen nothing of themselves or of one another, except the shadows thrown by the fire-light on the wall of the Cave facing them, would they?

Not if all their lives they had been prevented from moving their heads.

And they would have seen as little of the objects carried past.

Of course.

Now, if they could talk to one another, would they not suppose that their words referred only to those passing shadows which they saw?

Necessarily.

And suppose their prison had an echo from the wall facing them? When one of the people crossing behind them spoke, they could only suppose that the sound came from the shadow passing before their eyes.

No doubt.

In every way, then, such prisoners would recognize as reality nothing but the shadows of those artificial objects.

Inevitably.

Now consider what would happen if their release from the chains and the healing of their unwisdom should come about in this way. Suppose one of them was set free and forced suddenly to stand up, turn his head, and walk with eyes lifted to the light; all these movements would be painful, and he would be too dazzled to make out the objects whose shadows he had been used to see. What do you think he would say, if someone told him that what he had formerly seen was meaningless illusion, but now, being somewhat nearer to reality and turned towards more real objects, he was getting a truer view? Suppose further that he were shown the various objects being carried by and were made to say, in reply to questions, what each of them was. Would he not be perplexed and believe the objects now shown him to be not so real as what he formerly saw?

Yes, not nearly so real.

And if he were forced to look at the fire-light itself, would not his eyes ache, so that he would try to escape and turn back to the things which he could see distinctly, convinced that they really were clearer than these other objects now being shown to him?

Yes.

And suppose someone were to drag him away forcibly up the steep and rugged ascent and not let him go until he had hauled him out into the sunlight, would he not suffer pain and vexation at such treatment, and, when he had come out into the light, find his eyes so full of its radiance that he could not see a single one of the things that he was now told were real?

Certainly he would not see them all at once.

He would need, then, to grow accustomed before he could see things in that upper world. At first it would be easiest to make out shadows, and then the images of men and things reflected in water, and later on the things themselves. After that, it would be easier to watch the heavenly bodies and the sky itself by night, looking at the light of the moon and stars rather than the Sun and the Sun's light in the day-time.

Yes, surely.

Last of all, he would be able to look at the Sun and contemplate its nature, not as it appears when reflected in water or any alien medium, but as it is in itself in its own domain.

No doubt.

And now he would begin to draw the conclusion that it is the Sun that produces the seasons and the course of the year and controls everything in the visible world, and moreover is in a way the cause of all that he and his companions used to see.

Clearly he would come at last to that conclusion.

Then if he called to mind his fellow prisoners and what passed for wisdom in his former dwelling-place, he would surely think himself happy in the change and be sorry for them. They may have had a practice of honouring and commending one another, with prizes for the man who had the keenest eye for the passing shadows and the best memory for the order in which they followed or accompanied one another, so that he could make a good guess as to which was going to come next. Would our released prisoner be likely to covet those prizes or to envy the men exalted to honour and power in the Cave? Would he not feel like Homer's Achilles, that he would far sooner "be on earth as a hired servant in the house of a landless man" or endure anything rather than go back to his old beliefs and live in the old way?

Yes, he would prefer any fate to such a life.

Now imagine what would happen if he went down again to take his former seat in the Cave. Coming suddenly out of the sunlight, his eyes would be filled with darkness. He might be required once more to deliver his opinion on those shadows, in competition with the prisoners who had never been released, while his eyesight was still dim and unsteady; and it might take some time to become used to the darkness. They would laugh at him and say that he had gone up only to come back with his sight ruined; it was worth no one's while even to attempt the ascent. If they could lay hands on the man who was trying to set them free and lead them up, they would kill him.

Yes, they would.

Study Questions

1. To recapitulate: This is an allegory of what Plato sees as reality. What does it mean? Who are the prisoners? Where is the cave? What does it mean to see the sun?

2. What did Plato have in mind when he let Socrates speak the final sentences?

3. In what way might this worldview correspond to elements in the worldview of the Christian tradition? Are there significant differences?

4. Can you think of a modern story (film or novel) that speculates about the nature of reality? (Does it ask questions such as "Is reality the way we see it?" "What are we on this earth for?" and "Is there life after death?") Does it agree or disagree with Plato's version?

Narrative

The Truman Show

ANDREW NICCOL (SCREENWRITER)

PETER WEIR (DIRECTOR)

Film, 1998. Summary.

This film is one of those stories we can interpret in a number of ways. That it is a satire on the entertainment industry and its mixing of reality and fiction is the easy interpretation, but some also see it as an allegory about the freedom of the human spirit in a world that is overly regulated. It could also be one man's fantasy of being the center of the universe. But in essence *The Truman Show* is about seeking and finding true reality beyond the illusion that presents itself as everyday life, and as such it becomes a story with a Socratic twist, a parallel to Plato's "Myth of the Cave."

Truman Burbank is a young insurance salesman who lives with his wife, a nurse, in the small, pleasant island community of Seahaven, the kind of place where everybody knows everyone else — at least they all know Truman. It's a friendly town, and Truman has never been anywhere else. When he was a boy his father drowned during an outing in their sailboat: Surprised by a storm, Truman's dad fell overboard and disappeared in the waves. This traumatic experience gave Truman a fear of deep water, so the mere thought of going on the ferry to the mainland, or driving across the bridge, makes him anxious. Nevertheless, he has travel dreams: He wants to go to Fiji. As a boy he wanted to be an explorer, but his teacher was quick to tell him that all the places have already been discovered, so why would he want to go anywhere? His best friend since childhood does his best to discourage Truman's longing for exotic places, and Truman's wife points out that they can't afford to just take off, they have obligations and must meet house payments and so on. In fact, everyone seems to be trying to make Truman stay in Seahaven.

When he was in high school, he fell in love with Sylvia, a beautiful, elusive girl who seemed to have something important on her mind, but somehow they were always prevented from seeing each other — until a fateful evening at the library when they were able to sneak out and make a run for it to the beach. But within minutes a vehicle showed up, presumably driven by her father, who snatched Sylvia away from him. She wasn't normal, he said, and shouted that they were moving to Fiji. So we understand the reason Truman wants to go to Fiji isn't just to see a faraway place — it is to look for Sylvia. Before her father took her away, she tried to convey to Truman that something was wrong — but he didn't understand what she meant.

Now, years later, he is beginning to feel that something *is* wrong. His wife is constantly telling him about new household products with unnatural enthusiasm, as if she is acting in a commercial. In his car on the way to work the radio malfunctions, and he hears a voice describing the route he is taking. He walks into a building at the spur of the moment and tries to enter the elevator, only to find that there is no back wall to the elevator — he can see clear through to a backstage area where people are having lunch.

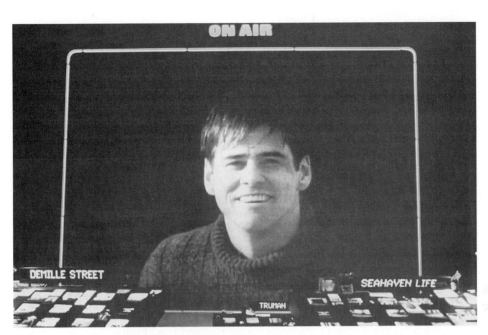

Truman (a *true man,* as opposed to all the other characters in the show) is on television 24/7, but he doesn't know it. The world is real to him, while everyone else knows it is a soundstage, a world of fakery. The only thing that isn't faked in the show is Truman himself and his emotional reactions. Once he realizes his world is not real, will he try to seek true reality, or be content with illusions and safety? Compare the question asked by Socrates in the Myth of the Cave: What is the philosopher supposed to do, once he realizes he has been stuck in a cave of illusions all his life?

But first and foremost, it is the chance encounter in the street with a homeless person who looks awfully familiar to him. He turns, takes a second look — and realizes that it is Dad, returned from the dead! But at that moment, strangers turn up and whisk the older man away on a bus.

This is the turning point for Truman: Is somebody trying to prevent him from talking to his father? Increasingly, he has the feeling that his entire reality is somehow staged and that people are not what they seem. And as viewers we know that he is right: Everything *is* staged except for Truman and his reactions, because Truman is the hero of *The Truman Show,* a live, twenty-four-hours-a-day television series broadcast to the entire world. This was the secret that Sylvia was trying to tell him but never quite managed to convey.

It is a hugely popular show. Truman has been on TV from the day he was born, without having the slightest idea that his reality isn't normal. And in a way it is "normal" — an idealized normality that doesn't exist for anyone else. His mother is an actor, his wife is an actor, even his best friend whom he has known since childhood — everyone is in on it except Truman. *The Truman Show* is the brainchild of the brilliant director Christoph, who watches over everything on the set high above Seahaven, in a control booth disguised as a perennially visible full moon. The control booth makes the sun rise and set electronically, changes the weather, and cues everyone on the set through ear-phones. The words of friendship spoken by his best friend are lines fed to the friend by Christoph. In a rare interview the great director is asked why Truman has never questioned his reality, and he answers that we all believe the reality that is presented to us.

But Truman's gullibility is coming to an end: When he realizes that the travel agent has no intention of selling him a ticket to Fiji, he packs his suitcase and heads for the bus depot, and buys a ticket to Chicago. But the bus isn't going anywhere—the bus driver is an actor who can't get the bus started—and Christoph isn't about to let Truman leave. There is nowhere to go; the set is enclosed. But Truman doesn't give up. One night, as the TV crew relaxes because they think he is asleep, what they're really watching is a dummy under a blanket, with a tape recorder producing snoring sounds. Truman has sneaked out. For the first time in his life he is not on camera.

Christoph mobilizes the entire island: All the actors are now engaged in looking for Truman, but he is nowhere to be found—until they think to look for him in the un-thinkable place: on the water, in a sailboat, headed for—Fiji? All over the world, view-ers watch with bated breath. Will Truman succeed in his quest? Will he escape his confining, designed world? Even Sylvia is watching, praying that Truman will make it. Christoph does what he can to thwart Truman, even ordering his reluctant engineers to whip up a nearly fatal storm. In spite of his deep-seated fear of water, Truman hangs in there, and outlasts Christoph's rage. He continues on his way toward the horizon—which comes up sooner than expected: All of a sudden the bow of his boat goes right through the sky, a beautifully painted backdrop. He has been sailing around in a huge tank on the soundstage.

Immediately ahead is a flight of stairs, leading up to a door. Truman steps off the boat, walks to the stairs along the edge of the world, and ascends to the door. And now Christoph, desperate, addresses him over the speaker system, a disembodied loving voice coming from above. He tells Truman about how long he has been observing him as a boy and a young man, all the kinds of experiences a parent would remember—and how well he knows him and his fears. Nothing bad can ever happen to him in Seahaven—the real world is a dangerous place. The door is open to the dark, mysteri-ous real world. Is Truman going to go through it and disappear, or will he act true to his conditioning and go back?

Study Questions

1. What are the similarities between Plato's "Myth of the Cave" and *The Truman Show,* and what are the differences? In Plato's myth the perfect world is outside the cave. Where is it in the film? You may also want to explore the concept of one person being deluded versus humanity as such being deluded. Is this exclusively Truman's story, or are we all "Trumans," stuck on the soundstage as in Plato's cave?

2. What is the significance of Truman's first name? What does it mean in the context of the story?

3. If you could choose, would you rather have a pleasant life based on a lie, or a difficult, unpredictable life founded on a true perception of the world?

Narrative

The Store of the Worlds

ROBERT SHECKLEY

Short story, 1959. Summary and Excerpt.

What is a "good life"? For many people today it means a life of no financial worries, of material goods and successful pursuit of pleasures. Socrates believed that a good life must involve intellectual and moral awareness: "The unexamined life is not worth living," he said. In order to live a full and fruitful life, one should stay aware and alert, not take things for granted, question authority, acquire knowledge, and certainly also make a point of enjoying oneself. For Socrates a good life would be one spent thinking; analyzing; trying to be a fair, just, and decent human being; and not letting the moments of life go to waste.

This little story written at the height of the Cold War, with its constant fear of sudden global nuclear annihilation, offers a version of what a good life is that may come as a surprise to you. And then again, perhaps not. For Mr. Wayne's fantasy of a perfect life doesn't involve fame or fortune, just the chance to enjoy more of an ordinary life that is gone forever. In the wake of September 11, I think many of us understand the moral of this little story — as does anyone who has come face-to-face with the loss of the daily life he or she has taken for granted.

Mr. Wayne is on a clandestine errand: Making certain he hasn't been followed, he slips into a small, obscure shack, clutching a parcel. Inside the primitive shack is the man he has come to see, Mr. Tompkins. Mr. Tompkins's activity is illegal, and yet word has spread about it; Wayne would like to know more. Tompkins explains.

> What happens is this, you pay me my fee. I give you an injection which knocks you out. Then, with the aid of certain gadgets which I have in the back of the store, I liberate your mind. . . . Your mind, liberated from its body, is able to choose from the countless probability-worlds which the Earth casts off in every second of its existence.

In every second of Earth's existence, Tompkins explains, alternate realities have been created: All the ways things could have happened, but didn't, in our own reality. You can spend a year in any alternate reality you choose! But the fee is high: Just about everything you own, plus ten years off your life. It will have the complete feel of reality, and the method of choosing will not even be conscious; your choice will be guided by your deepest unconscious desires. Tompkins is still working on a way to make it permanent, but so far he can manage only a year, and that is so strenuous to the body that the customer loses ten years of lifetime.

Mr. Wayne is fascinated, and tempted, but the price frightens him, so he asks if he can think it over. All the way home on the train to Long Island he ponders. But when he arrives home, he has other things to think about: His wife Janet needs to discuss household problems with him, his son wants help with his hobby, and his young daughter wants to tell about her day in kindergarten. Janet notices that he seems preoccupied, but he has no intention of telling her that he went to see the weirdo at the Store of the Worlds.

Next day his attention is completely absorbed by things at the office: Middle East events cause a panic on Wall Street, so he has to put all thoughts of the Store on the back burner. On weekends he goes sailing with his son; his daughter catches the measles; the boy wants to know about atomic bombs and hydrogen bombs and cobalt bombs and all the other kinds, and Wayne explains to the best of his ability. Sometimes on summer nights he and Janet go sailing on Long Island Sound, and it is cool and lovely. Occasionally he thinks about the Store; but autumn comes, and there are other everyday things to deal with. In mid-winter there is a fire in the bedroom, and the repairs put all luxuries out of his reach. Working at the office, worrying about the political tensions around the world, taking care of his son when he comes down with the mumps — all of a sudden it is spring again — a whole year has passed. . . .

"Well?" said Tompkins. "Are you all right?"

"Yes, quite all right," Mr. Wayne said. He got up from the chair and rubbed his forehead.

"Do you want a refund?" Tompkins asked.

"No. The experience was quite satisfactory."

"They always are," Tompkins said. . . . "Well, what was yours?"

"A world of the recent past," Mr. Wayne said.

"A lot of them are. Did you find out about your secret desire? Was it murder? Or a South Seas island?"

"I'd rather not discuss it," Mr. Wayne said, pleasantly but firmly.

"A lot of people won't discuss it with me," Tompkins said sulkily. "I'll be damned if I know why."

"Because — well, I think the world of one's secret desire feels sacred, somehow. No offence . . . Do you think you'll ever be able to make it permanent? The world of one's choice, I mean?"

The old man shrugged his shoulders. "I'm trying. If I succeed, you'll hear about it. Everyone will."

"Yes, I suppose so." Mr. Wayne undid his parcel and laid its contents on the table. The parcel contained a pair of army boots, a knife, two coils of copper wire, and three small cans of corned beef.

Tompkins's eyes glittered for a moment. "Quite satisfactory," he said. "Thank you."

"Good-bye," said Mr. Wayne. "And thank *you.*"

Mr. Wayne left the shop and hurried down to the end of the lane of grey rubble. Beyond it, as far as he could see, lay flat fields of rubble, brown and grey and black. Those fields, stretching to every horizon, were made of the twisted corpses of cities, the shattered remnants of trees, and the fine white ash that once was human flesh and bone.

"Well," Mr. Wayne said to himself, "at least we gave as good as we got."

That year in the past had cost him everything he owned, and ten years of life thrown in for good measure. Had it been a dream? It was still worth it! But now he had to put away all thought of Janet and the children. That was finished, unless Tompkins perfected his process. Now he had to think about his own survival.

With the aid of his wrist geiger he found a deactivated lane through the rubble. He'd better get back to the shelter before dark, before the rats came out. If he didn't hurry he'd miss the evening potato ration.

Study Questions

1. What was the world of Mr. Wayne's secret desire? What might the author want to convey with this story? Does it seem more relevant to you because of 9/11? Why or why not?

2. How might Socrates comment on this story? Has Mr. Wayne examined his life, thus making it worth living?

3. Describe what you would call "a good life."

4. Today we are close to having access to Mr. Tompkins's invention through computerized *virtual reality;* given the choice of alternate realities, which would you choose to spend a year in? Would you consider the lesson of "The Store of the Worlds"?

5. Is this a didactic story? Why or why not?

Chapter Nine

Aristotle's Virtue Theory

After Plato's death in 347 B.C.E., leadership of the Academy fell to his nephew, Speusippus. History believes that another man had expected to take over, and with good reason, for he was by far the best student ever to be associated with the Academy. This man was Aristotle, who had studied for twenty years with Plato. Scholars now think that because of the amount of traveling Plato did, Aristotle may never have been especially close to his teacher; it seems certain that the closeness between Socrates and Plato was never repeated between Plato and Aristotle.

Because Aristotle was not a native-born Athenian but was born in Stagira in northern Greece (in 384 B.C.E.), he did not have the rights of Athenians and had no recourse when he was not chosen as the new leader of the school. He left Athens, presumably in anger. He traveled to Asia Minor, got married, and began his studies in biology. In 343 he went to Macedonia, where he became a tutor for the young prince, the son of King Philip. (In three short years, this boy would become the regent of Macedonia and later of an immense realm covering most of the classical world. He would come to be known as Alexander the Great.) By 335 Aristotle was back in Athens and the head of his own school, the Lyceum, and for twelve years—not a particularly long span, as academic careers go—he taught students and wrote books about issues in philosophy, science, and what we today would call social and political science that were of interest to him.

Empirical Knowledge and the Realm of the Senses

Making claims about someone's influence on history can be a risky business, because such claims tend to be exaggerated. In Aristotle's case, however, it is quite safe to say that he is the one person in antiquity who has had the most influence on Western thinking and that even in modern times few people have rivaled his overall historical importance. As Plato left his legacy in Western philosophy and theology, Aristotle opened up the possibility of scientific, logical, empirical thinking—in philosophy as well as in the natural sciences.

It is no wonder that Plato made no contribution in this area. He wouldn't have been interested in natural science, because its object is the world of the senses, far removed from the Forms. Although Aristotle was a student of Plato and did believe in the general reality of Plato's Forms, he believed that Forms are *not* separate from material things; as a matter of fact, Aristotle believed the Forms have no existence outside their objects. If we're enjoying the view of a waterfall cascading off a cliff face, we are at the same time, Aristotle believed, directly experiencing the Forms of cliff, of waterfall, and of falling. If we're in love with someone and think the person

Aristotle (384–322 B.C.E.), Greek philosopher and naturalist, here shown teaching the young Alexander. If one were to pick one scholar as the most influential in Western cultural history, it would have to be Aristotle. Not only did he leave influential writings in a multitude of fields such as biology, metaphysics, logic, ethics, drama, and politics, he also introduced the concept of empirical science to the ancient world. It is said about Aristotle that he knew everything there was to know at the time, and that may well be an accurate description.

is beautiful, we are experiencing the Form of beauty right there in his or her face. And if we are studying a tree or a fossil, the Form that gives us knowledge about the history of that tree or fossil is right there. In other words, knowledge can be sought and found directly from the world of the senses. Compared to Socrates' remark in *Phaedrus* (which you may remember from the previous chapter) that he never ventured outside the city because trees and countryside could not teach him anything, Aristotle would most definitely look to those trees for knowledge.

During the Renaissance, Raphael painted this vision of Plato's Academy, titled *The School in Athens*—not a true representation of daily life in the school, but rather a highly symbolic image of two schools of thought. Two figures are approaching the steps in the center: Plato and Aristotle. Plato, the older man, is on the left. On the left side of the painting are some of Plato's students; but most are historical figures, including some from Raphael's own day, who have subscribed to the Platonic way of thought. Plato is pointing upward to the world of Forms, his image of true reality, whereas the younger man next to him, Aristotle, is stretching out his hand toward us, palm downward. He seems to say that it is in this world we can find true knowledge, not in any intellectual realm removed from the senses. On the right we find the Aristotelians of history, the scientists. And on the far right, Raphael has chosen to place himself, peeking straight out at us.

This turn in Aristotle's thinking—from Forms being separate to being insepa-rable from the thing or experience—is what made it possible for him to think in terms of empirical research (gathering evidence, making hypotheses, and testing the-ories on the basis of experience). Legend holds that Alexander the Great, on his ex-ploits deep into Persia and Afghanistan, had samples of flora and fauna collected and sent to his old teacher. Aristotle would have been delighted to receive such samples and would have studied them carefully, because he believed in the possibility of em-pirical knowledge.

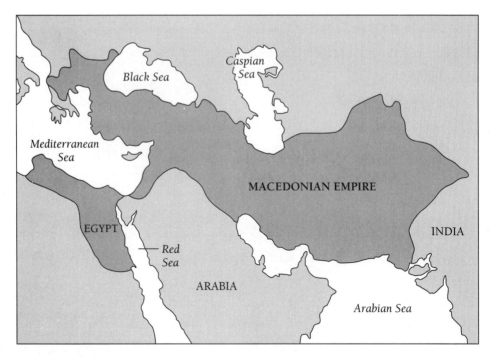

The realm conquered by Alexander the Great (356–323 B.C.E.) was immense by the standards of the time period and even of today; however, it was short-lived. On Alexander's death his generals divided the spoils and had to deal with local insurrections. Nevertheless, the memory of Alexander was kept alive in cultures as far apart as Egypt and northern India; in the mountainous reaches of Afghanistan, Pakistan, and northern India the name "Sikander" (Alexander) became a legend: For example, the Afghan city of Kandahar, which figured in the U.S. war on terrorism, is named after Alexander. In Egypt a dynasty was founded by his general Ptolemy, and a city was named after him which centuries later would become the new center of civilization, the city of Alexandria.

Aristotle the Scientist

Aristotle was instrumental in founding the sciences—not the exact disciplines as we know them today, but sciences in the sense that the concepts of *logic* and *observation* were combined. The extent of his influence, however, goes beyond that. It is hard for us to imagine that there was an era when a human being actually could "know everything," in the sense of having access to all available knowledge at the time, and yet it seems that Aristotle was such a person. He was the author of what we know as classical logic; he laid down the foundations of the classifications in biology; he developed theories of astronomy; he was interested in politics, rhetoric (the art of verbal persuasion), and drama; he wrote books on the proper structure of tragedy and of comedy; he developed theories of the nature of the soul, of God, and of other metaphysical questions. Indeed, the term *metaphysics* derives from Aristotle: He supposedly wrote a book on physics and then another book without a title about the nature of reality. Because it came after the book on physics, his followers called it the "book after physics," *ta meta ta physica.*

His book about ethics may prove to have the most enduring influence of them all. But he also wrote about the justification of slavery and the nature of woman as a lower being. Aristotle thus presents ideas in his writings that are deeply offensive to most modern Western readers, but philosophers usually choose to read his more controversial writings as historical documents rather than as blueprints for how to live our lives. In many ways Aristotle was not what we call a critical thinker; indeed, Socrates would not necessarily have approved of him, for he often refrains from analyzing a viewpoint (such as the status and nature of women) but rather limits himself to mentioning it. He seems to assume that some things are obvious; most people who lived during his time probably agreed with him.

A great many of Aristotle's writings are lost to us. Aristotle, like Plato, wrote dialogues, and the Roman orator Cicero held them in high regard, but only some fragments remain. For the most part, they're lecture notes and course summaries that he used in his classes; some were written for general audiences and some for more advanced students. Some of the works are supplemented by notes taken by his students.

Aristotle and Virtue

Virtue and Excellence

In the first part of Chapter 8 we saw that the Greek conception of virtue was slightly different from our colloquial use of the word. Although calling someone virtuous may for some imply a certain amount of contempt, no such meaning was implied by the ancient Greeks. If you were virtuous, you would not be considered dull or withdrawn from life, because being virtuous meant, above all, that you managed your skills and your opportunities well. To be virtuous meant to act with *excellence* — we might even say with *virtuosity,* because this term retains some of what the Greeks associated with virtue.

Nowhere is that more apparent than in Aristotle's philosophy: You might say that virtue lies in the difference between doing something and doing it well. To Aristotle, everything on this earth has its own virtue, meaning that if it "performs" the way it is supposed to by its nature, then it is virtuous. For one thing, this means that virtue is not reserved for humans; for another thing, it means that everything that exists, including humans, has a purpose. There is virtue to a sharp knife, a comfortable chair, a tree that grows straight, and a healthy, swift animal. For young, growing entities such as saplings and babies one might talk about *potential virtue.*

Teleology: The Concept of Purpose

One concept that is essential for understanding Aristotle's ideas on virtue comes from his metaphysics: the concept of *teleology.* In Greek, *telos* means goal or purpose, and a teleological theory or viewpoint assumes that something has a purpose or that the end result of some action is all-important. Examples of teleological theories exist even today; we encounter them often in everyday discussions about "the meaning of life." Modern science, however, has preferred to leave the question of the purpose of the universe behind. Plato also believed in the purpose of things, but Aristotle

Box 9.1   THE FOUR CAUSES

For Aristotle every event has four causes, of four factors that work on it and bring it into being. These are the *material cause,* or the "stuff" the thing is made of; the *efficient cause,* the force that has brought it into being; the *formal cause,* the shape or idea (the Form) of the thing; and the *final cause,* the purpose of the thing. Consider this illustration (for which I give credit to one of my students):

- Material cause: flour, water, and so on
- Efficient cause: me, the baker
- Formal cause: the idea of muffins
- Final cause: to be eaten!

The material cause and the efficient cause are fairly straightforward from a modern point of view: We have a general idea what Aristotle means when he says the material cause of a thing is the actual physical material that makes it what it is. But what about the efficient creative force? For a muffin, the creative force is the baker; for a wolf, it would be the wolf's parents; for a river, it would be mountain springs and precipitation. (Later religious traditions inspired by Aristotle have chosen to read God as the cre-

ative, efficient force.) But the formal and final causes are less intuitive. In the formal cause we see the last surviving element of Plato's theory of Forms in Aristotle's philosophy, but the Form is not outside the object in some intellectual realm; it is right there in the object itself. (Consider the painting by Raphael on p. 367: Aristotle is pointing downward, almost as if saying, "*This world* is where you find true reality.") A successful muffin displays the perfect Form of muffin, whereas a misshapen muffin is only a weak representation of the muffin Form.

For Aristotle, the final cause was by far the most important cause from a philosophical point of view, because it allows us to understand the purpose of a thing — in other words, its essential qualities and nature. We do not understand the nature of a thing — natural or manufactured — until we understand its purpose. It follows that Aristotle believed everything has a purpose given to it by nature; if the object realizes its potential, it has fulfilled its purpose and is a success. A sharp knife, a fast rabbit, and a smart human being would be examples of potential purpose actualized because each has become what it was supposed to be.

built his teleology into a complete metaphysical theory of "causes." (For Aristotle's four causes, see Box 9.1.)

For Aristotle, everything that exists has a purpose, built into the fabric of reality from the very beginning. The idea of a purpose seems reasonable when we look at manufactured objects, because these objects must surely have started with an idea, a purpose, in the mind of their maker. When we wallpaper our bathroom we do it for a purpose: to make the place nicer or perhaps to get a better price for our house. If a cutler makes a knife, its purpose is to cut well, not to just make a dent. When you bake muffins you intend them to be edible, whether they turn out that way or not. But can't we have human actions without a purpose? Aristotle would say no, especially if we are creating an object; its purpose is a given thing.

What about nature-made objects? Does a tree have a purpose, a wolf, an ant, a river? Today we would hesitate before saying "yes," because after all, who are we to make such assumptions? If we say the purpose of a tree is to give us shade, or apples, we are assuming that it is here for us humans and not just for its own sake in the order of things. Even if we say the wolf's purpose is to cull the herd of caribou, we still hesitate to say that someone "designed" it that way, with a purpose in mind. Today, if we tend to use the term *purpose* or *function* to describe how things work in nature, we should probably remind ourselves once in a while that, scientifically, we are referring to how things work within the ecosystem, without implying that there is an underlying designed purpose to nature. (Aristotle himself was not particularly interested in the relations between things in nature, such as an ecosystem, but was more concerned with the separate characteristics of natural phenomena.) There may well be such a purpose, as well as a designer, but scientists today generally believe that such assumptions fall outside the scope of science. Few scientists, regardless of how they feel privately, would willingly mix up personal religious opinions and professional theories. Aristotle, however, had no such compunction about making statements that reflected anthropocentrism (the view that everything happens for the sake of humans) or speculations about the general structure of the universe (for he believed he understood it). For Aristotle, everything in nature does have a purpose, although it may not be easy to determine just what that purpose is. How *do* we go about determining what the purpose is? We investigate what the thing in question *does best*. Whatever this is will be the special characteristic of that thing. If the thing performs its purpose or function well, then it is *virtuous*.

The Human Purpose

For Aristotle, there is no question that a specifically human purpose in life exists. Each limb and organ of the body has a purpose, he says—the eye for seeing, the hands for grasping—so we must conclude that the person, as a whole, has a purpose above and beyond the sum of the body parts. (For Aristotle this was an obvious conclusion; today we are not so quick to conclude anything about purposes. See Box 9.2.)

The idea that humans are born for a reason and with a purpose is irresistible even to many modern minds. We ask ourselves, "What is the reason for my being here on this earth?" "Why was I born?" We hope to find some answer in the future — some great deed we will do, a work of art we will create, the children we plan to raise, the influence we will exert on our profession, or the money and fame we plan to acquire. Some believe their greatest moment has come and gone, like an astronaut who has been on the moon—how do you top that? Such people may spend the rest of their lives searching for a new purpose.

Our belief in destiny, in one form or another, influences our perception of the purpose of our lives. But this is only half of Aristotle's concept of *telos,* because it applies only on a *personal* level. Aristotle is talking not only about the person becoming what he or she is supposed to become but also about the human being *as such* becoming what human beings are supposed to become. In other words, Aristotle believed not only that a telos exists for an individual but also that it exists for a species. How do we know what the purpose of an individual as a member of a species is? We investigate what that creature or thing does best—perhaps better than any

Box 9.2   TELEOLOGICAL EXPLANATIONS

We use teleological explanations quite often even today, although generally they are not acceptable as a scientific form of explanation. If we were to explain why giraffes have long necks, we might say something like "So they can reach tall branches." Saying "so they can" implies that somehow giraffes are designed for that purpose or else that they have stretched and stretched over the ages until they can finally reach those branches. (There actually was such a theory in the nineteenth century, prior to Charles Darwin. Its proponent was Jean Lamarck, and the theory is referred to as "inheritance of acquired characteristics.") Even though we all know that giraffes do eat leaves off of tall branches, it would not suit modern science to assume that that is their *purpose*. Darwin, with his theory of *natural se-*

lection, proposed a new point of view: that giraffes don't come equipped with a purpose, nor does any other creature, but we all adapt to circumstances, and those who adapt the best survive and have offspring. We therefore must imagine the ancestors of giraffes as being rather short-necked, with some born with longer necks as a result of mutation. Because the ones with long necks could reach the leaves that the others couldn't reach, they were successful during times of hardship when many of the others perished. They gave birth to long-necked offspring, who gave birth to offspring with even longer necks, and so on. This is a *causal explanation*; it looks to reasons in the past to explain why something is the way it is today, instead of looking toward some future goal.

other creature or thing. The purpose of a bird must involve flying, although there are flightless birds. The purpose of a knife must involve cutting, although there are movie prop knives that don't cut a thing. The purpose of a rock? To do whatever it does best: lie there. (This is true Aristotle, not a joke.) And the purpose of a human? To *reason*. We can't evaluate a person without taking into consideration the greater purpose of being human, which is to *reason well*.

> Now if the function of man is an activity of soul which follows or implies a rational principle . . . [and we state the function of man to be a certain kind of life, and this to be an activity or actions of the soul implying a rational principle . . . and if any action is well performed when it is performed in accordance with the appropriate excellence: if this is the case,] human good turns out to be activity of soul in accordance with virtue, and if there are more than one virtue, in accordance with the best and most complete.
>
> But we must add "in a complete life." For one swallow does not make a summer, nor does one day; and so too one day, or a short time, does not make a man blessed or happy.

Scholars are usually generous here in labeling reasoning the purpose of *humans*—for in Aristotle's terminology it is the "purpose of *man*." As we go deeper into Aristotle's works it becomes apparent that he is not using the word inclusively, to cover males and females, as was to become the intellectual habit in the eighteenth, nineteenth, and most of the twentieth centuries: He means *males*. For Aristotle, men are the creatures who have the true capacity for reasoning; women have their own purpose (such as childbearing) and their own virtues. In this, Aristotle seems to have joined forces with the public opinion of the times, although not with the opinion

Box 9.3   IS THERE A HUMAN PURPOSE?

Aristotle inspired an entire school of thought long after he was dead. The Catholic church came upon his writings some fifteen hundred years after his death, and Saint Thomas Aquinas incorporated several of Aristotle's ideas into his Christian philosophy in the thirteenth century, including the idea that humans have a purpose. For Aquinas this purpose included life, procreation, and the pursuit of knowledge of God (see Box 8.5 on natural law). Other thinkers are not so certain that humans have a purpose; Jean-Paul Sartre (1905–1980) believed there is no such thing as human nature and that anyone who says there is is only looking for an identity to hide behind so that he or she won't have to make difficult choices.

of his own teacher, Plato, who believed that the role of women depended on what they were well suited for, individually. (See Box 9.3 for what others have said about the human purpose.)

The purpose for man, Aristotle would say, is to think rationally, on a regular basis, throughout his life, as a matter of habit—in other words, to develop a rational *character.* And this, according to Aristotle, is the same as *moral goodness.*

For modern thinkers this is a surprising twist: that moral goodness can be linked with being good *at something* rather than just being good, period. Moral goodness seems for us to have more to do with not causing harm, with keeping promises, with upholding the values of our culture, and so on. For Aristotle, though, there is no difference between fulfilling one's purpose, being virtuous, doing something with excellence, and being morally good. It all has to do with his theory of *how* one goes about being virtuous.

Aristotle recognizes two forms of virtue, *intellectual* and *moral.* When our soul is trying to control our desires, we engage our moral virtues. But when our soul concentrates on intellectual and spiritual matters, we engage our intellectual virtues. When we think about objects of this world that are subject to change and try to make appropriate decisions, we engage our practical wisdom, our *phronesis.* But when we think about higher matters—the eternal questions of philosophy—we use our theoretical wisdom, our *sophia* (*philosophy* is a combination of *philo* = "love of" and *sophia* = "wisdom"). One may excel in other virtues, but the highest virtue of them all is *sophia,* actualizing the uniquely human potential for abstract thought. So the intellectual virtues involve being able to learn well, think straight, and act accordingly. The moral virtues also involve the use of the intellect, because the only way humans can strive for perfection is to engage their intellect in developing a keen sense of the needs of the moment.

The Golden Mean

Ancient Greece gave us the concept of moderation, or the "Golden Mean." Over the entrance to the temple of Apollo at Delphi were inscribed "Know Thyself" and

"Nothing in Excess." Socrates incorporated the idea of moderation in his teachings, as did several other thinkers, but above all it is at the heart of Aristotle's idea of virtue: an action or feeling responding to a particular situation at the right time, in the right way, in the right amount, for the right reason — not too much and not too little. By using the Golden Mean, Aristotle believes he describes the "good for man" — where a human can excel, what a human is meant to do, and where a human will find happiness. We will return to the subject of happiness shortly.

In his *Nicomachean Ethics,* named for his son Nichomachus, Aristotle compares the Golden Mean with an artistic masterpiece; people recognize that you can't add anything to it or take anything from it, because either excess (too much) or deficiency (too little) would destroy the masterpiece. The mean, however, preserves it. This may remind some readers of a joke among artists: "How many artists does it take to make a great painting? Two — one to paint it, and the other to hit the painter over the head when the painting is done." Why the bash on the head? Because there comes a time, if the work is good enough, when more paint would be too much, and sometimes the artist doesn't recognize that moment. Aristotle would reply that the *virtuous* artist will know this moment — indeed, this is precisely what constitutes a great artist. If this is the case for art, then it must apply to moral goodness: We are morally good if we are capable of choosing the proper response to every situation in life, not too much and not too little:

> Virtue, then, is a state of character concerned with choice, lying in a mean, i.e., the mean relative to us, this being determined by a rational principle by which the man of practical wisdom would determine it. Now it is a mean between two vices, that which depends on excess and that which depends on defect; and again it is a mean because the vices respectively fall short of or exceed what is right in both passions and actions, while virtue finds and chooses that which is intermediate.

Aristotle tells us that every action or feeling must be done in the right amount. In many ways this is quite modern and a very down-to-earth approach to our daily problems. We all have to make big and little decisions every day: How much gratitude should I show when someone does a favor for me or gives me a present I didn't expect? How much is the right amount of curiosity to express about my friend's personal life? (I don't want to appear to be snooping, and I don't want to appear cold, either.) How much should I study for my final? (I know when I've studied too little, but what exactly is studying too much?) How long should I leave the roast in the oven in order for it to be done to perfection when the kids like it gray and my spouse likes it bloody? How much love should I feel, and show, in a new relationship? We face these types of problems every day, and we rarely find good answers to them. In this sense Aristotle shows a feeling for what we might call the "human condition," common human concerns that remain the same throughout the ages. Very few philosophers have done as much as he to try to give people some actual advice about these mundane matters. Thus, even though Aristotle's ideas derive from an ancient, alien world of slavery and other policies that are unacceptable to us today, there are features of his works that make his writings relevant for modern times and modern people. (See Box 9.4 for a specific application of his ideas.)

Box 9.4   THE RIGHT DECISION AT THE RIGHT TIME

Imagine three women on a bridge: Heidi, Jill, and Jessica. Below them a dark river is rushing along, sweeping a little boy toward them, carrying him to certain doom. Heidi looks down at the swirling water and imagines all the things that could go wrong if she were to attempt a rescue: the submerged rocks, how heavy her shoes and jeans will get if she jumps in, the fact that she just got over a bad cold, and the fact that she doesn't swim well. Besides, she remembers, she has to make it to the library before closing time. While she has been doing all this thinking, Jill has already jumped in the river to save the boy. She jumped without thinking, however, and hit her head on one of the submerged rocks and knocked herself out. Jessica sees the boy, and fast as lightning she calculates the swiftness of the river, the position of the rocks, her own swimming prowess—and she runs down the little staircase to the riverbed, throws in the life preserver that is hanging on the wall, saves the boy, and pulls ashore the unconscious Jill for good measure. Or maybe she sheds her shoes and jumps in and saves the boy. Or shouts to some men who are out fishing and asks them to give her a hand. The main thing is that she *thinks*, and then *acts*, at the right time, in the proper amount. That is courage to Aristotle. Jill acted rashly. Heidi may have had the right intentions, but she did not act on them.

You must act on your intentions and succeed in order to be called virtuous.

But what if some time in the future, by some odd coincidence, Heidi finds herself in the same situation again? A bridge, a drowning child—or some other situation where she might be in a position to help by making the right split-second decision. Her previous failure might help her do better this time around. Aristotle believes we become virtuous through doing virtuous acts; and, if Heidi has learned anything from watching Jessica, then she, too, might do the right thing this time. (But she has to remember that no two situations are exactly alike. In another situation acting exactly as Jessica did could be to act either rashly or too timidly.) Similarly, Jill might have learned from the situation; next time around she might be too timid, but eventually she, too, might get it right. Now Jessica: Can we rely on her to always make the right choice from now on? Most of us would not have such lofty expectations and would forgive her for a future mistake, but for Aristotle it was clear: When you have ascended to the level of a virtuous person, then your future actions will generally also be virtuous, because you have developed virtuous habits. One brave deed does not make a person brave (as one swallow does not make a summer). If Jessica slips and makes a wrong judgment call, then she is not so virtuous after all.

Does Aristotle actually tell us what to do? Not really. He warns us that we each are prone to go toward one extreme or the other and that we must beware of such tendencies, but the only help we can find on the road to virtue is the idea that we must try and try again.

There are three questions one might want to ask. The first is, As this is supposed to be a theory of *character*, why does it seem to talk about actions and conduct and what to *do*? The answer is that for Aristotle, this *is* a question of character, because he is not so much interested in our response to singular situations as he is in our response in general. If we perform a considerate or courageous act only once, he would not call us considerate or courageous; the act must be done on a regular basis,

An application of Aristotle's theory of virtue: Three women on a bridge see a drowning child being swept along by the waters. One woman is rash and jumps in without looking; the other is too cautious and frets so much that the time for action is past. But the third one reacts "just right": She has developed a courageous character; she chooses an appropriate action and acts at the right time to save the child.

as an expression of the kind of person we strive to be. In other words, we have to acquire some good habits. This means we can't hope to be virtuous overnight—it takes time to mold ourselves into morally good people, just as it takes time to learn to play a musical instrument well. The second question one might ask is, What does this have to do with the specific human virtue of rational thinking? The answer lies in the fact that the way we find out what the mean is in every situation is through reasoning, and the more times we have done it and acted correctly as a result, the better we can build up this habit of responding correctly. Now let's ask the third question: Does this mean we are supposed to do *everything* in the right amount, not too much and not too little? It is easy to imagine eating in the right amount and exercising in the right amount, but what about acts like stealing? Lying? Or committing murder? Must we conclude that we can steal and lie and murder too much but also too little? That we will be virtuous if we steal, lie, and murder in the right amount? Hardly, and Aristotle was aware of this loophole; he tells us that some acts are just wrong by themselves and cannot be done in the right amount. Similarly, some acts are right in themselves and cannot be done too often. One such thing is justice: You can't be "too just," because being just already means being as fair as you can be.

Box 9.5 THE CLASH BETWEEN CLASSICAL
AND CHRISTIAN VIRTUES

For a modern Western person the idea that it is legitimate to take pride in an accomplishment is not strange; we understand why Aristotle says we should not humiliate ourselves by making ourselves less than we are. But his idea that we have a right to feel proud about things that aren't our own doing, like being born of a certain class and race, is more problematic. To the traditional Christian mind, in fact, the entire idea of legitimate pride is a grave misconception. As much as Aristotle became an inspiration to medieval Christianity, there is a marked discrepancy between most of Aristotle's virtues and the Catholic lists of the cardinal virtues and the cardinal sins. For the Christian it is a cardinal sin to feel pride, because our accomplishments come through the grace of God and are not our own doing. This is expressed in the Latin words *Soli Dei Gloria,* the honor (glory) is God's alone. The cardinal virtues are justice, prudence, temperance, fortitude, faith, hope, and charity. The cardinal sins are pride, lust, envy, anger, covetousness, gluttony, and sloth.

How exactly do we find the mean? After all, it is not an absolute mean; we cannot identify the exact midpoint between the extremes the way we would measure the exact amount of calories allowed in a diet. It is far more complex than that, and Aristotle warns us that there are many ways to go wrong but only one way to "hit the bull's-eye" in each situation. It takes a full commitment, involving the entire personality, over a lifetime of training. In his lectures Aristotle appears to have used a chart of virtues. Let us look at a few of them.

If someone is in danger, that person can react in three ways: with too little courage (in which case he is a coward), with the right amount of courage, or with too much courage (in which case he is being foolhardy).

Let's consider the act of pleasure seeking. If you overdo it, you are intemperate — but suppose you are not capable of enjoying pleasures at all? That is not a virtue, and Aristotle doesn't know what to call such a person except "unimpressionable." The virtue is to know in what amount to enjoy one's pleasures; that Aristotle calls *temperance.* Thus for Aristotle there is no virtue in staying away from pleasures, for "temperance" does not mean "abstinence." The key is to enjoy them *in moderation.*

Suppose we look at the art of spending money. For Aristotle there is a virtuous way to spend money, too. If you spend too much you are prodigal, and if you spend too little you are a miser. Spending just the right amount at the right time on the right people for the right reason makes you *liberal.*

For the Greek mind, for the man of the polis, *pride* is a natural virtue, and so it is for Aristotle. You can, however, overestimate your honor and become vain, or you can underestimate it and become humble. The virtuous way to estimate yourself and your accomplishments is through *proper pride.* (See Box 9.5 for a discussion of the differences between Aristotle's virtues, such as pride, and the traditional Christian list of cardinal virtues and vices.)

Is there a virtuous way to feel *angry*? Absolutely—by having a good temper or, as we might say today, being even-tempered. Being hot-tempered is a vice, but so is being meek. If you have been wronged, Aristotle believes, you ought to be angry in proportion to the offense against you.

Let us now consider the virtue of *truthfulness*. We probably would agree with Aristotle that this is a good thing, but what is his idea of a deficiency of truthfulness? Not *lying,* as we might expect, but *irony,* or as it is often translated, "mock-modesty" (in other words, downplaying the situation). Aristotle obviously would not have enjoyed Socrates' ironical bantering. The excess of truthfulness? Bragging. To the modern reader the excess of truthfulness might be something different, such as being *rude* by telling someone, "You sure gained weight over the holidays!" But for Aristotle it is not a matter of not harming others by lying or by being rude but a matter of assessing the situation properly, neither underplaying nor overplaying the truth. Here we touch on a hidden element of Aristotle's virtue theory: *Who is the theory intended for?* Not necessarily young people who need to get their lives straightened out. It is, instead, directed at future politicians. The young noblemen and sons of wealthy landowners who had the leisure time to go to school were expected to become the pillars of Athenian society. What Aristotle is teaching them is, in many ways, to be good public figures. That is why it is necessary to know how much money to spend, in large sums. That is why it is important to know the extent of your pride and your anger. Of course, Aristotle's virtues are also applicable to other people, but some of them—such as the virtues of wit or humor—carry a direct message to those young men who plan to enter public life. Most of us probably would like our partners to have a sense of humor. But imagine how important it is for a public figure not to be a boor, not to be a buffoon, and to have a ready wit. Aristotle recognized this fact. (See Box 9.6 for additional discussion of virtues.)

There are, then, three dispositions: two vices, one on either side, and virtue in the middle. How do we find the virtue? It may be difficult, depending on our own personal failings. If we have a hard time controlling our temper, we might try for a while to be so cool that nothing makes us angry, just to get out of the habit of being irascible; in other words, we might shoot *past* the target of good temper until we feel we can control ourselves and find the mean. If we tend to overindulge in desserts, we might try to lay off sweet things completely for a while. This is not the ideal situation, but Aristotle advises us to experiment until we get it right. Besides, if we find ourselves at one extreme, it is hard for us to see the difference between the other extreme and the virtue: A chocolate lover finds the chocolate hater and the person who has just a few bites of chocolate each week equally dull and unsympathetic. Indeed, some extremes are closer to the mean, the virtue, than others. Being a coward is probably more opposed to being courageous than to being foolhardy. So if you don't know what path to choose, at least stay away from the extreme that is more opposed to the mean than the other extreme. We all have to watch out for our own personal failings, and we also have to watch out for temptations, because if we let ourselves indulge in too many pleasures we lose our sense of moderation and proportion. These matters are not easy, and Aristotle knew that we must judge each situation separately.

Box 9.6   VARIATIONS ON ARISTOTLE'S THEME
OF THE GOLDEN MEAN

Virtues on Aristotle's list include magnificence (spending large sums of money correctly), friendliness, modesty, and righteous indignation (a sense of justice). And Aristotle's approach can be applied to many situations we find ourselves in on an everyday basis; you might want to discuss this additional list of virtues and vices and add your own suggestions.

ADDITIONAL VIRTUES AND VICES

EXCESS (VICE)	MEAN (VIRTUE)	DEFICIT (VICE)
Uncritical	Loyal	Disloyal
Passive	Patient	Impatient
Intrusive/Lacks judgment	Compassionate	Unfeeling
Feeling perpetually indebted	Grateful	Ungrateful
Takes everything too seriously	Responsible	Irresponsible
Stubborn	Persevering	Quitter
Rude	Honest	Lying
Strict	Sets rules with exceptions	Lenient
Worries all the time	Aware of real concerns	Don't worry, be happy
Drives too fast	Goes with traffic at speed limit	Drives too slowly
Studies too hard	Studies and passes test	Studies too little

And so on and so forth! Can you think of a vice (one not mentioned by Aristotle) that has no mean? Can you think of a virtue that has no excess?

In Chapter 7 you read about a theory that it is right and appropriate for a victim of a crime to feel *resentment* toward the perpetrator, as well as for the community to feel *moral indignation* on behalf of the victim. Since Aristotle believes there is a Golden Mean for the feeling of anger—somewhere between being prone to rage versus being cold or meek—and he also believes that *righteous indignation* is a virtue, his thinking is in harmony with this theory. Where, within the virtuous middle range, might the proper resentment/indignation response be for a person hit by a computer virus? For a rape victim? For a community targeted by bioterrorism?

Does Aristotle then propose a set of guidelines for what virtue is that can be applied in all situations? Nothing beyond the general range of the Golden Mean and an appeal to intuition, reasoning, and good habits. In other words, the virtuous person will know how to be virtuous! This has caused some ethicists to call Aristotle an ethical relativist, because virtue is, in a sense, relative to the situation. But labeling Aristotle an ethical relativist is wrong. He never states that morals are completely culture-dependent or that each social group determines what counts as their moral

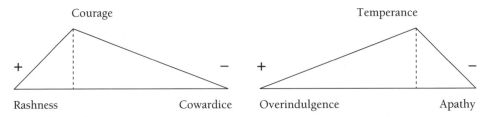

For Aristotle the mean between the extremes is not an absolute middle; in other words, depending on the situation, the persons involved, and the virtue itself, the mean may be closer to one extreme than the other, and Aristotle advises us to stay away from the vice that is the furthest from the mean. If you imagine yourself at one of the extremes, you also can imagine that it might be hard to tell exactly where the mean is; that is why Aristotle says we must find it through trial and error. A mean that might be viewed as closer to the vice of excess than to deficiency would be *courage,* which can be said to be closer to rashness than to cowardice; a virtue that is closer to the vice of deficiency than the vice of excess might be *temperance.*

code. On the contrary, Aristotle is quite adamant about virtues having a rock-bottom value for each situation; it is just that situations may differ, and one may be called upon to do more in one context than in another. If we want to apply a modern term to Aristotle, we might dare to call him a soft universalist (albeit with values typical for his day and age): Our responses to situations must remain flexible, and we each have our own ideals and failings, but the right, virtuous response reveals itself in being appropriate to the situation and falls within a range that is recognized by other people of virtue.

Is there such a thing as a perfectly virtuous person for Aristotle? Yes, it appears that he thought it was possible. Furthermore, he seems to have believed that if you are virtuous in one respect but fail miserably in another, then you have lost out completely. If you deviate only slightly, though, you are still a virtuous person — a person who is good at being human and at realizing the human potential.

Happiness

Being virtuous makes you happy — this is Aristotle's sole reason for designing the development of a virtuous character. But if the goal is happiness, why does he warn us about indulging in too many pleasures? Because pleasure and happiness are not identical, as most ancient thinkers would agree. We have to ask what exactly Aristotle means by happiness.

Happiness is what's "good for man," according to Aristotle. For most of us a good life means a happy life, but a good person means a moral person. For Aristotle there was no conflict. We can be happy only if we're good, but in what way? The highest realizable goods are to live well, to be happy, to do well; what is good for man can't be something that harms him, and indulgence in too many pleasures can certainly be harmful. A further requirement of true happiness is that it must be steadfast; if we rely too much on pleasures, we'll find that they cease to give us a thrill after a while, so pleasure can't be the same as happiness. Nor can fame or fortune, because those things are certainly ephemeral — we can lose both overnight. So what is the thing that can be ours forever, that nobody can take away, and that is not harmful but beneficial to us as human beings? Good reasoning, or, as the ancient Greeks would put it, *contemplation*. This can be ours forever, and, as anyone who has struggled with an intellectual problem and solved it knows, it can even be exhilarating. For Aristotle, then, the ultimately happy life is the life of the thinker. But Aristotle is a realist, too — he adds that, although the truly happy life may be a life of contemplation, it doesn't hurt to have friends, money, and good looks!

What about happiness as a reward for good behavior, in the afterlife? For Plato, the goal of a human life seemed to be a comprehension of the world of Forms and ultimately a reunification with that world in an afterlife. Aristotle seems to have had a different view of spirituality: As far as we can tell, he had no belief in an afterlife. In his theory of the soul he states that the soul is the *form* of a human while the body is one's *matter,* but form cannot exist separate from matter, so when the body dies, the soul ceases to exist in any personal way, even if (as he also says) the form of a human being may be immortal. In any event, whatever we are while we are alive will cease to exist when we die; therefore, happiness for Aristotle is exclusively a phenomenon for the living and must be achieved in this world for a person's life to have fulfilled its purpose. While Plato's metaphysics (as we have seen in Chapter 8) could easily be incorporated into a religion that focused on life after death, Aristotle's metaphysics offers no "pie in the sky." Thus it is all the more extraordinary that Aristotle's philosophy became one of the great pillars of support for Christianity as it evolved in the High Middle Ages.

Was Aristotle himself happy in his lifetime? It appears that during his twelve years in Athens running his own school, he enjoyed contemplation, he had money, and he had friends. (Whether he was good-looking we just don't know, since no images of Aristotle have been preserved, but he reputedly liked to dress in the latest styles.) But with the death of his former student Alexander the Great in 323 B.C.E. at the age of thirty-two, it all came to an abrupt end. The anti-Macedonian feelings that were mounting in the realm controlled by Alexander's troops (including the city-state of Athens) no longer could be kept in check, and because Aristotle was considered pro-Macedonian, the Athenian city council decided to get rid of him. Ironically, their method was to charge him with the same offense that had been leveled against Socrates, of offending the gods. But whereas Socrates chose to stay and die for his principles, Aristotle packed up and left Athens for good, so that "Athens wouldn't sin twice against philosophy." He died the year after of a stomach ailment.

Here we might want to ask ourselves, According to his own system of seeking the mean between extremes, did Aristotle in the end display courageous behavior, or was his behavior "deficient"? It is tempting to compare his choice with Socrates', and many would probably say that the comparison does not come out in Aristotle's favor. But here we should remember that the relationship Socrates had with the city of Athens was vastly different from that of Aristotle with the city-state; it had been Socrates' hometown, he had been concerned for its welfare all his life, and he had fought for it as a soldier. Aristotle was, for all intents and purposes, a foreigner, a "migrant worker" in the philosophy trade. He may have felt a certain loyalty to Athens from having spent over thirty years of his life in the city, but there was general discrimination against noncitizens, and Aristotle can't have been immune to that. He himself might have said that leaving was the perfectly rational, virtuous thing to do: the right action at the right time, for the right reason, not too much and not too little.

Aristotle's Influence on Aquinas

Aristotle's school, the Lyceum, kept operating until well into the third century C.E., but with the advent of Christianity his works were by and large forgotten in the Western world, and even the location of his school was forgotten until 1997, when it was rediscovered by archaeologists. Primarily in Alexandria, it was the Platonic spirit that survived to put its mark on the new world religion. In the Middle East, though, Aristotle's works were studied continually. As the scientific spirit declined in the West, Arabic scholars kept Aristotelian research alive until the advent of another new world religion, Islam, in which Aristotle's philosophy has remained influential. It was not until well into the next millennium that an interest in Aristotle was rekindled in the Christian world. Eventually his theories found their way back into Western philosophy through the works of Saint Thomas Aquinas (1225–1274). In the late Middle Ages and through the Renaissance, Aristotle eclipsed Plato as a philosopher and was known in European intellectual circles (as he had been for centuries in the Arabic world) as "The Philosopher."

It was Aristotle's concept of teleology that became particularly fascinating for Aquinas: If everything has a purpose, then surely it was designed by God. And if we humans, with our free will, decide to follow God's purpose for us, then it must mean we are following God's will, and we are doing right; on the other hand, if we decide to go against God's purpose, we are doing wrong. So what is God's purpose for us? Aquinas identified four specific goals that together made up what has become known as Aquinas's *natural law:* (1) We are obliged to preserve our own lives. (2) We are obliged to procreate within marriage. (3) We are obliged to live as good citizens among other people. (4) We are obliged to seek knowledge, primarily about God and his creation. These four rules are natural to us because we have been designed that way, says Aquinas. It doesn't mean these rules can't be broken—people commit suicide, people have babies outside of wedlock or take measures to avoid getting pregnant, some people care little about living in harmony with others, and some show no interest in seeking knowledge about God. However, they are going against God's will—a will that, for Aquinas, is knowable and understandable to humans, because this will is rational, and humans have been endowed with reason so we can understand God's rules. So if we decide not to follow our built-in purpose, it is because of a sinful willpower. (Aquinas's natural law is not to be confused with the *laws of nature* we are familiar with from science. Such scientific laws are descriptive, while Aquinas's natural law is normative: You can't break the law of gravity, but you can break the law of procreation.)

What happens to people who break these rules of the natural law? Aquinas is convinced that they will not get away with it — they might in this life, but certainly not in the next. That is why there is also *divine law,* for those offenses that God knows about but other humans haven't discovered. On this earthly plane there is also of course *human law*, so that criminal offenses that are discovered can be punished. And the entire universe is run by God according to eternal rules, the *eternal law*.

You may recognize some of Aquinas's views on natural law as contemporary Catholic doctrine. For example, it is Aquinas's rule of self-preservation that forbids suicide, and his rule of procreation that forbids abortion, contraception, and homosexual relationships (because all procreation must take place naturally between married couples, without hindrance, and in no other way). This was not always so: Aquinas's teachings were for centuries considered controversial by the church, and not until a church council in 1914 was it decided that they would from then on be considered official Catholic doctrine. So we can say that Aristotle long after his death not only made an everlasting mark on Western science and philosophy, as well as Middle Eastern philosophy, but to this day he has also been influential within Christianity.

Some Objections to Greek Virtue Theory

As mentioned earlier, the particular brand of ethical theory known as virtue ethics that we find in the Greek tradition by and large disappeared from view with the rise of modern philosophy. This was not merely because the texts were forgotten; this was a concerted effort by scholars to find a better approach to ethics, because as the centuries passed it was becoming clear, for a number of reasons, that the Greek theories of virtue had several shortcomings. For one thing, Thomas Aquinas found it difficult to reconcile Aristotle's virtues not just with Christian virtues but also with the Christian respect for *God's laws*. In the Christian approach to morals, following commandments is far more important than striving toward virtues, and belief in the human ability to shape one's own character autonomously is considered to be a sin of pride. You become what you ought to be by God's grace, not merely by your own effort.

Philosophy, after parting ways with theology in the sixteenth and seventeenth centuries, began to look critically at virtue ethics from a secular point of view, for, as we have seen, Aristotle was talking about the virtues of a ruling class, virtues that could not be disputed by someone with a different point of view. The modern, political vision of equality does not enter into the Aristotelian moral theory, and from both a Christian and a social viewpoint an egalitarian approach had become indispensable for an acceptable moral theory by the eighteenth century. For those scholars believing in "natural rights" for all people, it was necessary to set up a moral theory that everyone could follow regardless of status, birth, or intelligence, and such a theory could be based only on laws that were clear and reasonable. Virtues were criticized as being too vague and logically problematic, because what happens if two virtuous people disagree about what to do? How can one persuade the other? There is no recourse to reason in that case except to declare one person less virtuous than the other, so virtue ethics is not a tool in itself for solving conflicts. Such a problem does not arise if you have a clear set of moral and civil laws to refer to. This is what is needed if we regard each other as equals—not a theory with a static view of what makes a person virtuous. The rejection of virtue theory in favor of a rule- or duty-oriented moral theory was, therefore, considered a step forward in moral egalitarianism.

There is a more fundamental problem embedded in classical virtue theory: its basis in *teleology*. It was natural for Plato and Aristotle to assume that as human actions had a purpose, so did humans themselves have a purpose, and that purpose was to let their rationality shine because that was what human nature was all about. And because this is the human purpose, what is good for humans must begin and end with rationality. But that gives rise to a series of questions: (1) Must what is good for someone always be linked with what he or she does best? Suppose a man is excellent at forging paintings. Does that mean his life should include this as a purpose, in order to make him happy? Aristotle and Plato would reject this on the basis that forging paintings is bad in itself, but that is surely a lame answer, because it assumes that we know beforehand which purposes are acceptable and which aren't. However, even if we stick to the idea of rationality, it is not all that obvious that this is the human purpose. (2) Why must we talk about a human "purpose" at all? Science as well as philosophy today do not, as a rule, talk about purposes of nature, including human nature. A purpose requires that *someone* has that purpose; individuals may have purposes, but we hesitate to claim that nature has a purpose or even that there is a higher power with a purpose. This is outside the realm of science and also that of contemporary moral philosophy. (3) Even if humans are very good at being rational, they are not excellent at it, at least not everybody, and even the select few geniuses can't be rational all the time. We are instead good at *being able* to act rationally some of the time, and with these qualifications it is hard to claim that rationality is our overriding purpose. And (4) Why should there be just one purpose for humans? A knife can be used to cut, to throw, to clean your nails (don't try this at home), to hang on the wall, and any number of other things. A tree surely has more functions than to supply humans with shade and fruit—it provides oxygen, its leaves fertilize the ground, it provides a home for birds and squirrels and maggots, it supplies a subject for an art class to paint—and makes more trees. Why should we assume that each thing or species has one function that defines it? Humans surely have a multitude of functions. It is doubtful, then, whether a theory of virtue should, indeed, involve the question of function or purpose at all. Contemporary theories of virtue tend to steer clear of this ancient, problematic issue, as we will see shortly.

Study Questions

1. Explain Aristotle's theory of the four causes.

2. What is Aristotle's Golden Mean? Does it imply that the virtuous person is an average person of average talents and intelligence?

3. Explain Aristotle's theory of virtue in detail, using at least three examples. At least two of the examples must be Aristotle's own.

4. In the end, Aristotle was accused of the same crimes as Socrates, but, unlike Socrates, Aristotle chose exile. Evaluate Aristotle's choice: Was he himself displaying courage? Was he a coward? Was he rash? How do you think Aristotle would have defended his course of action?

Primary Readings and Narratives

The two Primary Readings are excerpts from Aristotle's *Nicomachean Ethics*. The first is from Book II, in which Aristotle explains the doctrine of the Golden Mean. The second is from Book III, in which he elaborates on the virtue of courage. The first Narrative is the ancient Greek myth of the flight of Icarus, illustrating Aristotle's theory that the virtuous person always seeks the middle way, avoiding the extremes of excess and deficiency: Flying on wings made of feathers and wax, Icarus disregarded his father's advice to take a middle course. The next Narrative explores the theme of courage; it is an excerpt from *Njal's Saga,* the Icelandic epic that takes place in the late Viking Age. In the excerpt, Njal, his wife Bergthora, and their little grandson face death with stoic courage, choosing to perish together. This is followed by a brief revisitation of *Lord Jim.* The fourth Narrative is an excerpt from a twentieth-century short story by Isaac Bashevis Singer, "A Piece of Advice," in which a nasty, temperamental man learns virtue by developing the habit of pleasant behavior. In a parallel story, another nasty man experiences a character transformation by doing nice things for others: the Academy-Award-winning film *As Good As It Gets*. In both cases, each man becomes less selfish by pursuing better habits *for their own sake.*

Primary Reading

Nicomachean Ethics

ARISTOTLE

Excerpt from Book II, fourth century B.C.E. **Translated by W. D. Ross.**

This excerpt contains some of Aristotle's most famous writings on virtue: he explains the relationship between virtue and conduct in Chapter 4, and in Chapter 6 he outlines the general theory of the Golden Mean. The excerpt from Chapter 7 gives us most of Aristotle's own list of virtues as examples of the relationship between the mean flanked by two extremes, too much and too little.

4   The question might be asked, what we mean by saying that we must become just by doing just acts, and temperate by doing temperate acts; for if men do just and temperate acts, they are already just and temperate, exactly as, if they do what is in accordance with the laws of grammar and of music, they are grammarians and musicians.

   Or is this not true even of the arts? It is possible to do something that is in accordance with the laws of grammar, either by chance or at the suggestion of another. A man will be a grammarian, then, only when he has both done something grammatical and done it grammatically; and this means doing it in accordance with the grammatical knowledge in himself.

Again, the case of the arts and that of the virtues are not similar; for the products of the arts have their goodness in themselves, so that it is enough that they should have a certain character, but if the acts that are in accordance with the virtues have themselves a certain character it does not follow that they are done justly or temperately. The agent also must be in a certain condition when he does them; in the first place he must have knowledge, secondly he must choose the acts, and choose them for their own sakes, and thirdly his action must proceed from a firm and unchangeable character. These are not reckoned in as conditions of the possession of the arts, except the bare knowledge; but as a condition of the possession of the virtues knowledge has little or no weight, while the other conditions count not for a little but for everything, i. e. the very conditions which result from often doing just and temperate acts.

Actions, then, are called just and temperate when they are such as the just or the temperate man would do; but it is not the man who does these that is just and temperate, but the man who also does them as just and temperate men do them. It is well said, then, that it is by doing just acts that the just man is produced, and by doing temperate acts the temperate man; without doing these no one would have even a prospect of becoming good.

But most people do not do these, but take refuge in theory and think they are being philosophers and will become good in this way, behaving somewhat like patients who listen attentively to their doctors, but do none of the things they are ordered to do. As the latter will not be made well in body by such a course of treatment, the former will not be made well in soul by such a course of philosophy.

6   Virtue, then, is a state of character concerned with choice, lying in a mean, i. e. the mean relative to us, this being determined by a rational principle, and by that principle by which the man of practical wisdom would determine it. Now it is a mean between two vices, that which depends on excess and that which depends on defect; and again it is a mean because the vices respectively fall short of or exceed what is right in both passions and actions, while virtue both finds and chooses that which is intermediate. Hence in respect of its substance and the definition which states its essence virtue is a mean, with regard to what is best and right an extreme.

But not every action nor every passion admits of a mean; for some have names that already imply badness, e. g. spite, shamelessness, envy, and in the case of actions adultery, theft, murder; for all of these and suchlike things imply by their names that they are themselves bad, and not the excesses or deficiencies of them. It is not possible, then, ever to be right with regard to them; one must always be wrong. Nor does goodness or badness with regard to such things depend on committing adultery with the right woman, at the right time, and in the right way, but simply to do any of them is to go wrong. It would be equally absurd, then, to expect that in unjust, cowardly, and voluptuous action there should be a mean, an excess, and a deficiency; for at that rate there would be a mean of excess and of deficiency, an excess of excess, and a deficiency of deficiency. But as there is no excess and deficiency of temperance and courage because what is intermediate is in a sense an extreme, so too of the actions we have mentioned there is no mean nor any excess and deficiency, but however they are done they are wrong; for in general there is neither a mean of excess and deficiency, nor excess and deficiency of a mean.

7   We must, however, not only make this general statement, but also apply it to the individual facts. For among statements about conduct those which are general apply more widely, but those which are particular are more genuine, since conduct has to do with individual cases, and our statements must harmonize with the facts in these cases. We may take these cases from our table. With regard to feelings of fear and confidence courage is the mean; of the people who exceed, he who exceeds in fearlessness has no name (many of the states have no name), while the man who exceeds in confidence is rash, and he who exceeds in fear and falls short in confidence is a coward. With regard to pleasures and pains—not all of them, and not so much with regard to the pains—the mean is temperance, the excess self-indulgence. Persons deficient with regard to the pleasures are not often found; hence such persons also have received no name. But let us call them 'insensible'.

With regard to giving and taking of money the mean is liberality, the excess and the defect prodigality and meanness. In these actions people exceed and fall short in contrary ways; the prodigal exceeds in spending and falls short in taking, while the mean man exceeds in taking and falls short in spending. (At present we are giving a mere outline or summary, and are satisfied with this; later these states will be more exactly determined.) With regard to money there are also other dispositions—a mean, magnificence (for the magnificent man differs from the liberal man; the former deals with large sums, the latter with small ones), an excess, tastelessness and vulgarity, and a deficiency, niggardliness; these differ from the states opposed to liberality, and the mode of their difference will be stated later.

With regard to honour and dishonour the mean is proper pride, the excess is known as a sort of 'empty vanity', and the deficiency is undue humility; and as we said liberality was related to magnificence, differing from it by dealing with small sums, so there is a state similarly related to proper pride, being concerned with small honours while that is concerned with great. For it is possible to desire honour as one ought, and more than one ought, and less, and the man who exceeds in his desires is called ambitious, the man who falls short unambitious, while the intermediate person has no name. The dispositions also are nameless, except that that of the ambitious man is called ambition. Hence the people who are at the extremes lay claim to the middle place; and we ourselves sometimes call the intermediate person ambitious and sometimes unambitious, and sometimes praise the ambitious man and sometimes the unambitious. The reason of our doing this will be stated in what follows; but now let us speak of the remaining states according to the method which has been indicated.

With regard to anger also there is an excess, a deficiency, and a mean. Although they can scarcely be said to have names, yet since we call the intermediate person good-tempered let us call the mean good temper; of the persons at the extremes let the one who exceeds be called irascible, and his vice irascibility, and the man who falls short an inirascible sort of person, and the deficiency inirascibility.

There are also three other means, which have a certain likeness to one another, but differ from one another: for they are all concerned with intercourse in words and actions, but differ in that one is concerned with truth in this sphere, the other two with pleasantness; and of this one kind is exhibited in giving amusement, the other in all the circumstances of life. We must therefore speak of these too, that we may the better see that in all things the mean is praiseworthy, and the extremes neither praiseworthy nor right, but worthy of blame. Now most of these states also have no names, but we must try, as in the other cases, to invent names ourselves so that we may be clear and easy to follow. With regard to truth, then, the intermediate is a truthful sort of person and the mean may be called truthfulness, while the pretence which exaggerates is boastfulness and the person characterized by it a boaster, and that which understates is mock modesty and the person characterized by it mock-modest. With regard to pleasantness in the giving of amusement the intermediate person is ready-witted and the disposition ready wit, the excess is buffoonery and the person characterized by it a buffoon, while the man who falls short is a sort of boor and his state is boorishness. With regard to the remaining kind of pleasantness, that which is exhibited in life in general, the man who is pleasant in the right way is friendly and the mean is friendliness, while the man who exceeds is an obsequious person if he has no end in view, a flatterer if he is aiming at his own advantage, and the man who falls short and is unpleasant in all circumstances is a quarrelsome and surly sort of person.

Study Questions

1. According to Aristotle, can we become virtuous just by doing the right thing? Can a person be virtuous without doing the right thing?

2. Examine the virtue of proper pride. The modern equivalent of humility might be called low self-esteem. Do you think there is such a vice as too much self-esteem? Why is pride considered a sin by the Catholic tradition?

3. Set Aristotle's list of virtues and vices up in a schema with "too little" to one side, virtue (the mean) in the middle, and "too much" to the other side. Are there virtues missing that you think ought to be essential to a virtue ethics? If yes, which ones?

 Primary Reading

Nicomachean Ethics

ARISTOTLE

Excerpt from Book III. Translated by W. D. Ross.

You may remember that the first virtue on Aristotle's list was *courage,* and we shall look at the theme of courage for the next few pages. Here Aristotle goes into detail examining what he considers true courage.

That it is a mean with regard to feelings of fear and confidence has already been made evident; and plainly the things we fear are terrible things, and these are, to speak without qualification, evils; for which reason people even define fear as expectation of evil. Now we fear all evils, e. g. disgrace, poverty, disease, friendlessness, death, but the brave man is not thought to be concerned with all; for to fear some things is even right and noble, and it is base not to fear them—e. g. disgrace; he who fears this is good and modest, and he who does not is shameless. He is, however, by some people called brave, by a transference of the word to a new meaning; for he has in him something which is like the brave man, since the brave man also is a fearless person. Poverty and disease we perhaps ought not to fear, nor in general the things that do not proceed from vice and are not due to a man himself. But not even the man who is fearless of these is brave. Yet we apply the word to him also in virtue of a similarity; for some who in the dangers of war are cowards are liberal and are confident in face of the loss of money. Nor is a man a coward if he fears insult to his wife and children or envy or anything of the kind; nor brave if he is confident when he is about to be flogged. With what sort of terrible things, then, is the brave man concerned? Surely with the greatest; for no one is more likely than he to stand his ground against what is awe-inspiring. Now death is the most terrible of all things; for it is the end, and nothing is thought to be any longer either good or bad for the dead. But the brave man would not seem to be concerned even with death in all circumstances, e. g. at sea or in disease. In what circumstances, then? Surely in the noblest. Now such deaths are those in battle; for these take place in the greatest and noblest danger. And these are correspondingly honoured in city-states and at the courts of monarchs. Properly, then, he will be called brave who is fearless in face of a noble death, and of all emergencies that involve death; and the emergencies of war are in the highest degree of this kind. Yet at sea also, and in disease; the brave man is fearless, but not in the same way as the seamen; for he has given up hope of safety, and is disliking the thought of death in this shape, while they are hopeful because of their experience. At the same time, we show courage in situations where there is the opportunity of showing prowess or where death is noble; but in these forms of death neither of these conditions is fulfilled.

What is terrible is not the same for all men; but we say there are things terrible even beyond human strength. These, then, are terrible to every one—at least to every sensible man; but the terrible things that are not beyond human strength differ in magnitude and degree, and so too do the things that inspire confidence. Now the brave man is as dauntless as man may be. Therefore, while he will fear even the things that are not beyond human strength, he will face them as he ought and as the rule directs, for honour's sake; for this is the end of virtue. But it is possible to fear these more, or less, and again to fear things that are not terrible as if they were. Of the faults that are committed one consists in fearing what one should not, another in fearing as we should not, another in fearing when we should not, and so on; and so too with respect to the things that inspire confidence. The man, then, who faces and who fears the right things and from the right motive, in the right way and at the right time, and who feels confidence under the corresponding conditions, is brave; for the brave man feels and acts according to the merits of the case and in whatever way the rule directs. Now the end of every activity is conformity to the corresponding state of character. This is true, therefore, of the brave man as well as of others. But courage is noble. Therefore the end also is noble; for each thing is defined by its end. Therefore it is for a noble end that the brave man endures and acts as courage directs.

Of those who go to excess he who exceeds in fearlessness has no name (we have said previously that many states of character have no names), but he would be a sort of madman or insensible person if he feared nothing, neither earthquakes nor the waves, as they say the Celts do not; while the man who exceeds in confidence about what really is terrible is rash. The rash man, however, is also thought to be boastful and only a pretender to courage; at all events, as the brave man is with regard to what is terrible, so the rash man wishes to *appear*; and so he imitates him in situations where he can. Hence also most of them are a mixture of rashness and cowardice; for, while in these situations they display confidence, they do not hold their ground against what is really terrible. The man who exceeds in fear is a coward; for he fears both what he ought not and as he ought not, and all the similar characterizations attach to him. He is lacking also in confidence; but he is more conspicuous for his excess of fear in painful situations. The coward, then, is a despairing sort of person; for he fears everything. The brave man, on the other hand, has the opposite disposition; for confidence is the mark of a hopeful disposition. The coward, the rash man, and the brave man, then, are concerned with the same objects but are differently disposed towards them; for the first two exceed and fall short, while the third holds the middle, which is the right, position; and rash men are precipitate, and wish for dangers beforehand but draw back when they are in them, while brave men are keen in the moment of action, but quiet beforehand.

As we have said, then, courage is a mean with respect to things that inspire confidence or fear, in the circumstances that have been stated; and it chooses or endures things because it is noble to do so, or because it is base not to do so. But to die to escape from poverty or love or anything painful is not the mark of a brave man, but rather of a coward; for it is softness to fly from what is troublesome, and such a man endures death not because it is noble but to fly from evil.

Study Questions

1. Aristotle is often assumed to have said that "a brave man is never afraid." Is this a fair statement?

2. What, according to Aristotle, is the most courageous behavior? Do you agree with him?

3. Would Aristotle consider Socrates' choice to stand trial a brave decision? Why or why not?

4. After September 11 a debate arose in the media about whether hijacking a plane and deliberately flying it into a building, causing death and anguish to civilians, was a "cowardly act." In many people's opinion the terrorist actions were the very picture of cowardice, using innocent poeple as weapons against other innocent people. A dissenting view came from television talk-show host Bill Maher, who suggested that deliberately flying an airplane into a building was not cowardly (and for that remark he

lost several sponsors). Media magnate Ted Turner chimed in, calling the hijackers "brave" but "a little nuts." In your view, were the terrorists brave or cowardly? Is there a third possibility? For a solution you might want to turn to Chapter 10 and the section on Philippa Foot, who suggests that a virtue without good intentions is no virtue at all.

Narrative

The Flight of Icarus

Ancient Greek Myth.

This myth illustrates an element in Aristotle's virtue theory that most Greeks were familiar with, because it corresponds to the classic Greek ideal of moderation, or what the Greeks called *sophrosyne;* in the *Nicomachean Ethics* we know it as the mean between extremes, not too much and not too little. The story of Icarus, part of Greek mythology, has been used often as a symbol in Western literature over the past several hundred years.

Wanted for the murder of his nephew, the great artisan Daedalus hid out on Crete, where he built King Minos a labyrinth to house the monster Minotaur (a creature with a bull's head and a man's body). Here Daedalus lived for years, fell in love with one of Minos' slaves, and had a son by her, Icarus. When Icarus was a young man, Daedalus decided to leave Crete. But Minos did not want to lose his master craftsman and so locked Daedalus and his son up in the labyrinth; they escaped with the help of Minos' wife. It was difficult to get off the island, because Minos kept all his ships under military guard, but Daedalus had an idea: He fashioned a pair of feather wings for himself and another pair for Icarus. The quill feathers were threaded together, but the smaller feathers were held together with wax. Daedalus was quite emotional when he told Icarus how to use the wings on the perilous journey, admonishing his son not to fly too high to avoid having the wax be melted by the sun and not to fly too low so that ocean water wouldn't soak his feathers. Then he told his son, "Follow me!" and they set out across the ocean toward the northeast. They had already traveled a considerable distance when Icarus, for whatever reason, disobeyed his father. He began rising toward the sun, enjoying the air currents and the sweep of his great wings.

When Daedalus looked back to see if his son was still following close behind him, there was nobody—but far below, on the waves, floated the feathers of Icarus' wings. He had risen too close to the sun, and the wax on his wings had melted, plummeting him toward the water below; Icarus had drowned. His father circled around and around

Pieter Bruegel the Elder, *The Fall of Icarus* (c. 1558). The inventor Daedalus made wings of feathers and wax for himself and his son Icarus, so they could escape from Crete, but Icarus flew too close to the sun, and the wax melted. If you look closely, you can see the legs of poor Icarus in the water (right-hand corner). Bruegel was so fascinated by this story that he painted it twice, both times with the farmer in the foreground. This is the original painting; the second is nearly identical except that Daedalus is shown flying above the cliffs. The Roman poet Ovid, who retold the story, specifically mentioned in his *Metamorphoses* that the fall was witnessed by a plowman, a shepherd, and a fisherman, and that is why Bruegel put them in his painting. What do you think the significance might be of the artist's having placed the tragedy of Icarus off to the side?

until the body of his son rose from the waters; then he picked it up and carried it to a nearby island where he buried it.

Study Questions

1. Is this story meant to be taken literally? Why or why not?

2. Bruegel's painting shows the fall of Icarus, but you have to look hard to find him. Why do you think the artist didn't make Icarus the focal point of the painting?

3. In Western literature the story of Icarus has often been used as a metaphor for overextending yourself, or being overconfident. It has been taken as a warning not to reach above your station in life, to "know your place." Is this lesson exactly the same as the original story teaches? (What would Aristotle say? What lesson might a parent be trying to teach his or her child when telling this story?)

4. Is this a didactic story? Why or why not?

Narrative

Njal's Saga

Prose epic, ca. 1280. Author unknown. Summary and Excerpt.

This story is set in the latter part of the Viking Age (700–1000 C.E.). It isn't a story of Vikings, however, but of their relatives, who stayed in Iceland to farm the land. The area was settled by the Norsemen (mostly Danes and Norwegians) in about 800, and by the time *Njal's Saga* was written it was a land of great unrest; blood feuds and various intrigues led to the Danish takeover of the country, which for four hundred years had been independent. *Njal's Saga* is one of many *sagas,* which are historical epics about past life in Iceland.

Nordic mythology teaches that the world as well as the gods eventually will perish in a natural disaster. Thus the Norsemen (the farmers as well as the Vikings) held to the belief in a gloomy fate looming ahead. Even though Christianity was by that time the official religion, the old view of life being ruled by fate still had a hold on people's minds.

This very brief outline cannot explain the complex plot of the saga and can only hint at the inevitable tragic ending. Njal, his wife, Bergthora, and their four sons are carrying on a blood feud with neighbors, not because either party is evil but because over the years events have led in that direction. Through misunderstandings and gossip, the enmity between Njal's family and their neighbors grows, even though Njal does his best to avert it by talking sense to everybody. His negotiations backfire, though, and things get worse. At the *Alting* (the place of arbitration) it becomes clear that all hope of peace is lost, and Njal goes home and prepares for a siege. His adversary, Flosi, arrives with a hundred men, and Njal asks his sons to help him defend the house from inside. The enemy are quick to take advantage of the situation and set fire to the farmhouse.

> There was an old woman at Bergthorsknoll called Sæunn. She knew a lot about many things and had second sight. She was very old by this time, and the Njalssons called her senile because she talked so much; but what she predicted often came true. One day she snatched up a cudgel and made her way round the house to a pile of chickweed that lay there, and started beating it and cursing it for the wretched thing that it was. Skarp-Hedin [one of Njal's sons] laughed at this, and asked her why she was so angry with the chickweed.
>
> The old woman replied, "This chickweed will be used as the kindling when they burn Njal and my foster child Bergthora inside the house. Quickly, take it away and throw it into some water or burn it."
>
> "No," said Skarp-Hedin "for if that is what is ordained, something else will be found to kindle the fire even if the chickweed is not here."
>
> The old woman kept nagging them all summer to take the chickweed indoors, but they never got round to doing it. . . .

Months later, Flosi has now shown up with his force of 100 men, and Njal has fortified himself and his household inside the farmhouse. Now the chickweed which figured in Sæunn's predictions becomes a weapon:

. . . They [Flosi and his men] brought the chickweed up and set fire to it, and before those inside knew what was happening, the ceiling of the room was ablaze from end to end. . . .

Njal said to them, "Be of good heart and speak no words of fear, for this is just a passing storm and it will be long before another like it comes. Put your faith in the mercy of God, for He will not let us burn both in this world and the next."

. . . Now the whole house began to blaze. Njal went to the door and said, "Is Flosi near enough to hear my words?"

Flosi said that he could hear him.

Njal said, "Would you consider making an agreement with my sons, or letting anyone leave the house?"

"I will make no terms with your sons," replied Flosi. "We shall settle matters now, once and for all, and we are not leaving until every one of them is dead. But I shall allow the women and children and servants to come out. . . ."

. . . Flosi said to Bergthora, "You come out, Bergthora, for under no circumstances do I want you to burn."

Bergthora replied, "I was given to Njal in marriage when young, and I have promised him that we would share the same fate."

Then they both went back inside.

"What shall we do now?" asked Bergthora.

"Let us go to our bed," said Njal, "and lie down."

Then Bergthora said to little Thord [their grandson], Kari's son, "You are to be taken out. You are not to burn."

The boy replied, "But that's not what you promised, grandmother. You said that we would never be parted; and so it shall be, for I would much prefer to die beside you both."

She carried the boy to the bed. Njal said to his steward, "Take note where we lay ourselves down and how we dispose ourselves, for I shall not move from here however much the smoke or flames distress me. Then you can know where to look for our remains."

The steward said he would.

An ox had recently been slaughtered, and the hide was lying nearby. Njal told the steward to spread the hide over them, and he promised to do so.

Njal and Bergthora lay down on the bed and put the boy between them. Then they crossed themselves and the boy, and commended their souls to God. These were the last words they were heard to speak. The steward took the hide and spread it over them, and then left the house. . . .

Study Questions

1. Do you think Njal, Bergthora, and the little boy display courage, or are they just giving up?

2. Would removing the chickweed have prevented the arson?

3. For the old Norsemen and -women, the name and reputation you leave behind when you die is all-important. How do you think Njal and Bergthora were regarded after they died?

4. Would Aristotle recognize their final act as courageous? Why or why not?

Narrative

Lord Jim (see Chapter 2, p. 82)

You may remember the story of *Lord Jim,* summarized at the end of Chapter 2 as an il-lustration of Aristotle's theory of tragedy and drama. It also serves as an excellent illus-tration of Aristotle's virtue of courage, and it is recommended that you take a second look at the Narrative and discuss the following questions:

1. Is Jim a coward, or is he courageous? Is it possible to be both?

2. Do you think we all are like Jim in the sense that we all have a moral breaking point that, when we reach it, reveals the frailty of our character?

3. How would Aristotle rate Jim? Is he in the end a virtuous person?

4. Although the virtue of *honor* is not on Aristotle's list, it was an important concept in his day. Today it may not seem terribly important to many in the Western world, but in the time period of Lord Jim, the concept of personal honor was at least as important as when Aristotle was alive. Do you agree with the author (Joseph Conrad) that it is more hon-orable for Jim to confess his failings during the inquest than to keep quiet and follow the lead of his superiors? Is Jim an honorable man? Why or why not?

Narrative

A Piece of Advice

ISAAC BASHEVIS SINGER

Translated by Martha Glicklich and Joel Blocker.
Short story, 1958. Summary and Excerpt.

This story takes place in a pre–World War II Polish-Jewish village; Singer (1904–1991), who won the Nobel Prize in literature in 1978 for his "impassioned narrative art," drew on his Polish-Jewish background for most of his stories.

Baruch lives with his wife's family in the village of Rachev; it is a much grander household than his own childhood home was because his father-in-law is a wealthy man and likes to live in style. The father-in-law is a good man in many ways, and a learned man, but he has one major fault: He has a terrible temper. Unwilling to forgive and for-get, he harbors resentments over any little offense. One time Baruch borrowed a pen from him and forgot to return it, and this sent his father-in-law into such a fit of rage that he struck Baruch in the face. This upset the family terribly because a father-in-law does not have that kind of authority over his son-in-law, but Baruch, being an easygoing young man, was quite willing to forgive the older man. The differences between the two men are noticeable: The older man is fastidious, and Baruch is lazy; his father-in-law is always sharp and on top of things, while Baruch is terribly forgetful and sometimes can't even find his way home because he doesn't pay attention to where he is. But after the incident with the pen Baruch's father-in-law approaches him — a rare event — and asks his advice on how to control his anger, for he has alienated all his business partners. Baruch suggests that they go to see the Rabbi of Kuzmir, a neighboring town. At first the older man scoffs at the thought, but later he agrees to go.

They arrive in Kuzmir on a Friday afternoon (at the beginning of the Sabbath) after a long journey through the winter snows, and Baruch's father-in-law goes to talk with Rabbi Chazkele; for three quarters of an hour he is alone with the rabbi, and then he emerges, irate, calling the rabbi a fool, an ignoramus, to the embarrassment of his son-in-law. What was the rabbi's advice that so infuriated Baruch's father-in-law? That he must become a flatterer. For a week he must flatter everyone he meets, going through the motions of saying nice but insincere things to all of them regardless of who they might be. And that, to the father-in-law, is worse than murder. But Baruch suspects there must be a deeper meaning to the odd piece of advice. The older man wants to go home immediately, but since it is the evening of the Sabbath they can't leave for home (because one does not travel on the Sabbath, between sunset on Friday and sunset on Saturday). So they stay in Kuzmir to celebrate the Sabbath and listen to the prayers of Rabbi Chazkele. Both Baruch and his father-in-law are deeply moved by the rabbi's chanting, and by his words.

> The rabbi commented on the law. And what he said was connected with what he had told my father-in-law at their meeting. "What should a Jew do if he is not a pious man?" the rabbi asked. And answered: "Let him play the pious man. The Almighty does not require good intentions. The deed is what counts. It is what you do that matters. Are you angry perhaps? Go ahead and be angry, but speak gentle words and be friendly at the same time. Are you afraid of being a dissembler? So what if you pretend to be something you aren't? For whose sake are you lying? For your Father in Heaven. His Holy Name, blessed be He, knows the intention and the intention behind the intention, and it is this that is the main thing."
>
> How can one convey the rabbi's lesson? Pearls fell from his mouth and each word burned like fire and penetrated the heart. It wasn't so much the words themselves, but his gestures and his tone. The evil spirit, the rabbi said, cannot be conquered by sheer will. It is known that the evil one has no body, and works mainly through the power of speech. Do not lend him a mouth — that is the way to conquer him. Take, for example, Balaam, the son of Beor. He wanted to curse the children of Israel but forced himself to bless them instead, and because of this, his name is mentioned in the Bible. When one doesn't lend the evil one a tongue, he must remain mute.
>
> Why should I ramble on? My father-in-law attended all three Sabbath meals. And when, on the Sabbath night, he went to the rabbi to take leave of him, he stayed in his study for a whole hour.
>
> On the way home, I said, "Well, father-in-law?" And he answered: "Your rabbi is a great man."

The road back to Rachev was full of dangers. Though it was still midwinter, the ice on the Vistula had cracked—iceblocks were floating downstream the way they do at Passover time. In the midst of all the cold, thunder and lightning struck. No doubt about it, only Satan could be responsible for this! We were forced to put up at an inn until Tuesday—and there were many Misoagids staying there. No one could travel further. A real blizzard was raging outside. The howling in the chimney made you shiver.

Misoagids are always the same. These were no exception. They began to heap ridicule upon Hasids—but my father-in-law maintained silence. They tried to provoke him but he refused to join in. They took him to task: "What about this one? What about that one?" He put them off good-naturedly with many tricks. "What change has come over you?" they asked. If they had known that he was coming from Rabbi Chazkele, they would have devoured him.

What more can I tell you? My father-in-law did what the rabbi had prescribed. He stopped snapping at people. His eyes glowed with anger but his speech was soft. And if at times he lifted his pipe about to strike someone, he always stopped himself and spoke with humility. It wasn't long before the people of Rachev realized that my father-in-law was a changed man. He made peace with his enemies. He would stop any little brat in the street and give him a pinch on the cheek. And if the water carrier splashed water entering our house, though I knew this just about drove my father-in-law crazy, he never showed it. "How are you, Reb Yontle?" he would say. "Are you cold, eh?" One could feel that he did this only with great effort. That's what made it noble.

In time, his anger disappeared completely. He began to visit Rabbi Chazkele three times a year. He became a kindly man, so good-natured it was unbelievable. But that is what a habit is like—if you break it, it becomes the opposite. One can turn the worst sin into a good deed. The main thing is to act, not to ponder. He even began to visit the ritual bath. And when he grew old, he acquired disciples of his own. This was after the death of Rabbi Chazkele. My father-in-law always used to say, "If you can't be a good Jew, act the good Jew, because if you act something, you *are* it. Otherwise why does any man try to act at all? Take, for example, the drunk in the tavern. Why doesn't he try to act differently?"

The rabbi once said: "Why is 'Thou Shalt Not Covet' the very last of the Ten Commandments? Because one must first avoid doing the wrong things. Then, later on, one will not desire to do them. If one stopped and waited until all the passions ceased, one could never attain holiness."

And so it is with all things. If you are not happy, act the happy man. Happiness will come later. So also with faith. If you are in despair, act as though you believed. Faith will come afterwards.

Study Questions

1. Is this an example of virtue ethics or ethics of conduct? Explain your answer.

2. Do you think someone can become a better person by constantly doing the right thing, even if his or her inclination is to do something else entirely? What might Aristotle say?

3. Comment on this quote: "One could feel that he did this only with great effort. That's what made it noble." What might Kant say to this? After you've read Chapter 10, return to this question and discuss what Philippa Foot might answer.

Narrative

As Good As It Gets

MARK ANDRUS AND JAMES L. BROOKS (SCREENWRITERS)
JAMES L. BROOKS (DIRECTOR)

Film, 1998. Summary.

Melvin Udall is a famous writer of romance novels. He is also a terrible person; he is an "equal opportunity offender," having epithets and other insults ready for anyone who crosses his path—blacks, Jews, foreigners, women, homosexuals, anyone at all. His gay neighbor's little dog irritates him, so he stuffs the dog down the disposal chute. Melvin is utterly obnoxious and self-centered. When eating at his favorite restaurant, he will only sit at one specific table and be served by one specific waitress, Carol; he even insults other customers so that they will leave and he can claim "his" table. In addition, he won't use the restaurant's silverware but carries a sealed plastic set. We begin to realize that Melvin is not just obnoxious, he is sick; he suffers from obsessive-compulsive disorder. But the disorder in itself doesn't excuse or explain away Melvin's selfishness and rudeness.

Melvin wants to continue his life with as few variations as possible: being careful not to step on cracks while walking from his Manhattan apartment to the restaurant and back; having no physical contact with anyone; eating at the restaurant, being served by and exchanging casual remarks with Carol; and spending his time alone and uninterrupted, writing his best-selling novels about people who experience the grand passion of their lives. But around him, things begin to change dramatically: His gay neighbor, Simon, an artist, is attacked and left for dead by one of his models and his pals. While Simon is in the hospital with terrible injuries, his good friend, an art dealer named Frank who is black, calls on Melvin to lend a helping hand. He figures Melvin owes Simon. They have exchanged words previously, when Simon had tried to confront Melvin about his dog (who came back safe from the chute experience) and Melvin closed the door in Simon's face. Frank then confronts Melvin and threatens him into behaving decently to Simon. Melvin is terrified of him, and when Frank insists that Melvin take the dog for a while, Melvin has no choice but to comply. And with this little change, a crack has opened in Melvin's armor.

As the weeks go by, Melvin doesn't just get used to the dog but dotes on him, feeding him bacon from the restaurant. When Simon gets back from the hospital, bruised and broke, he is devastated to find that his terrible neighbor is now his dog's favorite.

How do Aristotle, Isaac Bashevis Singer, and the movie *As Good As It Gets* (TriStar, 1998) propose transforming a cantankerous, mean-hearted, and selfish person into a kind and caring human being? By making him do things that a kind and caring person would, thus developing kind and caring habits. In this scene Melvin (Jack Nicholson) and Carol (Helen Hunt) share a tender, tentative moment in the midst of helping a mutual friend, although Melvin's transformation is not yet complete.

Other things change: One day Carol is no longer at work, and Melvin, being obsessive about who serves him, finds out why: Her little son Spence, who has asthma, has been getting worse. So Melvin makes a point of visiting her to try to persuade her to go back to work. Realizing the gravity of her son's condition, he arranges for a physician to make house calls to do for Spence what Carol's HMO hadn't done — make him better — thus freeing Carol to return to the restaurant and serve his meals. Carol tries to thank Melvin by writing him a long letter, but Melvin doesn't know how to accept gratitude and refuses to read it.

Frank talks Melvin into driving Simon to Baltimore to see his estranged parents; Simon is about to lose his apartment and needs financial help. Melvin doesn't want to travel alone with Simon and asks Carol to come along. The threesome embark on a strange journey that results in Simon becoming able to paint again and to get his confidence back, Melvin admitting to himself that he is in love with Carol, and Carol disliking Melvin more than ever, because she had been close to falling in love with him until he began acting in his old selfish, insensitive way. Upon their return to New York, Simon and Carol have become the best of friends — and Melvin reveals that he has arranged for Simon to share his big apartment. Now what remains is for Melvin to convince Carol that she loves him and that life with him will be good.

This story almost has the character of a fable—the mean boy who became a good boy, the lost young woman who found love, the friendless man who found a friend in his enemy—but all of it is saturated with humor and sarcasm, so very little sentimentality is allowed to linger. But what is the connection to virtue ethics? Here is a man of despicable character, rude and selfish, who is changed—by what? *By changing his habits.* By doing things differently, he becomes a different person. Compare this to the story by Isaac Bashevis Singer, and remember Aristotle's advice that "it is by doing just acts that the just man is produced."

Study Questions

1. Is Melvin a believable character? Is it likely that an insensitive, selfish person could become a better person by doing good deeds, even though they are done reluctantly and without good intentions?

2. Is Carol being too suspicious? How would you describe her character, referring to Aristotle's concept of the Golden Mean?

3. Compare Melvin and Baruch's father-in-law in Singer's story. What are the similarities? What are the differences?

4. Is it good enough to become a different and better person by having a change of habits forced on you, or is it better if you choose to change your habits yourself? Reread the first Primary Reading, Aristotle's *Nicomachean Ethics,* and explain what Aristotle would say. What do you yourself think? Has your character ever improved by being forced into a situation?

Chapter Ten

Contemporary Perspectives

*I*n the introduction to Chapter 8, I mentioned that the idea of a good character as one of the key elements in a moral theory was eclipsed by the general notion that all that matters is *doing the right thing*. With the advent of Christianity, virtue ethics was rejected in favor of an *ethics of conduct*—asking the kind of questions introduced in Part 2 of this book. As we saw earlier, this was in part a result of a greater social awareness: There is more fairness in asking everybody to follow rules of conduct than there is in trying to make people adapt to vague principles of how to be, and there is a greater chance of developing rational arguments for your position regarding rules of conduct than there is of getting others to agree to your viewpoint concerning what is virtuous. In recent years, though, philosophers have turned their attention to the ancient thoughts about character building, and virtue theory is now experiencing a revival. (See Box 10.1 for a brief overview of virtue ethics and character.) This trend has been hotly contested by scholars such as J. B. Schneewind, who believe the original reasons for adopting ethics of conduct are still valid.

The revival of virtue theory has been primarily a British and American phenomenon, and we will look at some of the proponents of this new way of approaching ethics. In continental philosophy (European philosophy excluding the British tradition), there was a separate renewal of interest in Aristotle and his virtue theory in the twentieth century, but in a sense a version of virtue theory has been in effect in continental philosophy ever since the nineteenth century, and we will take a look at this tradition, too. Because virtue theory is now associated with the new British/American theory, we will call its continental counterpart the "Quest for Authenticity."

Ethics and the Morality of Virtue

As we have seen, there is a subtle difference between morality and ethics, and in the debate about virtue this difference becomes very clear. In an *ethics of virtue* the issue is to ask yourself what kind of person you want to be, to find good reasons to back up your view and to listen to possible counterarguments, and then to set forth to shape your own character, all the while being ready to justify your choice of virtue rationally or to change your mind. An ethics of virtue doesn't specify what *kind* of virtue you should strive for, although it is usually assumed that it will be something benevolent or at least nothing harmful. The important thing is that you realize you *can* mold your character into what you believe is right. The question of whether your chosen virtue really is a morally good choice is not necessarily part of the issue.

Box 10.1   CAN WE CHANGE OUR SPOTS?

Opponents of virtue ethics often claim that in order for people to be praised for what they do, or blamed for it, it must be assumed that they are *responsible* for their actions. But are we responsible for our character and disposition? Virtue theory asks us to look primarily at people's character. Suppose we ask someone to give to charity, and she doesn't have a generous disposition. Can we then blame her for her lack of virtue? If we can't, then virtue ethics is useless as a moral theory. It may praise people for dispositions that they already have, but it doesn't tell us how to improve ourselves. Virtue theory's response to this is that certain people have certain dispositions, and in that respect some are more fortunate than others, morally speaking; some people are just naturally thoughtful and generous, or courageous, or truthful. The rest of us have to work on these things. Just because we lack a good disposition doesn't mean we can't work on improving it, and just because we have a tendency toward a certain disposition doesn't mean we can't work on controlling it.

However, a *morality of virtue* focuses precisely on this issue: Which virtue is desirable to strive for, and which is no virtue at all? Parents of young children generally know that telling stories can be an excellent way to teach moral virtues, but lately politicians as well as educators have also taken notice. The politician and writer William H. Bennett has published several collections of stories with morals — didactic stories — meant to be read to young children; the best known of these collections is simply titled *The Book of Virtues* and contains stories from the Western cultural heritage, as well as from other cultures, all with a short added moral explanation. (Box 10.2 discusses stories that warn against following nonvirtuous role models.)

In the last half of the twentieth century, virtue ethics made another entrance on the stage of British and American philosophy. For some thinkers it was an absolute necessity to make the switch from an ethics of conduct to virtue ethics, because, as virtue ethicists say, you can do the right thing and still be an unpleasant person; however, if you work on your character, you will become a good person *and* do the right thing without even having to think about it. For others, virtue ethics has become a much-needed supplement to an ethics of conduct. Some see virtue ethics as a way for people to explore the issue of a good character; others view it as a way to teach what a good character should be all about.

The Political Aspect of Conduct versus Character

In the last decade of the twentieth century the political debate in the United States became polarized in a new way — which actually turned out to be a polished and updated version of the older polarization between *conduct* and *character*. Republican politicians brought up the issue of character: Is the candidate trustworthy? Does he or she have integrity? Does he or she keep promises? In short, is the candidate a virtuous person — in his or her private life as well? Democratic politicians responded

Box 10.2   NEGATIVE ROLE MODELS

Virtue theory usually focuses on heroes and saints who are to be emulated, but little attention is given to those characters who perhaps teach a deeper moral lesson: the negative role models. Whether we look to real-life figures or fictional characters, moral lessons can be learned by observing the destiny of "bad guys," provided that they don't get away with their misdeeds. (Twisted souls can of course learn a lesson from the evildoer who does get away with it, but that is another matter.) From childhood we hear of people who did something they were not supposed to do and suffered the consequences. Most of these stories are issued as a warning: Don't "cry wolf," because in the end nobody will believe you. Look what happened to Adam and Eve, who ate the fruit of the one tree they were not supposed to touch. Look what happened to the girl who stepped on a loaf of bread so she wouldn't get her feet wet. She was pulled down into the depths of hell (in a Hans Christian Andersen story). When we grow up we learn the lesson of politicians who turned out to be crooked, of televangelists who didn't practice what they preached, of rich and famous people who have serious drug problems. Movies and novels also bombard us with negative models: Darth Vader (*Star Wars*) sells out to the Dark Side, so we learn to beware of people who have lost their integrity. Charles Foster Kane (*Citizen Kane*) forgets his humanity and dies lonely, his heart longing for the time when he was a small boy. The Count of Monte Cristo loses his own humanity through an obsession with revenge. Madame Bovary loses control of her life because she fantasizes too much. Through exposure to such characters we get a warning; we live their lives vicariously and find that bitterness lies at the end. Films such as *Money for Nothing, A Simple Plan, Goodfellas,* and *Fargo* show us that the life of selfish pursuits carries its own punishment. There are, however, works that fail to bring home the moral lesson because they are either too pompous or simply misinformed. Such a film is *Reefer Madness,* which is now a cult classic and which elaborates on the brain damage awaiting marijuana smokers. Another antidrug film but with a far superior story and impact is *Drugstore Cowboy:* It doesn't preach, but it shows us in terrible and detached detail the downhill slide of addicts and dealers of dope.

by pointing to the public policies of the candidate: What has he or she accomplished politically so far? What social policies does the candidate support, and with what success rate has he or she had them implemented? This is not just an interesting revival of the philosophical question of conduct versus character; this goes to the heart of how we view the importance of values. Do we think the question of personal character and integrity is the most important form of ethics—perhaps even the only form of ethics? Or do we believe that the personal standards of someone who serves the public are less important than his or her social conscience and efforts to change things for the better? For some politicians, the entire question of character has in itself become a matter of a person's outlook on social policies rather than a question of personal values: A person of good character is a person who supports certain social policies. The complete polarization of opinion as to what counts as moral values in politics came to a head in 1998 with the debate surrounding the impeachment of

Zits by Jerry Scott and Jim Borgman

© 1997 ZITS Partnership. Reprinted with permission of King Features Syndicate.

Virtue ethics recommends that we emulate role models; however, in this culture we also encourage individuality and the characteristics that make people unique and natural. Immanuel Kant warns about holding siblings up as role models, because this may create resentment rather than inspiration to be good. In *Zits,* the teen Jeremy is inundated with conflicting advice to be like someone else but also to be himself—is it any wonder he is confused?

President Bill Clinton. The situation is illustrated by the comment of a Democratic politician who said he couldn't judge the *private* morals of the president but that the president had the highest *public* morals of anyone he had ever met.

Virtue theory has turned its spotlight especially on the private lives of politicians. Whereas politics in Europe by and large (with the exception of some major scandals) is conducted without reference to the private lives of politicians, and the media in the United States until the late 1980s rarely paid attention to the sex lives of people in office, everything changed with the unraveling of Gary Hart's presidential campaign in 1988. The press caught Hart having an extramarital affair, and the media attention caused him to withdraw from the race. Did he do this because he thought the people would reject as untrustworthy a politician who cheats on his wife? For some, the very fact that Hart was breaking a moral law was enough to disqualify him. But for others, the issue was very different. Many people said they weren't looking for a politician without flaws—simply for one with *good judgment.* And someone who would take such chances during his campaign is hardly displaying good judgment. So perhaps it was the lack of monogamous virtue that felled Hart, and perhaps it was the lack of the virtues of sound judgment and self-control. Many saw the events leading up to President Clinton's impeachment as sharing the same features: a lack of the virtues of judgment and self-control.

Others regard the ideals and policies supported by a politician as the real virtues of that person. Increasingly, however, we have seen that a display of poor judgment concerning a private matter will spill over and affect a politician's career, regardless of his or her policies: In the late spring and summer of 2001 the media, during a slow news period, focused obsessively on a California congressman, Gary Condit, not because of his politics, but because a young woman, Chandra Levy, was missing, and it was revealed that he had been "close friends" with her. When Condit gave a high-profile TV interview it was clear to most viewers that he was intensely uncomfortable with the situation for whatever reason, and talk began circulating that it might be a good idea for Condit not to run for reelection in 2002. But he did run and was soundly defeated. In other words, the issue of character has entered the court of public opinion, probably as a permanent feature.

As with so many of the moral issues we have looked at, an extreme either/or turns out to be a *false dichotomy* — a false either/or with other possible alternatives. If we assume that character is important, why should we assume that a person's stand on social issues is less important? And if we assume that social views count, then why shouldn't character count as well? A person can have a perfectly squeaky-clean character and yet be completely ineffective as a decision maker or negotiator or even have little grasp of or interest in social policies and the needs of society. And a highly effective politician, well liked and radiating understanding of social and economic problems in the population, can turn out to have a personal life that is in shambles because of a lack of character. At times, though, it does seem all-important that a political leader have character and integrity — even if there is disagreement about his or her policies.

The emerging pattern shows that each group focuses on what it considers most important: For conservatives it is character and for liberals a variety of social policies, such as the right to abortion, affirmative action, gun control, school lunches, welfare, and other causes related to the general question of "What to do?"

Have Virtue, and Then Go Ahead: Mayo, Foot, and Sommers

Bernard Mayo

In 1958 the American philosopher Bernard Mayo suggested that Western ethics had reached a dead end, for it had lost contact with ordinary life. People don't live by great principles of what to do ("Do your duty" or "Make humanity happy"); instead, they measure themselves according to their moral qualities or deficiencies on an everyday basis. Novelists have not forgotten this, says Mayo, because the books we read tell of people who try hard to be a certain way — who sometimes succeed and sometimes fail — and we, the readers, feel that we have learned something.

An ethics of conduct is not excluded from virtue ethics, says Mayo — it just takes second place, because whatever we *do* is included in our general standard of virtue: We pay our taxes or help animals that are injured in traffic because we believe in the virtues of being a good citizen and fellow traveler on planet Earth. In other words, if we have a set of virtues we believe we should live by, we will usually do the right thing as a consequence. However, an ethics of conduct without virtue may not be benevolent at all; it is entirely possible to "do your duty" and still be a bad person—you do it for gain or to spite someone (a good example of such a person is Dickens's Ebenezer Scrooge in *A Christmas Carol,* who may appear to be a pillar of society, but only because it is profitable to him). You can do something courageous without actually being courageous, says Mayo (although Aristotle would insist that if you do it often enough you actually *become* courageous, and utilitarians would insist that it doesn't matter why you do something, as long as it has good results).

So how should we choose our actions in an everyday situation? Mayo says we shouldn't look for specific advice in a moral theory (Do such and such); we should, instead, adopt general advice (Be brave/lenient/patient). This will ensure that we have the "unity of character" a moral system of principles can't give us. Mayo advises us to select a role model, either an ideal person or an actual one. Be just, be a good American—or be like Socrates or Buddha or choose a contemporary role model such as Jane Goodall or Maya Angelou. There are heroes and saints throughout history we can choose from, not necessarily because of what they have done, but because of the kind of people they were.

So when Mayo suggests that we learn from factual *exemplars* such as Martin Luther King, Jr., Mother Teresa, or perhaps our parents, he is not saying we should emulate their actual doings but rather that we should live in their "spirit" and respond to everyday situations with the strength that a good character can give. This is a much more realistic approach to morality than is reflected in the high ideals of principles and duty that an ethics of conduct has held up for people. People have felt inadequate because nobody can live up to such ideals, says Mayo, but everyone can try to be like someone they admire. Critics of this enthusiasm for role models have pointed out that just emulating someone you admire doesn't in itself solve your moral dilemmas: (1) What if your idea of a role model doesn't correspond to what other people consider models of decent behavior? This is one of the traditional problems with virtue ethics: Who gets the final word about what is to count as virtue? It provides no easy method for solving moral disputes. (2) What if your role model turns out not to be so perfect after all? If he or she is still alive, you have to assume that anyone can make a wrong turn, even someone you have chosen to emulate. Are you supposed to keep a critical distance or just follow your model every step of the way? And even if your role model is a historical figure (who can't make any new mistakes), there is always the risk that new material will surface, showing another and less virtuous side to that person. Are you then supposed to drop your hero or find ways to defend him or her? (3) The most serious complaint may be the one that comes from several philosophers (from different time periods) who find fault with the very idea that one can be virtuous by just imitating someone else (Mayo, of course, didn't invent that idea; he just made it part of a modern philosophy of virtue). One is Kant, and you can find his thought-provoking criticism in Box 10.3. Another is the French philosopher Jean-Paul Sartre, who insisted that we ought to take responsibility for every single thing we do in order to be true to ourselves and become authentic human beings. Taking such responsibility precludes settling for just copying what others do, because that approach would give us a false sense of who we are and a false sense of security—by making us believe we can go through

Box 10.3   KANT'S REJECTION OF ROLE MODELS

Bernard Mayo points out that Kant rejected the idea of imitating others as a moral rule and called it "fatal to morality." Kant deplored holding up an example of an ideal, rather than striving for the ideal itself. Mayo thinks striving for the ideal itself is too much to ask of ordinary people. If we read Kant's *Lectures on Ethics* we find an interesting argument for why it is not a good idea to point to *people* as worth emulating: If I try to compare myself with someone else who is better than I am, I can either try to be as good or I can try to diminish that other person; this second choice is actually much easier than trying to be as good as the other person, and it invariably leads to *jealousy*. So when parents hold up one sibling for the other to emulate, they are paving the way for sibling rivalry; the

one who is being set up as a paragon will be resented by the other one. Kant suggests that we should recommend goodness as such and not proffer individuals to be emulated, because we all have a tendency to be jealous of people we think we can't measure up to. So the Kantian rejection of role models is not merely an abstract preference for an ideal but a realistic appreciation of family relationships and petty grudges. It may even serve as a valid psychological explanation for why some people have a profound dislike for so-called heroes and make consistent efforts to diminish the deeds of all persons regarded as role models by society. Such an attitude may just be another reaction against being told that someone else is a better person than you are.

life and be good persons just by imitating others. In Sartre's terminology, we would then be living a life of inauthenticity.

Philippa Foot

Opponents of virtue theory ask how we can call beneficial human traits "virtues" when some humans are *born* with such traits and others don't have them at all. In other words, human responsibility for these dispositions doesn't enter into the picture at all. Good health and an excellent memory are great to have, but can we blame those who are sick and forgetful for not being virtuous?

The British philosopher Philippa Foot counters this argument in her book *Virtues and Vices* (1978) by stressing that virtues aren't merely dispositions we either have or don't have. A virtue is not just a beneficial disposition but a matter of our *intentions*. If we couple our willpower with our disposition in order to achieve some goal that is beneficial, then we are virtuous. So having a virtue is not the same as having a skill; it is having the proper intention to do something good—and being able to follow it up with an appropriate action.

For Foot, virtues are not just something we are equipped with. Rather, we are equipped with some tendency to go astray, and virtue is our capacity to *correct* that tendency. Human nature makes us want to run and hide when there is danger; that is why there is the virtue of courage. And we may want to indulge in more pleasure than is good for us; that is why there is the virtue of temperance. Foot points out that virtue theories seem to assume human nature is by and large sensual and fearful, but there actually may be other character deficiencies that are more prevalent and more interesting to try to correct through virtue—such as the desire to be put upon and dissatisfied or the unwillingness to accept good things as they come along.

But what about people who are *naturally* virtuous? The philosophical tradition has had a tendency to judge them rather oddly. Suppose we have two people who make the decision to lend a hand to someone in need. Person A likes to do things for others and jumps at the chance to be helpful. Person B really couldn't care less about other people but knows that benevolence is a virtue, so he makes an effort to help in spite of his natural inclination. For Kant the person who makes an effort to overcome his or her inclination is a *morally better person* than the one to whom virtue comes easily. But surely there is something strange about that judgment, because in real life we appreciate the naturally benevolent person so much more than the surly one who grudgingly tries to be good for the sake of a principle. As a matter of fact, those are the people we *love,* because they *like* to do things for the sake of other people. Many schools of thought agree that it takes a greater effort to overcome than to follow your inclination, so it must be more morally worthy. Aristotle, however, believed that the person who takes pleasure in doing a virtuous action is the one who is truly virtuous.

Foot sides here with Aristotle: The person who likes to do good, or to whom it comes easily, is a morally better person than the one who succeeds through struggle. Why? Because the fact that there is a struggle is a sign that the person is *lacking in virtue* in the first place. Not that the successful struggler isn't good, or virtuous, but the one who did it with no effort is just a little bit better, because the virtue was already there to begin with. Foot's own example, in *Virtues and Vices,* is honesty:

> For one man it is hard to refrain from stealing and for another man it is not: which shows the greater virtue in acting as he should? . . . The fact that a man is *tempted* to steal is something about him that shows a certain lack of honesty: of the thoroughly honest man we say that it "never entered his head," meaning that it was never a real possibility for him.

In addition, Foot offers a solution to another problem plaguing virtue ethics: Can we say that someone who is committing an evil act is somehow doing it with virtue? Say that a criminal has to remain cool, calm, and collected in order to open a safe or has to muster courage in order to fulfill a contract and kill someone. Is this person virtuous in the sense of having self-control or courage? Foot borrows an argument from the one ethicist who is most often identified with an ethics of conduct, even though his work also includes the topic of virtue—Kant: *An act or a disposition can't be called good if it isn't backed by a good will.* Foot interprets it this way: If the act is morally wrong, or, rather, if the *intentions* behind the act are bad, then coolheadedness and courage *cease to be virtues.* Virtue is not something static; it is a dynamic power that appears when the intention is to do something good. The "virtue" value is simply switched off when the good intention is absent. And here we have an answer to the study question raised at the end of Chapter 9, after Aristotle's text on courage: *Can a terrorist be courageous?* Should we acknowledge that the September 11 hijackers were somehow brave, in spite of their evil intentions? Foot would probably say no: A virtue is nullified if it is done with an evil intention. The hijackers may have experienced some kind of spiritual fortitude, but it doesn't deserve the name *courage* if we view courage as a virtue. And saying that their intention may have been to do something good for somebody other than the victims doesn't count, in any moral theory: not in the religion of Islam, which forbids the killing of innocents; nor in Christianity or Judaism, which forbid the same thing; nor in utilitarianism, which sees the immensity of the massacre and psychological turmoil that followed throughout the world as unjustified by any local cause the hijackers may have had; nor in Kant's theory, which says we should never use any other person merely as a means to an end; nor in virtue theory, which, as we can now see, holds that it is *motivation* that determines whether or not a character trait can be called virtuous.

We find parallels in other situations in which there may not be any evil or criminal element. Hope, for example, is generally supposed to be a virtue, but if someone is being unrealistic and daydreams about wish fulfillment, hope is no longer a virtue. And temperance may be a virtue, but not if a person is simply afraid to throw herself into the stream of life. In that case it is a shield and not a virtue.

Critics of Foot's positive attitude toward the person who is naturally good with few selfish inclinations often point to Kant's argument against the storekeeper who decides not to cheat customers (similar to the version of the argument you know from Chapter 6): To say you like your customers so much that you would never cheat them is not enough, because what if you stopped liking your customers? Similarly, the person who has never been tempted because susceptibility to temptation is not in her or his nature may seem a higher moral person to Foot; but perhaps it is just because that person has never come across temptation before, and in that case it is easy enough to be virtuous. True virtue, say Kant's followers, shows itself precisely in the face of temptation — and not in its absence. However, when we have the choice between a store where they have a strict policy against cheating but the personnel are cold and grumpy and the store where they've known us for years and ask us how we're doing, don't we prefer to shop at the friendly place rather than at the unfriendly, but morally correct, place? Kant may think we should choose the unfriendly place, but Foot disagrees: We prefer friendliness, not principles. But what makes being friendly morally superior to being principled, in Foot's view? Remember, Kant rejected the storekeeper's third option because someone who wouldn't cheat his or her customers because of a sunny disposition toward them is really just doing what he or she wants, out of self-gratification, not out of principles. Of course it is possible to be of a sunny disposition *and* be principled, but that is not the issue here. The issue is whether a sunny disposition is enough to make someone a moral person or whether having a character that isn't tempted is morally superior to being a person who encounters temptation and fights it. Foot says yes: The storekeeper who wouldn't dream of cheating her customers is a better person than the one who has had a moment's temptation and rejected it, because temptation simply wasn't a factor. Foot's assumption is that it takes a weak character to be tempted. But,

Christina Hoff Sommers (b. 1950), American philosopher, coeditor of *Vice and Virtue in Everyday Life* (1985), and author of *Who Stole Feminism?* (1994) and *The War Against Boys* (2000), argues for a return to virtue ethics in order for people in modern society to regain a sense of responsibility rather than leave it to social institutions to make decisions on moral issues.

realistically, perhaps all that was missing was exposure and opportunity? So perhaps Kant has a point after all.

Christina Hoff Sommers

Which, then, are the virtues to which we should pay attention? Foot leaves the question open to an extent, because people tend to differ about what exactly is good for others and desirable as a human trait. Another ethicist, however, prefers to be more direct; her aim is not so much to defend virtue ethics as such but to focus on specific virtues and moral failings in our Western world. Christina Hoff Sommers tells of the woes an ethics professor of her acquaintance would experience at the end of a term. In spite of the multisubject textbooks they had read and the spirited discussions they had engaged in, the professor's students somehow got the impression that there are no moral truths. Everything they had studied about ethics had been presented in terms of rules that can be argued against and social dilemmas that have no clear solutions. More than half of the students cheated on their ethics finals. The irony of cheating on an ethics test probably did not even occur to these students.

What is lacking in our ethics classes? asks Sommers. It can't be good intentions on the part of instructors, because since the 1960s teachers have been very careful to present the material from all sides and to avoid moral indoctrination. (Even this text, as you have noticed, contains sporadic mention of the difference between doing ethics and *moralizing*.) Somehow, though, students come away with the notion that because everything can be argued against, moral values are a matter of taste. The teacher may prefer her students not to cheat, but that is simply her preference; if the student's preference is for cheating as a moral value ("Cheat but don't get caught"), then so be it. The moral lesson is learned by the student, and the chance for our society to hand down lessons of moral decency and respect for others has been lost because of a general fear of imposing one's personal values on others.

What does Sommers think should be done? She suggests that instead of teaching courses on the big issues such as abortion, euthanasia, and capital punishment,

Here is another stab at doing philosophy from Calvin, who is voicing rare scruples about cheating on an ethics test (scruples which apparently were not shared by the students of Christina Hoff Sommers's colleague). Is Hobbes right that "simply acknowledging the issue is a moral victory"?

we should talk about the little, everyday, enormously important things, such as honesty, friendship, consideration, respect. These are virtues that, if not learned at a young age, may never be achieved in our society. Sommers mentions that, in ethics courses of the nineteenth century, students were taught how to be good rather than how to discuss moral issues. When asked to name some moral values that can't be disputed, Sommers answered,

> It is wrong to mistreat a child, to humiliate someone, to torment an animal. To think only of yourself, to steal, to lie, to break promises. And on the positive side: it is right to be considerate and respectful of others, to be charitable and generous.

For Sommers it is not enough to investigate virtue ethics—one must practice it and teach it to others. In this way virtue *theory* becomes virtue *practice*. If we study virtue theory in school, chances are we will find it natural to seek to develop our own virtues. Sommers believes a good way to learn about virtues is to use the same method that both Bernard Mayo and philosopher Alasdair MacIntyre (see Box 10.4) advise: to read stories in which someone does something decent for others, either humans or animals. Through stories we "get the picture" better than we get it from

Box 10.4   MacINTYRE AND THE VIRTUES

The American philosopher Alasdair MacIntyre believes that our moral values would be enriched if we followed the examples of older cultures and let *tradition* be part of these values. We don't exist in a cultural vacuum, he says, and we would understand ourselves better if we'd allow a historical perspective to be part of our system of values. This doesn't mean that everything our ancestors did and thought should become a virtue for us, but a look back to the values of those who came before us adds a depth to our modern life that makes it easier to understand ourselves. And how do we understand ourselves best? As the tellers of stories of history, of fiction, and of our own lives. We understand ourselves in terms of the story we would tell of our own life, and by doing this we are defining our *character.* So virtue and character development are essential to being a moral person and doing what is morally good. But virtues are

not static abilities for MacIntyre any more than they are for Philippa Foot. Virtues are linked with our aspirations; they make us better at *becoming* what we want to be. It is not so much that we have a vision of the good life; rather, we have an idea of what we want to accomplish (what MacIntyre calls "internal goods"), and virtues help us accomplish these goals. Whatever our goal, we usually will be more successful at reaching it if we are conscientious and trustworthy in striving for it. Whatever profession we try to excel in, we will succeed more easily if we try to be courageous and honest and maintain our integrity. With all the demands we face and all the different roles we have to play—in our jobs, sexual relationships, relations to family and friends—staying loyal and trustworthy helps us to function as one whole person rather than as a compilation of disjointed roles.

philosophical dilemmas or case studies. Literary classics can tell us more about friendship and obligation than a textbook in moral problems can. For Sommers, there are basic human virtues that aren't a matter of historical relativism, fads, or discussion, and the better we all learn them, the better we'll like living in our world with each other. These virtues are part of most people's moral heritage, and there is nothing oppressive about teaching the common virtues of decency, civility, honesty, and fairness.

Too often we tend to think that certain issues are someone else's problem; the state will take care of it, whether it is pollution, homelessness, or the loneliness of elderly people. For Sommers this is part of a virtue ethics for grown-ups: *Don't assume that it is someone else's responsibility.* Don't hide from contemporary problems—take them on and contribute to their solution. Do your part to limit pollution. Think of how you can help homeless people. Go visit someone you know who is elderly and lonely. Virtues like these will benefit us all and are the kind we must learn to focus on if we are to make a success out of being humans living together.

This vision of personal virtues is probably the most direct call to a resurgence of moral values that has been produced so far within the field of philosophy. Of course, it doesn't even come close to the call for a revival of values that is heard every day in our contemporary society, usually from religious groups. Sommers, however, is arguing not for a revival of religious values but for a strengthening of basic concepts of personal responsibility and respect for other beings. Her claim is that few ethicists dare to stand by values and pronounce them good in themselves these days for fear of being accused of indoctrinating their students. For Sommers the list of values cited above is absolute: They can't be disputed. But we still might want to ask a fundamental question: How exactly does Sommers's call to virtuous living differ from old-time moralizing? Perhaps she is right that most people would agree her values are good, but there still seems to be something missing: the little safety valve that *reason* provides—in other words, a way to convince others who disagree with you about virtues and values. *How* do we convince college students that cheating is a bad thing? It can't be done simply by teaching them that honesty is a virtue; this might work for young children, but adolescents and adults need *reasons*. A moral story (such as Charles Dickens's *A Tale of Two Cities*) may tell us that self-sacrifice is a "far, far better thing" to practice than anything else, but I can easily disagree and dismiss it as propaganda. What has seemed indisputable at other times in history may seem unacceptable now. What seems indisputable to us may seem unacceptable to another culture. Sommers still needs to show that reason can provide evidence for why something is a virtue, even if it may seem obvious to most of us.

The Quest for Authenticity: Kierkegaard, Heidegger, Sartre, and Levinas

Within what is called "contemporary continental philosophy"—by and large European philosophy after World War I—one school of thought holds there is only one way to live properly and only one virtue to strive for: that of *authenticity*. This school of thought is *existentialism*. Although existentialism developed primarily at the hands of Jean-Paul Sartre as a response to the experience of meaninglessness in the day-to-day struggle of World War II, it has its roots in the writings of the Danish philosopher Søren Aabye Kierkegaard. In this section we take a look at Kierkegaard, Martin Heidegger, and Sartre, and in addition we will look at a philosopher, also coming out of the existential tradition, who in more recent years has emerged as a forceful voice for ethics as fundamental to human existence: Emmanuel Levinas. Whereas Kierkegaard's form of authenticity is ultimately conceived as a relationship between *oneself and God,* Heidegger's authenticity deals with one's relationship to *one's own form of existence,* and Sartre's authenticity deals with *one's relationship to oneself as a person making moral choices,* Levinas focuses on the relationship between *oneself and the Other*—our fellow human beings.

Kierkegaard's Religious Authenticity

During his lifetime (1813–1855), Kierkegaard was known locally, in Copenhagen, as a man of leisure who had a theology degree and spent his time writing convoluted and irritating attacks on the Danish establishment, including officials of the Lutheran church. Few people understood his points, because he was rarely straightforward in his writings and hid his true opinions under layers of pseudonyms and irony. The idea that there might be a great mind at work, developing what was to become one

Søren Kierkegaard (1813–1855), Danish philosopher, writer, and theologian, believed that there are three major stages in human spiritual development: the aesthetic stage, the ethical stage, and the religious stage. Not everyone goes through all stages, but true selfhood and personal authenticity can't happen until one has put one's complete faith in God.

of the most important lines of thought in the twentieth century, was obvious to no one at the time, in Denmark or elsewhere. As a matter of fact, Kierkegaard was working against the general spirit of the times, which was focused politically on the development of socialism and scientifically on the ramifications of Darwinism. People weren't ready to listen to ideas such as the value of personal commitment, the psychological dread that accompanies the prospect of total human freedom of the will, the relativity of truth, and the value of the individual. As it happened, though, such ideas were to become key issues for French and German existential philosophers a couple of generations after Kierkegaard's death.

There are two major, very different ways of approaching the strange writings of Søren Kierkegaard. You can dismiss him as a man who had a difficult childhood and as a consequence developed an overinflated ego with no sense of proportion as to the importance of events. In other words, you can view his writings as simply the product of an overheated brain that pondered the "great mystery" of Søren Kierkegaard's life and times. Or you can view his writings as words that speak to all humanity from a uniquely insightful point of view, which just happens to have its roots in events in Kierkegaard's own life. Among current scholars this second approach has become the prevailing one.

What was so eventful about Kierkegaard's life? Nothing much, compared to the lives of other famous people; but, contrary to most people, Kierkegaard analyzed everything that happened to him for all it was worth and with an eerie insight. He was born into a family of devout Lutherans (Lutheranism is the state religion in the Scandinavian countries and has been since the Protestant Reformation) and was the youngest boy born to comparatively old parents. Several of his older siblings died young, and for some reason both Søren and his father believed that Søren would not live long, either. His father's opinion had an extreme influence on the boy—an influence that Kierkegaard later analyzed to perfection, years before Freud described conflict and bonding between fathers and sons.

When his father was young and a shepherd in rural Denmark, he was overcome by hunger and cold one bleak day on the moors, and he stood up on a rock and cursed God for letting a child suffer like that. Shortly after this incident his parents sent him to Copenhagen as an apprentice, and his hard life was over. This was a psychological shock to him, because he had expected punishment from God for cursing him, and he waited for the punishment most of his life. He grew rich while others lost their money, and for that reason he expected God to punish him even more severely. The first tragic thing that happened to him was that he lost his young wife; however, two months later he married their maid, who was already pregnant at the time.

When Søren's older siblings died, his father thought that God's punishment had struck again, but otherwise his luck held while his guilt grew. It is possible that he then got the idea of letting his youngest son somehow make amends for him — take on the burden and strive for a reconciliation with God. In the Lutheran tradition there is no such thing as making a confession to your minister in order to "get things off your chest" — you alone must face your responsibility and handle your relationship with God. This means that you have direct access to God at any time, in your heart; you have a direct relationship to God. Your faith is a personal matter, and for Kierkegaard in particular the concept of faith was to become extremely personal.

Søren turned out to be an extraordinarily bright child, and his father devoted much time to his education, in particular to the development of his imagination. The two made a habit of taking walks — in their living room. Søren would choose where they were going — to the beach, to the castle in the woods, down Main Street — and his father would then describe in minute detail what they "saw." It was intellectually and emotionally exhausting for the boy, and scholars have ridiculed the father for his fancy, but today it is recognized by many that the combination of imagination and intellectual discipline is just about the best trait a parent can develop in a child, although one might say that this was a rather extreme way of going about it.

Kierkegaard was a young adult when his father died, and he understood full well the immense influence his father had on him. He wrote the following in *Stages on Life's Way* (1845), though he didn't let on that he was writing about himself:

> There was once a father and a son. A son is like a mirror in which the father beholds himself, and for the son the father too is like a mirror in which he beholds himself in the time to come. . . . the father believed he was to blame for the son's melancholy, and the son believed that he was the occasion of the father's sorrow — but they never exchanged a word on this subject.
>
> Then the father died, and the son saw much, experienced much, and was tried in manifold temptations; but infinitely inventive as love is, longing and the sense of loss taught him, not indeed to wrest from the silence of eternity a communication, but to imitate the father's voice so perfectly that he was content with the likeness . . . for the father was the only one who had understood him, and yet he did not know in fact whether he had understood him; and the father was the only confidant he had had, but the confidence was of such a sort that it remained the same whether the father lived or died.

So Kierkegaard *internalized* the voice of his father; as Freud would say, he made his father's voice his own *Superego*. This had the practical effect of prompting Kierkegaard finally to get his degree in theology (which his father had wanted him to do, but which he hadn't really wanted himself). Kierkegaard also internalized his father's

Edvard Munch, *The Scream* (1893). This image, which exists in more than fifty original versions, is the epitome of the feeling of angst. Munch described in his diary the moment that inspired him to do this work: "I was walking along the road with two friends — the sun was setting — all of a sudden the sky turned crimson — my friends walked on, and I froze, shaking with anguish — and I felt that through nature was passing a vast, endless scream." (Ulrich Bischoff, *Edvard Munch 1863–1944*, Köln: Benedikt Taschen GmbH & Co, 1989. Translated by Nina Rosenstand.)

guilt and rather gloomy outlook on life. (See Box 10.5 for another event that may have been influenced by his father.) Kierkegaard believed that everyone, even a child, has an intimate knowledge of what anguish feels like; he believed that you feel dread or anguish when you look to the future — you dread it because you realize you must make choices. This feeling, which has become known by the Danish/German word, *Angst,* is comparable, Kierkegaard says, to realizing that you're far out on the ocean and you have to swim or sink, act or die, and there is no way out. The choice is yours, but it is a hard choice, because living is a hard job. Suppose you refuse to make your own decisions and say, "Society will help me," or "The church will help me," or "My uncle will help me"? Then you have given up your chance to become a real person, to become *authentic,* because you don't accomplish anything spiritual unless you accomplish it yourself, by making the experience your own. Each person is an individual, but only through a process of individuation — choosing to make one's own decisions and take responsibility for them in the eyes of God — can a person achieve selfhood and become a true human individual. The truth you experience when you have reached this point is *your truth alone,* because only you took that particular path in life. Other people can't take a shortcut by borrowing "your truth" — they must find the way themselves. We can't, then, gain any deep insights about life from books or from teachers. They can point us in the right direction, but they can't spoon-feed us any truths.

This attitude is reflected in Kierkegaard's cryptic and disturbing assertion that *truth is subjective,* an idea that is vehemently disputed by scientists and philosophers alike. Some philosophers believe Kierkegaard meant there is no objective knowledge at all; we can never verify statements such as "2 + 2 = 4," "The moon circles the earth," and "It rained in Boston on April 6, 2002," because all such statements are, presumably, just a matter of subjective opinion, or what we call *cognitive relativism.* This would mean that we could never set any objective standard for knowledge. Although other philosophers, such as Friedrich Nietzsche, have actually worked toward such a radical viewpoint, Kierkegaard is not among them. He never says that *knowledge* is subjective, and to understand what he means we have to look more closely at what he says. His actual words are *"Subjectivity is Truth,"* and Kierkegaard scholars believe this to mean the following: There is no such thing as "Truth" with a capital *T* that we can just scoop up and call our own. The "meaning of life" is not something we can look up in a book or learn from anybody else, because *it just isn't there unless we find it ourselves.* There is no *objective* truth about life, only a *personal* truth, which will be a little bit different for each individual. It will not be vastly different, though, because when we reach the level at which we are truly personal, we will find that it corresponds to other people's experiences of individuation, too. In other words, the personal experience becomes a *universal* one — but only if you have gone through it yourself. This is the ultimate meaning of life and the ultimate virtue: to become an authentic human being by finding your own meaning. If you settle for accepting other people's view of life, you are no better than the evil magician Noureddin (or Jaffar, in the Disney movie version) in the story of Aladdin; he has no personal magic or talent himself, so he tries to steal it from the one who has, Aladdin.

Box 10.5   A KIND OF LOVE AND MARRIAGE
THAT WASN'T: REGINE OLSEN

An event of great importance in Søren Kierke-gaard's life was when he fell deeply in love for the first and only time. The girl's name was Regine Olsen, and she was the daughter of a minister. Regine and Søren became engaged, and he engaged himself in a new intellectual scrutiny: What was this feeling? Was it constant or a fluke? What might go wrong? Was it right for him to try to do something "universal" that everybody did, like get married and have chil-dren, or would it somehow interfere with his father's plans for him to be a sacrifice to God? Regine, a kind and loving girl, was utterly puz-zled at Søren's reluctance to accept that they were just young people in love. When they were together he was in a good mood and was confi-dent about their future together, but, when he was alone, the doubts started closing in on him. It appears that he felt he was not quite worthy of her, for some reason—perhaps because in years past he had visited a brothel, or perhaps because he couldn't quite explain his father's influence on him to her. Mostly, though, it was the shock of the physical attraction he felt to-ward her that distracted him, he thought, from becoming truly spiritual. During this period he began to understand one aspect of the Don Juan character: He realized that he loved Regine the most *when he was not with her* but was fanta-sizing about her. Once they were together his ardor cooled considerably. Eventually he de-cided that it was better for both of them if they broke up, but because nineteenth-century mores demanded that the woman, not the man, break off the engagement if her character were to remain stainless, he had to try to force Regine to break the engagement. This he did by being as nasty to her as he could, even though he still loved her. He embarked on a program he him-self had devised, alternating between playing the fool and the cynic; once when she asked him if

Regine Olsen, Søren Kierkegaard's fiancée, a gentle Copenhagen girl who did her best to understand the intellectual scruples of her boyfriend, who could not reconcile his devotion to God with the idea of physical attraction to a woman and a subsequent bourgeois marriage. This photo was taken a few years after Kierkegaard finally broke up with her. (Photo of Regine Schlegel [*née* Olsen] courtesy of The Royal Library, Copenhagen.)

he never intended to marry, he answered as nas-tily as he could, "Yes, in ten years when I've sown all my wild oats; then I'll need a young girl to rejuvenate me." For a long time he persisted in being rude to her, and she continued to for-give him, because she was very much in love with him. In the end he himself broke up with her, however, and she appears to have talked about killing herself. Kierkegaard wanted her to despise him, and a short time later she actually became engaged to a friend of theirs. After that, Kierkegaard never tired of talking about woman's fickle, stupid, and untrustworthy nature.

For Kierkegaard himself, truth is a religious truth: One must take on the concept of sin and responsibility and seek God's forgiveness directly, as an individual. But this is hard for most people to do, because we are born with quite another character. Typically humans are born into the *aesthetic stage:* the stage of sensuous enjoyment. Children obviously have a very strong interest in the joys of their senses, but if this persists into adulthood it can result in unhealthy character development, symbolized by the Don Juan type who loves to pursue the girl, but once he has seduced her he loses interest. She wants to get married, and he wants *out.* He leaves, only to fall in love with and pursue some other girl, and on it goes. Today we would say this is a person who *can't commit.* Kierkegaard makes the same basic observation but explains that this happens because the Don Juan type is steeped in sensuous enjoyment, which sours on itself: Too much of the same is not a good thing, but a person who is stuck in the aesthetic stage doesn't have any sense of what is morally right or wrong. Such knowledge usually comes as people mature and enter the *ethical stage* (although some people are stuck in the aesthetic stage forever).

In the ethical stage people realize that there are laws and conventions, and they believe that the way to become a good person is to follow these conventions. A fictional character from nineteenth-century middle-class Copenhagen becomes Kierkegaard's prototype for the ethical stage: Judge William, the righteous man who tries to be a good judge and a good husband and father. Scholars don't quite agree on how to evaluate this good and kind man, because the fact is that we are rarely certain when Kierkegaard is being serious and when he is being sarcastic. Kierkegaard also cites Socrates (whom he greatly admired) as an example of an ethical person. Although Socrates is commonly recognized as a truly courageous and virtuous man who strove to live (and die) the right way, Judge William doesn't come across as a heroic person; we even get the impression that he is actually a pompous, self-righteous, bourgeois bore who has his attention fixed on "doing the right thing" merely because society expects it of him. So it seems Kierkegaard wants to tell us that it isn't enough to follow the rules and become what everyone else thinks you ought to be; that way you exist only in the judgment of others. You have to take on responsibility for judging yourself, and the way you do that is by making a *leap of faith* into the *religious stage.* It isn't enough to judge your own life in terms of what makes sense according to society's rules and rational concepts of morality; what you must do in order to become an authentic person is leave the standards of society behind, including your love for reason and for things to make sense, and choose to trust in God, like Abraham, who made that same choice when he brought his son Isaac to be sacrificed, even though it didn't make sense to him. Reason and the rules of society can't tell you if the insight you reach as a religious person is the truth.

So why is Socrates not a perfect person? Why did he stay within the ethical stage and make no leap of faith to the religious stage, according to Kierkegaard? Because the leap was not available to him, since he didn't belong to the Judeo-Christian tradition. Socrates is an example of how far you can reach if you stay within the boundaries of reason. However, in the religious stage there is no objective measure of meaning. At this stage you take responsibility for yourself, but at the same time you give up your fate and place it in the hands of God. Finally you can become a true

Martin Heidegger (1889–1976), German philosopher and poet and a member of the National Socialist Party, believed authentic life is a life open to the possibility of different meanings. The feeling of *Angst* can help jolt us out of our complacency and help us see the world from an intellectually flexible point of view.

human being, a complete individual and person, because only in the religious stage can you realize what it means to say that "Subjectivity is Truth."

Heidegger's Intellectual Authenticity

Martin Heidegger is an enigmatic and controversial philosopher. He is enigmatic because he aims to make people break through the old boundaries of thinking by inventing new words and categories for them to think with. This means there is no easy way to read Heidegger; you must acquaint yourself with an entirely new vocabulary of key concepts and get used to a new way of looking at reality. In spite of his rather inaccessible style, though, Heidegger has become something of a cult figure in modern European philosophy. He is controversial because he was a member of the Nazi Party during World War II (see Box 10.6).

Heidegger sees human beings as not essentially distinct from the world they inhabit, in the same sense that traditional epistemology does: There is no "subject" on the inside of a person and no "object" of experience on the outside. Rather, humans are thrown into the world at birth, and they interact with it and in a sense "live" it. There is no such thing as a person who is distinct from his or her world of experience — we *are* our world of experience. This idea of interaction with the world from the beginning of life is one that Heidegger took over from his teacher and mentor Edmund Husserl, but he adds his own twist to it: What makes humans special is not that they are on the inside and the world is on the outside, but that they experience their *existence* differently than all other beings do. Humans *are there* for themselves; they are aware of their existence and of certain essential facts about that existence, such as their own mortality. So Heidegger calls humans "Being-there" (*Dasein*) rather than "humans." Things, on the other hand, don't know they exist, and to Heidegger neither do animals; an animal may know it is hungry, or in pain, or in heat, but it doesn't know its days are numbered, and that makes the difference. Our humanity consists primarily of our continuous awareness of death, our "Being-toward-death" (*Sein-zum-Tode*). On occasion we let ourselves get distracted, because this awareness is quite a burden on our minds, and we let ourselves forget. We become absorbed

Box 10.6   HEIDEGGER AND THE NAZI CONNECTION

At the time of Hitler's takeover of Germany in 1933, Martin Heidegger's philosophy professor, Edmund Husserl, was head of the philosophy department at the University of Freiburg. Husserl was already a famous philosopher, having developed the theory of *phenomenology*, a philosophical theory of human experience. Its main thesis is that there is no such thing as a consciousness that is empty at first and then proceeds to order and analyze the objects of sense experience; instead, our mind is already engaged in the process of experiencing the world from day one. We can't separate the concepts of the experiencing mind and the experience of the mind, and, because it is impossible for philosophy to say anything about a nonexperiencing mind and the unexperienced object-world, phenomenology sees its primary task as describing, as clearly as possible, the phenomenon of experience itself. Husserl had been the essential inspiration for many of Heidegger's writings; in fact, he had taken Heidegger under his wing when Heidegger was a young scholar. Husserl was Jewish, though, which meant that he was targeted for persecution by the new Nazi leaders. He was fired from his university position and eventually died as a result of Nazi harassment. Heidegger, his former student and protégé, profited from these events by taking over Husserl's position as department chair; indeed, it seems that he never raised any protest against the treatment of his old professor. At this time Heidegger joined the Nazi Party for, as he explained later, purely professional reasons: He couldn't have kept his university position without becoming a party member. This appears to be stretching the truth, for Heidegger never did anything at all to distance himself from the Nazi ideology during the war years. Today people are divided in their views on Heidegger; some feel that because of his Nazi association, his philosophy is tainted and must somehow contain elements of Nazi thinking. Others believe that Heidegger was essentially apolitical, although he was not very graceful about it; they think his philosophy should be viewed independent of his personal life.

in our jobs, our feelings, the gossip we hear, the nonsense around us. According to Heidegger, we often refer to what "They" say, as if the opinion of those anonymous others has some obvious authority. We bow to what "They" say and believe we are safe from harm and responsibility if we can get absorbed by this ubiquitous "They" (*Das Man*) and don't have to think on our own. In other words, we try to take on the safe and nonthinking existence-form of things — we objectify ourselves.

This does not make an authentic life, however, and in any event it is doomed to failure, because we can't forget so completely. Humans just can't become things, because we are the ones who understand the relationship between ourselves and things. When we do the dishes we understand what plates are for, what glasses are for, and why they must be cleaned. We understand the entire "doing dishes" situation. When we prepare a presentation on our computer we understand what a report is, what a computer is, and why the two have anything to do with ourselves, even if we may not understand what the report is for or how the computer works. In the end, humans are different because we can ask, What is it for? and understand the interconnections of the world we live in. We are asking, thinking creatures, and in order to regain our awareness of that fact, we must face our true nature. We may pretend to be nothing but victims of circumstances (I have to do the dishes; there is no other choice), but we also can choose to realize that we interact with our world and affect it. In *Being and Time* (1927), Heidegger calls this phenomenon (in his exasperating style) "An-already-thrown-into-the-world-kind-of-Being who is existing-in-relationship-to-existing-entities-within-that-world" (*Sich-vorweg-schon-sein-in* [*der-Welt*] *als Sein-bei* [*innerwelt-lich begegendem Seindenen*]). But he also describes it, in a slightly more down-to-earth fashion, as the structure of *care*. "Being-theres" always "care" about something, Heidegger says. This doesn't mean humans care *for* others, or *for* things—it merely means we are always *engaged* in something (the state of being engaged in something Heidegger called care—*Sorge*). Sometimes this involves caring for others, but mostly it involves engaging in our own existence: We fret, we worry, we look forward to something, we're concerned, we're content, we're disappointed about something—our health, our promotion, our family's well-being, our new kittens, or the exciting experiences we anticipate on our next vacation. We are always engaged in some part of our reality, unless we get caught up in another and deeper element of human nature: a *mood*, such as dread or anguish—Angst.

Heidegger's concept of *Angst* is related to Kierkegaard's: It does not involve fear of something in particular; it is, rather, the unpleasant and sometimes terrifying insecurity of not knowing where you stand in life and eventually having to make a choice—perhaps with little or no information about your options. For Kierkegaard this experience is related to a religious awakening, but for Heidegger the awakening is metaphysical: You realize that all your concerns and all the rules you live by are *relative,* in the deepest sense; you realize that you have viewed the world a certain way, within a certain frame, and now for some reason the frame is breaking up. A woman may feel angst if she loses her tenured job at a university, not just because she is worried about how she will provide for her family but because her worldview—her professional identity and sense of security—has been undermined. A young man may feel angst if he learns he has an incurable disease—not just because he is afraid to die but because "this isn't supposed to happen" to a young person. Children may feel angst if they are drawn into a divorce battle between their parents. A hitherto religious person may feel angst if he or she begins to doubt the existence of God, because this is the breakup of the ultimate framework. And humans may feel angst when they realize that their worldview is somehow not a God-given truth.

People whose attitude toward the world is *inauthentic* may experience the most fundamental form of angst. Heidegger himself states that if a Being-there is open to the possibility of different meanings in his or her reality, then he or she is living an authentic life. If, however, a Being-there does not want to accept the possibility that something may have a different meaning than he or she has believed up until now, then he or she is inauthentic. A typical trait of those who are inauthentic is that they become absorbed in just reacting to the things in their world—in driving the car, loading the laundry into the dryer, working on the computer, shopping, watching TV. Such persons think the predigested opinions of others or of the media are sufficient for getting by; they let themselves become absorbed in "The They," *das Man.*

But what does authenticity mean? Is it a call to "get in touch with yourself" by pulling away from the world? Or is it just a banal reminder to "stay open-minded"? Even worse, is it a built-in feature of being human, something we can't escape? Some Heidegger scholars see it not just as a call to reexamine yourself or to avoid hardening of the brain cells; to them authenticity is a fundamentally different attitude from one by which we allow the readily available worldviews of others to rule our lives. Being authentic means, for Heidegger, that you stop being absorbed by your doings and retain an attitude that "things may mean something else than what I expect." Only through this kind of intellectual flexibility can we even begin to think about making judgments about anything else, be they facts or people. So authenticity is, in a sense, remaining "open-minded," but it also involves performing a greater task by constantly forcing yourself to realize that reality is in flux, that things change, including yourself, and that you are part of a world of changing relationships. And *this* causes angst, because this means you have to give up your anchors and security zones as a matter of principle. In the end, angst becomes a liberating element that can give us a new and perhaps better understanding of ourselves and the world, but it is hard to deal with while we are in the midst of it.

Sartre's Ethical Authenticity

For some people angst is simply an existential fact, something we have to live with all our days. Jean-Paul Sartre is one of those persons. Sartre is the best known of the French existentialists of the mid-twentieth century; others include Albert Camus, Gabriel Marcel, and Simone de Beauvoir.

Sartre studied phenomenology (the discipline of the phenomenon of human consciousness and experience) in Berlin during the years between the two world wars, and he was well acquainted with the theories of Edmund Husserl and Martin Heidegger. During World War II Sartre was held by the Nazis as a prisoner of war, but he escaped and joined forces with the French Resistance movement. These experiences in many ways influenced his outlook on politics and on life in general: His political views were socialist and at times even Marxist, to a certain degree. Always politically active, Sartre may well be considered the most influential philosopher in twentieth-century Europe and possibly elsewhere, too—perhaps not as much because of his philosophical or literary writings (for Sartre was also a dramatist and novelist) as because of his intellectual inspiration. The existential movement may not have reflected a completely faithful version of the Sartrean philosophy, but it is certain that in his own century Sartre inspired the most extensive philosophical movement ever to reach people outside the academic world—the movement of existentialism.

Although existentialism as a fad in the 1950s became stereotyped as the interest of morose young people who dressed in black, chain-smoked late at night in small cafés, and read poems to each other about the absurdity of life, Sartre's existentialism had a whole other and more substantial content. Partly inspired by his experiences during the war, Sartre came to believe that there is no God, and, because there

French philosopher and writer Jean-Paul Sartre (1905–1980) was recognized as the most influential thinker in the existentialist movement. His best-known works of philosophy are the lecture "Existentialism as Humanism" (1945) and the much larger, much more intellectually challenging *Being and Nothingness* (1943).

is no God, there are no absolute moral rules, either. The concept that God's nonexistence makes everything permissible was not new at the time; it was well known to Western readers of Dostoyevsky and his novel *The Brothers Karamazov* as well as to readers of Friedrich Nietzsche. (See Box 10.7 for a discussion of Nietzsche's contributions to existentialism.) But it was given a new twist by Sartre. Instead of saying, as many other atheists did, that we can find our values in our own human context and rationality, Sartre held that without the existence of a God, there are no values, in the sense that there are no *objective* values. There is no master plan and, accordingly, nothing in the world *makes sense;* all events happen at random, and *life is absurd.* So what do we do? Give a shrug, and set about to make merry while we can? No, we must realize that because no values exist outside ourselves, we, as individuals in a community, become the *source* of values. And the process by which we create values is the process of *choice.*

When a person realizes that he or she has to make a choice and that the choice will have far-reaching consequences, that person may be gripped by *anguish* — Sartre uses the image of a general having to choose whether to send his soldiers to their death. It is not a decision that can be made lightly by a person of conscience, and such a person may worry about it a great deal, precisely because he doesn't know beforehand whether he will make the right decision. If he realizes the enormity of the situation and still makes his choice as best he can, shouldering whatever consequences may develop, he is living with *authenticity.* However, suppose the general says to himself, "I *have* to send the soldiers out, for the sake of my country/my reputation/the book I want to write." Then he is acting inauthentically: He is assuming that he *has no choice.* But for Sartre we always have a choice. Even the soldier who is ordered to kill civilians still has a choice, although he may claim he will be executed if he doesn't follow orders and thus has no choice. For Sartre there are some things that are worse than death, such as killing innocent civilians. So claiming that one's actions are somehow *determined* by the situation is inauthenticity or, as Sartre calls it, *bad faith.* Bad faith can be displayed in another way, too: Suppose the general is so distraught at having to make a choice that he says, "I just won't choose — I'll lock myself in the bathroom and wait until it is over." In that case, Sartre would say, the

Box 10.7   NIETZSCHE AND EXISTENTIALISM

The German philosopher Friedrich Nietzsche (1844–1900), one of the truly controversial figures in Western philosophy, is often credited with being one of the contributors to the French existentialism of the twentieth century. Sartre's view that life is absurd because there is no God has an early counterpart in Nietzsche's statement that "God is dead"; by this Nietzsche did not mean that Christ had died, or that there is no God, but that faith in God was waning if not gone altogether, and as a result the guarantees of stable, universal values provided by a faith in God had disappeared. For Nietzsche there are no absolute values in the absence of God; there are no values at all except those we as humans decide on. Whereas, for Sartre, the values we must decide on are the values that make us into beings who take responsibility for our lives as well as for the lives of others who look to us for guidance, Nietzsche suggested that the old Christian value system of loving one's neighbor and turning the other cheek must be scrapped, because it is the morality of a weak person, a "slave" who fears his "master," the strong-willed, self-made individual.

For Nietzsche, the "slave-morality" began in ancient times when slaves hated and feared their masters and resented anyone who wielded power over them. Whereas the values of the master would include pride, courage, and loyalty to one's clan, the values of the slave population included a fellowship with other slaves against the master. Because pride and courage are "master"-values, the slave prizes equality and meekness. Nietzsche speculates that when slavery was finally abolished in the ancient world, the former slaves took their value system with them and made it into social and religious ideals: social equality, resentment against anyone who stands above the crowd, and turning the other cheek in meekness. Nietzsche sees the slave-morality as a form of spiritual slavery to majority opinion. In

its place, he advocates a new "master-morality" in which values reflect respect for one's equal but disdain for weaker individuals; the person who is strong enough to create his own values in the face of absurdity has the right to forge ahead and make whatever life he wants for himself. (The use of the gender-specific *he* and *himself* here is deliberate: Nietzsche saw the powerful individual as male and displayed a generally misogynist approach to women in his writings.) For Nietzsche this meant a liberation from the hypocrisy of the late nineteenth century, in which, as he saw it, Europe was suffering from the fear of excelling, of anybody being stronger or more clever than a neighbor; he saw it as an opportunity for a gifted individual (an "Overman") to seize the day and create a life worth living. (Sometimes Nietzsche's term *Übermensch* is translated as "Superman," but many Nietzsche scholars tend to avoid that translation, since it so easily, and wrongly, associates to the familiar flying figure in a red cape. Instead the more direct translation, *Overman*, is used.) Nietzsche abhorred political despotism and would never have wanted his idea of the Overman to be transformed into an ideology of a "master race" because he saw the Overman as an individual, not a member of a group. But this is what happened when certain German politicians of the early twentieth century did a deliberately selective reading of his works. Early Nazi thinkers saw Nietzsche's ideas of the Overman as legitimizing the idea that some people (meaning some *races*) are nobler and more valuable than others, and many of Nietzsche's thoughts were worked into Nazi ideology. This association with the Nazis tainted Nietzsche's writings for many readers in the second half of the twentieth century, although he himself would probably have greatly disapproved of what Nazi thinkers got out of his philosophy.

(continued)

Box 10.7   NIETZSCHE AND EXISTENTIALISM *(continued)*

Nietzsche's thoughts on the Overman are generally referred to as a *transvaluation of values:* Through rejecting the herd mentality of the majority, the individual can reach an authentic set of values for himself. French existentialism has a clear line to Nietzsche's idea that life is absurd because God is dead, and there are no absolute values, but they part ways on the question of how to decide on a value system; there is no connection between French existentialism and Nietzsche's ideas of the right of the gifted individual to create his own values without taking other people into consideration.

general is deluding himself, because he is already making a choice — *the choice not to choose* — and thus he is in even less control of the consequences of his choice than if he actually had chosen a course of action. In our hearts we know this, and Sartre maintains we can never deceive ourselves 100 percent. There will always be a part of us that knows we are not like animals or inert things that can't make choices, simply because we are human beings, and human beings make choices, at least from time to time. (See Box 10.8 for Henri Bergson's view of choice — and the ethical choices he made.) Animals and things can exist without making choices, but humans can't, because humans are aware of their own existence and their own mortality; they have a relationship to themselves (they exist "for themselves," *pour soi*), whereas animals and things merely float through existence (they exist "in themselves," *en soi*). In *Being and Nothingness* (1943), Sartre says:

> Thus there are no *accidents* in a life; a community event which suddenly bursts forth and involves me in it does not come from the outside. If I am mobilized in a war, this war is *my* war; it is in my image and I deserve it. I deserve it first because I could always get out of it by suicide or by desertion; these ultimate possibilities are those which must always be present for us when there is a question of envisaging a situation. For lack of getting out of it, I have *chosen* it. This can be due to inertia, to cowardice in the face of public opinion, or because I prefer certain other values to the value of the refusal to join in the war (the good opinion of my relatives, the honor of my family, etc.). Any way you look at it, it is a matter of choice. . . . If therefore I have preferred war to death or dishonor, everything takes place as if I bore the entire responsibility for this war.

How does bad faith manifest itself? Sartre's famous example involves a young woman on a date. The woman's date makes a subtle move on her — he grasps her hand — and she doesn't quite know what to do. She doesn't want to offend him or to appear to be prudish, but she really doesn't know whether she wants to have a relationship with him, either. So she does nothing. She somehow manages to "detach" herself from the situation, as if her body really doesn't concern her, and, while he moves in on her, her hand seems not to belong to her at all. She looks at his face and pretends that she has no hand, no body, no sexuality at all. This, says Sartre, is bad faith: The woman thinks she can turn herself into a thing by acting

Box 10.8   HENRI BERGSON: LET YOUR TRUE SELF EMERGE

The French philosopher Henri Bergson (1859–1941) is not considered an ethicist per se, but his theories of consciousness and time perception involve an unusual concept of authenticity. For Bergson, humans live most of their lives subject to the demands of circumstances and customs and to the internalized opinions of others. Once in a while, however, their true selves break through. We can't live our lives without a certain amount of custom and regard for immediate circumstances, but if we are to remain true to what we really are, we need to listen to the murmurs of our own self that are hiding behind the facade of our civilized lives. And how do we know there is such a true self? We all have agonized over some decision, weighing the pros and the cons, coming up with the most logical answer or the one that will please us or seems to be the morally right thing to do. Then, sometimes, to our own surprise, we end up doing something else entirely. Afterward, when we are asked why, we answer that we just "had to do it"—we "couldn't help ourselves." This, says Bergson, is our true self emerging. It may happen to a person who has decided to marry someone, received all the gifts, ordered all the catering, and is standing at the altar—the person says NO! when she meant to say yes. If you experience, in the midst of your everyday life, a sense that all of a sudden there is *something you must do before it is too late,* such as running away with the circus, learning the art of fencing, going to Paris, or having a baby, this, says Bergson, is your true self trying to get your attention, and this is true authenticity—all the rest is a veneer. There are two major problems with Berg-

son's view. The first is that we have no assurance that this "deeper self" is actually a *good* self; the urge that comes over us may be to kill or betray someone. So it is doubtful that Bergsonian authenticity can actually be called a "virtue." The second problem is that Bergson thought this deeper self was proof that we have freedom of the will, but the whole point is that we have *no control* over what that self wants, and this is hardly what we normally mean by having a free will. Bergson's philosophy became immensely influential for just about all the French thinkers of the twentieth century, either as an inspiration or in creating a critical reaction. Sartre himself was greatly influenced by Bergson, and so was Emmanuel Levinas.

As a private person Bergson seems to have been a man of much integrity; in 1917 he went to the United States in order to fulfill a moral duty, as he saw it—to put an end to World War I. He also was utterly devoted to his daughter, who was hearing-impaired. In 1941 he lined up in the rain to be registered as a Jew by the Nazis during the Paris occupation; he contracted pneumonia, and it caused his death. He had wished to convert to Catholicism, but in view of Hitler's persecution of the Jews he decided to remain a member of the Jewish faith as a gesture of solidarity. These are the deeds of what we would call a person of moral virtue, so let us suppose we asked Bergson whether he did these things as a conscious, free decision. We might have received the answer that other people of moral virtue have given in similar situations: I did what I did because I could not do otherwise.

thinglike, but it is an illusion, because through it all she knows that sooner or later she has to say yes or no. What should she do in order to be authentic? She should realize that she has to make up her mind, even if she can't foresee whether she will want to have a relationship or not. Making up her mind will then create a new situation for her to react to, even though it is essentially unforeseeable. This openness to the unforeseen is part of being authentic. When we make a choice, Sartre says, we are taking on the greatest of responsibilities, for we are choosing not only for ourselves and our lives but for everyone else, too. Whatever choice we make sends out the message to everyone else that "this is okay to do." Therefore, through our choices we become role models for others. If we choose to pay our taxes, others will notice and believe that it is the right thing to do. If we choose to sell drugs to little children, somebody out there will see it and think it is a good idea. (Interestingly, doing something just because someone else is doing it is not enough for Sartre; as we saw in the section on Mayo's theory of role models, true authenticity must come from personal choices and not from just following role models.) Whatever we choose, even if we think it will concern only ourselves, actually will concern all of humanity, because we are endorsing our action as a general virtue. This is why choices can be so fraught with anxiety—and for Sartre this anxiety never goes away. We must live with it, and with the burden of the choice, forever. We are free to choose, but we are not free to refrain from choosing. In other words, *we are condemned to be free*.

So can we at least find comfort in the company of other people, close friends, lovers, or relatives who also have to face hard choices? For Sartre this presents no real solution; the presence of the Other—another person, different from myself—only reminds me of my absolute responsibility to make choices. And besides, the very presence of the Other is problematic in itself: When another person looks at me, and our eyes meet, he or she is always trying to dominate me, as I am trying to dominate him or her. For Sartre every human relationship is a game of dominance using the gaze as a tool of power, and this is especially the case for relationships between lovers. Essentially, we are alone with our choices and responsibilities.

But how can we make a choice if the world is absurd and all of our actions are meaningless? When we first experience the absurdity of existence we may feel nauseated, dizzy from the idea that reality has no core or meaning. But then we realize we must create a meaning; we must choose for something to matter to us. For Sartre the social conditions of France became a theme that mattered to him, but you might choose something else—your family, your job, or your Barbie doll collection. Any kind of life project will create values, as long as you realize that the world is still absurd in spite of your project! If you think you are "safe" with your family or your job or your doll collection—if you think you've created a rock-solid meaning for your life—then you've fallen back into bad faith. This is the case with the waiter (another of Sartre's examples) who wants so badly to become the perfect waiter that he takes on a "waiter identity" that provides answers to everything: how to speak, what to say, how to walk, where to go. The waiter has not chosen a project; he has turned himself into a thing, an "in itself" that doesn't have to choose anymore. Living authentically means living in anguish, always on the edge—confronting the absurdity of life and courageously making choices in the face of meaninglessness. When something you care about appears, then you will know what to do. The French philosopher and novelist Simone de Beauvoir, Sartre's significant other and his collaborator on the subject of existentialism, puts it like this: "Any man who has known real loves, real revolts, real desires, and real will knows quite well that he has no need of any outside guarantee to be sure of his goals."

Box 10.9   THE ART OF BEING HUMAN: ERIK ERIKSON

The quest for authenticity may be a primarily continental philosophy, but the ideal of being true to oneself is very much part of the Anglo-American tradition, too. William Shakespeare says, in *Hamlet,*

> This above all: to thine own self be true,
> And it must follow, as the night the day
> Thou can'st not then be false to any man.

In American psychology the idea of authenticity has had its own proponent, the influential German-born analyst Erik Erikson (1902–1994). Erikson believed that a psychologically mature human being has gone through several stages of personality development. In passing from stage to stage, a person may experience a sense of loss of self, an "identity crisis" (a term coined by Erikson), especially during adolescence. If the person can resolve the crisis successfully, he or she is on the way to becoming a stronger and more balanced human being. If the crisis remains with the person, he or she will develop psychological problems later in life. People who have managed to emerge successfully from each crisis eventually will achieve "ego integrity," an inner harmony and balance of the mind that gives the ego a sense of meaning and fulfillment. Persons with ego integrity don't agonize over "what might have been." Such persons don't dwell on how their parents did them wrong, how bad choices were made by others that affected their lives, or how short life is. Such persons take responsibility for their actions but aren't weighed down by guilt about things over which they have no control. Persons who lose their ego integrity experience fear of death and despair at lost chances and start up new projects in their panic over the brevity of life. A person doesn't need to be well educated in order to achieve ego integrity — people who have achieved it can be found in all cultures — but cultures can help individuals through their crises by supporting their transition and welcoming them on the other side. Erikson says that healthy children will not fear life if their elders have integrity enough not to fear death.

It is conceivable that the concept of ego integrity might change with changing times and places. In some cultures we might find it to mean a reconciliation with *fate* — accepting what life has handed you and learning to love it, as hard as that might be. Or it might mean putting your faith in the will of God and not asking why. In other cultures, though, this might be considered "bad faith." True ego integrity would then consist of a courageous realization of the unpredictability of everything and of not losing courage when facing an uncaring universe.

Suppose you decide you'll do something about your life *tomorrow*? That *next year* you'll write that novel? Or go back to college? Suppose you decide you *should have* married someone else, had children, gone to see the Pyramids, or become a movie actor? Then there is not much hope for your authenticity, says Sartre, because your virtue lies only in what you accomplish, not in choices you make about things you are *planning* to do. If you never start that book, you have no right to claim you are a promising writer. If you never tried to become an actor, then you can't complain that you're a great undiscovered talent. We are not authentically anything but what we *do,* and we are hiding from reality if we think we are more than that. Like Aristotle, Sartre links the value of our virtue with the success of our conduct: Intentions may be good, but they aren't enough. (For an American outlook on authenticity, see Box 10.9).

The Lithuanian-French philosopher Emmanuel Levinas (1905–1995) believed that ethics is the deepest and most primary human experience: We see the other person looking at us and we hear him or her talking to us, and we understand that this is someone whose life is precious and irreplaceable. The Other commands us not to kill, and we feel obliged to place his or her needs above our own.

Levinas and the Face of the Other

Emmanuel Levinas (1905–1995) was born the same year as Sartre, but whereas Sartre became a philosopher of the mid-twentieth century, Levinas was a late bloomer and became one of the leading voices of French philosophy only in the last decades of the twentieth century. His most important works are *Totality and Infinity* (1961; translated into English, 1969) and *Otherwise Than Being or Beyond Essence* (1974; translated into English, 1981). In many ways his experience parallels that of Sartre. He, too, became interested in the philosophies of Husserl and Heidegger in Germany; indeed, his interest preceded Sartre's by more than a decade, and it was Levinas, not Sartre, who introduced these ideas to the French public with books on Husserl and Heidegger. (According to Simone de Beauvoir, Sartre, when reading Levinas's book on Husserl, exclaimed, "This is the philosophy I wanted to write!"—although Sartre afterward claimed he could do it better.) Like Sartre, Levinas was a prisoner of war during World War II, doing forced labor for the Nazis; also like Sartre, he developed a highly personal philosophy based on his early interest in German phenomenology. Both became recognized as distinguished scholars within the field of philosophy. But here the similarities end. Sartre was French by birth, whereas Levinas—born a Lithuanian—became French by choice. Whereas Sartre's Catholic belief in God came to an end, Levinas never lost his Jewish faith. Whereas Sartre developed his existential philosophy based on the fundamental anguish of the choice—an essentially lonely enterprise—Levinas sees the bottom line of all human existence as the encounter with the Other, not in a competition for dominance, as Sartre sometimes would express it, but in coming face-to-face with another human being and realizing that the Other is alive, looking at *you*, speaking to *you*, needing *you* to recognize him or her as someone who is fundamentally different from you and fundamentally vulnerable. Levinas maintains that "ethics precedes ontology": Understanding the needs of the Other and *my* own responsibility for the needs of the Other comes before any philosophy about existence. That is why Levinas has described ethics as "First Philosophy": This is the foundation and the beginning point, which we are normally not even aware of but where we encounter what is really important in life: the face of the Other.

As we have seen, many modern theories of ethics state that everyone ought to be treated as *equal*. Bentham talks about how each person has one vote in terms of his or her pain and pleasure; Kant claims that all persons should be viewed as ends in themselves; Rawls points out that justice consists of treating all persons with fairness regardless of who they are. The Golden Rule is in effect even in philosophical systems that are otherwise opposed to each other. For Levinas there is nothing wrong with the political quest for equality, but this quest is not fundamental to ethics; what is fundamental is another experience altogether. When I meet another human being, another face, the ethical reaching out to that person consists in realizing precisely that we are *not* equal. Levinas is not saying I am "better" than the Other. On the contrary, the Other counts more than I: The Other, no matter who he or she is, is a person in need, always "poor" and asking for my help and understanding; first and foremost the Other is telling me, "You must not kill." As Levinas says in a dialogue with Richard Kearney:

> The approach to the face is the most basic mode of responsibility. As such, the face of the other is verticality and uprightness; it spells a relation of rectitude. The face is not in front of me (*en face de moi*) but above me; it is the other before death, looking through and exposing death. Secondly, the face is the other who asks me not to let him die alone, as if to do so were to become an accomplice in his death. Thus the face says to me: you shall not kill. . . . In ethics, the other's right to exist has primacy over my own, a primacy epitomized in the ethical edict: you shall not kill, you shall not jeopardize the life of the other. The ethical rapport is asymmetrical in that it subordinates my existence to the other.

Of course, this is not really a description of most actual encounters between people; fortunately, we rarely find ourselves in situations in which we are begging for our lives. But for Levinas this encounter is the underlying foundation beneath all human encounters: The face is naked, the eyes are pleading, the voice speaks. For Levinas, the true ethical moment happens when we are being addressed by the Other. In response, it is not enough to say, "Well, he or she is just the same as I am, we are all humans." That, to Levinas, is not going far enough, or it is going too far: That would be making us all into some collective form of being, some anonymous humanity. Instead, we are supposed to say, "He/she is completely different from what I am, so his/her life is my responsibility." This is the unequal, asymmetrical situation, the *alterity* (otherness) of the Other, which makes the other human individual our responsibility. In particular it is the Other's voice that calls to us, more so than looking into his or her eyes. Sartre's existential philosophy has often alluded to the power of the *gaze,* the eyes trying to dominate the other person's, but Levinas sees the typical encounter between humans as not only a visual but also an aural experience: You hear the voice speak to *you,* and you respond by being there for the other person. And when you respond with your whole being in acceptance that the Other is there, demanding attention, then you become special to the Other, you become *irreplaceable*. For Levinas, humans in an ethical relationship with each other recognize the Other as irreplaceable, "non-substitutable." The loss of the Other can't be

Box 10.10   KIERKEGAARD, LEVINAS, AND ABRAHAM

You may remember a section in Chapter 2 dealing with the biblical story of Abraham about to sacrifice his son Isaac to God. To briefly recapitulate: Abraham believes that God has told him to sacrifice his and Sarah's only son, so he takes young Isaac up on the mountain, letting Isaac carry the firewood; Isaac is wondering where the sacrificial lamb is, but Abraham explains that God will provide. On the top of the hill, they build the sacrificial altar, and Abraham straps his son down and is ready to slaughter him when the voice of God intervenes and rewards Abraham for his faith in God's command. Kierkegaard (whom you now know better than you did in Chapter 2) said that Abraham's attempt to sacrifice his son violated the ethics of the community, but believing that he served God's purpose took Abraham to a higher stage — to the religious stage, which he had to ascend to by a leap of faith — bringing him into direct contact with God. Levinas, on the other hand, believes

that Kierkegaard misunderstood the entire situation: The important moment is not that Abraham disregards his beloved son for God's sake, but that Abraham through the voice of Isaac himself is called back from the brink, back to the ethical demands of life and fatherhood; in a sense, Isaac's face intervenes on his own behalf. Levinas says that for Kierkegaard ethics is the rigid rules of the community that have to be overcome in order to be religious. For Levinas, however, ethics is the Other's voice speaking to one. Essentially, Levinas sees Abraham as someone who almost made a monumental mistake, but he sees Kierkegaard as having made the mistake of believing that the leap of faith was a matter between the individual and God alone and that to get there one had to leave behind the world of the others with their rules and morals. For Levinas, ethics, and in a sense also faith itself, takes place between one person and the Other.

made up for by finding another. (Box 10.10 explains how Levinas would look at the story of Abraham and Isaac in terms of the face of the Other.)

So is this the way things actually are between people, or is it the way Levinas thinks they ought to be? In other words, is he being descriptive or normative? Elegantly, Levinas answers that the encounter is something that happens before we even think in such categories: The encounter with the Other is not merely an actual situation but the framework within which human encounters take place, so it is the way we actually meet, deep down before we start speculating about existence and responsibility and all the rest, but it is also in a sense the way one ought to meet each individual person — because (sadly) not everyone sees other people as unique individuals who are supposed to be held higher than one holds oneself; some people even see others as "merely a means to an end."

The ultimate disregard for the Other is to Levinas represented by the Nazi Holocaust (in which he lost his entire Lithuanian family). The Holocaust represents the utter evil of putting people through torture and to death not for their convictions but for their ancestry. The fact that Heidegger had been involved with the Nazi Party made Levinas say, in later years, that "one can forgive many Germans, but there are some Germans it is difficult to forgive. It is difficult to forgive Heidegger." And, yet, the dreadful event of the Nazi death camps, where, in Levinas's words, God was not present but the devil was, in some roundabout way did not destroy his belief in God; he says,

> Before the twentieth century, all religion begins with the promise. It begins with the "Happy End." It is the promise of heaven. Well then, doesn't a phenomenon like Auschwitz invite you, on the contrary, to think the moral law independent of the Happy End? That is the question. . . . It is easier to tell myself to believe without promise than it is to ask it of the other. That is the idea of asymmetry. I can demand of myself that which I cannot demand of the other.
>
> Interview with Wright, Hughes, and Ainley, in Bernasconi and Wood (1988).

So ethics becomes the highest form of religious faith: Without the relief of a promise of heaven, we must be there for the Other, serve the Other for no reward at all. According to Levinas, "Faith is not a question of the existence or non-existence of God. It is believing that love without reward is valuable."

With his philosophy that we look to the Other as someone we must give our love to but who doesn't have to return it (an ethic that is sometimes used to describe the relationship between parent and child), Levinas's ethics stands as a complete renewal within the European tradition of autonomy, finding personal integrity in a relationship of the individual not to oneself but to someone else. In this he comes closest of all the modern European philosophers to an ethics of virtue, seeing the ultimate virtue as the willingness to serve the Other; as a thinker within the modern tradition of authenticity, he regards the asymmetrical relationship to the Other as the truly authentic relationship. Levinas's philosophy, which today perhaps more than any other philosophy stands for kindness and sacrifice of one's self for the sake of others, is nevertheless not without controversy.

Some critics see his thinking as a kind of throwback to a time when ethics were expressed in personal, even religious, terms, and further, in terms of male and female. And for some critics this throwback is a serious weakness. In a disarmingly innocent way, in his early writings Levinas insisted that the Other is, essentially, feminine (something that Sartre, by the way, has also been criticized for asserting): "The feminine is other for the masculine being not only because of a different nature but also inasmuch as alterity is in some way its nature."

In later years he modified his position, but it still generates discussion. Levinas's critics see this as just another statement in the long line of sexist philosophies in which a male point of view pronounces women to be "deviant" or "different" or "really kind of strange," and which assumes that women accept this as an objective truth. Seen in the light of this old tradition, it is small wonder that many women philosophers, most notably Simone de Beauvoir (see Chapter 11), have accused Levinas of being reactionary, deliberately taking a man's point of view, seeing himself as the Absolute and the woman as the Other.

But even if Levinas could be said to hold the opinion that woman is completely different from man, it does not mean he thinks woman is inferior to man; on the contrary, according to his theory of the Other, if anything is absolute, it is precisely the Other. In his later years, Levinas would talk about the feminine virtues of the home, of the welcoming feminine touch, the quality of "discretion" of the feminine face as opposed to the male face with its authority and self-assertion, but always in positive terms (however, whether you regard "feminine" as inferior or superior, it is still sexism to a *classical* feminist). A feminist philosopher, Tina Chanter, suggests that Levinas is in fact praising the feminine qualities as true *human* qualities; "feminine" does not mean biologically female to Levinas, says Chanter, and "masculine" doesn't mean "male"; rather, each term stands for features in all of us. This interpretation (in some ways similar to the gender philosophy of the psychoanalyst Carl Jung) may give another dimension to Levinas's controversial words about the Other as feminine.

Study Questions

1. Evaluate the question of character versus conduct in politics. Which do you think is of the highest importance for a person running for (or elected to) office to have: personal integrity or a view on government that you agree with? Is there an alternative? Explain.

2. Discuss the question of character versus conduct in personal matters: Philippa Foot claims, with Aristotle, that a person who has a good character is slightly better than a person who has to control himself or herself. Kant would say the opposite. Explain these viewpoints. Which do you agree with more and why?

3. Bernard Mayo wants us to emulate role models. Can you think of a person — a historical figure, a living person, or a fictional character — whom you would like to emulate? Explain who and why. What are some of the problems involved with the idea of emulating role models?

4. Levinas is reluctant to include animals as being with "faces." Do you agree that ethics can be extended to animals only as a secondary move patterned after ethics toward humans? Or should ethics toward animals be a primary form of ethics? Can Levinas's own theory be redesigned to include animals?

Primary Readings and Narratives

The first two Primary Readings are short excerpts from the writings of Søren Kierkegaard, one from *Johannes Climacus* and one from *Either/Or,* Volume II. The third Primary Reading is an excerpt from an interview with Emmanuel Levinas, conducted by three graduate students, Tamra Wright, Peter Hughes, and Alison Ainley, and published as "The Paradox of Morality: An Interview with Emmanuel Levinas." All three Narratives explore, in one way or another, the existential themes of choice, angst, authenticity, and responsibility. The first is a summary of an episode from Woody Allen's film *Hannah and Her Sisters* about a hypochondriac in the throes of existential angst. The second is a summary of Jean-Paul Sartre's classic play *No Exit* about three souls condemned to live in each other's company forever, in hell. The third is a summary of the film *A Few Good Men,* which raises the moral question of whether "I was just carrying out an order" is ever an acceptable excuse.

Primary Reading

Johannes Climacus

SØREN KIERKEGAARD

Written 1842–1843, first published 1912. Excerpt translated by Nina Rosenstand.

Kierkegaard used to speak through many aliases, and some we are not supposed to take seriously; Johannes Climacus became one of his most serious and personal aliases, and here we read about Johannes's childhood, which exactly resembles Kierkegaard's own.

His father was a very strict man, apparently dry and prosaic, but under this coat of coarse weave he hid a glowing imagination which not even his advanced years managed to conceal. When Johannes on occasion would ask permission to go out, he was most often refused; however, on one occasion his father offered, as a form of compensation, to take a walking tour up and down the floor. This was at first glance a poor substitute, and yet this turned out to be like the coarse coat: It hid something else entirely. The suggestion was accepted, and the decision where to go was left entirely to Johannes. So they left by the gate, walked to a nearby castle in the woods, to the beach, or up and down the streets, anywhere Johannes wanted, because for his father nothing was impossible. While they were walking up and down the floor, his father would describe everything they saw; they said hello to people passing by, coaches rolled noisily past, drowning out his father's voice; the fruits of the vendor woman looked more inviting than ever. He related everything so accurately, so vividly; he described so immediately in the most minute detail things that were familiar to Johannes, and whatever Johannes didn't know he described in such elaborate and educational manner that he, after having walked with his father for half an hour, was just as tired as if he had been outside an entire day. . . . For Johannes it was as if his father was the Good Lord, and he himself was his favorite who was allowed to come up with silly ideas to his heart's content; for he was never turned down, his father was never perturbed, everything was included and happened to Johannes's satisfaction.

Primary Reading

Either/Or

SØREN KIERKEGAARD

Excerpt from Volume II, 1843. Translated by Nina Rosenstand.

In this text, written shortly after Kierkegaard broke up with Regine Olsen, he speaks with the voice of Judge Williams, admonishing a friend who refuses to make choices (about

> The choice itself is decisive for the content of one's personality. . . . If you imagine a first mate on his ship at the moment when it has to make a turn, then he might say, I can do either this or that. However, if he is not a poor navigator, he will also be aware that the ship is all the while moving ahead at its regular speed, and that he thus only has an instant where it is immaterial whether he does one thing or the other. So it is with a human being: Should he forget to take account of the speed, there comes at last a moment when it is no longer a question of an either-or, not because he has chosen, but because he has refrained from choosing—which is the same as saying, because others have chosen for him, because he has lost his own self.

Study Questions

1. Do you approve of Kierkegaard's father's teaching technique? Explain. Are there similarities between his technique and virtual reality? Are there differences?

2. Who do you think Kierkegaard identifies most with, the friend who doesn't want to choose, or Williams? Or perhaps both?

3. Compare the second excerpt with Sartre's theory of the existential choice.

 Primary Reading

The Paradox of Morality: An Interview with Emmanuel Levinas

Interview conducted in 1986 by Tamra Wright, Peter Hughes, and Alison Ainley. Excerpt.

Three graduate students from the University of Warwick interviewed Levinas after taking a seminar on one of his books, *Totality and Infinity*. In the section on Levinas you read about one of the controversial points in his philosophy, his remarks about the feminine. Here you have a hint of another controversy: Levinas's statements about the face of another human being as the fundamental ethical experience; does this imply that we can't have an ethical relationship to a nonhuman—an animal, for instance?

> *Is the face a simple or a complex phenomenon? Would it be correct to define it as that aspect of a human being which escapes all efforts at comprehension and totalization, or are there other characteristics of this phenomenon which must be included in any definition or description of the face?*

The face is a fundamental event. Among the many modes of approach and diverse ways of relating to being, the action of the face is special and, for this reason, it is very difficult to give it an exact phenomenological description. The phenomenology of the face is very often negative.

What seems essential to me is, for example, the manner in which Heidegger understood the *Zeug*—that which comes to hand, the instrument, the thing. He understood it as irreducible prototype. The face is similar in that it is not at all a representation, it is not a given of knowledge, nor is it a thing which comes to hand. It is an irreducible means of access, and it is in ethical terms that it can be spoken of. I have said that in my analysis of the face it is a demand; a demand, not a question. The face is a hand in search of recompense, an open hand. That is, it needs something. It is going to ask you for something. I don't know whether one can say that it is complex or simple. It is, in any case, a new way of speaking of the face.

When I said that the face is authority, that there is authority in the face, this may undoubtedly seem contradictory: it is a request and it is an authority. You have a question later on in which you ask me how it could be that if there is a commandment in the face, one can do the opposite of what the face demands. The face is not a force. It is an authority. Authority is often without force. Your question seems to be based on the idea that God commands and demands. He is extremely powerful. If you try not doing what he tells you, he will punish you. That is a very recent notion. On the contrary, the first form, the unforgettable form, in my opinion, is that, in the last analysis, he can not do anything at all. He is not a force but an authority. . . .

Is it necessary to have the potential for language in order to be a "face" in the ethical sense?

I think that the beginning of language is in the face. In a certain way, in its silence, it calls you. Your reaction to the face is a response. Not just a response, but a responsibility. These two words [*réponse, responsabilité*] are closely related. Language does not begin with the signs that one gives, with words. Language is above all the fact of being addressed . . . which means the saying much more than the said.

In the word "comprehension" we understand the fact of taking [*prendre*] and of comprehending [*comprendre*], that is, the fact of englobing, of appropriating. There are these elements in all knowledge [*savoir*], all familiarity [*connaissance*], all comprehension; there is always the fact of making something one's own. But there is something which remains outside, and that is alterity. Alterity is not at all the fact that there is a difference, that facing me there is someone who has a different nose than mine, different colour eyes, another character. It is not difference, but alterity. It is alterity, the unencompassable, the transcendent. It is the beginning of transcendence. You are not transcendent by virtue of a certain different trait.

In totalization there is certainly the fact of inclusion, of adding up. Men can be synthesized. Men can easily be treated as objects. We speak to the other who is not encompassed, who, on the contrary, is the one who offers his face to you.

The analysis can go further. I'm not saying that it is completed. The idea that is very important to me is frailty, the idea of being in a certain sense much less than a thing. One can kill, annihilate. It is easier to annihilate than to possess the other.

For me, these two starting points are essential: the idea of extreme frailty, of demand, that the other is poor. It is worse than weakness, the superlative of weakness. He is so weak that he demands. This, of course, is the beginning of the analysis, because the way in which we behave concretely is different. It is more complex. In particular because, what seems to me very important, is that there are not only two of us in the world. But I think that everything begins as if we were only two. It is important to recognize that the idea of justice always supposes that there is a third. But, initially, in principle, I am concerned about justice because the other has a face. . . .

If animals do not have faces in an ethical sense, do we have obligations towards them? And if so, where do they come from?

It is clear that, without considering animals as human beings, the ethical extends to all living beings. We do not want to make an animal suffer needlessly and so on. But the prototype of this is human ethics. Vegetarianism, for example, arises from the transference to animals of the idea of suffering. The animal suffers. It is because we, as human, know what suffering is that we can have this obligation.

The widespread thesis that the ethical is biological amounts to saying that, ultimately, the human is only the last stage of the evolution of the animal. I would say, on the contrary, that in relation to the animal, the human is a new phenomenon. And that leads me to your question. You ask at what moment one becomes a face. I do not know at what moment the human appears, but what I want to emphasize is that the human breaks with pure being, which is always a persistence in being. This is my principal thesis. A being is something that is attached to being, to its own being. That is Darwin's idea. The being of animals is a struggle for life. A struggle for life without ethics. It is a question of might. Heidegger says at the beginning of *Being and Time* that *Dasein* is a being who in his being is concerned for this being itself. That's Darwin's idea: the living being struggles for life. The aim of being is being itself. However, with the appearance of the human—and this is my entire philosophy—there is something more important than my life, and that is the life of the other. That is unreasonable. Man is an unreasonable animal. Most of the time my life is dearer to me, most of the time one looks after oneself. But we cannot admire saintliness. Not the sacred, but saintliness: that is, the person who in his being is more attached to the being of the other than to his own. I believe that it is in saintliness that the human begins; not in the accomplishment of saintliness, but in the value. It is the first value, an undeniable value. Even when someone says something bad about saintliness, it is in the name of saintliness that he says it.

Study Questions

1. What does Levinas mean by saying, "The face is a hand in search of recompense, an open hand. That is, it needs something. It is going to ask you for something"?

2. Do you agree with Levinas that "there is something more important than my life, and that is the life of the other"? Why or why not?

3. Do you agree with Levinas that the prototype for all ethics, including ethical treatment of animals, is human ethics, based on the experience of the human face? Why or why not?

Narrative

Hannah and Her Sisters

WOODY ALLEN (SCREENWRITER AND DIRECTOR)

Film, 1986. Summary.

Can a comedy deal seriously with issues such as angst and the absurdity of life? Absolutely, at least when the director is Woody Allen. We will look primarily at the character played by Allen — Mickey, a hypochondriac who is always running to doctors believing he has some form of terminal illness. While his friends engage in stealthy extramarital affairs and other self-realization projects, Mickey finds that he is experiencing some dizziness and has lost some hearing in one ear, so he goes to see his doctor. He fully expects the doctor to shrug it off as an imagined disease as usual, but this time the doctor suggests X rays, because, although it might be just a minor problem, it also might be a brain tumor.

Mickey is plunged into the abyss of despair; he tries to make deals with God. He can't believe it is happening, and yet he believes it. On the X ray there is an ominous spot, and the doctor schedules a CAT scan. The idea of death, as often as he has played around with it, now seems both real and unfathomable: "You're in the middle of New York City, this is your town, you're surrounded by people and traffic and restaurants — how can you just one day — vanish?"

Finally, in the doctor's office, the doctor has all the charts and X rays out and shows him with clinical exactitude where the tumor is, saying there is nothing that anyone can do about it. The hypochondriac's worst nightmare is coming true.

And yet — a split second later — we find that he has just *imagined* the doctor speaking the words of doom; now the doctor comes in and says what Mickey was hoping to hear, that they can't find out why he has a minor hearing loss, but it is not a tumor. Mickey should be revived and elated, right? At first he is, but the close call has profoundly disturbed his equilibrium; he comes to the realization that life is absurd and meaningless because it can be threatened, and regarded, so casually. If we can be gone in an instant, what's the point of living? he asks. His release from *fear* has actually deepened his existential angst, for now he sees that there are no guarantees, no master plan, and no ready-made meaning for him to hold on to. If life is going to come to an end anyway, why bother doing anything? Nothing is worthwhile anymore; the hypochondriac has become a *nihilist*.

If only he could believe in God. . . . Mickey seeks help from religious experts, from Catholic priests to Hare Krishna converts (much to his Jewish mother's chagrin — couldn't he just give his own religion a try?). And yet one day Mickey is feeling better. He meets an old acquaintance, his ex-wife's nutty sister, and tells her the story: Recently he had reached the bottom of the abyss and was toying with the idea of killing himself. He actually held a rifle to his head, pondering the question of life and death, when the gun went off, shattering a window! He had held the trigger so tightly that it just went off, but because of his sweaty palms it slipped out of his hands. In a state of total confusion he went out, walked the streets of New York, and ended up in a revival movie theater where they were showing an old Marx Brothers comedy. Here he recaptured the meaning of life: "What if the worst is true—there is no God and you only go around once. Don't you want to be part of the experience?"

So Mickey finds meaning in absurdity, and he finds marriage and children with his ex-wife's nutty sister.

Study Questions

1. Do you think such an experience as Mickey's is common?
2. Has Mickey learned Sartre's lesson about living with absurdity, or hasn't he?
3. How would Sartre suggest that Mickey solve his problem of existential angst? Would Erik Erikson have a suggestion? What might Levinas suggest, if anything?

 *Narrative*

No Exit

JEAN-PAUL SARTRE

Play, 1966. Summary.

For Sartre there is no life after death, for there is no God to send the soul to one realm or the other. But as a dramatist and a novelist Sartre played with the idea of hell nevertheless. In the drama *No Exit* three characters find themselves in a locked room with no windows: a middle-aged man, Garcin; a young woman, Estelle; and a lesbian woman, Inez. They all know that they are dead and in hell, and they are highly surprised that there is no torture chamber—merely a room decorated in bad taste. They don't know each other, but they are forced to spend an unforeseeable amount of time together in this room, interrupted only occasionally by a prison guard, the "valet." For a while they can "glimpse" the life of the living, but that soon fades, and all they have is each other. Each pretends to wonder what the others have done to be sent to hell, but, as Inez says, they are all "murderers." Estelle killed her baby, Inez killed her lover's husband (or at least drove him to his death), and Garcin killed the spirit in his wife by his cruelty to her. What tortures Garcin most, though, is that he is a deserter. He, who always thought he would live and die bravely, never had a chance to prove himself, he says—he died too soon. But Inez corrects him:

> One always dies too soon—or too late. And yet one's whole life is complete at that moment, with a line drawn neatly under it, ready for the summing up. You are—your life, and nothing else.

Estelle is beginning to find Garcin attractive (she is used to men fawning over her). Inez is falling in love with Estelle, and Garcin is himself attracted to Estelle but prefers that each of them stay in their own corner rather than hurt each other. But the stage is set, and they can't help interacting. All three try to manipulate each other; they team up, two against the third one. They constantly scrutinize each other (for in hell you have no eyelids you can close). They need each other for comfort and support, but they have no trust in each other. They realize that there is no need for torture instruments and devils—they are each other's torturers. The room and the other two people in it *are* hell for them: Their punishment is spending an eternity with each other in a hostile triangle. In the end Garcin succeeds in opening the locked door to their room, but now all three are reluctant to leave, because for each that would mean the other two had won the dominance game. All three stay to torment each other, forever.

On the symbolic level Sartre is—probably—not talking about any real life after death, but about the human condition. He is saying we make life a hell for each other, because we are so very good at manipulating each other, and every human relationship, even that between lovers, has at its core a battle for power and dominance. Sartre concludes with one of his most famous lines: "Hell is—other people."

Study Questions

1. Would you agree with Sartre that "Hell is other people"?

2. Do you think Garcin, Estelle, and Inez might apply Sartre's own principles of existentialism to cope with their life in hell? How?

Narrative

A Few Good Men

AARON SORKIN (SCREENWRITER)
ROB REINER (DIRECTOR)

Based on the play by Sorkin. Film, 1992. Summary.

On the U.S. Marine base in Cuba, a young private, Santiago, is attacked in the middle of the night, bound and gagged and left in his room. An hour later he dies of what looks like poisoning: The rag used to gag him may have been soaked with a chemical. Two fellow marines, Corporal Dawson and Private Downey, are arrested for murder.

A Navy officer, the young lawyer Joanne Galloway, is interested in the case and requests that the Marines be transferred to Washington, D.C., for trial; she suspects that the case involves a so-called Code Red, an order given by a superior to discipline a subordinate soldier. Her request to become their counsel is denied, however, and another

The 1992 film *A Few Good Men* (Castle Rock) asks the question Is following orders ever a sufficient excuse? Paralleling the existential demand that each person take responsibility for his or her actions, the film shows soldiers coming to grips with demands of personal moral integrity that run counter to their training and their code. Here we see a clash between lawyer styles: Joanne Galloway (Demi Moore) confronts Daniel Kaffee (Tom Cruise) outside Navy headquarters early in the film, before they reach a stage of cooperation and mutual respect.

young Navy lawyer, Dan Kaffee, gets the case because of his outstanding record for plea bargaining. Joanne and Dan experience instantaneous dislike for each other; she thinks he is callous, and he thinks she is stuck-up. Dan goes to see the two Marines in the holding facility and comes face-to-face with another worldview: the Marine code. Although Dan himself is part of the armed forces, he regards his job as a career choice, not a lifestyle, but both young Marines see their Marine identity as a chosen way of life according to the code: Unit, Corps, God, and Country. While they show Dan all the respect their training requires (which he doesn't want), they have little respect for him as a person.

Joanne, unwilling to be left out, persuades a relative of one of the young Marines that he needs separate counsel and becomes his lawyer. Together, she, Dan, and Dan's aide now go to Guantanamo Bay in Cuba to question Santiago's superior officers. Information has surfaced that Santiago had been sending out numerous requests to be transferred to another post; his most recent request included a proposition to an officer who outranks the highest-ranking officer at Guantanamo, Colonel Jessep. If he is transferred, he said, he will testify about an illegal shooting incident between a Marine and a Cuban soldier across the fence between the base and Cuban territory. For this reason and because, as Dawson explains, Santiago didn't follow the chain of command but went directly to Jessep's superiors with his complaint, the lawyers assume that Santiago was harassed and killed.

On the base Dan and Joanne view Santiago's quarters, with his bloodstained bed, his closet full of clothes, and other personal items; they talk with Santiago's officers, who insist that strict orders had been given to the Marines not to lay a hand on Santiago. In addition, Jessep tells them that Santiago was about to be transferred that same morning, but regretfully the transfer came too late to save him. Dan seems satisfied with the explanations, but Joanne (who outranks him) insists on asking Jessep some tough questions about Code Red. Highly irritated, Jessep informs her that on the record he discourages the illegal code, but off the record it is an invaluable training instrument for disciplining soldiers who are out of line, who don't know how to be a member of the unit.

Back in Washington, Dan and Joanne now confront Downey and Dawson and ask them if they were given a Code Red order, and they admit that Kendrick, one of Jessep's officers, gave the order to them in private after telling the other Marines not to touch Santiago. A lawyer friend of Dan's, the Marine prosecutor in the case, suggests a deal: Have Downey and Dawson plead guilty and get two years; if they plead innocent, the whole machinery of justice will be used against them, and they will be locked up for life. Dan takes the deal to the Marines and is astounded when they refuse, but Dawson and Downey don't think they have done anything wrong: They have followed orders and acted like Marines ought to act, and if they plead guilty, they will have acted without honor. And furthermore, what would they do after spending time in jail? What kind of life would be available to them? Dan is now exasperated; he decides to withdraw from the case and get the Marines another lawyer. Sam, Dan's associate, is repulsed at the Marines' attitude and asks Joanne why she likes them so much; she answers, "Because they stand on a wall, and they say, 'Nothing is going to hurt you tonight, not on my watch.'"

Next day the trial begins, but Dan, to the surprise of his friends, enters a not-guilty plea instead of requesting another defense lawyer. Dan succeeds in showing that Santiago's death may have been due to a heart condition, not to poisoning, but otherwise the defense has very little material.

Out of the blue a missing person resurfaces: Colonel Jessep's second-in-command, Lieutenant Colonel Markinson, who has been incommunicado, contacts Dan in secret. He knows the truth about Santiago, and he considers himself to blame for not speaking up and preventing the tragedy from happening. Jessep never ordered any transfer, because he wanted Santiago "trained," and Markinson suspects that Jessep himself ordered the Code Red. Dan and Joanne quickly put Markinson in a hotel with a guard to protect him, as a key witness, but it does them no good: When Markinson learns that Dan plans to put him on the stand, he writes a letter to Santiago's family, apologizing for not having been strong enough to save their son's life, puts on his dress uniform, and shoots himself. Without Markinson as a witness, and with the surprise revelation that Downey never even heard any Code Red order from anyone but his corporal, Dawson, Dan is ready to give up. That evening, drunk and depressed, he has a flash of insight: Santiago's room hadn't been touched when they saw it at the base, and all his clothes and personal items were there, with no evidence of packing. Even so, without Markinson their only recourse is to put Jessep on the stand. They hope that they can play upon Jessep's anger at civilians and other non-Marines and make him confess to ordering the Code Red.

Jessep arrives in court, full of disdain for Dan, the Navy, and the entire situation. Dan does his best to provoke Jessep and involve him in contradictions: If Jessep gives an order (such as "Don't touch Santiago") will it then be followed? Jessep insists that following orders is a matter of life and death in the Marines. But then, says Dan, why would Santiago need to be transferred? He wouldn't be in any danger if the order was to leave him alone. Jessep's anger is mounting, and he blows up in Dan's face, yelling that the Marines stand on the wall, protecting him and others, because they know how to take orders. And Dan, seizing the moment, asks the question: Did Jessep order the Code Red? Proudly and defiantly, Jessep yells back that indeed he did; silence envelops the courtroom, and Jessep is the only one who doesn't understand that a major event has taken place. When he is being restrained and arrested by the MPs he still doesn't understand that his admission at once let the Marines off the hook for murder and declared his own guilt. The verdict is soon reached: Dawson and Downey are found not guilty of murder and conspiracy—but guilty of conduct unbecoming a Marine, with a dishonorable discharge. The lawyers are relieved, but Private Downey understands nothing. Why are they being punished, when they had been good Marines and had followed orders? Dawson, on the other hand, understands completely, and says to Downey that they are Marines and are supposed to fight for the weak, for those who can't fight for themselves. They should have fought for Santiago.

Study Questions

1. The film assumes that Marines don't have the right to question the orders of a commanding officer; this, in fact, appears to be no longer true. In your opinion, should a soldier have the right to question the orders of his or her commanding officer? If no, why not? If yes, under what kind of circumstances?

2. Identify the elements of the film that Sartre would call examples of "bad faith."

3. Identify the elements of the film that Levinas might call the encounter with the Other.

4. As Sam, Dan's associate, remarks, the defense that "I was just following orders" didn't work at the Nazi trials after World War II, and it didn't work for the officer accused of the My Lai massacre of civilians in Vietnam. Can you imagine a situation in which a person's defense that he or she was following orders would be acceptable? Why or why not?

5. Is this film fair to members of the Marine Corps? Why or why not?

Chapter Eleven

Different Gender, Different Ethics?

*J*f you ask a woman in the Western world today whether she is a feminist, chances are she will say no; if you ask her whether she believes that women and men should have equal opportunities, that women should not be discriminated against based on their gender, and that women and men should get equal pay for equal work, chances are she will say yes, and so will most men. This, according to classical feminism, qualifies anyone who agrees as a feminist, because these are the goals of classical feminism. But the word has today been weighed down by additional connotations to the extent that many people don't want to be associated with the idea of feminism; the term "feminazis," coined by talk show host Rush Limbaugh, hasn't helped any. Are feminists the same as "feminazis"? Not according to Limbaugh himself, who says he reserves the term "feminazis" for those he considers radicals. But the term has caused some people to assume that all feminists somehow want to rule the world. If you believe that we should end sex discrimination and help create a friendly, cooperative working environment as well as private partnership for men and women based on equality, however, you are in fact a feminist, regardless of whether you are male or female.

Feminism and Virtue Theory

Originally, feminism was associated with acquiring political and social rights for women: the right to work, to own property, to vote, to get a divorce, and other rights considered irrelevant for women by most thinkers with political influence until well into the nineteenth century. Later in the chapter we take a brief look at that development. During its struggle for political equality, feminism rarely regarded itself as a separate moral theory; the male-dominated (often called *patriarchal* by feminists) world would often point to women's sensibilities as those of a higher moral view (think of the role of the schoolmarm in Western movies, exercising her civilizing influence), but because that was usually coupled with an assumption that women were unfit for life in the rough and heartless real world of men, early feminists usually placed little emphasis on this notion. However, a connection not just to ethics as such but to virtue theory as well has become apparent in the past decades.

For modern virtue theory the important question is, How should I be? In other words, What is the character I should strive for? The moral rules of "doing unto others," of "universalizing one's maxim," of "maximizing happiness for as many as possible," and of "treating everyone with impartial fairness" take second place to virtues such as loyalty to family and friends, generosity, compassion, and courage. A moral vice may, under such circumstances, very well turn out to be related to a famous rule of moral conduct: If you act only when you can imagine others being allowed to do the same thing (Kant's categorical imperative), then your child or friend may die while you wonder about allowing all others to defend their child or friend. If you insist on treating everyone with impartial fairness (John Rawls's "original position"), you have an equal obligation to a starving person on the other side of the world and to your niece down the street; you have no right to prefer helping your niece. Virtue ethics, however, discards that approach as a breach of loyalty and family responsibility and insists that you *should* help your niece before you spread yourself thin helping strangers. And you can be accused of the same vice if you are trying to make strangers happy (the principle of utility) at the expense of the needs of your family.

This is where the connection to modern feminism comes in. You have already read, in Chapter 7, that Rawls was criticized for assuming we can pretend to be just strangers to each other in order to achieve fairness. In this chapter we will take a look at the modern feminist theory that is the basis for that criticism, a theory which suggests that women and men tend to view the entire field of ethics from different viewpoints. Whereas men (who have written most of the theories about ethics, law, and justice so far) tend to think of morality in terms of *rules of conduct*, justice, and fairness, says the theory, women tend to think of morality in terms of relationships, of staying friends, and of caring for those who are close to you or for whom you have accepted responsibility. In other words, women tend to think in terms of the *virtues* of caring, loyalty, and compassion. This theory is advanced by the psychologist Carol Gilligan, and we look at her ideas in further detail below. But first we must take a look at the idea of gender equality: What is it, do we have it now, and what has been done to achieve it?

What Is Gender Equality?

The purpose of feminism throughout its history, with a few exceptions (such as the 1960s women's organization SCUM, Society for Cutting Up Men, which may or may not have been meant as a joke), has been to achieve equality for the sexes. Today many refer to this goal as *gender equality* (see Box 11.1 for an explanation of sex versus gender). You know from Chapter 7 that the principle of equality does not imply that everyone is the same, but that everyone should be treated as equals unless special circumstances apply. But what exactly does that entail when applied to the two sexes? Below we look at the concepts of cultural as well as biological equality.

Gender and Language

Throughout the Enlightenment and on into the twenty-first century it has been customary to use words of the masculine gender to refer to both males and females. For many of us it is surprising to learn that the term *man* in some political statements, such as the American Declaration of Independence ("All men are created equal"), may not have been intended to cover women or people of color—an issue that is being discussed among constitutional scholars today.

Box 11.1   SEX OR GENDER?

By consensus, the term that is most commonly used today when people talk about sexual differences that go beyond mere biological functions is *gender.* Although this used to be a strictly grammatical term, it now is used instead of the biological term *sexual* as a sociopolitical term.

It is not true, of course, that the term *men* can *always* be used to include women; it doesn't make any sense to say, for instance, that half of all men have ovaries and half don't. Today, the use of the terms *he* and *men* to include women is considered by many to be discriminatory. And despite the fact that very few men or women ever intended discrimination by using the word *he* for a man or a woman and *man* for all humankind, we now are moving away from what is known as "gender-specific" language toward "gender-neutral" language, because many believe that even when used with the best intentions, gender-specific terms subconsciously tell us that being male is somehow more important than being female and that certain social roles are best performed by men. The real reason for being sensitive about gender and language is, of course, to achieve gender equality. (Box 11.2 provides a discussion of issues involved in gender-neutral language.)

Textbooks and cultural documents are continually being reworded to accommodate our new sensitivity toward gender and language. The Catholic church has officially endorsed the use of non-gender-specific language in religious documents and biblical translations. Gender-specific words such as *mailman, chairman, housewife,* and *maid* are being changed to *mail carrier, chairperson, homemaker,* and *maintenance assistant* in order to signify that these terms cover both genders. Writers and speakers alike are instructed to avoid the use of *he* as a generic term and instead use *he or she, they, one,* or *you.* College students are urged to avoid gender-specific language in their term papers. Perhaps you think this is a subject of little importance — that it is merely a matter of semantic misunderstanding. But consider this. If you are male and you hear a statement such as, "Now is the time for every man to stand up for what he believes in," there is a good chance you will feel somehow compelled to think hard about what you believe in. If you are female, you *may* feel the same way, but chances are you will feel, subconsciously, that somehow this statement does not apply to you; you may even think, "Yes, it is about time *they* pulled *themselves* together!" If even a few women feel excluded when they read or hear language that uses the masculine gender — excluded either in the sense of feeling left out or in the sense of not having to get involved — then that is enough reason to change the way we phrase things.

Is Biology Destiny?

When we ask whether or not sexual equality exists, we really are asking one of two questions: (1) Does cultural and social equality exist? or (2) Does biological equality? The first question is relative to the historical time period: Today we have reason

Box 11.2   THE ISSUE IS MANHOLE COVERS

People often seem to feel that we are getting too radical in our elimination of gender-specific terms. It may make sense to do away with words such as *chairman* and *fireman* and use *chairperson* and *firefighter* instead, but what about all the words in the English language that just happen to include a gender-specific term but for which there is no graceful substitute? Will *freshman* now be *freshperson*? Do we have to say *personhole* cover instead of *manhole* cover? How about *manpower*? And *manned space missions*? (And, jokesters might ask, how about *man*-ipulate? and *his*-tory?) Other languages present similar challenges, but some languages have less of a problem finding a common word for humanity. German has a specific term for "human being"—*Der Mensch*—which is different from the terms for man and woman but which still includes a gender-specific term (*Mensch*, which is masculine in gender). In Danish the word for "human being" is a gender-neutral term, *Et Menneske*. And in Sweden, the term for "human being" is *En Människa*, a grammatically feminine word! To make matters even

more interesting, there is a word in ancient Icelandic, *man*, that means slave/maid/mistress! Apparently that word has no connection with the ancient Germanic word for man (*Madr*), which is the source for the term *man* in English.

So, getting back to the manhole covers, what should we do? Change some words and not others? Leave *manhole covers* alone, but change *manned mission* to *crewed mission*? Change them all? Leave them all the way they are? Two things are at stake here: the self-esteem of half the English-speaking population versus the comfort of those used to an established language. We can choose between four major courses of action: (1) Forcibly change language to some degree (and we have seen that this can be done within a generation). (2) Wait until a new gender-neutral terminology evolves by itself, in response to the changing times. (3) Make a distinction between sexist and nonsexist terms and change only the blatantly sexist ones. (4) Insist on keeping the traditional terms no matter what. What would you suggest?

---

to say that we have not reached total equality yet, but we hope to do so in the future. (In the past, in Western society, the answer would have been a flat no.) But if we ask the second question, we have to ask a follow-up question: What do we mean by "biological equality"? Do we mean that men and women are the same? Or similar? That they will do similar things in similar situations? Or perhaps that they have a similar genetic makeup, even if there are cultural differences?

The bottom line is the difference between a descriptive and a normative approach. A descriptive theory of equality compares capabilities and pronounces people to be "similar" or "dissimilar." A normative theory of equality may or may not look at the "facts" presented by the descriptive theory but states that people *ought* to be treated a certain way—(1) the same, or (2) similarly under similar conditions, or (3) differently. And if a normative theory asserts that equality is a good thing, it will present a theory for how to achieve it.

Sexual equality, as an idea, is a complex issue (the same is true of racial equality). We must ask, Is sexual equality a biological fact? What does that mean? And is that important for an ethical policy? Let us look at what it means first. Are men and women biologically equal? We all know that, physically, most men are taller and stronger than most women, but that doesn't mean individual women can't be taller and stronger than individual men. In nature there is such a thing as *sexual dimorphism,* meaning that the two sexes of a species look very different, with one sex usually being much bigger than the other. (A consequence of dimorphism is usually that the bigger sex dominates the smaller sex, and that one individual of the bigger sex can have many mates of the smaller sex, but not vice versa. Where the sexes are of the same size there are usually lifelong monogamous relationships and equal partnerships.) So do humans have sexual dimorphism? Not nearly to the extreme that gorillas do but slightly more than bonobo chimpanzees do; gorilla society is male-dominated, but bonobo chimpanzees, our closest relatives on this earth, have a gender-equal society with a tendency toward matriarchy. Biologically, there is no reason to assume that it is natural for one human gender to dominate the other, but neither can we conclude that we have an obvious natural tendency to be completely equal partners.

But are we then biologically equal when it comes to the *intellect*? The viewpoints on male and female intelligence are diverse, stretching from the old assumption that men are logical and women are not, to the assumption shared by many modern people that if we are intellectually different at all it is merely a subtle difference, to the view that women's intellectual style is superior to that of men. What exactly would intellectual equality mean? That we reach the same results when faced with the same problem, or that we reach the same results *the same way* when faced with the same problem? Recent studies of the human brain have revealed that men and women actually use their brains differently when dealing with the same math problems, but they generally reach the same results in the same amount of time.

But whether we talk about physical or intellectual equality, some philosophers would call out a warning: Looking for actual equality is one thing, and perhaps a positive one, but if we intend our policy of gender equality to rest on a foundation of what we think is *actual, biological equality,* then we may be in trouble, because what if scientists someday prove that biologically we really are not the same at all? Then our reason for gender equality has disappeared, and we may slide back into some form of gender discrimination against women or against men. Better to forget about looking for actual similarities and concentrate on making a policy based on *what we would like to see happen:* In other words, instead of using *descriptive* means to make us politically equal, let us use normative means, spelling out how we ought to treat each other. Remember from Chapter 5 that if we try to go from fact to policy, from an "is" to an "ought," then we are committing the *naturalistic fallacy,* basing a policy on mere fact without adding a moral premise. But that doesn't mean we can't take biology into consideration when we establish policies. The idea of sexual, or rather *gender,* equality is so important to us now that we have antidiscrimination laws against "sexism." In other words, we believe that regardless of whether equality between the genders is a natural fact, it should be a cultural and sociological institution.

Women's Historical Role in the Public Sphere

Gender equality is, of course, a novel idea in terms of Western history. Until the mid-nineteenth century it was common practice in Western culture to assume that male and female natures were essentially different in their functions, aspirations, and potential, and that male nature was somehow more *normal* than female nature. It was not thought of as necessarily *better,* for, as I mentioned earlier, many men seemed to believe that women had higher moral standards; but it was considered more important in the sense that male nature was more representative of the human species than female nature was. What was this assumption based on? Today we might say *prejudice,* but it can't be dismissed as easily as that, because for a great many thinkers, objectivity was an important ideal. They tried to describe things as they saw them, not as they believed things ought to be, nor as they might appear to an undiscerning eye. And what they saw was that few women had any role to play in public life: There were few women politicians, few women artists, few women scientists. But why were there so few women in public life? The answer is tentative; not all the facts are in yet. It seems obvious, though, that a person's contribution to what we call public life is greatly dependent on that person feeling called or welcome as a contributor. If no one expects or wants you to become a good politician or mathematician or sculptor, you might not think of trying. Encouragement and expectation are major factors in such choices. On the other hand, if it appears that you are *destined* for a certain task, you might not question that, either. For most women (until the arrival of dependable birth control), motherhood, several times over, was their destiny. And for those familiar with the demands of large families, it does not come as news that the person in charge of the *private sphere,* the home, has precious little time for anything else, unless she can afford domestic help. Indeed, throughout history—Western history as well as world history—most cultural contributions by individual women were made by those who did not play the role of homemaker.

An interesting question is why women's contributions to the private sphere are rarely discussed. It's certainly true that when women could not own property, vote, or hold a job without the permission of a guardian, many women still had considerable power within the four walls of their home. They managed the bookkeeping and purchases, planned and prepared meals for the household, educated the children, and kept things running on the farm—a full-time job in itself. Why were these management skills not considered important? In an odd way, they were; it is probably our modern-day prejudice to think that they weren't. A young woman chosen as a spouse was expected to have these skills, and "woman's work" was a vitally important social factor. But in terms of the public sphere, women had no place and were not considered potential contributors until almost the end of the nineteenth century. (This assertion, of course, refers to women from middle- and upper-middle-class backgrounds; many working-class women have, for as long as there has been a working class, generally participated in the public sphere, simply because they have had no choice. If a widow with small children didn't enter the workforce, her children might starve to death—and she, too.) Even today, many people accept the idea that the public sphere is the vital one—perhaps because work in the public sphere is *paid for* and work in the private sphere generally is not. However, asking the question whether women's work has been valued may in itself be choosing the viewpoint of the public sphere in which men have traditionally determined values; women have traditionally always valued one another's work, learned from it, criticized it, improved it, and shared it. From a traditional woman's point of view, the question of public (male) recognition for her work may not be the most important question: What might matter more is receiving recognition and appreciation for her work from her peers in the community, other women.

Another factor must be mentioned here. In early times having women remain outside the public sphere was thought by most men (and women, too) to be a way of *protecting* women; they were spared the unpleasantness and insecurity of the world of affairs. This is the viewpoint of the Arab fundamentalist culture, where much the same pattern prevails today. Some critics believe it can be interpreted as a way of treating women as *property* (namely the property of their fathers and husbands)—as an investment in the next generation and as a working resource.

This pattern of women being excluded from the public sphere may seem so ancient that we believe it has always existed. However, a theory advanced by many feminist scholars today is that the subjection of women to men (which we know as a historical fact going back at least three thousand years) may not have been the ancient order of things. You may remember that John Stuart Mill was an early advocate of women's rights (see Chapter 5 and p. 455). In his book *The Subjection of Women* (1869) he says that we don't know what it would be like for women not to be subjected to men because they always have been. But he may well have been wrong, because archaeological evidence (artifacts and written documents) now points to the possibility of women having had far more influence in early Middle Eastern and African cultures than we used to think. In what is now Turkey there appear to have been civilizations more than ten thousand years ago who revered a mother goddess of fertility; in Greek and Middle Eastern legends we find ancient myths of a creator goddess and powerful priestesses and queens. Similarly, African legends suggest a strong memory of a mother goddess and of women who had much social power in their communities. Whether we should call these ancient cultures *matriarchal* is open to question, because we have no evidence that they were *ruled* by women, but there is tentative evidence that until some gradual cultural change toward patriarchy happened around thirty-five hundred years ago, women in the Old World had higher social standing than they did later. Part of this social standing may have derived from the local religions' belief in a creator goddess rather than a creator god.

Further challenges to the universality of patriarchy have come from other parts of the world: In the American Indian tradition, women were considered respected, full members of the community with rights to have their own opinions and to choose a husband and divorce him. Furthermore, in Eastern tribes it was not uncommon for the chief to be a woman. However, according to American Indian historian Paula Gunn Allen, the European settlers rarely reported this fact, and history books have most often referred to these chiefs as being male. At various times and places in human history, women seem to have had considerably more social influence than they have had in the Western world of the past several thousand years except for the past four decades.

A place where goddess worship may have lasted longer than most other places, and where women may have had comparatively more influence, was Ireland prior to the advent of Christianity with Saint Patrick in 435. And for centuries after

Christianity took hold, the high public standing of women that was a legacy of the goddess religion remained a factor in Ireland. Saint Brigit of Kildare (453–525) was raised by the pagan Druid priesthood but was attracted to Christianity. She was ordained as a bishop by mistake, instead of as a nun, as a result of the wrong oath being administered. It initiated a new tradition, and from then on until the Vikings arrived several hundred years later, women in Ireland could become bishops. Irish bishops generally had a more gender-egalitarian view of women than the rest of Europe did, and when in 900 a European bishops' council convened to decide whether women had souls, the yes votes won — by one vote. That vote came from an Irish bishop.

In the European convents of the early Middle Ages, women were receiving an education that allowed them to become medical practitioners, illustrators, composers, and writers, aside from having clerical powers equal to the male clergy of the monasteries. One such woman was Hildegard of Bingen (1098–1179), a German abbess. She was given to the church at the age of eight, and began having visions at an early age. She wrote a number of books on God's plan for humanity, two about her visions, and another two on science and nature. She composed liturgical songs, and wrote what is recognized as the first morality play about the battle between good and evil, *Ordo Virtuem*. She founded her own convent, Rupertsberg, where her music was performed. Toward the end of her life she offered her writings to the new University of Paris, only to suffer the indignity of having them rejected on the grounds that she was a woman.

In the twelfth to fourteenth centuries, women lost ground within the church. New policies deprived abbesses of their right to hear confessions, and convents that had functioned as hospitals and social safety nets for the community were closed down or transformed into isolated cloisters. No secular schools had been founded yet, and young women were now barred from a religious education. The reason may seem strangely arbitrary to a modern person: In order to be accepted by the church, receive an education, and communicate with God, the young acolyte's head had to be shaved into a tonsure. But according to Scriptures, women not only weren't allowed to shave their heads, they were supposed to hide their hair under a veil when in the presence of God. And since you can't have a tonsure, and thus be eligible for a religious education, while having a full head of hair and wearing a veil, the tonsure policy kept women out of schools.

First-, Second-, and Third-Wave Feminism

We often hear feminism referred to as "first wave," "second wave," and "third wave." These chronological terms form a time line for awareness of women's social situation. The first wave generally refers to the feminist movement in Europe and the United States from its early beginnings in the seventeenth century to the accomplishment of its most urgent goal, the right for women to vote. In 1869 women in Wyoming gained the right to vote, but general suffrage for women wasn't obtained in the United States until 1920. In the meantime, New Zealand women had been included as voters in 1893; in 1902 Australia followed suit. Norway joined the list in 1913, and Denmark in 1915. So, too, did Canada, England, Germany, and Austria after

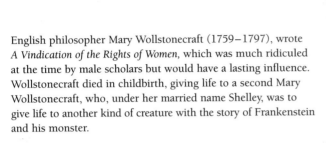

English philosopher Mary Wollstonecraft (1759–1797), wrote *A Vindication of the Rights of Women*, which was much ridiculed at the time by male scholars but would have a lasting influence. Wollstonecraft died in childbirth, giving life to a second Mary Wollstonecraft, who, under her married name Shelley, was to give life to another kind of creature with the story of Frankenstein and his monster.

World War I, in 1918. Sweden gave women the right to vote in 1921, but it wasn't until 1944 that French women could go to the polls, and Mexico followed in 1947. Switzerland waited until 1971, and in 1994 black women gained full suffrage in South Africa. What began as furtive discussions four hundred years ago has still not reached full global implementation.

Early Feminism in France and England

A very early speaker for the rights of women was the French thinker Poulain de la Barre, who in 1673 argued that men and women are fundamentally similar because they have the same powers of reasoning. Poulain believed women should have access to all occupations in society, even as generals in the army and leaders of Parliament. Few people paid much attention to Poulain, however; he remained both unique and unknown as a seventeenth-century feminist. During the French Revolution (begun in 1789) things changed considerably in France. Many sided with the thinker Madame d'Epinay, who believed that women and men have the same nature and the same constitution and will display different virtues and vices only if they are brought up that way; any differentiation is due to social pressure, nothing else. Her ideas inspired the philosopher the Marquis de Condorcet, who in 1792 suggested that education should be available to women because both men and women were, primarily, members of the human race. Condorcet's opponent, Talleyrand, who was inspired by the social critic Jean-Jacques Rousseau, managed to put a stop to these ideas, which, it seems, were too radical even for the revolutionaries. Thus the view of Rousseau, which had become popular in the late eighteenth century—that men should live in a democracy of equals but that their women belonged at home as intelligent but subordinate partners to their spouses—became the official view of the gender issue in France of the early nineteenth century.

In eighteenth-century England there were voices—male as well as female—that argued for the possibility of a different order. The British philosopher Mary Wollstonecraft (1759–1797) was one of the few women of the eighteenth century who directly addressed women's situation. (See Box 11.3 for a short list of other

Box 11.3   WOMEN MORAL PHILOSOPHERS

Carol Gilligan is right in saying that the famous and influential moral theories within the Western philosophical tradition have until recently all been expressed by male thinkers. This does not mean, however, that there have been no women moral thinkers in Western history aside from Mary Wollstonecraft and Harriet Taylor Mill; here is a small selection from a list of more than thirty names in the *Encyclopedia of Ethics* of women ethicists (Western as well as Eastern) from the earliest years of philosophy to the nineteenth century. I don't wish to imply that women's contributions to ethics until the twentieth century can be contained in a box. However, most of these names are not generally well known, and prior to the twentieth century women thinkers had very little influence in philosophy. This list demonstrates that there were women who could and did think and write during times when women were discouraged or even banned from taking part in intellectual life. In all probability there were many

more thinking and writing women than history has recorded.

Phintys of Sparta (c. 420 B.C.E.) held that it was not unfitting for women to philosophize and that courage, justice, and wisdom were common to women as well as men; in the tradition of Greek moral thinking (which you will recognize from Aristotle, who was not born yet when Phintys wrote her book, *On the Moderation of Women*), she recommends moderation in all things as a virtue for women.

Makrina of Neocaesaria (c. 300 C.E.) so impressed her brother, the Bishop of Nyssa, that he cited her moral philosophy in his own writings. Makrina was familiar with Plato's philosophy and taught that women were created in God's image and had rational souls; with a rational soul, one is capable of becoming morally virtuous and thus eligible for entry into heaven after death, she believed.

Murasaki Shikibu (978–c. 1031) was a Japanese courtier who, in her novel *Genji Monogatari*

women ethicists before the twentieth century.) In *A Vindication of the Rights of Women* (1792) she suggests not only that it is unfair to women to socialize them to be uneducated, unthinking creatures who are only eager to please but also that it is unfair to men, because although a man may fall in love with that kind of woman, he certainly won't want to live with her. After all, what will the two have in common once the seduction is over and they are married? No, Wollstonecraft wrote, women should have the same opportunities as men. If they don't measure up, men will have reason to claim superiority, but to apply two different value systems—one that says what is proper for men and one that says what is proper for women—is to make a mockery out of the concept of virtue itself:

> I wish to persuade women to endeavour to acquire strength, both of mind and body, and to convince them that the soft phrases, susceptibility of heart, delicacy of sentiment, and refinement of taste, are almost synonymous with epithets of weakness, and that those beings who are only the objects of pity and that kind of love, which has been termed its sister, will soon become objects of contempt. . . . Besides, the woman who strengthens her body and exercises her mind will, by managing her family and practicing various virtues, become the friend, and not the humble dependent of her husband.

(*The Tale of Genji*), which is considered the first real novel, led her main character, the woman Ukifune, to a realization of freedom and moral responsibility in the face of existential dread. Today this story is seen as an early exploration of the key themes of existentialism as they were later defined in the Western world of the twentieth century.

Christine de Pizan (1365–1431) wrote a book, *Cité des Dames* (*The City of Women*), in which she envisioned women living in a community to protect themselves from physical and moral harm. She argued that oppression of women was counterproductive to the improvement of society and that women should strive to avoid activities that dull their intellect, since they were limited by certain social roles.

Marie le Jars de Gournay (1565–1645) was the editor of Montaigne's *Essays* and wrote in a work of her own, *Egalité des Hommes et des Femmes* (*Equality Between Men and Women*), that women are equal to men in their capacity for moral reasoning and action. She believed that sexual differences are related exclusively to reproduction and have otherwise no bearing on male or female nature.

Mary Astell (1666–1731) worked on a synthesis of the traditions of Locke and Descartes and believed that reason ought to govern our passions. The only way to accomplish that, she said, was to have universal education for women as well as for men.

Antoinette Brown Blackwell (1825–1921) was the first ordained American woman. She was a prolific writer of philosophy and theology and maintained that women and men make moral judgments differently; in a forerunner of Gilligan's argument about an ethic of justice and an ethic of care, Blackwell claimed that women bring compassion to justice and caring to the concept of rights.

In the nineteenth century John Stuart Mill, inspired by his longtime intellectual friend (and later wife) Harriet Taylor, wrote about how women's as well as men's characters are molded by society:

> All women are brought up from the earliest years in the belief that their ideal of character is the very opposite to that of men; not self-will, and government by self-control, but submission, and yielding to the control of others. All the moralities tell them that it is the duty of women, and all the current sentimentalities that it is their nature, to live for others.

Under different social circumstances, Mill says, we would see women acting no longer as the full-time slaves of their husbands but as independent individuals with original intellectual ideas to contribute to society. If women are capable of fulfilling social functions, they should be free to do so. If it is impossible for a woman to do certain things because of her nature, then what need is there to prohibit her from doing them? The old saying "'ought' implies 'can'" applies: You can't tell someone she ought (or ought not) to do something unless she is actually able to do it. Mill does believe that male and female qualities in general are not the same—that men and women are usually good at different things—but that from a moral point of view these qualities should be considered equally important. So what might Mill say about the current controversy as to whether women soldiers should be allowed in combat? Probably that most women would prefer not to and would not qualify but that those who want to and who do qualify should be allowed to do so.

Feminism in America

The philosophy and goals of the first wave of feminism in the United States were straightforward: rights for women to self-determination; rights to inherit and own property, even in marriage (as opposed to the ownership of one's inherited or earned property passing to one's husband); rights to raise one's children; and above all the right to vote. The philosophy of the second wave is more complex, because during this period women had achieved the right to vote but not gender equality in any real measure—not in education nor in the job market, politics, or the private sphere. The goals of many second-wave feminists became equal pay for equal work, equal job and education opportunities, and an end to the treatment of women as though they were children without the ability to take care of themselves. The third wave is the hardest to define philosophically. Many young people believe that the second wave has paved the way for true equality, and they expect relationships between men and women to reflect this political equality. Some third-wave feminists want to attack the problem of gender discrimination radically; others believe that the work has been accomplished and that men and women are now free to explore whatever gender roles suit them. Here we take a look at some highlights of the first, second, and third waves.

Challenges to the Euro-American patriarchal system by individual women, as well as women's groups, happened sporadically through the 1700s and the first half of the 1800s, but the first Women's Rights Convention in Seneca Falls, New York, in 1848 is generally regarded as the beginning of the American women's movement. Led by Lucretia Mott and Elizabeth Cady Stanton, the convention resulted in a Declaration of Sentiments that stated "all men and women are created equal." Stanton later became the first woman candidate for Congress (1866), although women would not get the right to vote for another fifty-four years. The former slave Sojourner Truth gave speeches to white women's groups and others in which she stressed both the importance of women's rights and the urgency of the abolition of slavery. During the Civil War white women in the North organized to seek fair treatment for women workers, as well as abolition. Susan B. Anthony collected signatures for passage of the Thirteenth Amendment to abolish slavery. She also worked hard for an amendment to give women suffrage (the right to vote) and was tried and convicted for voting illegally. She and Elizabeth Cady Stanton formed the National Woman Suffrage Association in 1869. In 1869 women in Wyoming gained the right to vote, fifty years before they did in the rest of the nation. In 1893 the National Council of Jewish Women was formed, as was the National Association for Colored Women in the following year.

From the end of the 1800s to the early 1900s, many women were engaged in the temperance movement, working to get alcohol banned. The primary reasoning behind the temperance movement was that alcohol destroyed families by making drunks out of the breadwinners: fathers and husbands. These efforts often went hand in hand with the suffrage movement. Interestingly, the anti-alcohol movement succeeded before the suffrage movement did; Prohibition began in 1917 with the Eighteenth Amendment, three years before women achieved the right to vote.

We shouldn't forget that during those last few years of the first wave, what was on most people's minds was the Great War, World War I. The involvement of the United States from 1917 to 1918 not only meant anguish for women who saw their sons, fathers, husbands, and boyfriends go to war, it also had a homefront effect. Women all over the Western world took on men's jobs, partly to support themselves and their families but also to meet the needs of society. This was a major revelation both to women and to the political powers (although the same effect had happened to a lesser degree during the Civil War), because it conclusively proved that women could hold technical and intellectual jobs previously thought of as "male." One direct result of this was the Nineteenth Amendment of 1920, which granted women the right to vote.

After 1920 the women's movement quieted down, as though the effort of securing the right to vote had used up all its energy. The Great Depression of the 1930s created huge obstacles for women who wanted to work outside the home, because they were resented for taking jobs away from unemployed men. Even so, individual women campaigned for greater equality and freedom for women, and groups such as the National Council of Negro Women were founded. In Hollywood, movies were made depicting the problems of women in the workforce. The films in which Katharine Hepburn and Spencer Tracy starred together in the 1930s and 1940s often showed both the funny and the serious aspects of men and women getting used to each other as working partners.

World War II repeated the phenomenon of women taking jobs in the male workplace to feed their families and serve their country. "Rosie the Riveter," a fictional woman working in the fighter plane industry, became a symbol for the new woman (the movie *Swing Shift* tells the story of this time period very well). But after World War II there was a gigantic push to get women out of the job market and back in the home in order to open up jobs for returning servicemen. Indeed, many of the ideals of gender equality were all but forgotten with the birth of the baby boom generation.

The second wave of feminism in the United States was ushered in with the 1963 publication of Betty Friedan's book *The Feminine Mystique*. (In France, a similar reaction followed the publication of Simone de Beauvoir's *The Second Sex* in 1949.) The following year, the Civil Rights Act, which prohibited discrimination in employment because of race, also banned sex discrimination. In the 1960s the challenges to traditionally male institutions and occupations increased: The National Organization for Women (NOW) was organized in 1966, the concept of "women's liberation" became part of the culture of the 1960s and 1970s, and formal charges of sex discrimination in workplaces reached the courts. In 1972 the Equal Rights Amendment was passed by the House of Representatives but was later defeated in the Senate. What many feminists consider the landmark achievement of the era was the Supreme Court's Roe v.

Wade decision in 1973 that women have the freedom to choose abortion in the first trimester. (In the second and third trimesters, states may impose special limitations.)

For most feminists of the second wave, the primary goal was the creation of an equal-opportunity society without discrimination because of one's sex—a society in which women, as well as men, would be able to freely choose their way of life. For many feminists of this period, such a society seemed possible only if the structures of patriarchy were toppled, and those structures were often perceived as not just male-dominated but also middle-class-dominated. In other words, for many feminists of the second wave, women's liberation was also a political battle against the *capitalist economy*, and many second-wave feminists have identified themselves as Marxists.

Many feminists of the 1960s and 1970s focused on the traditional upbringing of boys and girls and speculated that bringing up children to think of themselves as *persons* rather than as either "boys" or "girls" would lead to the elimination of many male and female stereotypes within a few generations. Men would be accustomed to doing work around the house without feeling they were being emasculated or that they were "helping" rather than contributing their fair share; women would feel at home and welcome in the public sphere and comfortable about choosing a life without children and/or marriage. For politically engaged feminists regardless of party affiliation, a primary goal was to get women elected to office—a rarity in the 1960s and 1970s. For all the second-wave feminists, though, a common goal was complete and discrimination-free access for women to any education or profession they might be interested in and qualified for. Most second-wave feminists went through years of battling traditions in education, in the workplace, and even within their own families to change the perception that there were things women shouldn't do and places women shouldn't go. Part of the battle was against the traditional assumption that women were more fragile and less intelligent than men. This is why a second-wave feminist, to this day, may balk at having the door held for her or her chair pulled out at the table by a man. These small protests, which sometimes puzzle third-wave feminists (that is, many college students today), should be seen in their proper perspective. If a man holds the door for a woman today, it is generally seen as a gesture of courtesy. However, in the long tradition challenged by second-wave feminists, holding the door meant for them that men found women in need of help because of their second-class status. These were hard-fought battles, and the fact that the perception of what women can do has changed so dramatically testifies to the fact that they are also hard-earned victories.

Some identify the beginning of the third wave of feminism with the publication of Carol Gilligan's *In A Different Voice* (1982); others find the publication of Susan Faludi's *Backlash: The Undeclared War Against American Women* (1991) to be the defining moment. Many point to the Senate hearings of 1991 in which Supreme Court nominee Clarence Thomas was accused of sexual harassment by law professor Anita Hill, formerly Thomas's aide. (Box 11.4 discusses the topic of sexual harassment.) The hearings launched sexual harassment into mainstream American culture as a social and legal concept, and the American public noted that (1) The committee hearing the charges was an all-male roster; it lacked any female perspective.

Box 11.4   WHAT IS SEXUAL HARASSMENT?

Since the 1970s sexual discrimination has been unacceptable in most Western cultures, but it is only within the past few decades that *sexual harassment* has been identified as a related but separate problem. Unfortunately there is little clarity about what exactly sexual harassment means. Does it mean that someone at your workplace or your school corners you and touches you? Or cracks sexist or obscene jokes in your presence? Does it mean that someone compliments you on your looks? Or that someone from your workplace or your school asks you out? What seems like sexual harassment to one person may not look like it to another, and that is why there are now guidelines for the perplexed. According to the California Fair Employment and Housing Act, sexual harassment consists of:

- Unwanted sexual advances
- Offering employment benefits in exchange for sexual favors
- Making or threatening reprisals after a negative response to sexual advances
- Visual conduct: leering, making sexual gestures, displaying of sexually suggestive objects or pictures, cartoons, or posters
- Verbal conduct: making or using derogatory comments, epithets, slurs, and jokes
- Verbal sexual advances or propositions
- Verbal abuse of a sexual nature; graphic verbal commentaries about an individual's body; sexually degrading words used to describe an individual; suggestive or obscene letters, notes, or invitations
- Physical conduct: touching, assault, impeding or blocking movements

From this list it is obvious that cornering and touching an employee is sexual harassment, regardless of whether the cornered person is male or female. But what about asking someone out? That should depend on whether the advance is considered sexual and whether or not it is wanted, and that would certainly be a case-by-case judgment. And could complimenting someone on her, or his, looks be construed as "verbal abuse"? Under certain circumstances it might, and this is what frustrates so many people, mostly men who are used to showing friendliness by complimenting female employees. In order to determine whether or not sexual harassment has taken place, review boards often ask the person making the complaint if he or she perceived the situation as being one of sexual harassment; it is thus the *perception* of the victimized person that will stand in many cases, not the *intention* of the perceived victimizer.

In order to avoid all such situations some simple rules of the road are suggested: If you are in a superior position, at school or in the workplace, don't go out with someone in a position that you may be able to influence, because it can be seen as a "benefit/reprisal" situation of pressure, with the other person's job or grades on the line. In addition, others may view your date as now having an unfair advantage in terms of grades or the job. Some schools are moving toward banning all relationships between instructors and students, as some workplaces are banning relationships between coworkers, to avoid misunderstandings, ill will after relationships end, and (let's be realistic) lawsuits — because, as the guidelines based on the Fair Employment and Housing Act read, "If harassment occurs, an employer may be liable even if management was not aware of the harassment."

(2) An overwhelming number of women came forth with similar experiences of having been harassed sexually by teachers, professors, bosses, and other male persons of authority—something that had not been publicly discussed prior to the hearings. As a result of the hearings, a large number of women decided to run for office in the 1992 election—1992 incidentally having been designated "the Year of the Woman" by the United Nations—and both the House and the Senate saw such an increase in women members that restrooms for women had to be installed.

Whereas the aim of the first wave of feminism was the achievement of suffrage and the second wave focused on a discrimination-free society, there is no defining idea (as yet) behind third-wave feminism. Some third-wavers believe that equality really has been achieved and that it is now up to individual women and men to learn to get along even better. Others believe the work has just begun. Radical feminists of the 1990s have striven to identify the roots of the sex-discrimination problem and believe that although patchwork improvements have been made, the patriarchy is still in place and must be addressed or uprooted. Other third-wavers have decided to focus on specific issues rather than on the big picture and engage themselves in feminist environmentalism, easier access to child care for working women, combating economic and racial discrimination along with sexual discrimination, and so forth.

There is no sharp line between second- and third-wave feminism. Generally, it is a generational reference. Feminists who were young in the 1950s, 1960s, and 1970s are thought to belong to the second wave; feminists who were young in the 1980s and 1990s are thought to belong to the third wave. But of course any individual can decide at any time to address any particular feminist issue. An older woman who has been living a life as a traditional homemaker without being touched or troubled by issues of sex discrimination may, perhaps because of widowhood, be thrown late in life into awareness of sex discrimination for the first time, and thus effectively become a second-wave feminist decades after other women of her own generation did.

Facets of Feminism Today

Today the idea of gender equality has several facets. Feminists generally agree that there should be gender equality, but they don't necessarily agree on what is female and male human nature, nor on what exactly our policies should be in order to combat gender discrimination. The philosophies of feminism are in a process of development, responding to the pressures of the past and present and the challenges of the future. One facet is *classical feminism,* which calls for men and women to be considered as *persons* first and gendered beings second. Another is *difference feminism,* which holds that women and men possess fundamentally different qualities and that both genders should learn from each other. A facet of feminism that sometimes has received bad press is *radical feminism;* although some radical feminists indeed seem to be militant or extremist, the main point of radical feminism is not to mount the barricades but to seek out and expose the *root* of the problem of gender discrimination ("root" is *radix* in Latin; hence, radical feminism). And then there is a breakout form of feminism severely criticized by many feminists that labels itself *equity femi-*

SALLY FORTH *by GREG HOWARD and CRAIG MacINTOSH*

© 1997 Greg Howard. Reprinted by permission of King Features Syndicate.

Classical feminism taught that if gender differences are perpetuated, it is to the detriment of women's freedom. One of the traditions discarded by classical feminists was chivalry: men holding doors for women, pulling out chairs, and so on. The underlying assumption, said classical feminism, was that women are too weak or stupid to do things themselves, so chivalry was, in effect, demeaning to women. Now, in the age of third-wave feminism, opinion is divided as to traditional male chivalry. What do you think—can men be chivalrous to women without being sexists? Should women also hold doors for men? Would that be a veiled comment on a man's weakness?

nism: An equity feminist holds that the battle for equality has been won, that we should not think of women as victims of patriarchy any longer, and that we can now adopt any kind of gender roles we like because gender discrimination is by and large a thing of the past. (Box 11.5 discusses equity feminism.)

Classical Feminism: Beauvoir and Androgyny

For those taking the view that men and women should be considered as persons first, gender differences are primarily cultural. Biological differences are significant only in terms of procreation, they say; apart from birthing and breastfeeding infants, which can be done only by women, the sexual differences are irrelevant. Culture has shaped men and women, and a cultural change could therefore allow for another type of gender: the *androgynous* type.

In her groundbreaking work *The Second Sex,* Simone de Beauvoir, one of the most powerful voices for equal education and equal opportunities in the twentieth century, accuses the philosophical tradition of seeing man as the "typical" human being, so woman thus becomes "atypical." For man, woman becomes "the Other," an alien being who helps man define himself through her alienness, and with whom he communicates on an everyday basis but who never becomes "one of the boys." Woman, who has been placed in this situation for millennia, has also come to believe she is atypical. The female anatomy is seen as a psychologically determining factor, whereas the male anatomy is not. In other words, women do what they do because they are women; men do what they do because they are normal. But this is a *cultural* fact, not a natural one, says Beauvoir. And the only way a woman can

Box 11.5   CHRISTINA HOFF SOMMERS'S EQUITY FEMINISM

In a highly controversial book, *Who Stole Feminism?* (1994), Christina Hoff Sommers (see Chapter 10) argues that feminism has been split into two movements: the "equity feminists," wanting equal opportunity for women and men, and the "gender feminists," "resenter feminists," or "feminist radicals," who, as Sommers sees it, have male-bashing as their main agenda. Sommers sees herself as an equity feminist. She also uses the terms "new feminists" and "gynocentric feminism" to describe the type of feminism she believes has done the movement a grave disservice by creating an atmosphere of general mistrust of men and of women who work with, support, or admire them. Here Sommers doesn't align herself exactly with any of the facets of feminism that we have discussed; although radical feminism comes closest to what she calls gender feminism, Sommers also finds that difference feminism has elements of misandry in that women's approaches are considered superior to those of men. And classical feminism, although being the form of feminism that probably comes closest to what Sommers calls equity feminism, also has elements of gender feminism for Sommers: Simone de Beauvoir,

she says, had no intention of letting women choose gender roles freely but wanted to dictate the proper upbringing and life choices for women. Among contemporary gender feminists, Sommers counts Susan Faludi, Marilyn French, Carolyn Heilbrun, and Catharine MacKinnon. Sommers writes:

> Once I get into the habit of regarding women as a subjugated gender, I'm primed to be alarmed, angry, and resentful of men as oppressors of women. I am also prepared to believe the words about them and the harm they cause to women. I may even be ready to fabricate atrocities. . . . Resenter feminists like Faludi, French, Heilbrun and MacKinnon speak of backlash, siege, and an undeclared war against women. But the condition they describe is mythic—with no foundation in the facts of contemporary American life.

Since women now have their political and personal freedom, says Sommers, they should be making use of it, instead of judging the authenticity of each other's attitudes:

> But women are no longer disenfranchised, and their preferences are being taken into account.

become *authentic* is to shed her role as "deviant" and become a true human being by rejecting the traditional female role. Society can assist in this process by treating little boys and girls the same—by giving them the same education and the same subsequent opportunities. Here we must remember that Beauvoir was engaged in issues other than feminism; she was, with her partner Jean-Paul Sartre, one of the strongest voices in the philosophical existentialist movement of the mid-twentieth century (see Chapter 10). Existentialism posits that there is no human nature; any attempt at claiming we *have to* do or be something is nothing but a poor excuse for not wanting to make a choice: *bad faith*. If we carry this over into Beauvoir's theory of feminism, we understand what she means when she says that a woman must shed her culturally given role as the second sex: There is no female human nature any more than there is any human nature in general; we must fight the cultural traps of gen-

Nor are they now taught that they are subordinate or that a subordinate role for them is fitting and proper. . . . Since women today can no longer be regarded as the victims of an undemocratic indoctrination, we must regard their preferences as "authentic." Any other attitude toward American women is unacceptably patronizing and profoundly illiberal.

The feminists Sommers criticizes generally respond that Sommers herself has misunderstood the goals and nature of feminism; while the overt oppression of previous times is over, it has now become covert, internalized, and it lives in the hearts of the critics of feminism, women as well as men. Although opportunities have opened to women, many women still grow up believing that the masculine cultural world is their only option; it takes a long time for such wounds to heal, and they don't heal without active interference. For that reason, and for their own sake, women must be shown that equality is still far away. So when Sommers says women have the right to choose a life in which they work at home, raising children, or work in a male-dominated environment or when she says they have the right to enjoy romance literature in which men are strong and women are seduced, then Sommers must herself have internalized the traditional male view of what a woman's proper place is, according to some critics.

Sommers responds by claiming that gender feminism simply does not represent the viewpoint of most women today—women who are politically aware and concerned with gender equality—in other words, feminists. Most women today, says Sommers, have access to the professions of their choice and want to lead lives in which they have friendly relations with male coworkers and loving relations with male partners. Many want families, and some even want to live the traditional life of a homemaker, and they are not interested in being represented by women who tell them they have a false consciousness. As a fellow equity feminist, Sommers cites the author and fellow philosopher Iris Murdoch, who believed in a "culture of humanity," not in a "new female ghetto" of misandric feminism.

der roles and their assumption that this is how we have to be, because that is nothing but a poor excuse for not making our own choices. (However, if we should *want to* make the choice of traditional gender roles, Beauvoir would have little patience with us, since she believed the choice of gender freedom is best made if the traditional option of stay-at-home-mom is not available to women. Many contemporary feminists find that this hardly constitutes true freedom of choice.)

It is against the background of the traditional male philosophical approach to the gender question that Beauvoir criticizes Emmanuel Levinas and his view of the Other as essentially feminine (see Chapter 10). To Beauvoir, this is nothing but old-fashioned reactionary male-oriented thinking, because for a classical feminist like her, the attitude of seeing the sexes as fundamentally different also means that one is generally dominating the other; when Levinas praises feminine qualities as the nurturing and welcoming element in both men and women, the classical feminist still sees this as discrimination (against men as well as against women) because it persists in stereo-typing the typically feminine as nurturing.

Until women begin to think of themselves as a group, Beauvoir says, they will believe that they are abnormal human beings. And as long as men and women re-ceive different educations and different treatment from society, woman will not feel responsible for the state of the world but will regard herself as men regard her — as an overgrown child. Of course women are weak, Beauvoir says. Of course they don't use male logic (here we must remember that she is talking about uneducated women before World War II). Of course they are religious to the point of superstition. Of course they have no sense of history, and of course they accept authority. Of course they cry a lot over little things. They may even be lazy, sensual, servile, frivolous, utilitarian, materialistic, and hysterical. They may, in short, be all that some male thinkers thought they were. *But why are women all these things?* Because they have no power except by subterfuge. They have no education, so they have never been taught about the cause and effect of history and the relative powers of authority. They are caught up in a never-ending stream of housework, which causes them to be practically oriented. They nag because they realize they have no power to change their situation. They are sensual because they are bored. In *The Second Sex* Beauvoir says, "The truth is that when a woman is engaged in an enterprise worthy of a human being, she is quite able to show herself as active, effective, taciturn — and as ascetic — as a man." (See Box 11.6 for Beauvoir's influence on modern philosophy.)

So if we change our culture, we will change what has for so long been consid-ered female nature — and with it, probably also male nature. We will create people who are responsible human beings above all and who will respect each other for that reason. This philosophy was adopted by many late-twentieth-century feminists, in-cluding Germaine Greer, Gloria Steinem, and Joyce Trebilcot.

The quest for *androgynism* has taken on several shapes. A moderate, modern viewpoint advocates a common upbringing for all children, one that avoids using pink for girls and blue for boys and makes use of toys that don't perpetuate typical male/female roles. Proponents of this viewpoint advocate a general change in lan-guage from gender-specific terms to gender-neutral terms.

Two versions of androgynism as a political goal have been advocated, and Joyce Trebilcot analyzes both. One proposes a society in which men and women *share all the best characteristics of the traditional gender roles*; and if a woman *doesn't* want to hold a job (typically a male role) or if a man prefers *not* to care for his sick chil-dren (typically a female role), then society must teach them the necessity of sharing these duties. This version is sometimes referred to as *monoandrogynism.* The other version, *polyandrogynism,* suggests that gender roles be left as open as possible, with no demand that the duties be shared. If a man wants to fulfill the traditional male role, he is free to do so. If a woman wants to live the life of a traditional male, she can. If a man wants to stay home and care for the kids, fine. If a woman wants to do the same thing, so be it. Both theories assume that gender roles are cultural artifacts; however, polyandrogynism allows for the possibility that people just might be bio-logically different from one another. Trebilcot herself opts for polyandrogynism.

Box 11.6   THE OTHER: SIMONE DE BEAUVOIR

Simone de Beauvoir (1908–1986), a feminist and existentialist, was long considered a minor thinker by the philosophical community. One reason was that she was Jean-Paul Sartre's "significant other," and her books, such as *The Second Sex,* show considerable influence from Sartre's ideas. However, most philosophers now recognize that many of the fundamental ideas of existentialism came about through discussions between Sartre and Beauvoir, and many ideas first published by Sartre may well have originated during these discussions. There is even some suspicion that Sartre occasionally may have published ideas by Beauvoir under his own name. True or not, this new attitude reveals a changing perspective on women in philosophy. In the twenty-first century, Beauvoir's influence in the area of gender inequality has turned out to be just as viable as Sartre's philosophy. Beauvoir is primarily interested in the existence of woman as a cultural phenomenon; she analyzes woman's subjugation in a man's world—a situation that was far more common in the mid-twentieth century than now. She hopes that instead of a world where woman is considered deviant and man normal, we will have a society of *human beings,* not just males and females,

and people will interact with each other equally as productive, authentic beings. Beauvoir has come under heavy criticism from some feminists for not realizing that she herself regards man as the norm and wants women to be treated and to act like men, rather than rejoice in their inherent female nature. It appears that Beauvoir herself decided to live a child-free life in order to escape the female stereotype.

An ultraradical version of androgynism assumes that there are profound biological differences between men and women and suggests that we eradicate them. Thus if women are the only humans capable of giving birth, we must *change human biology* so that this becomes an option for men also.

The question is, Can we choose our gender at all? Obviously we can't choose our *sex* (not without going through major surgery, anyway). But the term *gender* also encompasses our *social roles* as male and female. Can we, then, decide which social role we wish to adapt—which gender we wish to be—or do biological factors exist that prevent people from exercising gender choice? In other words, is our gender determined by our biology to a greater extent than people who advocate androgyny realize?

Psychologists of the 1960s and 1970s generally assumed that sex roles were purely a matter of upbringing, or *nurture.* The theory of *psychosexual neutrality,* inspired

CATHY © 1997 Cathy Guisewite. Reprinted with permission of Universal Press Syndicate. All rights reserved.

The psychologist John Gray theorizes in his best-selling self-help book *Men Are from Mars, Women Are from Venus* that men and women have very different approaches and expectations. Difference feminism agrees. Classical feminism, on the other hand, assumes that if we minimize gender differences in a child's upbringing, a new generation of people who are persons first and gendered beings second will appear. Here is a classical feminist, Cathy, with a classical feminist dilemma: how to buy for children without perpetuating gender stereotypes. Does cartoonist Cathy Guisewite touch on a real problem? If so, what can be done about it?

by the theory of behaviorism, which arose earlier in the century, held that a child can be molded into being male or female, but is born neither except by virtue of the genitals; if a person seems stereotypically male, it is because of his upbringing, and not a biological fact. This theory also suggests that if we'd like our children to be less stereotypically male or female than tradition expects, we just have to give them a more unisex upbringing. But the theory of psychosexual neutrality has come under severe criticism within the past few years: Cases that had been reported as successful molding of children born with ambiguous genitalia (formerly called hermaphrodites, they're now referred to as *intersexual* children) are now under scrutiny for simply having assigned a sex to the child and assuming that upbringing and hormone treatment would take care of the rest.

A disturbing story is that of David Reimer, who lost his penis to a botched circumcision as an infant in the late 1960s and was raised as a girl, Brenda. In spite of the parents' well-meaning efforts to convince Brenda that she was a girl, she never felt comfortable, and upon discovering the truth at the age of fourteen, promptly discarded the female persona for that of David. He has since had reconstructive surgery. The case of Brenda/David as well as cases of intersexual children do seem to point toward *nature* being more important in forming a person's sexual identity than *nurture* is. (See Box 11.7 for a discussion of homosexuality and gender choice.) But we shouldn't discount the influence of nurture completely: The manner in which we express our sexuality and whether or not we become "typically" male or female may well be a matter of our upbringing, at least to some extent.

Difference Feminism: Gilligan and the Ethic of Care

The idea that nature will prevail over nurture has given a boost to the theory of *difference feminism,* which emerged in the 1980s to claim that women and men should be viewed as equal, but fundamentally different. By the beginning of the 1980s women had been in the workforce long enough for people to begin to evaluate the situation, and although some women felt good about working in what used to be a "man's world" and conforming to its standards (to a greater or lesser degree), others felt that somehow those standards were damaging to their female identity. Few provisions for child care existed, there was little understanding of family demands, and the overriding atmosphere was one of competition and isolation rather than cooperation and teamwork. For these women, survival in the male-dominated public sphere was possible only if they were willing to give up some of their female values. Difference feminism proposed that the feminist agenda could include not just equal opportunity and equal pay for men and women but an acknowledgment that many women want something different than men do and some of women's capabilities lie in areas other than those of most men.

Interestingly enough, this was not the first time such ideas have been advanced— Western history, and certainly the history of philosophy, is rich with statements about the nature of women being different from that of men. Some famous examples include Aristotle, who believed that women were deformed men; Kant, who found it thoroughly improper for a woman to display any interest in intellectual or technological

Box 11.7   CAN GAYS CHOOSE NOT TO BE GAY?

In talking about the possibility of choosing gender roles, it is reasonable to discuss the issue of homosexuality and the gay lifestyle. There is still considerable political and moral opposition to homosexuals in Western societies, in some more than in others. In some societies homosexuals can now marry; in others homosexuality is still illegal. Why is there a traditional opposition to homosexuality in Christian countries? It is because of several traditional Christian assumptions, such as (1) homosexuality is a *moral choice,* and one that goes against nature (nature calls for procreation), so homosexuality is morally wrong; and (2) homosexuals are primarily seducers of adolescents, who will then become homosexual. In the early 1990s scientists reached the *tentative* conclusion (based on brain autopsies) that male homosexuality is not a matter of choice but of biology. In that case both of the above objections would be invalid, because (1) gay men don't choose their lifestyle or sexual orientation but are born with it (so it is *natural* for them); and (2) boys can't be se-

duced to become homosexuals; they either are born that way or not. (Besides, being gay does not imply that one is primarily interested in young boys.) But there is as yet no extensive research about lesbianism, nor about bisexualism. The advantage for homosexuals of a conclusive result pointing to biological factors is obvious: There could be no more reason for discrimination based on the belief that homosexuality is an "immoral choice." But such a finding might open the door for new areas of discrimination: Might we see parents take their young children to the doctor to have them "screened" for homosexuality, and if they test positive, ask to have them "cured"? In this way homosexuality would be labeled a *defect,* a disease. Some homosexuals might say they would prefer to be heterosexual if that were possible, but certainly not all would. Joyce Trebilcot would say that in a polyandrogynous society the question of what your sexual orientation ought to be would never come up in the first place.

pursuits, even if she might be good at them; Rousseau, who saw a woman as a man's helpmate and little else; and Nietzsche, who admired women for being more "natural" than men but vilified them for being inconsistent. Theories such as these all state that women and men have different abilities and thus different places in society. However, these theories were not advanced with any notion of gender equality. John Stuart Mill was the first influential philosopher to suggest that although men and women have different capacities, they should nevertheless be given equal opportunities and equal respect for their abilities. It is this concept toward which the new feminism looks.

In general, the values we've celebrated for so long as good human behavior have been predominantly male values, say the new feminists, because the male person has been considered the "real" person, whereas women have been thought of as slightly deviant. The man is the typical human being. In older textbooks on human development, the earlier forms of hominids, such as *Homo habilis* and *Neandertal,* have usually been depicted as males ("Neandertal man"). Only recently in textbooks and articles have humans been symbolized by both male and female figures. Even recent theories of psychology seem to use boys and men as their research material

Carol Gilligan (b. 1936), American psychologist and author of *In a Different Voice.* Like Simone de Beauvoir, Gilligan believes that throughout Western history men have been considered the "normal" gender and women have been viewed as not-quite-normal. However, unlike Beauvoir, Gilligan does not argue for a monoandrogynous society, believing instead that men and women are fundamentally different in their approach to life — different but equal.

rather than girls and women, and the medical community must now face the problems resulting from years of conducting research with primarily male subjects. The statistics regarding women and certain diseases (heart disease, for example) are unreliable, and the administration of medicine to women is often decided on the basis of research on male subjects. This is not just a matter of a slanted ideology; it is a very practical problem. Women have for a long time been judged by the standards of men, as though women were what Aristotle claimed so long ago — deficient males. Difference feminism wants to replace the image of one of the genders being more "normal" than the other with an image of both genders, with all their unique characteristics, being equally representative of the human race. This shift involves upgrading the female tasks of motherhood, housekeeping, caring for family members, and so on, tasks that for some people seemed to fall by the wayside in the first rush to get women into the workforce. Typical female virtues that arise from concentrating on these tasks are generosity, caring, harmony, reconciliation, and maintenance of close relationships. The virtues that typically have been considered male are justice, rights, fairness, competition, independence, and adherence to the rules.

Psychologist Carol Gilligan has been a major inspiration in the gender debate. Her book *In a Different Voice* (1982) analyzes reactions of boys and girls, men and women, and concludes that there is a basic difference in the *moral attitudes* of males and females. In one of her analyses she uses an experiment by a well-known contemporary psychologist, Lawrence Kohlberg; it is called the *Heinz dilemma.* An interviewer using Kohlberg's method asked two eleven-year-old children, Jake and Amy, to evaluate the following situation: Heinz's wife is desperately ill, and Heinz can't afford medication for her. Should Heinz steal the medication? Jake has no doubts; he says yes, Heinz should steal the medication, because his wife's life is more important than the rule of not stealing. Amy, though, is not so sure. She says no, he shouldn't steal the medication, because what if he got caught? Then he would have to go to jail, and who would look after his sick wife? Perhaps he could ask the pharmacist to let him have the medication and pay later. The interviewer concluded that Jake had a clear understanding of the situation: It would be just that the wife should receive the medication, because her rights would override the law of not stealing. The interviewer thought that Amy's comprehension of the situation was fuzzy at best. Jake understood what it was all about: rights and justice.

Gilligan rereads Amy's answer and comes up with another conclusion entirely: Although Jake answered the question *Should Heinz steal the drug or not?* Amy heard it differently: *Should Heinz steal the drug, or should he do something else?* In effect, the children were answering different questions, and Amy's response makes as much sense as Jake's. But Amy is not concerned with the issues of rights and justice as much as she is with what will happen to Heinz and his wife; she even takes the humaneness of the pharmacist into consideration. In other words, she thinks in terms of *caring.* She acknowledges that there are laws, but she also believes people can be reasoned with. The interviewer, Gilligan says, didn't hear this in Amy's answer because he was looking for the "justice" answer. Gilligan concludes that boys and men tend to focus on an *ethic of justice,* while girls and women look toward an *ethic of care.*

Gilligan's influence on modern thinking about gender issues has been enormous, although other philosophers, psychologists, and linguists have also approached them in similar ways. You may remember the debate in Chapter 7 about justice, in which John Rawls suggested that we adopt "the original position," pretending that we don't know who we are when our policy takes effect; you may also remember the responses from Wolgast and Friedman that we can't just assume we are strangers who don't know each other, because part of being a social person is precisely that we have caring relationships with others and don't just exist in some abstract legal universe. This is, in essence, similar to Gilligan's criticism of a traditional ethic of justice as being the traditional male approach to moral questions and emphasizes that we can't just pretend we don't have our own gender.

Does this mean Gilligan is claiming that all women are always caring? That is a matter of interpretation. Some readers see her theory as a description of what we might call the "female condition": Because of either nature or upbringing or both, most women *are* caring human beings. Others see this as a preposterous statement. Not all women are caring, and few women, even if they are generally caring persons, are caring all the time. Gilligan's theory of the ethics of care does not have to be read as a description of how women really act, though; with its emphasis on values it is a theory about how most women believe they *ought to act.* It is a theory of women's normative values—we might call it a theory about the *caring imperative*—not a theory about some inevitable female nature.

What does the Gilligan theory add up to? For many women it means that their experiences of attachment and their focus on relationships are normal and good and not "overly dependent," "clinging," or "immature;" it means an upgrading of what we consider traditional female values. The point of Gilligan's book is to prompt the mature woman to understand rights and the mature man to understand caring, so we all can work and live together in harmony. Her hopes may not be realized for decades to come, however, for although some may argue that they know some very caring men and some very justice-oriented women, it seems Gilligan is right in claiming that most women in the United States grow up believing that caring is what is most important, and most men grow up believing that individual rights and justice are the ultimate ethical values.

There are risks involved in Gilligan's theory. Some think we may end up elevating female values far above male values. In that case we will have reversed an unfair system but created another unfair system by declaring women "normal" and men "slightly deviant." A more pressing problem is the following: If we say it is in a woman's nature to be understanding and caring, we may be forcing her right back into the private sphere from which she just emerged. Men (and also women) may say, Well, if most women aren't able to understand "justice," then we can't use them in the real world, and they'd better go home and do what nature intended them to do: have babies and care for their man. Similarly, if a job calls for "caring" qualities, employers may be reluctant to hire a man, because men are not "naturals" at caring. So instead of giving people more opportunities, Gilligan may actually be setting up new categories that could result in policies that exclude women from "men's work" and men from "women's work." It is not enough to say that the qualities of one gender are not supposed to outweigh the qualities of the other, because we all know that even with the best intentions, we tend to rank one set of differences higher than the other. We may all be equal, but remember George Orwell's *Animal Farm?* In this novel, which is a metaphor for political despotism, Orwell warns against some being considered "more equal than others." Critics have claimed that what Gilligan is doing is throwing a monkey wrench into the philosophy of gender equality, and her "ethic of care" theory may result in statements such as this: "We need a new executive with a good head for legal rules — but we can't hire a woman, of course, even though she seems otherwise qualified, because science says that women have a lousy sense of justice." In short, there is a danger that a psychological theory of gender may shift from describing what seems to be the case to prescribing a set of rules about who ought to do what.

Although her theory of the ethic of care may raise problems in the future, there is no doubt that Gilligan has touched on something a vast number of women have been able to relate to. I'll let this anecdote illustrate her talent for seizing the situation: A few years ago she gave the keynote address at an ethics conference at the University of San Diego. Gilligan, who is a petite woman, arrived at the podium in the great lecture hall — and completely disappeared behind the imposing lectern, designed in a more traditional age for taller male scholars. No provisions had been made for shorter speakers. Causing a storm of applause, she reappeared on the other side of the lectern and grabbed the microphone, calmly commenting, "There is obviously still work to be done!"

Recently Gilligan and other feminists engaged in a written debate in the *Atlantic Monthly* with Christina Hoff Sommers (see Box 11.5 and Chapter 10) who by then had acquired a solid reputation among some feminists as being no feminist at all. Sommers had just published a book, *The War Against Boys,* in which she claimed that because of what she calls gender feminism, young boys are now facing a hard time in school. Contrary to the standard wisdom that girls are overlooked in the classroom in favor of the more assertive boys, Sommers says it is in fact the girls who nowadays are getting all the attention from the teachers, and are being held up as role models as smarter and better behaved than the boys. This makes boys lose self-esteem. Sommers's claims caused consternation and disbelief among readers of the

Atlantic Monthly, where her views were first published. But she has also found an audience who agree that conditions in schools have changed dramatically over the past decades to the benefit of girls, and we need to look at the possibility that in some cases it may have come at a price: the shortchanging of boys.

Radical Feminism: Uprooting Sexism

The term *radical* alone is often enough to make some people tune out. We are used to the term meaning "extremism." For some, a radical feminist is a stereotypical male-basher. But we must be cautious here, because much depends on how we interpret the term *radical*. If we read it as "extremist feminism," then it will generally be used by nonfeminists to describe anything they disagree with as being too extreme. The feminists themselves who are tagged with the label may think of themselves as mainstream. It is thus a relative concept, and often used in a disparaging sense, meaning any feminism that goes further than you're willing to accept ("Equal pay for equal work" could sound like radical feminism to some traditionalists). To be sure, there are feminists who think in more sweeping terms than others. Some see sexual intercourse with men as inherently humiliating for women. And there are misandric feminists who assume that all men are incapable of wanting or working for gender equality, just as there are misogynist men who think ill of all women. But most of those who today call themselves radical feminists have a different agenda: They take the term *radical* in its original Latin meaning, going to the *root (radix)* of the matter. Such radical feminists ask, How did gender discrimination arise? What were the structures that kept it in place? And do we still have elements of those structures today? The answers are generally: *It arose in patriarchy;* those structures have kept gender discrimination alive to this day. A child is still considered to be of the father's family more than of the mother's; yet a mother is still considered to be the primary caregiver of a child taken ill at school, even though the father's profession might be less demanding than hers and his workplace closer to the child's school. A woman is still expected to take her career less seriously than a man is, and some continue to consider a woman's career contributions as less important than a man's. Sexual liberty is still considered more acceptable for boys and men than for girls and women. Commercials persist in depicting women in the kitchen and men at the workbench. Little girls' toys are still in the pink section in the toy stores, and little boys' toys are still action figures from a world with practically no equal women participants. The radical feminist doesn't necessarily want boys to play with dolls or girls to play Mortal Kombat, but she or he wants us to understand *where these choices are coming from* and to decide to discard any tradition that sees women as lesser beings than men.

A famous radical feminist, Andrea Dworkin, wrote in her book *Right-Wing Women: The Politics of Domesticated Females* (1983):

> To achieve a single standard of human freedom and one absolute standard of human dignity, the sex-class system has to be dismembered. The reason is pragmatic, not philosophical: Nothing less will work. However much everyone wants to do less, less will not

free women. Liberal men and women ask, Why can't we just be ourselves, all human beings, begin now and not dwell in past injustices, wouldn't that subvert the sex-class system, change it from the inside out? The answer is no. The sex-class system has a structure; it has deep roots in religion and culture; it is fundamental to the economy; sexuality is its creature; to be 'just human beings' in it, women have to hide what happens to them as women because they are women—happenings like forced sex and forced reproduction, happenings that continue as long as the sex-class system operates. The liberation of women requires facing the real condition of women in order to change it. 'We're all just people' is a stance that prohibits recognition of the systematic cruelties visited upon women because of sex oppression.

Dworkin says that one of the toughest challenges to women is to realize that all women have a common condition, even women you don't like, women you don't want to be compared to. The common condition is that women are, in Dworkin's words, "subordinate to men, sexually colonized in a sexual system of dominance and submission, denied rights on the basis of sex, historically chattel, generally considered biologically inferior, confined to sex and reproduction: this is the general description of the social environment in which all women live."

The goal of radical feminism is thus to raise the individual awareness of what the patriarchal tradition has done to us, men as well as women. We must try to undo the social and psychological damage done by centuries of male-dominated culture—by making women aware of how much in their personal and professional lives has been dominated and designed by men. Radical feminism sees women's minds as by and large shaped by men's accomplishments and thinking, and unless women learn to focus on women's talents and accomplishments, they/we will always have a "false consciousness": We think we understand, but all we have to work with are mind tools and concepts invented by men. Another radical feminist, Gerda Lerner, says that women have until recently been excluded from the "power of naming and defining." Men have defined the problems deemed worthy of attention, as well as the vocabulary with which they should be described. Being able to put a name to a problem is part of solving it, and if women are deprived of naming their own problems, the problems remain unrecognized. For that reason, sex discrimination isn't uprooted simply by listening to the private wishes and professional ideas of women, because these wishes and ideas may be favored by the male tradition we all grew up within. Radical feminism insists that both women and men must be educated to see this tradition as one of oppression and be encouraged to create a new one based on a female perspective.

Study Questions

1. Give a brief account of the similarities and differences between classical, difference, radical, and equity feminism. Can these facets overlap? Explain.

2. Can a third-wave feminist be a classical feminist? Can a first-wave feminist be a difference feminist? Can a second-wave feminist be a radical feminist? Explain.

3. Which brand of feminism do you think is the most relevant today? Are you a feminist? If yes, why? If no, why not?

4. Outline the advantages and problems associated with difference feminism.

Primary Readings and Narratives

The first Primary Reading is an excerpt from Simone de Beauvoir's *The Second Sex*. The second is an excerpt from Carol Gilligan's *In a Different Voice*. The third is an excerpt from the linguist Deborah Tannen's *Talking from 9 to 5* in which she explores the phenomenon of sexual harassment from a male and female point of view. The first Narrative is a summary and excerpt from the classic play by Henrik Ibsen, *A Doll's House*, in which a nineteenth-century housewife, treated as a beloved but mischievous child by her husband, proves to be very much an adult person. The second Narrative is a summary of Laura Esquivel's novel *Like Water for Chocolate*, in which we get to know the women in the De la Garza family. The third Narrative is a summary of and excerpts from Beauvoir's short story "A Woman Destroyed," in which the title character's husband leaves her for another woman. The final Narrative is a summary of the film *Thelma and Louise*, about two women who unintentionally embark on a crime spree and end up finding themselves.

 Primary Reading

The Second Sex

SIMONE DE BEAUVOIR

Excerpt, 1949.

In this excerpt, Beauvoir demonstrates her commitment to what we have called classical feminism: If boys and girls were raised as human beings rather than two different species, sexism would no longer exist. The "castration complex" and the "Oedipus complex" are references to Sigmund Freud's psychoanalytic theories that little girls feel inferior to boys because they have no penis (and believe they have been deprived of one). Here you should remember that the style of child-rearing Beauvoir criticizes is, for most educated people in the Western world, a thing of the past. Her critical assessment of the traditional upbringing of boys and girls has been a powerful factor in changing that tradition.

A world where men and women would be equal is easy to visualize, for that precisely is what the Soviet Revolution *promised*: women raised and trained exactly like men were to work under the same conditions and for the same wages. Erotic liberty was to be recognized by custom, but the sexual act was not to be considered a "service" to be paid for; woman was to be *obliged* to provide herself with other ways of earning a living; marriage was to be based on a free agreement that the spouses could break at will; maternity was to be voluntary, which meant that contraception and abortion were to be authorized and that, on the other hand, all mothers and their children were to have exactly the same rights, in or out of marriage; pregnancy leaves were to be paid for by the State, which would assume charge of the children, signifying not that they would be *taken away* from their parents, but that they would not be *abandoned* to them.

But is it enough to change laws, institutions, customs, public opinion, and the whole social context, for men and women to become truly equal? "Women will always be women," say the skeptics. Other seers prophesy that in casting off their femininity they will not succeed in changing themselves into men and they will become monsters. This would be to admit that the woman of today is a creation of nature; it must be repeated once more that in human society nothing is natural and that woman, like much else, is a product elaborated by civilization. The intervention of others in her destiny is fundamental: if this action took a different direction, it would produce a quite different result. Woman is determined not by her hormones or by mysterious instincts, but by the manner in which her body and her relation to the world are modified through the action of others than herself. The abyss that separates the adolescent boy and girl has been deliberately opened out between them since earliest childhood; later on, woman could not be other than what she *was made,* and that past was bound to shadow her for life. If we appreciate its influence, we see clearly that her destiny is not predetermined for all eternity.

We must not believe, certainly, that a change in woman's economic condition alone is enough to transform her, though this factor has been and remains the basic factor in her evolution; but until it has brought about the moral, social, cultural, and other consequences that it promises and requires, the new woman cannot appear. At this moment they have been realized nowhere, in Russia no more than in France or the United States; and this explains why the woman of today is torn between the past and the future. She appears most often as a "true woman" disguised as a man, and she feels herself as ill at ease in her flesh as in her masculine garb. She must shed her old skin and cut her own new clothes. This she could do only through a social evolution. No single educator could fashion a *female human being* today who would be the exact homologue of the *male human being;* if she is raised like a boy, the young girl feels she is an oddity and thereby she is given a new kind of sex specification. Stendhal [a nineteenth-century French novelist] understood this when he said: "The forest must be planted all at once." But if we imagine, on the contrary, a society in which the equality of the sexes would be concretely realized, this equality would find new expression in each individual.

If the little girl were brought up from the first with the same demands and rewards, the same severity and the same freedom, as her brothers, taking part in the same studies, the same games, promised the same future, surrounded with women and men who seemed to her undoubted equals, the meanings of the castration complex and of the Oedipus complex would be profoundly modified. Assuming on the same basis as the father the material and moral responsibility of the couple, the mother would enjoy the same lasting prestige; the child would perceive around her an androgynous world and not a masculine world. Were she emotionally more attracted to her father—which is not even sure—her love for him would be tinged with a will to emulation and not a feeling of powerlessness; she would not be oriented toward passivity. Authorized to test her powers in work and sports, competing actively with the boys, she would not find the absence of the penis—compensated by the promise of a child—enough to give rise to an inferiority complex; correlatively, the boy would not have a superiority complex if it were not instilled into him and if he looked up to women with as much respect as to men. The little girl would not seek sterile compensation in narcissism and dreaming, she would not take her fate for granted; she would be interested in what she was *doing,* she would throw herself without reserve into undertakings. . . .

I shall be told that all this is utopian fancy, because woman cannot be "made over" unless society has first made her really the equal of man. Conservatives have never failed in such circumstances to refer to that vicious circle; history, however, does not revolve. If a caste is kept in a state of inferiority, no doubt it remains inferior; but liberty can break the circle. Let the Negroes vote and they become worthy of having the vote; let woman be given responsibilities and she is able to assume them. The fact is that oppressors cannot be expected to make a move of gratuitous generosity; but at one time the revolt of the oppressed, at another time even the very evolution of the privileged caste itself, creates new situations; thus men have been led, in their own interest, to give partial emancipation to women: it remains only for women to continue their ascent, and the successes they are obtaining are an encouragement for them to do so. It seems almost certain that sooner or later they will arrive at complete economic and social equality, which will bring about an inner metamorphosis.

However this may be, there will be some to object that if such a world is possible it is not desirable. When woman is "the same" as her male, life will lose its salt and spice. This argument, also, has lost its novelty: those interested in perpetuating present conditions are always in tears about the marvelous past that is about to disappear, without having so much as a smile for the young future. It is quite true that doing away with the slave trade meant death to the great plantations, magnificent with azaleas and camellias, it meant ruin to the whole refined Southern civilization. The attics of time have received its rare odd laces along with the clear pure voices of the Sistine *castrati,* and there is a certain "feminine charm" that is also on the way to the same dusty repository. I agree that he would be a barbarian indeed who failed to appreciate exquisite flowers, rare lace, the crystal clear voice of the eunuch, and feminine charm.

When the "charming woman" shows herself in all her splendor, she is a much more exalting object than the "idiotic paintings, overdoors, scenery, showman's garish signs, popular chromos," that excited [French poet Arthur] Rimbaud; adorned with the most modern artifices, beautified according to the newest techniques, she comes down from the remoteness of the ages, from Thebes, from Crete, from Chichén-Itzá; and she is also the totem set up deep in the African jungle; she is a helicopter and she is a bird; and there is this, the greatest wonder of all: under her tinted hair the forest murmur becomes a thought, and words issue from her breasts. Men stretch forth avid hands toward the marvel, but when they grasp it it is gone; the wife, the mistress, speak like everybody else through their mouths: their words are worth just what they are worth; their breasts also. Does such a fugitive miracle—and one so rare—justify us in perpetuating a situation that is baneful for both sexes? One can appreciate them at their true value; if these treasures cost blood or misery, they must be sacrificed.

Study Questions

1. Identify the characteristic elements of classical feminism in this excerpt.

2. Comment on Beauvoir's remark that one can appreciate the beauty of flowers, the charm of women, and "appreciate them at their true value; if these treasures cost blood and misery, they must be sacrificed."

3. What does Beauvoir mean by saying, "Let the Negroes vote and they become worthy of having the vote; let woman be given responsibilities and she is able to assume them"?

4. Evaluate the criticism that the gender-free model of upbringing Beauvoir envisions for boys and girls is really just patterned after the traditional upbringing of boys; does Beauvoir want women to become men in order to achieve social and political freedom?

Primary Reading

In a Different Voice

CAROL GILLIGAN

Excerpt, 1982.

In this excerpt, Gilligan refers to the psychoanalyst Erik Erikson, whom you encountered in Chapter 10. Erikson's theory of development focuses on the importance of the adolescent boy's separating himself from his parents to achieve a personal identity, before he can experience any intimacy. For the adolescent girl it is different, says Erikson; she doesn't experience the same kind of separation. However, it is the boy's development that becomes the typical individual development for Erikson, according to Gilligan. In this excerpt she also refers to how fairy tales may give similar portrayals of male and female psychology. Gilligan here introduces the experience of the ethic of care from the woman's point of view.

Erikson's description of male identity as forged in relation to the world and of female identity as awakened in a relationship of intimacy with another person is hardly new. In the fairy tales that [psychoanalyst] Bruno Bettelheim describes [in *The Uses of Enchantment*] an identical portrayal appears. The dynamics of male adolescence are illustrated archetypically by the conflict between father and son in "The Three Languages." Here a son, considered hopelessly stupid by his father, is given one last chance at education and sent for a year to study with a master. But when he returns, all he has learned is "what the dogs bark." After two further attempts of this sort, the father gives up in disgust and orders his servants to take the child into the forest and kill him. But the servants, those perpetual rescuers of disowned and abandoned children, take pity on the child and decide simply to leave him in the forest. From there, his wanderings take him to a land beset by furious dogs whose barking permits nobody to rest and who periodically devour one of the inhabitants. Now it turns out that our hero has learned just the right thing: he can talk with the dogs and is able to quiet them, thus restoring peace to the land. Since the other knowledge he acquires serves him equally well, he emerges triumphant from his adolescent confrontation with his father, a giant of the life-cycle conception.

In contrast, the dynamics of female adolescence are depicted through the telling of a very different story. In the world of the fairy tale, the girl's first bleeding is followed by a period of intense passivity in which nothing seems to be happening. Yet in the deep sleeps of Snow White and Sleeping Beauty, Bettelheim sees that inner concentration which he considers to be the necessary counterpart to the activity of adventure. Since the adolescent heroines awake from their sleep, not to conquer the world, but to marry the prince, their identity is inwardly and interpersonally defined. For women, in Bettelheim's as in Erikson's account, identity and intimacy are intricately conjoined. The sex differences depicted in the world of fairy tales, like the fantasy of the woman warrior in Maxine Hong Kingston's recent autobiographical novel [*The Woman Warrior*, 1977] which echoes the old stories of Troilus and Cressida and Tancred and Corinda, indicate repeatedly that active adventure is a male activity, and that if a woman is to embark on such endeavors, she must at least dress like a man. [. . .]

"It is obvious," Virginia Woolf says, "that the values of women differ very often from the values which have been made by the other sex." Yet, she adds, "it is the masculine values that prevail." As a result, women come to question the normality of their feelings and to alter their judgments in deference to the opinion of others. In the nineteenth-century novels written by women, Woolf sees at work "a mind which was slightly pulled from the straight and made to alter its clear vision in deference to external authority." The same deference to the values and opinions of others can be seen in the judgments of twentieth-century women. The difficulty women experience in finding or speaking publicly in their own voices emerges repeatedly in the form of qualification and self-doubt, but also in intimations of a divided judgment, a public assessment and private assessment which are fundamentally at odds.

Yet the deference and confusion that Woolf criticizes in women derive from the values she sees as their strength. Women's deference is rooted not only in their social subordination but also in the substance of their moral concern. Sensitivity to the needs of others and the assumption of responsibility for taking care lead women to attend to voices other than their own and to include in their judgment other points of view. Women's moral weakness, manifest in an apparent diffusion and confusion of judgment, is thus inseparable from women's moral strength, an overriding concern with relationships and responsibilities. The reluctance to judge may itself be indicative of the care and concern for others that infuse the psychology of women's development and are responsible for what is generally seen as problematic in its nature.

Thus women not only define themselves in a context of human relationship but also judge themselves in terms of their ability to care. Women's place in man's life cycle has been that of nurturer, caretaker, and helpmate, the weaver of those networks of relationships on which she in turn relies. But while women have thus taken care of men, men have, in their theories of psychological development, as in their economic arrangements, tended to assume or devalue that care. When the focus on individuation and individual achievement extends into adulthood and maturity is equated with personal autonomy, concern with relationships appears as a weakness of women rather than as a human strength. [. . .]

The discovery now being celebrated by men in mid-life of the importance of intimacy, relationships, and care is something that women have known from the beginning. However, because that knowledge in women has been considered "intuitive" or "instinctive," a function of anatomy coupled with destiny, psychologists have neglected to describe its development. In my research, I have found that women's moral development centers on the elaboration of that knowledge and thus delineates a critical line of psychological development in the lives of both of the sexes.

Study Questions

1. Examine "The Three Languages," the first fairy tale cited in the excerpt, and compare it to "Snow White" and "Sleeping Beauty" (which I assume you are familiar with). Explain how each can be said to contain a view of the male and female psyche. You may want to read the section on fairy tales in Chapter 2 again.

2. How does this excerpt on women's moral values relate to virtue theory?

3. Evaluate Gilligan's statement that "Women's deference is rooted not only in their social subordination but also in the substance of their moral concern. Sensitivity to the needs of others and the assumption of the responsibility for taking care lead women to attend to voices other than their own and to include in their judgment other points of view." How do you think Levinas (Chapter 10) would comment on this statement? What do you think Christina Hoff Sommers might say? And what is your own opinion?

Primary Reading

Talking from 9 to 5

DEBORAH TANNEN

Excerpt, 1994.

Deborah Tannen's book *Talking from 9 to 5* followed on the heels of her immensely popular *You Just Don't Understand* (1990), a book about male and female forms of communication within personal relationships. Drawing on her linguistic research into speech patterns and conversational styles, Tannen concludes that, as men and women, we have different expectations of each other, based on the friendships we developed as children: Girls are used to games in intimate groups. Boys are used to a hierarchy of play-mates. Girls will engage in "troubles talk," sharing their problems with their best friend in a seemingly equal environment. Boys tend to hide their problems except in the company of special close friends, for fear of appearing to be one-down, lower in the hierar-chy. And that's why men don't ask for directions, she says! In *Talking from 9 to 5,* Tannen explores the conversational styles in the workplace. Here she claims that fear of sexual harassment is shared by both men and women, but on different grounds, and to a dif-ferent degree.

Men Can Be Harassed Too — But It's Different

When the Clarence Thomas hearings took place, I was asked to appear on radio and tele-vision to talk about the role of language in sexual harassment. I had previously spent the major part of a year appearing on such shows and writing articles on the topic of women's and men's conversational styles and had rarely gotten a negative response. Nearly everyone seemed to appreciate my even-handed approach: Women's and men's styles are equally valid; each has its own logic; problems occur because of the differences in style. But when I made public statements about sexual harassment, I had to say that things were different for women and men. I received several letters of complaint from men who felt I was slighting them. "Men can be sexually harassed too," they accurately protested. Michael Crichton's novel *Disclosure* dramatizes this. But it also shows that, al-though the situation can occur, its fundamental elements are different from those that underlie harassment of women by men.

Maureen Dowd summarizes the premise of *Disclosure* in a book review:

> Meredith Johnson, the cool, beautiful blond who is the new boss at Digital Com-munications in Seattle, summons one of her division managers, Tom Sanders, to her office for their first business meeting.
>
> She has a chilled bottle of chardonnay waiting. Her skirt is riding up her thigh. She kicks off her heels and wiggles her toes. She crosses and uncrosses her legs several times, explaining that she doesn't wear stockings because she likes "the bare feeling." She half parts her full lips and looks dreamily at him through preternaturally long lashes. She tells him that he has "a nice hard tush." She asks for a neck massage.

Dowd comments about the Crichton book, "Here is the novel Hollywood has been wait-ing for: Sharon Stone as Bob Packwood." But compare her description of the novel's ac-tion with a description of Bob Packwood's behavior, according to an account in *The New York Times Magazine:*

> While running for reelection in 1980, Bob Packwood was eager to meet his cam-paign chairwoman for Lane County, Ore. The Senator invited Gena Hutton to din-

ner at the motel where he was staying in Eugene for a get-acquainted meeting. Hutton, a 35-year-old divorced mother of two, had brought along pictures of her children and even her cats.

Then it was time to go and Packwood offered to walk her to her car. "As I started to put the key in the car door," Hutton recalls, "he just reeled me around and grabbed me and pulled me close to him." For an instant, she thought he was offering a good-night hug. But then the Senator planted a full kiss on her lips, wriggling his tongue into her mouth.

Packwood's behavior toward Hutton was aggressive. He grabbed her, pulled her toward him, and pushed his tongue into her mouth. In contrast, the woman in the Crichton novel, although clearly abusing her power, is seductive: She doesn't begin by lunging at Tom, but by luring him to her. Rather than forcibly pulling him toward her and doing things to him, she invites him to move toward her and do things to her. ("She asks for a neck massage.")

Later in Dowd's summary, Meredith is described as physically attacking Tom: "She pushes him onto the couch and pinions him there." But this physical assault comes after the seductive behavior previously described, not out of the blue as in the alleged Packwood example. And if Tom Sanders does not push Meredith Johnson off him, it is not because he is not big and strong enough to fight her off, but because he is unwilling to ruin his career by hitting his boss. Gena Hutton, in contrast, was smaller in stature and weaker in strength than Bob Packwood, as is usually the case when a woman and a man have an encounter. Hutton did not accept Packwood's invitation to enter his motel room, but if she had, and if he had wanted to, he would probably have been physically capable of throwing her down and "pinioning" her, and she would probably have been physically incapable of fighting him off.

Behaviors associated with the sexes in our culture are differently apportioned. Men's sexual behavior is expected to be aggressive, women's seductive. Imagine the scene of the Crichton novel with the genders reversed:

> Tom Sanders, the cool, beautiful blonde who is the new boss at Digital Communications in Seattle, summons one of his division managers, Meredith Johnson, to his office for their first business meeting.
>
> He has a chilled bottle of chardonnay waiting. His trousers are riding up his calves. He kicks off his shoes and wiggles his toes. He crosses and uncrosses his legs several times, explaining that he doesn't wear socks because he likes "the bare feeling." He half parts his full lips and looks dreamily at her through preternaturally long lashes. He tells her that she has "a nice hard tush." He asks for a neck massage.

It would not be surprising if Meredith Johnson, observing Tom Sanders behaving this way, would burst out laughing or determine he had come unhinged. Even the initial description, "cool, beautiful blonde," is incongruous when applied to a man, because it is only with women that physical attractiveness is the key feature, which is why the word "beautiful" has come to be associated with women—except, perhaps, to describe a young man from the perspective of someone who might be drawn to him. A description of a male boss would more likely be in terms of his size and appearance of power.

Woman As Witch

It might seem puzzling, at first, that Michael Crichton's character Meredith, a woman boss who sexually harasses a man who works for her, is portrayed as young and beautiful. Dowd suggests it is Crichton's way of finessing the irony that "while women think power is sexy in men, men often find power threatening in women." In other words, had the "carnivorous supervisor" been a large, physically overpowering older woman, the image of her making sexual advances toward Tom would have been less titillating for readers, a problem that would not have arisen if the genders were reversed.

But there is another reason, I think, for the way Meredith is portrayed. And it too comes down to cultural stereotypes and collective memory. A cultural icon deeply associated with female characters in folk tales and popular culture is the witch. In her book *Reflections on Gender and Science,* Evelyn Fox Keller quotes a character in a play published in 1659, Walter Charleton's *Ephesian Matron,* who is railing against witches in the form of woman: "You are the true *Hiena's,* that allure us with the fairness of your skins; and when folly hath brought us within your reach, you leap upon us and devour us."

It is the fear of being devoured by a woman he is attracted to, fear inspired by the very attraction he feels, that can stir such atavistic anxiety in a man. The fear results from the loss of control entailed by attraction. In other words, it is precisely the beautiful, alluring woman who is terrifying to men (especially when she is "cool," impervious to losing control as a result of sexual attraction herself), in a way that a large, physically threatening woman would not be. Although such a woman might frighten an individual man in a real-life encounter, the thought of a large, unattractive woman trying to seduce a man would not strike terror in most men's hearts but would be more likely to make them laugh; rather than tapping into deep fears, it would simply seem incongruous and therefore funny.

The woman as witch is also, I think, at the heart of another popular literary work about sexual harassment written by a man: David Mamet's play *Oleanna.* In it, a college student named Carol destroys a professor named John by falsely accusing him of sexual harassment and then rape. The action takes place in the professor's office. In the first act, Carol is insecure and self-effacing, confessing that she is unable to follow the course material and terrified of failing. "I can't understand," she wails. "I sit in class, in the back, and I smile, but I don't know what anyone's talking about. I'm just stupid." The professor is touched. He fears it is his fault, not hers, that she doesn't understand, so he tries to make amends. He reassures her: He'll tutor her privately; she will get an "A." At the end of the act, in his attempt to comfort her, he puts his arm around her shoulders. In Act II, we learn that Carol has filed a sexual-harassment suit against John, just when his tenure (the key to a professor's career) is hanging in the balance.

It is easy to imagine a real-life situation in which a professor might put his arm around a student to comfort her, and she might take offense, though hard to imagine her going so far as to file a complaint. Later in the play, however, Carol ups the ante and threatens to accuse him of rape. The action that follows leaves the realm of reality and enters the world of nightmare. In Act II, Carol is transformed. She is articulate, self-assured, and on the attack. Now it is she who is standing, lecturing, interrupting, and he who is sitting, helpless, speechless.

When I first saw this play, I found Carol's transformation from Act I to Act II baffling. I could only regard it as incompetent playwriting. But the description of witches makes it comprehensible. The play captures what it is about the issue of sexual harassment that so frightens men. Like a witch, a woman can lure a man with the fairness of her skin and a pretense of weakness, then leap upon him and destroy him. (This is the same deep fear that is embodied in the story of Samson and Delilah.) The professor in Mamet's play explains that he has always felt that authorities were out to get him: parents who told him he didn't understand and made him feel stupid, bosses, and now the tenure committee. The play shows that the ability to yell "sexual harassment" gives women students that kind of power over him, since any one of them could, in theory, fabricate a charge and destroy him.

This is why women and men seem so often to be holding on to different legs of this elephant. The aspect of sexual harassment that taps into women's fears is the specter of assault, verbal or physical, by a man from whose clutches they cannot easily escape. This aspect is likely to be dismissed by many men. Indeed, some men find it insulting because they hear the statement "the *possibility* of violence against women is ubiquitous" as an (obviously unfounded) accusation that all men are rapists. The aspect that holds power for most men is the possibility of a false charge, a possibility that many women dismiss as unlikely to happen, since bringing charges is so damaging to the accuser. For their part, many women are insulted by men's concern, which they hear as an accusation that women are manipulative liars. In fact, it is far more common for women to be physically assaulted or sexually harassed than for them to bring false charges, but these realities do not change the power each fear holds for the individuals who identify with one party or the other.

I believe that most men do not wish to use their status and position to hurt and exploit women. But many good men worry, What would I do if someone brought a false charge against me? Not realizing that those who are guilty of serious sexual harassment are doing things they would not think of doing, they ask themselves, "What kind of remark have I made, in innocence, that could be misconstrued?" Again, the relative infrequency with which women make false charges is not relevant here; it suffices that the possibility is theoretically real, and there have been enough such cases to dramatize the possibility. In other words, each group tends to dismiss the other's deep fears as unlikely to occur. Their own fears, however, thrive on the awareness of possibility.

Study Questions

1. Compare the *Disclosure* summary with Tannen's spoof. What makes the difference, and why is the spoof funny? What does that tell us about the phenomenon of sexual harassment?

2. What is it men are afraid of, according to Tannen? What is it women are afraid of? Is she right? Explain.

3. Comment on the reference to the play *Oleanna* (also a film, 1994, directed by the playwright, David Mamet). Is the story told from the professor's or the student's point of view? How might that make a difference? How might a student view the issue of sexual harassment? How might a professor view it?

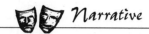 *Narrative*

 A Doll's House

HENRIK IBSEN

Play, 1879. Summary and Excerpt. Translated by William Archer. Two British film versions exist, both from 1973; one stars Claire Bloom and Anthony Hopkins; the other stars Jane Fonda and David Warner.

By the time the Norwegian playwright Henrik Ibsen wrote *A Doll's House,* isolated voices had been speaking out for the liberation of women for over a hundred years, but there was not a single country in the Western world where women had yet achieved the right to vote. When Ibsen's play was performed on the stages of Europe, the final act turned out to be a bombshell; Ibsen allows us to see Nora's situation from her own point of view and shows us that this viewpoint is heroic in its own way. In her quest to be regarded as a mature human being, Nora sent signals to men and women all over the Western world and made a considerable impact on the gender debate in Scandinavia at the end of the nineteenth and the beginning of the twentieth century. The story has been considered so compelling that the play is still performed today.

Some contemporary readers may prefer to look for literature about the condition of women written by *women,* not by *men.* But, for one thing, Ibsen's play has had historical importance in helping men as well as women see the traditional woman's role as a political question; for another thing, good writers gifted with clear powers of observation and an imaginative genius, such as Ibsen, are often quite capable of seeing a situation from the other gender's point of view.

The conflict between the feminine virtue of caring and the masculine focus on justice may seem new to many readers of Carol Gilligan, but in these excerpts you can see the outlines of that very same debate, anticipated by Ibsen more than a century ago.

Nora and Torvald Helmer are a happily married middle-class couple with three young children. Helmer regards his lively wife as another child, always happy and singing; his pet names for her are his songbird, his lark, his little squirrel. He accuses her of being a spendthrift, of always asking for more pocket money, but he forgives her because she is so sweet and amusing. And even to her friends she seems like a carefree, coddled woman with no worries other than choosing what clothes to wear for parties. But things are not what they seem on the surface. An old friend of Nora's comes to visit, and Nora tells her a deep secret of which she is very proud: Some years ago Helmer was very ill, and the doctor recommended an expensive trip to Italy as a cure. Helmer believes that Nora's father lent them the money, and he is now dead, so he can't tell. But Nora paid for the trip all by herself, with no income or fortune of her own: She took out a private loan, with high interest, and that is why she has been asking Helmer for so much pocket money, buying only the cheapest things for herself, and paying the loan off, always on time, with interest. And it won't be long now before the loan will be paid off: Helmer is being promoted to bank manager, and their finances will improve.

But disaster waits in the wings: An employee at the bank, Krogstad, turns up and begs her to ask her husband to let him keep his job. Why might he lose it? Because he has a criminal record; he has forged papers. And why would he come to Nora? Because Nora knows him well—he is the man who lent her the money for the trip to Italy. He threatens to tell Helmer, but what is worse, he has done some research. Nora's father cosigned the loan, as security—but the signature is dated days after her father died. The conclusion is obvious: Nora forged her father's signature, and now Krogstad threatens her with the law and tells her that his crime was no worse than her own.

Krogstad: May I ask you one more question? Why did you not send the paper to your father?

Nora: It was impossible. Father was ill. If I had asked him for his signature, I should have had to tell him why I wanted the money; but he was so ill I really could not tell him that my husband's life was in danger. It was impossible.

Krogstad: Then it would have been better to have given up your tour.

Nora: No, I couldn't do that; my husband's life depended on that journey. I couldn't give it up.

Krogstad: And did it never occur to you that you were playing me false?

Nora: That was nothing to me. I didn't care in the least about you. I couldn't endure you for all the cruel difficulties you made, although you knew how ill my husband was.

Krogstad: Mrs. Helmer, you evidently do not realise what you have been guilty of. But I can assure you it was nothing more and nothing worse that made me an outcast from society.

Nora: You! You want me to believe that you did a brave thing to save your wife's life?

Krogstad: The law takes no account of motives.

Nora: Then it must be a very bad law.

Krogstad: Bad or not, if I produce this document in court, you will be condemned according to law.

Nora: I don't believe that. Do you mean to tell me that a daughter has no right to spare her dying father trouble and anxiety?—that a wife has no right to save her husband's life? I don't know much about the law, but I'm sure you'll find, somewhere or another, that that is allowed. And you don't know that—you, a lawyer! You must be a bad one, Mr. Krogstad.

Krogstad: Possibly. But business—such business as ours—I do understand. You believe that? Very well; now do as you please. But this I may tell you, that if I am flung into the gutter a second time, you shall keep me company.

[*Bows and goes out through hall.*]

Nora: [*Stands a while thinking, then tosses her head.*] Oh nonsense! He wants to frighten me. I'm not so foolish as that. [*Begins folding the children's clothes. Pauses.*] But—? No, it's impossible! Why, I did it for love!

Later, Helmer talks to her about what a despicable man Krogstad is, and how vile his crime. Shortly after, Helmer fires Krogstad, in spite of Nora's pleas, and Krogstad shows up again. Now he wants more: Unless Nora makes Helmer reinstate him and give him a promotion, he will reveal all. And if Nora should think of drastic solutions, such as killing herself, her husband will still be told everything. Now Krogstad wants Helmer to know, so he can blackmail the two of them, instead of only her, and he leaves a letter for Helmer, telling him everything. Nora is desperate and tries to distract Helmer when he comes home by dancing for him, and she makes him promise that he will not open the letter until the next day. Meanwhile, she pleads with her friend and confidante to go to Krogstad and persuade him to stop his threats.

The following night Nora and Helmer are at a dance, and Nora dances as if it is her last night on this earth. Coming home, there is still the letter waiting for them, and Nora, deep in despair, is waiting, too: for a miracle, for without it she is going to kill herself.

But Helmer reads the letter, and is horrified: the woman he loved, a liar and a criminal! He blames her weakness of character and her father's bad influence and sees himself as a ruined man. He insists that Nora can no longer see her children—they must be protected from her evil influence. Nora threatens suicide, but Helmer scoffs at it: How is that going to help *him* and *his* ruin? And now it dawns on Nora that her motivation for forging her father's signature is utterly lost on Helmer; the miracle she was hoping for, and dreading, is far from happening.

But now comes the salvation: Nora's friend has succeeded in persuading Krogstad to drop the matter (through a personal sacrifice which Nora knows nothing about). Krogstad returns Nora's I.O.U. with an apologetic letter, and Helmer is ecstatic, exclaiming that now he is saved. And, magnanimously, he now sees Nora as a poor, misguided soul who has not understood what she has done, and he forgives her. All she needs now is his guidance, he says—from now on he'll be her will and her conscience, and everything will be as before.

Meanwhile Nora, stone-faced, has changed out of her masquerade dress and into her ordinary clothes. For her, the masquerade is over, and although he doesn't know it yet, it is, too, for him. She asks him to sit down, for she has much to talk over with him.

Helmer: You alarm me, Nora. I don't understand you.

Nora: No, that is just it. You don't understand me; and I have never understood you—till tonight. No, don't interrupt. Only listen to what I say.—We must come to a final settlement, Torvald.

Helmer: How do you mean?

Nora: [*After a short silence.*] Does not one thing strike you as we sit here?

Helmer: What should strike me?

Nora: We have been married eight years. Does it not strike you that this is the first time we two, you and I, man and wife, have talked together seriously?

Helmer: Seriously! What do you call seriously?

Nora: During eight whole years, and more—ever since the day we first met—we have never exchanged one serious word about serious things.

Helmer: Was I always to trouble you with the cares you could not help me to bear?

Nora: I am not talking of cares. I say that we have never yet set ourselves seriously to get to the bottom of anything.

Helmer: Why, my dearest Nora, what have you to do with serious things?

Nora: There we have it! You have never understood me. — I have had great injustice done me, Torvald; first by father, and then by you.

Helmer: What! By your father and me? — By us, who have loved you more than all the world?

Nora: [*Shaking her head.*] You have never loved me. You only thought it amusing to be in love with me.

Helmer: Why, Nora, what a thing to say!

Nora: Yes, it is so, Torvald. While I was at home with father, he used to tell me all his opinions, and I held the same opinions. If I had others I said nothing about them, because he wouldn't have liked it. He used to call me his doll-child, and played with me as I played with my dolls. Then I came to live in your house —

Helmer: What an expression to use about our marriage!

Nora: [*Undisturbed.*] I mean I passed from father's hands into yours. You arranged everything according to your taste; and I got the same tastes as you; or I pretended to — I don't know which — both ways, perhaps; sometimes one and sometimes the other. When I look back on it now, I seem to have been living here like a beggar, from hand to mouth. I lived by performing tricks for you, Torvald. But you would have it so. You and father have done me a great wrong. It is your fault that my life has come to nothing.

Helmer: Why, Nora, how unreasonable and ungrateful you are! Have you not been happy here?

Nora: No, never. I thought I was; but I never was.

Helmer: Not — not happy!

Nora: No; only merry. And you have always been so kind to me. But our house has been nothing but a play-room. Here I have been your doll-wife, just as at home I used to be papa's doll-child. And the children, in their turn, have been my dolls. I thought it fun when you played with me, just as the children did when I played with them. That has been our marriage, Torvald.

. . . .

Helmer: To forsake your home, your husband, and your children! And you don't consider what the world will say.

Nora: I can pay no heed to that. I only know that I must do it.

Helmer: This is monstrous! Can you forsake your holiest duties in this way?

Nora: What do you consider my holiest duties?

Helmer: Do I need to tell you that? Your duties to your husband and your children.

Nora: I have other duties equally sacred.

Helmer: Impossible! What duties do you mean?

Nora: My duties towards myself.

Helmer: Before all else you are a wife and a mother.

Nora: That I no longer believe. I believe that before all else I am a human being, just as much as you are — or at least that I should try to become one. I know that most people agree with you, Torvald, and that they say so in books. But henceforth I can't be satisfied with what most people say, and what is in books. I must think things out for myself, and try to get clear about them.

. . . .

Nora: I have waited so patiently all these eight years; for of course I saw clearly enough that miracles don't happen every day. When this crushing blow threatened me, I said to myself so confidently, "Now comes the miracle!" When Krogstad's letter lay in the box, it never for a moment occurred to me that you would think of submitting to that man's conditions. I was convinced that you would say to him, "Make it known to all the world"; and that then —

Helmer: Well? When I had given my own wife's name up to disgrace and shame — ?

Nora: Then I firmly believed that you would come forward, take everything upon yourself, and say, "I am the guilty one."

Helmer: Nora — !

Nora: You mean I would never have accepted such a sacrifice? No, certainly not. But what would my assertions have been worth in opposition to yours? — That was the miracle that I hoped for and dreaded. And it was to hinder that that I wanted to die.

Helmer: I would gladly work for you day and night, Nora — bear sorrow and want for your sake. But no man sacrifices his honour, even for one he loves.

Nora: Millions of women have done so.

So, in the end, Torvald is the one who understands nothing; he promises to love her, to do anything if she will only stay with him. But she sees him now as a stranger and prepares to leave. In her final words to him she says that in order to get together again, they would both have to change so much that "communion between them shall be a marriage." And Nora leaves, closing the door behind her.

Study Questions

1. What does Nora mean by the final line in this excerpt?

2. If you were in Nora's position, would your reaction be similar or different? Why? If you were in Helmer's position, would your reaction be similar or different? Why?

3. Examine the excerpts and find evidence of virtue ethics as opposed to an ethics of justice.

4. Ibsen refers to his characters as "Nora" and "Helmer" rather than "Nora" and "Torvald." What kind of effect might that have on the reader of the play? Do you think it is intentional?

5. You'll remember Flaubert's *Madame Bovary,* summarized in Chapter 4; Flaubert told of a vain and selfish woman who ruined her own and her husband's life by racking up debts for her own amusement. *A Doll's House,* from approximately the same time period and the same social world, is a story of another woman who also goes into debt. Compare the two stories: Are there significant similarities? Are there significant differences?

Narrative

Like Water for Chocolate

LAURA ESQUIVEL

Novel, 1989. Summary. Film version by Alfonso Arau (director) and Laura Esquivel (screenwriter), 1992.

One might get the impression that feminism claims all women are always caring and always in complete understanding with each other; but as we discussed earlier, not all women are caring or nurturing beings. Neither is it the case that women have a secret understanding that makes them friends or sisters; occasional enmity between women is a fact of life. However, as both classical and difference feminism claim, certain conditions shared by just about all women—such as a common biology and family roles—can be seen as laying down some ground rules for women's relationships with each other. One of these conditions is being raised in a male-dominated world; for difference feminists, the *caring imperative* is one of the ground rules. On the basis of these common conditions and rules, women should be able to understand each other to a great extent. A story that illustrates how common conditions make it possible to reach an understanding is the Mexican novel *Like Water for Chocolate.* In this story, which became a critically acclaimed film that won Academy Awards, Laura Esquivel tells of a matriarchal family consisting of the mother, three sisters, and the helpful ghost of a cook and of their relationships to each other and to the men in their lives. There are twelve chapters in the novel, one for each month of the year, and each with its own recipe attached to it, because this is a story of food and of cooking, of "mood meals" and how the intense emotions of a good cook can transform the lives of those eating her food.

Mama Elena and her daughters, Gertrudis, Rosaura, and Tita, live on a ranch in Mexico. The story takes place during the Mexican revolution in the early twentieth century, and the troops of rebel leader Pancho Villa play a part in the lives of the women.

Mama Elena is a strict woman who rules her household with an iron fist; "I've never needed a man for anything," she says. "All by myself, I've done all right with my ranch and my daughters." But there is little love between her and her youngest daughter, Tita, who feels that their cook, Nacha, is more of a mother to her. Together they spend their time in the kitchen, and Tita's toys are the pans and the stove and the traditional Mexican and pre-Columbian recipes of Nacha, who has Indian blood. Tita loves Nacha and the kitchen, but she also has another love: Pedro, a young man she has seen in the village. It was love at first glance for both of them, and now he has asked her mother for her hand in marriage; but that can never be, says Mama Elena, because Tita must, according to the family tradition, never marry or have children. As the youngest daughter, she must consecrate her life to taking care of her mother. And Tita asks, Who came up with this idea? And who will then take care of Tita when she grows old? And what about women who marry and can't have children? But all questions must be buried, because Mama Elena's rule is absolute. However, Mama Elena has an idea: If Pedro wants to get married, then Tita's sister Rosaura is available. The household is horrified (a maid says, "You can't just switch them, like tacos and enchiladas"), but nobody is more surprised than Tita when Pedro agrees to the marriage. She believed he would love her forever . . . but he explains to her, during a clandestine meeting, that this was the only way he could be with her forever, as part of the family.

During the wedding banquet something strange happens. Tita is dry-eyed, because she cried all her tears the day before when preparing the wedding cake, supported by Nacha. Tita's tears fell into the meringue icing, and when Nacha tasted it, she was seized by the most terrible longing. She remembered her fiancé of long ago, whom Doña Elena wouldn't allow her to marry, and she started crying so hard that she couldn't attend the wedding banquet the next day. As the wedding guests taste the cake, they, too, are gripped with longing; and furthermore they begin to throw up, so it is not the wedding Rosaura had dreamed of. And next morning they find Nacha dead, clutching a picture of her fiancé.

Life goes on at the ranch; Pedro has moved in, and Tita has become the head cook. To bring herself out of her grief for Nacha, Tita makes an ancient recipe based on rose petals — roses she received from Pedro, which she clutched so hard that they were stained with her blood. Again the meal has a profound effect: Pedro loves it, Rosaura doesn't want to eat it, but Gertrudis experiences an instant rush of sexual heat, which makes her perspire rose-scented sweat; a young man she likes, a soldier in Villa's army, is called from afar by the scent and carries her away to a new life.

After a while, Rosaura has her first baby, Roberto; nobody is in the house at the time but Tita, who takes charge of the delivery, and from then on the boy seems as close to her as if he were her own son. When Rosaura has no milk, milk miraculously wells up in Tita's breasts; always the nurturer, Tita is capable of feeding everybody, including her little nephew.

Someone else has now been introduced to the house: the doctor tending Rosaura, Dr. John Brown, an American physician. A widower, he falls in love with Tita and is appalled when he hears about the family tradition. In the course of events he does experience a close relationship with Tita, but in a way other than he had imagined: When Elena sends Rosaura, Pedro, and their baby to live in San Antonio, Tita loses all interest in life; and when the news that the little boy is dead reaches the ranch, Tita goes mad with grief and accuses her mother of having killed the boy, because she deprived him of Tita's care. Tita takes refuge in the pigeon coop in a state of madness, and Dr. Brown is called to remove her to an asylum; instead he takes her to his home and nurses her back to mental health. He is not alone, though. In a small room in the house Tita finds company, a silent old Indian woman who reminds her of Nacha and who shows her curative herbs and rekindles her interest in life. Soon she realizes that the woman is John Brown's long-dead grandmother, a Kikapu Indian called Morning Light. John, who does not see her, tells Tita of a theory his grandmother held: Each of us is born with a box of matches inside us, but we can't strike them by ourselves; we need oxygen (like the breath of a person you love) and a candle (like a beautiful experience). When the match is lit, we feel an intense emotion, which fades slowly until the next match is struck. This fire is the food for our soul. If you don't find out in time what sets off your explosions, the matches will dampen and you will never feel a spark. But you must take care not to light them all at the same time, because then you will be so dazzled that your soul will escape to its divine origin; your body will die.

Tita, feeling better, is visited by the maid from the ranch with oxtail soup from home, and Tita swears she will never return; but things have a way of happening: Arriving home, the maid is raped in a raid, and Elena, trying to defend her property, is shot and paralyzed from the waist down. Now Tita has to go home to take care of her mother. But everything Tita serves her tastes bitter to her, even if it tastes fine to the others, so Elena believes she is being poisoned. In order to counteract the poison she secretly swallows great amounts of emetics, which end up killing her. Cleaning up after her, Tita finds an old box with an old secret: Elena herself had been the victim of parental authority. She was never allowed to marry the man she loved, the son of a Mexican man and an African American woman. Gertrudis is actually this man's child, and only Rosaura and Tita are the daughters of the man Elena was forced to marry.

Rosaura and Pedro now have a little girl, Esperanza (and later we learn that she will be the mother of the storyteller); Tita hopes her sister will not perpetuate the family tradition, but Rosaura insists that Esperanza must never marry and will stay home to take care of her when she is old. Rosaura herself is becoming a nasty, smelly woman, and Pedro and Tita find secret opportunities for making love; but Tita is haunted by the ghost of Mama Elena, who is nagging her constantly. A turning point occurs when Gertrudis, now a general in the rebel army, comes to visit in the company of her beloved, and gives Tita the courage to confront Rosaura. In a terrible exchange of words they reveal what they think of each other, and that is the end of their friendship. Tita and Esperanza, on the other hand, grow very close to each other, like Nacha and Tita, in the old kitchen. (Eventually Tita will leave her book of recipes to her niece, and that is how Esperanza's child, the storyteller, can share them with us.)

John asks Tita to marry him, even though he knows she still loves Pedro; but Rosaura dies suddenly (we guess that she dies from just being so nasty that she has poisoned herself with evil), and Pedro is free. Will Tita and Pedro finally find happiness together? Or will Tita marry John? I suggest you read the book or watch the film and find out for yourself; and remember Morning Light's theory of the matches: If you don't strike them one by one, they may all go off at one time.

And the secret of the title, a mystery to moviegoers? Like water for making chocolate, when it feels as if life conspires against you, you're at the point of boiling!

Study Questions

1. Can this story be interpreted as a feminist narrative? If no, why not? If yes, which kind of feminism? You may want to consider the different roles played by Tita the nurturer and Gertrudis the warrior; what are the roles of Elena and Rosaura?

2. Evaluate the custom of the youngest daughter's being obliged to stay single in order to care for her aging parents. Can the custom be defended? Why or why not?

3. Do any of the characters exhibit an "ethic of care"? Explain your answer.

4. An existentialist such as Simone de Beauvoir might call the custom of the youngest (or eldest) daughter remaining single so she can take care of her parents an example of *bad faith*. What does that mean? Do you agree?

 Narrative

The Woman Destroyed

SIMONE DE BEAUVOIR

Short story, 1967. Summary and Excerpt. Translated by Patrick O'Brian.

As you know from Chapter 10, Jean-Paul Sartre was not only a philosopher but also a novelist and playwright. The fact that his longtime partner Simone de Beauvoir also wrote fiction is not quite as well known. Here we look at passages from her short story "The Woman Destroyed," about Monique, who has been married to Maurice for more than twenty years. Their two daughters are grown and no longer live at home, and Monique is under the impression that now she and Maurice will continue with the pleasant life they've established and which has become a habit. So it is a dreadful shock to her to discover that he has been having an affair with an acquaintance of theirs, Noëllie, for quite some time.

In these excerpts you will see Monique swing between extremes of blaming Noëllie, her husband, and herself for the situation that has developed. Maurice doesn't deny the relationship, and initially he doesn't want to lose either woman. He wants to have his cake and eat it, too.

> Maurice will see anything I say against Noëllie as the effect of my jealousy. It would be better to say nothing. But I really do find her profoundly disagreeable. She reminds me of my sister—the same confidence, the same glibness, the same phonily offhand elegance. It seems that men like this mixture of coquetry and hardness. When I was sixteen and she was eighteen Maryse swiped all my boyfriends. So much so that I was in a dreadful state of nerves when I introduced Maurice to her. I had a ghastly nightmare in which he fell in love with her. He was indignant. "She is so superficial! So bogus! Paste diamonds, rhinestones! You—you're the real jewel." Authentic: that was the word everyone was using in those days. He said I was authentic. At all events I was the one he loved, and I was not envious of my sister anymore; I was happy to be the person I was. But then how can he think a great deal of Noëllie, who is of the same kind as Maryse? He is altogether gone from me if he likes being with someone I dislike so very much— and whom he ought to dislike if he were faithful to our code. Certainly he has altered.

He lets himself be taken in by false values that we used to despise. Or he is simply completely mistaken about Noëllie. I wish the scales would drop from his eyes soon. My patience is beginning to run out. [. . .]

"I don't want any sharing: you must make your choice."

He had the overwhelmed look of a man who is saying to himself, *Here we are! It had to happen. How can I get myself out of this one?* He adopted his most coaxing voice. "Please, darling. Don't ask me to break with Noëllie. Not now."

"Yes, now. This business is dragging on too much. I have borne it too long by far." I looked at him challengingly. "Come now, which do you like best? Her or me?"

"You, of course," he said in a toneless voice. And he added, "But I like Noëllie too."

I saw red. "Admit the truth, then! She's the one you like best! All right! Go to her! Get out of here. Get out at once. Take your things and go."

I pulled his suitcase out of the wardrobe, I flung clothes into it higgledy-piggledy, I unhooked coat hangers. He took my arm: "Stop!" I went on. I wanted him to go; I really wanted it — it was sincere. Sincere because I did not believe in it. It was like a dreadful psychodrama in which they play at truth. It is the truth, but it is being acted. I shouted, "Go and join that bitch, that schemer, that dirty little shady lawyer."

He took me by the wrists. "Take back what you have said."

"No. She's a filthy thing. She got you by flattery. You prefer her to me out of vanity. You're sacrificing our love to your vanity."

Again he said, "Shut up." But I went on. I poured out everything I thought about Noëllie and him. Yes: I have a confused recollection of it. I said that he was letting himself be taken in like a pitiful fool, that he was turning into a pretentious, on-the-make vulgarian, that he was no longer the man I had loved, that once upon a time he had possessed a heart and given himself up to others — now he was hard and selfish and concerned only with his career.

"Who's selfish?" he cried. And he shouted me down. I was the one who was selfish — I who had not hesitated to make him give up a resident post, who would have liked to confine him to a small-time career all his life long so as to keep him at home, I who was jealous of his work — a castrating woman. [. . .]

Evening

I had an inspiration this morning: the whole thing is my fault. My worst mistake has been not grasping that *time goes by.* It was going by and there I was, set in the attitude of the ideal wife of an ideal husband. Instead of bringing our sexual relationship to life again I brooded happily over memories of our former nights together. I imagined I had kept my thirty-year-old face and body instead of taking care of myself, doing gymnastics and going to a beauty parlor. I let my intelligence wither away: I no longer cultivated my mind — *later,* I said, *when the children have gone.* (Perhaps my father's death was not without bearing on this way of letting things slide. Something snapped. I stopped time from that moment on.) Yes: the young student Maurice married felt passionately about what was happening in the world, about books and ideas; she was very unlike the woman of today, whose world lies between the four walls of this apartment. It is true enough that I tended to shut Maurice in. I thought his home was enough for him: I thought I owned him entirely. Generally speaking I took everything for granted; and that must have irritated him intensely — Maurice who changes and who calls things in question. Being irritating—no one can ever get away with that. I should never have been obstinate about our promise of faithfulness, either. If I had given Maurice back his freedom—and made use of mine, too, perhaps—Noëllie would not have profited by the glamour of clandestinity. I should have coped with the situation at once. Is there still time? [. . .]

It is only now that I realize how much value I had for myself, fundamentally. But Maurice has murdered all the words by which I might try to justify it: he has repudiated the standards by which I measured others and myself; I had never dreamed of challenging them—that is to say of challenging myself. And now what I wonder is this: what right had I to say that the inner life was preferable to a merely social life, contemplation to trifling amusements, and self-sacrifice to ambition? My only life had been to create happiness around me. I have not made Maurice happy. And my daughters are not happy either. So what then? I no longer know anything. Not only do I not know what kind of a person I am, but also I do not know what kind of a person I ought to be. Black and white merge into one another, the world is an amorphous mass, and I no longer have any clear outlines. How is it possible to live without believing in anything or in myself?

Study Questions

1. In your opinion, does Beauvoir want us to identify with Monique, or criticize her attitude, or perhaps a little bit of both? Identify the passages that support your view.

2. Compare these excerpts to the text excerpt from *The Second Sex* (p. 474). How might Beauvoir analyze Monique's situation and attitude from the viewpoint of her own classical feminism?

3. Monique seems to think she has no moral right to hold on to her husband. Do you agree? Why or why not?

Narrative

Thelma and Louise

CALLIE KHOURI (SCREENWRITER)
RIDLEY SCOTT (DIRECTOR)

Film, 1991.

Thelma and Louise are friends living ordinary lives in a small Arkansas town. Louise is single and works at a family restaurant. Thelma is married to a suspicious, jealous man. The two women decide to go away for a weekend together; their plans are to go to a cabin that Louise has use of. Thelma writes her husband a note and tapes it to the microwave oven.

Victims of circumstances and past traumas, Thelma (Geena Davis, left) and Louise (Susan Sarandon) try to escape not only the police but also their past roles and self-images on a trek from Arkansas to New Mexico and their ultimate destiny, in *Thelma and Louise* (MGM, 1990).

On the way to the cabin the two women stop at a country-western bar; Thelma hasn't had any fun in ages, and she wants to have a drink and enjoy the music. A local man asks her to dance; Louise finds him pushy and obnoxious, but Thelma thinks he is fun. The fun ends when Thelma goes outside to the parking lot for a bit of fresh air, and the man tries to rape her. His plan doesn't succeed, because Louise comes out of the bar with a pistol aimed straight at him.

As the women back toward their car, the man hurls insults at them. One of his remarks strikes too close to home for Louise, and she shoots him. He dies instantly, and the women hit the road.

This is the beginning of the story of Thelma and Louise, and it is the end of their ordinary life. They decide that they can't go home, and they can't go to the police; because there was no actual rape, Louise can't plead self-defense. As the days go by, they get deeper and deeper into a situation that has no solution. Louise's boyfriend offers his help without asking questions; to Louise his offer is both beautiful and tragic. She realizes he truly loves her, but she can't accept his love because she doesn't want to involve him in her problems. Their money is stolen by a man Thelma spends the night with; she leaves him alone in their motel room, and when she returns the money is gone. To get money, Thelma holds up a convenience store; the robbery is captured on a hidden camera.

A police officer from the women's hometown wants to help them out of their situation; he sees them as victims and knows what happened in the parking lot. But the more crimes they commit, the less they appear to be victims to other law officials. Louise and the officer talk on the phone several times, and it's clear each realizes that the other is bound by the circumstances of the situation.

At various times in their journey Thelma and Louise take on men who, as they see it, perpetuate patterns of intimidating women. One sexist trucker finally understands what it is to be harassed when they shoot out the tires on his truck and set it on fire. A police officer whose only offense is that he is about to run a check on them is forced into his trunk and left in the hot desert; Thelma uses her gun to put a few air holes in the lid of the trunk.

On one level the two friends are leading the life of fugitives; on another they are discovering both freedom and responsibility. They have never felt so alive as they have during this flight, which, incidentally, takes them from the flat landscape of southern Arkansas, through Oklahoma, and into the tall red rocks of the Southwest, the classic backdrop for outlaw Westerns. They are headed for Mexico, but Louise will not travel through Texas (which is hard to avoid if you're coming from Oklahoma). Louise was once raped in Texas, and that incident is at the core of her decision to run instead of return home and face charges.

In the end, Thelma and Louise realize that ultimate freedom is the freedom to make up your mind to act and take full responsibility for your actions.

Study Questions

1. Are Thelma and Louise heroes or villains?

2. What statement, if any, does the film make about modern men and modern women?

3. Is the film fair to modern women? To modern men?

4. In Chapter 2 you read about Western movies and their different ways of telling stories with moral issues. Many popular Westerns have had two male best friends — sometimes outlaws — as the main characters, such as *Butch Cassidy and the Sundance Kid.* Such films are referred to as "buddy Westerns." *Thelma and Louise* has been called a "buddy Western." Is that appropriate, even if they are women, and it takes place in modern times? Explain why or why not.

5. Would you say this story illustrates classical feminism? Difference feminism? Radical feminism? Or equity feminism? Explain.

Chapter Twelve

Case Studies in Virtue

*T*his chapter presents two classical virtues — *compassion* and *gratitude* — for closer examination. We look at how they have been perceived by some philosophers of the past and present and how they may affect our lives. Why these virtues? Why not also loyalty, honesty, courage, honor, and other virtues held dear by various traditions? Just for the simple reason that the topics of compassion and gratitude have provoked some fascinating contributions to the study of ethics and I would like to share these with you. And there is another simple reason: We have to limit our discussion to just a few samples. However, if you should feel inspired to continue the debate with other virtues as topics, I would wholeheartedly encourage it!

Compassion: Are We Born with It?

You may remember Thomas Hobbes's view that humans are by nature self-centered and that compassion is something humans show toward others in distress because they are afraid the same calamity might happen to them. In other words, when people show sympathy and pity toward one another either it is to make sure that others will help them if the same thing should happen to them, or else it is a kind of superstition, a warding off of the fate of others. There are scholars who think Hobbes's viewpoint was fostered by the political unrest of the seventeenth century, which might well have caused a thinker to focus on his own survival and to believe that self-love is the primary driving force.

In the eighteenth century, the Age of Reason, two philosophical giants shared a different idea. Both the Scottish philosopher David Hume and the Swiss philosopher Jean-Jacques Rousseau believed that humans are naturally compassionate toward one another. Hume held that even a selfish person will feel benevolence toward strangers whenever his self-interest is not involved. Rousseau claimed that the more we are corrupted by civilization, the more we tend to forget our natural inclination to help others and sympathize with them, because it is not an aberration of nature that makes people selfish — it is *civilization* itself. Rousseau certainly agreed that there are people who show compassion only because they are afraid something might happen to them and because they have only their own interests at heart, but this is not a natural thing, he said; it is caused by human culture. If we would seek only the natural capacities in ourselves, we would find the natural virtue of compassion still intact. The best way to reestablish contact with our original nature is to educate children as freely as possible so that they don't become infected with the evils of civilization.

Philosophers in the Western tradition were not the only ones to speculate about human nature and compassion; in the third century B.C.E. the Chinese philosopher Mencius (see below) claimed, as Rousseau would some two thousand years later, that humans are compassionate and benevolent by nature but have been corrupted by the circumstances of everyday life.

Philip Hallie: The Case of Le Chambon

Could Rousseau have been right that civilization is the cause of evildoing, or does "civilized" mean "compassionate"? An answer has been given indirectly by the American philosopher Philip Hallie (1922–1994), whom I once had the privilege of meeting. Hallie was an unusual philosopher, as today's philosophers go, because he was never afraid to talk about his own feelings and the feelings of others. You cannot understand evil unless you understand how it feels to those who are being victimized, he said, and you cannot understand goodness unless you ask those to whom goodness has been shown. Having been a U.S. soldier in World War II, Hallie had seen his share of bloodshed and cruelty, including the revelations of the Holocaust death camps. Deeply depressed about the apparent inability to fight evil without becoming as violent as one's enemy, Hallie was profoundly moved by learning about a concrete example of compassion that occurred in the midst of a civilization under the heel of barbarism. In the southern part of France there is a small village called Le Chambon-sur-Lignon, where the population has had a long history of being persecuted for their Huguenot faith. During World War II the people of the village came to the aid of Jewish refugees from all over France in a rescue effort that was matched only by the massive efforts of Danish citizens to save the Danish Jews by smuggling them across the water to neutral Sweden. The people of Le Chambon saved about six thousand lives (more than twice the number of their own population). The majority were Jewish children whose parents had already gone to the extermination camps. This took place all during the German occupation of France, even when southern France ceased to be a "free zone" governed by French collaborators.

As a contrast to the compassion of the French villagers, Hallie points to the sadism displayed during the Nazi reign. The Nazis regularly humiliated their prisoners; during marches prisoners were not allowed to go to the bathroom and had to perform their physical functions while on the march. Hallie describes this as an "excremental assault" and calls it an example of *institutionalized cruelty.* Hallie defines this type of cruelty as not only physical but also psychological. When a person's or a people's self-respect and dignity are attacked on a regular basis, the victims often begin to believe that somehow this cruelty is *justified* and that they really are no better than dirt. This is especially true when one population group commits this offense against another group. Thus cruelty becomes a social institution, endorsed by the victimizer and tolerated by the victim. Such instances of institutionalized cruelty can be seen not only in oppressive wartime situations but also in race relations throughout the course of history, in relations between the sexes, and in certain parent–child relations. The general pattern is a demeaning and belittling of one group by another, so that soon such behavior becomes routine.

Why does institutionalized cruelty occur? Because one group is more powerful than the other, either in terms of physical strength (it is bigger, is more numerous, or has more weapons) or in terms of economic, educational, or political clout (as when one group can hold property, get an education, and vote, and the other group can't). Power can even be verbal, as when one group has the monopoly of using slurs against the other.

How can it be helped? By changing the power balance, says Hallie. This, of course, is hard—it is hard to acquire the right to vote, to own property, to get an equal education. It is hard to build up physical strength. And it is hard to reverse the trend of slurs and other insults. Even if all this is achieved, though, the insidious effect of institutionalized cruelty is not over when the cruelty ceases, because *it leaves scars.* The prisoners who were liberated from Nazi extermination camps were never truly "free" again; they carried their scars with them forever. And just being "kind" to a victim doesn't help—it only serves as a reminder of how far he has sunk. What truly helps is a gesture similar to what the people of Le Chambon did for the Jewish refugees in the face of the Nazi occupation.

Hallie heard of Le Chambon and went there to talk to the people; most of them didn't think they had done anything exceptional. What these people did for the refugees was to show them compassion in the form of *hospitality.* They showed the refugees that they were equal to the villagers themselves, that they deserved to live in the villagers' own homes while their escape across the mountains to Switzerland was being planned. This, says Hallie, is the only effective antidote to institutionalized cruelty: hospitality offered as an act of compassion, in a way that makes it clear to the victims that their dignity is intact.

The story of Le Chambon has a twist that makes it even more exceptional. How did the rescue effort succeed in an occupied country with Nazi soldiers everywhere? It wasn't that the villagers were tremendously discreet—no group can hide six thousand people who pass through over a five-year period. It was because of the courage of the town minister, André Trocmé, and his masterly organization of the smuggling operation that Nazi curiosity was deflected for the longest time. Trocmé's cousin Daniel Trocmé, was arrested and executed by the Nazis, but this did not stop the rescue effort, because the villagers had an ally in a very unlikely person: the Nazi overseer of the village, Major Julius Schmäling. Schmäling's task was to keep the peace in the region—meaning, in Hallie's words, "to keep the French quiet while Germany raped the country and went about its business of trying to conquer the world." And Schmäling did keep the peace, but not through terror. Instead, he chose to ignore the steady stream of refugees and did not report the incidents to his superiors. One victim of the Nazis whom Schmäling could not save was one of the two doctors of Le Chambon, Le Forestier, who himself was not engaged in the underground movement. But one day he gave a ride to two hitchhikers from the underground, who hid their weapons in his Red Cross ambulance. When the ambulance was later searched by Nazi soldiers, the weapons were found and Le Forestier arrested. Intervention by Schmäling led the doctor's family to believe that he would only be sent to a work camp in Germany as a doctor, but in actual fact the Nazis intercepted the train taking the doctor to Germany. They took him off the train and executed him the following day with about 110 other people. The Trocmés found out the truth from Schmäling years after the war and realized that Schmäling, ever since that day, had agonized about the one life he hadn't been able to save.

In his posthumously published book *Tales of Good and Evil, Help and Harm* (1997), Hallie writes about the complex character of Schmäling: He and his wife tried for the longest time to avoid membership in the Nazi Party, but when it was finally imminent, Schmäling joined the army so that he wouldn't have to be a party member. Originally a schoolteacher in Munich, he had told his students that decency has no price, no market value, but as an overseer he was very efficient; otherwise he couldn't have stayed on the job. So that makes him a morally ambiguous man, says Hallie. "He served a government that systematically persecuted defenseless people, but he would not persecute them himself." And this refusal to persecute the weak did not go unnoticed by the people of Le Chambon: After the liberation of Paris in 1944, when Nazi officers were held accountable for their atrocities in trials all over France, Schmäling's trial was most unusual. As he walked up the aisle toward the judge, everyone rose to pay tribute to this man who had saved so many at the risk of his own life. When asked why he had not reported the Jewish children hiding in the village, he responded, "I could not stand by and watch innocent blood be shed." Schmäling spent some time in prison in France but later returned to Germany, where he lived in modest circumstances until his death in 1973. (See Box 12.1 for Hallie's views on one of the major Nazi leaders.)

To Hallie, virtue is this: the compassion one shows in reaching out to save others at the risk of one's own life. It it not necessarily the result of logical thinking—it may be an act of the heart. For Hallie there are degrees of moral behavior, though. If you just refrain from doing harm, you are following the *negative command,* "Do not cause harm." That is commendable, but there is a stronger command, a *positive command:* "Help others in need." It is much harder to follow a positive moral rule than a negative one, which just requires you to do nothing. The people of Le Chambon followed the harder path of the positive rule. In your opinion, what did Major Schmäling do? Did he follow the negative rule of no harmdoing, or did he, under the circumstances, also follow a positive rule of actively helping? At the end of this chapter we look at a powerful story of compassion similar to that of Le Chambon, an excerpt from Hallie's last book, and Steven Spielberg's film *Schindler's List.*

Richard Taylor: Compassion Is All You Need

In Chapters 3 through 7 we looked at a number of rules and principles regarding the nature of moral goodness and the proper conduct of human beings. Even in this section on virtue, most of the theories we have discussed involve using *reason* to evaluate the proper moral action. For some people, the way to do the right thing and have virtue is much simpler: We do the right thing *when our heart is in the right place;* moral goodness is simply a gut feeling that we all have, a conscience that speaks without words, an empathy that leads us to reach out in compassion to others. If we don't have that, we have no morality at all. For Richard Taylor, an American philosopher, reason has *no* role to play in making the right moral choice. Taylor belongs to

Box 12.1   IS IT BETTER TO CRY OVER YOUR VICTIM
THAN NOT TO FEEL SORRY?

In a celebrated paper the philosopher Jonathan Bennett claims that it is better to be a person guilty of wrongdoing who has compassion than it is to be an innocent person who has no compassion. An example of the first kind of person is Heinrich Himmler, who, as head of the Nazi SS (an elite guard unit), developed stomach troubles because of what he felt he had to do. The seventeenth-century American minister Jonathan Edwards was the other type of person; although he presumably served the needs of his flock, he believed everybody deserved to go to hell. Philip Hallie responds to Bennett's point of view by referring to an incident in Lewis Carroll's *Alice in Wonderland*. The Walrus and the Carpenter lure some little oysters to take a nice walk with them along the beach. After a while they all sit down on a rock, and the Carpenter and the Walrus begin to eat the oysters. The Walrus feels sorry for them and weeps, but he eats them nevertheless. The Carpenter couldn't care less about the oysters and is just concerned with eating them. Hallie asks, Are we really supposed to believe that the Walrus is a better creature than the Carpenter because he has sympathy for his victims? The Walrus ate as many oysters as he could stuff into his mouth behind his handkerchief. Likewise, Himmler killed more than 13 million people even though he was "feeling sorry" for them. For Hallie sympathy is no redeeming quality at all if it isn't accompanied by compassionate action.

a school of thought that says moral principles are, in effect, useless, because we can always find exceptions. You will remember that this was one of the issues we discussed in Chapter 6. But Taylor doesn't believe the alternative is a moral nihilism. On the contrary—in his book *Good and Evil* (2000) Taylor says:

> Moral principles are nothing but conventions, but they have the real and enormous value to life that conventions in general possess. They help us to get where we want to go. Without them social life would be impossible, and hence any kind of life that is distinctively human. Their justification is, therefore, a practical one and has nothing to do with moral considerations in the abstract. The moment such a principle ceases to have that value, the moment its application produces more evil than good, then it ceases to have any significance at all and ought to be scorned.

So if rational principles aren't the basis of ethics, then what is? It is the virtue of compassion, a phenomenon of the heart, not the brain. The eternal focus in ethics on reason needs an antidote, and Taylor finds it in an analysis of *malice versus compassion*.

Imagine a series of atrocities. A child pins a bug to a tree just to watch it squirm. Boys set fire to an old cat and delight in its painful death. Soldiers make a baby girl giggle before they shoot her and force an old man to dig his own grave before they beat him to death. What is so awful about these stories? It is not just that these victimizers did not live by the categorical imperative, says Taylor (referring to Kant). It is not that they didn't try to maximize general happiness for everyone involved (referring to utilitarianism). It is not that they were ignorant (Socrates) or didn't follow the Golden Mean (Aristotle). The horror we feel—and for Taylor it is the *same kind of horror* in all three cases—stems from the fact that these incidents are simply malicious. The acts are horrible not because the consequences are so terrible (the death of one bug, one cat, and two war victims may not have widespread effects) but because the intent was to cause suffering for the sake of someone else's pleasure or entertainment. These are not crimes against *reason* but crimes against *compassion*.

True moral value, then, lies in compassion, Taylor believes, and he illustrates this with three more tales. A boy comes up to an attic to steal something and rescues some pigeons that are trapped there, despite his father's strict command to leave the birds alone. When his father returns home he gives the boy a beating. A white sheriff beats up a black rioter during the race riots of the 1960s and then, breaking down in tears, cleans the man up and takes him home, after which he goes and gets drunk. An American soldier who is trapped on an island with a Japanese soldier during World War II finally finds the Japanese asleep but is not able to kill him. In each of these cases, Taylor says, these people had been taught moral principles that told them to do one thing ("Obey your father"; "Uphold the law through violence"; "Kill the enemy"), but their heart told them something else, and *their heart told them right.* According to Taylor,

> There are no heroes in these stories. . . . Goodness of heart, tenderness toward things that can suffer, and the loving kindness that contradicts all reason and sense of duty and sometimes denies even the urge to life itself that governs us all are seldom heroic. But who can fail to see, in these mixtures of good and evil, the one thing that really does shine like a jewel, by its own light?

In the end we can't trust our reason, but we can trust our heart; compassion is all we need in order to be moral human beings, compassion toward all living things. Even people who do the right thing can't be called moral if they don't have compassion—in other words, if they don't have the right intention.

This is a much more radical view than Hallie's, because it tells us to *disregard* our reason. Let us look at how that might work in practice. Taylor assumes that we all have this compassion in us—he appeals to our *moral intuition*. But what about the boys who set fire to the cat? Where was their natural compassion? And what about soldiers who kill defenseless civilians? Obviously, not everyone has this compassion, not even the people in Taylor's own examples. What can we do about people who have no compassion? Well, we can try to tell them stories about malice and compassion, but chances are that they will think it is a great idea to set fire to a cat and that the boy in the attic should have left the pigeons trapped. How can we appeal to people who are not responsive to compassion? If we were to ask Kant, Mill, Aristotle, or just about any moral thinker, he or she would say we must try to appeal to their *reason*. If we all had compassion there might not be any need for reason, but as we have seen, not everyone has it, and not everyone has it at the right time, at the right place, and for the right people. Therefore we must have something that might convince people who are lacking in compassion, and this is where reason has to come in. What arguments can we use? We might say, "How would you like it if someone did that to you?" In other words, we might appeal to their logical sense of univer-

Huck and Jim on the raft, from Mark Twain's *The Adventures of Huckleberry Finn*. While Jim is expressing his gratitude to Huck, Huck is torn between what his heart tells him — to help Jim — and what his head tells him — to turn Jim in.

salizability and invoke the Golden Rule. Or we might say, "If you do this you will get caught and punished." In this way we appeal to their sense of logic and causality; they can't possibly get away with any wrongdoing. If these two arguments don't convince them to do right, we might just lock them up — protect them from themselves, and us from them — until they display enough rationality to understand our arguments. Reason, then, is not a substitute for moral feeling (compassion), but it becomes the necessary argument when the moral feeling is absent or deficient. A moral theory that leaves room for only compassion is powerless when it comes to enforcing moral values and virtues.

There is one more problem with Taylor's idea that compassion is all we need, and to illustrate it we will turn to Mark Twain's novel *Huckleberry Finn*. In the story Huck, a young boy, helps Jim, a slave, escape from his owner, Miss Watson. Jonathan Bennett analyzes this famous literary incident — and Bennett is a philosopher who believes in reason as an important part of ethics. He concludes that Huck certainly did the right thing in helping Jim, but it still wasn't good enough, because he did it for the wrong reason. Let's review what happens in the story. Huck wants to help his friend Jim, but he realizes that by doing so he will be going against the morals of the town, which require him to return stolen property, which is what a runaway slave is. Because nobody has ever told Huck that owning people is wrong, he has no principle of equality to hold up against what Bennett calls the "bad morality" of the nineteenth-century town. So in the end Huck ends up lying to protect Jim without understanding exactly why, and he resolves not to adhere to any moral principles from then on because they are too hard to figure out. Bennett's conclusion is that Huck did the right thing, but for the wrong reason; he should have set up a new principle of his own, such as "It is wrong to own people" or merely "Jim is my friend, and one should help one's friends." This way Huck's sympathy for Jim would have been supported by his *reason,* and he would not have had to give up on morality because it was too puzzling.

To this we might add something: Mark Twain himself probably wouldn't have shared Bennett's conclusion, because for Twain Huck is a hero who does the right thing for the best of reasons — because he has compassion for a fellow human being (a human being whom many educated readers of Twain's own day and age might have chosen to turn in). Huck has virtue, even if he doesn't think very well. So Twain and Taylor would be in agreement there. But that doesn't make Huck's attitude any better, philosophically speaking, because it is just a stroke of luck that Jim is a good guy and worthy of Huck's compassion. Suppose the story had featured not the runaway slave Jim but a runaway chain-gang prisoner, Fred the axe murderer? Huck still might have felt compassion for this poor, frightened man and decided to help him go down the river and get rid of his irons. But later that night, Fred might have repaid Huck by killing him and an entire farm family farther down the river in order to get money and take possession of Huck's raft. This, tragically, is the fate of many a Good Samaritan. What Huck lacked was not compassion but *reason* to shape it, reason to help him choose when to act and when not to act — because surely not all people are deserving of our compassion to the extent that we should help them escape what society has determined is their rightful punishment. We may sympathize with mass murderers and understand that they had a terrible childhood, but that doesn't mean we should excuse their actions and help them go free.

This example serves another purpose, too. Not only does it show that we can't dispense with reason; it also shows that there is something else missing in virtue theory: If we focus solely on building a good character and developing the right virtues, such as loyalty, compassion, and courage, we still have to decide *what to do* once we've developed the virtues. We may have a wonderfully virtuous character but still be stuck with deciding between several mutually exclusive courses of action. Huck might ask himself (once he has decided to be loyal to Jim) what exactly is the best way to enact that loyalty: Is it to take Jim up north where nobody can own slaves, or is it to hide him until his owner stops looking for him? Might it be to help him escape with his family, hire him a lawyer, or what? Philosophers who object to virtue theory complain that even if we are virtuous, we still may not have a clue as to what to do in specific situations. A possible answer is that virtue ethics need not necessarily stand alone; even Aristotle talks about finding the right course for one's *actions,* not just for one's character. But if virtue ethics needs some rules of conduct in order to be a complete theory, then surely an ethics of conduct would do well to include elements from virtue ethics. We will take another look at the possibility of a combination of theories at the end of this chapter.

Box 12.2   LOVE AS A VIRTUE

When we talk about love as a virtue, we usually are not talking about passionate love. Passionate love does involve virtue; the passionate lover should not be self-effacing or too domineering, for example. However, that is not the issue here. The issue is love that we can *expect* of someone, and we usually can't expect to receive passionate love on demand. During the marriage ritual, when we promise to love and cherish each other, are we promising our partner that we will be passionately in love with him or her forever? Some undoubtedly see it this way, and they often are in for terrible disappointment if the passionate love of their relationship turns out not to last forever. Of course there are fortunate couples who remain passionately in love over the years or whose passion develops into even deeper feelings, but this is not something every couple can count on. The promise to love each other is rather a promise to *show* love, to show that you care about the other person's welfare and happiness and are 100 percent loyal to that person. This we *can* promise to do, even if passion might not last. So love can be a virtue between people who love each other. The Christian virtue of love does not imply any marital promises but is rather an impersonal reverence for other people. Because it also does not involve romantic passion, it can be a requirement in an ethical system, too.

Gratitude: How Much and When?

The Russian writer Ivan Turgenev tells the following story in his *Prose Poems* (1883): Once upon a time there was a party in heaven, and the Most High had invited all the virtues. Big and small virtues arrived, and everybody was having a good time, but the Most High noticed that two beautiful virtues didn't seem to know each other, so He went over and introduced them: "Gratitude, meet Charity; Charity, meet Gratitude." The two virtues were very surprised, because this was their very first encounter since the creation of the world. . . . Gratitude as a virtue usually implies that it is something that is *owed* to someone. The question is, Are we obliged to feel or show gratitude just because someone expects it, or are there guidelines for when we should express gratitude?

   For one thing, gratitude is a feeling, like love (see Box 12.2). Either you feel love or you don't, and nobody can make you feel it if you don't. (This is something that is known by anyone who has experienced unrequited love.) Similarly, we can't make people feel grateful toward us for something we have done for them; indeed, the more we point out how grateful they should be, the more distant and uncooperative they may become. So perhaps we should not talk about making people *feel* gratitude; perhaps we should talk instead about encouraging them to *show* it. Even if you don't *feel* grateful for the socks you got for Christmas, it would be virtuous to *show* gratitude to the person who gave them to you. Not everyone agrees with this viewpoint—I knew a European pedagogue who taught his children that they never had to say thank you or show gratitude for presents given to them, because they had not asked for those presents and to show gratitude without feeling was, in his view, hypocrisy. He may have been right, but life must have been hard for these children when they realized that few others play by the same rules as their father. There are limits to how far you can place yourself and your family outside the mainstream of your culture without getting your nose bloodied from time to time.

We Owe Our Parents Everything: Confucius, Mencius, and Lin Yutang

Most of the topics we have discussed in this book are part of the Western philosophical legacy, but other cultures around the world have their own philosophical traditions and moral values. Here we take a look at the moral philosophies of Confucius and his student Mencius and carry the theme into the twentieth century with the Chinese philosopher Lin Yutang. The subject is gratitude, and the natural recipients of our gratitude are the elderly.

Chinese culture was already ancient in 551 B.C.E. when Confucius was born. When he died in 479 B.C.E., his thoughts on the *superior man* had already changed life and politics in his country, and they were to remain influential, even during periods of opposition, until the twentieth century in China. For centuries the common Chinese attitude toward virtue and right conduct had been to ask the advice of the spirits through divination. However, a certain practical vision had by and large replaced this view by the time of Confucius—a realization that human endeavor was more effective than spiritual guidance. The more important questions became What exactly is a good person? and What is the best kind of human endeavor? The question was important, because whoever was best—a "man of virtue"—was considered to be the person best equipped to rule the country. Prior to Confucius, such a man was presumed to be a nobleman, but Confucius redefined the man of virtue, the superior man, as someone who is wise, courageous, and humane; someone who thinks well and acts accordingly; someone who models his behavior after virtuous men of the past; and someone who understands that life is a long learning process. The man of virtue exhibits his humanity by being benevolent, and he seeks not profit or revenge, but righteousness. His right conduct may show itself when he rectifies what is wrong or in particular in rectifying *names*, or titles (in other words, using the proper words to address others, in particular one's superiors). Studying proper conduct and developing proper character are the same as studying *the Way* (*Dao*, or *Tao*). The Way means the way to proper conduct and proper character—wisdom—and only through studying the Way do people become superior. How do we practice the Way? By developing good habits and continual good thinking. The evils to watch out for are, in particular, greed, aggressiveness, pride, and resentment. It truly is possible to become a superior man, according to Confucius, because people can be transformed by learning. Once we have learned enough about the Way to recognize it, we will know that there is virtue in *moderation*. (Like the Greeks, Confucius believed in the virtuous nature of the *mean* between the extremes of deficiency and excess; see Box 12.3.)

Confucianism is closer to virtue ethics than to an ethics of conduct, although proper conduct is also part of Confucius's philosophy. For the Confucian philosopher, ethics is not a matter of rigid definitions of what to do or how to be but a mat-

Box 12.3   CONFUCIUS AND ARISTOTLE

There are some extraordinary parallels between the virtue theory of Confucius and that of Aristotle; both men greatly influenced posterity, each in his own way. For both thinkers, good habits are the proper way to develop a good character. Both Confucius and Aristotle emphasized the link between good thinking and subsequent action, and both believed that the virtuous human being is one who recognizes the *mean*, the middle state of moderation. But there are also considerable differences. For Confucius the superior man is one who shuns pride and strives for humility; Aristotle would have considered such a man to have insufficient self-appreciation. Confucius also seems to have reached out to a more inclusive moral universe than Aristotle did, and this has caused some

scholars to compare him to Christian thinkers. Confucius is known to have expressed a version of the Golden Rule: Don't do to others what you wouldn't want them to do to you, sometimes called the "Silver Rule." (See Box 4.9.) We don't find this attitude in Aristotle's writings, because the general idea of *moral equality*, which is essential for the Golden Rule, is absent in Aristotle's code of ethics. Confucius's superior man also must appreciate *cooperation*— both between people and between people and Nature—whereas Aristotle stressed the hierarchy of rule. Both men, however, envisioned a state that is run according to the model of a well-functioning family, with the ruler as pater-familias at the head, deciding what is best for his family.

ter of virtues and behaviors that depend on circumstances. In order to know whether an action is appropriate, you must know how it affects others and whether it might be conducive or detrimental to the harmony of society. Virtue, *te,* consists of both personal character formation and good use of power by a government with good intentions. A person or a government that has achieved *te* is living according to *tao (dao)* and has also attained the basic virtues of *jen, li,* and *yi.* As with the term *tao,* there are no easy Western translations for these concepts: *Jen* means having a caring attitude toward others, including nonhuman beings; *li* means understanding and performing rituals correctly, but *li* is empty without *jen* (just knowing how to perform ceremonies correctly is meaningless if you don't have a caring approach); and *yi* is the understanding of what is proper and appropriate, not just in terms of etiquette but also in terms of whether something is reasonable and rational. So in order to have *li* (the understanding of rituals) you have to have *jen* (caring), but you must definitely also have *yi* (reasoned judgment) so you know what rituals are important and why. The classical Chinese society was burdened with many elaborate rituals and ceremonies, and Confucius allowed for one's critical sense to cut through and determine what was essential and practical and what was not, depending on the circumstances.

Confucius's ideas of the virtuous man and the well-run state became so influential that they were adopted as state religion in China for a period of several hundred years (618–907 C.E.) in spite of the fact that Confucius didn't concern himself with religious questions. He believed that because we know very little about death

Box 12.4   TAOISM

The Chinese philosopher Lao-Tzu was a contemporary of Confucius. The two men knew each other and disagreed politely on several essential points, the most important one being the usefulness of social action. For Confucius the superior man must try to effect change, to make life better for others. For Lao-Tzu this is a useless endeavor, because humans can't effect changes. Nature is a complex duality of opposite forces working together, the forces of yin and yang, he believed. These forces work according to a pattern that can't be observed by most humans, and things happen in their own time. The best humans can do is to contemplate this fact. This is the only access to the Way, or Tao: By doing nothing, by letting nature take its course, we are not obstructing this course; we are emptying our minds of the constant question What should I do next? And by letting our minds become still and perfectly empty, we are opening ourselves to the truth of the Way. The Tao of Lao-Tzu is far more mystical than that of Confucius, which is why his ideas have acquired their own label, Taoism. Virtue and proper conduct meld together in the concept of "doing nothing," or rather "not overdoing it," *wu wei*, which entails unselfishness and mental tranquility. Interestingly enough, this doesn't mean that you deliberately should refrain from doing things like taking a box of matches out of the hands of a three-year-old; indeed, not to do so would be a selfish, willful act. You *should* take the matches away from the child but without congratulating yourself that you've saved her life; after all, she may head straight for your medicine cabinet next. Do what you have to do, but don't think you can make a difference; eventually this will give you peace of mind. This is the hard lesson of Taoism.

and any life after death, we must focus our effort on this life and our relationships with other human beings. (Box 12.4 explains some differences between Confucianism and Taoism.)

Mencius (371–289 B.C.E.) followed in Confucius's footsteps but took Confucianism one step further. He believed not only that humans can learn to be good but also that they are good from the beginning; they just have been corrupted by life and circumstances. Mencius thought the proper method of finding our way back to our lost goodness is to look inside ourselves and recapture our nature — our conscience and our intuition. If we pay proper attention to our own good nature, it will grow and take over. Only through ourselves can we find the right way, and this process requires a certain amount of suffering. When we suffer, our character is developed. Mencius doubts that someone who has led an easy life can be truly virtuous. The virtues we are supposed to develop through suffering are independence, excellence, mental alertness, courage, and quietude of spirit. When we have reached such a mental equilibrium, we can help others achieve the same, because benevolence is the prime virtue.

The following admonishments are quoted from *The Book of Mencius,* a collection of sayings probably compiled by his followers. This excerpt shows that for Mencius the development of one's character is fundamentally the most important moral task.

Although one has duties (which is why there are rules for *conduct,* which one ought to follow), one is not able to fulfill these duties without being *virtuous*—in other words, without having retained one's moral character:

> What is the most important duty? One's duty towards one's parents. What is the most important thing to watch over? One's own character. I have heard of a man who, not having allowed his character to be morally lost, is able to discharge his duties towards his parents; but I have not heard of one morally lost who is able to do so. There are many duties one should discharge, but the fulfillment of one's duty towards one's parents is the most basic. There are many things one should watch over, but watching over one's character is the most basic. . . . Benevolence is the heart of man, and rightness his road. Sad it is indeed when a man gives up the right road instead of following it and allows his heart to stray without enough sense to go after it. When his chickens and dogs stray, he has sense enough to go after them, but not when his heart strays. The sole concern of learning is to go after this strayed heart.

The tradition of Confucius and Mencius continued into twentieth-century China and is noticeable to this day. A modern voice of this tradition is Lin Yutang (1895–1976). Aside from Mao Zedong, Lin Yutang may be the most influential of all modern Chinese writers in the West. He traveled extensively in the United States but never lost touch with his Chinese heritage and values. Even more than by Confucius, Lin Yutang was inspired by Mencius. Lin Yutang himself believed that Western philosophers were too fixated on the idea of reason and had forgotten what the ancient Greek thinkers saw as the most important element of their philosophy: human happiness. In his 1937 book *The Importance of Living,* he mentions with much modesty that he is uneducated in philosophy. His knowledge of both Chinese and Western philosophy is considerable, however. What is the importance of living? Knowing when to take things seriously and when to laugh at the solemnity of life; being so fortunate and living so long that one can become a serious intellectual and then return to a higher level of simple thinking and simple ways.

In several books Lin Yutang attempted to bridge the gap between East and West, especially at a time during the first half of the twentieth century when there wasn't much understanding between the two worlds. Writing about family values in a transitional period during which Chinese values were changing (the later Communist takeover forced a transfer of authority to the people as the feudal system was dissolved), Lin Yutang saw the greatest difference between East and West not in the area of politics or gender issues but in the way we treat our elderly—our parents in particular.

Whereas a Western man might think most about helping women and children, a Chinese man would think primarily about helping his parents and other elderly people. This is not because the elderly are thought of as being helpless; it is because they are *respected.* In the Chinese tradition, the older you are, the more respect you deserve. Lin Yutang describes this in *The Importance of Living:*

> In China, the first question a person asks the other on an official call, after asking about his name and surname, is "What is your glorious age?" If the person replies apologetically

Lin Yutang (1895–1976), the author of *The Importance of Living* (1937) and *The Wisdom of China and India* (1955), may be the modern Chinese thinker best known in the Western world. He worked hard to create a cross-cultural understanding between East and West, but he himself believed that some traditional Eastern values, such as respect for the elderly, are fundamentally different from modern Western values.

that he is twenty-three or twenty-eight, the other party generally comforts him by saying that he still has a glorious future and that one day he may become old. But if the person replies that he is thirty-five or thirty-eight, the other party immediately exclaims with deep respect, "Good luck!"; enthusiasm grows in proportion as the gentleman is able to report a higher and higher age, and if the person is anywhere over fifty, the inquirer immediately drops his voice in humility and respect.

Just as people under twenty-one in our culture may lie about their age in order to get into clubs that serve liquor, Chinese young people may pretend to be older in order to gain respect. But in the West there is a point at which most people don't want to seem older than they are; in fact, they might like to appear *younger* than they are. The Chinese traditionally want to appear *older* throughout their lives, because it is to their advantage. Lin Yutang saw the quest for youth in American culture as alien and frightening—and he was writing in the 1930s, when American teens still attempted to dress and act as "adults." Today, in the exaggerated youth cult that is part of the baby boomer legacy, the phenomenon has become even more extreme. As respect grows with age in the Chinese traditional culture, it seems to *diminish* with age in the West: Somehow we perceive ourselves and others as less powerful, beautiful, and valuable as we reach the far side of fifty or even forty. Lin Yutang quotes an American grandmother who says that it was the birth of her first grandchild that

Box 12.5 SELF-WORTH AND RETIREMENT

Lin Yutang chastises the West for its "throw-away" attitude toward the older generation. He praises respect and love for one's parents and grandparents as virtues that have to be learned. The West, however, has not always discarded its citizens at the onset of old age. In earlier farming communities in particular, elders not only were respected but were considered an important part of the community because of their *usefulness*. Perhaps they couldn't knead bread or plow the field anymore, but they still could look after the children and share their wisdom. In some parts of the Western world we still can find this type of relationship within a community. But as most people would agree, this is not the case in the larger cities of the West, where it is not customary for grandparents to live with their children. The general attitude seems to be that showing signs of aging is somehow a flaw. A British writer once wrote of Americans that they think death is optional—that if you die you must have done something wrong, like not having taken enough vitamins.

It would appear that part of our problem with accepting the aging process is that as Westerners we have developed the attitude that when we stop being *productive,* we stop being *valuable* as human beings. When a person retires, this feeling often is reinforced, because the person is all of a sudden excluded from part of his or her habitual environment—the workplace. Especially during the early and middle years of the twentieth century, when people would stay in their jobs for over forty years, retirement forced a reevaluation of the person's identity, and all too often the retiree felt that he or she had been *reduced* in value, had been deemed useless by society. This may be one reason it is not uncommon for people to fall ill and even die a short time after retirement, even if they had initially looked forward to it.

There are signs that this trend may change; there is a growing awareness that older people are still people, and because nowadays people usually don't stay at the same job as long as they did in previous generations they may depend less on their jobs for their sense of identity. Also, many retirees reenter the workforce part-time, either because they want to or, sadly, because they can't afford not to. Soon the oldest members of the baby boomer generation will be approaching retirement; perhaps they will refuse to be "thrown away." We may see more emphasis on the autonomy, competence, and worthiness of the retired or older person in the future.

"hurt," because it seemed to be a reminder of the loss of youth. (Box 12.5 discusses our attitude toward aging and how it affects retirement.)

American parents are afraid to make demands on their children, says Lin Yutang. Parents are afraid of becoming a burden, of meddling in their children's affairs, of being nosy. But in whose affairs would we meddle if not in the affairs of those who are closest to us? he asks. Parents do have a right to make demands of their children, he says; they do have a right to be cared for by their children. This is because *their children owe it to them.* We owe a never-ending *debt of gratitude* to our parents for raising us, for being there when we were teething, for changing those diapers and taking care of us when we were sick, and just for feeding and clothing us. (See Box 12.6 for further views.) Even among Chinese who immigrated to the United States, the

Box 12.6   THE DUTY TO TAKE CARE OF ONE'S PARENTS

For Lin Yutang, the duty to take care of one's parents is a quintessential feature of Chinese culture; as a legacy of Confucian virtue theory, which stresses respect for older people and caring for one's parents, it is a powerful cultural tradition even in today's China. However, the duty to care for aging parents is a near-universal moral rule, except in the less family-oriented lives of many modern city-dwellers. In more traditional cultures it is usually the oldest son who is expected to take care of his parents, as in China, but other traditions exist: From Chapter 11 you will remember *Like Water for Chocolate* and its criticism of the family tradition of the youngest daughter's staying unmarried in order to take care of her mother; it is, in fact, a widespread tradition in several parts of the world that the daughter, and often the youngest daughter, inherits the obligation of taking care of her aging parents. Whether we might call it a new tradition or simply the demands of circumstances, in our society it is quite often the daughter living closest to her aging parents who takes on the task of caring for them; this frequently places a particular strain on such middle-aged female caregivers, since they, in today's world, also are likely to work full-time outside the home and, in addition, may be in the process of raising teenage children.

guilt over not being with their parents in China is enormous, even if they have brothers and sisters who can perform the duty in their homeland.

According to the Chinese conception of virtue, letting his parents grow old and die without his support is the gravest sin a man can commit. This is true for a woman, too, but less so, because it is the duty of the firstborn boy to take care of his parents. Who is the daughter supposed to take care of? Her *husband's* parents. Herein lies the secret as to why it is so important for Chinese families to have male offspring—even today, when restrictions call for only one child per family. The state may take care of you in your retirement, but even so, life is not complete without a son to lean on in your old age. The pressure to have male babies is so intense that occasionally female babies are killed at birth so that the parents can try again to have a male child, or the birth of a girl is simply kept a secret: a difficult choice, since pregnancies are monitored by the state and abortions forced on women who already have one child. An alternative is paying a hefty fine for the second child. However, the one-child policy was under revision by the Chinese government by the spring of 1999. If parents choose to keep a little girl, the response from friends and colleagues is quite different than it would be if they had a boy. A boy is cause for celebration; a baby girl may prompt friends and colleagues to send cards of condolence to the parents.

The system, however, does provide for older people. Much to the shame of traditional Chinese, there are now some nursing homes for the elderly in the villages of China, but they are presumably more humane than the "human storage tanks" we have in our Western civilization because the elderly are still part of the community, and the problems of the village are presented to them in their capacity as advisers.

In this manner the traditional respect for the older people is maintained, at least on a symbolic level, even though the family patterns have been disrupted.

We Owe Our Parents Nothing: Jane English

A young American philosopher, Jane English (1947–1978), proposed a solution to the constant and very common squabbles between parents and their grown children. It seems rather radical: She suggests that we owe our parents nothing. This idea is not as harsh as it appears, however. English thinks the main problem between grown children and parents is the common *parental* attitude that their children somehow are indebted to them. This "*debt-metaphor*" can be expressed in a number of ways, such as, "We are paying for your schooling, so you owe it to us to study what we would like you to study"; "We've clothed you and fed you, so the least you could do is come home for Christmas"; or "I was in labor with you for thirty-six hours, so you could at least clean up your room once in a while." The basic formula is, "You owe us gratitude and obedience because of what we have done for you." For English this attitude undermines all filial love, because the obvious answer a kid can give is "I didn't ask to be born." And there is not much chance of fruitful communication after that. (As one of my students remarked, a parent can always fire back with "And you weren't wanted, either," but that would surely be the end of any parent–child friendship.)

So what should parents do? English said they should realize that there are appropriate ways of using the debt-metaphor and that applying it to a parent–child relationship is not one of them. An appropriate way to use the debt-metaphor is shown in the following example given by English in her essay "What Do Grown Children Owe Their Parents?":

> New to the neighborhood, Max barely knows his neighbor, Nina, but he asks her if she will take in his mail while he is gone for a month's vacation. She agrees. If, subsequently, Nina asks Max to do the same for her, it seems that Max has a moral obligation to agree (greater than the one he would have had if Nina had not done the same for him), unless for some reason it would be a burden far out of proportion to the one Nina bore for him.

English labels what Nina does for Max a "favor"—and favors incur *debts*. But once you have paid your debt—once Max has taken Nina's mail in—then the debt is discharged, and the matter is over. This is *reciprocity*, and it means that you must do something of a similar nature for the person you are in debt to. But what if Nina never goes out of town, so Max never has an opportunity to take in her mail and pay off the debt? Then he might mow her lawn, give her rides to work, or walk her dog. If she has no lawn or dog and likes to drive to work, then he might figure out something else to do for her, and chances are that they might become friends in the process. In that case another type of relationship kicks in, one that no longer is based on a reciprocal system of favors and debts. Instead, the relationship is based on a system of duties relating to *friendship*. (See Box 12.7 for further discussion.)

In friendship, according to English, the debt-metaphor ceases to be appropriate, because friends shouldn't think they owe each other anything. Although debts are discharged when a favor is reciprocated, friendships don't work that way; just because

Box 12.7   DATING, DEBT, AND FRIENDSHIP

Many of the problems of dating stem from a difference in attitude, says Jane English. One person thinks of the date in terms of a friendship, and the other one sees it as a debt-metaphor situation. Suppose Alfred takes Beatrice out for dinner and a movie, and at the end of the evening Alfred expects "something" in return for his investment. Alfred has chosen to view the situation as a favor-debt situation; he sees Beatrice as being indebted to him. Beatrice, however, is upset, because she viewed the situation as a friendship situation, with no favors and debts. In essence, Beatrice doesn't owe Alfred a thing, because Alfred's gesture was not presented as a "quid pro quo" situation to begin with but as an overture to friendship. The situation would have been more complex had Beatrice *agreed with Alfred* in the beginning that the dinner and movie were to be a "business arrangement" to be "paid off" later in the evening. A survey from some years back showed that, shockingly, a majority of California high school students, females as well as males, feel that dating is in fact a favor-debt situation. In that case we must say that if both participants agree, then so be it.

There is, however, a good old word for when someone sells physical favors for material goods; that word is *prostitution.* In such a situation the one who is "bought" becomes merely a means to an end.

What can you do if you want to make sure to avoid a favor-debt situation on a date? For one thing, you can insist on going Dutch. Both of you probably make the same kind of money these days, so why should one of you pay for the other? Remember, nobody should expect payment for doing someone an unsolicited favor (if the people involved aren't friends), and nobody should expect payment for doing any kind of favor if the people involved are friends. So either way you shouldn't expect anything of your date, and you shouldn't feel pressured by your date to repay anything. Be careful not to abuse this rule, though. One girl commented that "it's great to be able to be taken to a dinner and a movie and not have to do anything in return!" With this attitude, she reduces her date to becoming merely the means to an end, and that's not the idea.

you do something for your friend who has done something for you doesn't make you both "even." Friendships aren't supposed to be "tit for tat," and if they are, then the people involved aren't real friends. Friendship means that you are there for each other when needed and that you do things for each other because you *like* each other, not because you *owe* each other. The fact that there can be no debts doesn't mean that there are no obligations, however; on the contrary, friendship carries with it the never-ending obligation to be there for each other, at least while the friendship lasts. It implies a mutual sense of duty toward each other. With friendship, instead of reciprocity, there is *mutuality.*

Let us speculate a bit beyond what English herself writes: Suppose you borrow fifty dollars from a friend, and then you have a falling-out with her. Because there are no debts in a friendship and because obligations last only as long as the friendship does, you don't have to pay back the money, right? Wrong, because owing money is a true debt in our society and money must be paid back regardless of whether it is owed to friends or strangers. Similarly, you have to fulfill your part of a contract, regardless of whether it is with a friend, business partner, or stranger. Such transactions come under the proper use of the debt-metaphor and persist beyond the extent of friendships. (In fact, they often are the cause of the breakup of friendships.)

English believes we often fall into the trap of regarding friendship duties as debts. Most couples find themselves saying things like, "We've been over to Frank and Claire's four times now, so we owe them a dinner." For English this is a gross misunderstanding of what friendship is all about. You can go visit Claire and Frank a hundred times, and you still don't owe them a thing because they aren't doing you a "favor"; they ask you over because they like you. To most readers this may seem a trifle idealistic; after the twentieth dinner, Claire and Frank surely will think something is wrong and won't ask you over again. But English's idea is that you will be there if they need you and that you should contribute to the friendship in *some way or other*—she doesn't say how much you should contribute or in what way; how you contribute is up to you.

English says the relationship between parents and grown children should be modeled after the friendship pattern and not after the debt-metaphor pattern. Parents don't do their children a favor by raising them, and, accordingly, children don't owe any debt to them. But this doesn't mean grown children don't have *obligations* to their parents—they have the same obligations as they have to their friends. Those obligations are limitless as long as the relationship lasts; they cease when the relationship ends. No reciprocity can be evoked, such as "You fed and clothed me for eighteen years, so I'll take care of you for the next eighteen but not a minute longer." *Mutuality,* however, is expected at all times. (What is expected in terms of other relatives is discussed in Box 12.8.)

What is the basis for a good parent–child relationship, then? Above all, love and friendship. If these are present, all that must be considered are (1) the need of the parents and (2) the ability and resources of the grown child. The parents may be sick and in need, and their son may love them, but he also may be out of work and unable to help with the medical bills. In that case, helping to pay the bills would *not* be part of his obligations, but other things would, such as providing cheerful company, taking the trash out, or making other contributions.

Suppose the parents need help, but there is *no friendship* between the parents and the child. Then, essentially, the grown child is not obliged to help, especially if the end of the friendship (if in fact it ever existed) was the parents' choice. One might imagine that this would be the time for the parents to approach their estranged child and ask for a favor in the hope of reestablishing the friendship. English seems to assume that all the parents have to do is announce that they are sorry and would like to be friends again—but what if they follow this approach with immediate requests for support? Then their son or daughter might soon get the idea that there is a calculated reason behind this renewal of friendship. (This works both ways, of course; if the son or daughter has left home in anger and later decides that he or she needs help from home, an approach of remorse and offers of renewal of friendship followed by requests for support will look equally suspicious to the parents.)

For a solution we might want to turn to the American philosopher Fred Berger (whose theory we discuss in more detail shortly). In assessing the extent of the

Box 12.8   WHAT ABOUT RELATIVES?

Jane English's main concern is for parents and grown children to realize that their relationship ought to be like that between good friends, and in such a relationship there are limitless obligations. But do we have any obligations to people who aren't yet our friends (we may hardly know them) but aren't strangers, either, because they are more distant relatives? Should they rank as friends or strangers? English has no category for them, and yet many people are concerned about how much we can and should rely on the support of relatives other than those in our immediate family. When they come to visit, should we give up our bedroom to them? Can I, as a student, ask my mother's cousin in Paris if I can stay with her for a year while I study at the Sorbonne? How can we tell our aunt and uncle from Sweden/Los Angeles/Idaho/Mexico that it really is not convenient for them to stay six weeks in our apartment? Am I obliged to find a lawyer for my half-brother who is in trouble?

And so on. Many times we might *choose* to help, just as we might help a stranger, but often the old line "Blood is thicker than water" makes us feel that we do have a specific *duty* to our extended family. One solution might be to think of this duty as a "duty to do small favors"—like finding your relatives a good, cheap hotel or showing them around town and taking them out a few times—but not as a duty to provide very large favors, like letting them have the run of your home for six weeks. Instead of finding a lawyer for your half-brother who is in trouble, you might provide him with the number of a good legal agency but let him choose a lawyer himself and let him be financially responsible. By doing these small favors, a small debt to reciprocate now rests with the relative. If this debt is discharged to everyone's satisfaction—through reciprocal hospitality or perhaps through an annual Christmas card—you can all proceed to becoming friends.

gratitude you ought to show others for acts of kindness toward you, Berger says you should look for the *motivation*. Were these acts of kindness done for your sake, for the doer's, or both? If done for your sake alone, you should show gratitude; if done for the doer's own sake, you have no obligation; if done partly for your sake and partly for the doer's own sake, you should show some gratitude, but there is no need to go overboard. In a similar manner, we might ask, why are the parents approaching their grown child (or the children their parents)? Is it because of a genuine wish to reestablish contact, is it solely because they want assistance, or is the truth somewhere in between? If the approached party can determine the motivation with reasonable accuracy, then he or she can decide how to react.

What should parents say if they very much would like their grown child to take a certain course of action but realize that he or she does not owe it to them to do so? Not "You owe us" but something like "We love you, and we think you'd be happier if you did x." Or, suggests English, "If you love us, you'll do x." But is this second example a very good one? To most people this alternative would set off a tremendous guilt trip, because it plays on the notion that if you don't comply, you don't love your parents. Few people are able to follow their parents' advice all the time, no matter how much love and friendship there may be between them. One alternative approach, which was suggested by one of my students, is for the parents to explain the whole situation: "Because of our past experience, we believe it is best for you, but it's your choice."

Jane English never lived to develop her theory further; she died at the age of thirty-one while on a mountaineering expedition in Switzerland. In her short life she published several other thought-provoking papers, and one might wonder how this bright person might have felt about the same issue had she lived to become a parent of grown children.

Friendship Duties and Gratitude

English supplies some guidelines for how we should consider *friendship* as a virtue that applies to the relationship between parents and grown children; Lin Yutang believes the virtue that should be applied to such relationships is *gratitude*. But what about both friendship and gratitude in other types of relationships, like those between friends, or lovers, or neighbors? How far do our duties of friendship go? Are we obliged to help our friends in every way, to help them cheat on their tax returns, to lie to their spouse about where they were last night, to hide them from the police, to buy them drugs? The answer is of course no—even if they would do those things for us. Friendship may be a virtue, but it doesn't entail giving up one's other moral standards merely for the sake of friendship; besides, your friend is hardly displaying the virtue of friendship toward you, since by helping him or her you may be considered "aiding and abetting" someone in trouble with the law. A good friend doesn't ask that of another. But this doesn't mean you can't do *something* for your friends when they are in trouble, like be there for them to talk to or find them an appropriate counselor. (Box 12.9 discusses how the Golden Rule applies to such issues.)

A more mundane but equally tricky situation arises when someone does something nice for us that we didn't ask and then expects something in return. Jane English states that such "unsolicited favors" do not create any debt, so we don't have to reciprocate. However, the situation may be more complex than that: The favor extended may be in an emergency situation in which a person is not capable of requesting help (such as someone picking up a wallet a person has dropped and returning it, or giving someone first aid after an accident). Jane English doesn't address such issues. And what if a person doing an unsolicited favor for a stranger is truly trying to be nice? In that case, doing nothing in return seems rude, even if we didn't ask for the favor. Here Fred Berger answers that certainly we have an obligation, and that obligation is to *show gratitude*. A simple thank-you, verbal or written, may be all it takes. In some situations the person who did us an unsolicited favor (offered to give us a ride or gave us a present) may *insist* that we show gratitude and reciprocate by doing business with them, going out with them, or even having sex with them. In that case, Berger says, we have to look at the giver's *intentions*: Did he give us something or do us a favor just so that we would be indebted to him? In that case, we don't owe the person anything, not even gratitude, because he did it for *himself*, not for us.

So how do we know when we owe people gratitude? Certainly we owe it when we have *asked* them to do us a favor. As far as unsolicited favors go, though, we should

Box 12.9   DOES THE GOLDEN RULE ALWAYS WORK?

The Golden Rule has been mentioned several times in this text, and it is certainly one of the most widespread rules of ethics in existence, finding expression in religions and moral teachings throughout recorded history. But is it always the best solution to do unto others as you would have them do unto you? Suppose a friend wants you to put her up for a few weeks. She tells you she has been involved in a hit-and-run accident, and now she wants to hide from the police. You are reluctant to let her stay, but she assures you that she would do the same for you or even that you would want her to do the same for you if you were in trouble. But that may not be the case; you may see the situation in quite a different light. If you were in trouble you might need a friend, but you might not ask that friend to hide you; chances are you wouldn't have left the scene of the accident in the first place. (Staying at the scene is of course the only ethical course of action—besides, it's the law.) Your friend's perception of what she wants done for her is not the same as what you might want a friend to do for you. In everyday life we find lots of examples of this type of situation: Maria gives Cheryl a bread machine for Christmas because that's what Maria would like to get. But she didn't think to find out whether Cheryl might also like one, and in fact Cheryl doesn't like kitchen gifts. Paul and Lisa stay at Lee and Chi-Wah's house while they are abroad, and as a gesture of gratitude they mow the lawn, tear up all the wildflowers, and make the yard look "neat," because that's the way they would like it to look. But Lee and Chi-Wah love the wild and unkempt look and are heartbroken at the sight of their tidy, trimmed yard; being polite, however, they pretend to be grateful for all the yardwork. Often, such misplaced acts of kindness are caused by a self-centered attitude or a lack of perception, but they also may happen due to a fundamental difference in the approach to life. In her book *That's Not What I Meant,* the linguist Deborah Tannen describes a classic situation of misapplied Golden Rule approaches between partners who have different visions of correct behavior (or what Tannen calls different "styles"):

> Maxwell wants to be left alone, and Samantha wants attention. So she gives him attention, and he leaves her alone. The adage "Do unto others as you would have others do unto you" may be the source of a lot of anguish and misunderstanding if the doer and the done unto have different styles.

> It appears that if we are to act on the Golden Rule, we have to make certain that the others really want to "be done unto."

express gratitude when we can be reasonably certain that (1) they did it for our own sake—because they like and respect us, as Kant would say, as *ends in ourselves,* not because they viewed us as the *means to an end.* We also should make certain that (2) they did help us *on purpose* and didn't just blunder into the situation. Moreover, we have to ascertain that (3) they did it *voluntarily,* that no one else forced them to do it. In Berger's words, gratitude should be a response to benevolence, not benefits, and this applies to all relationships, even those between parents and children. We should express gratitude in proportion to the things that are done for our sake (to be sure, not everything parents do is done for the sake of the child). If something is done for other reasons, our duty to show gratitude diminishes proportionately. And, says Berger, when we do show gratitude to people who have done something for us, we show that we appreciate *them* as intrinsically valuable persons—as ends in themselves and not just as instruments for our well-being.

Suppose the people who do things for us like us and respect us but still hope to get something out of being nice to us? You'll recall that we discussed the issue of selfishness vs. altruism in Chapter 4, and we can apply that lesson here. We shouldn't disqualify others from deserving our gratitude just because they were hoping for some little advantage themselves; it is when we were considered solely a means to an end that our duty to show gratitude disappears.

Suppose you have good reason to feel grateful for something someone has done. Let's assume you are a poor student and your neighbors have seven kids. They cook up a huge dinner every night, and at the end of the month, when you are broke, they always invite you over for dinner. They say, "We have to cook anyway, so come on over." And you do, month after month. You keep waiting for the moment when the family may need your invaluable assistance with something, but the time never comes. So you keep eating their food and feeling like a moocher. What can you do? Well, you might do the dishes once in a while or help babysit. In other words, you can contribute to the mutuality of a friendship even if you aren't specifically asked to do so.

Let's return to the question How much gratitude should I feel? The answer, says Berger, lies in Aristotle's theory of virtue: just enough—not too much and not too little. As vague as it is, this is still the guideline most people instinctively use when they try to figure out how to respond to an act of kindness. We know that enslaving ourselves for the rest of our natural lives, giving up our firstborn, and other such measures would be too much. We also know that being rude and doing or saying nothing to show our appreciation is too little. (For vices of too much and too little, see Box 12.10.) But where exactly lies the right amount? This is, as with all the Aristotelian virtues, a case-by-case matter. Sometimes the right amount consists of a thank-you note, a bottle of wine, or a batch of chocolate-chip cookies. Sometimes it is house-sitting for six months, and sometimes it is going across country to give someone a helping hand. If we manage to hit the bull's-eye and find the right response, perhaps Aristotle is right, and we are on the way to becoming virtuous.

How to Receive Gratitude?

One aspect of the question of gratitude rarely touched on by philosophers is a matter that, in everyday life, is almost as important as the questions of when to be grateful and how much gratitude to show, and that is the virtue of gracefully *accepting gratitude*. Just as it takes skill to be a good giver, so it takes skill to be a good receiver, regardless of whether we talk about gifts, favors, or reciprocation. What if you are the person who did someone else a favor without expecting anything in return? In other words, you treated that someone as an end in himself or herself, and the mere fact that you were able to help is enough reward for you. But now the other person wants to thank you and do something for you in return. What do you do? Saying

Box 12.10   A SHORT VIEW OF VICES

No case study of virtues would be complete without sneaking a peek at the forbidden zone: the vices. In his list of virtues, Aristotle himself devotes much attention to the extremes of deficiency and excess, because without knowing when there is too much or too little of something, how do we know when there is just enough? Some people use this as an excuse for exploring the vices before settling for being virtuous, but virtue theory doesn't assume that such explorations are necessary; just knowing the limits of virtue may be sufficient. For our two virtues in this chapter the corresponding vices, in an Aristotelian approach, would be as follows:

- For *compassion:* The vice of excess might be for a person to be intrusive and nosy or lack an understanding of when others should be pitied; the vice of deficiency would be for a person to be coldhearted and unfeeling.
- For *gratitude:* The vice of excess might be to feel perpetually indebted; the vice of deficiency would, of course, be ingratitude.

As you will remember from our discussion about negative role models, the fascination for how *not* to be is at least as deep as our interest in being a good person. Vices keep inspiring authors from all parts of the world, and two of the most commonly used vices in works of fiction are *jealousy* and the *thirst for revenge.*

Jealousy should be distinguished from envy, which is wanting what another person has or is;

by jealousy we usually mean sexual jealousy: the feeling of gnawing anger and hurt at the thought (or prospect, or fact) of the one we love in an amorous situation with someone else. For some people any kind of jealousy is a vice, because it reduces the one we love to a piece of *property,* which we think we can own; others see it as a healthy expression of love, provided that it is not carried to excess through perpetual suspicion.

Thirst for revenge would for Aristotle probably be excessive, but the idea of revenge itself would not be a vice for the ancient Greek mind: It would rather be appropriate under specific circumstances of settling an offense; otherwise, one might seem meek and weak-hearted (and in this the ancient Greeks and the Vikings would have seen completely eye to eye). For the Christian tradition, however, revenge is supposed to be a matter for God to carry out; the old saying from the Bible is "Vengeance is mine, saith the Lord" (Rom. 12:19). As you may remember from Chapter 7, vengeance is not acceptable as a reason for punishment in the modern legal system. Retribution is a different phenomenon, a socially sanctioned action based on logic rather than emotion and designed to mete out justice in proportion to the crime. Revenge can easily spill over into a blood feud, resulting in the killing of innocents. At the end of this chapter you can read summaries of two classic stories about jealousy and two about the thirst for revenge.

you don't want any thanks may be telling the other person how you feel, but it may not be enough, because the other person may feel he or she *needs* to reciprocate; so you must be able to sometimes allow the other to do so, with the implicit understanding that it is not going to lead to a game of one-upmanship with returned favors. Sometimes a simple "You're welcome" is enough, while sometimes the proper way to accept gratitude may be to gracefully accept a favor or a gift in return, even if you did not do the original favor in order to get rewarded. And here Aristotle comes in handy again: Your guideline as to how big a favor you can accept in return for a favor should be the extent of the original favor ("just right"). At the end of the chapter we will look at *Grand Canyon,* a film which explores just that kind of situation: showing and accepting gratitude.

Virtue and Conduct: A Combination?

In Chapters 3–7 we explored the most influential theories of what has become known as ethics of conduct, and in Chapters 8–12 we have looked at classical and contemporary versions of virtue ethics. The majority of ethicists over the years have perceived their task as defining in the simplest terms possible, and with as few rules as possible, a moral theory that would have universal application, one that would be valid in all situations. As we have seen, no theory so far can be said to work equally well in all situations; all theories, when put to the test, show some flaws or problems. For all its positive elements, ethical relativism allows for a tolerance that objects to nothing, not even crimes against humanity; egoism, while recognizing the right of the individual to look after his or her own interests, fails to recognize that humans may actually be interested in serving the interests of others; utilitarianism, while seeking general happiness for all sentient beings, seems to allow for the few to be used, and even sacrificed, for the sake of the many; Kantian deontology wants to do the right thing but is so focused on duty that it may overlook bad consequences of doing one's duty—consequences that otherwise could have been avoided. And virtue ethics, which is intended as an alternative to these theories of conduct, hasn't quite solved the problem of when and how to use one's reason and rational argumentation in terms of defining moral standards, and it hasn't succeeded in coming up with a theory of action in which the general ideas of virtue can be brought into play in particular situations or in solving disagreements between people who consider themselves virtuous. For those who look for a good answer to moral problems, this can be more than discouraging, and some might even decide, like Huck Finn, that moral speculations are too confusing and it's better just to follow their gut feelings. But this would be taking the easy way out, and actually it is not a very satisfying solution. On occasion we all may have to justify an action, and "It seemed like a good idea at the time" is not an adequate answer. Furthermore, we may decide that ethicists haven't come up with a complete solution to moral problems, but that doesn't mean we don't have to keep on trying to solve them on an individual basis. Just because the experts haven't given us all the solutions on a silver platter doesn't mean we're exempt from seeking solutions on our own. There *are* alternative answers.

Most of the theories we have looked at originated in time periods when it was assumed that humans would someday know all the answers to everything. It also was assumed, from a scientific viewpoint, that a simple explanation was better and more pleasing than a complex one. To a great extent that is still true: A theory gains in strength if unnecessary elements are cut away (this phenomenon is often referred to as *Occam's razor,* from the British medieval philosopher William of Occam). But the late twentieth century also taught us that simple solutions may not always be available, or even desirable, because there may be many possible ways of looking at each situation. (A case in point is Deborah Tannen's example of different "styles" of behavior described in Box 12.9.) So we are not focused on seeking simple answers to complex issues in ethics any longer.

I often hear students remark, Why do all these philosophers have to be so single-minded about everything? Why can't their theories allow for nuances? It is a good question—but it is a question that is possible only because we have become a culture that allows for nuances and different perspectives. (Many theories do, in fact, allow for nuances, but it is unfortunately in the nature of introductory courses that some of those nuances tend to fall by the wayside in the effort to express a theory as clearly, and as briefly, as possible.) This culture probably wouldn't have arrived at such an openness had it not been for the progression in moral theory (the phenomenon the Australian philosopher Peter Singer referred to as "the expanding circle," as you may remember from Chapter 4). Elements in theories that may now seem too narrow and absolutist at some point in time expanded or broke a narrower and more rigid system of values. It seems that we are now ready for something of a more complex nature: an expansion that allows for assuming the possibility that we can have certain basic values in common and at the same time allows for a relativistic tolerance of other values. We may be looking for what was introduced in Part 2 as *soft universalism:* the theory that deep down, we can agree on certain core values that are based on our common humanity. However, this is not going to be easy, because we have to agree on *which* values are supposed to be the ones we have in common, and here our different cultural upbringing and ethnic diversity may come into play.

Some philosophers have been trying for a long time to redesign the traditional theories (such as utilitarianism, deontology, or virtue theory) to make them more logical, more responsive to present-day sensitivities, or more tolerant of exceptions. But we can choose another path: seeking the best advice from a multitude of theories. The approach of Fred Berger to the question of compassion is an example of this approach: He uses both Aristotle's theory of the mean between extremes and Kant's theory of ends in themselves in order to explore the subject of compassion. In other words, he allows for several different theories to be used at the same time, letting them work together to achieve a functional solution. This is a very pragmatic approach, and some might even call it a very American approach, because Americans are (presumably) typically interested in whether or not something *works*.

This approach may work if we don't expect too much. Letting the vast spectrum of ethical viewpoints and traditions become available as options will certainly be no easy road, primarily because we can't just decide to take the best elements of all theories and lump them together in the hope that they may work. For one thing, they may well contradict each other; for another, if we choose a theory for its advantages, we're stuck with its disadvantages, too. We can't just decide to add deontology to utilitarianism, for example, and assume that a smooth theory will emerge; we may have doubled our range of solutions, but we have also doubled our problems.

It is, however, probably the only viable solution for a future theory of ethics. We need theories of conduct, and we need theories of virtue, from more than just a few cultural groups; besides, most of us already use a pluralistic approach on a day-by-day basis. Sometimes we consider consequences as vitally important (especially in matters of life and death); sometimes we think keeping promises and other obligations is more important than worrying about consequences; sometimes we feel we're entitled to look after ourselves and our own interests; and sometimes we are focused on developing a good character — based on compassion, courage, or another virtue. Often we do combine these views in specific situations. But we have to be able to decide when one viewpoint or aspect is more appropriate than another, and we have to try to avoid contradicting ourselves by putting together principles that are in obvious opposition to each other. You can't claim at the same time that consequences don't count and that consequences are all-important. What you *can* claim is that there are times when consequences are supremely important (such as calling and waiting for the ambulance to come for your neighbor who keeled over with a heart attack, even if you have to break your movie date in order to do that), and at other times a principle may be more important than certain consequences (such as a jury turning in a guilty verdict based on clear evidence, even if it may result in rioting). So despite the reluctance of many ethicists to mix and match moral theories, we do it on an everyday basis, and we can train ourselves to do it better by making sure we don't just make loopholes for ourselves, but genuinely try to address and evaluate the various aspects of real-life ethics as they arise in real situations: duty theory, consequentialism, virtue ethics, respect for other moral traditions — and, on occasion, some legitimate self-interest (provided that it doesn't seriously disregard the interests of others).

Another possibility inherent in soft universalism is its support for a multitude of moral viewpoints in a modern society — an approach called *ethical pluralism* by some. We have already seen that soft universalism can serve as the theoretical underpinning of multiculturalism, provided that all groups seek common ground. The same thing goes for ethical pluralism: If by that concept we mean a culture consisting of disparate and mutually exclusive viewpoints — groups not conversing, isolating themselves within their group identities — then soft universalism and ethical pluralism have little in common. But if by ethical pluralism we mean a diverse society that wishes to create an environment with mutual respect and interest in sharing the responsibilities and joys of the community, then soft universalism can lend a hand, with its credo that we can show respect for a variety of moral viewpoints, as long as we agree that we can find some common values underlying the differences. In the end, the view of soft universalism is that those common values are founded in our common humanity, in the fact that we live in groups and bond with other human beings but are also competitive individuals within our groups. So the challenge of soft universalism is to provide justification for why certain values are to be considered common ground. It must set up a system of justification for which moral values should be considered valid at all times (such as the United Nations' list of human rights, for example), which values should be considered a matter of cultural preference and tradition, and which values should be considered globally unacceptable (such as "Some people are born to be free, and others are born to be slaves"). A new theory of ethics must embrace all such elements if it is to offer genuine solutions to the problems of a highly complex world.

Study Questions

1. What does Philip Hallie mean by negative and positive commands? Explain. Do you agree with him that positive commands are harder to live up to than negative commands?

2. Evaluate Richard Taylor's view that morality is a matter not of rational principles but of having your heart in the right place. Explore the pros and cons of such a view.

3. Evaluate the respect for the elderly as expressed in the philosophies of Confucius, Mencius, and Lin Yutang. Are such values completely alien to Western culture? Do you think modern Western culture would be improved by incorporating such ideas? Why or why not?

4. Contrast the conclusions of Jane English and Lin Yutang concerning the parent–grown child relationship.

5. Discuss the issue of dating: Is it a favor/debt or a friendship situation? Is there a way of resolving the problem of different expectations for dating partners in the twenty-first century?

Primary Readings and Narratives

The first Primary Reading is an excerpt from Philip Hallie's *Tales of Good and Evil, Help and Harm*. The second Primary Reading, an excerpt from Lin Yutang's essay "On Growing Old Gracefully," discusses traditional ideas of gratitude within the family; the summaries of the films *Eat Drink Man Woman* and *Grand Canyon* illustrate how this virtue can be practiced in modern life.

To illustrate the virtue of compassion, praised as the true universal virtue by Western as well as non-Western thinkers, I have chosen the parable of the Good Samaritan, the Hindu tale "King Yudisthira and the Dog," and the film *Schindler's List*. These stories explore not only when one should show compassion but also whom one should show compassion toward — in other words, who counts as a member of one's moral universe.

As we've seen, however, lessons in virtuous living are often told through negative examples, through stories about vice and about people of frail or evil character. The vice of jealousy, "the green-eyed monster which doth mock the meat it feeds on," is epitomized in Shakespeare's *Othello*, which is summarized here. The theme is also explored in other cultures, and we look at a story from the Pueblo Indians of New Mexico. In addition, we have short summaries of two famous stories of vengeance: *The Count of Monte Cristo,* and *The Searchers.* Thirst for revenge is usually considered a vice, but you'll also remember from Chapter 7 that some thinkers consider emotion to be legitimate, at least to some degree, when considering punishment. You might keep that in mind, and ask yourself what makes thirst for vengeance a vice.

Primary Reading

Tales of Good and Evil, Help and Harm

PHILIP HALLIE

Excerpt, 1997.

Most of the old ethical theories and commandments present ethics as a friend of life and an enemy of death. And so those theories and commandments praise help and condemn harm. They celebrate the spreading of life with two sorts of ethical rules or ideals: negative and positive. The negative rules are scattered throughout the Bible and other ethical documents, but Moses brought the most memorable ones down to the West from Mount Sinai: Thou shalt not murder, thou shalt not betray. . . . These rules say no to the deliberate extinction of life and joy. On the other hand, positive rules are also spread across many ethical documents. For instance, the Bible enjoins us to be our brother's keeper. These rules say yes to the protection and spreading of life.

The naysaying ethic forbids our doing certain harmful things, and the yeasaying one urges us to help those whose lives are diminished or threatened. To follow the negative ideals you must have clean hands; but to follow the positive ones you can be less hygienic — you can dirty your hands doing something helpful. If you would be your brother's keeper you must go out of your way. The negative ethic is the ethic of decency, of restraint. It is terrible to violate it — to be a murderer or a liar — but obey it and you could be a dead person. A corpse does not kill and does not betray. Moreover, you could obey the no ethic by being silent, and it was the silent majority in Germany and in the world who fed the torturers and the murderers with their silence. The murderers and the torturers drank the silence like wine, and it made them drunk with power.

On the other hand, the yes ethic demands action. You must be alive if you would meet its demands; sometimes you must even put your life on the line. You must go out of your way, sometimes very *far* out of your way. In combat I had to become a killer in order to help stop Germany in its tracks. I had to violate the no ethic in order to help stop the many tortures and murders that Nazi Germany was perpetrating in Central Europe.

. . . My experience had led me to believe that human beings are doomed either to be clean-handed and helpless or murderous and helpful. I knew no one who was both clean and noble.

But in that story about the village of Le Chambon I found people who were both. Here were people in this slaughterhouse of a world who avoided hating and hurting life and at the same time prevented murder. . . .

. . . .

If evil has to do with the twisting and diminution of human life, then the government [Schmäling] ably served was evil. In a mountainous part of France where there were many French guerrilla fighters, he helped keep the French from stabbing his fellow Germans in the back and hindering the cruel march of Nazism. He helped an evil cause ably, and importantly.

But if goodness has to do with the spreading of human life, and the prevention of hatred and cruelty and murder, then he was surely good. Good and evil have much to do with perspectives, points of view. If you want to know whether cruelty is happening and just how painful it is, do not ask the torturer. Do not ask someone like Obergruppenführer [Lieutenant General] Otto Ohlendorff, the head of the special troops assigned to kill unarmed civilians in Eastern Europe. The victimizer does not feel the blows, the victim feels them. Do not ask a sword about wounds; look to the person on whose flesh the sword falls. Victimizers can be blinded by simple insensitivity, by a great cause, by a great hatred, or by a hundred self-serving "reasons." Victims too can be desensitized, but usually they are the best witnesses to their pain. They feel it in their flesh and in their deepest humiliations and horrors.

And if you want to know about goodness, do not ask only the doers of good. They may be doing what they do out of habitual helpfulness or for some abstract cause. They may not realize exactly how they are helping the people they have helped: They may not be looking deeply into the eyes and minds of the beneficiaries of their good deeds.

But usually the beneficiaries of those deeds know. Usually they have this knowledge in their flesh and in their passions. And usually if they do not have this knowledge, goodness is not happening, the joy of living is not being enhanced and widened for them. Do-gooders can in fact do great harm. The points of view of victims and beneficiaries are vital to an understanding of evil and of good.

Study Questions

1. What is the difference between naysaying ethics and yeasaying ethics? Explain. What does this have to do with the story of the people of Le Chambon?

2. What does Hallie mean by saying, "To follow the negative ideals you must have clean hands; but to follow the positive ones you can be less hygienic — you can dirty your hands doing something helpful"? Explain, and evaluate Hallie's viewpoint: Is he right? Why or why not?

3. What is Hallie's final verdict on Schmäling? Was he good or evil? Explain.

4. Whose perspective does Hallie suggest that we seek in order to find out about goodness?

Primary Reading

On Growing Old Gracefully

LIN YUTANG

Excerpt from **The Importance of Living,** *1937.*

In this excerpt Lin Yutang talks about the duty of the adult male toward his parents and about the process of aging, which, to him, ought to be a stage characterized by both happiness and wisdom.

Every one realizes . . . that orphanages and old age pensions are poor substitutes for the home. The feeling is that the home alone can provide anything resembling a satisfactory arrangement for the old and the young. But for the young, it is to be taken for granted that not much need be said, since there is natural paternal affection. "Water flows downwards and not upwards," the Chinese always say, and therefore the affection for parents and grandparents is something that stands more in need of being taught by culture. A natural man loves his children, but a cultured man loves his parents. In the end, the teaching of love and respect for old people became a generally accepted principle, and if we are to believe some of the writers, the desire to have the privilege of serving their parents in their old age actually became a consuming passion. The greatest regret a Chinese gentleman could have was the eternally lost opportunity of serving his old parents with medicine and soup on their deathbed, or not to be present when they died. For a high official in his fifties or sixties not to be able to invite his parents to come from their native village and stay with his family at the capital, "seeing them to bed every night and greeting them every morning," was to commit a moral sin of which he should be ashamed and for which he had constantly to offer excuses and explanations to his friends and colleagues. This regret was expressed in two lines by a man who returned too late to his home, when his parents had already died:

> The tree desires repose, but the wind will not stop;
> The son desires to serve, but his parents are already gone.

. . . It seems a linguistic misfortune that hale and hearty old men in America tell people that they are "young," or are told that they are "young" when really what is meant is that they are healthy. To enjoy health in old age, or to be "old and healthy," is the greatest of human luck, but to call it "healthy and young" is but to detract from that glamour and impute imperfection to what is really perfect. After all, there is nothing more beautiful in this world than a healthy wise old man, with "ruddy cheeks and white hair," talking in a soothing voice about life as one who knows it. The Chinese realize this, and have always pictured an old man with "ruddy cheeks and white hair" as *the symbol of ultimate earthly happiness.* Many Americans must have seen Chinese pictures of the God of Longevity, with his high forehead, his ruddy face, his white beard — and how he smiles! The picture is so vivid. He runs his fingers through the thin flowing beard coming down to the breast and gently strokes it in peace and contentment, dignified because he is surrounded with respect, self-assured because no one ever questions his wisdom, and kind because he has seen so much of human sorrow. To persons of great vitality, we also pay the compliment of saying that "the older they grow, the more vigorous they are." . . .

I have no doubt that the fact that the old men of America still insist on being so busy and active can be directly traced to individualism carried to a foolish extent. It is their pride and their love of independence and their shame of being dependent upon their children. But among the many human rights the American people have provided for in their Constitution, they have strangely forgotten about the right to be fed by their children, for it is a right and an obligation growing out of service. How can any one deny that parents who have toiled for their children in their youth, have lost many a good night's sleep when they were ill, have washed their diapers long before they could talk and have spent about a quarter of a century bringing them up and fitting them for life, have the right to be fed by them and loved and respected when they are old? Can one not forget the individual and his pride of self in a general scheme of home life in which men are justly taken care of by their parents and, having in turn taken care of their children, are also justly taken care of by the latter? The Chinese have not got the sense of individual independence because the whole conception of life is based upon mutual help within the home; hence there is no shame attached to the circumstance of one's being served by his children in the sunset of one's life. Rather it is considered good luck to have children who can take care of one. One lives for nothing else in China.

Study Questions

1. Explain the quote: "Water runs downwards and not upwards." What does this have to do with the relationship between parents and children?

2. Evaluate Lin Yutang's view of gratitude toward parents: Is it dependent on parental love? Why or why not? Is that an important issue?

3. When evaluating two opposing viewpoints in this chapter, Lin Yutang's and Jane English's, whose approach do you find more appealing? Explain why.

Narrative

The Parable of the Good Samaritan

From the New Testament, Luke 10:30–37, King James Version.

For readers with a Christian background, the story of the Good Samaritan is the archetypal story of compassion. The Good Samaritan is one of the parables of Jesus of Nazareth, and it is intended to be taken as an allegory.

A certain man went down from Jerusalem to Jericho, and fell among thieves, which stripped him of his raiment, and wounded him, and departed, leaving him half dead. And by chance there came down a certain priest that way: and when he saw him, he passed by

Arrival of the Good Samaritan at the Inn (1866) by Gustave Doré. The Good Samaritan has rescued
a victim of a highway assault and here is taking him to be cared for. The Samaritan pays for the
victim's keep and treatment out of his own pocket and lets the innkeeper know that if the costs
add up to more, he will pay for that, too.

on the other side. And likewise a Levite, when he was at the place, came and looked on
him, and passed by on the other side. But a certain Samaritan, as he journeyed, came
where he was: and when he saw him, he had compassion on him. And went to him,
and bound up his wounds, pouring in oil and wine, and set him on his own beast, and
brought him to an inn, and took care of him. And on the morrow when he departed, he
took out two pence, and gave them to the host, and said unto him, Take care of him; and

whatsoever thou spendest more, when I come again, I will repay thee. Which now of these three, thinkest thou, was neighbor unto him that fell among the thieves? And he said, He that shewed mercy on him. Then said Jesus unto him, Go and do thou likewise.

To the modern reader, the story illustrates that the Good Samaritan is the one who is truly good, because he acts with compassion while others, who are supposed to know the difference between right and wrong, do nothing. For contemporaries of Jesus, however, the story may have meant something slightly different. A Samaritan was, for the Jews of Israel, a social outcast; the Samaritans were a population politically and ethnically distinct from the Hebrews, and people from Samaria had hardly any standing at all. The Jews, then, would have seen Jesus' purpose in telling the story as not so much instructing us to be compassionate as instructing us to recognize who our *neighbor* is (our neighbor is any person who acts with compassion toward us). The lesson is, "Even" a Samaritan can be our neighbor. But of course the overriding lesson is to "go and do likewise."

Study Questions

1. Explain what Jesus seems to mean by using the term *neighbor.* Is this story meaningful for Christians only, or might it also appeal to people of other faiths, agnostics, and atheists? Explain.

2. What might an ethical egoist say about this story? Why? Would you have a critical response, or would you agree? Why?

3. A university study conducted years ago tested people's willingness to stop and help someone in distress. A group of students were told to go to a lecture about the parable of the Good Samaritan, and on their way they encountered a man who appeared to be in severe pain. Apparently the topic of the lecture didn't make any difference: Many of those students who thought they were early for the talk stopped to help, whereas few of the students who thought they were late stopped. Do you think it would make a difference to you, if you found yourself having to choose between helping or hurrying on, whether you remembered this story?

Narrative

King Yudisthira and the Dog

Summary. A story from the epic Indian poem the Mahabharata, *fourth century* C.E.

When King Yudisthira was an old man and felt that he had served his people well, he decided to withdraw from the world. With his four brothers and his beloved wife Drapaudi he set out on foot toward the high Mount Meru to seek entrance to the gates of the City of Heaven. Soon they discovered that a dog was following them.

The mountain was steep, and the road was very long; on the way the old king saw one brother die, and then another, and another, until he had lost all four brothers. In the end even Drapaudi lost her life. But the dog was still with him, following him quietly and faithfully all the way to the gates of heaven.

There they were met by the god Indra, who welcomed the old king and was about to let him in; but the king had a question first: What about his wife and his brothers? Indra assured him that they had already arrived in heaven and were waiting for him. But the king's next request was more problematic, because he insisted that the faithful dog deserved to be let in the gates with him. Indra was taken aback and refused to consider the possibility of granting a dog immortality, especially since dogs were considered unclean. He asked the king if it could really be that he would be willing to give up his immortal bliss for the sake of an animal? Yes, said Yudisthira, because he had always lived according to three vows: never to desert someone who is frightened and who seeks his protection, or who is destitute, or who is too weak to protect his own life. "And now there is a fourth," said Yudisthira: never to abandon someone who shows devotion to you. Never abandon a friend. And he bent down to pat the dog, but suddenly, right before his eyes, the dog was changing, and growing, and taking on the shape of a god. And there, before him, stood Dharma in all his splendor, the god of Justice and Righteousness.

Indra smiled and said to Yudisthira, "You have shown compassion for another creature instead of choosing to spend eternity with the gods. Compassion for the humble is the highest virtue of all, and you shall be honored in heaven." And so the king entered heaven accompanied by Dharma and was met by his wife and his four brothers.

Study Questions

1. Evaluate the moral lesson: Is it a virtue to give up a lifelong goal or benefit for the sake of another? Why or why not?

2. It has sometimes been speculated by various writers that "all dogs go to heaven": that if there is such a thing as heaven, then pets, in their innocence and loyalty, deserve to get there more than most people do. Mark Twain, who was a cat lover, once said he believed that the pets we have loved and lost are patiently waiting for us at the gates of heaven. How do you feel about the idea that *if* there is another life beyond this one, then pets belong there, too? Explain.

3. Do you think Yudisthira might have preferred to keep the dog rather than have him transformed into the god Dharma?

4. A *Twilight Zone* episode from 1962, "The Hunt," tells the same story, but with a twist. Old Mr. Simpson and his dog find themselves dead and arrive at a gate; the gatekeeper says that it is the entrance to heaven and that the old man is welcome, but dogs aren't allowed. The dog growls, and Simpson in anger turns his back on heaven, taking his dog down the road again—but farther down the road he meets an angel sent to find him and bring him and his dog to the real heaven. The gate he had just visited was actually the entrance to hell. Simpson asks the angel why hell doesn't allow any dogs, and the angel answers, "You see, Mr. Simpson, a man, well he'll walk right into hell with both eyes open—but even the devil can't fool a dog!"

   Compare the two versions: Are there significant differences? Which one appeals more to you? Why?

Narrative

Schindler's List

STEVEN ZAILLIAN (SCREENWRITER)
STEVEN SPIELBERG (DIRECTOR)

Film, 1993. Based on the 1982 book by Thomas Keneally.

All the story summaries in this book come with a strong suggestion: that you experience the stories in their original version because the summaries are only intended to highlight certain moral problems and can in no way do justice to the experience of reading the book or watching the film. This is especially true of the award-sweeping *Schindler's List,* based on a true story from Poland in World War II. The historical fact of the Holocaust is (or ought to be) familiar to everyone, but even if we think we know what happened, the experience of *hearing and seeing* people suffering (even in a Hollywood version) is more powerful than any words can convey. For the sake of the moral of the story I have to tell you the entire story line, but I have of course omitted a great many details.

The year is 1939; the place is Kraków, Poland; the Nazi army has by now taken Poland, and Polish Jews are being moved to the 600-year-old Kraków ghetto. Deprived of the right to make a living, the Jews are trying to adjust. A German Gentile, Oskar Schindler, approaches the *Judenrat* (the Jewish Council) with a suggestion: Their investments and his business sense could make the start of a new factory. But Itzhak Stern, a member of the council, turns him down. We see Schindler getting cozy with top Nazi officials, showing himself to be a high roller and making friends, all for the sake of future business connections.

Two years later the overcrowded ghetto becomes a prison for Kraków's Jewish population; everybody of Jewish heritage is moved into the old city, and Schindler profits from the situation: He takes over the beautiful apartment belonging to a Jewish businessman. And now he again approaches the council with his suggestion; this time they are desperate for food and other goods unavailable to them, so investors agree to help Schindler set up his factory, making enamelware crockery. Stern becomes his production manager and immediately sees a way to help people in the ghetto by hiring them as skilled workers for the factory, people who have never done manual labor before — a rabbi, a musician, a history professor — because if they can't prove that they can contribute to the war effort, they will be deported.

Schindler sends for his wife from his hometown and proudly tells her that he is about to get rich — that all his previous failed business ventures lacked an essential ingredient that is now present: war. He is selling his crockery to his Nazi friends and making money hand over fist.

When Stern leaves his identification papers behind and is stopped without them, the Nazis are quick to put him on a train to Auschwitz. As the train pulls out, Schindler turns up and saves him by threatening the young Nazi officers with an end to their careers; Stern is grateful, but it is clear that Schindler didn't do it for Stern's sake. He says, "What if I'd got here five minutes later? Then where would I be?"

Philip Hallie talks about the *institutionalized cruelty* of Nazi Germany and of the antidote of hospitality provided by the people of Le Chambon; another example of an antidote against the Nazi horrors is the true story of Oskar Schindler, told by Steven Spielberg in his 1993 film *Schindler's List* (Universal Pictures). By hiring Jews as workers in his factory, Schindler was able to cheat the Nazi extermination machinery of more than 1,100 men, women, and children. Here Schindler (Liam Neeson) argues desperately with an SS guard at the Auschwitz death camp that the children of his workers are also needed at his factory because their small hands can polish the inside of artillery shell casings.

For the others being sent to Auschwitz there is no salvation; we see their suitcases opened by Nazi officials, the contents placed on shelves, their jewelry collected—and their gold teeth as well.

A new commander arrives at Plazov, the nearby labor camp: He is Amon Goeth, a ruthless and barely sane man who delights in shooting people at the slightest provocation or merely as target practice. On his order the Nazi storm troopers commence the liquidation of the Kraków ghetto: Everybody is rounded up and either shot on the spot or moved to Plazov. From a hilltop overlooking the ghetto, Schindler watches the horror of the mass murder. From afar he notices a little girl in a red coat (*Schindler's List* is a black-and-white film; the girl's coat is one of only a few items of color); we see his reaction when he understands that the girl will not survive.

Back in his factory, Schindler is all alone; the workers are gone. So he goes to Goeth to get his workers back, complaining that he is losing money. Goeth demands a cut of his profit and lets him have his workers back, all except Stern.

Up until now profit may have been the true drive behind Schindler's actions, but when he is approached by a young woman begging him to take in her parents as "workers" so they won't be killed, he agrees (after first refusing). We begin to see a change in him; he is beginning to see his Jewish workers, the "Schindler Jews," as people. Goeth is in no such frame of mind, though—he tells his maid, one of the young Jewish women, that he likes her, even if "she is not a person in the strictest sense of the word." When he is tempted to kiss the frightened young woman, he accuses her of almost seducing him and cuts her up with a piece of broken glass.

More prisoners are arriving at Plazov, and Goeth wants to make room for them; his method is to sort the healthy from the unhealthy, and so he forces the entire camp to take off their clothes and run around in a circle, naked, under the eyes of the camp doctors. Anyone looking less than completely fit is taken aside and shot. When the survivors are allowed to dress, they are elated—but their joy is short-lived: In the meantime, the Nazis have rounded up the children and are now taking them away to be exterminated. A few children manage to hide, some of them inside the latrine.

After a period of more heartbreaks, Stern tells Schindler that he has been put in charge of the final "evacuation" to Auschwitz, with himself on the last train. Schindler is resigned to going home with his money and calling it quits, but as he is packing up all his money, he thinks of a use for it: He approaches Goeth and asks if he can *buy* his workers' lives, to have them transferred to another camp in order to set up a new factory. Goeth drives a hard bargain and agrees; now Schindler and Stern together must make a list of names of people to be saved: as many names as Schindler can afford. In the end, the list includes more than 1,100 Jews, and Stern tells him, "The list is life"— all around it is death. So the Schindler Jews are taken to the safe haven of Schindler's hometown in Czechoslovakia; but only the men and boys arrive. The train with the women and the girls has been sidetracked, through a clerical error—to Auschwitz.

By bribing the overseer at Auschwitz with diamonds, Schindler buys his women workers back but has to put up a fight to save their daughters. Finally the families are reunited, and for the remaining seven months of the war the factory produces useless artillery shells, for Schindler does not want to contribute to the killing. By the time the war ends, Schindler has no more money; he has spent his entire fortune saving 1,100 people. Saying good-bye to his Jewish friends (he is now considered a war criminal and must flee), he breaks down, thinking that he might have saved just a few more people if he had sold his car and his jewelry, but Stern and the others give him a letter, signed by everyone, and a gold ring with a quote from the Talmud: "Whoever saves one life saves an entire world." They collected the gold by extracting their own gold teeth and melting them down.

Study Questions

1. Explain the quote from the Talmud: "Whoever saves one life saves an entire world."

2. How does the compassion shown by Schindler compare with the virtue of hospitality shown by the people of Le Chambon (see the discussion of Philip Hallie)?

3. Does the fact that Schindler originally hired the Kraków Jews for profit detract from his efforts to save them? Why or why not? (Here you might use Berger's criteria for gratitude.)

4. Compare the scene in which the prisoners are forced to run naked in front of the Nazi officers with Hallie's theory of institutionalized cruelty.

Narrative

Eat Drink Man Woman

HUI-LING WANG, JAMES SCHAMUS, AND ANG LEE (SCREENWRITERS)
ANG LEE (DIRECTOR)

Film, 1994.

I chose this film for its conflict between the old Confucian virtue of gratitude toward parents (in particular the virtue of children's sacrificing their happiness for the sake of their parents) and the virtue of seeking and creating happiness wherever you can find it.

The master chef Chu is preparing one of his fantastic meals — not at the restaurant where he has been working for many years, but at his home in Taipei, Taiwan. Everything is prepared with serious dedication, even though Chu has a problem: He has lost his sense of taste. His three grown daughters, whom he is cooking for, don't hesitate to point out if there is something amiss with the recipes; quarreling is not unusual in their home, and before she died, their mother used to quarrel with their father herself. It seems that the only way Chu knows how to express himself is through cooking, and it is through his efforts with his meals that we realize how much he cares for his daughters, especially the middle daughter, Jia-Chien.

Jia-Chien is a modern young woman: She is an airline executive, she has a once-in-a-while lover, and she is preparing to move out of her childhood home. We learn that she grew up in her father's restaurant kitchen and learned all the elaborate recipes, but her father wanted her to get a "real job," so she had to give up her dreams of becoming a great chef. The youngest daughter, Jia-Ning, is working as a waitress and trying very hard to steal her best friend's boyfriend away from her. The oldest daughter, Jia-Jen, a math teacher, has had a sad life: Nine years ago her boyfriend, a young student of chemistry, broke up with her and went to the United States, and she has never been able to get over it. Now she has converted to Christianity and believes she must resign herself to staying single in order to take care of their father.

Chu may love his daughters, but he does not understand them. After work at the restaurant (where he salvaged a botched dinner for important customers), he and his old friend, Old Wen, get drunk together and talk about life. Wen says, "Eat, drink, man, woman — food and sex — basic desires — can't avoid them!" Chu complains, "All my life, every day, all I do. . . . is that all there is? Is this the good life?" And Old Wen replies, "We're still alive, still cooking, thank God."

Dinners in the Chu household are the times when family announcements are made, and Jia-Chien announces that she is moving out, thus stealing her father's thunder, for he had an announcement to make, too, but we don't get to hear it. And it looks as if things are going well for her: She is about to be promoted to a position in Amsterdam. A new colleague is introduced to her at work, a young man who has lived for years in the United States, and she finds herself attracted to him but is horrified when she realizes that he is her sister's former boyfriend, the man who broke her heart. She is even more horrified when she confronts him with the old story and learns that he has no idea

The film *Eat Drink Man Woman* (Central Motion Pictures, 1994) explores updated versions of Confucian values in a modern Taiwanese family: When the oldest daughter believes that her father needs her, she gives up any idea of marriage (at least for a while); when, later, the middle daughter suspects that her father is ill, she gives up a career opportunity to stay with him. Here the middle daughter (Chien-Lien Wu) and her father (Sihung Lung) share a moment of understanding over an excellent dinner for two.

who her sister is—the girl he used to date was her sister's best friend, Jin-Rong. So now Jia-Chien knows that her sister made the whole thing up.

Jin-Rong herself married someone else and is now getting divorced from him. They live close by Mr. Chu's house. She has a little daughter, Shan-Shan, and Mr. Chu finds himself becoming protective toward the little girl; he watches her get on the bus to school, a tiny child disappearing among pushy big adults, and we can tell that his heart goes out to her. Since her mother is not a good cook, he begins to prepare a lunchbox with elaborate little dishes for Shan-Shan; he takes Jin-Rong's food home and eats it (it is not very good). It soon turns out that Jin-Rong has found out, but she is not angry — she is very grateful that Mr. Chu cares about her little girl. Changes are happening in Jin-Rong's household, too: Her mother is returning after having lived in the United States for many years. Mrs. Liang smokes, gossips, and loves to visit with Mr. Chu, and Chu's daughters soon believe they know what is happening: perhaps a permanent arrangement between their father and Mrs. Liang?

Old Wen collapses at work and is taken to the hospital, where Jia-Chien visits with him. Here he tells her that her father represses his emotions but that he loves her and is very proud of her. The next time she goes to visit Old Wen he has left for home, but further down the hallway she sees a familiar figure: her father, walking into the cardiovascular unit. At this moment her attitude toward her father changes: She believes he is keeping up a brave front, but that his days are numbered, and when Old Wen dies on his first day back at work the reality of her father's age and the brevity of life overwhelms her. So when her promotion to the Amsterdam office comes through, she turns it down, to the surprise of her coworkers: She thinks her father needs her more.

Family developments continue, all announced during dinners: Jia-Ning has become pregnant and moves in with her new boyfriend; Jia-Jen falls in love with the new coach at her school and marries him in secret; and that leaves Chu and Jia-Chien alone in the big old house, except for visits from Mrs. Liang, her daughter, Jin-Rong, and little Shan-Shan. But now Chu has an announcement to make, and he prepares a most elaborate dinner for everybody: the daughters and the two new husbands, Jin-Rong, her daughter and her mother. During the dinner he toasts his daughters, one toast after another, because he is trying to gather enough courage to say what must be said. The daughters, as well as Mrs. Liang, believe they know what he is going to say. Most believe that he will announce his engagement to Mrs. Liang; Jia-Chien believes the bad news about his health will finally come out. But Chu has something else on his mind. Proudly (and a bit drunkenly) he proclaims that he has sold the old house, shows Mrs. Liang his new health certificate to prove he is in great shape, and asks, formally, for her daughter's, Jin-Rong's, hand in marriage. Jin-Rong, the same age as his oldest daughter, Jia-Jen, sits modestly by his side, facing the incredulous family, and Mrs. Liang falls off her chair in a fainting spell. That was not the news she had expected. The evening ends in general emotional upheaval.

A few months later: Jin-Rong is pregnant and happy in their new house. Chu comes to visit the almost-empty old house for the last time and have a last meal there — but this time it is Jia-Chien who is cooking: Using her skills to prepare a meal the way her father has taught her, she proves that she really is a marvelous cook. And as they sit there, the two of them together, her father gently criticizing her food, he realizes that he can *taste* her soup — that his palate is functioning again and that for the first time in years he can taste food.

Study Questions

1. How does the filmmaker use food as a symbol in this film? (You might compare it with *Like Water for Chocolate,* which also uses food symbolically.)

2. Describe the Confucian traditions in the film, and contrast them with the modern elements.

3. If you believed that your aging mother or father needed you, would you give up a promotion/transfer you had wanted in order to become a caregiver and stay at home for the remainder of your parent's life? Why or why not? How would Lin Yutang respond? How would Jane English respond?

Narrative

Grand Canyon

LAWRENCE KASDAN AND MEG KASDAN (SCREENWRITERS)
LAWRENCE KASDAN (DIRECTOR)

Film, 1991.

This film provides a discussion of the idea of gratitude toward strangers: how much, when, and why?

Mack and Claire are a white middle-aged couple living in Los Angeles. On his way home from a game one night, Mack tries to get around the traffic and finds himself in a run-down neighborhood with broken windows and other evidence of gang violence. And here his car dies on him. From a phone booth he calls a service station, acutely aware that he is on dangerous and unfamiliar turf, and runs back to his car, where a group of armed young black males approach him and threaten him. What exactly they want is something Mack does not find out (it could be his car, his wallet, or perhaps his life), because like an angel from heaven a savior arrives: the towtruck driver, Simon (a black man). Soft-spoken and polite, he persuades the gang to leave. He then hooks Mack's car to his truck and takes Mack to his garage. Outside, after Mack has called home, he has a curbside talk with Simon about the dangers of modern life, and Simon tells him about an experience he had when visiting the Grand Canyon: It is so big, so old, and so impersonal that one's ego shrinks to nothing; he felt like "a gnat landing on the ass of a cow." For Simon the world is a cold place to live in, and one can't count on one's luck.

Mack returns home, grateful for being safe and alive. Simon returns to his sister's home on a street with heavy gang activity.

In the following days several things happen that are out of the ordinary for Mack and Claire: Mack's friend Davis, a self-centered producer of violent films, who has commented to Mack that all people feel fear and attempt to hide their fear, is shot by a mugger and has to undergo extensive surgery. In the hospital bed he experiences an epiphany and denounces all future contributions to the world of violence. From now on he will make only positive films dealing with the life energy. Claire, who visits him, is elated, because she has been a harsh critic of his for years, and, besides, she is undergoing her

The 1991 film *Grand Canyon* (Twentieth Century Fox) is a story about the harsh realities of living in Los Angeles (or any other big city) and about learning to recognize and accept that good things as well as bad happen to us, even if they may not follow a logical pattern. One theme running through the film is the question of gratitude — how to show it and how to acknowledge it. Simon (Danny Glover, right) has just rescued Mack (Kevin Kline) from a gang encounter, and here they are exchanging views of life.

own transformation: On her usual jogging route through their pleasant neighborhood, she discovers a baby girl, hidden under some bushes; driven by some compelling force — perhaps the life energy that Davis talked of — she takes the baby home and keeps her for nine hours without notifying the police. When Mack comes home he is taken aback by her displaying such a lack of judgment, and they turn the baby over to the authorities, but Claire insists that if the baby is not claimed, she wants to adopt her. This is not Mack's idea of a rational move, since he himself is happy that their son is a teenager and no longer a baby. Claire tries to explain that perhaps it is not good to be so rational all the time; perhaps things happen for a reason, and we must see them through. Meanwhile, she is having nightmares about homeless people, about seeing her husband and son leave, and about losing sight of the baby in the bushes.

But Mack himself is not being all that rational, either, and his own attitude has come as a surprise to him: He finds himself thinking constantly about Simon and what Simon did for him and finds himself compelled to look Simon up. He invites Simon for breakfast and learns more about his life, his deaf daughter, and his sister's predicament. And Mack, to a puzzled Simon's slight embarrassment, offers to find his sister an apartment in a new neighborhood. Simon declines politely, saying that he doesn't deserve any thanks, but now we hear why Mack has been so preoccupied with Simon's helping hand. Some time ago Mack was walking on the "Miracle Mile" in L.A., deep in his own thoughts. He was about to step off the curb to cross the street when a hand grabbed him from behind and held him back, and instantly a large vehicle sped by where he would have been standing. The woman who had stopped him just walked on, and all he could think of doing was to say, "Thank you." Since then he has been thinking about it, and knowing that his life was saved that day, he feels terrible for not having done more in appreciation. So now he wants to make sure that he shows appreciation to Simon, but Simon wants none of it. He thinks that Mack was just lucky, and sometimes people are not so lucky; if you live long enough, he says, something terrible is bound to happen to you. So he wants no favors in return, and when Mack asks him why, he says, "Sometimes it's hard, even dangerous, reaching in and mucking around with other people's lives—sometimes there's a reason for them doing what they're doing." But later, when the sister is approached by an insurance salesman who wants her to take out policies on her children's lives, she decides to move, and Mack helps her find a place in a safer neighborhood.

And now Mack is on a roll: Somehow feeling that he can do even more for Simon, he sets him up on a blind date with an African American coworker, Jane. Against their expectations, they find themselves falling in love and credit Mack with having a deep understanding of both of them, or perhaps, as Simon says, "We are the only two black people he knows!"

Not everything is working out smoothly: Simon's teen nephew feels uncomfortable in the new neighborhood, which is predominantly white, especially since he is pulled over by the police merely for running through the streets; Claire has problems convincing Mack that her wish to adopt the little girl is not just because their son is growing up and she is approaching middle age. And Davis "recovers" from his phase of planning nonviolent films; he explains to Mack that movies don't create violent situations, but just imitate them, and besides, since there is now a chasm, a "Grand Canyon," between the haves and the have-nots, creating more and more violence, film producers have a duty to show it like it is until the chasm is gone.

How will it end? Will Claire get to adopt her baby girl? Will Simon and Jane continue seeing each other? Will Simon and Mack become friends? See for yourself; suffice it to say that the film serves as a fine illustration not only of the problem of gratitude but also of the issue of whether reason or emotion should be the determining factor in one's moral deliberations and life choices.

Study Questions

1. How would you evaluate Mack's attempt to show his gratitude? Is he doing too much (butting in) or too little, or is he achieving the mean? What would Fred Berger say?

2. Is Simon a good "receiver" of gratitude? Why or why not?

3. Even though this film is used as an example of gratitude, it also works to illustrate the discussion about reason versus emotion (or moral intuition). Do you agree with Claire that we should not strive to be completely logical all the time, or would you agree with Mack's viewpoint, that we must remain rational in order to have some control over our lives? Is there a middle way? What would Richard Taylor say? What would

Jonathan Bennett say? What might Martha Nussbaum (Chapter 1) say? Could this be a gender issue? Why or why not?

4. What does the metaphor of the Grand Canyon mean in this film?

5. Do you think (with Claire and Simon) that there may be a reason for the things that happen to us? Explain.

Narrative

Othello

WILLIAM SHAKESPEARE

Play, 1604–05; film, 1952, 1965, 1986, 1995, 2001. Summary.

In Venice a beautiful young woman, Desdemona, falls in love with Othello, a Moor. ("Moor" usually indicates Arab or Muslim but can also mean black, and Othello is described as a black man; however, he has often been played by white actors wearing dark makeup. An exception is the film version from 1995.) Desdemona's family is against the match, but Desdemona prevails and marries Othello, who meanwhile has been promoted to a high military position. Enter Iago, who is in love with Desdemona and jealous of Othello's success. He bets that the two will tire of each other because they are so different, but he thinks of ways to help the situation along. What if Othello could be made to believe that his wife is being unfaithful to him? A young lieutenant of Othello's, Cassio, seems to fit the picture. Desdemona, who wants to be a good friend to Othello's friends, is kind to Cassio; Iago begins to drop hints to Othello that there is hanky-panky going on. Without knowing of Iago's plan, his wife, Emilia, who is a good friend of Desdemona's, lends a helping hand by obtaining from Desdemona a handkerchief that Othello has given her. Iago plants the handkerchief among Cassio's possessions. Othello refuses to believe Iago's assertions, but when Desdemona can't produce the handkerchief he considers it proof that Iago is telling the truth. He becomes increasingly distant and critical toward his wife, who doesn't understand the change that has come over him. Desdemona begins to think her parents were right—that perhaps she and Othello are too different to have a successful marriage.

Othello persuades Iago to kill Cassio. Iago succeeds only in wounding him seriously, but Desdemona grieves when she hears of Cassio's misfortune, because she thinks of Cassio as a good friend. Othello takes Desdemona's reaction as further proof that Cassio is her lover and decides, at Iago's urging, to kill Desdemona. Why would Iago suggest this, when he is himself in love with her? Because she is not interested in him, and if he can't have her, he vows that nobody else will.

As Emilia discovers the truth about the situation and rushes to Othello to tell him, he is already in the process of murdering his wife. Desdemona insists that she is innocent and begs for a little more time, begs to live for half an hour, just long enough for a prayer, but he will not listen and strangles her. Emilia bursts in and tells Othello the truth; Iago is right behind Emilia, however, and he kills her. Officials show up and arrest Othello. Cassio himself tells the truth about the handkerchief—that he merely found it among his possessions one day but never was given it by Desdemona. Othello, full of despair over his lack of faith in his wife, stabs himself and dies. Iago is taken away to answer for his crimes.

(See the Study Questions following *The Faithful Wife and the Woman Warrior*.)

 Narrative

The Faithful Wife and the Woman Warrior

A Tiwa (Pueblo) Indian story, reported by Elsie Clews Parsons, 1940. Summary.

Two Apache warrior friends are going off on a raid against an enemy tribe. Blue Hawk is married to the chief's daughter, and Red Hawk is single. Once they are away from the village, Red Hawk suggests that Blue Hawk's wife sleeps around when he is not there, because that's how women are. Blue Hawk insists that his wife is true to him. Red Hawk says he'll bet that if he goes back alone, Blue Hawk's wife will sleep with him. Blue Hawk accepts the bet, and the two return to the vicinity of the village, where Blue Hawk hides while Red Hawk rides in alone.

Red Hawk tries to make Blue Hawk's wife interested in him, but she just ignores him. He turns to an old woman of the village and asks if there is any way she can help him see the young wife when she has no clothes on. The old woman complies and goes to Blue Hawk's wife, pretending to be poor and in need of shelter. The young woman feels sorry for her and takes her in. During the night the old woman observes that the young woman's anatomy is peculiar: She has a long, gold braid coming out of her stomach and a black spot on her backbone. The old woman returns to Red Hawk and tells him what she saw. Red Hawk rides out to Blue Hawk and confronts him with the details of his wife's body as proof that he slept with her. Blue Hawk believes him and is depressed. The two men return to the village. Blue Hawk gives Red Hawk all his possessions, much to the surprise of his wife. He then fills a big trunk with supplies and asks his wife to jump in the trunk, too. He explains that they are going on a trip and the trunk will protect her skin from the sun. Once they are away from the village, Blue Hawk dumps the trunk in the nearest river and goes back to the tribe with no explanation of where his wife has gone. This upsets her father, who guesses that foul play has occurred. He arranges for Blue Hawk to fall into a deep hole.

Blue Hawk's wife is not dead, however; she is rescued by a fisherman and enters a new phase of her life. Disguised as a man, she becomes a famous warrior. With the help of witchcraft she kills all enemies of her tribe and returns to her father's village. She reveals her true identity and asks for Blue Hawk, who is still in the hole and near death from starvation. She embraces him, tells her side of the story, and asks that Red Hawk and the old woman, as well as two wild ponies, be brought forth. Red Hawk and the woman are tied to the ponies; the horses are then let free, and the two culprits are torn to pieces.

Study Questions

1. Compare *Othello* and "The Faithful Wife." Is there a significant difference between Shakespeare's vision of jealousy and that of the American Indian storyteller? Are there any significant similarities?

2. Is jealousy a vice in itself? Why or why not? Is jealousy ever appropriate, and what kind of action might it in that case suggest?

3. The French writer La Rochefoucauld once said, "*Il y a dans la jalousie plus d'amour propre que d'amour*" (In jealousy there is more of self-love than love). Do you agree? Why or why not?

Narrative

The Count of Monte Cristo

ALEXANDRE DUMAS

Novel, 1844. Film, 1934, 1954, 1961, 2002. Summary. Television film, 1975.

This story has been made into a film numerous times by French and American filmmakers, but as yet no film has succeeded in capturing the *entire* plot of the book. Neither will this outline, for the plot is extremely intricate.

The story begins in France, where Napoleon is in exile for the first time. Edmond Dantès is a young man, handsome, in love, and about to become captain of a ship, the *Pharao*. On the day before his wedding all his plans come to an abrupt halt: He is arrested for a crime he is not aware of and transported to Castle If, the prison island in the harbor of Marseille. There he stays and stays; he almost goes mad trying to figure out what happened to him. Several years into his incarceration he meets another prisoner, the mad Abbé Faria, who, trying to escape, managed only to dig his way into Edmond's cell. The Abbé is a learned man, and upon their meeting Edmond's true education begins. The Abbé teaches him languages, chemistry, history, science, politics, economics, and intrigue. Through the Abbé's insight Edmond learns who is to blame for his downfall: Fernand, who wanted Edmond's girlfriend, Mercedes, for himself; and Danglars, who didn't want Edmond to become captain because he wanted the job for himself. These two men put together a letter denouncing Edmond as a Bonapartist (supporter of Napoleon). Villefort, the prosecutor, was also part of the plan; he knew that Edmond was innocent but condemned him to oblivion, because if he let Edmond go, it would implicate Ville-fort's father as a Bonapartist and put an end to Villefort's own career.

Faria dies, but just before his death he tells Edmond why everyone considers him, Faria, to be mad: It is because he claims to know of a treasure on the island of Monte Cristo. Edmond escapes from prison by donning the burial garments meant for the Abbé and pretending to be him. He figures he can dig his way out of the soft earth, but to his horror he is not buried in a cemetery; he is thrown into the ocean. He is picked up by smugglers, and he embarks on a new life. First he visits Monte Cristo and finds the trea-sure, which does indeed exist. Then he sets out to gain his revenge (or what he sees as divine retribution), fourteen years after having been thrown into prison.

It takes years and careful planning. Certain that God has chosen him as his instrument of retaliation, Edmond (who is now the Count of Monte Cristo) seeks out his old enemies, who have all done well for themselves. Fernand has married Mercedes and is a war hero. Danglars is a rich banker, and Villefort holds a position similar to that of attorney general. Piece by piece the Count's revenge falls into place. He inflicts defamation, ruin, and death on the three culprits and their families, until he realizes that in the process he has caused innocent lives to be lost. He understands that no man can play God, and he tries to make amends to the blameless survivors. One of these is Mercedes, who recognized him from the start. She tells the Count that she is as guilty as any of the three, because she didn't wait for Edmond but believed him dead. Edmond, however, is through with revenge; he lets Mercedes and her grown son go, and he awards them a pension and a small house—his own home in Marseille, the very house they were to have been married in.

Study Questions

1. Do you believe that Edmond's vengeful actions were justified? How might Edmond's approach be criticized?

2. If you can't expect society to retaliate against a crime on your behalf, is it all right to take matters into your own hands? Why or why not?

3. Some scholars think there is a difference between revenge and retribution. Are they right? Why or why not?

Narrative

The Searchers

FRANK S. NUGENT (SCREENWRITER)

JOHN FORD (DIRECTOR)

Film, 1956. Based on a novel by Alan Le May.

Ethan Edwards returns from the Civil War to his brother's ranch and to his brother's wife, Martha, with whom he has been in love for a long time. He gets reacquainted with his brother's family, two daughters and a son, and with the grown foster son, Marty, who is part

In *The Searchers* (Warner Bros., 1956) Ethan Edwards (John Wayne) discovers that his brother and sister-in-law have been murdered and that his niece Debbie has been kidnapped by the Comanches. Here Ethan finds Debbie's shawl and her doll in the family graveyard where she had been told to hide out in the event of Indian attacks. He vows to find her, no matter how long it takes. He is sure that he will find her, "just as sure as the turnin' of the earth." It soon becomes apparent, however, that Ethan not only wants to find his niece but also wants vengeance for the murders. As time goes by, he plots to kill Debbie herself because, in his view, she has been "contaminated" by living with the Indians.

American Indian. An Indian raid lures Ethan and Marty away from their home the following day; they realize too late that it was a trick. In the meantime the Comanches have killed the family and taken the youngest daughter, Debbie, prisoner. For eight years Ethan and Marty look for the girl all over the western United States. The search changes Ethan: Now he wants to find Debbie in order to kill the Indians, but to Marty's horror he also intends to kill Debbie, who he believes has been "contaminated" by living with the tribe (this reflects the general opinion held by whites at the time). Marty tries to reason with Ethan, to no avail. After years of obsessive searching they finally catch up with Debbie and the Comanche tribe, who are by now quite aware of the two searchers. Debbie comes to warn them of an ambush, and Ethan, true to his word, tries to kill her, but Marty prevents it. Debbie escapes, and the two find her again only after staging a raid on the Indian village and killing the chief, Scar, who was responsible for the murder of Ethan's brother, the rape and murder of Martha, and the abduction of Debbie. Marty manages to get Debbie out in time, and he himself kills Scar. Moments later Ethan is on the scene and finds the body of Scar; he takes out his knife and scalps the dead chief. And now he looks around for Debbie. Debbie is running toward the hills as fast as she can, but Ethan is on horseback; Marty, on foot, tries to intercept Ethan but is summarily brushed aside, and Ethan starts up the hill after Debbie. There is now no way Marty can save her from Ethan.

Will Ethan kill Debbie, or will something happen that will save her? See the film for yourself; it is one of the best Westerns ever made and perhaps one of the best American films ever. The surprise ending caused French film director Jean-Luc Godard to call it "one of the most moving moments in film history."

Toward the very end of the film we see Ethan framed by a doorway, with the desert behind him; he is alone, and he turns around, away from civilization, and returns to the wilderness. He has been estranged from civilization too long to belong with other human beings. He has no home anymore.

Study Questions

1. Is Ethan Edwards a racist?

2. What is he really avenging?

3. Why is Ethan trying to kill Debbie? What do you think might make him change his mind?

Chapter Thirteen

Applied Ethics: A Sampler

*T*his final chapter is a result of several reader requests for more detailed discussions of issues involving applied ethics, drawing on the previous chapters on ethics of conduct and virtue ethics. In general, this book is designed not to cover the field of applied ethics as such, but rather to discuss theories of ethics using stories as examples, and occasionally to explore issues in applied ethics. This chapter does reflect issues I spend extra time on in my own classes: *media ethics, animal rights,* and *the death penalty.* In addition, because of the watershed events of September 11, we have talked at length about the *Just War* concept, and chances are you may be interested in discussing this subject, too. As such, Chapter 13 is intended to complement Chapter 7, with its focus on rights and justice, and Chapter 12, with its focus on two virtues.

Of course there are many areas within applied ethics that space concerns prevent me from addressing in further detail, such as abortion, euthanasia, gun control, and free speech on the Internet. I hope you will feel inspired to discuss these and other subjects further on your own, drawing on the theories you have been introduced to in this book.

Media Ethics

The media seem to be showing an increasing interest in reporting issues of moral controversy. This certainly reflects their perennial interest in "good copy" (news that sells papers or commercial air time); if people weren't interested in hearing about such matters, it wouldn't be good copy. Most frequently these stories of moral controversy involve transgressions by the rich and famous. In recent years, though, general reporting of differences of opinion about what's right and wrong has become more common. Issues such as abortion and euthanasia are high on the list of media topics, and whenever candidates vie for office, their opinions on such matters, as well as on matters of gender and racial politics, are closely examined.

The question of moral standards in the news profession itself is an especially important one: Is it ethical, for example, for a journalist to make public a matter of national security? And does the public always have a "right to know"? Journalists who gain access to sensitive material and publish it may be said not only to report the news but also to create conditions for more "news" to report. In other words, they may play an active role in situations that they supposedly are merely reporting.

The Right to Know

The public's "right to know" has become questionable in the aftermath of hugely publicized court cases and human tragedies of the 1990s. After examining the effects of televised high-profile trials, some now question the wisdom of allowing cameras in the courtroom because their presence may actually affect the trial, at least turning it into a circus, as it did in O. J. Simpson's criminal trial in 1995. And does the public really have a "right" to see TV close-ups of relatives grieving over grisly photos of murder scenes? Sensationalism in the mainstream media seems to have become the order of the day. Decades ago, the tabloid ("yellow") press was where you'd find subjects with salacious content, and not much evidence of journalistic concern for verifying facts.But according to some media commentators, the line between mainstream and tabloid media has blurred, to the extent that people have been demonized in the "court of public opinion" with the help of the mainstream media, relying primarily on leaks and rumors. And once the story has hit the press, the genie can't be put back in the bottle. Hasty accusations of wrongdoing published by the media, although later proven to be untrue, may hang over a person's head for years, perhaps for life. When the media decided to go with the story that Richard Jewell, the suspect in the 1996 bombing of Olympic Park in Atlanta, had a history of aberrant behavior, the story was disseminated nationwide. When he was later exonerated (and took the media to court for libel), it wasn't front-page news. And most of us just happen to remember sensational headlines on front pages rather than the follow-ups on page 13.

One moral problem for the media is sensationalism; another is stretching the truth, or downright *lying*. And lately, the credibility of certain news media (if not all of them) has been damaged by instances such as these: In June 1998 a *Boston Globe* columnist, Patricia Smith, was forced to resign because she had invented characters in her columns—which were supposed to depict real people and real events. Another *Globe* journalist, Mike Barnicle, was also forced to resign after using borrowed material without mentioning the source. Within the same month, CNN and *Time* magazine were quick to break a news story that U.S. forces used nerve gas to kill defectors from the United States during the Vietnam War. Shortly after, CNN and *Time* had to issue retractions and apologies and have since been sued for defamation: There was no corroborating evidence to support the story. With the surfacing of other examples of the media jumping to conclusions or simply fabricating stories, the public seems to have lost faith in the journalism profession. According to a *Newsweek* poll in the late 1990s, 62 percent of 752 people surveyed said they trust the media less now than they used to.

The linguist and author Deborah Tannen (see also Chapters 11 and 12) suggests in her 1998 book *The Argument Culture* that the media have become argument-crazy: Every issue must be presented with an opposing point of view in order to get a "good fight" going, even when people agree about the subject and no real opposing point of view exists. This means that controversial stories get front-page coverage and that if there is no controversy, the media will look for an opposing point of view until someone is willing to supply it. This is what is sometimes called the *adversarial* method. Although this method is excellent at exploring truly opposed, equally challenging viewpoints, it is no help as a problem solver if it invents problems for the sake of stirring up debate. Tannen suggests that although the press is not supposed to take on the docile role of a *lapdog,* it seems to have given up its role as the nation's

In the film *15 Minutes,* a television station acquires a videotape depicting the murder of a popular police detective. A tabloid-TV journalist (Kelsey Grammer) makes the decision to air the video as an exclusive, because, as he says, "If it bleeds, it leads." In the scene depicted here, the journalist has acquired yet another tape, this one showing the killer's confession. Do you think a TV station would deliberately air a murder? In an accelerated, sensationalist news environment, might the scenario of *15 Minutes* become possible—here or abroad?

watchdog for a much less attentive but louder role as an *attack dog,* picking fights for the fun of it. Interestingly, Tannen's book was virtually ignored by the conflict-oriented television talk-show circuit.

Media Ethics in Wartime

Whatever we may have thought of the public's right to know, and the media's right to find out, under those conditions that we regarded as "normal" before September 11, a wartime media ethics has a different makeup—although not fundamentally different. The idea that the public has a right to know certain things, even in wartime, is at the very heart of the notion of freedom of the press—which of course is a constitutional right, embedded in the First Amendment; on the other side of the issue, however, looms the concept of national security.

An extreme illustration of the clash between the media and wartime interests is the U.S. troops secretly landing on the beach in Somalia in 1998 under cover of darkness—until huge floodlights illuminated the entire scene, welcoming them to Africa: CNN and other television crews were on the shore already, functioning as a welcoming committee. The world did indeed get to see a live military beach land-ing, but the American troops lost the element of surprise. For many, the conflict be-tween the people's "right to know" and legitimate military concerns came into sharp focus at that moment, especially since CNN is a network that is watched globally — by foe as well as by friend.

On the first day of what became known as the war on terrorism, September 11, television stations exercised a self-restraint that was admirable to many who other-wise tended to be critical of the media: After the first television stations had shown footage of people jumping to their deaths from the burning WTC towers, national TV stopped showing that footage. While coverage of the terrorist attacks during the first hours was heavy and indiscriminate, the media soon developed an approach of discretion in showing actual footage of the carnage at Ground Zero. As one jour-nalist remarked on the air, they had plenty of footage depicting victims, but it wouldn't be right to show it on TV. Presumably this was done partly out of respect for the victims and their families, but also out of the realization that in addition to the heartbreaking images of the falling towers, it would have brought further pain and anguish to the viewers. In retrospect, one might also suspect that the decision deprived terrorists and their sympathizers of an extra opportunity to gloat. While this decision was not based on national security concerns at the time, one can still call the decision a key moment in wartime media ethics: While some violent im-ages may be newsworthy, airing them serves no purpose other than sensationalism. (Box 13.1 explores the issue of media airing of on-camera deaths.) Later that fall, other media restraints were observed at the request of the government, such as the decision not to show unedited televised interviews or statements by terrorists under the assumption that they might contain covert messages to other terrorists. And, having learned the lessons of the Gulf War and the ill-fated engagement in Somalia with its live television coverage, the Pentagon chose to conduct the war on terror-ism without detailed advance briefings. But since this is a free society, and all gov-ernment actions must be accessible to the public, in due time, when national security is no longer an issue, any and all information about the war on terrorism (as well as any other conflict or issue of national interest) must be made known to Ameri-can citizens.

An additional issue of media conduct arose with the anthrax scare in the fall of 2001. Five people died from inhalation anthrax delivered, as far as is known, through the mail, and thousands of others were inconvenienced and frightened by having to take antibiotics. Since the first anthrax letters were received by members of the media in Florida and New York City, the networks took the situation as a personal threat and treated the issue as major news (even as the only news, at times) — to the extent that many Americans asked themselves whether the story was perhaps being blown out of proportion, creating an atmosphere of fear (and thus helping the cul-prits achieve their goal of terror) rather than informing the public about the situa-tion and the very slight risk anyone had of encountering anthrax. At a town meeting hosted in San Diego by Peter Jennings of ABC News, members of the press were asked about the choices they make when bringing such stories to the forefront, and

Box 13.1   HOW FAR WOULD TELEVISION GO?

How far will the media go in order to secure an exclusive story? And how far is too far? If a tabloid show—or News at 11, for that matter—had the opportunity to show, uncut, the video of the murder of a well-known person, would they choose to show it? As you have read in this chapter, on September 11 the media chose to stop broadcasting footage of people jumping from the burning World Trade towers. But does that mean that footage will never be seen again? Those of us who have a cynical streak predict the producers of future television specials might not be so sensitive to the feelings of the survivors and the families of the victims. In the media's defense, one could note that they have had lots of opportunities to show tape of people dying over the years, but unless broadcasters have been surprised by a live TV event taking a bad turn (such as the shooting of Lee Harvey Oswald on live TV), they have exhibited professional restraint and have refrained from airing such scenes. But many forget that CBS, on *60 Minutes,* chose to air a videotape of the assisted-suicide death of one of Dr. Jack Kevorkian's patients, and local TV stations around the country have occasionally aired deaths on live camera: police shootings, suicidal people jumping off bridges, and the like. We know that *Wall Street Journal* reporter Daniel Pearl's murder by terrorists in Pakistan in 2002 was videotaped by his tormentors. CBS had already aired a 30-second portion of the tape, showing an interrogation of Pearl, and the entire video could be seen on certain Websites. Can we be sure it won't be aired in its entirety on TV, here or elsewhere? Should it? In the Narrative section we take a look at a film, *15 Minutes,* in which the host of a tabloid show on a New York television station makes the decision to air a videotaped murder on TV. You decide how unrealistic, or undesirable, that scenario is.

several journalists responded that they just report the facts; they don't invent them or doctor them—but that can surely be dismissed as a media myth: Before journalists report the facts, they select *which* facts to report (having decided what counts as a fact), and they choose *how* and *when* to report them. A debate about media ethics must be based on an understanding of that process.

How much a journalist should report and an editor release, and when, of course depends on the situation. Aristotle's theory of the Golden Mean provides a good starting point for solving the media ethics problem. For each situation there is one correct answer, somewhere within the middle range. Sometimes the media need to freely share information, as unpleasant as it may be, in the interest of the public's right to make decisions based on informed consent. At other times the proper amount of coverage called for is the bare minimum, either because no more information is available at the time (and excessive speculation may hurt more than help the public), or because the dissemination of the information might threaten the security of the country. Crying wolf is poor journalistic ethics, but so are apathy and indifference. It is a brilliant journalist or editor who knows the difference in each single instance.

NON SEQUITUR   by WILEY

Much of the criticism of the press in the past few years, and especially in the wake of 9/11, is that it has become a fear-monger because a good dose of anxiety ("Anthrax found in a post office! More news at 11!") keeps people glued to their television sets or makes them buy more papers and magazines. Is that a fair criticism? Do the media just report the news, or do they also select what news to report, and when and how to report it? Where do we draw the line between the media giving out information, including warnings and alerts, and whipping up panic?

Just War Theory

World War II has been referred to as "the last good war," meaning the last one that had identifiable good and evil sides. But even World War II was, in the beginning, not considered clear-cut at all to many Americans; even after the Japanese attack on Pearl Harbor (December 7, 1941), some argued that more violence was not a proper response to violence. In addition, victories over the Nazis and imperial Japan during the war didn't come without their cost in civilian lives.

For many Americans—young as well as older people—during the Vietnam War, the very idea that a war could be "just" was an oxymoron. During the late sixties and early seventies the war in Vietnam was widely perceived as an *unjust war* since the principles being fought for were unclear or downright objectionable to many, involving mainly politics. Conscription was in effect, and many of the young men drafted against their will saw the war they were being asked to fight as not being a matter of national self-defense. Conscientious objectors found the entire idea of a just war self-contradictory.

When the United States and its allies engaged in the Gulf War against Iraq, liberating occupied Kuwait, some people who, two decades before, had stood against the idea of the Vietnam War had mixed emotions: Liberating another country from an occupational force seemed a noble enough cause, but then there was the question of oil, and the availability of it for an oil-dependent nation. The suspicion remained for many that the underlying motivation for U.S. involvement was tainted with self-interest. Of course, it is a good question exactly why it is supposed to be suspect for a country to pursue its own interests; it becomes questionable only when that self-interest prevents other countries from pursuing *their* own interests.

(You'll remember the harm principle from Chapter 5; you'll also remember from Chapter 4 and Chapter 12 that an action that is motivated not just by self-interest but also by concern for others cannot be labeled as straight egoism.)

The U.S. military response to the terrorist attacks of September 11 changed a lot of things, including some people's perception of what constitutes a just war. Here was an attack on American soil, against civilians, directed from outside the United States by forces who had already expressed their wish to "kill all Americans," an attack that was (as most Americans saw it) unprovoked and utterly unjustifiable. British prime minister Tony Blair declared on September 12 that regardless of whatever grievances and grudges anyone might have against the United States, nothing could justify those acts of aggression. Later that same fall, U.S. secretary of state Colin Powell expressed the same idea: In his view, no amount of anger or frustration could be justifications for acts of terrorism.

At the time of this writing, it is too soon to judge whether the war on terrorism has been successful, and at what cost, but many believe that unless international terrorism is stopped or at least made far more difficult to accomplish, we must face the possibility that our society and our way of life will be perennially in jeopardy, if not lost outright to the terrorist threat—and with that threat being a fixture on the horizon, we must expect a long, hard, expensive battle if we cherish what it means to live in a free society. (Box 13.2 takes up the question of patriotism, and Box 13.3 explores the question of "terrorist" versus "freedom fighter.") I hope you will take the opportunity to discuss the current situation, however it looks to you at the time you read this.

So is there such a thing as a just war? For a *pacifist,* the answer is no: Nothing on this earth—no attack on our loved ones, no danger to our life or our country—warrants raising our hand or using weapons of any kind against another human being. If you're a pacifist, say critics, you can't make an exception such as "I don't believe in war, but I'd of course want to defend my family," for two reasons: (1) If you have proclaimed that you reject the idea that force can solve a problem, then it doesn't matter if we talk about it on a grand or a small scale: Force is impermissible, period. (2) If you believe that it is okay for you to resort to force in order to save your family from harm, what about those who don't have family members to save *them* from harm? That is traditionally the state's role: to protect its citizens from enemies, both domestic and foreign. When it is engaged in protection against harm caused by a foreign force, we call it war. And if you find it acceptable for an individual to protect his or her family from harm, then, logically, you should accept that the state takes on a similar action to protect its citizens.

So, according to the critics, the only consistent viewpoint for a pacifist is to reject the notion of using force to defend one's family against harm. Other forms of defense are acceptable, such as calling 911 (but if you don't approve of violence, you can't allow the police to use violence to save your family, either). Or you can put yourself in harm's way and use passive resistance, hoping that harm to your family will be deflected onto you, or that the harm-doer will think twice. In the 1930s and 1940s, Mohandas K. Gandhi (1869–1948), known by the reverent title of Mahatma, headed a movement to make the British pull out of their colony of India and give it

Box 13.2   PATRIOTISM: TOO MUCH, TOO LITTLE,
OR JUST THE RIGHT AMOUNT?

In the wake of September 11, we saw flags go up by the thousands in just about every neighborhood in the country—in windows, displayed on walls and car bumpers, and flown from flagpoles and car antennae. To some, this was one of the few upsides of 9/11: that people discovered, or rediscovered, a love of their country. To others, it was an oppressive display of excessive nationalism, what used to be called *jingoism*. In my classes we discussed the issue at length, and a viewpoint emerged among my students that the news media hadn't explored: that many put flags up not because they hadn't loved their country before and all of a sudden discovered they did, or that they wanted to shove their patriotism in others' faces, but simply because *it made them feel better* at a time when we all felt the ground shaking under us. One cable station on September 11 showed the image of a young woman weeping hopelessly into a giant Stars and Stripes hanging down over her head, holding on to it as if she were drowning. Was that undue sentimentality or oppressive patriotism—or was it simply reaching out for something fundamental and constant in a time of crisis? Sometimes emotional gestures should be seen in their own context rather than as exclusively political symbols. Some of us held on to our parents, spouses, and children, to our pets, even to stuffed animals. Some of us held on to our flag. In the days that followed, some TV networks took the line that wearing a flag pin was a personal statement, undermining the professional objectivity of their journalists, and banned flags in the newsrooms; other news media supported the view that the flag is a national symbol, appropriate as a display in wartime, and not just a personal political statement, and hung the Stars and Stripes, or allowed their reporters to decide whether or not to wear flag pins.

But what exactly is patriotism, and when is it too much, too little, or just the right amount? In the 1970s the opinion was voiced among philosophers that patriotism is like racism and sexism: It is an unfounded preference for one's own country just because it is one's own country, just like sexism is a preference for one's own sex and a disregard for the other sex, and racism is a preference for one's own race and a disregard for other races. One of the visions of Marxism, for example, is people shedding their national affiliations and boundaries and becoming international, because the plight of workers is pre-

its independence. His method, passive resistance, provided an alternative for countless people—in India as well as elsewhere—who would like to express their disapproval of an idea or a policy without resorting to violence. Gandhi's approach helped bring about Indian independence in 1946, but in 1948 he himself became a victim of violence, being gunned down by an assassin. Martin Luther King, Jr., met with the same fate in 1968 after being a lifelong admirer of Gandhi's philosophy of passive resistance and advocating the same method in his civil rights movement. King's commitment continues to inspire people who seek to create political change without resorting to any form of violence.

But critics of pacifism point out: (1) If you put yourself in harm's way to save your family without personal use of force and lose your life, and your act of sacrifice

sumably the same everywhere. The final words of the original French song and rallying cry for Communism from 1871, *The Internationale,* are "The Internationale unites the human race." Less radical views of patriotism have been suggested, based on the criticism that it makes no sense to say we aren't allowed to love our country more than other countries—just as it would make no sense to say we shouldn't love our own family more than we love strangers. In a paper from 1989, "In Defense of 'Moderate Patriotism,'" Steven Nathanson (whom you will also meet in the section on the death penalty) argues against critics of patriotism that "Patriotism is a virtue as long as the actions it encourages are not themselves immoral . . . That a morally acceptable form of patriotism is possible can be seen by comparing patriotism to love or family loyalty. People may (and, one hopes, typically do) have a special interest and concern for their parents, spouses, and children. They really do care more about those 'near and dear' than about strangers. Yet, so long as this concern is not an exclusive concern, there is nothing the matter with it." In other words, it is acceptable to be a patriot as long as one is mainly expressing a love for one's country and homeland and isn't implying that one's country is always automatically right—in other words, this view rejects the notion of "My country, right or wrong," but allows for a personal sense of affiliation and love for one's roots. But isn't it also possible to feel and express *pride* in one's country, without thereby buying in to the idea that one must therefore be proud of every single aspect of one's country's history? Can't we be proud of, say, the Bill of Rights and the space program, without necessarily being proud of the internment of Japanese Americans during World War II, or the McCarthy period in the 1950s, which spawned a witch hunt of anyone who might have had communist or socialist sympathies? Part of the American tradition is the right to question authority—to ask good questions and expect them to be answered. One might say that it is a matter of pride in one's tradition, of patriotism, to keep asking good questions. Something that is deeply American and an ingrained feature in both the political left and the right is to want the United States to be the best that it can be, because we love this country and wish it well. Conservatives don't have a monopoly on patriotism, and neither do liberals.

doesn't save your family, nothing has been gained. (2) You may have the right to refuse to use any form of force or violence yourself, but if you have responsibility for others, such as small children, your right does not extend to them, because they are under your protection, morally and legally.

If you are not a pacifist and believe in the concept of a just war, the alternative isn't simply to be a "hawk," a "war-monger," or a belligerent, violent person. On the contrary: The doctrine of just war is based on the assumption that the ideal condition is peace; war is seen as the last resort to restore peace. Once that is a given, several other conditions must be in place in order to call a war just (*jus bellum*). These rules were worked out in the late Middle Ages by the so-called Schoolmen or scholastics, building on Roman law and early Christian thinkers such as Augustine

Box 13.3   TERRORIST OR FREEDOM FIGHTER?

A terrorist is someone who terrorizes others in order to obtain a goal, usually of a political nature, and usually by means of violence or threat of violence. That's the easy definition. Terrorism has been used as a political weapon by political subgroups in the West particularly since the 1970s, when left-wing terrorist groups emerged in Germany and the United States, with stated goals of overthrowing the government. In the last decades we have also seen right-wing terrorists, such as abortion clinic bombers and snipers; left-wing terrorism has branched off into *eco-terrorism,* terrorist attacks on behalf of the environment. Generally, most people in democratic cultures frown on the use of fear and violence as a means of making a political point, and this attitude was only strengthened by the 9/11 attacks. But after 9/11 a saying was quite often heard in political discussions: "One person's terrorist is another person's freedom fighter." Does this expression merit consideration? Given the fact that Osama bin Laden, the supposed mastermind behind 9/11, received support from the United States back in the days when he was fighting in Afghanistan with underground Afghani troops against the Soviet occupational forces, the question is legitimate. Perhaps all that matters is from whose perspective one sees it? When we approve of their fight, they become freedom fighters, and when we disapprove, they're terrorists? But we don't have to accept this relativistic definition if we can decide on a distinction. Some, including myself, suggest that you can be a freedom fighter with a political goal, and even use violence and fear to obtain your goal, as long as your target is an occupational or other oppressive force within a country you call your own, and violence is not directed deliberately against civilians. (And of course you can be a freedom fighter without resorting to violence at all. Gandhi was such a freedom fighter, and so was Martin Luther King, Jr. I doubt that anyone today would call them terrorists, although their nonviolent, passive-resistance policy did strike fear in the hearts of opponents.) A terrorist directs his or her acts of violence not only against military and/or occupational forces, but against civilians. The only way a terrorist can claim to be a freedom fighter is to claim that there are no innocents among his or her targets, which was indeed a claim made by bin Laden on video in the fall of 2001, but it was a claim that most Americans found hard to accept, since we distinguish between military and civilian targets and victims, and there were no military victims anywhere except at the Pentagon on 9/11. An argument sometimes used by people targeting what most of us would call civilians is that if you don't actively rebel against your government, then you are an accomplice in its transgressions, so you are not a civilian. But the September 11 attacks didn't follow that definition, either, since there were children (who don't make political decisions) among the victims—and apparently there was no attempt to weed them out, or ascertain whether any adults on board the planes or at the World Trade Center harbored ill feelings toward the U.S. government (and should thus have been excluded as targets).

Of course, there is still some leeway in the interpretation of what qualifies as an occupational or oppressive force, but not nearly as much when it comes to a definition of civilians. In the Primary Readings the philosopher Jan Narveson explains what he thinks characterizes a terrorist.

and Ambrose, and they have become the foundation for military ethics in the West ever since. Here we look at an overview of these rules, as they are taught in military ethics courses:

- **Last resort** As stated above, a war can only be just if all other ways of restoring peace have been exhausted, such as negotiations, economic sanctions, etc.

- **Just cause** If going to war is the only way a country can defend its values and lives of innocent citizens against aggression and restoring peace, then the cause is considered just. In modern-day terms, identified by Michael Waltzer in his influential book *Just and Unjust Wars* (1977), this boils down to a response to an aggression, and a defense of rights.

- **Legitimate, competent authority** War can only be declared by a competent governmental authority. Some overenthusiastic general can't start a war on his or her own.

- **Comparative justice** The values and rights that are being defended must be so important that their defense outweighs the horrors of war.

- **Right intention** The intention must be to defend the rights in question, and not have some ulterior motive as gaining territory, or enhancing business.

- **Probability of success** There has to be a reasonable assumption that the war will accomplish its goal, and there has to be:

- **Proportionality of ends** The costs of the war must not exceed the presumed benefits. Some victories are too costly, as any utilitarian will tell you. The term for such a victory is *Pyrrhic,* from Pyrrhus, the king of Epirus who won a battle against the Romans in 279 B.C.E., but sustained such huge losses that it put the value of the victory in doubt.

These are the rules that have to be in place when war is declared; in addition, there are rules that must be followed while conducting the war, "justice in war" (*jus in bello*). Over the past few centuries there has been a tendency to emphasize justice in war rather than just war, because the "just cause" concept is hard to define: After all, any nation (or terrorist group) can claim that their values are at risk, and then march off to war. Instead, scholars have focused on limiting the damage done by war through these two rules:

- **Proportionality of means** While some harm will of course be caused, one should avoid causing unnecessary damage.

- **Discrimination** The term *discrimination* here means discerning, or "discriminating" between combatants and non-combatants. This rule was added to Just War theory in the Middle Ages; prior to those days Western thinking did not discriminate between soldiers and civilians (as some would argue that certain non-Western cultures do not do until this day). Since everyone knows that wars usually involve civilian casualties, especially modern wars, the last rule doesn't exclude the loss of innocent non-combatants altogether, but they can't be *deliberately* targeted. Having some civilian casualties — on the enemy side, but also on one's own side — is considered acceptable as long as the overall result furthers the goal of peace. This falls under the principle of the *double effect,* which you read about in Chapter 7, a principle based on Catholic theology: An action which is prohibited under normal circumstances can be permitted if part of the outcome is (1) unintended, (2) doesn't exceed the goal in magnitude, and (3) unavoidable in order to accomplish its goal.

Even if two warring nations do follow these rules (which of course is not a given), there are still plenty of gray areas where one group can interpret the rules differently than another. And just wars can involve unjust acts. Some would cite the internment of Japanese Americans during World War II as an example of an unjust action during a just war.

What do modern thinkers have to say about the notion of just war? The conservative and liberal viewpoints are surprisingly similar. Only pacifism stands off on its own. In October 2001, novelist Barbara Kingsolver expressed the pacifist viewpoint in an op-ed piece in the *Los Angeles Times,* "No Glory in Unjust War on the Weak":

> I am somebody's mother, so I will say that right now. The issue is, people are getting hurt [in the war on terrorism]. We need to take a moment's time out to review the monstrous waste of an endless cycle of retaliation. The biggest weapons don't win this one, guys. When there are people on Earth willing to give up their lives in hatred and use our own domestic airplanes as bombs, it's clear that we can't out-technologize them. You can't beat cancer by killing every cell in the body — or you could, I guess, but the point would be lost. This is a war of who can hate the most. There is no limit to that escalation. It will only end when we have the guts to say it really doesn't matter who started it, and begin to try and understand, then alter the forces that generate hatred.

In contrast, and coincidentally in the same issue of the same paper, commentator Marc Cooper, identifying himself as a liberal, stated,

> The left must recognize that these forces [the terrorists] cannot be neutralized by nonviolent moral suasion or international law alone. As some of the left have argued, the WTC attacks demand a "just response" that includes limited, targeted, and effective military action aimed at lessening the threat of future terrorist attacks and restoring a sense of domestic security. For those who are squeamish about taking out Osama bin Laden's network and its Taliban defenders, let them reflect on just how much further American politics will slide to the right if there are a half-dozen more major terror attacks here at home.

When we look to discussions of a just war and terrorism by contemporary philosophers, most papers and books written before September 11 have one thing in common: They imagine a future enemy to be a nation with an identifiable government, rarely a shadowy association of international terrorists. At the time of this writing, philosophical commentaries on the war on terrorism have yet to be published. At the end of the chapter you will find a selection of text excerpts on the subject predating 9/11, and you must decide for yourself whether you think they apply to the post–September 11 situation. In war-torn eighteenth-century Prussia, Kant wrote one of his last works, "Perpetual Peace." With a clarity that wasn't apparent to readers until after World War II, Kant envisioned the slippery slope of escalating wars of the future leading to a war of mutual extermination and admonished that the only way civilization will survive is for all governments to become republican (that is, a democracy instead of various forms of dictatorship that regard their citizens as merely a means to an end). You will remember the concept of the kingdom of ends from Chapter 6, and this is what Kant was dreaming of: a world where people respect one another and their laws, where no nation abuses its own citizens, where nations will join together in a federation of free states, and where strangers are considered people, too. While some might say Kant's vision is both a trifle naive and incomplete, one might hope there is a profound truth to his observation that truly democratic countries, where each citizen knows he or she has constitutionally protected rights, are less likely to generate wars of aggression — or have individuals embark on terrorist ploys against their own government or other nations — than countries where the individual has few or no rights and feels like a pawn in the political games of others. An active global effort toward democracy might thus go a long way toward preventing future terrorist actions as well as future wars.

Animal Welfare and Animal Rights

In Chapters 5 and 6 we touched on the issue of animals as candidates for moral respect. Chapter 5 introduced you to Descartes's idea that animals cannot feel pain because they have no minds, and Bentham's and Mill's view that since animals obviously can feel pain and experience pleasure, consideration for animals should be included in whatever moral decisions we make that might affect them. Today, research by animal behaviorists has established that nonhuman animals are capable of feeling physical pain. In addition, animal studies in the wild as well as under more controlled conditions in animal behavior labs support the old anecdotal assumption that animals can also feel emotions, and the criticism, raised repeatedly throughout the twentieth century, that animal researchers are just "anthropomorphizing" their subjects is rarely heard now. Animal researchers and writers are increasingly affirming the observations of David Hume and Charles Darwin that if animals act as if they feel emotions similar to fear, joy, and sadness, then it is the simplest and most likely explanation that they do in fact feel such similar emotions — although we will have a hard time showing exactly how similar, until the day when we can hook up animals (and people) to monitors and read their minds electronically and chemically, or in fact talk to the animals themselves and ask them, as some ape researchers are already doing. (The question of animal *intelligence* is considered in Box 13.4.)

The Utilitarian Approach

Within the utilitarian philosophy the recognition that animals can feel pain — physically, and even emotionally — obviously doesn't mean we as humans are not allowed to cause animals pain or distress, any more than it means we are not allowed to cause other humans pain: When great results can be obtained for a majority (of humans and/or animals), then causing pain to sentient creatures is morally acceptable and even commendable. For this reason, classical utilitarians such as Bentham and Mill and most utilitarians today rarely use the term "animal rights." Rather, modern utilitarians talk about "animal welfare." As you'll remember from Chapter 7, Bentham thought the notion of human rights was "nonsense upon stilts," and obviously a utilitarian would view animal rights in the same light, inasmuch as a utilitarian doesn't believe it serves any good purpose to talk about rights that are absolute and can never be infringed on, if the protection of such rights would be detrimental to the majority in a society.

Box 13.4   RATIONAL ANIMALS?

The question of animal intelligence has been a challenge ever since Aristotle claimed that animals can think in a practical sense, but only humans can think rationally and abstractly. What does it take to think rationally? You'll remember that our working definition of rationality in Chapter 6 was the ability to identify a goal and take the shortest route to it (and that definition itself was questionable). For Kant the true test of a rational being is whether he or she can understand the categorical imperative: Could you allow yourself to do something you wouldn't accept as a universal law? Most of us, however, have a less strict view of what it is to think rationally. If someone solves a problem through trial and error, we usually view it as a rational method, but it is even better if someone can envision a solution to a problem without having encountered the problem before, and solve it on the first try simply by having thought about it abstractly.

Most of us are probably willing to accept that nonhuman animals have some sort of mental activity whereby they associate time and place, link past fears and joys with present persons and places, and anticipate events in the near future, such as dinner. But can nonhuman animals solve abstract problems, and even conceive of a kind of categorical imperative? Throughout the twentieth century this question was so controversial that most scholars steered clear of it for fear of ridicule; in 1900 a horse in Germany, Clever Hans, believed by his owner and numerous scientists to be able to do math because he could thump out the correct answers to math questions when asked, was revealed to be "simply" a good reader of human body language, and research into animal intelligence carried the stigma of Clever Hans with it well into the last half of the twentieth century. But since new research into animal intelligence was made public

during the 1980s and 1990s, many researchers have been less reluctant to consider nonhuman animals as having a rudimentary capacity for rational thinking and even for language comprehension. Close observation and interaction with dolphins, orca whales, monkeys, pigs, and even birds have led to a new appreciation of the possibility of nonhuman animal reasoning. In particular, research into the behavior and language capacity of nonhuman great apes (bonobo chimpanzees, chimpanzees, gorillas, and to a lesser extent orangutans) has made it conceivable that the great apes have a grasp of abstract rational thinking as well as trial-and-error thinking.

Of the great apes, the bonobo chimpanzee Kanzi may be the most famous example of nonhuman animal intelligence today, although his sister Panbanisha now seems to surpass him in linguistic talent. They both live at the Georgia State University Language Research Center under the tutelage of psychologist Sue Savage-Rumbaugh. Having taught himself how to use a lexigram (an electronic "talking" board with symbols for English words) by watching the humans try, unsuccessfully, to teach his mother its use, he answers questions or tells his human friends what he wants, including watching videos where humans in ape costumes are featured. Panbanisha has been raised in the human-language environment and has learned to use the lexigram as well. Kanzi's feats include understanding new sentences and reacting accordingly (such as "Put the key in the refrigerator"), as well as displaying logical thinking, going through a series of actions to achieve a goal (such as cutting a string to get into a box with a key that opens another box with a treat). Panbanisha has shown an interest in copying the words she sees on the computer screen and has reportedly taken up writing words in En-

The bonobo chimpanzee Kanzi is today perhaps the most outstanding, and controversial, example of a nonhuman being using and understanding language and demonstrating rational thought—at the approximate level of a human child of three (and occasionally even older). Never having been trained to understand human language or use a lexigram (a talking board with symbols signifying nouns, verbs, and names), Kanzi picked up both skills as an infant from watching his mother in training. Here, at sixteen years of age, Kanzi is working with his lexigram, answering questions for Sue Savage-Rumbaugh at Georgia State University's Language Research Center.

glish on the floor with chalk. In addition, Panbanisha now serves as an interpreter for her and Kanzi's mother, who never learned the use of the lexigram.

Would Kant recognize these behaviors as evidence of rational thinking, and welcome Kanzi and Panbanisha as persons instead of things? That would depend on whether it is possible for the apes to grasp the concept of universalization: Might they understand the idea of "Don't do that—how would you like it if we did that to you?" Kanzi's and Panbanisha's language comprehension is now presumably at the level of a three-year-old human child's. If we are ready to recognize a small child as having some grasp of rational thought, and understanding the preceding sentence, and are willing to call a three-year-old child a person, why not be as open-minded about the personhood of an ape if he or she is on the approximate same intellectual level? For some thinkers, the entire ape language experiment hinges on whether it's merely some smart animals "aping" human behavior for rewards, or whether apes can really communicate freely (within limits) in a human language.

(continued)

Box 13.4   RATIONAL ANIMALS? *(continued)*

Since one of the first apes who learned American Sign Language, Washoe, taught her son the ASL signs and communicated with him using signs even when they thought themselves to be unobserved by humans, and Panbanisha is now teaching her young son how to use the lexigram, the answer seems to be yes.

But what about the apes who haven't learned human language? Might they still have rational thought activity? In other words, is it possible to think without language? In the Primary Readings you'll find a text by Savage-Rumbaugh, who argues that thinking without words is a natural phenomenon among apes as well as among humans.

John Stuart Mill does talk about rights, in particular the rights to security, liberty, and justice, but you will also remember from Chapter 7 that he says, "particular cases may occur in which some other social duty is so important, as to overrule any one of the general maxims of justice." A utilitarian believes we should take animal pain and pleasure into consideration whenever there are no overriding concerns that would justify causing pain for the sake of achieving good consequences for the many. As we saw in Chapter 5, a typical utilitarian response to animal experiments would be to frown on the use of animals in research on household products or cosmetics, because the contentment or protection each individual human would gain from the pain of animal experiments—a safer hairspray, a milder detergent—does not outweigh that pain, especially since humans can choose to avoid products that make your eyes sting and dry out your hands. However, when the focus shifts to medical experiments possibly resulting in the cure for terminal or debilitating illnesses, many utilitarians change their minds: The beneficial outcome of such research, which uses a limited number of animals, could be so overwhelming that there is no excuse not to perform such experiments. (You will recognize the problem from the film *Extreme Measures,* summarized in Chapter 5, even though the film addresses the problem of *human* test subjects.)

The Kantian Approach

As you will remember from Chapter 6, Kant excludes animals from moral consideration as ends in themselves because, to him, they are not rational creatures. Rational creatures are capable of understanding moral rules and, above all, moral duties and responsibilities. Kantians believe that only those who are capable of entering into a mutual relationship involving moral responsibilities are eligible for rights, and since animals are not perceived as having such capabilities, the deontological tradition reserves rights for humans. So what happens to human beings who, for some reason, are not capable of taking on duties and responsibilities? Some modern Kantians, such as the philosopher Carl Cohen, choose to solve that problem by saying that as long as most people are capable of rational thinking and understanding duties, then respect should also be extended to the few who aren't. However, even if it may appear as though an animal is capable of understanding its "duties," what this understanding really amounts to is training based on rewards or punishment—not a true understanding of moral duties—so from a Kantian point of view, animals are by their very nature excluded from having rights. This is what Cohen and others refer to as *contractarianism:* If your mind is capable of comprehending the obligations involved in a contract—written or oral—then you are a rational being and should be treated with respect. A creature that doesn't understand the implications of a contract can't have duties, and consequently can't have any rights, either. This doesn't mean we can't or shouldn't choose to be kind to animals, because there is no excuse for causing needless suffering, but although we may take on the responsibility of caring for an animal, our pet has no moral claim on us.

Rights and Interests

From the viewpoint that having rights entails having an understanding of duties, the path to animal rights ought to remain blocked. However, there is an alternative viewpoint linking rights not with *duties,* but with *interests.* You were introduced to the ideas of Australian philosopher Peter Singer in Chapter 4, and you may remember the title of one of his books, *The Expanding Circle.* The circle Singer would like to see expanded is our moral universe: Who counts as a morally important being? Singer sees our view of who counts as having expanded from the family or the tribe to nations and to all humans. Singer and others would now like to see this circle expanded further to include the great apes and possibly other intelligent, social species, such as whales, dolphins, and wolves, in what is called "the community of equals," as stated in the Declaration on Great Apes. The argument used by many thinkers advocating rights for animals is that if a living being is capable of having interests, then these beings should have at least some moral standing (they should be taken into our moral universe). But what does it mean to have an interest? It may seem as if our cars have an interest in regular maintenance, because otherwise they break down. But presumably our cars don't suffer when they break down (only we, the owners, do). So the capacity for suffering and the interest in not suffering must be included in the basic description of a being with moral standing. But is an interest something that some individual really wants, or is it something that is good for that individual? And if interests imply rights, does it mean that individuals with interests have a right to have the interest fulfilled? For Singer it is the capacity for interests that makes an individual eligible for rights, but that capacity doesn't mean those individuals have a right to have their wishes (or even their needs) fulfilled; however, they have a right to have their needs taken into consideration as morally relevant. In concrete terms, Singer's suggestions for "rights for the great apes" would include the right not to be tortured, not to be deprived of their freedom, and not to be killed, but it would not include any right to a steady supply of jellybeans (if that's what some individual ape might prefer). Some critics have remarked that it is unusual for a utilitarian philosopher such as Singer to use a concept such as *rights* instead of *welfare,* since traditionally any right for a utilitarian must be superseded by overriding social concerns. But Singer's philosophy of the ethical treatment of animals comes as close to the concept of rights as is possible for a utilitarian, since he believes the possibility that these rights would ever be overridden by other concerns is remote. For Singer, harming an animal would be permissible only in extreme cases such as saving all of humanity.

Other thinkers sharing Singer's view that beings with interests should have rights include Joel Feinberg and Steve Sapontzis. For Feinberg it is obvious that individual animals have interests, perhaps more interests than some humans who are severely mentally impaired, so individual animals should have rights. However, an entire species can't have "interests," so Feinberg doesn't favor the rights of endangered *species,* only those of *individuals,* nonhuman or human. But, says Feinberg, if the criterion for being a member of the moral universe is that you can make moral claims against someone else, then animals already have such rights, because they can be represented in court by humans protecting their interests.

Sapontzis looks at the issue from both a utilitarian and a Kantian point of view: If we agree that animals probably have an overall narrower range of interests than humans, that is still not a sufficient reason to disregard such interests. In "The Moral Significance of Interests," he writes: "It certainly does not follow on utilitarian grounds that because an individual has a narrower range of interests he may be treated as a tool for the gratification of the interests of a being with a wider range of interests. If that did follow, renaissance men could eat specialists and peasants for dinner." Utilitarians aren't obliged to treat humans and animals in *the same* way, just to take their interests into equal consideration (so there won't be a question of giving animals the right to vote or to a good, well-rounded education, as some critics are fond of speculating).

What if we apply Kantianism to the issue of animal interests? Sapontzis points to the wealth of new research in animal intelligence, as well as to our common experiences with animals: It is about time, he says, that we put the debate over whether animals are rational behind us; of course they are — not to the degree of human rationality, but rational nevertheless. They may not be able to use the categorical imperative, but they are courageous, loyal, and devoted, and if we want to extend moral worth to humans with the same qualities, then we must let many animals into the moral fold, too. As Sapontzis says, "Anyone still inclined to believe that only humans are rational should adopt a dog and get to know him personally."

What if you still think that granting rights to animals is too big a step, since humans, after all, have such a wide range of moral interactions that animals may never comprehend or participate in? You may consider a solution suggested by the philosopher Mary Ann Warren: *partial rights.* Because many animals do have the same rudimentary intellectual capabilities as small children and the same (or an even greater) capacity for suffering, they should have some moral standing, but since human capacities for both reasoning and suffering are more extensive, they may override the rights of animals. Animals can probably never be morally autonomous the way humans can, but moral autonomy need not be the only criterion for having rights. It is, however, an important factor. So Warren suggests that humans should be the only beings granted full, equal rights (at least until we find other morally autonomous creatures), but nonhuman animals can be the bearers of partial rights, to be superseded by human rights only in extreme cases.

Trees and Other Elements of Nature

In Hans Christian Andersen's fairy tale "Little Ida's Flowers," a little girl, Ida, is upset that the flowers in the vase, which were so beautiful the day before, are now all wilted. But a college student living with her family comforts her: The flowers are just tired, because they have been to the King's Ball all night. Flowers have a life of their own at night, he tells her, and sometimes they even leave their stalks and fly off to seek new adventures—butterflies are really flowers in flight! A sour old government official grumbles, "Why teach the child a lot of nonsense?"

As adults, we know this story to be a metaphor for the magic of childhood, which should be the birthright of any child. But suppose the story were true? Suppose the flowers could tell us whether they wanted to be in the sun or the shade, and suppose the tree communicated that it would prefer that we not lower the waterline, because doing so would kill it. In a sense these things do happen; plants do "communicate" with us to let us know their needs—not in a conscious sense, but quite mechanically. When they need water they droop; when they need sun they look pale and get long and scraggly. So it seems that plants do have interests, even if they aren't aware of it. Does that mean we should think of including them in our moral universe as beings with some standing?

This is a question that some scholars predict will be bothering us long after we've settled the question of animal rights—and, as with animal rights, it will have far-reaching consequences. It provokes the same question we asked when considering our treatment of animals: If we decide not to be cruel to these living things, for whose sake are we doing it? For the sake of people or animals? If we decide to grant the right to life to plants, are we doing it because people like to look at trees or because trees like to continue to grow?

In 1974 Christopher D. Stone wrote a paper, "Should Trees Have Standing? Towards Legal Rights for Natural Objects." Many dismissed the paper as complete nonsense at the time, but it has gained in influence since then. Stone states that every time we have opted to include another group in our welfare concern, such as slaves, women, minorities, children, or animals, the decision has been met with ridicule before it has achieved common acceptance. He proposes that we now expand our moral universe to cover not only individual animals but also entire species and natural objects such as lakes and streams, mountain meadows, marshes, and so on (which really can't be said to have interests since they are not "alive"):

> Whenever it carves out "property" rights, the legal system is engaged in the process of *creating* monetary worth. . . . I am proposing we do the same with eagles and wilderness areas as we do with copyrighted works, patented inventions, and privacy: *make* the violation of rights in them to be a cost by declaring the "pirating" of them to be the invasion of property interest. If we do so, the net social costs the polluter would be confronted with would include not only the extended homocentric cost of his pollution [. . .] but also cost to the environment *per se.*

What Stone suggests here is a grand solution not only to the problem of whose rights should be protected but also to the problem of *how* they should be protected.

He proposes fining polluters because pollution is *bad for nature,* regardless of whether it might affect a local human population or visitors to a polluted wilderness area. It would take us too long to discuss in detail the concept of giving rights to plants and natural objects such as rocks and streams (and of course we'd want to include cultural objects such as historical buildings, old baseball fields, statues, favorite movie locations, and so on). The question is how far we want to go, not in assigning protection for the environment—because we can take that as far as we want to go—but in assigning rights per se, regardless of human interest in the subject. If nobody cares about a certain meadow or about the building in downtown Los Angeles where they filmed *Blade Runner* (the Bradbury building, incidentally), then should we give it rights on the basis that someone may someday care, or because it has acquired those rights just by hanging around?

If we do want to assign rights to plants, where do we stop? It is all well and good to preserve a stately row of trees, but what about preserving a scraggly row of carrots on the grounds that they have a right to life? What we have here is a *slippery slope argument,* a logical fallacy claiming that some idea will invariably lead to a series of increasingly unacceptable consequences (such as: "If you refuse to wear fur because of concern for living creatures, then you shouldn't eat meat, either; as a matter of fact, you shouldn't fight the roaches and ants in your kitchen because they, too, are living creatures, nor should you use antibiotics or antibacterial mouthwash out of concern for the living bacteria"). A slippery slope is usually advanced as a satirical criticism of some idea (here, refusing to wear fur) by pointing to ridiculous consequences (another term for this type of argument is a *reductio ad absurdum,* a reduction to absurdity). To respond to a slippery slope argument, we can take one of three paths: (1) abandon our original idea, because the consequences now seem silly; (2) agree that we should take the consequences seriously; or (3) *draw the line* between one part of the slope and another by arguing that there is a moral difference between, for example, eating meat and killing roaches, which spread disease. Concerning the question of giving rights to trees, one could argue that there is a moral difference between granting rights to trees (if that is one's conviction) and granting rights to carrots. However, if we choose to draw the line, it is up to us to have good arguments as to why there is a moral difference between one step of the slope and the next.

The Death Penalty

When the question of punishing criminals comes up today, it is usually related to the issue of sentencing children as adults or that of the death penalty. The issue of trying children in adult court was examined briefly in Chapter 7, and here we explore the issue of capital punishment. In order to get the most out of the debate it is recommended that you have the punishment discussion from Chapter 7 fresh in your mind, particularly the five categories of punishment: deterrence, rehabilitation, incapacitation, retribution, and vengeance.

THE WIZARD OF ID   Brant parker and Johnny hart

By permission of Johnny Hart and Creators Syndicate, Inc.

With a particularly dark sense of humor, this *Wizard of Id* strip deals with capital punishment—a topic that isn't usually a source of laughter. The strip creates a perverted application of a utilitarian principle of punishment: As long as punishment has good consequences (such as deterrence or rehabilitation), then the issue of guilt or innocence is of minor importance.

Two Philosophers on Capital Punishment

Most philosophers up until the twentieth century have had no compunction about arguing in favor of the death penalty. Two voices coming from two different traditions have been particularly influential, and you are familiar with both of them: John Locke, in seventeenth-century England, stated that humans have rights even before the social contract, in the state of nature. These are the three negative rights, to *life, liberty, and property.* But since there is no government in the state of nature to enforce these rights, one must take on that task oneself. Therefore, if a person has infringed on your rights, you are free to punish the perpetrator (if you can catch him or her, that is). And, says Locke, if someone in the state of nature has taken a life, then he has given up his own right to life and can be hunted down and killed like a wild animal. Locke believes such action will have two effects: (1) *deterrence*—those who see how a killer is treated will think twice about doing the same thing—and (2) *retribution,* restoring the balance that was disrupted by the murder. So Locke uses both a forward-looking and a backward-looking argument in favor of killing a killer.

The other familiar voice in favor of the death penalty is Immanuel Kant, speaking to us from eighteenth-century Prussia. Kant argues that capital punishment is a rational response to a capital crime—and he argues exclusively in favor of *retribution:* If we execute a criminal in order to obtain some good social consequences such as safe streets, then we are in effect using the killer as merely a means to an end—we are using him or her as a stepping stone to safe streets. Indeed, executing an *innocent* person would probably have the same kind of deterrent effect. Instead, Kant insists that there should be one reason, and one reason only, for punishing a person: because of his or her *guilt.* And in order for us to proceed according to the principle of *lex talionis,* we should punish the guilty in proportion to the crime, not with an eye toward any further social consequences. This means the only proper punishment for murder is death—even if good social consequences might actually come out of imprisoning the killer for life or letting him or her go free after a period of rehabilitation.

We see how seriously Kant takes this principle by his example: If a society decides to disband but still has people waiting on death row, then the last action of that society should be to execute its convicted murderers, even if there will be no society afterward to enjoy the safer streets. Furthermore, it is only right and proper to execute a murderer for his crime—and in a sense it is showing the convicted killer the utmost *respect* as a human being: Instead of using him for some social purpose (such as deterrence), or trying to rehabilitate him under the assumption that he didn't know what he was doing, we give him credit for actually having made up his own mind to commit a crime—and then we hold him accountable for it.

It wasn't until the nineteenth century that strong voices began to speak up against capital punishment as such, and not merely in opposition to executions for lesser crimes such as burglary. In the twentieth century opposition to the death penalty became known as *abolitionism* (whereas "abolition" in the nineteenth century referred to abolishing slavery in America).

Today's Capital Punishment Criteria

From 1968 to 1976 the death penalty was not available in the United States, but since 1976 individual states have been able to decide whether they want to make certain crimes punishable by death, as long as their laws meet guidelines established by the U.S. Supreme Court.

What crimes are today punishable by death in the thirty-eight states that allow capital punishment? Theoretically, treason is, but the death penalty is only evoked under rare circumstances, as with the execution of Julius and Ethel Rosenberg for espionage in 1953—still a controversial judicial decision, especially since 2001, when a witness for the prosecution admitted that he lied on the stand. In previous decades, murder, even if committed in a state of rage or panic, might lead to the gas chamber or the electric chair, but today one or more "special circumstances" have to apply, depending on the state legislation. In California, for example, some of the special circumstances are killing more than one person; raping and killing a person; stalking a victim before killing him or her; killing a police officer, a judge, or a jury member; killing with poison; and killing while carjacking. Richard Allen Davis, who abducted, sexually assaulted, and killed twelve-year-old Polly Klaas in Petaluma, California, in 1993, is on death row: He pleaded not guilty but was convicted. Brandon Wilson, who killed nine-year-old Matthew Checci in 1998 in Oceanside, California, after following him into a restroom (stalking), is now on death row. These are cases in which the California law of special circumstances applies. In other death penalty states, other rules may apply. In the state of Washington, for example, a killer of multiple victims must be shown to have had a "common scheme" in killing them, such as robbery. The simple fact of there being more than one victim isn't enough in itself to warrant the death penalty; Washington legislators have been debating changing the law in the wake of the capture of several serial killers.

Abolitionist Arguments

Abolitionists make the following general arguments:

1. The death penalty is an uncivilized, cruel, and unusual form of punishment, depriving the criminal of the ultimate right: the right to life. Abolitionists often cite the fact that among Western nations, the United States is the only country that still executes its citizens, and abolitionist nations around the world usually refuse to extradite a murderer to the United States if he or she may be executed. Proponents of the death penalty, called *retentionists* because they want to *retain* the penalty, reply that of all Western nations, the United States is the only country in which serial killers operate on a regular basis and that the homicide rate is generally higher than in other Western nations, so special measures have to be taken.

2. Executing a murderer is no better than stooping to the level of the murderer, making murder state-sanctioned. Retentionists reply that this is a false analogy: The murderer kills innocent people, whereas the state executes someone who has been found guilty.

3. As it is administered today, at least in certain states, the death penalty shows patterns of discrimination: The poor, the uneducated, and African American men are more likely to receive the death penalty than are people from other population groups, regardless of the crime rate. Retentionists reply that this is not an argument against the death penalty as such, only against the way it has been administered — which admittedly has been discriminatory. But such slanted approaches can be avoided in the future, and according to a recent report from the Justice Department such approaches are virtually a thing of the past, at least in federal cases. Be that as it may, the general perception among abolitionists as well as many retentionists is that the discrimination issue is still far from having been resolved.

4. Mistakes have been made and innocent people executed — twenty-three known innocents in this country in the twentieth century. A person wrongly incarcerated cannot have the years he or she spent behind bars restored, but he or she can be compensated financially. An innocent person who has been executed can't be compensated in any way, because everything has been taken from him or her. To many, this argument is the strongest abolitionist point, leading to the adage that it is better that many guilty go free than that one innocent person be punished.

5. Some abolitionists argue that you can choose to be a retentionist only if you are ignorant, sadistic, or emotional, and that once you bothered to examine exactly what goes on at an execution, and to distance yourself from your emotional response to the victims, then you would become an abolitionist. (These arguments are set forth in the abolitionist book *Who Owns Death? Capital Punishment, the American Conscience, and the End of Executions* [2000] by Robert Jay Lifton and Greg Mitchell.) Retentionists answer that even botched executions are no argument against the death penalty as such, only against incompetence; that most retentionists don't *like*

the thought of putting people to death and regard capital punishment as a necessary evil; and relating to the suffering of the victims is extremely relevant to the entire issue of punishment. You'll remember the argument from Berns, Strawson, and Whiteley in Chapter 7 that if we are incapable of feeling some form of morally righteous indignation and anger on behalf of the victim—and all the more so on behalf of a murder victim—then we have in effect lost respect and empathy for other human beings.

Retentionist Arguments

Retentionists make the following arguments:

1. Only capital punishment can fit the severity of the crime of murder, and a person who murders has forfeited his or her own right to life. In other words, the issue for many retentionists is *justice,* and the only adequate justice they see for a capital crime is one of retribution. The murderer deserves to die; the victim's family deserves closure; and society deserves to have the books balanced: Commit a crime, and you will pay for it in proportion to the crime. Abolitionists reply that the whole issue of proportionality ("an eye for an eye") has been distorted by retentionists. Only in murder cases do they invoke the principle—does anyone ever talk about "an eye for an eye" when the issue is burglary? Does the court go in and take something from the home of the thief as punishment? Or how about carjacking, embezzlement, or prostitution? How do you punish someone proportionately to that? In the Primary Readings you'll find an excerpt by Stephen Nathanson arguing against the proportionality principle.

2. The only way to protect the public effectively from future killings is to eliminate the murderer (the argument of *incapacitation*). An abolitionist may argue that keeping a murderer in prison for life without the possibility of parole is just as effective, but the retentionist will answer that the prison has not yet been built that is 100 percent escape-proof. Even science fiction contains escape scenarios from asteroid penal colonies! And even if prisons were escape-proof, we may still have gubernatorial decisions pardoning murderers. A serial killer of children may appear to be completely rehabilitated in prison and given a pardon, but recidivism in these cases is very high. Here an abolitionist may point to the slippery slope, implying that perhaps any criminal who can't be rehabilitated should be executed regardless of his or her crime. Or perhaps we should even try to anticipate what criminal tendencies a first-time offender has and execute him or her on the basis of what he or she will probably do later on! But though some retentionists would welcome a broadening of capital punishment to cover rapes and child molestation, no serious philosophers of law argue that a person should be punishable for something he or she has not done yet, and most retentionists reserve capital punishment for murders with special circumstances.

3. Some retentionists argue that a conviction followed by execution is a deterrent (whereas almost everyone agrees that the longer the time lag between conviction and execution, the less deterrent effect the execution has). It will certainly be a specific deterrent for that criminal, because he or she is not going to commit mur-

der again! In the general sense of the word, others will be deterred by the threat of sure and swift punishment. Some retentionists cite swift justice as a formidable deterrent in countries where civil liberties are not on the main political agenda: If you know you will have your hand amputated if you steal, are you really going to take the chance? But other retentionists claim that civil liberties and rights are too high a price to pay for safe streets. The effectiveness of general deterrence is undecided statistically: Some statistics show some deterrence factor after an execution; other statistics actually portray the crime rate as going up after executions. (Deterrence seems to be a fact in noncapital crimes. However, it is hotly debated whether the "three strikes and you're out" law in California and similar laws in other states have had any deterrent effect.) Abolitionists sometimes point out that if a person has killed once and knows that he or she is likely to get caught, convicted, and executed, then what is to deter the murderer from killing again, perhaps witnesses? They can suffer the penalty only once. And retentionists answer back by saying that a murderer in prison for life might well (and often does) go on murdering in prison, knowing that there can be no stricter penalty than the one he or she is already suffering, so the only way to prevent further killings is to retain and use the death penalty.

The five reasons for punishment discussed in Chapter 7 all have a role in the death penalty debate. As we just saw, *deterrence* can be used as a retentionist argument. The effect is usually assumed to be that others are deterred from committing the same crime; the intention is less to deter the criminal from doing it again (specific deterrence). (See *The Wizard of Id* on page 567, a spoof of a retentionist utilitarian argument: The wrong man may be executed, but the real killer learns a valuable lesson.) *Incapacitation* can likewise be a retentionist argument, but what about *rehabilitation*? Rehabilitation is not relevant here, for obviously an executed person doesn't learn not to commit the same crime again. *Retribution,* on the other hand, is highly relevant, for a retributivist will usually argue that the death penalty is the ultimate form of justice: It fits the crime, provided that society can be certain it has caught and convicted the guilty person. *Vengeance,* the supposedly nonlegitimate reason for punishment, is generally the most prevailing retentionist view among laypeople, who often argue that a murderer ought to die because he or she ought to suffer the way the victim suffered and that the suffering of the murderer will make society feel better. An abolitionist will generally argue that a life term can be as effective a deterrent as death, that a life term also incapacitates a murderer, and that there is always a chance that a murderer can be rehabilitated. Few retributivists are abolitionists, but it is possible to argue that a life term is the proportionate punishment for a murder, so we can have proportionality and still have respect for life, even the life of a murderer; vengeance is never an option for an abolitionist, who generally sees the death penalty as an expression of primitive social revenge.

It has been customary among scholars to view this insistence on how we *feel* as a primitive trait, but before we reject all references to emotions in the death penalty debate outright, we should remember that several philosophers have recently argued that emotions are not altogether irrelevant in our moral decision process. Martha Nussbaum (Chapter 1) argues that emotions can have their own logic; Richard Taylor (Chapter 10) says that the fundamental morality of compassion comes from the heart, not the brain; Walter Berns (Chapter 7) says a society that punishes without feeling anger toward the criminal doesn't care for its victims; Diane Whiteley (Chapter 7) argues that a proper understanding of justice includes a sense of moral indignation over harm done to a victim. No thinkers today argue that punishment should take place along exclusively emotional lines, because in that case we'd probably quickly see the punishment exceed the severity of the crime, but maybe justice should not be completely separated from emotions, either. Should we be seeking a Golden Mean between impartial justice that punishes according to a set scale with neither rage nor compassion and a system of justice that allows a measure of emotion to enter into the picture, as an outlet for society's righteous anger against a perpetrator, as well as an opening for mercy when an unusual set of circumstances warrants it? Or is that a dangerous step toward legitimatizing revenge?

The DNA Issue

Recently, a number of people serving life sentences or waiting on death row have been exonerated and released as the result of DNA testing. These reversals have prompted both retentionists and abolitionists to question the procedures that convicted these people in the first place. In Idaho, Charles Fain was on death row eighteen years for raping and killing a nine-year-old girl. When DNA analyses cleared him in 2001, he magnanimously said that he had no hard feelings, but was just looking forward to resuming his life after years of incarceration. It appears that the small town where he had been convicted had conveniently pounced on him as a newcomer to the area, even though he had an alibi. And in Oklahoma City it was revealed in 2001 that a forensic chemist whose testimony had contributed to 23 people being sent to death row and 11 already executed, had lied on the stand on at least six occasions. Given such cases, one doesn't have to be an abolitionist to wonder how many other executions may have involved a less-than-fair trial. But a retentionist will state that such cases still don't provide a compelling argument against the death penalty as such, only against the way it has been administered, and retentionists as well as abolitionists are generally in favor of introducing mandatory DNA testing of suspects in a wide array of criminal cases so the risk of convicting an innocent person can be minimized.

However, not all crime scenes contain DNA from the perpetrator; only if the criminal leaves blood, saliva, hair with follicles, body tissue, or semen at the crime scene can DNA be used to rule out other suspects, and point to one suspect in particular. And it is equally important to realize that DNA is not the only important evidence that can convict a criminal. Eyewitnesses *can* be reliable and, contrary to the popular conception, circumstantial evidence can sometimes be extremely strong.

When a suspect was apprehended in December 2001 in Seattle and charged with the Green River serial killings of the early 1980s, most people who had followed the case were astonished that an arrest had actually been made. The case had dragged on so long, with several suspects but not enough evidence, that only a few dedicated police detectives were still on the case. But these clear-thinking officers had collected a saliva sample from one of the suspects years earlier on the off chance that science at some time in the future could do something with it, and in the late

1990s the DNA technology was available. When the Washington State lab got around to testing the sample in 2001, the perseverance of the detectives paid off: There was a DNA match between semen found on three Green River victims and the saliva sample. In San Diego a DNA match was found between semen on two little boys murdered in the 1980s and a man who was already serving a sentence for rape and assault, but who was free at the time of their deaths, and now he will stand trial for their murder. It seems that with the new, faster DNA tests there is no legal or moral downside: Innocent people are being set free, and killers are being matched up with their victims even decades after their murders. In addition, it isn't just the criminal's DNA left at the crime scene that can help convict him or her—the victim's DNA speaks loudly, too. If the victim's blood, for example, has been found in the suspect's home or on his or her clothes, it provides important evidence, such as in the case of seven-year-old Danielle van Dam, abducted from her San Diego home in the middle of the night and murdered in the spring of 2002. Her blood found in the suspect's motor-home and on his clothes gave the judge reasonable cause to order him to stand trial. He was found guilty in August 2002.

You may have wondered why it is that police and lawyers talk about DNA matches as being one in 5, 6, or even 10 billion, since there are "only" 6 billion humans on the planet these days. How can there be a match between a suspect and another nonexistent person? The fact of the matter is that talking about matches of one to several billion is just another way of saying that the DNA points *exclusively* to the accused. The roundabout way of saying it is, in effect, a consequence of a scientific problem you are well acquainted with from Chapter 3, the problem of induction. Since DNA research is an empirical science, a good scientist can't make statements about anything being 100 percent certain, but referring to the actual statistical possibility of another person being born with the exact same DNA (which would be, presumably, 10 billion to one), you can make a statement in court that translates into common English as a complete and indisputable identification of a criminal, even better than with a fingerprint.

If the American criminal justice system in the future *can* eliminate most of the doubt as to someone's guilt or innocence through DNA analysis, would that also eliminate the abolitionist argument that the death penalty sometimes kills innocents? In cases where no DNA evidence exists, there would still be a danger of an innocent person being executed. And it is the principle of the state taking a life that the abolitionist is protesting more than anything. But for reluctant retentionists the increased certainty of guilt might pave the way for a *greater* confidence in the justification of capital punishment.

Even with these new scientific safeguards against convicting the wrong person, however, there appears to be a growing unease in the United States about the very nature of the death penalty, at least at the legislative level. Case in point: In 2000 the state of Illinois declared a moratorium on the death penalty, and in the spring of 2002 a fourteen-member panel recommended a major reform of capital punishment in the state, including a statewide DNA database, an independent forensic lab, videotaping of interrogations, and a ban on executing mentally retarded murderers. The bipartisan commission stopped short of recommending an end to capital punishment, but a narrow majority on the panel concluded that since no system can guarantee that no innocent person is ever sentenced to death, the death penalty should be abolished in the state of Illinois. Maryland imposed a one-year moratorium on capital punishment in 2002, and studies of the question of the death penalty and fairness were undertaken in New Jersey and Virginia.

Stories and Issues: A Final Word

In this chapter we have examined four issues within the field of applied ethics. Of course there are many more issues with a moral dimension that concern us in today's world, such as euthanasia, abortion, and gun control. I hope that you will make use of the theories we have explored throughout this book to embark on discussions of some of these other issues as well, since you now have the theoretical background to weigh in with more than how you *feel* about an issue. As we have seen numerous times in this book, feelings about moral issues need not be irrelevant, but feelings can't take the place of rational arguments—primarily because an appeal to feelings rarely solves conflicts, but an appeal to logic might. In addition, I hope you will approach the world of stories with an enhanced appreciation for issues raised in television shows, in movies, and in literature, be it stories about cloning and genetic engineering, media ethics and responsibilities, human relations involving compassion and gratitude, or perhaps stories of courage in wartime and peacetime. In this book we've used summaries and excerpts of such stories to illustrate and explore some intricate moral issues, and I hope you've felt inspired to seek out and experience the original stories in their entirety by yourself, because a summary or even an excerpt doesn't do a good story justice. My hope is that as the access to a moral theory has perhaps been made easier or more relevant by a movie or a novel, so, too, might a good background knowledge of moral theories enhance your enjoyment of a fictional story. I know it has for me. There are lots of issues out there, nationally and globally, and lots of stories about them. Enjoy the exploration!

Study Questions

1. If you were a journalist, how might you describe the proper balance between the public's right to know and the need for national security? Would it make a difference if you were not a journalist but a member of law enforcement? Or a schoolteacher? Or a military person?

2. In your view, can a war be just? Explain in detail, referring to the text.

3. What is patriotism? Can we apply Aristotle's concept of the Golden Mean and talk about too much, the right amount, and too little patriotism? Explain.

4. Should animals have rights? If no, explain why not. If yes, explain whether your view is based on their ability to suffer, their ability to think, both, or neither.

5. Which, in your view, is the strongest argument in favor of the death penalty? Which is the strongest argument against it? In your view, should we retain or abolish capital punishment? Explain.

Primary Readings and Narratives

The first Primary Reading is an excerpt from John Rawls's book *The Law of Peoples,* in which he explores the theory of a just war. The second is an excerpt about terrorism from Jan Narveson's essay "Morality and Violence: War, Revolution, Terrorism." The third is an excerpt from Sue Savage-Rumbaugh's book *Kanzi: The Ape at the Brink of the Human Mind.* Two excerpts from books about the death penalty— one an abolitionist view, the other retentionist—conclude the Primary Readings: Stephen Nathanson's *An Eye for an Eye? The Morality of Punishing by Death,* and John Douglas and Mark Olshaker's *Journey into Darkness.* The Narratives are the film *15 Minutes,* about media ethics; the short story "The Jigsaw Man," about a utilitarian form of capital punishment; and the film *Dead Man Walking,* about Sister Helen Prejean's work with a death row inmate.

Primary Reading

The Law of Peoples

JOHN RAWLS

Excerpt, 1999.

John Rawls, whom you met in Chapter 7 as well as in this chapter, hopes in his *Law of Peoples* to outline a *realistic utopia* according to the principles of justice, recognizing that peoples should view each other as free and independent. He sees five kinds of domestic societies: *Reasonable, liberal peoples* and *decent peoples* ("nonliberal societies whose basic institutions meet certain specified conditions of political right and justice") together form the category of *well-ordered peoples;* then there are *outlaw states; societies burdened by unfavorable conditions;* and *societies of benevolent absolutisms* (societies that recognize human rights but don't allow their citizens a political voice). Here Rawls explores the right of well-ordered peoples to go to war.

Role of Nonideal Theory

To this point we have been concerned with ideal theory. In extending a liberal conception of justice, we have developed an ideal conception of a Law of Peoples for the Society of well-ordered Peoples, that is, liberal and decent peoples. That conception is to guide these well-ordered peoples in their conduct toward one another and in their designing common institutions for their mutual benefit. It is also to guide them in how to deal with non-well-ordered peoples. Before our discussion of the Law of Peoples is complete, we must therefore consider, though we cannot do so wholly adequately, the questions arising from the highly nonideal conditions of our world with its great injustices and widespread social evils. On the assumption that there exist in the world some relatively well-ordered peoples, we ask in nonideal theory how these peoples should act toward non-well-ordered peoples. We take as a basic characteristic of well-ordered peoples that they wish to live in a world in which all peoples accept and follow the (ideal of the) Law of Peoples.

Nonideal theory asks how this long-term goal might be achieved, or worked toward, usually in gradual steps. It looks for policies and courses of action that are morally permissible and politically possible as well as likely to be effective. So conceived, nonideal theory presupposes that ideal theory is already on hand. For until the ideal is identified, at least in outline — and that is all we should expect — nonideal theory lacks an objective, an aim, by reference to which its queries can be answered. Though the specific conditions of our world at any time — the status quo — do not determine the ideal conception of the Society of Peoples, those conditions do affect the specific answers to questions of nonideal theory. For these are questions of transition, of how to work from a world containing outlaw states and societies suffering from unfavorable conditions to a world in which all societies come to accept and follow the Law of Peoples.

There are [. . .] two kinds of nonideal theory. One kind deals with conditions of noncompliance, that is, with conditions in which certain regimes refuse to comply with a reasonable Law of Peoples; these regimes think a sufficient reason to engage in war is that war advances, or might advance, the regime's rational (not reasonable) interests. These regimes I call *outlaw states*. The other kind of nonideal theory deals with unfavorable conditions, that is, with the conditions of societies whose historical, social, and economic circumstances make their achieving a well-ordered regime, whether liberal or decent, difficult if not impossible. These societies I call *burdened societies*.[1]

I begin with noncompliance theory, and recall that the fifth initial principle of equality of the Law of Peoples gives well-ordered peoples a right to war in self-defense but not, as in the traditional account of sovereignty, a right to war in the rational pursuit of a state's rational interests; these alone are not a sufficient reason. Well-ordered peoples, both liberal and decent, do not initiate war against one another; they go to war only when they sincerely and reasonably believe that their safety and security are seriously endangered by the expansionist policies of outlaw states. In what follows, I work out the content of the principles of the Law of Peoples for the conduct of war.

Well-Ordered Peoples' Right to War

No state has a right to war in the pursuit of its *rational,* as opposed to its *reasonable,* interests. The Law of Peoples does, however, assign to all well-ordered peoples (both liberal and decent), and indeed to any society that follows and honors a reasonably just Law of Peoples, the right to war in self-defense.[2] Although all well-ordered societies have

---

[1] There are also other possibilities. Some states are not well-ordered and violate human rights, but are not aggressive and do not harbor plans to attack their neighbors. They do not suffer from unfavorable conditions, but simply have a state policy that violates the human rights of certain minorities among them. They are therefore outlaw states because they violate what are recognized as rights by the Society of reasonably just and decent Peoples, and they may be subject to some kind of intervention in severe cases. [. . .]

[2] The right to war normally includes the right to help to defend one's allies.

this right, they may interpret their actions in a different way depending on how they think of their ends and purposes. I will note some of these differences.

When a liberal society engages in war in self-defense, it does so to protect and preserve the basic freedoms of its citizens and its constitutionally democratic political institutions. Indeed, a liberal society cannot justly require its citizens to fight in order to gain economic wealth or to acquire natural resources, much less to win power and empire.[3] (When a society pursues these interests, it no longer honors the Law of Peoples, and it becomes an outlaw state.) To trespass on citizens' liberty by conscription, or other such practices in raising armed forces, may only be done on a liberal political conception for the sake of liberty itself, that is, as necessary to defend liberal democratic institutions and civil society's many religious and nonreligious traditions and forms of life.[4]

The special significance of liberal constitutional government is that through its democratic politics, and by following the idea of public reason, citizens can express their conception of their society and take actions appropriate to its defense. That is, ideally, citizens work out a *truly* political opinion, and not simply an opinion about what would best advance their own particular interests, of whatever kind, as members of civil society. Such (truly political) citizens develop an opinion of the rights and wrongs of political right and justice, and of what the well-being of different parts of society requires. As in *Political Liberalism,* each citizen is regarded as having what I have called "the two moral powers"—a capacity for a sense of justice and a capacity for a conception of the good. It is also assumed that each citizen has, at any time, a conception of the good compatible with a comprehensive religious, philosophical, or moral doctrine. These capacities enable citizens to fulfill their role as citizens and underwrite their political and civic autonomy. The principles of justice protect citizens' higher-order interests; these are guaranteed within the framework of the liberal constitution and the basic structure of society. These institutions establish a reasonably just setting within which the background culture[5] of civil society may flourish.

Decent peoples also have a right to war in self-defense. They would describe what they are defending differently from the way a liberal people would; but decent peoples also have something worth defending. For example, the rulers of the imagined decent people, Kazanistan, could rightly defend their decent hierarchical Muslim society. They allow and respect members of different faiths within their society, and they respect the political institutions of other societies, including non-Muslim and liberal societies. They also respect and honor human rights; their basic structure contains a decent consultation hierarchy; and they accept and abide by a (reasonable) Law of Peoples.

The fifth kind of society listed earlier—a *benevolent absolutism*—would also appear to have the right to war in self-defense. While a benevolent absolutism does respect and honor human rights, it is not a well-ordered society, since it does not give its members a meaningful role in making political decisions. But *any* society that is nonaggressive and that honors human rights has the right of self-defense. Its level of spiritual life and

---

[3] Of course, so-called liberal societies sometimes do this, but that only shows they may act wrongly.

[4] See *A Theory of Justice,* sec. 58, pp. 380ff.

[5] See *Political Liberalism,* p. 14.

culture may not be high in our eyes, but it always has the right to defend itself against invasion of its territory.

Study Questions

1. What are the two kinds of nonideal theories, and what is Rawls's purpose in introducing the concept?

2. When do well-ordered peoples have a right to go to war, according to Rawls? Would you agree? Why or why not?

3. What are "the two moral powers"? What roles do they play in society, and how do they complement each other?

 Primary Reading

Morality and Violence: War, Revolution, Terrorism

JAN NARVESON

Essay published in the anthology **Matters of Life and Death,** *1993. Excerpt.*

Jan Narveson, a libertarian philosopher, explores the nature and function of terrorism in this essay written years before September 11, 2001, but well within the modern era of terrorist acts. He asks the question whether terrorism is ever justified, and whether terrorists deserve to air their grievances and be heard.

In recent times, the use of political terrorism has been much too prominent for comfort. As the term suggests, terrorism has a major psychological dimension. Hooded figures appear out of nowhere, spraying an airport with bullets from automatic weapons; car bombs go off; civilian hostages are taken. These things do physical damage, indeed; but their main purpose is to frighten us, thus (so the terrorist reasons) to compel us or our leaders to accept a political program or act that we would not otherwise accept. "Terror" arises because the terrorist is intentionally indiscriminate: anyone can be targeted, and even those not targeted can easily be in the way of an assassin, especially one whose modus operandi is the time bomb or other means lacking immediate control. The fact that damage to the innocent might well ensue doesn't worry the terrorist at all—but it *does* worry us.

Terrorism is, then, a sort of war, waged on behalf of political causes; but unlike ordinary wars, which are "up front," this war is in the shadows. And it is so because those fomenting it are too weak to wage open warfare, where it is clear who the combatants are. So terrorism is (quite reasonably) seen as underhanded, "sneaky," disreputable.

This characterization calls for an important distinction between two very different contexts of employment of terror. On the one hand we have "insurgent" terrorism, that used by groups on the *outside* of official political power, as exemplified by the Red Army in Germany and Italy, the Irish Republican Army, several Palestinian organizations, and so on. On the other hand we have "state" terrorism, employed by those very officials themselves: the Stalinist regime with its "Gulag Archipelago," the dread SS troops of the Nazis, the Czarist secret police, assassination squads in some Latin American countries. What these two kinds of terrorism have in common is their shadowy, extralegal (or in the case of state terrorism, often spuriously legal) character, so that victims can't predict what will happen to them nor appeal to regular sources of redress. But they differ drastically in the extent of their effects.

Of the two, state terrorism is the overwhelmingly greater in the extent of evils done. Millions of victims fell to Eastern European Communism, Nazism, and other evil regimes, as against thousands at the hands of "insurgents." Condemnation of state terrorism is easy. There is no question about whether to disapprove of regimes that resort to such methods to secure themselves in power and defend their policies: they are simply evil, ghastly monstrosities masquerading as real governments devoted, however fuzzily, to the good of their people. For that reason we will talk only of insurgent terrorism from here on, hoping that we will have sufficiently averted the risk of leaving the reader with the impression that this is the only sort there is.

Insurgent terrorists are characteristically weak. If they could command real armies with a serious chance of winning, they would engage the forces of the state in open battle. As it is, they can do little real damage — the number of victims of this kind of terrorism is comparatively small. (Even in Ireland, the total number of deaths from terrorism doesn't nearly equal the rate from auto accidents, say.) This type of terrorist is, then, in a kind of strategic dilemma. Can he create enough fear to win the concessions he aims for? But there is a problem. He cannot do anything else, being too weak. And a rare outburst will not do the trick. On the other hand, a really substantial campaign of terror, if he can manage that, will have at least two drawbacks from his point of view: first, it will put the established order's counterterrorism facilities in high gear, which could easily be fatal to the Movement. Second, if terrorism becomes the order of the day, people become calloused and blasé, as in Lebanon: the terrorist no longer inspires the sort of terror by which alone he can hope to be effective. Terrorists become a terrible nuisance, but that is all.

The trouble in this regard is that the terrorist trades on what is in fact an irrational tendency in human nature — the tendency to magnify unexpected and "mysterious" evils out of their true proportion. And the cure is a dose of rationality, plus a modicum of courage. The life expectancy of the average citizen is very little reduced by terrorism, whereas the expected evil if we accede to the terrorists' demands is great. The statesman, therefore, won't be cowed, but will soldier on.

There are other problems inherent in the use of terrorist methods as well. To forward their cause, terrorists must publicize the fact that it was they who threw the bomb, or whatever. But such publicity sets people on the road to tracking them down and destroying them, for terrorist groups are never strong enough to resist real armies or well-organized and well-armed police. Besides, those who resort to terrorist tactics inspire hatred, which is hardly a propitious environment for an aspirant to political power. If we know what these evil people can do when they are weak, what could we expect if they were strong? Our motivation to make sure they do not become so is redoubled with every victim.

Is terrorism ever justified? Are there any circumstances and any causes which would allow moral resort to such tactics? One is tempted to answer in the negative. Unfortunately, terrorism has been disconcertingly effective in the past: in Ireland, earlier in this century; in Israel in the late 1940s; and on many other occasions. And while we may take the view that no possible end could justify such evil means, this may be just lack of perspective. The German officers' plot to assassinate Hitler in 1944 was of the same general kind of terrorism, but few of us think it was morally unjustified.

Insofar as terrorism has worked, why has it? For two rather different reasons, I believe. On the one hand, those in charge have concluded that they're better off knuckling under to the threats than attempting further to resist them. On the other, and I believe more importantly, those in charge have concluded that their own position is untenable. Sometimes what they conclude is that it is *morally* untenable. The terrorists are seen, after all, to be supporting the just cause.

Clearly that should not happen. Terrorism is prima facie unjust, as is all violence. If people resort to using terrorist methods, why do they do so? It must be because they see no chance of their proposals being adopted by the powers that be if they confine themselves to more civilized methods. But if their proposals are just, they should be acceptable to people, and hence popular. Either those proposals are not so good after all, or the state against whom the terrorist methods are being used is unjustly subjugating its populace. In the latter case, if terrorist methods are used in a selective manner, against the officials of the regime rather than the general populace, there may be some expectation of success, since the populace may be presumed to sympathize with the aims of the terrorists. The efforts of officials to track down the terrorists and root them out will be thwarted by a populace not inclined to cooperate with them. A government that rules only by force can perhaps be brought down by determined persons using such tactics. The cost of doing so is high, of course. But there may be literally no other way, in which case the question is whether the result is worth the cost. Many of those killed will surely be innocent even if they are officials of the regime, not to mention others who are not connected with nor sympathetic to it. One who throws bombs and the like has a lot to answer for, and the answers had better be good ones. But it is difficult to argue that the use of terrorist tactics cannot possibly be morally justified, for the same reason that military means cannot be ruled out when all else (or at least, enough else) fails. Thus, we have noted the existence of terror inspired in a populace by its own government: people snatched from their beds and dragged off to the gulag, or tortured and shot in miserable dungeons, opposition members disappearing without a trace. Governments that rule by these methods are, one may plausibly argue, the most purely and absolutely evil of all human agencies on earth. Such regimes do not deserve the support of their people or of anyone else, and almost any sort of rebellion that has any chance of success against them is likely to be justified. Indeed, the fact that a regime is seen as a *terrorist regime* in that sense, ruling exclusively by force, is itself a principal cause of counterterrorism by insurgents. The least we can do is be aware of, and publicize as much as possible, the facts about such regimes, hoping to inspire some kind of redress by whatever means—and be thankful that democratic governments, whatever their other vices, are at least largely free of such tactics. (We should also not complacently think that they are entirely free of them, nor that the relatively civilized impositions of democratic governments on their citizens are of no account.)

In conclusion, we cannot condemn terrorists absolutely, without giving their cause a hearing. Indeed, the impossibility of *getting* a sufficient hearing by standard means is probably one of the main causes of the resort to terrorism. And if our hearing finds that they have a point, then we must do something about it; else we leave the terrorists in the situation of saying, "Well, that's our point: we *must* act like this, for otherwise we just continue to suffer." But beyond that? Clearly we must not knuckle under to the terrorists' threats simply because they are threats. To do that is to give way to greater evils to come.

Study Questions

1. Define the two types of terrorism according to Narveson's guidelines. Do the terrorist attacks of September 11 fall within either category? Explain.

2. What, to Narveson, is it in particular that terrorists trade on? And what is the antidote? In light of September 11, do you agree? Why or why not?

3. What should a civilized nation do to combat terrorism, according to Narveson? How does that compare to the war on terrorism? Do you agree with Narveson? Why or why not?

4. Narveson argues that we should not altogether refuse to listen to the grievances of terrorists. In light of September 11, do you agree? Why or why not? In your view, are there any grievances that would legitimate the deliberate targeting of civilians? Explain.

Primary Reading

Kanzi: The Ape at the Brink of the Human Mind

SUE SAVAGE-RUMBAUGH AND ROGER LEWIN

1994. Excerpt.

Sue Savage-Rumbaugh's work with Kanzi at Georgia State University's Language Research Center during the first fourteen years of his life is documented in the book *Kanzi*. He was born in 1980 and has by now surpassed many of the linguistic skills described in the book, as has his sister Panbanisha. In this excerpt Savage-Rumbaugh argues that because behavioral science has forced animal behaviorists to avoid anthropomorphic language at all costs (language comparing animals to humans), important insight into the obvious similarities between apes and humans in terms of thought and feeling has been overlooked.

The physical world that surrounds us is of a different order from the animal world. The greater the degree of development of the nervous system, the more these two worlds differ in kind. The purpose of complex nervous systems is to permit flexible actions, unique to each situation. To the extent that organisms take in environmental information and make decisions about future actions, they become increasingly different from inanimate matter and require different paradigms for their study.

Once organisms have developed nervous systems sufficiently complex to postulate presumed goals and/or intentions for other living creatures, a world based on the moment-by-moment interpretations of the intent of others will arise. That is, it will be the presumed intent behind the behavior, rather than the specific actions themselves, that will mold the response of the observer. Certainly, humans and apes have entered the world of interpreted intent, and I suspect that a number of other animals have done so as well.

Some students of animal behavior have sought to escape the limitations posed by the laboratory by engaging in fieldwork. They rightly argue that by observing an animal in its natural habitat, one does not arbitrarily constrain the range of options available to it. The view that the behavior of animals is fundamentally different from that of man nonetheless manages to hold sway, even among those who do field observations. This is, in part, because a special language has been devised to describe and label behaviors of animals in nature. This devised language carefully avoids using any terms that we would apply to similar human behaviors. The taboo against using terms reserved for humans to describe the behavior of animals becomes most apparent when we observe apes. If a chimpanzee frowns and presses his lips together in a display of anger, either feigned or real, fieldworkers do not say he was mad; they say he displayed a bulged lips face. When he smiles and hugs another animal after a fisticuffs, they say he displayed an open-mouth bared-teeth grin and an arm around. Field researchers are admonished to speak in this manner in order to avoid the bugbear of anthropomorphism—the act of attributing human emotions to animals.

Consequently, out of fear that we might see a humanlike emotion where it does not exist, we design ways of speaking that permit us to talk about animal behavior without attributing any humanlike emotion to the animals whatsoever. We therefore approach the study of the animal mind with the unwritten assumption that it would be an error of the greatest magnitude if we were to conclude wrongly, in any circumstance, that an animal (even one that shares 99 percent of our DNA) felt as we do when angry or happy. Thus, even when we observe the animal in nature, the way we are taught as scientists to ask our questions, to structure our data, and to discuss what we see, constrains the conclusions we permit ourselves to find.

What if we were to assume at least partial continuity of emotional expression and intelligence between animals and man and thus permit ourselves to talk about animal behavior in a new light? We might risk the error of sometimes attributing capacities that did not exist, but we would surely find humanlike capacities that do exist but are currently hidden from us by the blinders we press over our eyes. Would the error of sometimes erroneously attributing capacities that did not exist be greater than that of never discovering any emotional or intellectual capacities that were continuous with our own? I think not. At the very least, if one scientist made a mistake and attributed some capacity to an animal that was far beyond its true ability, another scientist would come along and correct this mistake. As the situation currently stands, we don't even have the right to make the mistake. We should be able to ask questions about how animals perceive their worlds, their roles in those worlds, and what kinds of events or relationships alter these perceptions. It seems to me that this is what a science of animal behavior should be about.

I am not the first to suggest that we need to look at animal behavior through a different lens. Donald Griffin has been urging us to do so since the 1970s. Why are so many behavioral scientists still unable to break out of their constraints? The problem lies in part in the omniscience we attribute to the human mind, an omniscience that we believe is made possible by the gift of language. Even students of behavior who would not deny minds to animals nonetheless maintain there is no way of gaining access to the animal mind; consequently, they believe the issue is, like that of religious experience, beyond science. I suggest that we expand our ways of doing science to encompass such questions.

The essence of the difference between the human and the animal mind is often claimed to be that man can reflect upon his actions while animals, lacking words, cannot. Crucial to this view is the underlying and unspoken premise that language is the only possible means of reflection. Without language how can we ask an animal what it is thinking? And without language how can it tell us? And if it cannot tell us, how can we legitimately assume that it is thinking?

Once, while riding in the car through the woods with Kanzi's sister Panbanisha, I noted she appeared to be very quiet and pensive. I was moved to ask her what she was thinking—a question I generally avoid since I have no means of validating the answer, nor even of determining if an ape understands the question. Occasionally, when I have posed this question in the past, I have generally been ignored. However, at this moment Panbanisha looked literally lost in thought, and so I dared. She seemed to reflect upon the question a few seconds and then answered [via lexigram] "Kanzi." I was very surprised, as she almost never uses Kanzi's name. I replied, "Oh, you are thinking about Kanzi, are you?" and she vocalized in agreement, "Whuh, whuh, whuh."

Similarly, one time I was riding in a car with Heather, one of the [human] children in our project, through the very same area of woods. Heather was two years of age and just beginning to form sentences. She, like Panbanisha, typically ignored questions like "What are you thinking about?" But, like Panbanisha, at this moment she appeared lost in thought and so I dared to inquire. She replied "Mommy." I asked, "Do you wish your Mommy was here?" and she nodded her head.

I cannot be certain that either Panbanisha or Heather was really thinking. Currently there is no way to establish scientific consensus regarding the inner thoughts of another person. Yet it seems that credence should be given to the fact that both Heather and Panbanisha, on occasions when they appeared pensive, elected to answer the question. On other occasions, when they were engaged in other activities, the question was ignored as though it were nonsensical. These observations suggest that it is possible that children and apes think in a reflexive sense, even before they are competent language users. Could it be that they think in some way other than with words?

Thought, or the manipulation of one's mental model of the world, surely must take place in the absence of language, utilizing neurological machinery that services the channels of perception through which the world is viewed. It requires but a moment's reflection to recognize that humans engaged in complex nonverbal activities—such as in dance, music, sculpting, and athletic skills—depend on wordless thought. To suggest otherwise "is a notion that only a college professor or other professional wordsmith could have ever taken seriously."

Mary Midgley, the British philosopher of science, puts the issue more generally: "If language were really the only source of conceptual order, all animals except man would live in a totally disordered world. They could not be said to vary in intelligence, since they could not have the use of anything that could reasonably be called intelligence at all. . . . The truth seems to be that—even for humans—a great deal of the order in the world is pre-verbally determined, being the gift of faculties we share with other animals." Nonhuman animals quite evidently live in ordered worlds, an outcome of their own cognitive processes. Without such mental ordering, the management of the myriad interactions among other members of a community and the efficient exploitation of a diverse resource base would be nearly impossible. There is no question that language enhances thought processes, permitting a more intricate and powerful manipulation of mental worlds. But this is surely an extension of faculties already in place, not the establishment of something novel. Spoken language, and the thoughts it mediates, is built on the same neurological foundation that underlies thinking in nonhuman animals.

Study Questions

1. Why has behavioral science enforced an avoidance of "anthropomorphic language" in descriptions of animal behavior? What has the effect been, according to Savage-Rumbaugh?

2. What is Savage-Rumbaugh trying to tell us with her stories of Panbanisha and Heather? Do you think she is right in her assessment of their inner life?

3. In your view, can apes think without words? Can you? If so, what might that entail for our future treatment of apes and other intelligent nonhuman animals? What might Immanuel Kant say to this discussion?

Primary Reading

An Eye for an Eye? The Morality of Punishing by Death

STEPHEN NATHANSON

Excerpt. 1987.

Stephen Nathanson, a philosophy professor at Northeastern University, argues for abolitionism. He sees the death penalty as an affront to the humanity of everyone, including the criminal, and a state-sanctioned way to continue the cycle of violence.

According to the *lex talionis* or principle of "an eye for an eye" we ought to treat people as they have treated others. What people deserve as recipients of rewards or punishment is determined by what they do as agents. [. . .] Applied strictly, it would require that we rape rapists, torture torturers and burn arsonists whose acts have led to deaths. [. . .] This is not its only defect. In many other cases, the principle tells us nothing at all about how to punish [. . .] what would we decide to do to embezzlers, spies, drunken drivers, airline hijackers, drug users, prostitutes, air polluters, or persons who practice medicine without a license? If one reflects on this question, it becomes clear that there is simply no answer to it. We could not in fact design a system of punishment simply on the basis of the "eye for an eye" principle.

In order to justify using the "eye for an eye" principle to answer our question about murder and the death penalty, we would first have to show that it worked for a whole range of cases, giving acceptable answers to questions about amounts of punishment. Then, having established it as a satisfactory general principle, we could apply it to the case of murder. It turns out, however, that when we try to apply the principle generally, we find that it either gives wrong answers or no answers at all. Indeed, I suspect that the principle of "an eye for an eye" is no longer even a principle. Instead, it is simply a metaphorical disguise for expressing belief in the death penalty. People who cite it do not take it seriously. They do not believe in a kidnapping for a kidnapping, a theft for a theft, and so on. Perhaps "an eye for an eye" once was a genuine principle, but now it is merely a slogan. Therefore, it gives us no guidance in deciding whether murderers deserve to die.

In reply to these objections, one might defend the principle by saying that it does not require that punishment be strictly identical with crimes. Rather, it requires only that a punishment produce an amount of suffering in the criminal which is equal to the amount suffered by the victim. [. . .] Unfortunately, this reply really does not solve the problem. [. . .] Just how much suffering is produced by an airline hijacker or a spy? And how do we apply the principle to prostitutes or drug users, who may not produce any suffering at all? We have rough ideas about how serious various crimes are, but this may not correlate with any clear sense of just how much harm is done.

Furthermore, the same problem arises in determining how much suffering a particular punishment would produce for a particular criminal. People vary in their tolerance of pain and in the amount of unhappiness that a fine or jail sentence would cause them. Recluses would be less disturbed by banishment than extroverts. Nature lovers will suffer more in prison than people who are indifferent to natural beauty. A literal application of the principle [of "an eye for an eye"] would require that we tailor punishments to individual sensitivities, yet this is at best impractical. [. . .]

What is the symbolic message that we would convey by deciding to renounce the death penalty and to abolish its use?

I think that there are two primary messages. The first is the most frequently emphasized and it is usually expressed in terms of the sanctity of human life, although I think we could better express it in terms of human dignity. One way we express our respect for the dignity of human beings is by abstaining from depriving them of their lives, even if they have done terrible deeds. In defense of human well-being, we may punish people for their crimes, but we ought not to deprive them of everything, which is what the death penalty does.

[. . .] But, one might ask, hasn't the murderer forfeited whatever rights he might have had to our respect? Hasn't he, by his deeds, given up any rights that he had to decent treatment? Aren't we morally free to kill him if we wish? [. . .] Certainly, when people murder or commit other crimes, they do forfeit some of the rights that are possessed by the law-abiding. They lose a certain right to be left alone. It becomes permissible to bring them to trial and, if they are convicted, to impose an appropriate—even a dreadful—punishment on them.

Nonetheless, they do not forfeit all their rights. [. . .] No matter how terrible a person's deeds, we may not punish him in a cruel and unusual way. We may not torture him, for example. His right not to be tortured has not been forfeited. Why do these limits hold? Because this person remains a human being, and we think there is something in him that we must continue to respect in spite of his terrible acts. [. . .]

[The second symbolic message:] We want to avoid the cycle of violence that can come from retaliation and counter-retaliation. Violence is a contagion that arouses hatred and anger, and if unchecked, it simply leads to still more violence. The state can convey the message that the contagion must be stopped, and the most effective principle for stopping it is the idea that only defensive violence is justifiable. Since the death penalty is not an instance of defensive violence, it ought to be renounced.

Study Questions

1. Is Nathanson right that the death penalty is not an instance of defensive violence? Why or why not?

2. Nathanson doesn't believe in the idea of proportional justice (an eye for an eye) as a defense of the death penalty. Can you think of a defense of the death penalty (a retentionist argument) that doesn't imply the principle of "an eye for an eye"?

3. Nathanson wants to abolish the death penalty to send symbolic messages of respect for humans and stop the cycle of violence. Can you think of a symbolic message implied in the retentionist position?

Primary Reading

Journey into Darkness

JOHN DOUGLAS AND MARK OLSHAKER

Excerpt. 1997.

John Douglas is not a professional philosopher, although his years as a profiler for the FBI have prompted him to philosophize about the nature of crime and punishment. Here he argues for a limited use of the death penalty, reserved for extreme cases, from the perspective of the victims and their families rather than from that of the rights of the criminal. In other words, Douglas is a retentionist.

Capital punishment is one of those issues like abortion. Not many of us are ever going to change anyone's opinion about it, one way or the other. If you are against the death penalty on moral grounds, I think a case can be made for putting away the worst of these monsters for life with no possibility they will ever be let out or paroled. But we know that there is no such thing. And frankly, in certain cases, I don't think it's enough.

As [special agent and profiler] Steve Mardigian put it, "The tremendous devastation against victims warrants that we do something appropriately serious. In my view, we have no reason to keep people capable of inflicting this kind of horror alive."

Some would argue that capital punishment is "legalized murder" and therefore an immoral act on the part of society. My personal feeling is that these offenders have made a choice to remove themselves from society and therefore it is a moral statement to say that society will not tolerate the perpetrator of this kind of horrible act in its midst.

Asserting that capital punishment is legalized murder does a tremendous injury, in my opinion, to the very concept of right and wrong, in that it trivializes the crucial distinction between the victim of the crime and its perpetrator—the innocent life and the one who chose for his own vile reasons to take that innocent life.

If you ask me if I'm personally prepared to throw the switch that would legally end the life on earth of [serial killers] Sedley Alley, Larry Gene Bell, Paul Bernardo, Lawrence Bittaker, or others of their ilk, my answer would be a resounding "Yes!" And for those who talk of forgiveness, I'll tell them I am sympathetic to the concept, but at the same time I do not feel I am authorized to forgive; it's not my place.

Had Sedley Alley *merely* (and I use this word with some trepidation) raped, beaten, and tortured Suzanne Collins, but left her alive and her mental faculties intact, then she, and only she, would have been in a position to forgive him if she so chose. And as far as I'm concerned, she remains the only one capable of forgiving him, but because of what actually did happen, she can only do so now *after* his jury-imposed sentence has been carried out. [. . .]

Now, on the subject of deterrence, I admit that there can be little doubt that as presently administered in the United States, the death penalty is not a general deterrent to murder in many, if not most, situations. Common sense should tell us that if you're a young urban criminal making your living off the drug trade where there are huge amounts of money at stake and your business competition is out there trying to kill you every day, the dim prospect of a possible death sentence and execution somewhere at the end of a fifteen year procedural morass—that is, if you get caught, if you don't plea bargain, if you draw a tough judge and a tough jury, if you don't get reversed, if they don't change the law, et cetera, et cetera—isn't much of a deterrent, or a risk, for that matter, compared to the occupational hazards you face on the street every day of your working life. So let's be realistic about that aspect of this argument.

If the death penalty were applied more evenly and uniformly, and if the period of time from sentence to execution were reduced to a reasonable matter of months rather than a protracted period of years or even the decades that people like the Collinses have had to endure, then perhaps it would become more useful in dissuading would-be offenders in certain types of murders. But frankly, this theoretical speculation doesn't concern me all that much. Meted out fairly and consistently, perhaps the death penalty could become a general deterrent; I'm not certain and I wouldn't be optimistic about it.

But of one thing I am certain: it is, by God, a specific deterrent. No one who has been executed has ever taken another innocent life. And until such time as we really mean it as a society when we say "imprisonment for life," I, and the families of countless victims, would sleep better at night knowing there is no chance that the worst of these killers will ever again be able to prey on others. Even then, I personally believe that if you choose to take another human life, you ought to be prepared to pay with your own. [. . .]

Then there's the argument that rather than killing these guys, we should keep them alive "for study." I'm not sure what people mean by this; I don't think they know, themselves. I suppose they mean that if we study enough of them long enough, we'll figure out why they kill and what we can do to stop them.

Now as it happens, my colleagues at Quantico and I are among the few professionals who actually have studied these people. If anyone has a stake, therefore, in keeping them alive for intellectual reasons, it's us. And here's my response to that: If they're willing to talk to me at all, there is plenty of time during the protracted appeals process. If they're only willing to talk—as Ted Bundy ultimately was—as a bargaining chip for staying alive longer, then what they tell me is going to be tainted and self-serving anyway. When you tell me we should keep someone like Bundy alive to study, I say, "Fine, keep him alive six hours longer; that's all I need." I really don't think we're going to get much more beyond that. [. . .]

But no responsible discussion of the death penalty can fail to include reflection on the fact that our legal system is imperfect and there is always the chance that the wrong man will be convicted. Inevitably, in any consideration of capital punishment, we must confront the example of David Vasquez. And much as we may hate to admit it, his copping of an Alford plea might have saved his life. [Douglas explains the Alford plea as "not a guilty plea but acknowledging that the prosecution has sufficient evidence to try and convict the defendant of a more serious crime."]

The fact that this was a rare, odd type of case in which the [innocent] defendant actually confessed, not once, but three times, should not give us too much comfort or reassurance. At the same time, I don't think this is a valid argument for scrapping the death penalty altogether.

What I think it is a valid argument for is the insistence on an overwhelming amount and degree of proof. And while some might argue that you can never be absolutely sure, I think in the kinds of cases I'm talking about, you can be sure enough that innocent people like Vasquez will not go wrongly to their deaths.

The types of offenders I most want to see face the ultimate penalty are the repeat, predatory, sexually motivated killers. By the time we catch them there is generally a mountain of solid, behaviorally consistent, forensic evidence against them. As with Cleophus Prince, if he did one of the murders, he did all of them. If there isn't a sufficiently formidable mountain of evidence, then don't execute. But if there is, as there was against

Bell, as there is against Alley and Bernardo and Bittaker and so many others, then do what needs to be done. [. . .]

So how do you prioritize all our concerns and all the things we might wish the criminal justice system to be? To me, it's innocent potential victims first, victims of violent crime and their families second, and defendants and their families last. First and foremost, I'll do anything I can to see to it that someone does not become the victim of someone who has already committed a similar crime. Failing that, I want to bring victims and their families to the forefront of the system, to give them the due that is rightly theirs. And then I want to make sure that defendants get a fair trial and convicted felons receive appropriate sentences for their crimes. None of these need be mutually exclusive.

Does this mean I think we need a police state? Of course not. It means simply what it says—that we need to keep our priorities straight if we hope to be a just and civilized society.

Study Questions

1. The debate about the death penalty is often polarized into a "criminal's rights" view versus a "victim's rights" view. Do these two viewpoints have to be opposed, or can you think of some common ground?

2. Douglas argues that the death penalty should be reserved for the kind of murderer who isn't likely to change, such as serial killers and child molester/killers. Would you agree that (1) there are people who are essentially unredeemable? (2) the best way for society to deal with them is killing them? Why or why not?

3. Does Douglas's view reflect the theory of retribution? Deterrence? Incapacitation? Revenge?

4. Often abolitionists argue that executions are nothing but state-sanctioned murder, that the right to life ought to be considered inalienable, and that the state stoops to the level of the murderer by taking the life of a citizen. How does Douglas respond? What is your opinion?

Narrative

15 Minutes

JOHN HERZFELD (SCREENWRITER AND DIRECTOR)

Film, 2001.

The American avant-garde artist Andy Warhol once said that in the future, everyone will be famous for fifteen minutes. He was referring to the mass-media hunger for news, feeding on brief stories about individual lives. You've seen this quote in Chapter 7, in *The Insider.*

Movie reviewers weren't very kind to the film bearing the promising title *15 Minutes,* and it wasn't much of a box office success, either, but I find that it is far better than its reputation, especially in raising the question of media responsibility. As you read in Box 13.1, opinions differ on how far a TV network might go in terms of securing an exclusive story. Would they choose to air a videotaped murder? *15 Minutes* speculates that some tabloid show might do just that, for the sake of ratings.

In addition, the theme of what might happen when a fascination for Hollywood and the movies goes bad links this film up with our discussion about Hollywood influence in Chapter 2.

Two men go through immigration in New York; one, Oleg, is a Russian with a Hollywood fixation. He explains to the immigration officer that he has come to America because he saw *It's a Wonderful Life.* The other is Emil, a Czech, who has acquaintances in New York who owe him money. On the way to visit Emil's acquaintances Oleg steals a video camera. When they reach their destination and it turns out that his friend can't pay Emil what he owes him, Emil kills him and his wife with a kitchen knife. Meanwhile, Oleg is filming the event in detail, the first step toward fulfilling his dream of becoming an American film director.

Emil, having no intention of letting a couple of murders stop him, seeks to cover up the crime by setting fire to the apartment — but someone is watching from an adjacent bathroom: a woman. She flees down the stairs but has left her purse behind. So Emil and Oleg set out to find her.

Meanwhile, we encounter the host of a New York tabloid show, Robert Hawkins. His producer is trying to tone down the violent style of his show, but Hawkins is adamant: If they don't run a violent story, someone else will — and besides, what is a better lead story? "If it bleeds, it leads," he says.

A frequent guest on his show is popular New York police detective Eddie Fleming. His face is on the cover of magazines, and he is quite aware of his own celebrity status — but not merely because he enjoys the attention. He explains that if his fame can buy him just a little extra goodwill from the public so more crimes can be solved, then that's what he'll use it for. He may be narcissistic, but he is also a pro.

The apartment where Emil committed the murders and set the fire is now burned out, and the New York Fire Department takes control of the scene. A young arson inspector, Jordy Warsaw, finds to his dismay that NYPD and star detective Fleming are already there. At first Fleming thinks it is an accident, but he bows to the younger man's expertise when he shows him evidence of its being arson, and thus a murder scene.

In the meantime, Oleg and Emil are watching TV in a cheap hotel room and see Hawkins interview a serial killer who has been deemed temporarily insane. Emil's reaction: "I love America — nobody is responsible for what they do!" In an attempt to find the female witness, they call an escort service, dialing a number they found on a card in her purse. The woman who shows up from the escort service isn't the witness — but they murder her when she won't give out the escort service's address. (And Oleg films the entire incident.) Later, when the police and Fleming investigate this new crime scene, they find that she has been murdered with the same knife that was used in the arson murders.

Fleming, at home, hears a noise outside, investigates, and sees nothing—but in the meantime Emil and Oleg make their way into his apartment, attack him, and tie him to a chair with duct tape while Oleg films it all. Emil, with the logic of a madman, explains his plan to Fleming: They will kill someone famous and film it—which will prove they're crazy, because who else but crazy men would film their crimes? Then a judge will sentence them to a mental hospital instead of prison, but in the hospital they will reveal that they are sane, and because of the American double-jeopardy law (you cannot be tried for the same crime twice), they will be set free, sell their film to Hollywood, and become rich.

Fleming, knowing himself to be in a desperate predicament, fights back every way he can, using the chair he is strapped into as a weapon, but in the end it does him no good: While Oleg films everything, Fleming is knifed by Emil and dies.

Now Hawkins is approached by Emil and Oleg. They have a story worth a lot of money: a tape of Fleming's death. Will he buy it? And will he air it? Indeed, Hawkins shows up at the arranged place and buys the tape. Oleg films the exchange of the tape and the briefcase full of cash. When Hawkins arrives back at the TV station, Fleming's police colleagues try to talk sense to him and beg him for the tape, but it is too late: Minutes later, it is being broadcast all over New York and beyond, with Hawkins's introduction stating that he, as a journalist, feels obliged to show it.

As Oleg and Emil are watching the broadcast in a restaurant, their fellow patrons are horrified by what they see on the giant TV in the middle of their dinner, and when they hear the two men quarreling over the movie rights, they recognize them from the televised tape. In short order Emil is caught; Oleg disappears into the crowd.

Several twists and turns of the plot lead us to a final resurfacing of Oleg. Enraged that Emil, having found a lawyer who will argue that he was legally insane and that Oleg planned the whole thing, is found incompetent and indeed will escape punishment, Oleg has a trump card: the tape where Emil tells Fleming of his plan, effectively proving that he was legally sane and responsible for his crimes. What does Oleg do with this tape? Will he succeed in becoming a famous American film director? Will Hawkins have a change of heart about what constitutes media ethics? I will leave that for you to experience on your own.

Study Questions

1. In your opinion, was Hawkins acting responsibly as a journalist when he chose to air Fleming's death scene? Why or why not? Remember that Hawkins says, "If it bleeds, it leads," but that he also says it is his duty as a journalist to show the tape. If you answered no, then what, in your view, might be the responsible action of a journalist faced with Hawkins's moral choice?

2. Oleg is obsessed with American movies, to the point that he wants to make his own. However, he also seems to think that Hollywood has given an accurate portrayal of American society. Hollywood films shown around the world may indeed give people a skewed view of life in America—but do you think there are many such as Oleg who believe this view is true? If so, what can be done about it?

3. Do you think it possible that a "reality show" such as *Survivor* might air scenes where its participants are injured or perhaps killed? Why or why not? Should they? Why or why not?

4. Emil is misinformed about the rules of double jeopardy: If a legally insane convict recovers his sanity, he can be tried as a sane person. But in order for someone to be judged insane, he or she has to be unaware of the difference between right and wrong. Might Emil, in a real-life situation, be found legally insane? Explain why or why not.

5. What does the title refer to in the context of the film?

Narrative

The Jigsaw Man

LARRY NIVEN

Short story, 1967. Summary.

This science-fiction story explores a topic that seemed far fetched in 1967 to most readers, illegal trade in organs. But reality seems to be catching up: For years Chinese dissidents who had escaped to the West told stories about the Chinese organ trade, but it wasn't until 2000 that the rumors were corroborated: Chinese prisons tailor executions of death row inmates according to the organs needed. Kidneys are especially popular; Chinese recipients pay less for them than foreign customers do, and such customers have been traced worldwide, including transplant recipients in the United States. Stories in the West about people turning up with kidneys missing may be an "urban legend," but a five-year-old Russian boy was close to being sold for parts by his grandmother in 2000, for $90,000. Niven not only speculates about the future, but also seems to express a viewpoint on capital punishment. Young Lew is in jail, awaiting his trial. He knows that the outcome will be a sentence of death. They have evidence enough to convict him, and many people are being convicted and executed these days. We are in the late part of the twenty-first century (in Larry Niven's "Known Space," a future history of Earth and the universe).

In jail, Lew is confronted with a grisly story: Two fellow inmates tell about their crime of organlegging. Organs for transplant are in high demand among wealthy people, and high prices are paid for illegally acquired organs. How does one acquire organs illegally? One kidnaps healthy people, murders them, and sells their organs. One of Lew's cellmates is the bodysnatcher; the other is the doctor performing the organ extractions. They are both scheduled for execution.

Are there no legal organ transplants in this future society? Of course there are. By this time a method has been developed to keep organs fresh indefinitely, and worthy recipients are always waiting for life-saving organs, but there are more people needing organs than there are organs made available through accidents. As a result, an alternative method has been in use for almost a century (since the 1990s): On death row are people whose death, some say, doesn't do society any good, so they are made to "atone" for what evil they did in life by having their organs serve others when they die. Organ harvesting of condemned murderers is part of the system of punishment now, so Lew's two cellmates know what awaits them: an injection, instant freezing, death, and organ extraction. However, society needs more organs than the murderers on death row can supply. So, while kidnapping was already punishable by death in some states, now other crimes have joined the list.

Suddenly there is activity in the cell: The two cellmates are pressing themselves up against the bars and invite Lew to join them: They are about to commit suicide in a way that will make the organ banks reject them. The doctor has a hollowed-out space in his leg with a bomb implanted, and in a gruesome display of blood and gore the two inmates are blown to pieces—but so is the outside wall! Lew manages to squeeze out the hole in the wall, but he is very far off the ground, up close to the roof of the building. Driven by fear, he manages to swing himself upward toward the roof, and he lands on a pedwalk moving from the jail to the adjoining building. From there he jumps to a ledge and breaks through a window, into an office. While looking for something he can use to make himself less conspicuous—a change of clothes, shaving gear, anything—he notices what building he is in. A hospital. The hospital where criminals are executed and their organs removed. He has landed in the organ bank. Moving from room to room, he tries to find a way out, but he is being tracked, and beams of tranquilizer sounds are hitting him. Desperately he looks around and realizes that he is in the room of organ tanks. Refusing to die for what he considers nothing, he grabs a chair and starts smashing tanks, and he keeps smashing tanks until he blacks out.

Final scene: Lew is in court, hearing prosecutor and defense argue about his case; to his amazement, nobody mentions the organ tanks. They have plenty on him as it is; extra charges are considered only as a backup. Lew knows that he will lose his life, but at least he also knows that he has put up a fight. And now we learn what Lew is accused of, with plenty of ironclad evidence: "The state will prove that the said Warren Lewis Knowles did, in the space of two years, willfully drive through a total of six red traffic lights. During that same period the same Warren Lewis Knowles exceeded local speed limits no less than ten times, once by as much as fifteen miles per hour."

Study Questions

1. How does this story illustrate the type of argument called a "slippery slope"?

2. In your view, can the trade in organs from executed criminals be justified? If so, how? If not, why not?

3. Is this story a criticism of a forward-looking reason for punishment or a backward-looking one? Explain.

4. How would a utilitarian respond to this story? How would a deontologist respond? Explain in detail.

Narrative

Dead Man Walking

TIM ROBBINS (SCREENWRITER AND DIRECTOR)

Film, 1995.

This story about a killer on death row and the nun who befriends him is based on factual events. The nun, Sister Helen Prejean, wrote an autobiographical book about her experiences as the spiritual adviser to death row inmates. The killer in the film, Matthew Poncelet, is actually a composite of two men.

Sister Helen lives and works in a rundown neighborhood in Angola, Louisiana, having dedicated her life to helping the poor. She receives a letter from Poncelet, a convicted murderer on death row. Reluctantly she pays him a visit at Angola State Prison against the advice of her superior, who also finds it inappropriate that she is not wearing a nun's habit. At their first meeting, Poncelet insists on his innocence and requests that Sister Helen help him with an appeal; he comes across as a braggart, an irresponsible person who even attempts to flirt with her. Sister Helen is an abolitionist and sees no legal or religious justification for the death penalty, but she is also appalled at the crime Poncelet has committed, if indeed he is guilty. He was convicted of having murdered two young lovers at night in the woods; the boy was shot to death, and the girl was raped and stabbed more than twenty times. Poncelet is placing all the blame on his accomplice and on the fact that they were drunk and on drugs. But the accomplice is not on death row; he had a better lawyer and was released after five years. In the course of the film, however, the audience learns through flashbacks that Poncelet is definitely guilty, along with his friend.

Sister Helen finds an appeals lawyer for Poncelet and visits Poncelet's mother. Here we realize that there are more victims in this case than the two teens who were murdered and their families; the killer's family members are, in their own way, also victims of his crime. They suffer not only feelings of shame and guilt and grief for a loved one who went wrong but also the scorn of the community.

During the hearing the lawyer puts up a passionate defense for abolitionism: The death penalty has been with us for a long time, he says; we think we have found a humane method, lethal injection, but it is still a barbaric thing for a state to do to an individual. It may look peaceful on the outside, but that is only because the condemned person's muscles have been paralyzed. The torment of the lungs and other organs is not noticed by onlookers.

But Poncelet's appeal fails, and his execution is scheduled to take place in six days. Now Poncelet requests that Sister Helen become his spiritual adviser. She realizes that if she is to become his spiritual adviser — the first female adviser to a condemned prisoner — her main task will be to make him admit to the dreadful thing he has done, to reach a full comprehension of his crime. The concern of the church is of course with the redemption of Poncelet's soul, because without a heartfelt admission of his guilt, his soul won't be saved. However, Sister Helen's effort to make him understand what he has done

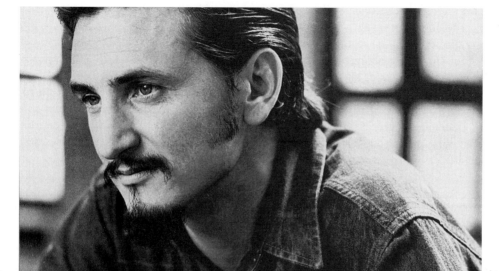

In the film *Dead Man Walking,* Matthew Poncelet (Sean Penn) has been found guilty of murder and is awaiting his execution, having exhausted all appeals. Sister Helen Prejean, his spiritual adviser, believes that her main duty to him is to help him to understand what he has done and to feel contrition, so that his soul will be saved. We see in flashbacks how Poncelet and his friend killed two young people at night in the woods. For many viewers the graphic murder scene justifies the death sentence, even though the filmmakers seem to want us to share Helen Prejean's abolitionist stance.

translates into more than a religious quest: It becomes an effort to make him into a whole human being rather than the brutal, whining subhuman she first encounters, someone who is willing to take responsibility for what he has done. But Poncelet is not a cooperative or a likable character: He is a racist, a member of the Aryan Brotherhood, and a vocal fan of Hitler—at least this is how he wants to come across to the media.

After the hearing, Sister Helen had been confronted by the families of the murdered teens, who asked how she could spend time with Poncelet and not with them. Now she makes a point of seeking them out, at first in some vague hope that she might "help" them. The boy's father makes her understand what a presumptuous idea that is and begins to tell her of his son's short life. In his grief and willingness to talk, she grasps the enormity of the tragedy that has befallen his family; not only have the parents lost their only child, but they are splitting up because of the strain caused by their son's murder. Some tenuous understanding is reached between her and the father of the boy; not so, however, with the parents of the murdered girl. When Sister Helen comes to visit them, they assume she has "changed sides"; when they realize she hasn't, they throw her out, unwilling or unable to understand what she is trying to do. They assume she must have a crush on the killer—a man they hate so much that they believe they will find no closure until he is dead.

The date of the execution is drawing near, and Poncelet is moved to the facility of execution, his measurements are taken, funeral arrangements are scheduled, his leg is shaved (to find a vein for the injection), and a final meeting with his family is set up. Sister Helen tries to make him admit to the killings to her, but he insists that it wasn't his fault. Not until their final private conversation does Poncelet open up to her, and in a chilling display of both humanity and depravity he tells her about what went on that night in the woods. In the last hours of his life, Poncelet does indeed take responsibility for what he has done, even though it may well have been his friend who was the instigator.

For his final walk to the death chamber, in slippers, diapered, and with one shaved leg, with the warden calling out, "Dead man walking!" to clear the way, Poncelet is not allowed to walk to his death with his boots on, the way he had hoped. Sister Helen is with him and tells him that Christ is with him, too. She wants Poncelet to look at her face "as they do this thing to you" so that he will see love as the last thing before he dies. Poncelet is taken to the isolated death chamber and strapped down, arms stretched out in the shape of a cross. He has final words for the families watching behind the glass with Sister Helen, begging them for forgiveness. He also has final words for the state: that killing is wrong, no matter who does it—himself or the government. And then the process of the lethal injection begins.

The film reflects Sister Helen Prejean's abolitionist view of the death penalty, and she was herself an adviser on the film. The final scenes are shocking to many viewers because of their sheer clinical detachment—as Poncelet's appeals lawyer says, they put him to death as they would an old horse. However, with its numerous flashbacks to the crime scene and the close-up attention to the victims' families, we aren't allowed to forget Poncelet's crime.

Study Questions

1. What is the strongest abolitionist argument you see in this film? What is the strongest abolitionist argument in the general death penalty debate, in your opinion?

2. What is the strongest retentionist argument in the death penalty debate, in your opinion?

3. Argue why you think Poncelet should or should not have been executed. If you have not reached an opinion, explore the issue, arguing first for, then against, his execution.

4. Why do you think Sister Helen chose to become Poncelet's spiritual adviser? Did she make the right choice, helping him more than the bereaved families? Why or why not?

5. What do you think Stephen Nathanson would say to this film? What would John Douglas say?

Glossary

abolitionism: Today: the viewpoint that the death penalty ought to be abolished. *See* retentionism.

absolution: Forgiveness; usually God's forgiveness.

absolutism: The ethical theory that there is a universal set of moral rules that can and should be followed by everybody.

absurdity: The existentialist concept that life is meaningless because there is no God to determine right and wrong (or because we can't know what God's values are, if God happens to exist).

act utilitarianism: The classical version of utilitarianism that focuses on the consequences of a single act.

ad hominem argument: A logical fallacy (a formally faulty argument) that assumes that because a person is who he or she is, his or her viewpoint must be wrong.

agnosticism: The view that God is unknown or that it cannot be known whether or not there is a God.

altruism: Concern for the interests of others. Extreme (ideal) altruism: concern for the interests of others while disregarding one's own interests. Moderate altruism (also known as Golden Rule altruism or reciprocal altruism): taking others' interests into account while being concerned for one's own interests as well.

ambiguity: Quality exhibited in an expression or statement that can be interpreted in different ways.

anamnesis: Greek: re-remembering. Plato's theory of remembering the truth about the Forms, forgotten at birth.

androgynism: Male and female nature in the same individual, either in terms of sex (biological) or gender (cultural).

android: An artificial intelligence; a robot made to resemble a human being. Literally: manlike. There is no accepted word for a female android, but the equivalent would be *gyneoid.*

angst: Existentialist term for anxiety or anguish, a feeling of dread without any identifiable cause. Most frequently felt when one has to make important decisions. Different from *fear,* where the object of the emotion is known.

anthropocentrism: Viewing everything from an exclusively human perspective.

anthropology: The study of humans. Physical anthropology: the study of human biology and biological prehistory. Cultural anthropology: the study of human cultures.

anthropomorphism: Literally: making into a human shape. Projecting human characteristics into the behavior of other animals.

anxiety: *See* angst.

approximation: To approach something with as much accuracy as the conditions allow.

arbitrary: Coincidental, without meaning or consistency.

asceticism: Denying oneself physical pleasures and indulgence.

ataraxia: Epicurus's highest form of pleasure, having peace of mind due to freedom from pain.

atheism: The conviction that there is no God.

authenticity: Being true to yourself, having personal integrity. Existentialism: not succumbing to the idea that you have no free choice. *See* bad faith.

auto-icon: An image of oneself that consists of oneself. Bentham's term for his own planned future position as a stuffed corpse on display.

autonomy: Independence; a state achieved by those who are self-governing. Autonomous lawmaker: Kant's term for a person using the categorical imperative without regard for personal interest, arriving at something he or she would want to become a universal law. Moral autonomy: being capable of and allowed to make moral decisions on your own.

backward-looking justice: Correcting past wrongs.

bad faith: Existentialist term for the belief that you have no choice; the belief that you can transform yourself into a thing with no will or emotions.

begging the question: A logical fallacy whereby a person who is supposed to prove something assumes from the start that it is a fact.

Being-there: Heidegger's term for human beings, or at least for beings who are self-aware.

benevolence: Interest in the well-being or comfort of others.

bibliotherapy: Using books, usually stories of fiction, in therapy sessions to facilitate patients' understanding of themselves and their situation and options.

care: (1) Heidegger's concept of human existence, involving a *Care-structure,* being engaged in living; (2) Gilligan's concept of ethics as it is typically viewed by women — *an ethics of care* rather than an *ethics of justice.*

catalyst: A person or agent that causes something to happen.

categorical imperative: Kant's term for an absolute moral rule that is justified because of its logic: If you can wish for your maxim to become a universal law, your maxim qualifies as a categorical imperative.

catharsis, cathartic: Cleansing. *See* Aristotle's theory of drama, Chapter 2.

causality, causal explanation: The chain of cause and effect. Aristotle's theory of causation: material cause (the material aspect of a thing), efficient cause (the maker of a thing), formal cause (the idea of a thing), and final cause (the purpose of a thing).

character arc: A concept used in screenwriting and narrative theory. A character in the story undergoes a certain development leading to a conclusion.

chauvinism: Originally: excessive feeling of nationalism, from the Frenchman Chauvin. Today it usually means male chauvinism (sexism from a male point of view).

classical feminism: The feminist view that women and men ought to be considered persons first and gendered beings second.

cloning: Creating a genetic copy of another individual, either through a process where multiple twins are created, or a process where a cell nucleus is taken from the original individual, implanted in an emptied ovum, and allowed to develop into an embryo. If the embryo is terminated within ten to fourteen days, *stem cells* may be harvested. If an embryo can survive and be carried to term, a cloned individual is the result. Cloning will not result in a perfect copy of another individual, physically or mentally, because of the variety of circumstances surrounding the growth process that can't be duplicated.

cognitive, cognition: The faculty of knowing, examining something rationally.

communitarianism: A moral and political theory that the individual receives his or her identity from his or her community and can flourish only within the community. The theory is found in the ancient Greek tradition but is also evident in traditional African tribal cultures. Modern communitarians mentioned in this book include Alasdair MacIntyre and Elizabeth Wolgast. In addition, Hillary Rodham Clinton has declared herself a communitarian with the publication of her book, *It Takes a Village.*

conceptualize: Make a vague notion into a concept with a clear definition that can be used in a description or an argument.

condition of possibility: What makes something possible, or what makes it come into being.

consequentialism: A theory that focuses exclusively on the consequences of an action. Utilitarianism is the best-known consequentialist theory, but ethical egoism also qualifies as an example of consequentialism.

Continental philosophy: Philosophical traditions from the European continent (excluding British traditions).

contractarianism: The theory that only humans can have rights, because only humans can enter into agreements (contracts) and recognize duties springing from those agreements.

correlative: A term or a concept that is understood in its relation to other concepts. The fallacy of the suppressed correlative: If terms are correlative, like *hot/cold,* and *tall/short,* they help define each other. If one is suppressed, the other ceases to have any meaning.

counterfable/countermyth: A story/fable/myth told deliberately to prove another story, type of story, or idea wrong.

criminal justice: Punishment of people found guilty of crimes.

criterion: A test, rule, or measure for distinguishing between true and false, relevant and irrelevant. A standard for a correct judgment. Plural: *criteria.*

Crusades, the: Military expeditions undertaken by European Christians from the eleventh through the thirteenth centuries to recover the Holy Land from the Muslims.

cultural diversity: The recognition of a variety of ethnic and racial groups within a given region (all the way from a neighborhood to planet Earth).

cultural imperialism: A critical term for the attitude of imposing one's cultural accomplishments and moral convictions on other cultures.

cultural relativism: The theory that different societies or cultures have different moral codes. A descriptive theory.

cynicism: Distrust in evidence of virtue or disinterested motives. Pessimism. Originally a Greek school of thought believing that virtue, not pleasure or intellect, was the ultimate goal of life. Deteriorated into the idea of self-righteousness.

debt-metaphor: English's term for using the terms *owing* and *debt* in situations where they may or may not be appropriate. Appropriate use: a situation in which favors are owed. Inappropriate use: a situation of friendship or family relationship.

deduction: The scientific and philosophical method of identifying an item of absolute truth (an axiom) and using this as a premise to deduce specific cases that are also absolutely true.

deontology: Duty-theory. An ethical theory that disregards the importance of consequences and focuses only on the rightness or wrongness of the act itself.

descriptive: Describing a phenomenon without making an evaluative or judgmental statement. Opposite of normative.

deterrence: A concept of criminal justice: punishing criminals with the intent to deter them (*specific* deterrence) or others (*general* deterrence) from committing the same crime.

dialectic method: Socrates' method of guiding his students to their own realization of the truth through a conversation, a dialogue. Also called the Socratic method.

dichotomy: An "either-or" statement. A false dichotomy: an either-or statement that ignores other possibilities.

didactic: Done or told for the purpose of teaching a lesson.

difference feminism: The feminist view that women and men are fundamentally different, morally and psychologically.

dilemma: The situation of having to choose between two courses of action that either exclude each other or are equally unpleasant.

distributive justice: Fair distribution of social goods.

divine command theory: A theological theory that God has created the laws of morality; in other words, something is right because God commands it. Opposed to *natural law theory,* which claims that God commands something because it is right. *See* also natural law theory.

double effect: A principle primarily found within Catholic ethics: An action that is otherwise prohibited can be permitted, provided that it is an *unintended* side effect to some other, necessary action; that the effect of the primary action is *proportionately very serious,* and the effect of the secondary action is *unavoidable.* The principle is used to justify rare cases of euthanasia and abortion, among others.

dualism: The metaphysical theory that reality consists of matter and mind. Also used as a term for any theory of opposite forces.

egalitarian: A theory that advocates social equality.

Ego: Freud's term for the human experience of the self. *See* also Superego and Id.

ego integrity: Erikson's term for mental equilibrium, accepting one's past, and not playing the "what if" game with oneself.

elitism: The belief that a certain advantage (for instance, knowledge, education, or wealth) should be reserved for a small part of the population, an elite.

empiricism: The philosophical school of thought that claims humans are born without knowledge, that the mind is an empty slate (*tabula rasa*) at birth, and that all knowledge comes through the senses.

end in oneself: Kant's term for a person. Persons (rational beings) should be regarded as dignified beings who have their own goals in life; they should not be used as a means to an end only. *See* means to an end, merely.

end justifies the means, the: The statement of a consequentialist: Only the consequences count, not how they are brought about.

Enlightenment, the: In the European and American cultural tradition, the eighteenth century saw a new focusing on the rights of the individual, the importance of education, and the objectivity of science. Also called the *Age of Reason* or the Western Enlightenment; rationality was considered the ultimate cultural goal by scientists, philosophers, and many politicians.

epistemology: Theory of knowledge. One of the main branches of traditional philosophy.

equilibrium: In this book: A well-balanced mind, capable of fair judgment.

equity feminism: The feminist view that the battle for equality has been won and that further insistence on women's inequality only serves to make women into victims.

essence: A thing's inner nature. "Essence precedes existence": the traditional philosophical conception of reality, including human nature; the theory that there is a design or purpose that nature must follow.

ethical egoism: The theory that everybody ought to be egoistic/selfish/self-interested.

ethical pluralism: Several moral systems working simultaneously within one culture.

ethical relativism: The theory that there is no universal moral code and that whatever the majority of any given society or culture considers morally right is morally right for that culture. A normative theory. *See also* cultural relativism.

ethicist: A person professionally or vocationally involved with the theory and application of ethics.

ethics: The study, questioning, and justification of moral rules.

ethics of conduct: The study of moral rules pertaining to decisions about what course of action to take or "what to do."

ethics of virtue: The study of moral rules pertaining to the building of character or "how to be."

ethos: The moral rules and attitudes of a culture.

eudaimonia: Greek: well-spirited, contentment, happiness. Aristotle's term for the ultimate human goal.

Eurocentric: A critical term meaning that American culture is overly focused on its European roots. Possibly a misnomer, since Americans rarely focus on European traditions, politics, and history, but rather on the European *legacy* for mainstream American culture.

euthanasia: Mercy killing; doctor-assisted suicide. Literally: "good death," from Greek. Voluntary euthanasia: requested by the patient. Involuntary euthanasia: (a) The patient is killed against her or his will; (b) The patient cannot communicate his or her wish, so the decision is made by the family (also called nonvoluntary euthanasia). Active euthanasia: helping someone to die at his or her request. Passive euthanasia: withholding treatment that will not help a terminally ill patient.

evidence: A ground or reason for certainty in knowledge. Usually empirical evidence; facts gathered in support of a theory.

exemplar: A model, an example for others to follow.

existence precedes essence: Existentialist belief that humans aren't determined by any essence (human nature) but exist prior to any decision about what and how they ought to be.

existentialism: A Continental school of thought that believes all humans have freedom of the will to determine their own life.

extrinsic value: *See* instrumental value.

fable: A short narrative with a moral, introducing persons, animals, or inanimate things as speakers and actors.

fallacy: A flaw in one's reasoning; an argument that does not follow the rules of logic.

falsification, principle of: The concept that a valid theory must test itself and allow for the possibility of situations in which the theory doesn't apply. In a sense, part of the verification process of a theory is being able to hypothetically falsify it.

fatalism: The theory that life is determined by a higher power and that our will can't change our destiny.

faux pas: French: a misstep, a social blunder.

fecundity: Being fruitful, having good consequences.

first-wave feminism: Feminism from the eighteenth century until approximately 1920. *See* second- and third-wave feminism.

Forms, theory of: Plato's metaphysical theory of a higher reality that gives meaning and existence to the world we experience through our senses. This higher reality is accessible through the mind. Example: a perfect circle; it doesn't exist in the world of the senses, but it does exist in the intelligible world of Forms.

fortitude: Strength of mind and courage in the face of adversity.

forward-looking justice: Creating good future social consequences. *See also* consequentialism.

fundamentalism: A religious approach to reality that interprets the dogmas and sacred scriptures of the tradition literally.

gender-neutral: Not gender-specific. Usually used when referring to language. Examples: Scientists must do their research well. Nurses should take good care of their patients.

gender-specific: Applying to one sex only. Examples of gender-specific language: A scientist must do *his* research well. A nurse should take good care of *her* patients.

genetic engineering: Scientific manipulation of the DNA code of an individual (human, animal, or plant), usually to enhance certain desired characteristics or eliminate congenital diseases.

genetic fallacy, the: Assuming that something can be fully explained by pointing to its original/first condition.

genocide: The murder of all or most of a population.

genre: A literary type of story (or film), such as horror, western, or science fiction.

Golden Mean, the: The Greek idea of moderation. Aristotle's concept of virtue as a relative mean between the extremes of excess and deficiency.

good will: For Kant, having good will means having good intentions in terms of respecting a moral law that is rational and deserves to be a universal law.

greatest-happiness principle, the: *See* utility.

hard universalism: *See* absolutism.

harm principle, the: John Stuart Mill's idea that one should not interfere with other people's lives unless those people are doing harm to others.

hedonism: Pleasure-seeking. The paradox of hedonism: The more you look for pleasure, the more it seems to elude you. Hedonistic calculus: Bentham's pros-and-cons system, in which pleasures are added and pains subtracted to find the most utilitarian course of action.

heterogeneous: Consisting of dissimilar or diverse elements.

hierarchy: A structure of higher and lower elements, ordered according to their relative importance.

homogeneous: Consisting of similar elements.

human condition, the: What it means to be a human being, usually in terms of inevitable facts: having physical and spiritual needs, being a social creature, and being subject to illness and aging.

hyphenated: A political term for the distinction between one's national or ethnic ancestry and one's American identity, such as *Swedish-American*. To be "hyphenated" indicates for some people that one's loyalties are divided. Today it is common to omit the hyphen, as in *Swedish American*.

hypothetical imperative: A command that is binding only if one is interested in a certain result. An "if-then" situation.

Id: Freud's term for the Unconscious, the part of the mind that the conscious self (the Ego) has no access to but that influences the Ego.

idealism: The metaphysical theory that reality consists of mind only, not matter.

immutability: Something that remains stable and can't be changed.

inalienable: Incapable of being taken or given away.

incapacitation: A concept of criminal justice: punishing a criminal with the intent of making the public safe from his or her criminal activity. May refer to incarceration as well as other forms of punishment, including capital punishment.

induction: The scientific and philosophical method of collecting empirical evidence and formulating a general theory based on those specific facts. The problem of induction: Because one never knows if one has collected enough evidence, one can never achieve 100 percent certainty through induction.

institutionalized cruelty: Hallie's term for cruelty (psychological or physical) that has become so established, it seems natural to both victimizer and victim.

instrumental value: To have value for the sake of what further value it might bring. Also known as extrinsic value; good as a means to an end. *See* means to an end.

intersexual: A person with both male and female genitalia.

intrinsic value: To have value in itself without regard to what it might bring of further value. Good in itself, good as an "end in itself." *See* end in oneself.

intuition: Usually, an experience of understanding that is independent of one's reasoning. Can also mean the moment of understanding, an "Aha" experience. Moral intuition: a gut-level feeling of right and wrong.

ipso facto: By the fact itself.

irony: Ridicule through exaggeration, praise, or understatement.

jus bellum: Just war: a war conducted in self-defense according to set rules.

jus in bello: Justice in war. Rules for proper conduct of war.

kingdom of ends: Kant's term for a society of autonomous lawmakers who all use the categorical imperative and show each other mutual respect.

leap of faith: Kierkegaard's concept of the necessary step from the ethical to the religious stage. It involves throwing yourself at the mercy of God and discarding all messages from your rational mind or your self-interested emotions.

lex talionis: The law of retaliation; an eye for an eye. A retributivist argument for punishment.

liberalism: A political theory that supports gradual reforms through parliamentary procedures and civil liberties.

libertarianism: (1) A theory of government that holds the individual has a right to life, liberty, and property; that nobody should interfere with these rights (negative rights); and that the government's role should be restricted to protecting these rights. (2) A theory that humans have free will independent of mechanistic causality.

master morality: Nietzsche's view of the morality of strong individuals in ancient times; includes respect for the enemy, loyalty to friends and kin, and scorn for weaker individuals. Leads to the concept of the Overman (Superman), the strong individual who has gone beyond the moral rules and sets his own standards of good and evil.

materialism: The metaphysical theory that reality consists of matter only, not mind.

matriarchy, matriarchal: A society in which women have great social influence and the words of older women within the family carry much weight. Sometimes taken to mean a society ruled by women.

maxim: Kant's term for the rule or principle of an action.

means to an end: Something used to achieve another goal, an end. *See* instrumental value.

means to an end, merely: Kant's term for using others as a stepping-stone for one's own purpose.

mental state: Any mind activity or mental image.

metaethics: The approach to ethics that refrains from making normative statements but focuses on the meaning of terms and statements and investigates the sources of normative statements.

metaphor: An image or an illustration that describes something in terms of something different. A figurative image such as "My boyfriend is a tiger."

metaphysics: The philosophical study of the nature of reality or of being.

misanthropy: Misgivings about, hatred of, or lack of trust in the goodness of human nature.

misogyny: Misgivings about, hatred of, or lack of trust in female human nature. There is no traditional equivalent term for mistrusting male human nature, but such a term might be *misandry*.

monism: A type of metaphysics that holds that there is one element of reality only, such as materialism or idealism.

monoculturalism: As opposed to multiculturalism. The concept of a dominant culture, viewing its history and cultural practices as the only significant contributions to the culture in question.

moral agent: A person capable of reflecting on a moral problem and acting on his or her decision.

morality, morals: The moral rules and attitudes that we live by, or are expected to live by.

mores: The moral customs and rules of a given culture.

multiculturalism: The policy of recognizing cultural diversity to the extent where all cultures within a given region are fairly represented in terms of public life and education. Sometimes includes gender as cultural diversity. *See also* cultural diversity, pluralism, and particularism.

myth: A story or a collection of stories that give identity, guidance, and meaning to a culture. Usually these are stories of gods and heroes, but they may involve ordinary people, too. In common language myth has come to mean "falsehood" or "illusion," but this is not the original meaning.

narrative: A story with a plot. Narrative structure: perceiving events as having a logical progression from a beginning through a middle to an ending.

narrative time: The time frame within which a story takes place. The experience of sharing this time frame as one reads or watches the story unfold.

natural law: A view introduced to the Catholic church by Thomas Aquinas that what is natural for humans (in other words, what God has intended) is good for humans. What is natural for humans includes: preservation of life, procreation, socialization, and pursuit of knowledge of God.

natural rights: The assumption that humans (and perhaps also nonhumans) are born with certain inalienable rights.

naturalistic fallacy: The assumption that one can conclude from what is natural/a fact ("what is") what should be a rule or a policy ("what ought to be"). Not all philosophers think this is a fallacy.

negative command: Hallie's term for a moral command involving a prohibition, such as "Don't lie" or "Don't cause harm." *See* positive command.

negative rights: Rights not to be interfered with; usually includes the right to life, liberty, and property. Originally an element in John Locke's political philosophy; has become a defining element of modern Libertarian philosophy.

neo-classicism: A style of art and architecture in the seventeenth and eighteenth centuries that revived classical Greek and Roman forms. Also, any spiritual and philosophical movement that tries to recover the classical ideals of moderation and order.

nihilism: From the Latin *nihil*, nothing. The attitude of believing in nothing. Moral nihilism: the conviction that there are no moral truths.

normative: Evaluating and/or setting norms or standards. Opposite of descriptive.

objectification: Making an object, a thing, out of someone: disregarding their human dignity. Also reification, making a thing out of someone.

objective: The kind of knowledge that is supported by evidence and that has independent existence apart from experience or thought.

ontology: A philosophical discipline investigating the nature of existence.

original sin: The Christian belief that the disobedience of Adam and Eve are inherited by all humans from birth, so all humans are born sinful.

Other, the: A philosophical concept meaning either something that is completely different from yourself and all your experiences or someone who is different from you and is thus hard to understand.

Overman, or Superman: Nietzsche's term for the individual who has recognized his will to power and created his own system of values based on an affirmation of life.

pacifism: The belief that war and violence are morally wrong, regardless of the circumstances.

parable: A short narrative told to make a moral or religious point.

particularism: The branch of multiculturalism that believes people not belonging to the dominant culture should retrieve their self-esteem by learning about the traditions and accomplishments of their own cultural group rather than those of the dominant group or any other group. Also called exclusive multiculturalism.

paterfamilias: The male head of the household.

patriarchy: A society ruled by men, or a society in which men have great social influence.

philanthropy: Greek: loving humans. Doing good deeds, being charitable.

philology: The study of language, its structure and history.

phronesis: Aristotle's term for practical wisdom, our everyday decision-making process.

pleasure principle: Freud's term for the oldest layer of the human mind, which caters selfishly to our own pleasure. For most people it is superseded by the reality principle, at least most of the time.

pluralism: The branch of multiculturalism that believes racial and ethnic discrimination in a population of cultural diversity can be abolished by a shared orientation in each other's cultural traditions and history. Also called inclusive multiculturalism. Also: any theory or culture that includes several different viewpoints.

positive command: Hallie's term for a moral command to actively do something rather than merely refraining from doing something wrong (a negative command). Example: "Help another being in distress."

positive rights: Rights of entitlement. The theory that each individual has a right to the basic means of subsistence against the state, such as food, shelter, clothing, education, welfare, health services.

preconceived notion: An idea that is formed prior to actual knowledge or experience and that you don't think of questioning.

prerational: Before the use of reason; instinctive; belonging to human nature prior to the development of reason.

prescriptive: *See* normative.

presocial: Before the existence of society.

principle of utility: *See* utility.

procreation: Having offspring, giving birth.

protagonist: The hero of the story.

psychological egoism: The theory that everyone is selfish, self-interested.

psychosexual neutrality: The behaviorist theory that human sexuality is a matter of upbringing (nurture) rather than a hardwiring of the brain (nature).

radical feminism: The feminist view that the root cause of male dominance of women and discrimination against women must be examined.

rational being: Anyone who has intelligence and the capacity to use it. Usually stands for human beings, but may exclude some humans and include some nonhuman beings.

rationalism: The philosophical school of thought that claims humans are born with some knowledge, or some capacity for knowledge, such as logic and mathematics. Opposite of empiricism.

reality principle: Freud's term for the knowledge that we can't always have things our own way.

reductio ad absurdum: A form of argument in which you reduce your opponent's viewpoint to its absurd consequences.

rehabilitation: A concept of criminal justice: punishing a criminal with the intent of making him or her a better socialized person at the end of the term of punishment.

reification: *See* objectification.

relevance: Direct application to a situation; pertinence.

Renaissance: Literally: rebirth. The European cultural revival of the arts and sciences in the fourteenth through sixteenth centuries. This period marked the end of the Middle Ages.

replicant: Term used in the film *Blade Runner* for androids. *See* android.

restorative justice: Rehabilitation of criminals, and restitution to the victims.

retentionism: The viewpoint that the death penalty ought to be retained (kept as an option).

retribution: A concept of criminal justice: the logical dispensing or receiving of punishment in proportion to the crime. Sometimes known as "an eye for an eye," *lex talionis*. To be distinguished from vengeance, which is an emotional response that may exceed the severity of the crime.

retributive justice: Punishment of criminals in proportion to their crime.

revisionism: Advocacy of revision of former values and viewpoints. Today: refers mostly to a cynical revision of heroic values of the past.

rhetoric: The art of verbal persuasion.

Romanticism, the Romantic Movement: A movement among artists, philosophers, and social critics in the late eighteenth and nineteenth centuries, partly based on the idea that emotion is a legitimate form of expression and can give access to higher truths without necessarily involving the intellect.

rule utilitarianism: The branch of utilitarianism that focuses on the consequences of a type of action done repeatedly, and not just a single act. *See* act utilitarianism.

satire: The use of sarcasm in a criticism of conditions one doesn't approve of.

second-wave feminism: Feminism in the United States and Europe from the mid-1950s on. Some consider second-wave feminism to have ended by the mid-1980s; others see it as continuing.

selfish gene: The twentieth-century theory that humans as well as animals have a disposition that favors themselves, but also the survival of their genes. Occasionally, animals (or humans) will sacrifice themselves so that their closely related relatives or offspring may survive.

Silver Rule, the: Do not do to others what you would not like them to do to you. A negative version of the Golden Rule, Do unto others as you would have them do unto you.

skepticism: The philosophical approach that we cannot obtain absolutely certain knowledge. In practice it is an approach of not believing anything until there is sufficient evidence to prove it.

slave morality: Nietzsche's concept of the morality of the "herd," people who in his view resent strong individuals and claim that meekness is a virtue.

slippery slope argument: A version of the *reductio ad absurdum* argument; you reduce your opponent's view to unacceptable or ridiculous consequences, which your opponent will presumably have to accept or else abandon his or her theory. Your opponent's argument must "slide down the slope" of logic. A way to defeat the slippery slope argument is to "draw the line" and defend your viewpoint on the basis that there is a difference between the "top of the slope" and the "bottom of the slope."

social contract: A type of social theory, popular in the seventeenth and eighteenth centuries, that assumes humans in the early stages of society got together and agreed on terms for creating a society.

soft universalism: The ethical theory that although humans may not agree on all moral rules or all customs, there are a few bottom-line rules we can agree on, despite our different ways of expressing them.

sophia: Greek: wisdom. Aristotle's term for theoretical wisdom, the highest intellectual virtue.

spatial: Associated with space.

straw man (straw dummy) argument: A logical fallacy that consists of attacking and disproving a theory invented for the occasion.

subjective opinion: One that is not supported by evidence, or is dependent on the mind and experience of the person.

subjectivism: Ethical theory that claims that your moral belief is right simply because you believe it; there are no intersubjective (shared) moral standards.

Superego: Freud's concept of the human conscience, the internalized rules of our parents and our society.

teleology: A theory of purpose. A teleological theory such as Aristotle's may assume that everything has a purpose. Also used to designate theories interested in the outcome of an action, that is, consequentialist theories.

temperance: In virtue theory this means moderation. In a modern context it may mean abstinence from alcohol.

temporal: Associated with time. Temporal being: a being living in time and understanding himself or herself in terms of a past, a present, and a future.

theology: The study of God and God's nature and attributes.

third-wave feminism: Feminism from the mid-1980s to the present day.

totalitarianism: A form of government that views the state as all-important and the lives of its citizens as disposable.

transgenic: Genetic engineering of an animal or a plant (or, theoretically, a human) with some genes from another species.

universal law: Kant's term for a moral rule that can be imagined as applying to everybody in the same situation and accepted by other rational beings.

universalizability: A maxim that is acceptable as a universal law.

universalization: The process by which one asks oneself whether one's maxim could become a universal law: "What if everybody did this?"

utilitarianism: The theory that one ought to maximize the happiness and minimize the unhappiness of as many people (or sentient beings) as possible.

utility: Fitness for some purpose, especially for creating happiness and/or minimizing pain and suffering. Principle of utility: To create as much happiness and minimize suffering as much as possible for as many as possible. Also: the greatest-happiness principle.

Utopia: Literally, no place. Sir Thomas More's term for a nonexistent world, usually used as a term for a world too good to be true. Utopia can also mean "good place." A bad place is known as "Dystopia."

vengeance: Revenge. When used as a concept of criminal justice: an emotional response to punishment.

vicariously: To experience something through the experiences of others.

Way, the: Chinese: Tao (Dao). The morally and philosophically correct path to follow.

yin and yang: The two cosmic principles of Taoism, opposing forces that keep the universe in balance.

Selected Bibliography

Works of Nonfiction

Ammitzbøll, Marianne. *Den skjulte skat.* Copenhagen: Olivia, 1995.

Andersen, Pauli. "Celleklumper eller mennesker." *Berlingske Tidende,* November 26, 2001.

Aristotle. *Nichomachean Ethics.* In *Introduction to Aristotle,* edited by Richard McKeon, translated by W. D. Ross. New York: Random House, 1947.

———. *Poetics.* In *Introduction to Aristotle,* edited by Richard McKeon, translated by Ingram Bywater. New York: Random House, 1947.

Arrison, Sonia. "New Anti-Terrorism Law Goes Too Far." Op-ed, *San Diego Union-Tribune,* October 31, 2001.

Austin, Jonathan D. "U.N. Report: Women's Unequal Treatment Hurts Economies." CNN.com, September 20, 2000.

Badinter, Elisabeth. *The Unopposite Sex.* Translated by Barbara Wright. New York: Harper & Row, 1989.

Beauvoir, Simone de. *The Second Sex.* Translated by H. M. Parshley. New York: Knopf, 1952.

———. *The Ethics of Ambiguity.* Translated by Bernard Frechtman. New York: Philosophical Library, 1948.

Bedau, Hugo A., ed. *Justice and Equality.* Englewood Cliffs, N.J.: Prentice-Hall, 1971.

Belenky, Mary Field et al. *Women's Ways of Knowing.* New York: Basic Books, 1986.

Benedict, Ruth. "Anthropology and the Abnormal." *Journal of General Psychology* 10 (1934).

Bentham, Jeremy. *Principles of Morals and Legislation.* In *The Utilitarians.* New York: Anchor Books, 1973.

———. *The Works of Jeremy Bentham,* vol. 2. Edited by John Bowring. Edinburgh, 1838–43.

Berger, Fred. "Gratitude." In *Vice and Virtue in Everyday Life,* edited by Christina Hoff Sommers and Fred Sommers. Fort Worth: Harcourt Brace Jovanovich, 1985.

Bergson, Henri. *Time and Free Will.* Translated by F. L. Pogson. New York: Harper, 1960.

Bernasconi, Robert, and Wood, David, eds. *The Provocation of Levinas.* New York: Routledge, 1988.

Bok, Sisela. *Strategy for Peace.* New York: Random House, 1989.

Bonevac, Daniel, ed. *Today's Moral Issues.* Mountain View, Calif.: Mayfield, 1992.

Bonevac, Daniel et al., eds. *Beyond the Western Tradition.* Mountain View, Calif.: Mayfield, 1992.

Booth, Wayne C. *The Company We Keep.* Berkeley: University of California Press, 1988.

———. "Why Ethical Criticism Fell on Hard Times." In *Ethics: Symposium on Morality and Literature* 98, no. 2 (January 1988). Chicago: University of Chicago Press.

Boss, Judith A. *Ethics for Life.* Mountain View, Calif.: Mayfield, 1998.

"Boy Sentenced to Watch *Saving Private Ryan.*" Associated Press, August 20, 1998.

Brickhouse, Thomas B., and Smith, Nicholas D. *Socrates on Trial.* Princeton, N.J.: Princeton University Press, 1989.

The Cambridge Companion to John Stuart Mill. Edited by John Skorupski. New York: Cambridge University Press, 1998.

Carmody, Denise Lardner, and Carmody, John Tully. *How to Live Well: Ethics in the World Religions.* Belmont, Calif.: Wadsworth, 1988.

Chan, W., ed. *A Source Book in Chinese Philosophy.* Princeton, N.J.: Princeton University Press, 1963.

Cohen, Carl. "The Case for the Use of Animals in Biomedical Research." *New England Journal of Medicine* 315 (October 2, 1986).

Confucius. *The Analects.* New York: Dover, 1995.

Cooper, Marc. "Liberals Stuck in Scold Mode." Op-ed, *Los Angeles Times,* October 14, 2001.

Coren, Stanley. *The Intelligence of Dogs.* New York: Macmillan, 1994.

Donn, Jeff. "Company Says It Cloned Human Embryo." Associated Press, November 25, 2001.

Douglas, John, and Olshaker, Mark. *Journey into Darkness.* New York: Pocket Star Books, 1997.

———. *Obsession.* New York: Scribner, 1998.

Dworkin, Andrea. *Right-Wing Women.* New York: Perigree, 1993.

Dworkin, Ronald. *Taking Rights Seriously.* Cambridge, Mass.: Harvard University Press, 1977.

Ehrenburg, Ilya. "Bøger." In *Evige Tanker,* edited by Anker Kierkeby. Copenhagen: Westmans Forlag, 1951.

The Elder Edda. A selection translated from the Icelandic by Paul B. Taylor and W. H. Auden. London: Faber and Faber, 1973.

Encyclopedia of Ethics. Edited by Lawrence C. Becker and Charlotte B. Becker. New York: Garland, 1992.

English, Jane. "What Do Grown Children Owe Their Parents?" In *Having Children: Philosophical and Legal Reflections on Parenthood,* edited by Onora O'Neill and William Ruddick. New York: Oxford University Press, 1979.

Erikson, Erik. *Childhood and Society.* New York: Norton, 1964.

Ethics as First Philosophy: The Significance of Emmanuel Levinas. Edited by Adriaan T. Peperzak. New York: Routledge, 1995.

Ethics for Military Leaders I–II. Edited by Anne Donovan, Donald E. Johnson, George R. Lucas, Jr., Paul E. Rousch, and Nancy Sherman. American Heritage Christian Publishing, 1997.

Feinberg, Joel. "Psychological Egoism." In *Ethical Theory,* edited by Louis P. Pojman. Belmont, Calif.: Wadsworth, 1989.

———. "The Rights of Animals and Unborn Generations." In *Philosophy and Environmental Crisis,* edited by William T. Blackstone. Athens: University of Georgia Press, 1974.

Fitzsimmons, Mike. Editorial on anti-terrorism law. KXLY, October 30, 2001.

Foot, Philippa. *Virtues and Vices.* Berkeley: University of California Press, 1978.

Freeman, Derek. *The Fateful Hoaxing of Margaret Mead.* Boulder, Colo.: Westview Press, 1999.

Friedman, Marilyn. "Feminism and Modern Friendship: Dislocating the Community." *Ethics* 99 (1989), University of Chicago Press.

Fuhrman, Mark. *Murder in Spokane.* New York: HarperCollins, 2001.

Genovese, E. N. *Mythology: Texts and Contexts.* Redding, Calif.: C.A.T. Publishing, 1991.

Gilligan, Carol. *In a Different Voice.* Cambridge, Mass.: Harvard University Press, 1982.

Graves, Robert. *The Greek Myths.* 2 vols. Penguin, 1960.

Gross, Hyman. *A Theory of Criminal Justice.* New York: Oxford University Press, 1979.

Guillo, Karen. "Study Finds No Death Penalty Bias." Associated Press, June 7, 2001.

Gyekye, Kwame. *An Essay on African Philosophical Thought: The Akan Conceptual Scheme.* New York: Cambridge University Press, 1987.

Hallie, Philip. "From Cruelty to Goodness." In *Vice and Virtue in Everyday Life,* edited by Christina Hoff Sommers and Fred Sommers. Fort Worth: Harcourt Brace Jovanovich, 1985, 1989.

———. *Tales of Good and Evil, Help and Harm.* New York: HarperCollins, 1997.

Harris, Jr., C. E. *Applying Moral Theories.* Belmont, Calif.: Wadsworth, 1986.

Heidegger, Martin. *Being and Time.* Translated by John Macquarrie and Edward Robinson. New York: Harper & Row, 1962.

Herodotus. *The Histories.* Translated by Aubrey de Sélencourt. New York: Penguin Books, 1996.

Hertel, Hans. *Verdens litteraturs historie,* vols. 1–7. Copenhagen: Gyldendal, 1985–93.

Hinman, Lawrence. *Ethics, A Pluralistic Approach.* Austin: Harcourt Brace, 1993.

Hobbes, Thomas. *English Works.* Vol. 3. Edited by Sir W. Molesworth. London: J. Bohn, 1840.

Hohlenberg, Johannes. *Søren Kierkegaard.* Copenhagen: Aschehoug Dansk Forlag, 1963.

Huffington, Arianna. "The Gary Conditization of the Terror Story." AriannaOnline, October 24, 2001.

Hume, David. *An Enquiry Concerning the Principles of Morals.* In *Enquiries Concerning Human Understanding and Concerning the Principles of Morals,* 3rd ed., edited by L. A. Selby-Bigge, revised by P. H. Nidditch. Oxford: Clarendon, 1975.

Illustreret Videnskab Nr. 3, March 1994. Copenhagen: Bonnier.

Issues in Feminism. Edited by Sheila Ruth. Mountain View, Calif.: Mayfield, 1998.

Jalbert, Shana. "U.S. Must Address Real Problems, Forget Military Might, Turner Says." *Brown* (University) *Daily Herald,* February 12, 2002.

Kalin, Jesse. "In Defense of Egoism." In *Ethical Theory,* edited by Louis P. Pojman. Belmont, Calif.: Wadsworth, 1989.

Kant, Immanuel. *Grounding for the Metaphysics of Morals.* Translated by James W. Ellington. Indianapolis: Hackett, 1981.

———. *The Metaphysics of Morals.* Introduction, translation, and notes by Mary Gregor. Cambridge: Cambridge University Press, 1991.

———. "On the Distinction of the Beautiful and Sublime in the Interrelation of the Two Sexes." In *Philosophy of Woman,* edited by Mary Briody Mahowald. Indianapolis: Hackett, 1983.

Kaplan, Alice. "The Trouble with Memoir." *Chronicle of Higher Education,* December 5, 1997.

Kearney, Richard. *Dialogues with Contemporary Continental Thinkers: The Phenomenological Heritage.* Manchester: Manchester University Press, 1984.

Kemp, Peter. "Etik og narrativitetens tre niveau'er." *Psyke & Logos,* Copenhagen, no. 1, vol. 17.

Kemp, Peter, Lebech, Mette, and Rendtorff, Jacob. *Den bioetiske vending.* Copenhagen: Spektrum/Forum Publishers, 1997.

Kemp, Peter. "Social Justice." In *The Good Society: Essays on the Welfare System at a Time of Change,* edited by Egon Clausen. Copenhagen: Ministry of Social Affairs, 1995.

———. *Das Unersetzliche: Eine Technologie-Ethik.* Berlin: Wichen-Verlag, 1992.

Kierkeby, Anker, ed. *Evige Tanker.* Copenhagen: Westmans Forlag, 1951.

Kierkegaard, Søren. *Johannes Climacus* (written 1842–43, first published 1912). Copenhagen: Gyldendal, 1967.

———. *Enten-Eller. Anden Deel.* Copenhagen: H. Hagerup's Forlag, 1950.

Kingsolver, Barbara. "No Glory in Unjust War on the Weak." Op-ed, *Los Angeles Times,* October 14, 2001.

Kittay, Eva Feder, and Meyers, Diana T., eds. *Women and Moral Theory.* Savage, Md.: Rowman & Littlefield, 1987.

Körner, Stephan. *Kant.* Harmondsworth, England: Penguin, 1955.

Kravets, David. "Court to Revisit Ruling on Abortion Opponent." *San Diego Union-Tribune,* October 4, 2001.

Kurtz, Stanley. "Free Speech and an Orthodoxy of Dissent." *Chronicle of Higher Education,* October 26, 2001.

Leake, Jonathan. "Scientists Teach Chimpanzee to Speak English." *The Sunday Times,* UK, July 25, 1999.

Le Guin, Ursula K. "It Was a Dark and Stormy Night." In *On Narrative,* edited by J. I. Mitchell. Chicago: University of Chicago Press, 1981.

Lerner, Gerda. *The Creation of Feminist Consciousness.* New York: Oxford University Press, 1993.

———. *The Creation of Patriarchy.* New York: Oxford University Press, 1986.

Levin, Richard. *The Question of Socrates.* New York: Harcourt, Brace & World, 1961.

Levinas, Emmanuel. *Ethics and Infinity: Conversations with Philippe Nemo.* Pittsburgh: Duquesne University Press, 1985.

Lifton, Robert Jay, and Mitchell, Greg. *Who Owns Death?: Capital Punishment, the American Conscience, and the End of Executions.* New York: Morrow, 2000.

Lin Yutang. *The Importance of Living.* London: Heinemann, 1937.

Lloyd, *Genevieve. The Man of Reason.* Minneapolis: University of Minnesota Press, 1984.

Louv, Richard. "Line Between Reality and Science Fiction Has Been Eroding." *San Diego Union-Tribune,* October 28, 2001.

———. "War on Terrorism Calls for Re-evaluation of Military Ethics." *San Diego Union-Tribune,* October 21, 2001.

McCormick, Patrick T. "Adult Punishment Doesn't Fit the Underage Criminal." *Spokesman-Review,* September 4, 2001.

MacIntyre, Alasdair. *After Virtue.* Notre Dame, Ind.: University of Notre Dame Press, 1981, 1984.

Mackie, J. L. *Ethics: Inventing Right and Wrong.* New York: Penguin, 1977.

McLemee, Scott. "What Makes Martha Nussbaum Run?" *Chronicle of Higher Education,* October 5, 2001.

Mahowald, Mary Briody, ed. *Philosophy of Woman.* Indianapolis: Hackett, 1983.

Malinowski, Bronislaw. "Myth in Primitive Psychology." In *Magic, Science, and Religion.* Garden City, N.Y.: Doubleday Anchor, 1954.

Maltin, Leonard. *Leonard Maltin's TV Movies and Video Guide.* New York: Signet, 1996.

Mayo, Bernard. "Virtue or Duty?" In *Vice and Virtue in Everyday Life,* edited by Christina Hoff Sommers and Fred Sommers. Fort Worth: Harcourt Brace Jovanovich, 1985, 1989.

Medlin, Brian. "Ultimate Principles and Ethical Thought." In *Ethical Theory,* edited by Louis P. Pojman. Belmont, Calif.: Wadsworth, 1989.

Mencius. Translated by D. C. Lau. Harmondsworth, England: Penguin, 1970.

Mill, John Stuart. *Autobiography.* New York: Columbia University Press, 1924.

———. *On Liberty.* In *The Utilitarians.* New York: Anchor Books, 1973.

———. *The Subjection of Women.* Cambridge, Mass.: MIT Press, 1970.

———. *Utilitarianism.* In *The Utilitarians.* New York: Anchor Books, 1973.

Mitchell, J. I., ed. *On Narrative.* Chicago: University of Chicago Press, 1981.

Mitrovich, George, and Winters, Timothy. "Separated by a Hyphen." Op-ed, *San Diego Union-Tribune,* October 11, 2001.

Morality in Criminal Justice. Edited by Daryl Close and Nicholas Meier. Belmont, Calif.: Wadsworth, 1995.

Morlin, Bill, and White, Jeanette. *Bad Trick: The Hunt for Spokane's Serial Killer.* Spokane, Wash.: New Media Ventures, 2001.

Mulhauser, Dana. "National Group Rallies Students Who Question Campus Feminism." *Chronicle of Higher Education,* October 5, 2001.

Narveson, Jan. "Morality and Violence: War, Revolution, Terrorism." In *Matters of Life and Death,* 3rd ed., edited by Tom Regan. New York: McGraw-Hill, 1993.

Nathanson, Stephen. *An Eye for an Eye? The Morality of Punishing by Death.* Savage, Md.: Rowman & Littlefield, 1987.

———. "In Defense of 'Moderate Patriotism,'" *Ethics,* vol. 99 (April 1989).

Nietzsche, Friedrich. *Beyond Good and Evil.* Translated by Helen Zimmern. Riverside, N.J.: Macmillan, 1911.

———. *On the Genealogy of Morals.* Translated by Walter Kaufmann and R. J. Hollingdale. New York: Random House, 1969.

Nussbaum, Martha. *Love's Knowledge.* New York: Oxford University Press, 1990.

O'Brian, William. *The Conduct of Just and Unjust War.* Westport, CT. Praeger Publishers, 1981.

O'Bryan, Aileen. *Navajo Indian Myths.* New York: Dover, 1993 (Republication of *The Diné: Origin Myths of the Navajo Indians.* Bulletin 163, Bureau of American Ethnology of the Smithsonian Institute, 1956).

Oden, Thomas C., ed. *Parables of Kierkegaard.* Princeton, N.J.: Princeton University Press, 1978.

Packe, Michael St. John. *The Life of John Stuart Mill.* New York: Capricorn, 1954.

Parekh, Bhikhu. "The Concept of Multicultural Education." In *Today's Moral Problems,* edited by Daniel Bonevac. Mountain View, Calif.: Mayfield, 1992.

Park, Michael Y. "Army Looks to Hollywood for Scenarios." Foxnews.com, October 8, 2001.

Plato. *Apology.* In *Dialogues of Plato.* Translated by Benjamin Jowett. New York: Washington Square Press, 1968.

———. *Euthyphro.* In *The Dialogues of Plato,* with an introduction by Erich Segal, translated by R. F. Allen. New York: Bantam Books, 1986.

———. *Plato's Phaedrus*. Translated by W. C. Helmbold and W. G. Rabinowitz. New York: The Liberal Arts Press, 1956.

———. *The Republic*. Translated by G. R. U. Grube. Indianapolis: Hackett, 1974.

———. *The Republic of Plato*. Translated by Francis MacDonald Cornford. London: Oxford University Press, 1945.

Pojman, Louis P., ed. *Ethical Theory*. Belmont, Calif.: Wadsworth, 1989.

Punishment and the Death Penalty: The Current Debate. Edited by Robert M. Baird and Stuart E. Rosenbaum. New York: Prometheus, 1995.

Race and the Enlightenment: A Reader. Edited by Emmanuel Chukwudi Eze. Oxford: Blackwell, 1997.

Rachels, James. *The Elements of Moral Philosophy*. New York: Random House, 1986, 1999.

Rand, Ayn. "The Ethics of Emergencies," "Man's Rights." In *The Virtue of Selfishness*. New York: Penguin, 1964.

Rawls, John. "Justice As Fairness." *Philosophical Review* 67 (April 1958).

———. *The Law of Peoples*. Cambridge, Mass.: Harvard University Press, 2001.

———. "Two Concepts of Rules." *Philosophical Review* 1–13, 1955.

Rendtorff, Jacob Dahl, and Kemp, Peter. *Basic Ethical Principles in European Bioethics and Biolaw*. Vol. 1, *Autonomy, Dignity, Integrity and Vulnerability*. Copenhagen: Centre for Ethics and Law, and Barcelona: Institut Borja de Bioètica, 2000.

Rescher, Nicholas. *Distributive Justice*. Indianapolis: Bobbs-Merrill, 1966.

Ricoeur, Paul. *Interpretation Theory*. Fort Worth: Texas Christian University Press, 1976.

———. "Narrative Time." In *On Narrative*, edited by J. I. Mitchell. Chicago: University of Chicago Press, 1981.

———. *Time and Narrative*. 3 vols. Chicago: University of Chicago Press, 1985–1989.

Rosenstand, Nina. "Arven fra Bergson: En Virknings-historie." In *Den Skapende Varighet*, edited by Hans Kolstad. Oslo, Norway: H. Aschehoug & Co., 1993.

———. "Everyone Needs a Stone: Alternative Views of Nature." In *The Environmental Ethics and Policy Book*, 2nd ed., edited by Donald VanDeVeer and Christine Pierce. Belmont, Calif.: Wadsworth, 1998.

———. *The Human Condition: An Introduction to Philosophy of Human Nature*. New York: McGraw-Hill, 2002.

———. "Med en anden stemme: Carol Gilligans etik." In *Kvindespind — Kønsfilosofiske Essays*, edited by Mette Boch et al. Aarhus, Denmark: Forlaget Philosophia, 1987.

———. *Mytebegrebet*. Copenhagen: Gads Forlag, 1981.

———. "Myths and Morals: Images of Conduct, Character, and Personhood in the Native American Tradition."

In *Tribal Mythologies*, edited by Helmut Wautischer. Aldershot: Ashgate, 1998.

Rousch, Paul E. "Justification for Resort to Force" in *Ethics for Military Leaders*, edited by Anne Donovan, David E. Johnson, George R. Lucas, Jr., Paul E. Rousch, and Nancy Sherman. American Heritage Christian Publishing, 1997.

"Russian Grandmother 'Wanted to Sell Child for Organs.'" CNN.com, November 28, 2000.

Sapontzis, Steve F. "The Moral Significance of Interests." *Environmental Ethics*, Winter 1982.

Sartre, Jean-Paul. Excerpt from *Being and Nothingness*. In *Reality, Man and Existence: Essential Works of Existentialism*, edited by H. J. Blackham. New York: Bantam, 1965.

———. *Existentialism Is a Humanism*. Translated by P. Mairet. New York: The Philosophical Library, 1949.

Savage-Rumbaugh, Sue, and Lewin, Roger. *Kanzi: The Ape at the Brink of the Human Mind*. New York: Wiley, 1994.

Saving Private Ryan: The Men. The Mission. The Movie. Edited by Linda Sunshine. New York: Newmarket Press, 1998.

Schmidt, Kaare. *Film-historie, kunst, industri*. Copenhagen: Gyldendal, 1995.

Schneewind, J. B. "The Misfortunes of Virtue." *Ethics* 101, October 1990. Chicago: University of Chicago Press, 1990.

"Sexual Harassment Is Forbidden by Law." San Diego State University pamphlet, November 1994.

Shapiro, Laura. "Guns and Dolls." *Newsweek*, May 28, 1990.

Shaw, William H. *Morality and Moral Controversies*. Englewood Cliffs, N.J.: Prentice-Hall, 1981.

Singer, Peter. *The Expanding Circle*. Farrar, Straus and Giroux, 1981.

Social Ethics. Edited by Thomas A. Mappes and Jane S. Zembaty. 4th ed. New York: McGraw-Hill, 1992.

Sommers, Christina Hoff. "Teaching the Virtues." *Imprimis*. Hillsdale College, Michigan, November 1991.

———. *Who Stole Feminism?* New York: Simon & Schuster, 1994.

———, and Sommers, Fred, eds. *Vice and Virtue in Everyday Life*. Fort Worth: Harcourt Brace Jovanovich, 1985, 1989.

Srinivasan, Kalpana. "Feds Accuse Entertainment Industry." Associated Press, September 11, 2000.

Steifels, Peter. "Emmanuel Levinas, 90, French Ethical Philosopher." Obituary, *New York Times*, December 27, 1995.

Steindorf, Sara. "A Novel Approach to Work." *Christian Science Monitor*, January 29, 2002.

Stone, Christopher. "Should Trees Have Standing? — Toward Legal Rights for Natural Objects." In *People, Penguins, and Plastic Trees: Basic Issues in Environmental Ethics*. Edited by Donald VanDeVeer and Christine Pierce. Belmont, Calif.: Wadsworth, 1986.

Stone, I. F. *The Trial of Socrates.* New York: Doubleday, 1988.

Stone, Oliver, and Sklar, Zachary. *JFK: The Book of the Film.* New York: Applause Books, 1992.

"Study of Monkeys Hints at a Thinking Ability Without Language." New York Times News Service, October 24, 1998.

"Sudanese Criticize Governor's Decree on Women." CNN.com, September 6, 2000.

Sullivan, Christopher. "Young Americans Sense a Turning Point." Associated Press, September 16, 2001.

Tannen, Deborah. *The Argument Culture.* New York: Random House, 1998.

———. *That's Not What I Meant!* New York: Ballantine, 1986.

———. *You Just Don't Understand.* New York: Morrow, 1990.

Taylor, Mark C. *Journeys to Selfhood: Hegel & Kierkegaard.* Berkeley: University of California Press, 1980.

Taylor, Paul W. *Principles of Ethics: An Introduction.* Belmont, Calif.: Wadsworth, 1975.

Taylor, Richard. *Good and Evil.* New York: Prometheus, 2000.

Trebilcot, Joyce. "Two Forms of Androgynism." *Journal of Social Philosophy,* January 1977.

Waal, Frans B. M. de. "Do Humans Alone 'Feel Your Pain'?" *Chronicle of Higher Education,* October 26, 2001.

———. *Good Natured: The Origins of Right and Wrong in Humans and Other Animals.* Cambridge, Mass.: Harvard University Press, 1996.

Warren, Mary Ann. "Human and Animal Rights Compared." In *Environmental Philosophy: A Collection of Readings,* edited by Robert Elliot and Arran Gare. State College: Pennsylvania State University Press, 1983.

Weiss, Rick. "Test-Tube Baby Born to Save Ill Sister." *Washington Post,* October 3, 2000.

Wesley, John. "Reel Therapy." *Psychology Today,* February 2000.

Wilgoren, Jodi. "Death Knell for the Death Penalty?" New York Times News Service, April 15, 2002.

Williams, Ian. "China Sells Organs of Slain Convicts." *Observer* (UK), December 10, 2000.

Williams, Bernard. *Morality: An Introduction.* New York: Harper & Row, 1972.

Wolgast, Elizabeth. *The Grammar of Justice.* Ithaca, N.Y.: Cornell University Press, 1987.

Wollstonecraft, Mary. *A Vindication of the Rights of Women.* Excerpt in *Philosophy of Woman,* edited by Mary Briody Mahowald. Indianapolis: Hackett, 1983.

Wright, Tamra, Hughes, Peter, and Ainley, Alison. "The Paradox of Morality: An Interview With Emmanuel Levinas." In *The Provocation of Levinas,* edited by Robert Bernasconi and David Wood. New York: Routledge, 1988.

Zack, Naomi. *Thinking About Race.* Belmont, Calif.: Wadsworth, 1998.

Works of Literature

Andersen, Hans Christian. *Eventyr og Historier.* 16 vols. Odense, Denmark: Skandinavisk Bogforlag, Flensteds Forlag.

Beauvoir, Simone de. *The Woman Destroyed.* Translated by Patrick O'Brian. New York: Putnam, 1969.

Bennett, William J. *The Book of Virtues.* New York: Simon & Schuster, 1993.

Conrad, Joseph. *Lord Jim: A Tale.* New York: Bantam, 1981.

Dostoyevsky, Fyodor. *The Brothers Karamazov.* New York: Signet Classic, New American Library, 1957.

Dumas, Alexandre. *The Count of Monte Cristo.* New York: Bantam, 1985.

Erdoes, Richard, and Ortiz, Alfonso, eds. *American Indian Myths and Legends.* New York: Pantheon, 1984.

Esquivel, Laura. *Like Water for Chocolate.* Translated by Carol and Thomas Christensen. New York: Doubleday, 1992.

Euripides, *Medea.* In classical mythology: *Images and Insights,* by Stephen L. Harris and Gloria Plazner. Translated by Moses Hadas. Mountain View, Calif., Mayfield, 1995.

Flaubert, Gustave. *Madame Bovary.* Translated by Lowell Lair. New York: Bantam, 1981.

Goethe, Johan Wolfgang von. *The Sorrows of Young Werther.* Translated by Elizabeth Mayer and Louise Bogan. New York: Vintage Books, 1973.

Graves, Robert. *The Greek Myths.* 2 vols. Harmondsworth, England: Penguin, 1960.

Grimm's Complete Fairy Tales. Garden City, N.Y.: Doubleday.

Huxley, Aldous. *Brave New World.* New York: Bantam, 1958.

Ibsen, Henrik. *A Doll's House.* In *The Collected Works of Henrik Ibsen,* vol. 7: *A Doll's House, Ghosts.* Introductions and translations by William Archer. New York: Scribner, 1906.

Jewkes, W. T., ed. *Man the Myth-Maker.* New York: Harcourt Brace Jovanovich, 1973.

Kafka, Franz. *The Basic Kafka.* New York: Simon & Schuster, 1979.

Lee, Spike, with Lisa Jones. *Do the Right Thing.* New York: Simon & Schuster, 1989.

Le Guin, Ursula K. "The Ones Who Walk Away From Omelas." In *The Wind's Twelve Quarters.* New York: Harper & Row, 1981.

Marriott, Alice, and Rachlin, Carol K., eds. *American Indian Mythology.* New York: Harper & Row, 1968.

Matheson, Richard. "Mantage." In *Shock I.* New York: Berkeley, 1961.

Niven, Larry. "The Jigsaw Man." In *Tales of Known Space: The Universe of Larry Niven.* New York: Ballantine, 1975.

Njal's Saga. Translated by Magnus Magnusson and Hermann Palsson. Baltimore: Penguin, 1960.

Poe, Edgar Allan. *Complete Tales and Poems.* New York: Barnes & Noble Books, 1992.

Rand, Ayn. *Atlas Shrugged*. New York: Signet, 1957.

Rushdie, Salman. *Haroun and the Sea of Stories*. New York: Penguin, 1990.

Sartre, Jean-Paul. *No Exit*. New York: Random House, 1989.

Shakespeare, William. *The Tragedy of Othello*. New York: New American Library, 1963.

Sheckley, Robert. "The Store of the Worlds," (1959). *More Penguin Science Fiction Classics*. Edited by Brian Aldiss. Hammandsworth, England. Penguin, 1963.

Shelley, Mary. *Frankenstein*. New York: Bantam, 1981.

Singer, Isaac Bashevis. "A Piece of Advice." From *The Spinoza of Market Street*. Translated from Yiddish into English by Martha Glicklich and Joel Blocker. New York: Fawcett Crest, 1958.

Tarantino, Quentin. *Pulp Fiction, A Quentin Tarantino Screenplay*. New York: Hyperion, 1994.

Tepper, Sheri S. *Sideshow*. New York: Bantam Books, 1993.

Walker, Alice. *Possessing the Secret of Joy*. New York: Simon & Schuster, 1993.

Wessel, Johann Herman. "Smeden og Bageren." In *De gamle huskevers*. Edited by Fritz Haack. Copenhagen: Forlaget Sesam, 1980.

Zicree, Marc Scott. *The Twilight Zone Companion*. New York: Bantam, 1982.

Selected Website Sources

Ape language research
http://www.mcg.edu/SOM/mdphd/fr_srumbaugh.htm
http://www.wm.edu/wmnews/062598/apes.html;
http://www.gsu.edu/~wwwlrc/

Atlantic Monthly websites, Christina Hoff Sommers debate
http://www.theatlantic.com

Bonobos
http://www.geographical.co.uk/geographical/features/may_2000_monkey.html

California's Three Strikes Law
http://www.rand.org/publications/RB/RB4009/RB4009.word.html

CNN-Speaking Freely: A Brief History of the Right to Free Speech in America
http://www.cnn.com.

Criminal justice ethics
http://www.lib.jjay.cuny.edu/cje/html/cje.html

Death penalty
http://law.fsu.edu/lawtech/deathpen/deathpen.html

Ethics Updates, edited by Lawrence Hinman
http://ethics.acusd.edu/index.html

Fired because of use of word
http://www.adversity.net/special/niggardly.htm

Gandhi
http://www.mkgandhi.org/

The Great Ape Project
http://arrs.envirolink.org/gap/international/gapglobal.html

Illinois death penalty report
http://www.cnn.com/2002/LAW/04/15/death.penalty.report/index.html

Immanuel Kant's "Perpetual Peace"
http://www.mtholyoke.edu/acad/intrel/kant/kant1.htm

Jeremy Bentham's Auto-Icon
http://www.ucl.ac.uk/Bentham-Project/info/jb.htm

Martin Luther King's "A Letter from (a) Birmingham Jail"
http://www.triadntr.net/~rdavis/milkbirm.html

Megan's Law
http://www.state.nj.us/lps/meganl.htm

The Molly and Adam Nash story
http://www.ama-assn.org/sci-pubs/amnews/pick_01/prse0115.htm

Moral brain area
http://www.news.excite.com/news/r/991019/21/health-mor10

Nathaniel Abraham
http://www.wsws.org/articles/2000/jan2000/abra-j14.shtml

Oklahoma City Death Penalty Controversey, ABC News, April 29, 2001
http://www.insightquest.org/death/gilchrist.htm

The Primates Home Page
http://www.geocities.com/willc7/index.html

Retributive and restorative justice
http://www.georgetown.edu/centers/woodstock/report/r-fea61a.htm

Robert Yates investigation files
http://www.krem.com

Sherrice Iverson's murder
http://www.iverson.org/
http://spyglass1.sjmercury.com/breaking/docs/063107.htm

The Society for the Study of Ethics and Animals
http://www.phil.vt.edu/ssea.html

Spokane serial killer
http://www.kxly.com/default.asp

Tuskeegee syphilis study
http://www.med.virginia.edu/hs-library/historical/apology/

U.S. Constitution
http://www.nwbuildnet.com/nwbn/usconstitutionsearch.html

"Who's a terrorist and who isn't?" AP article, 10/03/01
http://www.msnbc.com/news/636814.asp

Women's suffrage
http://www.rochester.edu/SBA/history.html

Women's suffrage, global
http://www.womenshistory.about.com/library/weekly/aa091600a.htm

Credits

Index

Page numbers in **boldface** refer to primary readings and narratives. Page numbers in *italics* refer to illustrations.